All the help you need. Anytime you need it.

Master the Next Generation Sunshine State Standards with your *Holt McDougal Mathematics* Student Edition and these great tools!

Holt McDougal Mathematics Florida Worktext

Provides in-depth coverage of every Benchmark through a five step process.

Explore It! Explore new concepts through hands-on and discovery-based activities.

Learn It! Learn concepts by completing interactive examples and Check It Out problems.

Summarize It! Summarize important concepts and complete graphic organizers using your own words.

Practice It! Practice lesson skills by completing exercises.

Apply It! Apply the lesson skills to solve real-world problems.

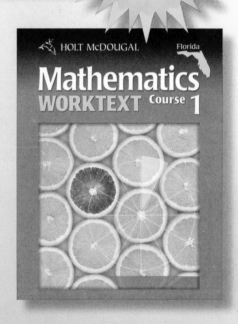

HOLT McDOUGAL   Florida
Mathematics
WORKTEXT Course **1**

 Online Edition

Everything you need for success at the click of a mouse.

- Complete Student Edition and Worktext
- Lesson Tutorial Videos
  Course 1: **231** videos
  Course 2: **272** videos
  Course 3: **269** videos
- Animated Math
- PowerPoint® Presentations
- Homework Help Online
- Intervention and enrichment exercises
- Online Tools
  Graphing calculator
  Virtual Manipulatives
  Multi–Language Glossary

www.thinkcentral.com

Award–winning. Entertaining. Enlightening.

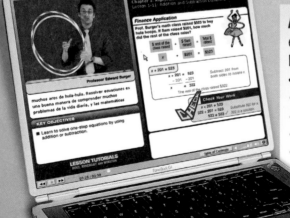

Lesson Tutorial Videos illustrate every lesson example in the Student Edition and Worktext.

- Teacher-at-your-fingertips
- Never get behind when you are absent
- Great way to review for tests
- Support for parent tutors
- Spanish closed captioning

HOLT McDOUGAL

Florida

Mathematics
Course 1

Jennie M. Bennett

Edward B. Burger

David J. Chard

Earlene J. Hall

Paul A. Kennedy

Freddie L. Renfro

Tom W. Roby

Janet K. Scheer

Cathy L. Seeley

Bert K. Waits

HOLT McDOUGAL
a division of Houghton Mifflin Harcourt

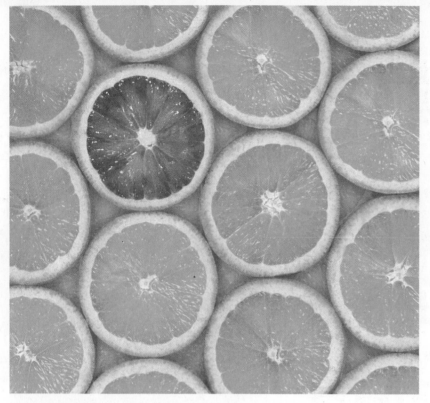

Cover Photography: (oranges background) © Image Source/Punchstock; (blood orange) © Teubner/Getty Images.

ISBN 978-0-554-01553-8

ISBN 0-554-01553-6

23456789 0868 15 14 13 12 11 10

50000000980653

Authors

Jennie M. Bennett, Ed.D., is a recently retired mathematics teacher at Hartman Middle School in Houston, Texas. She is past president of the Benjamin Banneker Association, the former First Vice-President of NCSM, and a former board member of NCTM. .

Edward B. Burger, Ph.D., is Professor of Mathematics at Williams College and is the author of numerous articles, books, and videos. He has won many prestigious writing and teaching awards offered by the Mathematical Association of America. Dr. Burger has made numerous media appearances and mathematical presentations around the world.

David J. Chard, Ph.D., is the Leon Simmons Endowed Dean of the School of Education and Human Development at Southern Methodist University. He has been a leader in the Council for Exceptional Children, a member of the International Academy for Research on Learning Disabilities, and the principal researcher for numerous U.S. Department of Education projects.

Earlene J. Hall, Ed.D., is the Middle School Mathematics Supervisor for the Detroit Public Schools district. She teaches graduate courses in Mathematics Leadership at University of Michigan Dearborn. Dr. Hall has traveled extensively throughout Africa and China and has made numerous presentations. She is a member of the NCTM 2009 Yearbook Panel.

Paul A. Kennedy, Ph.D., is a professor and Distinguished University Teaching Scholar in the Department of Mathematics at Colorado State University. Dr. Kennedy is a leader in mathematics education. His research focuses on developing algebraic thinking by using multiple representations and technology. He is the author of numerous publications and the recipient of many teaching and scholarship awards.

Freddie L. Renfro, MA, has 35 years of experience in Texas education as a classroom teacher and director/coordinator of Mathematics PreK-12 for school districts in the Houston area. She has served as a reviewer and TXTEAM trainer for Texas Math Institutes and has presented at numerous math workshops.

Tom W. Roby, Ph.D., is Associate Professor of Mathematics and Director of the Quantitative Learning Center at the University of Connecticut. He founded and co-directed the Bay Area-based ACCLAIM professional development program. He also chaired the advisory board of the California Mathematics Project and reviewed content for the California Standards Tests.

Janet K. Scheer, Ph.D., Executive Director of Create A Vision™, is a motivational speaker and provides customized K-12 math staff development. She has taught and supervised internationally and nationally at all grade levels.

Cathy L. Seeley has worked for over 35 years in K-12 education as a mathematics teacher, district mathematics coordinator, and state mathematics supervisor. She served as President of the National Council of Teachers of Mathematics and is currently a senior fellow with the Charles A. Dana Center at the University of Texas, working on state and national policy issues related to school mathematics.

Bert K. Waits, Ph.D., is a Professor Emeritus of Mathematics at The Ohio State University and cofounder of T^3 (Teachers Teaching with Technology), a national professional development program. Dr. Waits is also a former board member of NCTM and an author of the original NCTM Standards.

Florida Teacher Advisory Panel

Sally Andersen
Math Teacher
Swift Creek Middle School
Tallahassee, FL

Dawn Bourdette
Math Teacher
Silver Sands Middle School
Port Orange, FL

Jennifer Byrd
Math Teacher
Suwannee Middle School
Live Oak, FL

Carolyn Costello
Math Teacher/Department Chair
L.A. Ainger Middle School
Rotonda West, FL

Karen Fleeman
Math Teacher
South Fork High School
Stuart, FL

Danni Greenberg
District Resource Teacher
Hillsborough County Public
    Schools
Tampa, FL

Fred Kaouk
Math Teacher
Pineridge Middle School
Naples, FL

Delia H. Pogorzelski
Math Teacher
Raa Middle School
Tallahassee, FL

Marta P. Pratt
Gifted Math Teacher
Gulf Middle School
Cape Coral, FL

Rebecca A. Shine
Math Teacher
Andrew Jackson Middle School
Titusville, FL

Julie Stiens
Math Teacher
Benito Middle School
Tampa, FL

Dori White
Math Teacher
Sawgrass Springs Middle School
Coral Springs, FL

Tallahassee
Live Oak
Port Orange
Titusville
Tampa
Stuart
Rotonda West
Cape Coral
Coral Springs
Naples

Miami skyline

Florida Reviewers

Sally Andersen
Math Teacher
Swift Creek Middle School
Tallahassee, FL

Judy Broughton
Math Teacher
Poplar Street Middle School
North Little Rock, AR

Jennifer Byrd
Math Teacher
Suwannee Middle School
Live Oak, FL

Carolyn Costello
Math Teacher/Department
    Chair
L.A. Ainger Middle School
Rotonda West, FL

Troy Deckebach
Math Teacher
Wissahickon Middle School
Ambler, PA

Karen Fleeman
Math Teacher
South Fork High School
Stuart, FL

Maridith Gebhart
Math Teacher
Ramay Junior High School
Fayetteville, AR

Danni Greenberg
District Resource Teacher
Hillsborough County Public
    Schools
Tampa, FL

Ruth Harbin-Miles
District Math Coordinator–
    Retired
Instructional Resource Center
Olathe, KS

Kim Hayden
Intervention Specialist
Clermont County School District
Milford, OH

Rhoni Herrell
Math Teacher
DeWitt Waller Junior High
Enid, OK

Becky Lowe
Math Teacher
Bartlesville Mid-High
Bartlesville, OK

George Maguschak
Math Teacher/Building
    Chairperson
Wilkes-Barre Area
Wilkes-Barre, PA

Samantha McGlennen
Math Teacher/Department
    Coordinator
Summit Middle School
Fort Wayne, IN

Diane McIntire
Math Teacher–Retired
Garfield School
Kearny, NJ

Kenneth McIntire
Math Teacher
Lincoln School
Kearny, NJ

Tim Messal
Math Teacher/Department
    Chair
Woodside Middle School
Fort Wayne, IN

Vicki Perryman Petty
Math Teacher
Central Middle School
Murfreesboro, TN

Delia H. Pogorzelski
Math Teacher
Raa Middle School
Tallahassee, FL

Marta P. Pratt
Gifted Math Teacher
Gulf Middle School
Cape Coral, FL

Laronda Raines-Langham
Math Teacher
McAdory Elementary School
McCalla, AL

Rene Rush
Math Teacher
Colonial Heights Middle School
Colonial Heights, VA

Jennifer Sawyer
Math Teacher
Sawboro, NC

Shelly Schram
Math Teacher
East Grand Rapids Middle
    School
East Grand Rapids, MI

Richard Seavey
Math Teacher–Retired
Metcalf Junior High
Eagan, MN

Rebecca A. Shine
Math Teacher
Andrew Jackson Middle School
Titusville, FL

Gail Sigmund
Math Teacher–Retired
Charles A. Mooney Preparatory
    School
Cleveland, OH

Jeffrey Slagel
Math Department Chair–Retired
    South Eastern Middle
    SchoolFawn Grove, PA

Julie Stiens
Math Teacher
Benito Middle School
Tampa, FL

Paul Turney
Math Teacher
Ladue School District
St. Louis, MO

Dave Warren
Math Teacher
Meridian Middle School
Meridian, ID

Marilyn Wheeler
Math Teacher
Cityside Middle School
Zeeland, MI

The State Capitol in Tallahassee

Florida seagull

Florida flora

Sunshine State Standards and Benchmarks for Grade 6

Florida's mathematics benchmarks have the following coding scheme:

MA.	6.	A.	1.	1
Subject	Grade level	Body of Knowledge	Big Idea / Supporting Idea	Benchmark

Body of Knowledge Key:

A ~ Algebra

G ~ Geometry

P ~ Probability

S ~ Statistics

BIG IDEA 1

Develop an understanding of and fluency with multiplication and division of fractions and decimals.

MA.6.A.1.1 Explain and justify procedures for multiplying and dividing fractions and decimals.

MA.6.A.1.2 Multiply and divide fractions and decimals efficiently.

MA.6.A.1.3 Solve real-world problems involving multiplication and division of fractions and decimals.

The state bird is the mockingbird

The orange blossom is the state flower

BIG IDEA 2

Connect ratio and rates to multiplication and division.

MA.6.A.2.1 Use reasoning about multiplication and division to solve ratio and rate problems.

MA.6.A.2.2 Interpret and compare ratios and rates.

Continued

Bridges, Florida Keys

Florida alligator, Everglades National Park

BIG IDEA 3

Write, interpret, and use mathematical expressions and equations.

MA.6.A.3.1 Write and evaluate expressions that correspond to given situations.

MA.6.A.3.2 Write, solve, and graph one- and two-step linear equations and inequalities.

MA.6.A.3.3 Works backward with two-step function rules to undo expressions.

MA.6.A.3.4 Solve problems given a formula.

MA.6.A.3.5 Apply the Commutative, Associative, and Distributive Properties to show that two expressions are equivalent.

MA.6.A.3.6 Construct and analyze tables, graphs and equations to describe linear functions and other simple relations using both common language and algebraic notation.

SUPPORTING IDEAS

GEOMETRY AND MEASUREMENT

MA.6.G.4.1 Understand the concept of π, know common estimates of π (3.14; 22/7) and use these values to estimate and calculate the circumference and the area of circles.

MA.6.G.4.2 Find the perimeters and areas of composite two-dimensional figures, including non-rectangular figures (such as semicircles) using various strategies.

MA.6.G.4.3 Determine a missing dimension of a plane figure or prism, given its area or volume and some of the dimensions, or determine the area or volume given the dimensions.

Continued

Florida pine trees

Florida *the sunshine state*

NUMBER AND OPERATIONS

MA.6.A.5.1 Use equivalent forms of fractions, decimals, and percents to solve problems.

MA.6.A.5.2 Compare and order fractions, decimals, and percents, including finding their approximate location on a number line.

MA.6.A.5.3 Estimate the results of computations with fractions, decimals, and percents and judge the reasonableness of the results.

Florida Sunshine State Standards and Benchmarks for Grade 6

FL7

DATA ANALYSIS

MA.6.S.6.1 Determine the measures of central tendency (mean, median, and mode) and variability (range) for a given set of data.

MA.6.S.6.2 Select and analyze the measures of central tendency or variability to represent, describe, analyze and/or summarize a data set for the purpose of answering questions appropriately.

Continued

Miami skyline

LANGUAGE ARTS

LA.6.1.6.5 The student will relate new vocabulary to familiar words.

LA.6.4.2.2 The student will record information (e.g., observations, notes, lists, charts, legends) related to a topic, including visual aids to organize and record information and include a list of sources used.

Apalachicola National Forest

Florida orange trees

Florida panther

Daytona International Speedway

Preparing for Florida Standards Assessment

Holt McDougal Florida Mathematics provides many opportunities for you to prepare for your Florida Standards Assessment.

Florida Spiral Review

Use the Florida Spiral Review exercises for daily practice of standards-based questions in various formats.

Multiple Choice— choose your answer.

Gridded Response—write your answer in a grid and fill in the corresponding bubbles.

Short Response—write open-ended responses that are scored with a 2-point rubic.

Extended Response—write open-ended responses that are scored with a 4-point rubric.

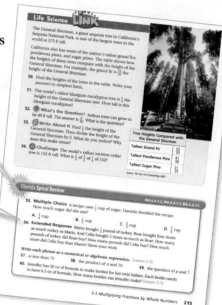

Test Tackler

Use the Test Tackler to become familiar with and practice test-taking strategies.

The first page of this feature explains and shows an example of a test-taking strategy.

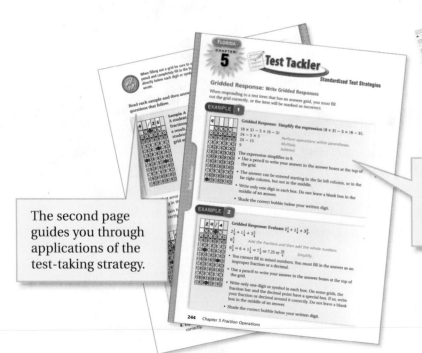

The second page guides you through applications of the test-taking strategy.

Mastering the Standards

Use **Mastering the Standards** to review standards taught in the current and previous chapters in test-taking formats.

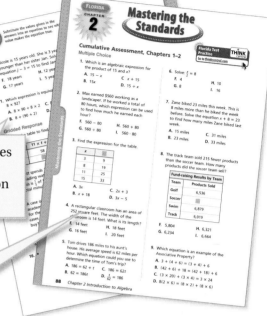

The **Hot Tip** provides test-taking tips to help you succeed on your tests.

These pages include practice with multiple choice, gridded response, short response, and extended response test items.

Countdown to Standards Assessment

Use the **Countdown to Standards Assessment** for daily standards practice in test-taking formats.

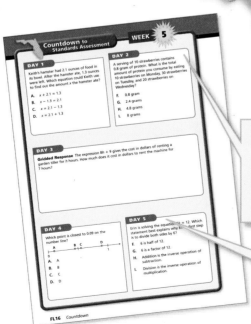

These are 24 pages of practice for your state test. Each page is designed to be used in a week so that all practice will be completed before the Florida state assessment is given.

Each week's page has five practice test items, one for each day of the week.

Countdown to Standards Assessment

DAY 1

Which equation shows an example of the Associative Property?

A. $7 \times (4 \times 12) = 7 \times (12 \times 4)$

B. $7 \times (4 \times 12) = (7 \times 4) \times 12$

C. $7 \times (4 \times 12) = 7 \times 48$

D. $7 \times (4 \times 12) = (4 \times 12) \times 7$

DAY 2

Which equation shows an example of the Distributive Property?

F. $(5 \times 7) + (5 \times 8) = 5 \times (7 \times 8)$

G. $(5 \times 7) + (5 \times 8) = 5 \times (7 + 8)$

H. $(5 \times 7) + (5 \times 8) = 5 + (7 \times 8)$

I. $(5 \times 7) + (5 \times 8) = 5 + (7 + 8)$

DAY 3

Which is the best estimate of 5.89×0.53?

A. 0.3 **C.** 12

B. 3 **D.** 25

DAY 4

Gridded Response Jerome uses metal strips to make rectangular frames that are 8.5 inches long and 4.25 inches wide. What is the total length in inches of the metal needed to make 5 frames?

DAY 5

Which of the following numbers has a value between 0 and $\frac{1}{2}$?

F. 0.09

G. 0.90

H. $\frac{2}{3}$

I. 1.1

DAY 1

Jeffrey used the following steps to find the product 25 × 7 × 4 mentally:

Step 1   25 × 7 × 4 = 25 × 4 × 7

Step 2   = 100 × 7

Step 3   = 700

Which property did Jeffrey use in Step 1?

A.   Commutative

B.   Associative

C.   Identity

D.   Distributive

DAY 2

Gridded Response Joan walked 6 miles in 2 hours. In the formula $d = r \times t$, d represents distance traveled, r represents rate, and t represents time. Use the formula to find Joan's rate in miles per hour.

DAY 3

Which expression gives the missing value in the table?

F. $3x$

G. $x + 4$

H. $2x + 2$

I. $4x - 4$

Lydia's Age	Sarah's Age
2	6
3	7
4	8
x	▨

DAY 4

Cougar Park is a rectangle with a length of 0.6 mile. Its area is 0.12 square mile. What is the width of the park?

A.   0.2 mile

B.   0.48 mile

C.   0.5 mile

D.   0.72 mile

DAY 5

Let m represent the number of miles Tomas biked last week. He biked 6 miles fewer this week. Which expression shows the number of miles he biked this week?

F. $6m$

G. $6 - m$

H. $m - 6$

I. $m + 6$

DAY 1

Gridded Response A sleeping bag is on sale for $39.97 after tax. Georgia buys two sleeping bags and pays for them with a $100 bill. How much change in dollars should Georgia receive?

DAY 2

The table shows the number of gallons a typical heart pumps in different amounts of time. What expression can you use to find the number of gallons a heart pumps in h hours?

Hours	Gallons
1	80
2	160
3	240
4	320

A. $h + 80$

B. $80 \div h$

C. $\frac{h}{80}$

D. $80h$

DAY 3

Sandy drove to her aunt's house. The expression $203 \div t$ represents her average speed in miles per hour, where t is in hours. If she took 3.5 hours to drive to her aunt's house, what was her average speed?

F. 45 miles per hour

G. 58 miles per hour

H. 54.5 miles per hour

I. 62 miles per hour

DAY 4

Ty buys 3 notebooks and a compass for school. The notebooks are $0.89 each, and the compass is $2.19. Which is the best estimate for the cost of these items?

A. $3

B. $5

C. $7

D. $9

DAY 5

There are s students in Mr. Chen's class. Each student brought in 10 pennies for a math project. Mr. Chen brought in 25 pennies for the project. What expression can you use to find the total number of pennies in the class?

F. $10s + 25$

G. $s + 10 + 25$

H. $25s + 10$

I. $25 \times 10s$

DAY 1

Chuck is 2 inches shorter than his sister, Jan. If j is Jan's height, what equation can you use to find Chuck's height c?

A. $j + 2 = c$

B. $c - j = 2$

C. $c = j - 2$

D. $c = 2j$

DAY 2

Cara wants to cover a wall with fabric. The wall is 19.25 feet by 49.75 feet. About how much fabric should Cara buy?

19.25 ft

49.75 ft

F. 450 square feet

G. 600 square feet

H. 850 square feet

I. 1,000 square feet

DAY 3

Alicia bought n notebooks that cost $3 each. She paid for the notebooks with a $20 bill. Assuming there is no sales tax, what expression shows the amount of change Alicia should receive?

A. $3n - 20$

B. $20 - 3 - n$

C. $3n + 20$

D. $20 - 3n$

DAY 4

Gridded Response There are several spiders in Joy's attic. Each spider has 8 legs, and there is a total of 72 spider legs in the attic. Solve the equation $72 = 8s$ to find how many spiders there are in the attic.

DAY 5

What expression gives the missing value in the table?

Kirk's Age	9	10	11	12	n
Sandra's Age	14	15	16	17	?

F. $n - 5$

G. $n + 5$

H. $5n$

I. $n \div 5$

DAY 1

Keith's hamster had 2.1 ounces of food in its bowl. After the hamster ate, 1.3 ounces were left. Which equation could Keith use to find out the amount x the hamster ate?

A. $x + 2.1 = 1.3$

B. $x - 1.3 = 2.1$

C. $x = 2.1 - 1.3$

D. $x = 2.1 + 1.3$

DAY 2

A serving of 10 strawberries contains 0.8 gram of protein. What is the total amount of protein you consume by eating 10 strawberries on Monday, 30 strawberries on Tuesday, and 20 strawberries on Wednesday?

F. 0.8 gram

G. 2.4 grams

H. 4.8 grams

I. 8 grams

DAY 3

Gridded Response The expression $8h + 9$ gives the cost in dollars of renting a garden tiller for h hours. How much does it cost in dollars to rent the machine for 7 hours?

DAY 4

Which point is closest to 0.09 on the number line?

A. A

B. B

C. C

D. D

DAY 5

Erin is solving the equation $6k = 12$. Which statement best explains why Erin's first step is to divide both sides by 6?

F. 6 is half of 12.

G. 6 is a factor of 12.

H. Addition is the inverse operation of subtraction.

I. Division is the inverse operation of multiplication.

DAY 1

The table shows the batting averages for four players after the first 6 games of the season. Which player has the greatest batting average?

A. Webster

B. Charles

C. Dan

D. Hector

Player	Average
Webster	0.098
Charles	0.400
Dan	0.667
Hector	0.298

DAY 2

The manager of a furniture store bought 25 vases at a total cost of $450. She plans to sell each vase for $23. What is the fewest number of vases she must sell in order to make a profit?

F. 19

G. 20

H. 23

I. 25

DAY 3

If Sarah wants to buy a dozen roses and two dozen irises, how much will she spend?

Flower prices (per dozen)	
Roses	$15.99
Irises	$6.75

A. $9.24

B. $22.74

C. $29.49

D. $31.98

DAY 4

Gridded Response Each side of Square A measures 6.4 centimeters. Each side of Square B measures 3.2 centimeters. How much greater in square centimeters is the area of Square A than Square B?

DAY 5

Kris has four pet turtles. Last week he measured each turtle. What is the order of the turtles from shortest to longest?

Turtle	Length (in.)
Bennie	5.67
Charley	5.75
Patty	5.07
Carly	5.5

F. Carly, Patty, Bennie, Charley

G. Patty, Bennie, Charley, Carly

H. Patty, Carly, Bennie, Charley

I. Bennie, Patty, Carly, Charley

DAY 1

Gridded Response A rectangle has a length of 15.6 meters and a perimeter of 56.88 meters. What is the width of the rectangle in meters?

DAY 2

Barb is making gift baskets for each of her teachers. Which expression gives the missing value in the table?

Gift Baskets	4	5	6	x
Number of Muffins	12	15	18	■

A. $x + 3$

B. $x + 4$

C. $2x$

D. $3x$

DAY 3

Monica is 5 years younger than twice her brother's age. Let b represent her brother's age. Which expression represents Monica's age?

F. $2b - 5$

G. $2(b - 5)$

H. $5 - \frac{1}{2}b$

I. $\frac{1}{2}b - 5$

DAY 4

The distance from Denver to Tulsa is 694 miles. Serena drives at an average speed of 51.1 miles per hour. About how many hours will the drive take?

A. 8 hours

B. 12 hours

C. 14 hours

D. 16 hours

DAY 5

For which equation is $n = 6$ NOT a solution?

F. $5 + n = 11$

G. $\frac{n}{2} = 12$

H. $48 = 8n$

I. $n - 6 = 0$

DAY 1

The formula $C = \frac{5}{9}(F - 32)$ gives the Celsius temperature (C) when the Fahrenheit temperature is F degrees. The average minimum temperature in January in Miami is 59 °F. What is the temperature in degrees Celsius?

A. 0.78 °C

B. 3 °C

C. 15 °C

D. 27 °C

DAY 2

Claire buys 1.5 pounds of asparagus. The asparagus costs $2.49 per pound. How much does Claire pay for the asparagus?

F. $3.74

G. $3.99

H. $4.45

I. $4.98

DAY 3

What is the solution of the equation $124 = v + 31$?

A. $v = 4$

B. $v = 93$

C. $v = 155$

D. $v = 3{,}844$

DAY 4

A magazine has p pages. A stack of 15 copies of the magazine has a total of 960 pages. What equation can you use to find the number of pages in the magazine?

F. $15 \div p = 960$

G. $p \div 15 = 960$

H. $15p = 960$

I. $960p = 15$

DAY 5

Gridded Response What is the area of the figure in square inches?

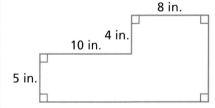

DAY 1

Let d represent the length of Lee's vacation in days. Which expression shows the length of her vacation in weeks?

A. $d + 7$

B. $7d$

C. $\frac{d}{7}$

D. $7 \div d$

DAY 2

If the relationship between x and y shown in the table is true for all values of x, what does y equal when x equals 39?

x	25	23	21	19
y	16	14	12	10

F. $y = 20$

G. $y = 30$

H. $y = 40$

I. $y = 48$

DAY 3

The shaded portion of the model at the right represents a fraction. What is this fraction written as a decimal?

A. 0.4

B. $0.\overline{4}$

C. 0.49

D. $0.\overline{5}$

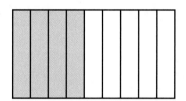

DAY 4

A geologist has four rock samples whose masses are 1.2 kilograms, 1.48 kilograms, 1.55 kilograms, and 1.6 kilograms. She needs a sample whose mass is as close as possible to $1\frac{1}{2}$ kilograms. Which sample should she use?

F. 1.2 kilograms

G. 1.48 kilograms

H. 1.55 kilograms

I. 1.6 kilograms

DAY 5

Gridded Response Let a represent the distance from Miami to Orlando, in miles. The expression $3a - 351$ gives the distance from Miami to Jacksonville. It is 232 miles from Miami to Orlando. How far is it in miles from Miami to Jacksonville?

DAY 1

Eric's science class grew plants from bean seeds. The table shows how much each student's plant grew in two weeks. Put the plants in order from least change to greatest change.

A. $\frac{1}{2}, \frac{5}{12}, \frac{3}{16}, \frac{1}{8}, \frac{4}{5}$

B. $\frac{1}{8}, \frac{3}{16}, \frac{5}{12}, \frac{1}{2}, \frac{4}{5}$

C. $\frac{1}{2}, \frac{4}{5}, \frac{1}{8}, \frac{5}{12}, \frac{3}{16}$

D. $\frac{1}{2}, \frac{1}{8}, \frac{3}{16}, \frac{4}{5}, \frac{5}{12}$

Student	Miguel	Eric	Jane	Trisha	Cindy
Plant Heights (in.)	$\frac{1}{2}$	$\frac{5}{12}$	$\frac{3}{16}$	$\frac{1}{8}$	$\frac{4}{5}$

DAY 2

The table shows the results of a survey of 40 people who were asked to choose their favorite fruit. Which fraction shows the number of people who named strawberry?

Fruit	Number of People
Apple	18
Orange	10
Strawberry	12

F. $\frac{1}{4}$

G. $\frac{3}{10}$

H. $\frac{9}{20}$

I. $\frac{11}{20}$

DAY 3

Which number is between $\frac{3}{4}$ and $\frac{11}{12}$?

A. $\frac{9}{12}$

B. $\frac{5}{6}$

C. $\frac{2}{3}$

D. $\frac{7}{12}$

DAY 4

Gridded Response About $\frac{1}{40}$ of the water on Earth is fresh water and therefore suitable for drinking. How can you write $\frac{1}{40}$ as a decimal?

DAY 5

The table shows the amount of water needed to cook $\frac{1}{6}$ cup of several different grains. Which grain requires the greatest amount of water?

Cooking Instructions	
Grain	**Amount of Water**
Buckwheat	$\frac{1}{3}$ cup
Millet	$\frac{5}{12}$ cup
Oats	$\frac{2}{3}$ cup
Wild Rice	$\frac{1}{2}$ cup

F. Buckwheat   H. Oats

G. Millet   I. Wild Rice

DAY 1

Gridded Response A rectangular painting with a perimeter of 146 inches has a width of 19 inches. What is the length of the painting in inches?

DAY 2

The baseball field is $2\frac{7}{8}$ miles from Burger Bonanza, $3\frac{1}{4}$ miles from Frozen Fun, and $2\frac{3}{5}$ miles from Hot Dog Hut. Which correctly shows the relationships among the distances?

A. $2\frac{3}{5} < 2\frac{7}{8} < 3\frac{1}{4}$

B. $3\frac{1}{4} < 2\frac{3}{5} < 2\frac{7}{8}$

C. $2\frac{7}{8} < 2\frac{3}{5} < 3\frac{1}{4}$

D. $3\frac{1}{4} < 2\frac{7}{8} < 2\frac{3}{5}$

DAY 3

Mitch made a long sandwich for a birthday party. A guest cut off $\frac{2}{3}$ of the sandwich. Then another guest cut off $\frac{1}{2}$ of the remainder. After these two cuts, the sandwich was 4 inches long. What was the original length of the sandwich?

F. 12 inches   H. 18 inches

G. 16 inches   I. 24 inches

DAY 4

Which equation expresses the relationship between d, the number of dozen eggs that you buy, and n, the total number of eggs in your purchase?

A. $n = 12d$

B. $d = 12n$

C. $n = \frac{d}{12}$

D. $n = d + 12$

DAY 5

Mike has $8\frac{3}{4}$ feet of fishing line and Tomas has $1\frac{1}{2}$ times as much. How many feet of fishing line do they have together?

F. $10\frac{1}{4}$ feet

G. $13\frac{1}{8}$ feet

H. $20\frac{1}{4}$ feet

I. $21\frac{7}{8}$ feet

DAY 1

What value is missing from the table?

x	1	2	3	4	5
y	4	7	10	■	16

A. 8

B. 12

C. 13

D. 14

DAY 2

For which equation is $y = 7$ a solution?

F. $4(y - 5) = 23$

G. $3y + 11 = 22$

H. $5(8 - y) = 5$

I. $17 = 6y - 15$

DAY 3

Gridded Response A square inch is a square with sides that measure 1 inch. A square yard is a square with sides that measure 1 yard. How many square inches are there in 1 square yard?

DAY 4

It takes $1\frac{3}{4}$ cups of sauce to make one pizza. How many cups of sauce are needed to make $5\frac{1}{2}$ pizzas?

A. $5\frac{3}{8}$ cups

B. $7\frac{1}{4}$ cups

C. $9\frac{5}{8}$ cups

D. $12\frac{5}{6}$ cups

DAY 5

In Orlando, FL, a taxi costs $2 for the first $\frac{1}{4}$ mile and $0.25 for each additional $\frac{1}{4}$ mile. How much will a 3.5-mile trip cost?

F. $4

G. $5.25

H. $7.50

I. $9

DAY 1

Margie took the following steps to find the quotient of $4\frac{1}{6}$ and $2\frac{1}{3}$. Which step is missing?

Step 1	$4\frac{1}{6} \div 2\frac{1}{3}$
Step 2	$\frac{25}{6} \div \frac{7}{3}$
Step 3	
Step 4	$\frac{75}{42} = 1\frac{11}{14}$

A. $\frac{25}{6} \cdot \frac{3}{7}$ **C.** $\frac{6}{25} \div \frac{7}{3}$

B. $\frac{6}{25} \cdot \frac{7}{3}$ **D.** $\frac{25}{6} \div \frac{3}{7}$

DAY 2

Allison took three quizzes. Her scores on the first two quizzes were 6 and 9. The mean of her three scores was 8. What was her score on the third quiz?

F. 6

G. 7

H. 8

I. 9

DAY 3

The table shows the number of electoral votes for several states. Given that the median number of electoral votes for these states is 4.5, how many electoral votes does Nebraska have?

A. 2

B. 4

C. 5

D. 7

State	Electoral Votes
Hawaii	4
Kansas	6
Nebraska	?
Vermont	3

DAY 4

Carla has $3\frac{1}{3}$ times as many stamps in her collection as Holly. Andy has $2\frac{1}{2}$ times as many stamps as Carla. If Andy has 300 stamps in his collection, how many stamps does Holly have?

F. 36

G. 90

H. 120

I. 2,500

DAY 5

Gridded Response In most places, it is possible to see only 2,000 stars in the nighttime sky due to light pollution. This is $\frac{4}{15}$ as many stars as you can expect to see in the sky at Bryce Canyon National Park in Utah. How many stars can you expect to see at Bryce Canyon?

DAY 1

Which two measures best describe the price of a baseball cap?

Prices of Baseball Caps at Four Stores			
$15	$16	$15	$26

A. mode and mean

B. mode and median

C. mode and range

D. median and mean

DAY 2

Gridded Response If $m = 2.5$ and $n = 4.2$, what is the value of $8m - 3.5n$?

DAY 3

Which expression is equal to $7(a + 2b)$?

F. $7a + 2b$

G. $14ab$

H. $7a + 14b$

I. $7a + 9b$

DAY 4

On the first day of July, Juan deposited $200 at his bank. On the first day of every month after that, he deposited $100. How much money did he have in his account n months after he started?

A. $(200 + 100)n$

B. $200 + 100n$

C. $200n$

D. $100(n + 1)$

DAY 5

The dance club has 11 more members than the soccer club. There are 34 students in the soccer club. What equation can you solve to find the number of students in the dance club?

F. $d + 11 = 34$

G. $d + 34 = 11$

H. $d - 11 = 34$

I. $d = 34 - 11$

DAY 1

The Hawks' mean score in two football games was 26. They scored 18 points in the first game. How many points did they score in the second game?

A. 8

B. 22

C. 34

D. 44

DAY 2

Beth runs 5 times per week. Last week, she ran 3 miles, 5 miles, 6.5 miles, 3 miles, and 5 miles. What is the median of this data?

F. 3 miles

G. 4.5 miles

H. 5 miles

I. 6.5 miles

DAY 3

The table shows how much a seedling grew each day for five days. On which days did the seedling grow less than $\frac{3}{4}$ inches?

A. Monday and Friday

B. Tuesday and Wednesday

C. Wednesday and Thursday

D. Thursday and Friday

Day	M	T	W	Th	F
Growth (in.)	$\frac{4}{5}$	$\frac{5}{6}$	$\frac{7}{10}$	$\frac{5}{8}$	$\frac{4}{5}$

DAY 4

Gridded Response In the chess club, 50% of the students are girls. Of the girls, 50% are playing in a tournament. There are 7 girls from the club playing in the tournament. How many students are in the club altogether?

DAY 5

Mr. Andrews drove 186 miles in 3 hours. Which operation can you use to find Mr. Andrews' rate of speed, in miles per hour?

F. Addition

G. Subtraction

H. Proportion

I. Division

DAY 1

The figure shows a pattern of tiles on the top of a table. Jared writes the ratio of black tiles to white tiles as n:6. What is the value of n?

A.   1

B.   2

C.   3

D.   12

DAY 2

A hot-air balloon rises at 42.1 feet per minute. It descends at twice the rate that it rises. If it descends at a constant rate, how many feet will the hot-air balloon descend in 20 minutes?

F.   842 feet

G.   1,684 feet

H.   2,105 feet

I.   4,210 feet

DAY 3

There are 26 students in Ha's science class. The ratio of boys to girls in the class is 5:8. How many more girls than boys are in the class?

A.   5

B.   6

C.   8

D.   10

DAY 4

Gridded Response What is the mean number of candles sold per month?

Candles Sold Per Month

Jan.   Feb.   Mar.   Apr.

🕯 = 5 candles

DAY 5

The ratio of girls to boys at a summer camp is $\frac{2}{3}$. There are 20 children at the camp. How many girls are there?

F.   2

G.   8

H.   12

I.   16

DAY 1

A rope is 17 feet long. Natasha cuts the rope into pieces that are each $1\frac{3}{8}$ feet long. What is the maximum number of such pieces that she can cut from the rope?

A. 9

B. 12

C. 13

D. 15

DAY 2

In the 2004 Olympics, the ratio of gold medals to silver medals won by the team from Hungary was 4:3. The ratio of silver medals to bronze medals won by the team was 2:1. The team won 3 bronze medals. How many gold medals did they win?

F. 4

G. 6

H. 8

I. 12

DAY 3

Coach Wang bought 3 large pizzas for the softball team. The shaded pieces represent how much of each pizza was eaten. To the nearest percent, how much of the pizzas was NOT eaten?

A. 7%   B. 29%   C. 33%   D. 71%

DAY 4

Powell Gardens in Kansas City has a nature trail that is 3.25 miles long. Rosa takes a photo at the beginning and end of the trail and every 0.25 mile along the way. How many photos does she take?

F. 4

G. 12

H. 13

I. 14

DAY 5

Gridded Response Frank took six history exams. On each exam, the highest possible score was 100. His scores on the first five exams were 90, 82, 90, 93, and 85. The range of his scores was 19. What was Frank's score on the sixth exam?

DAY 1

Marianne earns money baby-sitting. When she baby-sits 3 hours, she earns $21; for 5 hours, she earns $35; and for 6 hours, she earns $42. Suppose h is the number of hours Marianne baby-sits and m is the amount she earns. Which equation describes the situation?

A. $m = 3h$

B. $m = h + 18$

C. $m = 7h$

D. $m = \frac{h}{7}$

DAY 2

A machine can make 10 widgets in 6 minutes. A worker sets the machine to make 15 widgets. A bell rings every 30 seconds while the widgets are being made. How many times does the bell ring while the 15 widgets are being made?

F.   9

G.   12

H.   15

I.   18

DAY 3

Gridded Response What is the solution of the equation $\frac{3}{4}k = 36$?

DAY 4

Which statement correctly places the numbers $\frac{1}{2}$, 20%, and 2 in order from least to greatest?

A. $20\% < \frac{1}{2} < 2$

B. $\frac{1}{2} < 20\% < 2$

C. $\frac{1}{2} < 2 < 20\%$

D. $20\% < 2 < \frac{1}{2}$

DAY 5

What is the mean of the number of TVs repaired in June, July, and August?

F.   14

G.   21

H.   28

I.   63

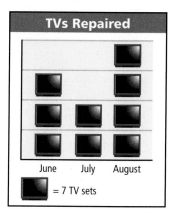

TVs Repaired

June   July   August

= 7 TV sets

DAY 1

In Derek's class, 18 of the 25 students belong to an after-school club. Which of the following describes the ratio of students NOT in an after-school club to students in an after-school club?

A. $\frac{7}{18}$

C. 25:18

B. 18 to 25

D. $\frac{7}{25}$

DAY 2

The radius of a circle is 18 inches. A snail crawls along the diameter of the circle at a rate of 3 inches per minute. How long does it take the snail to make the trip?

F. 3 minutes

G. 6 minutes

H. 9 minutes

I. 12 minutes

DAY 3

The picture shows the shirts Teresa owns. Teresa buys 6 more red shirts. How many blue shirts would she need to buy to keep the ratio of red shirts to blue shirts shown in the picture?

A. 2

C. 4

B. 3

D. 9

DAY 4

The ratio of male fish to female fish in an aquarium is 2:5. There are 6 male fish in the aquarium. How many fish are there altogether?

F. 14

H. 18

G. 15

I. 21

DAY 5

Gridded Response If 30 buses can carry 1,500 people, how many people can 5 buses carry?

DAY 1

Joan counted the number of robins she saw in her backyard each day last week.

9, 3, 6, 11, 8, 3, 7

Which two measures best describe the number of robins Joan saw each day?

A.   median and mean

B.   median and mode

C.   range and median

D.   mean and mode

DAY 2

Which expression best represents the value of y?

x	2	4	6	8	10
y	1	2	3	4	5

F. $x - 1$

G. $2x$

H. $\frac{x}{2}$

I. $x + 1$

DAY 3

In Katie's class, 65% of the students have a pet. What fraction of the class does NOT have a pet?

A. $\frac{7}{50}$

B. $\frac{7}{20}$

C. $\frac{1}{2}$

D. $\frac{13}{20}$

DAY 4

Gridded Response The width of a rectangle is 75% of the length. The length of the rectangle is 12 feet. What is the perimeter in feet of the rectangle?

DAY 5

If it takes Pat 4 hours to knit a child's cap, how many hours will it take to knit 3 caps?

4 hours   ? hours

F.   6 hours

G.   8 hours

H.   10 hours

I.   12 hours

DAY 1

What is the perimeter of the figure?

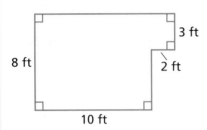

A. 23 feet

B. 28 feet

C. 35 feet

D. 40 feet

DAY 2

Before gym class, Mr. Reiger took 17 soccer balls out of the ball bin. There were 9 soccer balls left in the bin. Which equation can you use to find b, the number of balls that were in the bin before any were removed?

F. $b + 9 = 17$

G. $b - 9 = 17$

H. $b = 17 - 9$

I. $9b = 17$

DAY 3

Gridded Response The number of seconds it takes a machine to make a metal axle is given by the expression $6p^2 - 7.8$, where p is the weight of the metal in pounds. If the metal for an axle weighs 2.4 pounds, how long in seconds will it take the machine to make the axle?

DAY 4

What is the area of the shaded region?

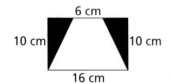

A. 25 square centimeters

B. 50 square centimeters

C. 110 square centimeters

D. 160 square centimeters

DAY 5

Jill drew a diagram of her room. What is the area of Jill's room?

F. 18 square feet

G. 36 square feet

H. 40 square feet

I. 80 square feet

DAY 1

An artist uses wood to make this circular disk. Approximately how much wood is needed to make the disk?

6 in.

A.   6 square inches

B.   9 square inches

C.   19 square inches

D.   28 square inches

DAY 2

A box of crackers is a rectangular prism with a volume of 128 cubic inches. The length of the box is 8 inches and the width is 4 inches. What is the height of the box?

F.   2 inches

G.   4 inches

H.   8 inches

I.   16 inches

DAY 3

Jimmy ran 0.82 mile. What distance in feet did he run?

A.   0.0001 foot

B.   433 feet

C.   4,329.6 feet

D.   6,439 feet

DAY 4

Ed calculated that the circumference of a circle is about 25.12 inches. What is the best estimate for the diameter of the circle?

F.   4 inches

G.   8 inches

H.   12.56 inches

I.   16 inches

DAY 5

Gridded Response What is the solution of the equation $\frac{n}{7} - 18 = 24$?

DAY 1

Gridded Response What is the area of the figure in square inches?

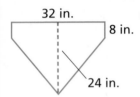

32 in.

8 in.

24 in.

DAY 2

A toy wheel has a diameter of $\frac{1}{3}$ foot. Which is the best estimate of the circumference of the wheel?

A. 0.5 foot

B. 1 foot

C. 1.5 feet

D. 2 feet

DAY 3

What is the area of this figure? Use 3.14 for π.

F. 127.68 square yards

G. 146.52 square yards

H. 542.16 square yards

I. 1,125 square yards

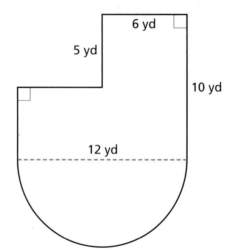

6 yd

5 yd

10 yd

12 yd

DAY 4

The rule for a certain function is to multiply by 2 and then subtract 3. What is the input value when the output value is 15?

A. 2

B. 3

C. 9

D. 15

DAY 5

Which equation describes the function in the table?

x	1	2	3	4
y	4	9	14	19

F. $y = x + 3$

G. $y = 4x$

H. $y = 3x + 1$

I. $y = 5x - 1$

DAY 1

A flower bed is 12 feet long and 4 feet wide. Judy covers 75% of the flower bed's area with mulch. How many square feet are covered with mulch?

A. 12 square feet

B. 24 square feet

C. 27 square feet

D. 36 square feet

DAY 2

Joe wants to add a baseboard all around the room shown in this diagram. How much wood does Joe need to buy?

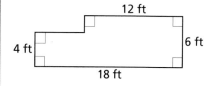

F. 24 feet   **H.** 54 feet

G. 48 feet   **I.** 128 feet

DAY 3

Solve the inequality. $x + 3 > 12$

A. $x > 0$

B. $x > 3$

C. $x > 9$

D. $x > 15$

DAY 4

Gridded Response Ted wants to make a small sandbox for his niece. The diagram shows the dimensions of the sandbox. How many cubic feet of sand will Ted need to fill the sandbox?

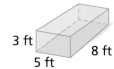

DAY 5

Julie earns $8 per hour shelving books in the library. On Saturday, she earned more than $50. Let n represent the number of hours she worked. Which expresses the relationship between the number of hours that she worked and her total earnings?

F. $8n = 50$

G. $50 > 8 \times n$

H. $8 = 50 + n$

I. $8n > 50$

Freedom Tower, Miami

Cape Canaveral

St. Augustine Lighthouse and Museum

Coral off Key Largo

Whole Numbers and Patterns

Table of Contents

Tools for Success

Reading and Writing Math

Reading Math 5
Writing Math 9, 13, 19, 23, 27
Vocabulary 6, 10, 16, 24

THINK central

Lesson Tutorial Videos 6, 10, 16, 20, 24
Animated Math 10, 16, 24
Homework Help Online 8, 12, 18, 22, 26

Mastering the Standards

Countdown Week 1
Florida Spiral Review 9, 13, 19, 23, 27
Test Tackler 36
Mastering the Standards 38

Chapter Resources
THINK central
Go to thinkcentral.com

Introduction to Algebra

Tools for Success

Reading Math 62, 63

Writing Math 43, 47, 51, 55, 59, 65, 69, 72, 76, 79

Vocabulary 44, 48, 62, 66

Lesson Tutorial Videos 44, 48, 52, 56, 62, 66, 70, 73, 77

Animated Math 48, 52, 62, 67, 70, 73, 77

Homework Help Online 46, 50, 54, 58, 64, 68, 71, 75, 78

Countdown Weeks 1, 2, 3, 4, 5

Florida Spiral Review 47, 51, 55, 59, 65, 69, 72, 76, 79

Mastering the Standards 88

Chapter Resources
THINK central
Go to **thinkcentral.com**

Decimals

Tools for Success

Reading Math 94

Writing Math 93, 97, 101, 105, 111, 114, 118, 121, 125

Vocabulary 98

Lesson Tutorial Videos 94, 98, 102, 108, 112, 115, 119, 122

Animated Math 94, 102, 122

Homework Help Online 96, 100, 104, 110, 113, 117, 120, 124

Countdown Weeks 6, 7, 8, 9

Florida Spiral Review 97, 101, 105, 111, 114, 118, 121, 125

Test Tackler 134

Mastering the Standards 136

Chapter Resources

Go to thinkcentral.com

Number Theory and Fractions

Tools for Success

Reading Math 141, 164
Writing Math 145, 149, 153, 159, 161, 163, 167, 171, 175, 179
Vocabulary 142, 146, 150, 156, 160, 164, 168

Lesson Tutorial Videos 142, 146, 150, 156, 160, 164, 168, 172, 176
Animated Math 142, 146, 156, 160, 164
Homework Help Online 144, 148, 152, 158, 162, 166, 170, 174, 178

Countdown Weeks 9, 10, 11
Florida Spiral Review 145, 149, 153, 159, 163, 167, 171, 175, 179
Mastering the Standards 188

Chapter Resources
Go to thinkcentral.com

Fraction Operations

Tools for Success

Reading and Writing Math

Writing Math 197, 201, 205, 209, 215, 219, 227, 231, 235

Vocabulary 194, 198, 224

THINK central

Lesson Tutorial Videos 194, 198, 202, 206, 212, 216, 220, 224, 228, 232

Animated Math 212, 216, 220, 228, 232

Homework Help Online 196, 200, 204, 208, 214, 218, 222, 226, 230, 234

Mastering the Standards

Countdown Weeks 11, 12, 13

Florida Spiral Review 197, 201, 205, 209, 215, 219, 223, 227, 231, 235

Test Tackler 244

Mastering the Standards 246

Chapter Resources

THINK central

Go to thinkcentral.com

FLORIDA

CHAPTER

6

Collecting and Displaying Data

Tools for Success

Reading Math 251, 263, 266
Writing Math 259, 265, 271, 275
Vocabulary 252, 256, 262, 266, 269, 272, 279

Lesson Tutorial Videos 252, 256, 262, 266, 269, 272, 276, 279
Animated Math 253, 256, 269, 276
Homework Help Online 254, 258, 264, 267, 270, 274, 277, 280

Countdown Weeks 13, 14, 15
Florida Spiral Review 255, 259, 265, 268, 271, 275, 278, 281
Mastering the Standards 290

Chapter Resources

THINK central

Go to thinkcentral.com

FLORIDA
CHAPTER
7

Proportional Relationships

Tools for Success

Reading Math 296, 304

Writing Math 295, 299, 303, 307, 313, 317, 321, 325, 329, 332, 335

Vocabulary 296, 304, 310, 322, 326, 330, 333

Lesson Tutorial Videos 296, 300, 304, 310, 314, 318, 322, 326, 330, 333

Animated Math 297, 305, 310, 314, 318, 322, 326, 330, 333

Homework Help Online 298, 302, 306, 312, 316, 320, 324, 328, 331, 334

Mastering the Standards

Countdown Weeks 15, 16, 17, 18, 19

Florida Spiral Review 299, 303, 307, 313, 317, 321, 325, 329, 332, 335

Test Tackler 344

Mastering the Standards 346

Chapter Resources
THINK central
Go to thinkcentral.com

FLORIDA
CHAPTER

8

Measurement and Geometry

Tools for Success

Writing Math 355, 359, 363, 367, 371, 377, 381

Vocabulary 352, 356, 374, 378

Lesson Tutorial Videos 352, 356, 360, 364, 368, 374, 378

Animated Math 356, 360, 374

Homework Help Online 354, 358, 362, 366, 370, 376, 380

Countdown Weeks 19, 20, 21

Florida Spiral Review 355, 359, 363, 367, 371, 377, 381

Mastering the Standards 390

Chapter Resources 

Go to thinkcentral.com

Measurement: Area and Volume

Tools for Success

Reading Math 395, 400

Writing Math 399, 403, 407, 411, 417, 421, 425, 429

Vocabulary 396, 414, 418, 426

Lesson Tutorial Videos 396, 400, 404, 408, 414, 418, 422, 426

Animated Math 401, 405, 414, 418, 422, 426

Homework Help Online 398, 402, 406, 410, 416, 420, 424, 428

Countdown Weeks 21, 22, 23

Florida Spiral Review 399, 403, 407, 411, 417, 421, 425, 429

Test Tackler 438

Mastering the Standards 440

Chapter Resources

Go to thinkcentral.com

Functions, Equations, and Inequalities

Tools for Success

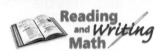

Writing Math 445, 449, 453, 460, 465, 469

Vocabulary 446, 450, 461

Lesson Tutorial Videos 446, 450, 456, 461, 466

Homework Help Online 448, 452, 458, 464, 468

Countdown Week 24

Florida Spiral Review 449, 453, 460, 465, 469

Mastering the Standards 478

Chapter Resources

Go to thinkcentral.com

Integers

Tools for Success

Reading Math 485

Writing Math 487, 491, 495, 498, 501, 504, 507, 511, 515

Vocabulary 484, 492, 512

Lesson Tutorial Videos 484, 488, 492, 498, 502, 505, 508, 512

Animated Math 498, 502

Homework Help Online 486, 490, 494, 500, 503, 506, 510, 514

Mastering the Standards

Florida Spiral Review 487, 491, 495, 501, 504, 507, 511, 515

Test Tackler 524

Mastering the Standards 526

Chapter Resources
THINK central
Go to **thinkcentral.com**

Student Resources

Scavenger Hunt

Holt McDougal Florida Mathematics is your resource to help you succeed. Use this scavenger hunt to discover some of the many tools Holt provides to help you be an independent learner. On a separate sheet of paper, fill in the blanks to answer each question below. In each answer, one letter will be in a yellow box. When you have answered every question, use the letters to fill in the blank at the bottom of the page.

1. Chapter 5's **Test Tackler** gives strategies for what kind of standardized test item?

2. What are you asked to solve in Chapter 4 **Game Time**?

3. What school subject is connected to math in the **Link** on page 307?

4. What **study strategy** is described on page 351?

5. What is the first key **vocabulary** term in the Study Guide: Preview for Chapter 6?

6. What is the topic of the **Real-World Connection** in Chapter 3?

7. What city is mentioned on page 2?

8. What is the last key **vocabulary** term in the Study Guide: Review for Chapter 6?

Math Humor

What did zero say to eight?

Focus on Problem Solving

The Problem Solving Process

In order to be a good problem solver, you first need a good problem-solving process. The process used in this book is detailed below.

UNDERSTAND the Problem

■ **What are you asked to find?** — Restate the problem in your own words.

■ **What information is given?** — Identify the facts in the problem.

■ **What information do you need?** — Determine which facts are needed to answer the question.

■ **Is all the information given?** — Determine whether all the facts are given.

■ **Is there any information given that you will not use?** — Determine which facts, if any, are unnecessary to solve the problem.

Make a PLAN

■ **Have you ever solved a similar problem?** — Think about other problems like this that you successfully solved.

■ **What strategy or strategies can you use?** — Determine a strategy that you can use and how you will use it.

SOLVE

■ **Follow your plan.** — Show the steps in your solution. Write your answer as a complete sentence.

LOOK BACK

■ **Have you answered the question?** — Be sure that you answered the question that is being asked.

■ **Is your answer reasonable?** — Your answer should make sense in the context of the problem.

■ **Is there another strategy you could use?** — Solving the problem using another strategy is a good way to check your work.

■ **Did you learn anything while solving this problem that could help you solve similar problems in the future?** — Try to remember the problems you have solved and the strategies you used to solve them.

Using the Problem Solving Process

During summer vacation, Nicholas will visit first his cousin and then his grandmother. He will be gone for 5 weeks and 2 days, and he will spend 9 more days with his cousin than with his grandmother. How long will he stay with each family member?

UNDERSTAND the Problem

Identify the important information.

- Nicholas's visits will total 5 weeks and 2 days.
- He will spend 9 more days with his cousin than with his grandmother.

The answer will be how long he will stay with each family member.

Make a PLAN

You can draw a diagram to show how long Nicholas will stay. Use boxes for the length of each stay. The length of each box will represent the length of each stay.

SOLVE

Think: There are 7 days in a week, so 5 weeks and 2 days is 37 days in all. Your diagram might look like this:

| Cousin | ? days | 9 days | = 37 days |

| Grandmother | ? days |

| Cousin | 14 days | 9 days | $37 - 9 = 28$ |

| Grandmother | 14 days | $28 \div 2 = 14$ |

So Nicholas will stay with his cousin for 23 days and with his grandmother for 14 days.

LOOK BACK

Twenty-three days is 9 days longer than 14 days. The total of the two stays is $23 + 14$, or 37 days, which is the same as 5 weeks and 2 days. This solution fits the description of Nicholas's trip given in the problem.

Using the Student Success System

Holt McDougal's Student Success System provides you with all the tools you need for in-depth understanding of the Next Generation Sunshine State Standards.

Textbook Tools

Learn

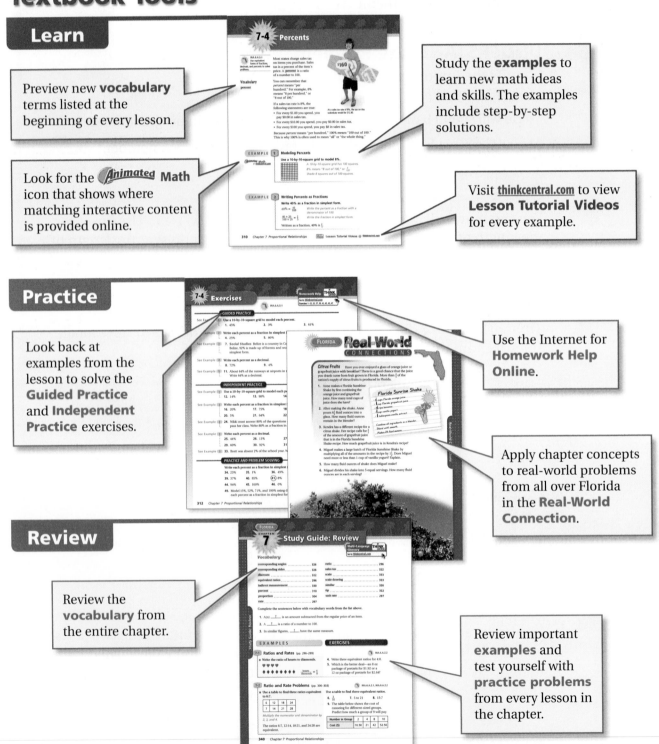

Preview new **vocabulary** terms listed at the beginning of every lesson.

Look for the **Animated** Math icon that shows where matching interactive content is provided online.

Study the **examples** to learn new math ideas and skills. The examples include step-by-step solutions.

Visit **thinkcentral.com** to view **Lesson Tutorial Videos** for every example.

Practice

Look back at examples from the lesson to solve the **Guided Practice** and **Independent Practice** exercises.

Use the Internet for **Homework Help Online**.

Apply chapter concepts to real-world problems from all over Florida in the **Real-World Connection**.

Review

Review the **vocabulary** from the entire chapter.

Review important **examples** and test yourself with **practice problems** from every lesson in the chapter.

The Worktext is a companion to your textbook that helps you gain in-depth knowledge of the standards using a 5-step process.

Worktext Tools

1 **Explore It!** Explore new concepts using models and other hands-on activities.

2 **Learn It!** Complete interactive examples and work Check It Out sample problems.

3 **Summarize It!** Summarize important concepts and complete graphic organizers using your own words.

4 **Practice It!** Complete exercises to practice standards taught in the lesson.

5 **Apply It!** Use lesson concepts to solve real-world problems.

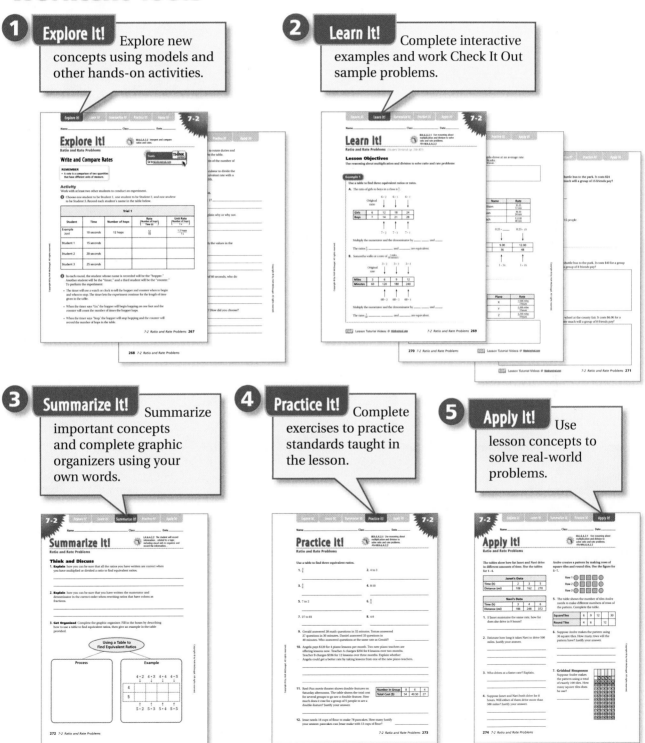

Whole Numbers and Patterns

Worktext
pages 1–2

Additional instruction, practice, and activities are available online, including:
- Lesson Tutorial Videos
- Homework Help
- Animated Math

THINK central

Go to <u>thinkcentral.com</u>

Why Learn This?

Numbers and patterns can be used to describe the world around us, such as the number of people who visit a beach or the pattern of the waves in the ocean.

Fort Lauderdale

Chapter Focus
- Use the order of operations to simplify expressions.
- Find possible rules for sequences.

Are You Ready?

Are You Ready? THINK central

Go to thinkcentral.com

✓ Vocabulary

Choose the best term from the list to complete each sentence.

1. The answer in a multiplication problem is called the _____?_____ .

2. 5,000 + 400 + 70 + 5 is a number written in _____?_____ form.

3. A(n) _____?_____ tells about how many.

4. The number 70,562 is written in _____?_____ form.

5. Ten thousands is the _____?_____ of the 4 in 42,801.

place value

estimate

product

expanded

standard

period

Complete these exercises to review skills you will need for this chapter.

✓ Compare Whole Numbers

Compare. Write < , >, or =.

6. 245 ▮ 219

7. 5,320 ▮ 5,128

8. 64 ▮ 67

9. 784 ▮ 792

✓ Round Whole Numbers

Round each number to the nearest hundred.

10. 567

11. 827

12. 1,642

13. 12,852

14. 1,237

15. 135

16. 15,561

17. 452,801

Round each number to the nearest thousand.

18. 4,709

19. 3,399

20. 9,825

21. 26,419

22. 12,434

23. 4,561

24. 11,784

25. 468,201

✓ Whole Number Operations

Add, subtract, multiply, or divide.

26. 18 × 22

27. 135 ÷ 3

28. 247 + 96

29. 358 − 29

✓ Simplify Numerical Expressions

Simplify each expression.

30. 3 × 4 × 2

31. 20 + 100 − 40

32. 5 × 20 ÷ 4

33. 6 × 12 × 5

Study Guide: Preview

Before

Previously, you

- compared and ordered whole numbers to the hundred thousands.
- used the order of operations without exponents.
- looked for patterns.

Now

You will study

- representing whole numbers by using exponents.
- using the order of operations, including exponents.
- how to choose a method of computation.
- how to recognize and extend sequences.

Why?

You can use the skills learned in this chapter

- to express numbers in scientific and standard notation in science classes.
- to recognize and extend geometric sequences.

Key Vocabulary/Vocabulario

base	base (en numeración)
exponent	exponente
numerical expression	expresión numérica
order of operations	orden de las operaciones
sequence	sucesión
term	término (en una sucesión)

Vocabulary Connections

To become familiar with some of the vocabulary terms in the chapter, consider the following. You may refer to the chapter, the glossary, or a dictionary if you like.

1. An *order* is the way things are arranged one after the other. How do you think an **order of operations** will help you solve math problems?

2. The word *numerical* means "of numbers." The word *expression* can refer to a mathematical symbol or combination of symbols. What do you think a **numerical expression** is?

3. A *sequence* is a list or arrangement that is in a particular order. What kind of **sequence** do you expect to see in this chapter?

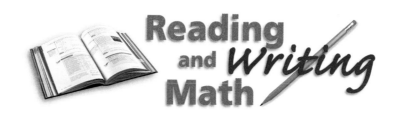

Reading and Writing Math

Reading Strategy: Use Your Book for Success

Understanding how your textbook is organized will help you locate and use helpful information.

As you read through an example problem, pay attention to the **margin notes,** such as Reading Math notes, Writing Math notes, Helpful Hints, and Caution notes. These notes will help you understand concepts and avoid common mistakes.

Reading Math
A group of four ta
marks with a line
through it means

Writing Math
To write a repeati
decimal, you can
show three dots

Helpful Hint
Estimating before
you add or subtra
will help you che

Caution!
When you write a
expression for dat
a table, check tha

The **Glossary** is found in the back of your textbook. Use it as a resource when you need the definition of an unfamiliar word or property.

The **Index** is located at the end of your textbook. Use it to locate the page where a particular concept is taught.

The **Skills Bank** is found in the back of your textbook. These pages review concepts from previous math courses, including geometry skills.

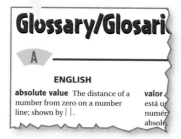

Glossary/Glosari

A

ENGLISH

absolute value The distance of a number from zero on a number line; shown by | |.

valor
está u
numér
absolu

Index

A

Aaron, Hank, 36
Abacus, 9
Absolute value, 762
Accuracy, 767

in sc
37
in sin
solvi
tiles, 63
variable
Algebra ti
Algebraic
writing
Alternate
Alternate
Alvin sub

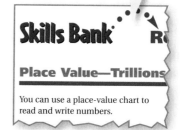

Skills Bank   R

Place Value—Trillions

You can use a place-value chart to read and write numbers.

Try This

Use your textbook.

1. Use the glossary to find the definitions of *function* and *ratio*.

2. Where in the Skills Bank can you review how to round decimals?

3. Use the Problem Solving Handbook to list the four steps of the problem-solving process and two different problem-solving strategies.

4. Use the index to find the pages where *Distributive Property* and *perimeter* appear.

Reading and Writing Math

1-1 Estimating with Whole Numbers

Prep for MA.6.A.5.3
Estimate the results of computations with fractions, decimals, and percents and judge the reasonableness of the results.
Review of MA.4.A.6.6

Vocabulary

estimate

compatible number

underestimate

overestimate

Sometimes in math you do not need an exact answer. Instead, you can use an *estimate*. **Estimates** are close to the exact answer but are usually easier and faster to find.

When estimating, you can round the numbers in the problem to *compatible numbers*. **Compatible numbers** are close to the numbers in the problem, and they can help you do math mentally.

"WELL, MAYBE UMPTEEN ZILLION WAS TOO GENERAL A COST ESTIMATE."

© Cartoon Stock

EXAMPLE 1 Estimating a Sum or Difference by Rounding

Estimate each sum or difference by rounding to the place value indicated.

5,439 + 7,516; thousands

A
$$\begin{array}{r} 5,000 \\ + 8,000 \\ \hline 13,000 \end{array}$$
 Round 5,439 down.
 Round 7,516 up.

The sum is about 13,000.

62,167 − 47,511; ten thousands

B
$$\begin{array}{r} 60,000 \\ - 50,000 \\ \hline 10,000 \end{array}$$
 Round 62,167 down.
 Round 47,511 up.

The difference is about 10,000.

> **Remember!**
> When rounding, look at the digit to the right of the place to which you are rounding.
> • If that digit is 5 or greater, round up.
> • If that digit is less than 5, round down.

An estimate that is less than the exact answer is an **underestimate**.

An estimate that is greater than the exact answer is an **overestimate**.

EXAMPLE 2

Estimating a Product by Rounding

Ms. Escobar is planning a graduation celebration for the entire eighth grade. There are 9 eighth-grade homeroom classes of 27 students. Estimate how many cups Ms. Escobar needs to buy for the students if they all attend the celebration.

Find the number of students in the eighth grade.

$9 \times 27 \rightarrow 9 \times 30$ *Overestimate the number of students.*

$9 \times 30 = 270$ *The actual number of students is **less than** 270.*

If Ms. Escobar buys 270 cups, she will have enough for every student.

EXAMPLE 3

Estimating a Quotient Using Compatible Numbers

Mrs. Byrd will drive 120 miles to take Becca to the state fair. She can drive 65 mi/h. About how long will the trip take?

To find how long the trip will be, divide the miles Mrs. Byrd has to travel by how many miles per hour she can drive.

miles ÷ miles per hour

$120 \div 65 \rightarrow 120 \div 60$ *120 and 60 are compatible numbers.*
    ***Underestimate** the speed.*

$120 \div 60 = 2$ *Because she **underestimated** the speed, the actual time will be **less than** 2 hours.*

It will take Mrs. Byrd about two hours to reach the state fair.

Think and Discuss

1. Suppose you are buying items for a party and you have $50. Would it be better to overestimate or underestimate the cost of the items?

2. Suppose your car can travel between 20 and 25 miles on a gallon of gas. You want to go on a 100-mile trip. Would it be better to overestimate or underestimate the number of miles per gallon your car can travel?

3. Describe situations in which you might want to estimate.

Homework Help

Go to **thinkcentral.com**
Exercises 1–12, 15, 17, 19, 21, 23, 25, 27

 Prep for MA.6.A.5.3

GUIDED PRACTICE

See Example **1**   Estimate each sum or difference by rounding to the place value indicated.

1. 4,689 + 2,469; thousands

2. 50,498 − 35,798; ten thousands

See Example **2**   **3.** The graph shows the number of bottles of water used in three bicycle races last year. If the same number of riders enter the races each year, estimate the number of bottles that will be needed for races held in May over the next five years.

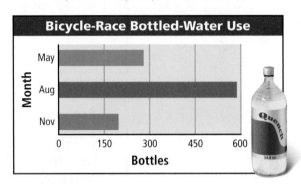

Bicycle-Race Bottled-Water Use

See Example **3**   **4.** If a local business provided half the bottled water needed for the August bicycle race, about how many bottles did the company provide?

5. Carla drives 80 miles on her scooter. If the scooter gets about 42 miles per gallon of gas, about how much gas did she use?

INDEPENDENT PRACTICE

See Example **1**   Estimate each sum or difference by rounding to the place value indicated.

6. 6,570 + 3,609; thousands

7. 49,821 − 11,567; ten thousands

8. 3,912 + 1,269; thousands

9. 37,097 − 20,364; ten thousands

See Example **2**   **10.** The recreation center has provided softballs every year to the city league. Use the table to estimate the number of softballs the league will use in 5 years.

See Example **3**   **11.** The recreation center has a girls' golf team with 8 members. About how many golf balls will each girl on the team get?

Recreation Center Balls Supplied	
Sport	Number of Balls
Basketball	21
Golf	324
Softball	28
Table tennis	95

12. If the recreation center loses about 4 table tennis balls per year, and they are not replaced, about how many years will it take until the center has none left?

PRACTICE AND PROBLEM SOLVING

Estimate each sum or difference by rounding to the greatest place value.

13. 152 + 269

14. 797 − 234

15. 242 − 179

16. 6,152 − 3,195

17. 9,179 + 2,206

18. 10,982 + 4,821

19. 82,465 − 38,421

20. 38,347 + 17,039

21. 51,201 + 16,492

22. 639,069 + 283,136

23. 777,060 − 410,364

24. 998,927 − 100,724

○ = WORKED-OUT SOLUTIONS
on p. WS2

Use the bar graph for Exercises 25–31.

25. On one summer day there were 2,824 sailboats on Lake Erie. Estimate the number of square miles available to each boat.

26. If the areas of all the Great Lakes are rounded to the nearest thousand, which two of the lakes would be the closest in area?

27. About how much larger is Lake Huron than Lake Ontario?

28. The Great Lakes are called "great" because of the huge amount of fresh water they contain. Estimate the total area of all the Great Lakes combined.

29. **?** **What's the Question?** Lake Erie is about 50,000 square miles smaller. What is the question?

30. **Write About It** Explain how you would estimate the areas of Lake Huron and Lake Michigan to compare their sizes.

31. **Challenge** Estimate the average area of the Great Lakes.

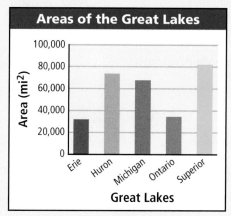

Area includes the water surface and drainage basin within the United States and Canada.

Florida Spiral Review   Prep for MA.6.A.5.3

32. **Multiple Choice** Which number is the best estimate for 817 + 259?

   A. 10,000   **B.** 2,000   **C.** 1,100   **D.** 800

33. **Short Response** The National Football League requires home teams to have 36 new footballs for outdoor games and 24 new footballs for indoor games. Estimate how many new footballs the Washington Redskins must buy for 8 outdoor games. Explain how you determined your estimate.

Find each product or quotient. (Previous Course)

34. $148 \div 4$ 35. 523×5 36. $1,054 \div 31$ 37. 312×8

Write each number in expanded form. (Previous Course)

38. 269   39. 1,354   40. 32,498   41. 416,703

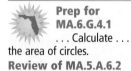

The most recent eruption of Mount Vesuvius took place in 1944.

Prep for MA.6.G.4.1
... Calculate ...
the area of circles.
Review of MA.5.A.6.2

Since 1906, the height of Mount Vesuvius in Italy has increased by about 7^3 feet. How many feet is this?

The number 7^3 is written with an exponent. An **exponent** tells how many times a number called the **base** is used as a factor.

Vocabulary

exponent

base

exponential form

Base → 7^3 = $7 \times 7 \times 7 = 343$ ← Exponent

So the height of Mount Vesuvius has increased by about 343 ft.

Animated Math @ thinkcentral.com

A number is in **exponential form** when it is written with a base and an exponent.

Exponential Form	Read	Multiply	Value
10^1	"10 to the 1st power"	10	10
10^2	"10 squared," or "10 to the 2nd power"	10×10	100
10^3	"10 cubed," or "10 to the 3rd power"	$10 \times 10 \times 10$	1,000
10^4	"10 to the 4th power"	$10 \times 10 \times 10 \times 10$	10,000

E X A M P L E **1** **Writing Numbers in Exponential Form**

Write each expression in exponential form.

A $4 \times 4 \times 4$

4^3 *4 is a factor 3 times.*

B $9 \times 9 \times 9 \times 9 \times 9$

9^5 *9 is a factor 5 times.*

E X A M P L E **2** **Finding the Value of Numbers in Exponential Form**

Find each value.

A 2^7

$2^7 = 2 \times 2 \times 2 \times 2 \times 2 \times 2 \times 2$

$= 128$

B 6^4

$6^4 = 6 \times 6 \times 6 \times 6$

$= 1,296$

EXAMPLE 3 PROBLEM SOLVING APPLICATION

If Dana's school closes, a phone tree is used to contact each student's family. The secretary calls 3 families. Then each family calls 3 other families, and so on. How many families will be notified during the 6th round of calls?

1. Understand the Problem

The **answer** will be the number of families called in the 6th round.

List the **important information:**
- The secretary calls 3 families.
- Each family calls 3 families.

2. Make a Plan

You can draw a diagram to see how many calls are in each round.

Secretary

1st round—3 calls

2nd round—9 calls

3. Solve

Notice that in each round, the number of calls is a power of 3.
1st round: 3 calls = 3 = 3^1
2nd round: 9 calls = 3 × 3 = 3^2

So during the **6**th round there will be 3^6 calls.
$3^6 = 3 \times 3 \times 3 \times 3 \times 3 \times 3 = 729$
During the 6th round of calls, 729 families will be notified.

4. Look Back

Drawing a diagram helps you visualize the pattern, but the numbers become too large for a diagram after the third round of calls. Solving this problem by using exponents can be easier and faster.

Think and Discuss

1. Read each number: 4^8, 12^3, 3^2.

2. Explain which has the greater value, 3^4 or 4^3.

Exercises

Homework Help

Go to thinkcentral.com
Exercises 1–32, 35, 37, 47, 49, 57, 59, 61

GUIDED PRACTICE

See Example ① Write each expression in exponential form.

1. $8 \times 8 \times 8$ **2.** 7×7 **3.** $6 \times 6 \times 6 \times 6 \times 6$

4. $4 \times 4 \times 4 \times 4$ **5.** $5 \times 5 \times 5 \times 5 \times 5$ **6.** 1×1

See Example ② Find each value.

7. 4^2 **8.** 3^3 **9.** 5^4 **10.** 8^2 **11.** 7^3

See Example ③ **12.** At Russell's school, one person will contact 4 people and each of those people will contact 4 other people, and so on. How many people will be contacted in the fifth round?

INDEPENDENT PRACTICE

See Example ① Write each expression in exponential form.

13. $2 \times 2 \times 2 \times 2 \times 2 \times 2$ **14.** $9 \times 9 \times 9 \times 9$ **15.** 8×8

16. $1 \times 1 \times 1$ **17.** $6 \times 6 \times 6 \times 6 \times 6$ **18.** $5 \times 5 \times 5$

19. $7 \times 7 \times 7 \times 7 \times 7 \times 7 \times 7$ **20.** $3 \times 3 \times 3 \times 3$ **21.** 4×4

See Example ② Find each value.

22. 2^4 **23.** 3^5 **24.** 6^2 **25.** 9^2 **26.** 7^4

27. 8^3 **28.** 1^4 **29.** 16^2 **30.** 10^8 **31.** 12^2

See Example ③ **32.** To save money for a video game, you put one dollar in an envelope. Each day for 5 days you double the number of dollars in the envelope from the day before. How much will be saved on the fifth day?

PRACTICE AND PROBLEM SOLVING

Write each expression as repeated multiplication.

33. 16^3 **34.** 22^2 **35.** 31^6 **36.** 46^5 **37.** 50^3

38. 4^1 **39.** 1^9 **40.** 17^6 **41.** 8^5 **42.** 12^4

Find each value.

43. 10^6 **44.** 73^1 **45.** 9^4 **46.** 80^2 **47.** 10^5

48. 19^2 **49.** 2^9 **50.** 57^1 **51.** 5^3 **52.** 11^3

Compare. Write <, >, or =.

53. 6^1 ▇ 5^1 **54.** 9^2 ▇ 20^1 **55.** 10^1 ▇ $1,000,000^1$

56. 7^3 ▇ 3^7 **57.** 5^5 ▇ 25^1 **58.** 100^2 ▇ 10^4

○ = **WORKED-OUT SOLUTIONS**
on p. WS2

You are able to grow because your body produces new cells. New cells are made when old cells divide. Single-celled bodies, such as bacteria, divide by *binary fission*, which means "splitting into two parts." A cycle is the length of time a cell needs to divide once.

59. In science lab, Carol has a dish containing 4^5 cells. How many cells are represented by this number?

60. A certain colony of bacteria triples in length every 15 minutes. Its length is now 1 mm. How long will it be in 1 hour? (*Hint:* There are four cycles of 15 minutes in 1 hour.)

Use the bar graph for Exercises 61–64.

61. Determine how many times cell type A will divide in a 24-hour period. If you begin with one type A cell, how many cells will be produced in 24 hours?

62. Multi-Step If you begin with one type B cell and one type C cell, what is the difference between the number of type B cells and the number of type C cells produced in 24 hours?

63. Write About It Explain how to find the number of type A cells produced in 48 hours.

64. Challenge How many hours will it take one C cell to divide into at least 100 C cells?

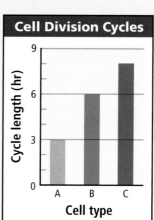

Cell Division Cycles

This plant cell shows the anaphase stage of mitosis. Mitosis is the process of nuclear division in complex cells called eukaryotes.

Florida Spiral Review Prep for MA.6.G.4.1, MA.6.A.5.3

65. Multiple Choice Which of the following shows the expression $4 \times 4 \times 4$ in exponential form?

A. 64   **B.** 444   **C.** 3^4 **D.** 4^3

66. Multiple Choice Which expression has the greatest value?

F. 2^5 **G.** 3^4 **H.** 4^3 **I.** 5^2

Order the numbers from least to greatest. (Previous Course)

67. 8,452; 8,732; 8,245   **68.** 991; 1,010; 984   **69.** 12,681; 11,901; 12,751

Estimate each sum or difference by rounding to the place value indicated. (Lesson 1-1)

70. 12,876 + 17,986; thousands   **71.** 72,876 − 15,987; ten thousands

Ready To Go On?
SECTION 1A

Quiz for Lessons 1-1 Through 1-2

 1-1 **Estimating with Whole Numbers**

Estimate each sum or difference by rounding to the place value indicated.

1. 61,582 + 13,281; ten thousands

2. 86,125 − 55,713; ten thousands

3. 7,903 + 2,654; thousands

4. 34,633 − 32,087; thousands

5. 1,896,345 + 3,567,194; hundred thousands

6. 56,129,482 − 37,103,758; ten millions

7. Marcus wants to make a stone walkway in his garden. The rectangular walkway will be 3 feet wide and 21 feet long. Each 2-foot by 3-foot stone covers an area of 6 square feet. How many stones will Marcus need?

8. Jenna's sixth-grade class is taking a bus to the zoo. The zoo is 156 miles from the school. If the bus travels an average of 55 mi/h, about how long will it take the class to get to the zoo?

9. Robin's class is contacting families from her school as part of a fundraiser. If there are 471 families at the school and 27 students in Robin's class, about how many families will each student contact?

 1-2 **Exponents**

Write each expression in exponential form.

10. $7 \times 7 \times 7$

11. $5 \times 5 \times 5 \times 5$

12. $3 \times 3 \times 3 \times 3 \times 3 \times 3$

13. $10 \times 10 \times 10 \times 10$

14. $1 \times 1 \times 1 \times 1 \times 1$

15. $4 \times 4 \times 4 \times 4$

Find each value.

16. 3^3

17. 2^4

18. 6^2

19. 8^3

20. To start reading a novel for English class, Sara read 1 page. Each day for 4 days she reads double the number of pages she read the day before. How many pages will she read on the fourth day?

Focus on Problem Solving

Solve

• Choose the operation: addition or subtraction

Read the whole problem before you try to solve it. Determine what action is taking place in the problem. Then decide whether you need to add or subtract in order to solve the problem.

If you need to combine or put numbers together, you need to add. If you need to take away or compare numbers, you need to subtract.

Action	Operation	Picture
Combining Putting together	Add	
Removing Taking away	Subtract	
Comparing Finding the difference	Subtract	

 Read each problem. Determine the action in each problem. Choose an operation in order to solve the problem. Then solve.

Most hurricanes that occur over the Atlantic Ocean, the Caribbean Sea, or the Gulf of Mexico occur between June and November. Since 1886, a hurricane has occurred in every month except April.

Number of Out-of-Season Hurricanes Since 1886	
Month	Number
Jan	1
Feb	1
Mar	1
May	14
Dec	10

Use the table for problems 1 and 2.

❶ How many out-of-season hurricanes have occurred in all?

❷ How many more hurricanes have occurred in May than in December?

❸ There were 14 named storms during the 2000 hurricane season. Eight of these became hurricanes, and three others became major hurricanes. How many of the named storms were not hurricanes or major hurricanes?

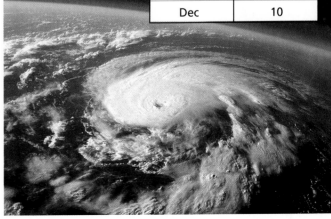

Focus on Problem Solving **15**

Order of Operations

**Prep for
MA.6.A.3.3** Works
backward with
two-step function rules to
undo expressions.
Review of MA.5.A.6.2

A **numerical expression** is a mathematical phrase that includes only numbers and operation symbols.

Numerical Expressions	$4 + 8 \div 2 \times 6$	$371 - 203 + 2$	$5{,}006 \times 19$

Vocabulary

numerical expression

simplify

order of operations

When you **simplify** a numerical expression, you find its value.

Erika and Jamie each simplified $3 + 4 \times 6$. Their work is shown below. Whose answer is correct?

When an expression has more than one operation, you must know which operation to do first. To make sure that everyone gets the same answer, we use the **order of operations**.

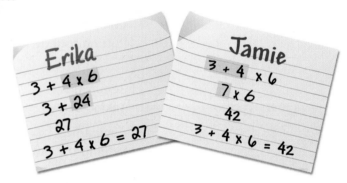

Remember!

The first letters of these words can help you remember the order of operations.

Please	*Parentheses*
Excuse	*Exponents*
My	*Multiply/*
Dear	*Divide*
Aunt	*Add/*
Sally	*Subtract*

ORDER OF OPERATIONS

1. Perform operations in **parentheses**.
2. Find the values of numbers with **exponents**.
3. **Multiply** or **divide** from left to right as ordered in the problem.
4. **Add** or **subtract** from left to right as ordered in the problem.

$3 + 4 \times 6$ *There are no parentheses or exponents. Multiply first.*

$3 + 24$ *Add.*

27 *Erika has the correct answer.*

EXAMPLE **1** **Using the Order of Operations**

Animated Math
@ thinkcentral.com

Simplify each expression.

A $9 + 12 \times 2$

     $9 + 12 \times 2$ *There are no parentheses or exponents.*

     $9 + \quad 24$ *Multiply.*

       33 *Add.*

[Video] **LESSON TUTORIAL VIDEOS @ thinkcentral.com**

Simplify each expression.

B $7 + (12 \times 3) \div 6$

$7 + (12 \times 3) \div 6$	
$7 + \quad 36 \quad \div 6$	*Perform operations within parentheses.*
$7 + \qquad 6$	*Divide.*
13	*Add.*

EXAMPLE 2 **Using the Order of Operations with Exponents**

Simplify each expression.

A $3^3 + 8 - 16$

$3^3 + 8 - 16$	*There are no parentheses.*
$27 + 8 - 16$	*Find the values of numbers with exponents.*
$35 \quad - 16$	*Add*
19	*Subtract.*

B $8 \div (1 + 3) \times 5^2 - 2$

$8 \div (1 + 3) \times 5^2 - 2$	
$8 \div \quad 4 \quad \times 5^2 - 2$	*Perform operations within parentheses.*
$8 \div \quad 4 \quad \times 25 - 2$	*Find the values of numbers with exponents.*
$2 \quad \times 25 - 2$	*Divide.*
$50 \quad - 2$	*Multiply.*
48	*Subtract.*

EXAMPLE 3 *Consumer Application*

Regina bought 5 carved wooden beads for $3 each and 8 glass beads for $2 each. Simplify $5 \times 3 + 8 \times 2$ to find the amount Regina spent for beads.

$5 \times 3 + 8 \times 2$

$15 \; + \; 16$

31

Regina spent $31 for beads.

Think and Discuss

1. Explain why $6 + 7 \times 10 = 76$ but $(6 + 7) \times 10 = 130$.

2. Tell how you can add parentheses to the numerical expression $2^2 + 5 \times 3$ so that 27 is the correct answer.

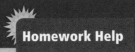

Homework Help
Go to thinkcentral.com
Exercises 1–21, 25, 27, 31, 39, 41, 43, 45

 Prep for MA.6.A.3.3

GUIDED PRACTICE

See Example 1   Simplify each expression.

1. $36 - 18 \div 6$ **2.** $7 + 24 \div 6 \times 2$ **3.** $62 - 4 \times (15 \div 5)$

See Example 2   **4.** $11 + 2^3 \times 5$ **5.** $5 \times (28 \div 7) - 4^2$ **6.** $5 + 3^2 \times 6 - (10 - 9)$

See Example 3   **7.** Coach Milner fed the team after the game by buying 24 Chicken Meal Deals for $4 each and 7 Burger Meal Deals for $6 each. Simplify $24 \times 4 + 7 \times 6$ to find the cost of the food.

INDEPENDENT PRACTICE

See Example 1   Simplify each expression.

8. $9 + 27 \div 3$ **9.** $2 \times 7 - 32 \div 8$ **10.** $45 \div (3 + 6) \times 3$

11. $(6 + 2) \times 4$ **12.** $9 \div 3 + 6 \times 2$ **13.** $5 + 3 \times 2 + 12 \div 4$

See Example 2   **14.** $4^2 + 48 \div (10 - 4)$ **15.** $100 \div 5^2 + 7 \times 3$ **16.** $6 \times 2^2 + 28 - 5$

17. $6^2 - 12 \div 3 + (15 - 7)$ **18.** $21 \div (3 + 4) \times 9 - 2^3$ **19.** $(3^2 + 6 \div 2) \times (36 \div 6 - 4)$

See Example 3   **20.** The nature park has a pride of 5 adult lions and 3 cubs. The adults eat 8 lb of meat each day and the cubs eat 4 lb. Simplify $5 \times 8 + 3 \times 4$ to find the amount of meat consumed each day by the lions.

21. Angie read 4 books that were each 150 pages long and 2 books that were each 325 pages long. Simplify $4 \times 150 + 2 \times 325$ to find the total number of pages Angie read.

PRACTICE AND PROBLEM SOLVING

Simplify each expression.

22. $12 + 3 \times 4$ **23.** $25 - 21 \div 3$ **24.** $1 + 7 \times 2$

25. $60 \div (10 + 2) \times 4^2 - 23$ **26.** $10 \times (28 - 23) + 7^2 - 37$ **27.** $(5 - 3) \div 2$

28. $72 \div 9 - 2 \times 4$ **29.** $12 + (1 + 7^2) \div 5$ **30.** $25 - 5^2$

31. $(15 - 6)^2 - 34 \div 2$ **32.** $(2 \times 4)^2 - 3 \times (5 + 3)$ **33.** $16 + 2 \times 3$

Add parentheses so that each equation is correct.

34. $2^3 + 6 - 5 \times 4 = 12$ **35.** $7 + 2 \times 6 - 4 - 3 = 53$

36. $3^2 + 6 + 3 \times 3 = 36$ **37.** $5^2 - 10 + 5 + 4^2 = 36$

38. $2 \times 8 + 5 - 3 = 23$ **39.** $9^2 - 2 \times 15 + 16 - 8 = 11$

40. $5 + 7 \times 2 - 3 = 21$ **41.** $4^2 \times 3 - 2 \div 4 = 4$

42. **Critical Thinking** Jon says the answer to $1 + 3 \times (6 + 2) - 7$ is 25. Julie says the answer is 18. Who is correct? Explain.

○ = **WORKED-OUT SOLUTIONS**
on p. WS2

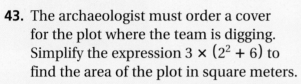

Archaeologists study cultures of the past by uncovering items from ancient cities. An archaeologist has chosen a site in Colorado for her team's next dig. She divides the location into rectangular plots and labels each plot so that uncovered items can be identified by the plot in which they were found.

43. The archaeologist must order a cover for the plot where the team is digging. Simplify the expression $3 \times (2^2 + 6)$ to find the area of the plot in square meters.

Tourists assist archaeologists at Shields Pueblo in Colorado.

44. In the first week, the archaeology team digs down 2 meters and removes a certain amount of dirt. Simplify the expression $3 \times (2^2 + 6) \times 2$ to find the volume of the dirt removed from the plot in the first week.

45. Over the next two weeks, the archaeology team digs down an additional 2^3 meters. Simplify the expression $3 \times (2^2 + 6) \times (2 + 2^3)$ to find the total volume of dirt removed from the plot after 3 weeks.

46. ✐ **Write About It** Explain why the archaeologist must follow the order of operations to determine the area of each plot.

47. ⭐ **Challenge** Write an expression for the volume of dirt that would be removed if the archaeologist's team were to dig down an additional 3^2 meters after the first three weeks.

Florida Spiral Review   Prep for MA.6.A.3.3

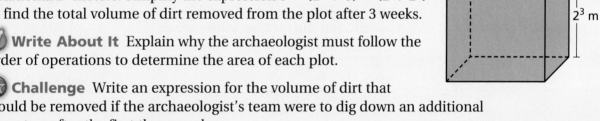

48. Multiple Choice Which operation should you perform first when you simplify $81 - (6 + 30 \div 2) \times 5$?

A. Addition   **B.** Division   **C.** Multiplication   **D.** Subtraction

49. Multiple Choice Which expression does NOT have a value of 5?

F. $2^2 + (3 - 2)$ **G.** $(2^2 + 3) - 2$ **H.** $2^2 + 3 - 2$ **I.** $2^2 - (3 + 2)$

50. Gridded Response What is the value of the expression $3^2 + (9 \div 3 - 2)$?

Write each number in standard form. (Previous Course)

51. $3,000 + 200 + 70 + 3$ **52.** $10,000 + 500 + 20 + 1$ **53.** $70,000 + 7$

Find each value. (Lesson 1-2)

54. 8^5 **55.** 5^3 **56.** 3^8 **57.** 4^4 **58.** 7^2

1-4 Choosing a Method of Computation

Prep for MA.6.A.1.1 Explain and justify procedures for multiplying and dividing fractions and decimals.
Review of MA.5.A.1.2

Earth has one moon. Neptune has 13 moons of which Triton is the largest. Scientists have determined that other planets in our solar system have as many as 63 moons. Mercury and Venus have no moons at all.

EXAMPLE 1 *Astronomy Application*

Choose a solution method and solve. Explain your choice.

A **How many known moons are in our solar system?**

It might be hard to keep track of all of these numbers if you tried to add mentally. But the numbers themselves are small. You can use paper and pencil.

$$
\begin{array}{r}
1 \\
2 \\
63 \\
60 \\
27 \\
+13 \\
\hline
166
\end{array}
$$

Planet	Moons
Mercury	0
Venus	0
Earth	1
Mars	2
Jupiter	63
Saturn	60
Uranus	27
Neptune	13

Source: The Planetary Society, 2006

There are 166 known moons in our solar system.

B **The average temperature on Earth is 59 °F. The average temperature on Venus is 867 °F. How much hotter is Venus's average temperature?**

Venus temperature − Earth temperature
    867   −   59

These numbers are small, and 59 is close to a multiple of 10. You can use mental math.

$(867 + 1) − (59 + 1)$ *Think: Add 1 to 59 to make 60. Add 1 to*
    $868 − 60$ *867 to compensate.*
        808

The average temperature on Venus is 808 °F hotter than the average temperature on Earth.

[Video] **Lesson Tutorial Videos** @ **thinkcentral.com**

Choose a solution method and solve. Explain your choice.

C The diameter of Jupiter is approximately 21 times as great as the diameter of Mars. What is the diameter of Mars?

diameter of Jupiter ÷ 21
142,984　　　　　÷ 21

These numbers are not compatible, so mental math is not a good choice.

You could use paper and pencil, but dividing a 6-digit number by a 2-digit number requires several steps. Using a calculator will probably be faster.

Carefully enter the numbers on a calculator.

142,984 ÷ 21 ENTER

142,984 ÷ 21 = 6,809

The diameter of Mars is approximately 6,808 km.

Check Use estimation to check the reasonableness of your answer. Round 142,984 to 140,000 and round 21 to 20 to get compatible numbers.

140,000 ÷ 20 = 7,000

The answer seems reasonable since 6,808 is close to the estimate of 7,000.

Think and Discuss

1. **Give an example** of a situation in which you would use mental math to solve a problem. When would you use paper and pencil?

2. **Tell** how you could use mental math in Example 1B if the problem were 867 + 59.

3. **Explain** why it is important to know different methods of computation.

Prep for MA.6.A.1.1

Homework Help

Go to **thinkcentral.com**

Exercises 1–6, 7, 13, 15, 17

GUIDED PRACTICE

See Example 1 **Choose a solution method and solve. Explain your choice.**

1. **Astronomy** What is the total number of astronauts who have space flight experience?

U.S.	Germany	France	Canada	Japan	Italy	Russia
244	9	8	7	5	3	88

2. **Sports** In the 2004 Summer Olympic Games, 929 medals were given. The U.S. team brought home the most medals, 103. How many medals were not won by the U.S. team?

3. A factory produces 126 golf balls per minute. How many golf balls can be produced in 515 minutes?

INDEPENDENT PRACTICE

See Example 1 **Choose a solution method and solve. Explain your choice. For 4 and 5, use the diagram at right.**

4. The highest score is a total of all the squares on the board. What is that score?

6	9	5
10	20	8
3	7	4

5. What score is higher, the total of the squares in the middle row or middle column?

6. If each store in a chain of 108 furniture stores sells 135 sofas a year, what is the total number of sofas sold?

PRACTICE AND PROBLEM SOLVING

Simplify the expression, and state the method of computation you used.

7. 5 + 24 + 7 + 1 + 64 + 2 + 8
8. 16 + 2 + 4 + 13 + 5 + 1 + 14
9. 417 + 13
10. 500 ÷ 50
11. 267 × 133
12. 634 − 546
13. 828 × 623
14. 742 − 167
15. 41 + 169
16. 499 − 201
17. 338 + 12
18. 400 + 237 + 23
19. 14,256 ÷ 54
20. 1,108 − 65

21. A satellite travels 985,200 miles per year. How many miles will it travel if it stays in space for 12 years?

22. The school cafeteria had 27 cases of juice before lunch. After lunch, there were 14 cases of juice left. How many cases of juice were used during lunch?

○ = **WORKED-OUT SOLUTIONS** on p. WS2

Sports

A standard marathon is approximately 26.2 miles (42.195 kilometers). A half marathon is about 13.1 miles (21.0975 kilometers).

23. Life-Science There are approximately 10,000 taste buds on the human tongue. Humans have about 400 times the number of taste buds of chickens. About how many taste buds do chickens have?

24. Sports The Clearwater Halfathon takes place in Clearwater, Florida. The table shows the number of people who finished the race in several years. How many more people finished the race in 2007 than in 2006?

Clearwater Halfathon	
Year	Number of Finishers
2006	329
2007	455
2008	376

25. Geography The area of Canada is 9,984,670 square kilometers. The area of the United States is 9,826,630 square kilometers.

a. What is the total area of Canada and the United States?

b. What is the difference in the areas of Canada and the United States?

26. What's the Question? An astronaut has spent the following minutes training in a tank that simulates weightlessness: 2, 15, 5, 40, 10, and 55. The answer is 127. What is the question?

27. Write About It Explain how you can decide whether to use pencil and paper, mental math, or a calculator to solve a subtraction problem.

28. Challenge A list of possible astronauts was narrowed down by two committees. The first committee selected 93 people to complete a written form. The second selected 31 of those people to come to an interview. If 837 were not asked to complete a form, how many were on the original list?

Florida Spiral Review

Rev. of MA.5.A.1.2, MA.5.A.6.2

29. Multiple Choice It takes Mars 687 days to revolve around the Sun. It takes Venus only 225 days to revolve around the Sun. How many more days does it take Mars to revolve around the Sun than it takes Venus?

A. 462 days   **B.** 500 days   **C.** 900 days   **D.** 912 days

30. Short Response Hector biked 13 miles on Monday, Wednesday, and Friday of every week for 24 weeks. Find the total number of miles he biked during the 24 weeks. Explain your answer.

Estimate each sum or difference by rounding to the greatest place value. (Lesson 1-1)

31. $685 + 230$ **32.** $52,087 - 35,210$ **33.** $9,210 - 796$ **34.** $14,325 + 25,629$

Simplify each expression. (Lesson 1-3)

35. $(2 + 7 - 5) \div 2$ **36.** $10(6 - 3)$ **37.** $5 + 8 \times 7 - 1$ **38.** $5 + (8 + 2) - 3$

1-5 Patterns and Sequences

Prep for MA.6.A.3.3 Works backward with two-step function rules to undo expressions.
Review of MA.4.A.4.1

Vocabulary

sequence

term

arithmetic sequence

Each month, Eva chooses 3 new DVDs from her DVD club.

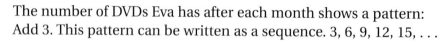

Eva's DVDs	
Month	**DVDs**
1	3
2	6
3	9
4	12

Position → (points to Month) Value of Term → (points to DVDs)

+3, +3, +3

The number of DVDs Eva has after each month shows a pattern: Add 3. This pattern can be written as a sequence. 3, 6, 9, 12, 15, . . .

A **sequence** is an ordered set of numbers. Each number in the sequence is called a **term**. In this sequence, the first term is 3, the second term is 6, and the third term is 9.

When the terms of a sequence change by the same amount each time, the sequence is an **arithmetic sequence**.

EXAMPLE 1 Extending Arithmetic Sequences

Animated Math @ thinkcentral.com

Identify a pattern in each arithmetic sequence and then find the missing terms.

A 3, 15, 27, 39, ▓, ▓, . . .

Look for a pattern.
A pattern is to add 12 to each term to get the next term.
39 + 12 = 51   51 + 12 = 63
So 51 and 63 are the missing terms.

3, 15, 27, 39, ▓, ▓, . . .
+12 +12 +12 +12 +12

Look for a relationship between the 1st term and the 2nd term. Check if this relationship works between the 2nd term and the 3rd term, and so on.

B 12, 21, 30, 39, ▓, ▓, . . .

Use a table to find a pattern.

Position	1	2	3	4	5	6
Value of Term	12	21	30	39	▓	▓

+9 +9 +9 +9 +9

A pattern is to add 9 to each term to get the next term.
39 + 9 = 48   48 + 9 = 57
So 48 and 57 are the missing terms.

Video Lesson Tutorial Videos @ thinkcentral.com

Not all sequences are arithmetic sequences.

Arithmetic Sequences		Not Arithmetic Sequences	
2, 4, 6, 8,... +2 +2 +2	20, 35, 50, 65,... +15 +15 +15	1, 3, 6, 10,... +2 +3 +4	2, 6, 18, 54,... ×3 ×3 ×3

In nonarithmetic sequences, look for patterns that involve multiplication or division. Some sequences may even be combinations of different operations.

EXAMPLE 2

Completing Other Sequences

Identify a pattern in each sequence. Name the missing terms.

A 4, 15, 8, 19, 12, 23, 16, ▦, ▦, ▦, . . .

$$4 \quad 15 \quad 8 \quad 19 \quad 12 \quad 23 \quad 16 \quad ▦ \quad ▦ \quad ▦$$
$$\quad +11 \quad -7 \quad +11 \quad -7 \quad +11 \quad -7 \quad +11 \quad -7 \quad +11$$

A pattern is to add 11 to one term and subtract 7 from the next.

$16 + 11 = 27 \qquad 27 - 7 = 20 \qquad 20 + 11 = 31$

So 27, 20, and 31 are the missing terms.

B

Position	1	2	3	4	5	6	7	8	9
Value of Term	1	6	2	12	▦	24	8	▦	16

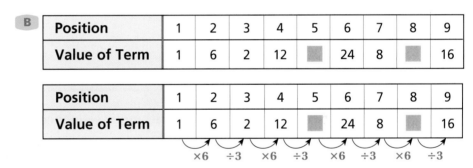

Position	1	2	3	4	5	6	7	8	9
Value of Term	1	6	2	12	▦	24	8	▦	16

×6 ÷3 ×6 ÷3 ×6 ÷3 ×6 ÷3

A pattern is to multiply one term by 6 and divide the next by 3.

$12 \div 3 = 4 \qquad 8 \times 6 = 48$

So 4 and 48 are the missing terms.

Think and Discuss

1. **Tell** how you could check whether the next two terms in the arithmetic sequence 5, 7, 9, 11, . . . are 13 and 15.

2. **Explain** how to find the next term in the sequence 16, 8, 4, 2, ▦, ...

3. **Explain** how to determine whether 256, 128, 64, 32, . . . is an arithmetic or nonarithmetic sequence.

Homework Help

Go to **thinkcentral.com**
Exercises 1–7, 17, 19, 21

GUIDED PRACTICE

See Example ① Identify a pattern in each arithmetic sequence and then find the missing terms.

1. 12, 24, 36, 48, ■, ■, ■, . . .   **2.** 105, 90, 75, 60, 45, ■, ■, ■, . . .

3.

Position	1	2	3	4	5	6
Value of Term	7	18	29	40	■	■

4.

Position	1	2	3	4	5	6
Value of Term	44	38	32	26	■	■

See Example ② Identify a pattern in each sequence. Name the missing terms.

5. 2, 9, 7, 14, ■, ■, . . .   **6.** 80, 8, 40, 4, ■, 2, 10, ■, . . .

7.

Position	1	2	3	4	5	6	7	8
Value of Term	1	6	3	18	■	54	27	■

INDEPENDENT PRACTICE

See Example ① Identify a pattern in each arithmetic sequence and then find the missing terms.

8. 9, 19, 29, 39, 49, ■, ■, ■, . . .   **9.** 98, 84, 70, 56, 42, ■, ■, ■, . . .

10.

Position	1	2	3	4	5	6
Value of Term	45	38	31	24	■	■

11.

Position	1	2	3	4	5	6
Value of Term	8	11	14	17	■	■

See Example ② Identify a pattern in each sequence. Name the missing terms.

12. 50, 40, 43, 33, ■, 26, ■, . . .   **13.** 7, 28, 24, 45, ■, ■, ■, . . .

14.

Position	1	2	3	4	5	6	7
Value of Term	120	60	180	90	■	■	405

15.

Position	1	2	3	4	5	6	7
Value of Term	400	100	200	50	■	■	50

◯ = **WORKED-OUT SOLUTIONS**
on p. WS2

Use the pattern to write the first five terms of the sequence.

16. Start with 1; multiply by 3. **17.** Start with 5; add 9. **18.** Start with 100; subtract 7.

19. **Social Studies** The Chinese lunar calendar is based on a 12-year cycle, with each of the 12 years named after a different animal. The year 2006 was the year of the dog.
   a. When will the next year of the dog occur?
   b. When was the last year of the dog?
   c. Will the year 2030 be a year of the dog? Explain.

Identify whether each given sequence could be arithmetic. If not, identify the pattern of the sequence.

20. 10, 16, 22, 28, 34, . . . **21.** 60, 56, 61, 57, 62, . . . **22.** 111, 121, 131, 141, 151, . . .

23. **Choose a Strategy** The * shows where a piece is missing from the pattern. What piece is missing?

   A. y   **B.** B   **C.** y   **D.** Y

24. Whole numbers raised to the second power are called perfect squares. This is because they can be represented by objects arranged in the shape of a square. Perfect squares can be written as the sequence 1, 4, 9, 16, . . .
   a. Find the next two perfect squares in the sequence.
   b. Explain how can you know whether a number is a perfect square?

25. **Write About It** Explain how to determine if a sequence is arithmetic.

26. **Challenge** Find the missing terms in the following sequence:
   ▮, 2^3, 27, 4^3, 125, ▮, 343, . . .

Florida Spiral Review   Prep for MA.6.A.3.3

27. **Multiple Choice** Identify the pattern in the sequence 6, 11, 16, 21, 26, . . .

   A. Add 5.   **B.** Add 6.   **C.** Multiply by 5.   **D.** Multiply by 6.

28. **Extended Response** Identify the first term and a pattern for the sequence 5, 8, 11, 14, 17, . . . Is the sequence arithmetic? Explain why or why not. Find the next three terms in the sequence.

Write each expression in exponential form. (Lesson 1-2)

29. $5 \times 5 \times 5 \times 5 \times 5 \times 5$ **30.** $10 \times 10 \times 10 \times 10 \times 10$ **31.** $7 \times 7 \times 7 \times 7 \times 7$

Choose a solution method and solve. Explain your choice. (Lesson 1-4)

32. As of 2006, Hank Aaron was Major League Baseball's career home run leader with 755 home runs. Sadaharu Oh was the career home run leader of Japanese baseball with 868 home runs. How many more home runs did Oh hit than Aaron?

Quiz for Lessons 1-3 Through 1-5

✓ **1-3** **Order of Operations**

Simplify each expression.

1. $3 \times 4 \div (10 - 4)$ **2.** $5^2 + 10 \div 2 - 1$ **3.** $4 + (12 - 8) \times 6$

4. $(2^3 + 2) \times 10$ **5.** $3 \times 3^2 + 13 - 5$ **6.** $10 \div (3 + 2) \times 2^3 - 8$

7. $4^2 - 12 \div 3 + (7 - 5)$ **8.** $10 \times (25 - 11) \div 7 + 6$ **9.** $(3 + 6) \times 18 \div 2 + 7$

10. Mrs. Webb buys 7 cards for $2 each, 3 metallic pens for $1 each, and 1 pad of writing paper for $4. Simplify $7 \times 2 + 3 \times 1 + 1 \times 4$ to find the total amount Mrs. Webb spends.

✓ **1-4** **Choosing a Method of Computation**

Choose a solution method and solve. Explain your choice.

11. How many Texas state parks are shown in the table?

12. How many more parks are there in the Prairies and Lakes region than in the Big Bend region?

Texas State Parks	
Region	**Number of Parks**
Big Bend	7
Gulf Coast	11
Hill Country	11
Panhandle Plains	12
Pineywoods	13
Prairies and Lakes	22
South Texas Plains	5

✓ **1-5** **Patterns and Sequences**

Identify a pattern in the arithmetic sequence and then find the missing terms.

13.

Position	1	2	3	4	5	6	7
Value of Term	5	14	23	32	▓	▓	▓

Identify a pattern in each sequence. Name the missing terms.

14. 4, 20, 15, 31, ▓, ▓, 37, …

15. 16, 32, 8, 16, ▓, ▓, ▓

16. 8, 11, 14, ▓, ▓, ▓

17. 50, 45, 40, ▓, ▓, ▓

18. 7, 14, 21, ▓, ▓, ▓

19. 63, 54, 45, ▓, ▓, ▓

20. A concert hall has 5 seats in the front row, 9 seats in the second row, 13 seats in the third row, and 17 seats in the fourth row. If this pattern continues, how many seats are in the sixth row?

Real-World CONNECTIONS

Tallahassee

FSU Women's Basketball In recent years, Florida State University in Tallahassee has fielded one of the nation's best women's basketball teams. In 2008, the Seminoles made their fourth straight appearance in the NCAA championship tournament.

1. The table shows the number of field goals and free throws that were made by some of the teams' players during the 2007–2008 season. Estimate the total number of free throws that were made by these players. Explain how you made your estimate.

FSU Women's Basketball: 2007–2008 Season			
Player	Two-Point Field Goals	Three-Point Field Goals	Free Throws
Tanae Davis-Cain	86	49	42
Mara Freshour	66	66	90
Christian Hunnicutt	25	10	17
Jacinta Monroe	135	0	67
Shante Williams	112	5	90

Florida State Women's Basketball

2. To find the total number of points a player scored, multiply the numbr of two-point field goals by 2, multiply the number of three-point field goals by 3, and multipy the number of free throws by 1. Then add these values.

   a. To find the number of points scored by Christian Hunnicutt, a fan writes the expression $25 \times 2 + 10 \times 3 + 17 \times 1$. Explain how to simplify this expression. Then find the number of points Christian Hunnicutt scored.

   b. Find the total number of points scored by each of the other four players. Which of the five players scored the greatest number of points?

3. In a 2007 game against the Indiana University Hoosiers, the Seminoles scored $3^4 + 2^2$ points. The two teams scored a total of 163 points. How many points did each team score?

Game Time

Palindromes

A *palindrome* is a word, phrase, or number that reads the same forward and backward.

Examples:

race car   Madam, I'm Adam.   3710173

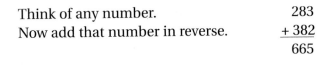

You can turn almost any number into a palindrome with this trick.

Think of any number.	283
Now add that number in reverse.	+ 382
	665

Use the sum to repeat the previous step and keep repeating until the final sum is a palindrome.	665
	+ 566
	1,231

$$1,231$$
$$+ 1,321$$
$$2,552$$

It took only three steps to create a palindrome by starting with the number 283. What happens if you start with the number 196? Do you think you will ever create a palindrome if you start with 196? One man who started with 196 did these steps until he had a number with 70,928 digits and he still had not created a palindrome!

Spin-a-Million

The object of this game is to create the number closest to 1,000,000.

Taking turns, spin the pointer and write the number on your place-value chart. The number cannot be moved once it has been placed.

After six turns, the player whose number is closest to one million wins the round and scores a point. The first player to get five points wins the game.

A complete copy of the rules and game pieces are available online.

Games

Go to **thinkcentral.com**

THINK central

Materials
- plastic DVD case
- card stock
- markers
- scissors
- glue stick
- library pocket
- index cards
- brass fastener
- large paper clip

PROJECT Picture This

Make a game in an empty DVD case to review concepts from this chapter.

Directions

1 Cut a piece of card stock that can be folded in half to fit inside the DVD case. Lay the card stock flat and draw a path for a board game. Be sure to have a start and a finish. **Figure A**

2 Close the game board and decorate the front. Glue a library pocket onto the front to hold the index cards. **Figure B**

3 On the index cards, write problems that can be solved using math from the chapter. Place the cards in the pocket.

4 Cut a piece of card stock to fit the other side of the DVD box. Glue directions for your game at the top. At the bottom, make a spinner the size of a DVD. Attach a brass fastener to the middle of the spinner, and then attach a paper clip to the fastener. **Figure C**

Putting the Math into Action

Play your game with a partner. Use buttons or coins as playing pieces. Players should take turns spinning the spinner and then be required to solve a problem correctly in order to move their piece.

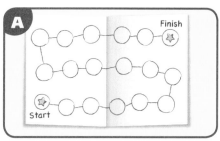

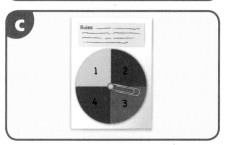

Study Guide: Review

Multi–Language Glossary

Go to thinkcentral.com

Vocabulary

Complete the sentences below with vocabulary words from the list above.

1. An ordered set of numbers is called a(n) ___?___. Each number in a sequence is called a(n) ___?___.

2. In the expression 8^5, 8 is the ___?___, and 5 is the ___?___.

3. The ___?___ is a set of rules used to evaluate an expression that contains more than one operation.

4. When you ___?___ a numerical expression, you find its value.

EXAMPLES

EXERCISES

1-1 **Estimating with Whole Numbers** (pp. 6–9)

 Prep for MA.6.A.5.3

- **Estimate the sum 837 + 710 by rounding to the hundreds place.**
  800 + 700 = 1,500
  The sum is about 1,500.

- **Estimate the quotient of 148 and 31.**
  150 ÷ 30 = 5
  The quotient is about 5.

Estimate each sum or difference by rounding to the place value indicated.

5. 4,671 − 3,954; thousands

6. 3,123 + 2,987; thousands

7. 53,465 − 27,465; ten thousands

8. Ralph has 38 photo album sheets with 22 baseball cards in each sheet. About how many baseball cards does he have?

1-2 Exponents (pp. 10–13)

 Prep for MA.6.G.4.1

■ Write 6 × 6 in exponential form.

6^2 *6 is a factor 2 times.*

Find each value.

■ 5^2

$5^2 = 5 \times 5$

$= 25$

■ 6^4

$6^4 = 6 \times 6 \times 6 \times 6$

$= 1296$

Write each expression in exponential form.

9. $5 \times 5 \times 5$ **10.** $3 \times 3 \times 3 \times 3 \times 3$

11. $7 \times 7 \times 7 \times 7$ **12.** 8×8

13. $4 \times 4 \times 4 \times 4$ **14.** $1 \times 1 \times 1$

Find each value.

15. 4^4 **16.** 2^4 **17.** 6^3

18. 3^3 **19.** 1^5 **20.** 7^4

21. 5^3 **22.** 10^2 **23.** 9^2

24. A certain colony of bacteria doubles in size every 5 minutes. If the colony began with 2 organisms, how many will there be after 20 minutes?

25. Patricia e-mailed a joke to 4 of her friends. Each of those friends e-mailed the joke to 4 other friends. If this pattern continues, how many people will receive the e-mail on the fifth round of e-mails?

1-3 Order of Operations (pp. 16–19)

 Prep for MA.6.A.3.3

■ Simplify $8 \div (7 - 5) \times 2^2 - 2 + 9$.

$8 \div (7 - 5) \times 2^2 - 2 + 9$

$8 \div 2 \times 2^2 - 2 + 9$ *Subtract in parentheses.*

$8 \div 2 \times 4 - 2 + 9$ *Simplify the exponent.*

$4 \times 4 - 2 + 9$ *Divide.*

$16 - 2 + 9$ *Multiply.*

$14 + 9$ *Subtract.*

23 *Add.*

Simplify each expression.

26. $9 \times 8 - 13$ **27.** $21 \div 3 + 4$

28. $6 + 4 \times 5$ **29.** $19 - 12 \div 6$

30. $30 \div 2 - 5 \times 2$ **31.** $(7 + 3) \div 2 \times 3^2$

32. Jerome bought 4 shirts for $12 each and 5 pairs of pants for $18 each. The tax for his purchase was $11. Simplify $4 \times 12 + 5 \times 18 + 11$ to find the amount Jerome spent for clothes.

33. The sixth-grade band students sell cases of fruit for a fund-raiser. Emily sold 18 cases of oranges for $12 each, 11 cases of apples for $10 each, and 5 cases of grapefuit for $14 each. Simplify $18 \times 12 + 11 \times 10 + 5 \times 14$ to find how much money she should collect in all.

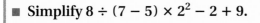

Study Guide: Review

1-4 **Choosing a Method of Computation** (pp. 20–23)

 Prep for MA.6.A.1.1

■ Choose a solution method and solve. Explain your choice.

The average annual rainfall in Washington, D.C., is 39 inches. How much rain does Washington, D.C., average in 8 years?

These numbers are not so big that you must use a calculator. Use pencil and paper to find the answer. $39 \times 8 = 312$ inches

Choose a solution method and solve. Explain your choice.

34. The average high temperature for Washington, D.C., in January is 42 °F. The record high temperature for Washington, D.C., is 104 °F. How much higher is the record temperature than the average high temperature in January?

35. There are 14 players on Emily's softball team. If each player's family bought 5 tickets to a tournament, how many tickets did Emily's team buy in all?

36. If the National Debt of the United States is \$8,951,056,150,180.66 and there are 302,634,238 people in the country, what is each person's share of the debt, rounded to the nearest penny?

37. At 5:00 A.M., the temperature was 41 °F. By noon, the temperature was 69 °F. By how many degrees did the temperature increase?

1-5 **Patterns and Sequences** (pp. 24–27)

 Prep for MA.6.A.3.3

Identify a pattern in the sequence. Name the missing terms.

■ 1, 3, 5, 7, ▨, ▨, ...
  +2 +2 +2 +2 +2

The pattern is to add 2 to each term. The missing terms are 9 and 11.

■ 6, 12, 11, 22, ▨, 42, ▨, ...
  ×2 −1 ×2 −1 ×2 −1

The pattern is to multiply one term by 2 and subtract the next by 1. The missing terms are 21 and 41.

Identify a pattern in each arithmetic sequence and then find the missing terms.

38. 4, 9, 14, 19, ▨, ▨, ...

39. 21, 19, 17, 15, ▨, ▨, ...

Identify a pattern in each sequence. Name the missing terms.

40. 16, 20, 18, 22, ▨, 24, ▨, ...

41. 1, 3, 9, 27, ▨, ▨, ...

42. 65, 70, 68, 73, ▨, 76, ▨, ...

Study Guide: Review

Chapter Test

Estimate each sum or difference by rounding to the place value indicated.

1. 8,743 + 3,198; thousands

2. 62,524 − 17,831; ten thousands

3. 23,218 + 37,518; ten thousands

4. 292,801 − 156,127; hundred thousands

Estimate.

5. Kaitlin's family is planning a trip from Washington, D.C., to New York City. New York City is 227 miles from Washington, D.C., and the family can drive an average of 55 mi/h. About how long will the trip take?

6. An auditorium can hold 572 people. If 109 people have come in through the north entrance, and 218 people have come in through the south entrance, about how many more people can fit in the auditorium?

Write each expression in exponential form.

7. $4 \times 4 \times 4 \times 4 \times 4$

8. $10 \times 10 \times 10$

9. $6 \times 6 \times 6 \times 6$

10. $1 \times 1 \times 1 \times 1 \times 1 \times 1 \times 1$

11. $3 \times 3 \times 3 \times 3 \times 3$

12. 8×8

Find each value.

13. 2^3

14. 5^2

15. 4^4

16. 11^2

Simplify each expression.

17. $12 + 8 \div 2$

18. $3^2 \times 5 + 10 - 7$

19. $12 + (28 - 15) + 4 \times 2$

20. $(7 + 8) \div 3 + 5^2$

21. $2^4 + (6 - 1) \div 5 - 8$

22. $2 \times (9^2 \div 9) + 9 - 2$

Choose a solution method and solve. Explain your choice.

23. During a performance, a middle school choir stands on risers in 4 rows. There are 11 singers in the first row, 13 in the second row, 14 in the third row, and 17 in the last row. How many singers are there in the choir?

24. Earth is approximately 93,000,000 miles from the Sun. Neptune is approximately 2,794,000,000 miles from the Sun. How many times the distance from Earth to the Sun is the distance from Neptune to the Sun?

25. The coldest temperature in a city was 11 °F. The warmest temperature that same year was 89 °F. What is the difference between the highest and lowest temperatures?

Identify a pattern in each sequence. Name the missing terms.

26. 8, 22, 36, 50, ■, ■, ■, . . .

27. 2, 10, 7, 15, ■, 20, ■, . . .

28. A tile pattern has 1 tile in the first row, 3 tiles in the second row, and 5 tiles in the third row. If this pattern continues, how many tiles are in the fifth row?

✏️ **Test Tackler**

Standardized Test Strategies

Multiple Choice: Eliminate Answer Choices

You can solve some math problems without doing detailed calculations. You can use mental math, estimation, or logical reasoning to help you eliminate answer choices and save time.

EXAMPLE 1

Which number is the closest estimate for 678 + 189?

A. 700   **C.** 1,000

B. 900   **D.** 5,000

You can use logical reasoning to eliminate choice A because it is too small. The estimated sum has to be greater than 700 because 678 + 189 is greater than 700.

Choice D may also be eliminated because the value is too large. The estimated sum will be less than 5,000.

Round 678 up to 700 and 189 up to 200. Then find the sum of 700 and 200: 700 + 200 = 900. You can eliminate choice C because it is greater than 900.

Choice B is the closest estimate.

EXAMPLE 2

Which of the following numbers is the standard form of four million, six hundred eight thousand, fifteen?

F. 468,015   **H.** 4,068,150

G. 4,608,015   **I.** 4,600,815,000

Logical reasoning can be used to eliminate choices. Numbers that have a place value in the millions must have at least seven but no more than nine digits. Choices F and I can be eliminated because they do not have the correct number of digits.

Both choices G and H have the correct range of digits, so narrow it down further. The number must end in 15. Choice H ends in 50, so it cannot be correct. Eliminate it.

The correct answer choice is G.

Some answer choices, called distractors, may seem correct because they are based on common errors made in calculations.

Read each item and answer the questions that follow.

Item A
Which number is the greatest?

A. 599,485   C. 5,569,003

B. 5,571,987   D. 5,399,879

1. Are there any answer choices you can eliminate immediately? If so, which ones and why?

2. Describe how you can find the correct answer.

City Middle School Populations	
Central Middle School	652
Eastside Middle School	718
Northside Middle School	663
Southside Middle School	731
Westside Middle School	842

Item B
The school district receives $30 a day in state funding for every student enrolled in a public school. Find the approximate number of students that attend all of the city middle schools.

F. 2,000   H. 3,600

G. 3,300   I. 4,000

3. Can F be eliminated? Why or why not?

4. Can H be eliminated? Why or why not?

5. Explain how to use mental math to solve this problem.

Item C
Simplify $8^2 - (4 + 6) \div 2$.

A. 27

B. 33

C. 59

D. 65

6. Are there any answer choices that can be eliminated?

7. Explain what error a student might have made if they answered A.

Item D
Stacey is beginning a new exercise program. She plans to cycle 2 kilometers on her first day. Each day after that, she will double the number of kilometers she cycled from the day before. Which expression shows how many kilometers she will cycle on the sixth day?

F. 2×6 H. 2^6

G. $2 + 2 + 2 + 2 + 2 + 2$ I. 6^2

8. Are there any answer choices you can eliminate immediately? If so, which choices and why?

9. Explain how you can use a table to help you solve this problem.

Item E
James is driving to his aunt's house. If he drives about 55 miles per hour for 5 hours, about how many miles will he have driven?

A. 12 miles   C. 60 miles

B. 300 miles   D. 600 miles

10. Which answer choice(s) can be immediately eliminated and why?

11. Explain how to solve this problem.

Cumulative Assessment, Chapter 1

Multiple Choice

1. Jonah has 31 boxes of baseball cards. If each box contains 183 cards, about how many baseball cards does Jonah have in his collection?

   A. 3,000 cards   **C.** 9,000 cards

   B. 6,000 cards   **D.** 12,000 cards

2. Which of the following does NOT have a value of 27?

   F. 3^3 **H.** $3 \times 3 + 18$

   G. $3^2 + 3 \times 7$ **I.** $9^2 \div 3$

3. What are the next two terms in the following sequence?

   $$6, 3, 12, 6, 24, \ldots$$

   A. 3, 12   **C.** 12, 48

   B. 6, 36   **D.** 18, 72

4. A student correctly simplified the expression $5^2 \div (7 - \blacksquare) + 10$ as 15. What number is missing from the expression?

   F. 2   **H.** 6

   G. 5   **I.** 7

5. Last month, Maria drove 2,548 miles for her job. She worked 18 days last month. Which is the best estimate for the average number of miles Maria drove for her job each day she worked?

   A. 100   **C.** 200

   B. 125   **D.** 43,000

6. Jane extends the pattern shown for several more rows. Which row has 19 circles?

   Row 1

   Row 2

   Row 3

   F. Row 6   **H.** Row 8

   G. Row 7   **I.** Row 9

7. The distance from Lydia's house to her sister's house is 360 miles. Lydia drives at an average speed of 60 miles per hour. How long will it take her to drive from her house to her sister's house?

   A. 6 hours   **C.** 420 hours

   B. 300 hours   **D.** 21,600 hours

8. What is $6 \times 6 \times 6 \times 6$ written in exponential form?

   F. 24^4

   G. 1,296

   H. 6^4

   I. $1000 + 200 + 90 + 6$

9. When the expression $5^2 \times (5 + 2) \,\blacksquare\, 7$ is simplified, the value is 25. What operation is missing from the expression?

   A. $+$ **C.** $\times$

   B. $-$ **D.** $\div$

10. Erik paid $24 for some muffins. The muffins were sold for $8 per dozen. How many muffins did Erik buy?

   F. 3   **H.** 36

   G. 12   **I.** 192

11. Which statement has the same value with or without the parentheses?

   A. $(2^3 + 4) \times 5 - 6$

   B. $24 - 3 \times (3 + 1) \div 2^2$

   C. $7 + (2 \times 3^2) - 1$

   D. $8 \div 2 \times (6^2 - 3)$

 When you read a word problem, underline the information you need to help you answer the question.

Gridded Response

12. What is the value of
$3 + 8 \times 6 - (12 \div 2^2)$?

13. Martha walked 4 minutes on Monday, 7 minutes on Tuesday, and 10 minutes on Wednesday. If the pattern continues, how many minutes will she walk on Saturday?

14. At 3:00 P.M., the water temperature in the pool was 88 °F. At 6:00 P.M., the water temperature was 83 °F. At 9:00 P.M., the water temperature was 78 °F. If the pattern continues, what will the water temperature be at 12:00 midnight in degrees Fahrenheit?

15. What is the sum of 3,820 and 4,373 when rounded to the nearest thousand?

16. The expression $\blacksquare^3 - (7 + 9) \div 2^3$ can be simplified to the value 25. What number is missing?

17. Matthew has 6 pairs of white socks and 3 pairs of black socks. What is the total number of socks Matthew has?

Short Response

S1. Megan deposited $2 into her savings account on the first Friday of the month. Each week she doubles her deposit from the week before.

   a. If this pattern continues, how much money will she deposit in week 4?

   b. What is the total amount in Megan's account after her fourth deposit? Explain how you found your answer.

S2. Create a numerical expression that can be simplified in four steps. Include one set of parentheses and an exponent. The same mathematical operation may be used no more than two times. Show how to simplify your expression.

S3. A wall displays a pattern of rows of tiles. The first row has 15 tiles, the second row has 18 tiles, the third row has 21 tiles, the fourth row has 24 tiles, and the pattern continues.

   a. Describe the pattern and determine how many tiles are in the sixth row.

   b. Explain whether any row of the pattern has exactly 400 tiles.

Extended Response

E1. Paul and Amelia each have a savings account. The table shows their total savings for four weeks.

Week	1	2	3	4
Paul's Savings ($)	8	17	26	35
Amelia's Savings ($)	19	27	35	43

   a. Identify a pattern for each person's savings.

   b. Find how much each person will have in their account after 8 weeks.

   c. Amelia and Paul continue the pattern. Explain whether Amelia will always have more money saved than Paul. If not, tell when Paul will have more money saved than Amelia.

CHAPTER 2

Introduction to Algebra

Worktext
pages 3–84

Additional instruction, practice, and activities are available online, including:

- Lesson Tutorial Videos
- Homework Help
- Animated Math

Go to **thinkcentral.com**

Why Learn This?

The Florida panther is one of the most rare and endangered mammals in the world. Expressions involving panther density are often given as the number of animals per 100 square miles.

Chapter Focus
- Write expressions and equations for given situations.
- Evaluate expressions.
- Solve one-step equations.

Are You Ready?

Are You Ready? THINK central

Go to **thinkcentral.com**

✓ Vocabulary

Choose the best term from the list to complete each sentence.

1. Multiplication is the ___?___ of division.

2. The ___?___ of 12 and 3 is 36.

3. The ___?___ of 12 and 3 is 15.

4. Addition, subtraction, multiplication, and division are called ___?___.

5. The answer to a division problem is called the ___?___.

dividend

factor

inverse

operations

product

quotient

sum

Complete these exercises to review skills you will need for this chapter.

✓ Multiplication Facts

Multiply.

6. 7×4 7. 8×9 8. 9×6 9. 7×7

10. 6×5 11. 3×8 12. 5×5 13. 2×9

✓ Division Facts

Divide.

14. $64 \div 8$ 15. $63 \div 9$ 16. $56 \div 7$ 17. $54 \div 6$

18. $49 \div 7$ 19. $30 \div 5$ 20. $32 \div 4$ 21. $18 \div 3$

✓ Whole Number Operations

Add, subtract, multiply, or divide.

22. $\begin{array}{r} 28 \\ + 15 \end{array}$ 23. $\begin{array}{r} 71 \\ + 38 \end{array}$ 24. $\begin{array}{r} 1,218 \\ + 430 \end{array}$ 25. $\begin{array}{r} 2,218 \\ + 1,135 \end{array}$

26. $\begin{array}{r} 72 \\ - 35 \end{array}$ 27. $\begin{array}{r} 98 \\ - 45 \end{array}$ 28. $\begin{array}{r} 1,642 \\ - 249 \end{array}$ 29. $\begin{array}{r} 3,408 \\ - 1,649 \end{array}$

30. 6×13 31. 8×15 32. 16×22 33. 20×35

34. $9\overline{)72}$ 35. $7\overline{)84}$ 36. $16\overline{)112}$ 37. $23\overline{)1,472}$

Before

Previously, you

- wrote numerical expressions involving whole numbers.

- solved problems using addition, subtraction, multiplication, and division of whole numbers.

Now

You will study

- writing algebraic expressions involving whole numbers.

- using addition, subtraction, multiplication, and division to solve one-step equations involving whole numbers.

- determining whether a number is a solution to an equation.

Why?

You can use the skills learned in this chapter

- to solve one-step equations involving decimals and fractions.

- to solve one-step inequalities.

Key Vocabulary/Vocabulario

algebraic expression	expresión algebraica
Associative Property	Propiedad asociativa
Commutative Property	Propiedad conmutativa
constant	constante
Distributive Property	Propiedad distributiva
equation	ecuación
solution of an equation	solución de una ecuación
variable	variable

Vocabulary Connections

To become familiar with some of the vocabulary terms in the chapter, consider the following. You may refer to the chapter, the glossary, or a dictionary if you like.

1. You may *commute* an equal distance each day—from home to school, or from school to work. What do you think the **Commutative Property** tells us about adding or multiplying two numbers?

2. *Algebra* is a type of math that uses letters to represent numbers. The word *algebraic* means "relating to algebra." What do you think an **algebraic expression** contains?

3. When something is *constant,* it does not change. If there is a **constant** in an expression, do you think the number changes? Explain.

4. When something is *variable,* it is able to vary, or change. What do you think a **variable** in an expression is able to do?

5. An *equation* shows that two expressions are equal. What mathematical symbol would you expect to see in an **equation**?

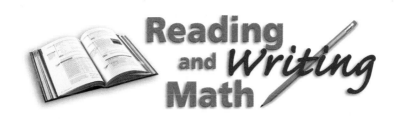 **Reading and Writing Math**

Writing Strategy: Use Your Own Words

Sometimes when you are reading about a new math concept for the first time from a textbook, the concept is difficult to understand.

LA.6.1.6.5 The student will relate new vocabulary to familiar words.

As you go through each lesson, do the following:

- Look for the key ideas.
- Rewrite explanations given as paragraphs as steps or a list.
- Add an example when possible.

What Lupe Reads

When you multiply two numbers, you can "break apart" one of the numbers into a sum and then use the Distributive Property.

What Lupe Writes

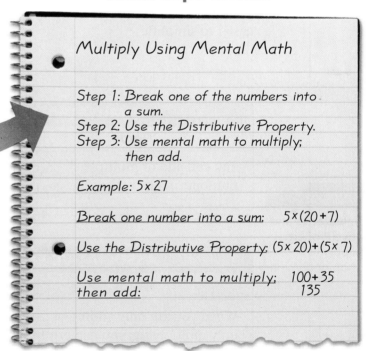

Multiply Using Mental Math

Step 1: Break one of the numbers into a sum.
Step 2: Use the Distributive Property.
Step 3: Use mental math to multiply; then add.

Example: 5×27

Break one number into a sum: $5 \times (20 + 7)$

Use the Distributive Property: $(5 \times 20) + (5 \times 7)$

Use mental math to multiply; $100 + 35$
then add: 135

Reading and Writing Math

> **Try This**

Rewrite the paragraph in your own words.

1. Sometimes in math you do not need an exact answer. Instead, you can use an estimate. Estimates are close to the exact answer but are usually easier and faster to find. When estimating, you can round the numbers in the problem to compatible numbers. Compatible numbers are close to the numbers in the problem, and they can help you do math mentally.

2-1 Properties and Mental Math

MA.6.A.3.5 Apply the Commutative, Associative, and Distributive Properties . . . expressions are equivalent.

Mental math means "doing math in your head." Shakuntala Devi is extremely good at mental math. When she was asked to multiply 7,686,369,774,870 by 2,465,099,745,779, she took only 28 seconds to multiply the numbers mentally and gave the correct answer of 18,947,668,177,995,426,462,773,730!

Many mental math strategies use number properties that you already know to make equivalent expressions that may be easier to simplify.

Vocabulary

Commutative Property

Associative Property

Distributive Property

Caution!

The Commutative and Associative Properties do not apply to subtraction or division.

COMMUTATIVE PROPERTY (Ordering)	
Words	**Numbers**
You can add or multiply numbers in any order.	$18 + 9 = 9 + 18$ $15 \times 2 = 2 \times 15$

ASSOCIATIVE PROPERTY (Grouping)	
Words	**Numbers**
When you are only adding or only multiplying, you can group any of the numbers together.	$(17 + 2) + 9 = 17 + (2 + 9)$ $(12 \times 2) \times 4 = 12 \times (2 \times 4)$

EXAMPLE 1 Using Properties to Add and Multiply Whole Numbers

A Simplify $12 + 4 + 18 + 46$.

$12 + 4 + 18 + 46$	*Look for sums that are multiples of 10.*
$12 + 18 + 4 + 46$	*Use the Commutative Property.*
$(12 + 18) + (4 + 46)$	*Use the Associative Property to make*
$30 \quad + \quad 50$	*groups of compatible numbers.*
80	*Use mental math to add.*

Video Lesson Tutorial Videos @ thinkcentral.com

Helpful Hint

The expressions in each row of Example 1B are equivalent expressions because they have the same value.

B Simplify 5 × 12 × 2.

5 × 12 × 2	*Look for products that are multiples of 10.*
12 × 5 × 2	*Use the Commutative Property.*
12 × (5 × 2)	*Use the Associative Property to group*
12 × 10	*compatible numbers.*
120	*Use mental math to multiply.*

To multiply a number by a sum, such as 6 × (10 + 4), you can use the order of operations, or you can use the *Distributive Property.*

DISTRIBUTIVE PROPERTY	
Words	**Numbers**
To multiply a number by a sum, multiply by each number in the sum and then add.	6 × (10 + 4) = (6 × 10) + (6 × 4) = 60 + 24 = 84

When you multiply two numbers, you can "break apart" one of the numbers into a sum and then use the Distributive Property.

EXAMPLE **Using the Distributive Property to Multiply**

Use the Distributive Property to find each product.

A 4 × 23

4 × 23 = 4 × (20 + 3)	*"Break apart" 23 into 20 + 3.*
= (4 × 20) + (4 × 3)	*Use the Distributive Property.*
= 80 + 12	*Use mental math to multiply.*
= 92	*Use mental math to add.*

B 8 × 74

8 × 74 = 8 × (70 + 4)	*"Break apart" 74 into 70 + 4.*
= (8 × 70) + (8 × 4)	*Use the Distributive Property.*
= 560 + 32	*Use mental math to multiply.*
= 592	*Use mental math to add.*

Think and Discuss

1. Give examples of the Commutative Property and the Associative Property.

2. Name some situations in which you might use mental math.

GUIDED PRACTICE

See Example **1** **Simplify.**

1. $13 + 9 + 7 + 11$ **2.** $19 + 18 + 11 + 32$ **3.** $25 + 7 + 13 + 5$

4. $5 \times 14 \times 4$ **5.** $4 \times 16 \times 5$ **6.** $5 \times 17 \times 2$

See Example **2** **Use the Distributive Property to find each product.**

7. 5×24 **8.** 8×52 **9.** 4×39 **10.** 6×14

11. 3×33 **12.** 2×78 **13.** 9×12 **14.** 2×87

INDEPENDENT PRACTICE

See Example **1** **Simplify.**

15. $15 + 17 + 3 + 5$ **16.** $14 + 7 + 16 + 13$ **17.** $6 + 21 + 14 + 9$

18. $5 \times 25 \times 2$ **19.** $2 \times 32 \times 10$ **20.** $6 \times 12 \times 5$

See Example **2** **Use the Distributive Property to find each product.**

21. 3×36 **22.** 4×42 **23.** 6×71 **24.** 2×94 **25.** 6×23

26. 5×25 **27.** 6×62 **28.** 7×21 **29.** 8×41 **30.** 3×74

PRACTICE AND PROBLEM SOLVING

Use mental math to find each sum or product.

31. $8 + 13 + 7 + 12$ **32.** $2 \times 25 \times 4$ **33.** $4 + 22 + 16 + 18$

34. $5 \times 8 \times 12$ **35.** $5 + 98 + 95$ **36.** $6 \times 5 \times 14$

37. $11 + 75 + 25$ **38.** $8 \times 11 \times 5$ **39.** $19 + 1 + 11 + 39$

40. Paul is writing a story for the school newspaper about the landscaping done by his class. The students planted 15 vines, 12 hedges, 8 trees, and 35 flowering plants. How many plants were used in the project?

41. **Earth Science** The high temperature on Sunday was 58 °F. It is predicted to rise 4 °F on Monday, then rise 2 °F more on Tuesday, and then rise another 6 °F by Saturday. Find the predicted high temperature on Saturday.

42. **Multi-Step** Janice orders new traction pads for her surf club. Use the receipt at right to find her total cost.

Description	Number	Unit Cost with Tax	Price
Traction Pads	7	$24.00	
		Shipping & Handling	$7.00
		Total	

○ = WORKED-OUT SOLUTIONS
on p. WS2

Multiply using the Distributive Property.

43. 9×17 **44.** 4×27 **45.** 11×18 **46.** 7×51

Determine if each pair of expressions is equivalent. If so, state the property shown.

47. 8×35 and $(8 \times 30)(8 \times 5)$ **48.** $14 + 7 + 6$ and $6 + 14 + 7$

49. $(9 \times 7) \times 6$ and $9 \times (7 \times 6)$ **50.** $24 \div 6 \div 2$ and $6 \div 24 \div 2$

51. Life Science Poison-dart frogs can breed underwater, and the females lay from 4 to 30 eggs. What would be the total number of eggs if four female poison-dart frogs each laid 27 eggs?

Use the table for Exercises 52 and 53.

52. Rickie wants to buy 3 garden hoses. How much will they cost?

53. The boys in Josh's family are saving money to buy 4 ceiling fans. How much will they need to save?

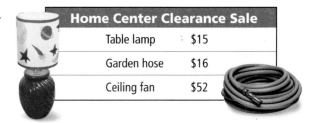

Home Center Clearance Sale	
Table lamp	$15
Garden hose	$16
Ceiling fan	$52

54. Critical Thinking Give a problem that you could simplify using the Commutative and Associative Properties. Then, show the steps to solve the problem and label the Commutative and Associative Properties.

55. What's The Error? A student wrote $5 + 24 + 25 + 6 = 5 + 25 + 24 + 6$ by the Associative Property. What error did the student make?

56. Write About It Why can you simplify $5(50 + 3)$ using the Distributive Property? Why can't you simplify $5(50) + 3$ using the Distributive Property?

57. Challenge Explain how you could find the product of $5^2 \times 112$ using the Distributive Property. Simplify the expression.

Florida Spiral Review MA.6.A.3.5

58. Multiple Choice Which expression does NOT have the same value as $7 \times (4 + 23)$?

A. 7×27 **B.** $(7 \times 4) + (7 \times 23)$ **C.** $7 \times 4 + 23$ **D.** $28 + (7 \times 23)$

59. Short Response Tia is making 5 posters. Each poster is 17 in. by 20 in. The expression $5 \times (17 \times 20)$ represents the total amount of poster board that she needs.

a. Use properties to show that the expression is equivalent to $(5 \times 20) \times 17$. Find the total amount of poster board that Tia needs.

b. What is the advantage of the expression from part a over the original expression? Explain.

Simplify each expression. (Lessons 1-2, 1-3)

60. $10^4 - 10^3 + 10$ **61.** $18 \div 3^2 + 8$ **62.** $(5 \times 2^3 - 1^5) \div 3 + 1$

Variables and Expressions

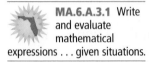

MA.6.A.3.1 Write and evaluate mathematical expressions . . . given situations.

Vocabulary

variable

constant

algebraic expression

evaluate

Inflation is the rise in prices that occurs over time. For example, you would have paid about $7 in the year 2000 for something that cost only $1 in 1950.

With this information, you can convert prices in 1950 to their equivalent prices in 2000.

1950	2000
$1	$7
$2	$14
$3	$21
$p	$p × 7

Input

Output

A **variable** is a letter or symbol that represents a quantity that can change. In the table above, p is a variable that stands for any price in 1950. A **constant** is a quantity that does not change. For example, the price of something in 2000 is always 7 times the price in 1950.

An **algebraic expression** contains one or more variables and may contain operation symbols. So $p × 7$ is an algebraic expression.

Algebraic Expressions	Numerical Expressions
$150 + y$	$85 ÷ 5$
$35 × w + z$	$10 + 3 × 5$

To **evaluate** an algebraic expression, substitute a number for the variable and then find the value by simplifying.

EXAMPLE 1 Evaluating Algebraic Expressions

Animated Math
@ thinkcentral.com

Evaluate each expression to find the missing values in the tables.

A

w	$w ÷ 11$
55	5
66	
77	

Substitute for w in $w ÷ 11$.

$w = 55$; $55 ÷ 11 = 5$

$w = 66$; $66 ÷ 11 = 6$

$w = 77$; $77 ÷ 11 = 7$

The missing values are 6 and 7.

Video **Lesson Tutorial Videos** @ thinkcentral.com

Evaluate each expression to find the missing values in the tables.

B

n	$4 \times n + 6^2$
1	40
2	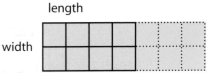
3	

Substitute for n in $4 \times n + 6^2$.
Use the order of operations.

$n = 1$; $4 \times 1 + 36 = 40$
$n = 2$; $4 \times 2 + 36 = 44$
$n = 3$; $4 \times 3 + 36 = 48$

The missing values are 44 and 48.

Writing Math

When you are multiplying a number times a variable, the number is written first. Write "$3x$" and not "$x3$." Read $3x$ as "three x."

You can write multiplication and division expressions without using the symbols $\times$ and $\div$.

Instead of . . .	You can write . . .
$x \times 3$	$x \cdot 3 \quad x(3) \quad 3x$
$35 \div y$	$\dfrac{35}{y}$

EXAMPLE 2 Evaluating Expressions with Two Variables

A rectangle is 2 units wide. What is the area of the rectangle if it is 4, 5, 6, or 7 units long?

You can multiply length and width to find area, which is measured in square units. Let ℓ be length and w be width.

ℓ	w	$\ell \times w$
4	2	8
5	2	
6	2	
7	2	

Make a table to help you find the number of square units for each length.
$\ell = 4$; $4 \times 2 = 8$ square units
$\ell = 5$; $5 \times 2 = 10$ square units
$\ell = 6$; $6 \times 2 = 12$ square units
$\ell = 7$; $7 \times 2 = 14$ square units

The rectangle will cover 8, 10, 12, or 14 square units.

Check
Draw a rectangle 2 units wide. Then count the total number of square units when the rectangle is 4, 5, 6, and 7 units long.

length

width

Think and Discuss

1. Name a quantity that is a variable and a quantity that is a constant.

2. Explain why $45 + x$ is an algebraic expression.

MA.6.A.3.1

GUIDED PRACTICE

See Example ① Evaluate each expression to find the missing values in the tables.

1.

n	n + 7
38	45
49	▪
58	▪

2.

x	12x + 2³
8	104
9	▪
10	▪

See Example ② **3.** A rectangle is 4 units wide. How many square units does the rectangle cover if it is 6, 7, 8, or 9 units long?

INDEPENDENT PRACTICE

See Example ① Evaluate each expression to find the missing values in the tables.

4.

x	4x
50	200
100	▪
150	▪

5.

n	2n − 3²
10	11
16	▪
17	▪

See Example ② **6.** A builder is designing a rectangular patio that has a length of 12 units. Find the total number of square units the patio will cover if the width is 4, 5, 6, or 7 units.

PRACTICE AND PROBLEM SOLVING

7. Estimation Bobby drives his truck at a rate of 50 to 60 miles per hour.
a. Approximately how far can Bobby drive in 2, 3, 4, and 5 hours?
b. Bobby plans to take an 8-hour trip, which will include a 1-hour stop for lunch. What is a reasonable distance for Bobby to drive?

8. Multi-Step Each table in the cafeteria seats 8 people. Find the total number of people that can be seated at 7, 8, 9, and 10 tables. If the average bill per person is $12, how much money can the cafeteria expect from 7, 8, 9, and 10 tables that have no empty seats?

9. Measurement When traveling in Europe, Jessika converts the temperature given in degrees Celsius to a Fahrenheit temperature by using the expression $9x \div 5 + 32$, where x is the Celsius temperature. Find the temperature in degrees Fahrenheit when it is 0 °C, 10 °C, and 25 °C.

10. Geometry To find the area of a triangle, you can use the expression $b \times h \div 2$, where b is the base of the triangle and h is its height. Find the area of a triangle with a base of 5 cm and a height of 6 cm.

○ = WORKED-OUT SOLUTIONS
on p. WS2

Evaluate each expression for the given value of the variable.

11. $3h + 2$ for $h = 10$ | **12.** $2x^2$ for $x = 3$ | **13.** $t - 7$ for $t = 20$

14. $4p - 3$ for $p = 20$ | **15.** $\frac{c}{7}$ for $c = 56$ | **16.** $10 + 2r$ for $r = 5$

17. $3x + 17$ for $x = 13$ | **18.** $5p$ for $p = 12$ | **19.** $s^2 - 15$ for $s = 5$

20. $14 - 2c$ for $c = 2$ | **21.** $10x$ for $x = 11$ | **22.** $4j + 12$ for $j = 9$

23. Money The zloty is the currency in Poland. In 2005, 1 U.S. dollar was worth 3 zlotys. How many zlotys were equivalent to 8 U.S. dollars?

24. Use the graph to complete the table.

Why does a Polish coin show Australia and a kangaroo? This coin honors Pawel Edmund Strzelecki, a Pole who explored and mapped much of Australia.

Cups of Water	Number of Lemons
8	
12	
16	
w	

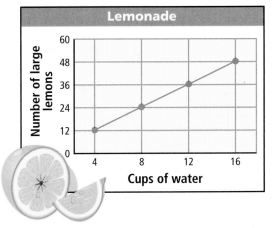

25. What's the Error? A student evaluated the expression $x \div 2$ for $x = 14$ and gave an answer of 28. What did the student do wrong?

26. Write About It How would you evaluate the expression $2x + 5$ for $x = 1, 2, 3,$ and 4?

27. Challenge Using the algebraic expression $3n - 5$, what is the smallest whole-number value for n that will give you a result greater than 100?

Florida Spiral Review MA.6.A.3.1, MA.6.A.3.5

28. Multiple Choice Evaluate $8m - 5$ for $m = 9$.

A. 67   B. 83   C. 84   D. 94

29. Gridded Response Evaluate the expression $4p + 18$ for $p = 5$.

30. Write an equivalent expression for $5 \times (2 \times 17)$ that is easier to simplify with mental math. Write the property you used and then simplify the expression. (Lesson 2-1)

31. Ralph wants to simplify the expression 14×21. What property allows him to rewrite the expression as $14 \times 20 + 14 \times 1$? Simplify the expression. (Lesson 2-1)

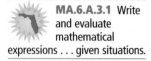

2-3 Translating Between Words and Math

MA.6.A.3.1 Write and evaluate mathematical expressions . . . given situations.

The distance from Charlotte, North Carolina, to Charlotte Harbor, Florida, is 675 miles. Beth drove *c* miles from Charlotte, NC, toward Charlotte Harbor, FL. How many more miles must Beth drive?

In word problems, you may need to identify the action to translate words to math.

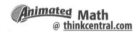 **Animated Math @ thinkcentral.com**

Action	Put together or combine	Find how much more or less	Put together groups of equal parts	Separate into equal groups
Operation	Add	Subtract	Multiply	Divide

To solve this problem, you need to find how many more miles Beth must drive. To find *how much more*, subtract.

$$675 - c$$

Beth must drive $675 - c$ more miles to reach Charlotte Harbor, FL.

EXAMPLE **1** *Social Studies Applications*

A The Nile River is the world's longest river. Let *n* stand for the length in miles of the Nile. The Amazon River is 4,000 miles long. Write an expression to show how much longer the Nile is than the Amazon.

To *find how much longer*, subtract the length of the Amazon from the length of the Nile.

$$n \qquad - \qquad 4{,}000$$

The Nile is $n - 4{,}000$ miles longer than the Amazon.

B Let *s* represent the number of senators that each of the 50 states has in the U.S. Senate. Write an expression for the total number of senators.

To *put together 50 equal groups of s*, multiply 50 times *s*.

$$50s$$

There are 50*s* senators in the U.S. Senate.

There are several different ways to write math expressions with words.

Operation	➕	➖	✖	➗
Numerical Expression	$37 + 28$	$90 - 12$	8×48 or $8 \cdot 48$ or $(8)(48)$ or $8(48)$ or $(8)48$	$327 \div 3$ or $\frac{327}{3}$
Words	• 28 **added** to 37 • 37 **plus** 28 • the **sum** of 37 and 28 • 28 **more than** 37	• 12 **subtracted** from 90 • 90 **minus** 12 • the **difference** of 90 and 12 • 12 **less than** 90 • **take away** 12 from 90	• 8 **times** 48 • 48 **multiplied** by 8 • the **product** of 8 and 48 • 8 **groups** of 48	• 327 **divided** by 3 • the **quotient** of 327 and 3
Algebraic Expression	$x + 28$	$k - 12$	$8 \cdot w$ or $(8)(w)$ or $8w$	$n \div 3$ or $\frac{n}{3}$
Words	• 28 **added** to x • x **plus** 28 • the **sum** of x and 28 • 28 **more than** x	• 12 **subtracted** from k • k **minus** 12 • the **difference** of k and 12 • 12 **less than** k • **take away** 12 from k	• 8 **times** w • w **multiplied** by 8 • the **product** of 8 and w • 8 **groups** of w	• n **divided** by 3 • the **quotient** of n and 3

EXAMPLE **2** **Translating Words into Math**

Write each phrase as a numerical or algebraic expression.

A 287 plus 932

$287 + 932$

B b divided by 14

$b \div 14$ or $\frac{b}{14}$

EXAMPLE **3** **Translating Math into Words**

Write two phrases for each expression.

A $a - 45$
• a minus 45
• take away 45 from a

B $(34)(7)$
• the **product** of 34 and 7
• 7 **multiplied** by 34

Think and Discuss

1. Tell how to write each of the following phrases as a numerical or algebraic expression: 75 less than 1,023; the product of 125 and z.

2. Give two examples of "$a \div 17$" expressed with words.

Homework Help THINK central

Go to **thinkcentral.com**
Exercises 1–27, 29, 31, 33, 37

MA.6.A.3.1

GUIDED PRACTICE

See Example 1

1. Social Studies The Big Island of Hawaii is the largest Hawaiian island, with an area of 4,028 mi^2. The next biggest island is Maui. Let m represent the area of Maui. Write an expression for the difference between the two areas.

See Example 2

Write each phrase as a numerical or algebraic expression.

2. 279 minus 125   **3.** the product of 15 and x **4.** 17 plus 4

5. p divided by 5   **6.** the sum of 9 and q **7.** 149 times 2

See Example 3

Write two phrases for each expression.

8. $r + 87$ **9.** 345×196 **10.** $476 \div 28$ **11.** $d - 5$

INDEPENDENT PRACTICE

See Example 1

12. Social Studies In 2005, California had 21 more seats in the U.S. Congress than Texas had. If t represents the number of seats Texas had, write an expression for the number of seats California had.

13. Let x represent the number of television show episodes recorded in a season. Write an expression for the number of episodes recorded in 5 seasons.

See Example 2

Write each phrase as a numerical or algebraic expression.

14. 25 less than k **15.** the quotient of 325 and 25

16. 34 times w **17.** 675 added to 137

18. the sum of 135 and p **19.** take away 14 from j

See Example 3

Write two phrases for each expression.

20. $h + 65$ **21.** $243 - 19$ **22.** $125 \div n$ **23.** $342(75)$

24. $\frac{d}{27}$ **25.** $45 \cdot 23$ **26.** $629 + c$ **27.** $228 - b$

PRACTICE AND PROBLEM SOLVING

Translate each phrase into a numerical or algebraic expression.

28. 13 less than z **29.** 15 divided by d

30. 874 times 23   **31.** m multiplied by 67

32. the sum of 35, 74, and 21   **33.** 319 less than 678

34. Critical Thinking Paula and Manda were asked to write an expression to find the total number of shoes in a closet. Let s represent the number of pairs of shoes. Paula wrote s and Manda wrote $2s$. Who is correct? Explain.

 35. Write About It Write a situation that could be modeled by the expression $x + 5$.

○ = **WORKED-OUT SOLUTIONS**
on p. WS3

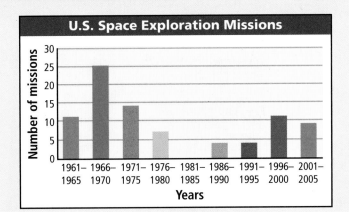

The graph shows the number of U.S. space exploration missions from 1961 to 2005.

U.S. Space Exploration Missions

36. Between 1966 and 1970, the Soviet Union had *m* fewer space missions than the United States. Write an algebraic expression for this situation.

37. Let *d* represent the number of dollars spent on space missions from 1986 to 1990. Write an expression for the average cost per mission during this time.

38. ✏️ **Write a Problem** Use the data in the graph to write a word problem that can be answered with a numerical or algebraic expression.

39. Critical Thinking Let *p* stand for the number of missions between 1996 and 2000 that had people aboard. What operation would you use to write an expression for the number of missions without people? Explain.

40. ⭐ **Challenge** Write an expression for the following: two more than the number of missions from 1971 to 1975, minus the number of missions from 1986 to 1990. Then simplify the expression.

41. Multiple Choice Which expression represents the product of 79 and *x*?

A. $79 + x$ **B.** $x - 79$ **C.** $79x$ **D.** $\frac{x}{79}$

42. Extended Response Tim is driving from Ames, Iowa to Canton, Ohio. He is 280 miles from Ames when he stops for gas. Write an expression to represent the number of miles Tim has left to drive. Explain. Translate your expression into two different word phrases.

Evaluate each expression for the given value of the variable. (Lesson 2-2)

43. $2y + 6$ for $y = 4$ **44.** $\frac{z}{5}$ for $z = 40$ **45.** $7r - 3$ for $r = 18$ **46.** $\frac{p}{7} + 12$ for $p = 28$

47. Which is NOT an example of the Commutative Property? Explain. (Lesson 2-1)

  I. $13 + 27 = 27 + 13$ **II.** $8 \times (4 \times 3) = 8 \times (3 \times 4)$ **III.** $8 \times (4 \times 3) = (8 \times 4) \times 3$

Translating Between Tables and Expressions

MA.6.A.3.1 Write and evaluate mathematical expressions . . . given situations.

Ray Robson is the youngest chess master in the history of the state of Florida. In 2008, he became the youngest IM, or *International Master*, in the United States. The table shows the number of pieces needed to play a number of games at the same time at a chess tournament.

Games	Pieces
1	32
2	64
3	96
n	$32n$

The number of pieces is always 32 times the number of games. For n games, the expression $32n$ gives the number of pieces that are needed.

EXAMPLE **Writing an Expression**

Write an expression for the missing value in each table.

A

Reilly's Age	Ashley's Age
9	11
10	12
11	13
12	14
n	▩

Ashley's age is Reilly's age plus 2.

$9 + 2 = 11$
$10 + 2 = 12$
$11 + 2 = 13$
$12 + 2 = 14$
$n + 2$

When Reilly's age is n, Ashley's age is $n + 2$.

B

Eggs	Dozens
12	1
24	2
36	3
48	4
e	▩

The number of dozens is the number of eggs divided by 12.

$12 \div 12 = 1$
$24 \div 12 = 2$
$36 \div 12 = 3$
$48 \div 12 = 4$
$e \div 12$

When there are e eggs, the number of dozens is $e \div 12$, or $\frac{e}{12}$.

You can look for a pattern in a table to help you write an expression.

EXAMPLE 2 Writing an Expression for a Sequence

Write an expression for the sequence in the table.

Position	1	2	3	4	5	n
Value of Term	3	5	7	9	11	

Look for a relationship between the positions and the values of the terms in the sequence. Use guess and check.

Guess $3n$.
Check by substituting 2.
$3 \times 2 \neq 5$ ✗

Guess $2n + 1$.
Check by substituting 3.
$2 \times 3 + 1 = 7$ ✔

The expression $2n + 1$ works for the entire sequence.
$2 \times 1 + 1 = 3, 2 \times 2 + 1 = 5, 2 \times 3 + 1 = 7,$
$2 \times 4 + 1 = 9, 2 \times 5 + 1 = 11$

The expression for the sequence is $2n + 1$.

Caution!

When you write an expression for data in a table, check that the expression works for *all* of the data in the table.

EXAMPLE 3 Writing an Expression for the Area of a Figure

A triangle has a base of 8 inches. The table shows the area of the triangle for different heights. Write an expression that can be used to find the area of the triangle when its height is h inches.

Base (in.)	Height (in.)	Area (in^2)
8	1	4
8	2	8
8	3	12
8	4	16
8	h	

$8 \times 1 = 8, \quad 8 \div 2 = 4$
$8 \times 2 = 16, \ 16 \div 2 = 8$
$8 \times 3 = 24, \ 24 \div 2 = 12$
$8 \times 4 = 32, \ 32 \div 2 = 16$
$8 \times h = 8h, \ 8h \div 2$

In each row of the table, the area is half the product of the base and the height. The expression is $\frac{8h}{2}$, or $4h$.

Think and Discuss

1. **Describe** how to write an expression for a sequence given in a table.

2. **Explain** why it is important to check your expression for all of the data in a table.

Exercises

Homework Help
Go to **thinkcentral.com**
Exercises 1–7, 9, 11, 13

MA.6.A.3.1

GUIDED PRACTICE

See Example 1   Write an expression for the missing value in each table.

1.

Go-Carts	1	2	3	4	n
Wheels	4	8	12	16	

See Example 2   Write an expression for the sequence in the table.

2.

Position	1	2	3	4	5	n
Value of Term	9	10	11	12	13	

See Example 3   **3.** A rectangle has a length of 5 inches. The table shows the area of the rectangle for different widths. Write an expression that can be used to find the area of the rectangle when its width is w inches.

Length (in.)	Width (in.)	Area (in²)
5	2	10
5	4	20
5	6	30
5	8	40
5	w	

INDEPENDENT PRACTICE

See Example 1   Write an expression for the missing value in each table.

4.

Players	Soccer Teams
22	2
44	4
66	6
88	8
n	

5.

Weeks	Days
4	28
8	56
12	84
16	112
n	

See Example 2   Write an expression for the sequence in the table.

6.

Position	1	2	3	4	5	n
Value of Term	7	12	17	22	27	

See Example 3   **7.** The table shows the area of a square with different side lengths. Write an expression that can be used to find the area of a square when its side length is s feet.

Length (ft)	2	4	6	8	s
Area (ft²)	4	16	36	64	

Make a table for each sequence. Then write an expression for the sequence.

8. 2, 4, 6, 8, . . .   **9.** 6, 7, 8, 9, . . .   **10.** 10, 20, 30, 40, . . .

11. **Earth Science** The planet Mercury takes 88 days to make a complete orbit of the Sun. The table shows the number of orbits and the number of days it takes to make the orbits. Write an expression for the number of days it takes Mercury to make n orbits.

Orbits	Days
1	88
2	176
3	264
n	■

12. **Multi-Step** The entry fee for a county fair is $10. Each ride at the fair costs $2. The table shows the total cost to go on various numbers of rides. Write an expression for the cost of r rides. Then use the expression to find the cost of 12 rides.

Number of Rides	1	3	5	8	10	r
Total Cost ($)	12	16	20	26	30	■

13. **Critical Thinking** Write two different expressions that describe the relationship in the table.

Position (n)	Value of Term
3	10

14. **Write About It** Explain how you can make a table of values for the expression $4n + 3$.

15. **Challenge** Can there be more than one expression that describes a set of data in a table? Explain.

Florida Spiral Review   MA.6.A.3.1

16. **Multiple Choice** Which expression describes the sequence in the table?

Position	1	2	3	4	5	n
Value of Term	6	11	16	21	26	■

A. $n + 5$ **B.** $5n + 1$ **C.** $6n$ **D.** $6n - 1$

17. **Multiple Choice** Evaluate the expression $2t - (t - 3)$ for $t = 4$. (Lesson 2-2)

F. 6   **G.** 7   **H.** 8   **I.** 9

18. **Short Response** Lucy has a dollar and some quarters in her pocket. She says the value of the money can be represented by the expression $0.25(q + 4)$, where q is the number of quarters. Jose says the expression should be $1 + 0.25q$. (Lessons 2-1, 2-2)

a. Evaluate each expression for $q = 3$.
b. Use properties to show that $0.25(3 + 4)$ is equivalent to $1 + 0.25(3)$.

 **Ready To Go On?**
SECTION 2A

Quiz for Lessons 2-1 Through 2-4

2-1 Properties and Mental Math

Simplify.

1. $4 + 21 + 9 + 6$ **2.** $5 \times 17 \times 2$ **3.** $45 + 19 + 1 + 55$ **4.** $2 \times 17 \times 10$

Use the Distributive Property to find each product.

5. 5×62 **6.** 9×41 **7.** 4×23 **8.** 7×14 **9.** 5×34

2-2 Variables and Expressions

Evaluate each expression to find the missing values in the tables.

10.

y	23 + y
17	40
27	▨
37	▨

11.

w	w × 3 + 10
4	22
5	▨
6	▨

12. Stephanie's CD holder holds 6 CDs per page. How many CDs does Stephanie have if she fills 2, 3, 4, or 5 pages?

2-3 Translating Between Words and Math

13. The small and large intestines are part of the digestive system. The small intestine is longer than the large intestine. Let n represent the length in feet of the small intestine. The large intestine is 5 feet long. Write an expression to show how much longer the small intestine is than the large intestine.

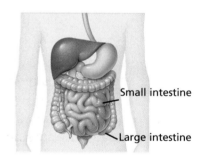
Small intestine
Large intestine

Write an algebraic expression or phrase.

14. 719 minus x **15.** t multiplied by 7 **16.** the sum of n and 51

17. $n + 19$ **18.** $72 - x$ **19.** $\frac{t}{12}$ **20.** $15s$

2-4 Translating Between Tables and Expressions

Write an expression for the missing value in the table.

21.

Position	1	2	3	4	5	n
Value of Term	8	16	24	32	40	▨

Make a table for each sequence. Then write an expression for the sequence.

22. 3, 4, 5, 6, . . . **23.** 4, 7, 10, 13, . . .

Focus on Problem Solving

Understand the Problem

• Identify too much or too little information

Problems often give too much or too little information. You must decide whether you have enough information to work the problem.

Read the problem and identify the facts that are given. Can you use any of these facts to arrive at an answer? Are there facts in the problem that are not necessary to find the answer? These questions can help you determine whether you have too much or too little information.

If you cannot solve the problem with the information given, decide what information you need. Then read the problem again to be sure you haven't missed the information in the problem.

LA.6.4.2.2 The student will . . . organize and record information . . .

Copy each problem. Circle the important facts. Underline any facts that you do not need to answer the question. If there is not enough information, list the additional information you need.

1 The reticulated python is one of the longest snakes in the world. One was found in Indonesia in 1912 that was 33 feet long. At birth, a reticulated python is 2 feet long. Suppose an adult python is 29 feet long. Let f represent the number of feet the python grew since birth. What is the value of f?

2 The largest flying flag in the world is 7,410 square feet and weighs 180 pounds. There are a total of 13 horizontal stripes on it. Let h represent the height of each stripe. What is the value of h?

3 The elevation of Mt. McKinley is 20,320 ft. People who climb Mt. McKinley are flown to a base camp located at 7,200 ft. From there, they begin a climb that may last 20 days or longer. Let d represent the distance from the base camp to the summit of Mt. McKinley. What is the value of d?

4 Let c represent the cost of a particular computer in 1981. Six years later, in 1987, the price of the computer had increased to $3,600. What is the value of c?

2-5 Equations and Their Solutions

MA.6.A.3.2 Write [and] solve . . . one-step linear equations . . .

An **equation** is a mathematical statement that two expressions are equal. You can think of a correct equation as a balanced scale.

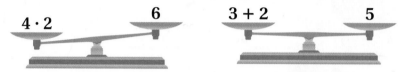

$4 \cdot 2$ 6 $3 + 2$ 5

Vocabulary

equation

solution

Equations may contain variables. If a value for a variable makes an equation true, that value is a **solution** of the equation.

You can test a value to see whether it is a solution of an equation by substituting the value for the variable.

 **Math**
@ thinkcentral.com

$$s + 15 = 27$$

$s = 12$ $s = 10$

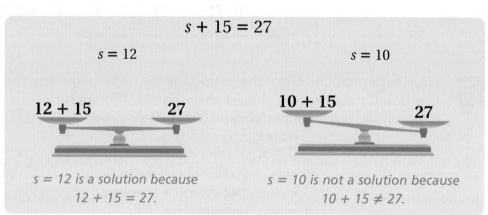

$12 + 15$ 27 $10 + 15$ 27

Reading Math

The symbol ≠ means "is not equal to."

s = 12 is a solution because 12 + 15 = 27.   *s = 10 is not a solution because 10 + 15 ≠ 27.*

EXAMPLE 1   **Determining Solutions of Equations**

Determine whether the given value of the variable is a solution.

A $a + 23 = 82$ for $a = 61$

$a + 23 = 82$

$61 + 23 \stackrel{?}{=} 82$ *Substitute 61 for a.*

$84 \stackrel{?}{=} 82$ *Add.*

84   82

Since $84 \neq 82$, 61 is not a solution of $a + 23 = 82$.

Determine whether the given value of the variable is a solution.

B $60 \div c = 6$ for $c = 10$

$60 \div c = 6$

$60 \div 10 \overset{?}{=} 6$ *Substitute 10 for c.*

$6 \overset{?}{=} 6$ *Divide.*

6	**6**

Because $6 = 6$, 10 is a solution of $60 \div c = 6$.

You can use equations to check whether measurements given in different units are equal.

For example, there are 12 inches in one foot. If you have a measurement in feet, multiply by 12 to find the measurement in inches: $12 \cdot \text{feet} = \text{inches}$, or $12f = i$.

If you have one measurement in feet and another in inches, check whether the two numbers make the equation $12f = i$ true.

EXAMPLE 2

Life Science Application

One science book states that a male giraffe can grow to be 19 feet tall. According to another book, a male giraffe may grow to 228 inches. Determine if these two measurements are equal.

$12f = i$

$12 \cdot 19 \overset{?}{=} 228$ *Substitute.*

$228 \overset{?}{=} 228$ *Multiply.*

Because $228 = 228$, 19 feet is equal to 228 inches.

Reading Math

An equation has an equal sign, but an expression does not. An equation can be solved, but an expression can only be evaluated or simplified.

Think and Discuss

1. Tell which of the following is the solution of $y \div 2 = 9$: $y = 14$, $y = 16$, or $y = 18$. How do you know?

2. Give an example of an equation with a solution of 15.

Homework Help

Go to **thinkcentral.com**
Exercises 1–21, 25, 27, 29, 35, 37, 39, 41

 MA.6.A.3.2

GUIDED PRACTICE

See Example **1** — Determine whether the given value of the variable is a solution.

1. $c + 23 = 48$ for $c = 35$ **2.** $z + 31 = 73$ for $z = 42$

3. $96 = 130 - d$ for $d = 34$ **4.** $85 = 194 - a$ for $a = 105$

5. $75 \div y = 5$ for $y = 15$ **6.** $78 \div n = 13$ for $n = 5$

See Example **2** — **7. Social Studies** An almanac states that the Minnehaha Waterfall in Minnesota is 53 feet tall. A tour guide said the Minnehaha Waterfall is 636 inches tall. Determine if these two measurements are equal.

INDEPENDENT PRACTICE

See Example **1** — Determine whether the given value of the variable is a solution.

8. $w + 19 = 49$ for $w = 30$ **9.** $d + 27 = 81$ for $d = 44$

10. $g + 34 = 91$ for $g = 67$ **11.** $k + 16 = 55$ for $k = 39$

12. $101 = 150 - h$ for $h = 49$ **13.** $89 = 111 - m$ for $m = 32$

14. $116 = 144 - q$ for $q = 38$ **15.** $92 = 120 - t$ for $t = 28$

16. $80 \div b = 20$ for $b = 4$ **17.** $91 \div x = 7$ for $x = 12$

18. $55 \div j = 5$ for $j = 10$ **19.** $49 \div r = 7$ for $r = 7$

See Example **2** — **20. Money** Kent earns \$6 per hour at his after-school job. One week, he worked 12 hours and received a paycheck for \$66. Determine if Kent was paid the correct amount of money. (*Hint:* \$6 per hour · hours = total pay)

21. Measurement The Eiffel Tower in Paris, France, is 300 meters tall. A fact page states that it is 30,000 centimeters tall. Determine if these two measurements are equal. (*Hint:* 1 m = 100 cm)

PRACTICE AND PROBLEM SOLVING

Determine whether the given value of the variable is a solution.

22. $93 = 48 + u$ for $u = 35$ **23.** $112 = 14 \times f$ for $f = 8$

24. $13 = m \div 8$ for $m = 104$ **25.** $79 = z - 23$ for $z = 112$

26. $64 = l - 34$ for $l = 98$ **27.** $105 = p \times 7$ for $p = 14$

28. $94 \div s = 26$ for $s = 3$ **29.** $v + 79 = 167$ for $v = 88$

30. $m + 36 = 54$ for $m = 18$ **31.** $x - 35 = 96$ for $x = 112$

32. $12y = 84$ for $y = 7$ **33.** $7x = 56$ for $x = 8$

34. Estimation A large pizza has 8 slices. Determine whether 6 large pizzas will be enough for 24 people, if each person eats 2 to 3 slices of pizza.

○ = WORKED-OUT SOLUTIONS
on p. WS3

35. **Multi-Step** Rebecca has 17 one-dollar bills. Courtney has 350 nickels. Do the two girls have the same amount of money? Justify your answer. (*Hint*: First find how many nickels are in a dollar.)

Replace each ▢ with a number that makes the equation correct.

36. $4 + 1 = ▢ + 2$

37. $2 + ▢ = 6 + 2$

38. $▢ - 5 = 9 - 2$

39. $5(4) = 10(▢)$

40. $3 + 6 = ▢ - 4$

41. $12 \div 4 = 9 \div ▢$

42. **Critical Thinking** Linda is building a rectangular playhouse. The width is x feet. The length is $x + 3$ feet. The distance around the base of the playhouse is 36 feet. Is 8 the value of x? Explain.

? 43. **Choose a Strategy** What should replace the question mark to keep the scale balanced?

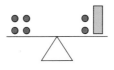 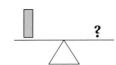

A. ●   **B.**   **C.**   **D.**

44. **Write About It** Explain how to determine if a value is a solution to an equation.

45. **Challenge** Is $n = 4$ a solution for $n^2 + 79 = 88$? Explain.

Florida Spiral Review   MA.6.A.3.2, MA.6.A.3.1

46. **Multiple Choice** For which equation is $b = 8$ a solution?

   A. $13 - b = 8$ **B.** $8 + b = 21$ **C.** $b - 13 = 21$ **D.** $b + 13 = 21$

47. **Multiple Choice** When Paul gets 53 more postcards, he will have 82 cards in his collection. Use the equation $n + 53 = 82$ to find how many postcards Paul has in his collection now.

   F. 135   **G.** 125   **H.** 29   **I.** 27

Evaluate each expression for $a = 3$ and $b = 6$. (Lesson 2-2)

48. $3ab + 10$ **49.** $b^2 - a^2$ **50.** $4(b + 2a)$ **51.** $\frac{b}{a}$

Write an expression for the sequence in the table. (Lesson 2-4)

52.

Position	1	2	3	4	5	n
Value of Term	4	7	10	13	16	▢

MA.6.A.3.2 Write [and] solve . . . one-step linear equations . . .

Vocabulary
inverse operations

Some surfers recommend that the length of a beginner's surfboard be 14 inches greater than the surfer's height. If a surfboard is 82 inches, how tall should the surfer be to ride it?

The height of the surfer *combined* with 14 inches equals 82 inches. To combine amounts, you need to add.

Let h stand for the surfer's height. You can use the equation $h + 14 = 82$.

The equation $h + 14 = 82$ can be represented as a balanced scale.

To find the value of h, you need h by itself on one side of a balanced scale.

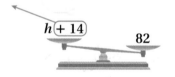

To get h by itself, first take away 14 from the left side of the scale. Now the scale is unbalanced.

To rebalance the scale, take away 14 from the other side.

Taking away 14 from both sides of the scale is the same as subtracting 14 from both sides of the equation.

$$\begin{array}{rcr} h + 14 = & & 82 \\ \underline{-14} & & \underline{-14} \\ h \quad = & & 68 \end{array}$$

A surfer using an 82-inch surfboard should be 68 inches tall.

Inverse operations undo each other. Addition and subtraction are inverse operations. If an equation contains addition, solve it by subtracting from both sides to "undo" the addition.

Video **Lesson Tutorial Videos @ thinkcentral.com**

EXAMPLE 1 **Solving Addition Equations**

Solve each equation. Check your answers.

A $x + 62 = 93$

$$
\begin{array}{rl}
x + 62 = & 93 \\
- 62 & - 62 \\
\hline
x = & 31
\end{array}
$$

62 is added to x.
Subtract 62 from both sides to undo the addition.

Check $x + 62 = 93$
$$31 + 62 \overset{?}{=} 93$$
$$93 \overset{?}{=} 93 \checkmark$$

Substitute 31 for x in the equation.
31 is the solution.

B $81 = 17 + y$

$$
\begin{array}{rl}
81 = & 17 + y \\
- 17 & - 17 \\
\hline
64 = & y
\end{array}
$$

17 is added to y.
Subtract 17 from both sides to undo the addition.

Check $81 = 17 + y$
$$81 \overset{?}{=} 17 + 64$$
$$81 \overset{?}{=} 81 \checkmark$$

Substitute 64 for y in the equation.
64 is the solution.

EXAMPLE 2 *Social Studies Application*

Tulsa, Oklahoma City, and Lawton are located in Oklahoma, as shown on the map. Find the distance d between Oklahoma City and Tulsa.

distance between Tulsa and Lawton	=	distance between Oklahoma City and Lawton	+	distance between Oklahoma City and Tulsa
175	=	75	+	d

$$
\begin{array}{rl}
175 = & 75 + d \\
-75 & -75 \\
\hline
100 = & d
\end{array}
$$

75 is added to d.
Subtract 75 from both sides to undo the addition.

The distance between Oklahoma City and Tulsa is 100 miles.

Think and Discuss

1. Tell whether the solution of $c + 4 = 21$ will be less than 21 or greater than 21. Explain.

2. Describe how you could check your answer in Example 2.

Homework Help THINK central

Go to **thinkcentral.com**
Exercises 1–17, 21, 23, 25, 27, 29, 31, 33

MA.6.A.3.2

GUIDED PRACTICE

See Example 1 Solve each equation. Check your answers.

1. $x + 54 = 90$ **2.** $49 = 12 + y$ **3.** $n + 27 = 46$

4. $22 + t = 91$ **5.** $31 = p + 13$ **6.** $c + 38 = 54$

See Example 2 **7.** Lou, Michael, and Georgette live on Mulberry Street, as shown on the map. Lou lives 10 blocks from Georgette. Georgette lives 4 blocks from Michael. How many blocks does Michael live from Lou?

INDEPENDENT PRACTICE

See Example 1 Solve each equation. Check your answers.

8. $x + 19 = 24$ **9.** $10 = r + 3$ **10.** $s + 11 = 50$

11. $b + 17 = 42$ **12.** $12 + m = 28$ **13.** $z + 68 = 77$

14. $72 = n + 51$ **15.** $g + 28 = 44$ **16.** $27 = 15 + y$

See Example 2 **17.** What is the length of a killer whale?

PRACTICE AND PROBLEM SOLVING

Solve each equation.

18. $x + 12 = 16$ **19.** $n + 32 = 39$ **20.** $23 + q = 34$

21. $52 + y = 71$ **22.** $73 = c + 35$ **23.** $93 = h + 15$

24. $125 = n + 85$ **25.** $87 = b + 18$ **26.** $12 + y = 50$

27. $t + 17 = 43$ **28.** $k + 9 = 56$ **29.** $25 + m = 47$

○ = WORKED-OUT SOLUTIONS
on p. WS3

Write an equation for each statement.

30. The number of eggs e increased by 3 equals 14.

31. The number of new photos taken p added to 20 equals 36.

32. Physical Science Temperature can be measured in degrees Fahrenheit, degrees Celsius, or kelvins. To convert from degrees Celsius to kelvins, add 273 to the Celsius temperature. Complete the table.

	Kelvins (K)	°C + 273 = K	Celsius (°C)
Water Freezes	273	°C + 273 = 273	▨
Body Temperature	310	▨	▨
Water Boils	373	▨	▨

33. History In 1520, the explorer Ferdinand Magellan tried to measure the depth of the ocean. He weighted a 370 m rope and lowered it into the ocean. This rope was not long enough to reach the ocean floor. Suppose the depth at this location was 1,250 m. How much longer would Magellan's rope had to have been to reach the ocean floor?

? 34. Write a Problem Use data from your science book to write a problem that can be solved using an addition equation. Solve your problem.

35. Write About It Why are addition and subtraction called inverse operations?

36. Challenge In the magic square at right, each row, column, and diagonal has the same sum. Find the values of x, y, and z.

7	61	x
y	37	1
31	z	67

Florida Spiral Review

MA.6.A.3.2, MA.6.A.3.1

37. Multiple Choice Pauline hit 6 more home runs than Danielle. Pauline hit 18 home runs. How many home runs did Danielle hit?

A. 3   **B.** 12   **C.** 18   **D.** 24

38. Multiple Choice Which is the solution to the equation $79 + r = 118$?

F. $r = 39$ **G.** $r = 52$ **H.** $r = 79$ **I.** $r = 197$

Evaluate each expression to find the missing values in the table. (Lesson 2-2)

39.

x	5	6	7	8
$9x$	45	▨	▨	▨

40.

y	121	99	77	55
$y \div 11$	11	▨	▨	▨

41. Which is NOT an example of the Associative Property? Explain. (Lesson 2-1)

    I. $3 \times 41 = 41 \times 3$ **II.** $2 + (4 + 7) = (2 + 4) + 7$ **III.** $9 \times (5 \times 3) = (9 \times 5) \times 3$

MA.6.A.3.2 Write [and] solve . . . one-step linear equations . . .

When Theodore Roosevelt became president of the United States, he was 42 years old. He was 27 years younger than Ronald Reagan was when Reagan became president. How old was Reagan when he became president?

Let a represent Ronald Reagan's age.

Ronald Reagan's age	–	27	=	Theodore Roosevelt's age
a	–	27	=	42

Recall that addition and subtraction are inverse operations. When an equation contains subtraction, use addition to "undo" the subtraction. Remember to add the same amount to both sides of the equation.

$$a - 27 = 42$$
$$\underline{+\ 27 \quad +\ 27}$$
$$a \quad = \quad 69$$

Ronald Reagan was 69 years old when he became president.

EXAMPLE **1** **Solving Subtraction Equations**

Solve each equation. Check your answers.

Animated Math
@ thinkcentral.com

A $p - 2 = 5$

$$p - 2 = 5 \qquad \text{\textit{2 is subtracted from p.}}$$
$$\underline{+\ 2 \quad +\ 2} \qquad \text{\textit{Add 2 to both sides to undo}}$$
$$p \quad = \quad 7 \qquad \text{\textit{the subtraction.}}$$

Check $p - 2 = 5$

$$7 - 2 \overset{?}{=} 5 \qquad \text{\textit{Substitute 7 for p in the equation.}}$$
$$5 \overset{?}{=} 5 ✔ \qquad \text{\textit{7 is the solution.}}$$

Video **Lesson Tutorial Videos** @ thinkcentral.com

Solve each equation. Check your answers.

B $40 = x - 11$

$$40 = x - 11$$
$$\underline{+\ 11 \qquad\quad +\ 11}$$
$$51 = x$$

11 is subtracted from x.

Add 11 to both sides to undo the subtraction.

Check $40 = x - 11$

$$40 \stackrel{?}{=} 51 - 11$$
$$40 \stackrel{?}{=} 40 \checkmark$$

Substitute 51 for x in the equation.

51 is the solution.

C $x - 56 = 19$

$$x - 56 = \quad 19$$
$$\underline{+\ 56 \quad\ +\ 56}$$
$$x \qquad = \quad 75$$

56 is subtracted from x.

Add 56 to both sides to undo the subtraction.

Check $x - 56 = 19$

$$75 - 56 \stackrel{?}{=} 19$$
$$19 \stackrel{?}{=} 19 \checkmark$$

Substitute 75 for x in the equation.

75 is the solution.

Think and Discuss

1. **Tell** whether the solution of $b - 14 = 9$ will be less than 9 or greater than 9. Explain.

2. **Explain** how you know what number to add to both sides of an equation containing subtraction.

Exercises

 MA.6.A.3.2

Homework Help THINK central

Go to thinkcentral.com
Exercises 1–15, 17, 19, 21, 23, 25, 27, 29

GUIDED PRACTICE

See Example **1** Solve each equation. Check your answers.

1. $p - 8 = 9$
2. $3 = x - 16$
3. $a - 13 = 18$

4. $15 = y - 7$
5. $n - 24 = 9$
6. $39 = d - 2$

INDEPENDENT PRACTICE

See Example **1** Solve each equation. Check your answers.

7. $y - 18 = 7$
8. $8 = n - 5$
9. $a - 34 = 4$

10. $c - 21 = 45$
11. $a - 40 = 57$
12. $31 = x - 14$

13. $28 = p - 5$
14. $z - 42 = 7$
15. $s - 19 = 12$

Video **Lesson Tutorial Videos @ thinkcentral.com**

Solve each equation.

16. $r - 57 = 7$ **17.** $11 = x - 25$ **18.** $8 = y - 96$

19. $a - 6 = 15$ **20.** $q - 14 = 22$ **21.** $f - 12 = 2$

22. $18 = j - 19$ **23.** $109 = r - 45$ **24.** $d - 8 = 29$

25. $g - 71 = 72$ **26.** $p - 13 = 111$ **27.** $13 = m - 5$

28. Geography Mt. Rainier, in Washington, has a higher elevation than Mt. Shasta. The difference between their elevations is 248 feet. What is the elevation of Mt. Rainier? Write an equation and solve.

29. Social Studies In 2004, the population of New York City was 5 million less than the population of Shanghai, China. The population of New York City was 8 million. Solve the equation $8 = s - 5$ to find the population of Shanghai.

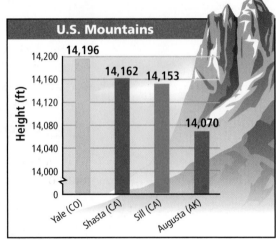

U.S. Mountains

Height (ft)

14,196

14,162

14,153

14,070

Yale (CO)   Shasta (CA)   Sill (CA)   Augusta (AK)

30. Write About It Suppose $n - 15$ is a whole number. What do you know about the value of n? Explain.

31. What's the Error? Look at the student paper at right. What did the student do wrong? What is the correct answer?

32. Challenge Write "the difference between n and 16 is 5" as an algebraic equation. Then find the solution.

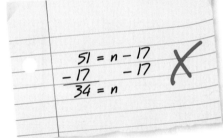

$$51 = n - 17$$
$$-17 \quad\quad -17$$
$$34 = n$$

33. Multiple Choice Which is a solution to the equation $j - 39 = 93$?

A. $j = 54$ **B.** $j = 66$ **C.** $j = 93$ **D.** $j = 132$

34. Short Response When 17 is subtracted from a number, the result is 64. Write an equation that can be used to find the original number. Then find the original number.

Write the property that is illustrated by each equation. (Lesson 2-1)

35. $4 \times (2 + 3) = 4 \times 2 + 4 \times 3$ **36.** $18 \times 2 = 2 \times 18$ **37.** $4 + (2 + 3) = (4 + 2) + 3$

Solve each equation. (Lesson 2-6)

38. $a + 3 = 18$ **39.** $y + 7 = 45$ **40.** $x + 16 = 71$ **41.** $87 = b + 31$

○ = **WORKED-OUT SOLUTIONS**
on p. WS3

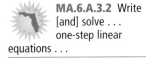

2-8 Multiplication Equations

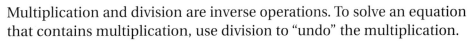

MA.6.A.3.2 Write [and] solve . . . one-step linear equations . . .

Nine-banded armadillos are always born in groups of 4. If you count 32 babies, what is the number of mother armadillos?

To put together equal groups of 4, multiply. Let m represent the number of mother armadillos. There will be m equal groups of 4.

You can use the equation $4m = 32$.

Multiplication and division are inverse operations. To solve an equation that contains multiplication, use division to "undo" the multiplication.

Caution!

$4m$ means "$4 \times m$."

$$4m = 32$$
$$\frac{4m}{4} = \frac{32}{4}$$
There are 8 mother armadillos.
$$m = 8$$

EXAMPLE 1   Solving Multiplication Equations

Animated Math
@ thinkcentral.com

Solve each equation. Check your answers.

A $3x = 12$

$3x = 12$ *x is multiplied by 3.*

$\dfrac{3x}{3} = \dfrac{12}{3}$ *Divide both sides by 3 to undo the multiplication.*

$x = 4$

Check $3x = 12$

$3(4) \overset{?}{=} 12$ *Substitute 4 for x in the equation.*

$12 \overset{?}{=} 12$ ✔   *4 is the solution.*

B $8 = 4w$

$8 = 4w$ *w is multiplied by 4.*

$\dfrac{8}{4} = \dfrac{4w}{4}$ *Divide both sides by 4 to undo the multiplication.*

$2 = w$

Check $8 = 4w$

$8 \overset{?}{=} 4(2)$ *Substitute 2 for w in the equation.*

$8 \overset{?}{=} 8$ ✔   *2 is the solution.*

EXAMPLE **2**

PROBLEM SOLVING APPLICATION

The area of a rectangle is 36 square inches. Its length is 9 inches. What is its width?

1 Understand the Problem

The **answer** will be the width of the rectangle in inches.

List the **important information:**

• The area of the rectangle is 36 square inches.

• The length of the rectangle is 9 inches.

Draw a diagram to represent this information.

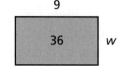

2 Make a Plan

You can write and solve an equation using the formula for area. To find the area of a rectangle, multiply its length by its width.

$$A = \ell w$$
$$36 = 9w$$

3 Solve

$36 = 9w$ *w is multiplied by 9.*

$\dfrac{36}{9} = \dfrac{9w}{9}$ *Divide both sides by 9 to undo the multiplication.*

$4 = w$

So the width of the rectangle is 4 inches.

4 Look Back

Arrange 36 identical squares in a rectangle. The length is 9, so line up the squares in rows of 9. You can make 4 rows of 9, so the width of the rectangle is 4.

Think and Discuss

1. Tell what number you would use to divide both sides of the equation $15x = 60$.

2. Tell whether the solution of $10c = 90$ will be less than 90 or greater than 90. Explain.

 MA.6.A.3.2

GUIDED PRACTICE

See Example **1** Solve each equation. Check your answers.

1. $7x = 21$ **2.** $27 = 3w$ **3.** $90 = 10a$

4. $56 = 7b$ **5.** $3c = 33$ **6.** $12 = 2n$

See Example **2** **7.** The area of a rectangular deck is 675 square feet. The deck's width is 15 feet. What is its length?

15 ft

INDEPENDENT PRACTICE

See Example **1** Solve each equation. Check your answers.

8. $12p = 36$ **9.** $52 = 13a$ **10.** $64 = 8n$

11. $20 = 5x$ **12.** $6r = 30$ **13.** $77 = 11t$

14. $14s = 98$ **15.** $12m = 132$ **16.** $9z = 135$

See Example **2** **17.** Marcy spreads out a rectangular picnic blanket with an area of 24 square feet. Its width is 4 feet. What is its length?

PRACTICE AND PROBLEM SOLVING

Solve each equation.

18. $5y = 35$ **19.** $18 = 2y$ **20.** $54 = 9y$ **21.** $15y = 120$

22. $4y = 0$ **23.** $22y = 440$ **24.** $3y = 63$ **25.** $z - 6 = 34$

26. $6y = 114$ **27.** $161 = 7y$ **28.** $135 = 3y$ **29.** $y - 15 = 3$

30. $81 = 9y$ **31.** $4 + y = 12$ **32.** $7y = 21$ **33.** $a + 12 = 26$

34. $10x = 120$ **35.** $36 = 12x$ **36.** $s - 2 = 7$ **37.** $15 + t = 21$

38. Estimation Colorado is almost a perfect rectangle on a map. Its border from east to west is about 387 mi, and its area is about 104,247 mi². Estimate the length of Colorado's border from north to south. (Area = length × width)

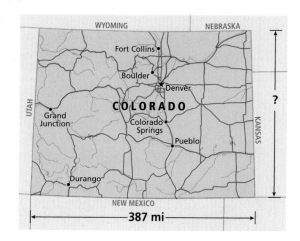

○ = **WORKED-OUT SOLUTIONS**
on p. WS3

Arthropods make up the largest group of animals on Earth. They include insects, spiders, crabs, and centipedes. Arthropods have segmented bodies. In centipedes and millipedes, all of the segments are identical.

Millipedes kept as pets can live for up to 7 years and grow to be up to 15 inches long.

39. Centipedes have 2 legs per segment. They can have from 30 to 354 legs. Find a range for the number of segments a centipede can have.

40. Millipedes have 4 legs per segment. The record number of legs on a millipede is 752. How many segments did this millipede have?

Many arthropods have compound eyes. Compound eyes are made up of tiny bundles of identical light-sensitive cells.

41. A dragonfly has 7 times as many light-sensitive cells as a housefly. How many of these cells does a housefly have?

42. Find how many times more light-sensitive cells a dragonfly has than a butterfly.

43. ✏️ **Write About It** A trapdoor spider can pull with a force that is 140 times its own weight. What other information would you need to find the spider's weight? Explain.

44. ⭐ **Challenge** There are about 6 billion humans in the world. Scientists estimate that there are a billion billion arthropods in the world. About how many times larger is the arthropod population than the human population?

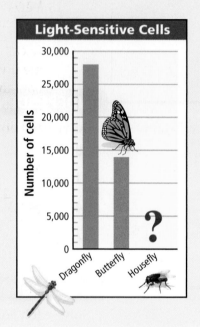

Light-Sensitive Cells

Number of cells

30,000
25,000
20,000
15,000
10,000
5,000
0

Dragonfly   Butterfly   Housefly

?

---

45. Multiple Choice Solve the equation $25x = 175$.

   A. $x = 5$ **B.** $x = 6$ **C.** $x = 7$ **D.** $x = 8$

46. Multiple Choice The area of a rectangle is 42 square inches. Its width is 6 inches. What is its length?

   F. 5 inches   **G.** 7 inches   **H.** 9 inches   **I.** 11 inches

47. This year, Tom is x years older than Hector. Last year, Hector was 17 years old. Write an expression for Tom's age this year. (Lesson 2-3)

Solve each equation. (Lessons 2-5 and 2-6)

48. $b + 53 = 95$ **49.** $a - 100 = 340$ **50.** $n - 24 = 188$ **51.** $w + 20 = 95$

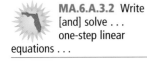

2-9 Division Equations

MA.6.A.3.2 Write [and] solve . . . one-step linear equations . . .

Recreational scuba divers go as deep as 130 feet underwater to view fish and coral. At this depth, the pressure on a diver is much greater than at the water's surface. Water pressure can be described using equations containing division.

Recall that multiplication and division are inverse operations. If an equation contains division, solve it by multiplying on both sides to "undo" the division.

EXAMPLE 1 **Solving Division Equations**

Animated Math
@ **thinkcentral.com**

Solve each equation. Check your answers.

A $\frac{y}{5} = 4$

$$\frac{y}{5} = 4 \qquad \text{y is divided by 5.}$$

$$5 \cdot \frac{y}{5} = 5 \cdot 4 \qquad \text{Multiply both sides by 5 to undo the division.}$$

$$y = 20$$

Check

$$\frac{y}{5} = 4$$

$$\frac{20}{5} \overset{?}{=} 4 \qquad \text{Substitute 20 for y in the equation.}$$

$$4 \overset{?}{=} 4 ✔ \qquad \text{20 is the solution.}$$

B $12 = \frac{z}{4}$

$$12 = \frac{z}{4} \qquad \text{z is divided by 4.}$$

$$4 \cdot 12 = 4 \cdot \frac{z}{4} \qquad \text{Multiply both sides by 4 to undo the division.}$$

$$48 = z$$

Check

$$12 = \frac{z}{4}$$

$$12 \overset{?}{=} \frac{48}{4} \qquad \text{Substitute 48 for z in the equation.}$$

$$12 \overset{?}{=} 12 ✔ \qquad \text{48 is the solution.}$$

Video Lesson Tutorial Videos @ thinkcentral.com

EXAMPLE 2 *Physical Science Application*

Pressure is the amount of force exerted on an area. Pressure can be measured in pounds per square inch, or psi.

The pressure at the surface of the water is half the pressure at 30 ft underwater.

pressure at surface = $\dfrac{\text{pressure at 30 ft underwater}}{2}$

The pressure at the surface is 15 psi. What is the water pressure at 30 ft underwater?

Let p represent the pressure at 30 ft underwater.

$15 = \dfrac{p}{2}$ *Substitute 15 for pressure at the surface.*
p is divided by 2.

$2 \cdot 15 = 2 \cdot \dfrac{p}{2}$ *Multiply both sides by 2 to undo the division.*

$30 = p$

The water pressure at 30 ft underwater is 30 psi.

Think and Discuss

1. Tell whether the solution of $\dfrac{c}{10} = 70$ will be less than 70 or greater than 70. Explain.

2. Describe how you would check the answer to Example 2.

3. Explain why $13 \cdot \dfrac{x}{13} = x$.

2-9 Exercises

MA.6.A.3.2

Homework Help THINK central

Go to **thinkcentral.com**
Exercises 1–18, 19, 21, 23, 25, 27

GUIDED PRACTICE

See Example 1 · Solve each equation. Check your answers.

1. $\dfrac{y}{4} = 3$ **2.** $14 = \dfrac{z}{2}$ **3.** $\dfrac{r}{9} = 7$ **4.** $\dfrac{s}{10} = \dfrac{4}{40}$

5. $12 = \dfrac{j}{3}$ **6.** $9 = \dfrac{x}{5}$ **7.** $\dfrac{f}{12} = 5$ **8.** $\dfrac{g}{2} = 1$

See Example 2 · **9.** Irene mowed the lawn and planted flowers. The amount of time she spent mowing the lawn was one-third the amount of time it took her to plant flowers. It took her 30 minutes to mow the lawn. Find the amount of time Irene spent planting flowers.

 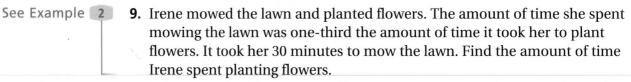 **Video** **Lesson Tutorial Videos @ thinkcentral.com**

See Example **1**

Solve each equation. Check your answers.

10. $\frac{d}{3} = 12$ **11.** $\frac{c}{2} = 13$ **12.** $7 = \frac{m}{7}$ **13.** $\frac{g}{7} = 14$

14. $6 = \frac{f}{4}$ **15.** $\frac{x}{12} = 12$ **16.** $\frac{j}{20} = 10$ **17.** $9 = \frac{r}{9}$

See Example **2**

18. The area of Danielle's garden is one-twelfth the area of her entire yard. The area of the garden is 10 square feet. Find the area of the yard.

PRACTICE AND PROBLEM SOLVING

Find the value of c in each equation.

19. $\frac{c}{12} = 8$ **20.** $4 = \frac{c}{9}$ **21.** $\frac{c}{15} = 11$ **22.** $c + 21 = 40$

23. $14 = \frac{c}{5}$ **24.** $\frac{c}{4} = 12$ **25.** $\frac{c}{4} = 15$ **26.** $5c = 120$

27. **Multi-Step** The Empire State Building is 381 m tall. At the Grand Canyon's widest point, 76 Empire State Buildings would fit end to end. Write and solve an equation to find the width of the Grand Canyon at this point.

28. **Earth Science** You can estimate the distance of a thunderstorm in kilometers by counting the number of seconds between the lightning flash and the thunder and then dividing this number by 3. If a storm is 5 km away, how many seconds will you count between the lightning flash and the thunder?

 29. **Write a Problem** Write a problem about money that can be solved with a division equation.

 30. **Write About It** Use a numerical example to explain how multiplication and division undo each other.

 31. **Challenge** A number halved and then halved again is equal to 2. What was the original number?

Florida Spiral Review MA.6.A.3.1, MA.6.A.3.2

32. **Multiple Choice** Carl has n action figures in his collection. He wants to place them in 6 bins with 12 figures in each bin. Solve the equation $\frac{n}{6} = 12$ to determine the number of action figures Carl has.

A. $n = 2$ **B.** $n = 6$ **C.** $n = 18$ **D.** $n = 72$

33. **Multiple Choice** Which equation does NOT have $k = 28$ as a solution?

F. $\frac{k}{14} = 2$ **G.** $\frac{k}{7} = 4$ **H.** $\frac{k}{28} = 1$ **I.** $\frac{k}{6} = 12$

34. Write an expression for the sequence in the table. (Lesson 2-4)

Laps	3	4	5	6	n
Time (min)	78	104	130	156	

Solve each equation. (Lesson 2-7)

35. $4r = 52$ **36.** $8k = 128$ **37.** $81 = 9p$ **38.** $119 = 17q$

Quiz for Lessons 2-5 Through 2-9

2-5 **Equations and Their Solutions**

Determine whether the given value of the variable is a solution.

1. $c - 13 = 54$ for $c = 67$ **2.** $5r = 65$ for $r = 15$ **3.** $48 \div x = 6$ for $x = 8$

4. Brady buys 2 notebooks and should get \$3 back in change. The cashier gives him 12 quarters. Determine if Brady was given the correct amount of change.

2-6 **Addition Equations**

Solve each equation. Check your answers.

5. $p + 51 = 76$ **6.** $107 = 19 + j$ **7.** $45 = s + 27$

8. A large section of the original Great Wall of China is now in ruins. As measured today, the length of the wall is about 6,350 kilometers. When the length of the section now in ruins is included, the length of the wall is about 6,850 kilometers. Write and solve an equation to find the approximate length of the section of the Great Wall that is now in ruins.

2-7 **Subtraction Equations**

Solve each equation. Check your answers.

9. $k - 5 = 17$ **10.** $150 = p - 30$ **11.** $n - 24 = 72$

12. The Kingda Ka roller coaster at Six Flags® Great Adventure in New Jersey is taller than the Top Thrill Dragster located at Cedar Point™ in Ohio. The difference between their heights is 36 feet. The Top Thrill Dragster is 420 feet high. Write and solve an equation to find the height of Kingda Ka.

2-8 **Multiplication Equations**

Solve each equation. Check your answers.

13. $6f = 18$ **14.** $105 = 5d$ **15.** $11x = 99$

16. Taryn buys 8 identical glasses. Her total is \$48 before tax. Write and solve an equation to find out how much Taryn pays per glass.

2-9 **Division Equations**

Solve each equation. Check your answers.

17. $10 = \frac{j}{9}$ **18.** $5 = \frac{t}{6}$ **19.** $\frac{r}{15} = 3$

20. Paula is baking peach pies for a bake sale. Each pie requires 2 pounds of peaches. She bakes 6 pies. Write and solve an equation to find how many pounds of peaches Paula had to buy.

Tampa

Lowry Park Zoo Tampa's Lowry Park Zoo is home to more than 2,000 animals from Florida and other similar habitats around the world. In 2007, 1.1 million visitors explored the 56-acre park.

1. In 2003, the Lowry Park Zoo added 4 African elephants from Swaziland to the park.

   Lowry Park Zoo, Tampa

   a. An African elephant drinks 30 gallons of water per day. How much water do the elephants from Swaziland drink each day?

   b. Let x represent the number of days. Write an expression for the number of gallons of water all of the elephants drink in x days.

   c. How many days does it take the elephants to drink 600 gallons of water? How do you know?

The graph gives data about several of the zoo's habitats. Use the graph for Exercises 2–3.

2. The number of species in Primate World is 27 less than the number of species in Safari Africa. Write and solve an equation to find the number of species in Safari Africa.

3. A duiker is a member of the antelope family. The number of species of duikers at the zoo is one-sixth the number of species in the Florida Boardwalk habitat. The number of species in the Florida boardwalk habitat is 3 more than the number of species in the Asian Gardens. How may duiker species are at the zoo?

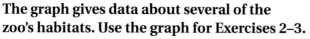

Lowry Park Zoo Habitats

Habitat Area

Wallaroo Station
Primate World
Birds of Prey
Asian Gardens

0 2 4 6 8 10 12 14 16
Number of Species

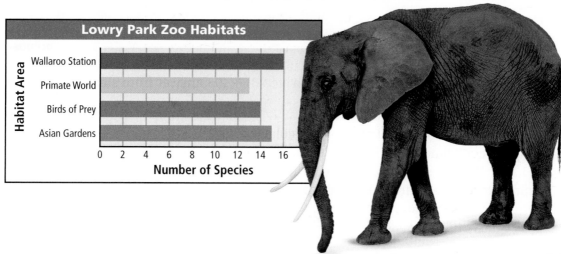

Game Time

Math Magic

Guess what your friends are thinking with this math magic trick.

Copy the following number charts.

1	10	19
2, 2	11, 11	20, 20
4	13	22
5, 5	14, 14	23, 23
7	16	25
8, 8	17, 17	26, 26

3	12	21
4	13	22
5	14	23
6, 6	15, 15	24, 24
7, 7	16, 16	25, 25
8, 8	17, 17	26, 26

9	15	21, 21
10	16	22, 22
11	17	23, 23
12	18, 18	24, 24
13	19, 19	25, 25
14	20, 20	26, 26

Step 1: Ask a friend to think of a number from 1 to 26.
Example: Your friend thinks of 26.

Step 2: Show your friend the first chart and ask how many times the chosen number appears. Remember the answer.
Your friend says the chosen number appears twice on the first chart.

2

Step 3: Show the second chart and ask the same question. Multiply the answer by 3. Add your result to the answer from step 2. Remember this answer.
Your friend says the chosen number appears twice.
The answer from step 2 is 2.

$3 \cdot 2 = 6$
$6 + 2 = 8$

Step 4: Show the third chart and ask the same question. Multiply the answer by 9. Add your result to the answer from step 3. The answer is your friend's number.
Your friend says the chosen number appears twice.
The answer from step 3 is 8.

$9 \cdot 2 = 18$
$18 + 8 = 26$

↑
Your friend's number

How does it work?

Your friend's number will be the following:

(answer from step 2) + (3 · answer from step 3) + (9 · answer from step 4)

This is an expression with three variables: $a + 3b + 9c$. A number will be on a particular chart 0, 1, or 2 times, so a, b, and c will always be 0, 1, or 2. With these values, you can write expressions for each number from 1 to 26.

a	b	c	$a + 3b + 9c$
1	0	0	$1 + 3(0) + 9(0) = 1$
2	0	0	$2 + 3(0) + 9(0) = 2$
0	1	0	$0 + 3(1) + 9(0) = 3$

Can you complete the table for 4–26?

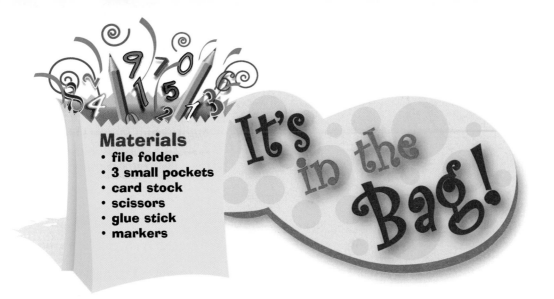

Materials
- file folder
- 3 small pockets
- card stock
- scissors
- glue stick
- markers

It's in the Bag!

PROJECT **Tri-Sided Equations**

Use a colorful file folder to prepare a three-sided review of algebra!

Directions

❶ Close the file folder. Fold one side down to the folded edge. Turn the folder over and fold the other side down to the folded edge. **Figure A**

❷ Open the folder. It will be divided into four sections. On the top section, cut off $\frac{1}{4}$ inch from each edge. On the bottom section, make a 1 inch diagonal slit in the top left corner and in the top right corner. **Figure B**

❸ Fold the folder so that the corners of the smaller top section fit into the slits. This will create your three-sided holder for notes. **Figure C**

❹ Write the definition of an equation on one side of your note holder. Write the order of operations on another side. Write examples of expressions on the third side.

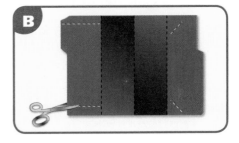

Taking Note of the Math

Glue a small pocket made from construction paper or card stock onto each side of your note holder. On rectangular slips of card stock, write problems that demonstrate your knowledge of equations, order of operations, and expressions. Store the note cards in the appropriate pockets.

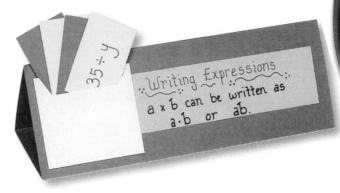

FLORIDA

CHAPTER

2

Study Guide: Review

Multi–Language Glossary

Go to thinkcentral.com

THINK central

Study Guide: Review

Vocabulary

algebraic expression	48	Distributive Property	45
Associative Property	44	evaluate	48
Commutative Property	44	inverse operations	66
constant	48	solution	62
equation	62	variable	48

Complete the sentences below with vocabulary words from the list above.

1. The ___?___ states that you can add or multiply numbers in any order.

2. A(n) ___?___ contains one or more variables.

3. A(n) ___?___ is a mathematical statement that says two quantities are equal.

4. In the equation $12 + t = 22$, t is a ___?___.

5. The expressions $4 \times (5 \times 13)$ and $(4 \times 5) \times 13$ are equivalent by the ___?___.

EXAMPLES

EXERCISES

2-1 **Properties and Mental Math** (pp. 44–47)

 MA.6.A.3.5

Simplify.

- $4 + 13 + 6 + 7$
  $4 + 6 + 13 + 7$
  $(4 + 6) + (13 + 7)$
  $10 + 20$
  30

- $5 \times 9 \times 6$
  $5 \times 6 \times 9$
  $(5 \times 6) \times 9$
  30×9
  270

- **Use the Distributive Property to find** 3×16.

  $3 \times 16 = 3 \times (10 + 6)$
  $\qquad = (3 \times 10) + (3 \times 6)$
  $\qquad = 30 + 18 = 48$

Simplify.

6. $9 + 5 + 1 + 15$ **7.** $8 \times 13 \times 5$

8. $31 + 16 + 19 + 14$ **9.** $6 \times 12 \times 15$

10. $17 + 12 + 8 + 3$ **11.** $16 \times 5 \times 4$

Use the Distributive Property to find each product.

12. 7×24 **13.** 9×15

14. 6×34 **15.** 8×19

2-2 Variables and Expressions (pp. 48–51)

MA.6.A.3.1

■ A rectangle is 3 units wide. How many square units does the rectangle cover if it is 5, 6, or 7 units long?

ℓ	w	$\ell \times w$
5	3	15
6	3	▨
7	3	▨

5 × 3 = 15 square units

6 × 3 = 18 square units

7 × 3 = 21 square units

The rectangle will cover a total of 15, 18, or 21 square units.

Evaluate each expression to find the missing values in the tables.

16.

y	$y \div 7$
56	8
49	
42	

17.

k	$k \times 4 - 6$
2	2
3	▨
4	▨

18. A rectangle is 9 units long. How many square units does the rectangle cover if it is 1, 2, 3, or 4 units wide?

2-3 Translating Between Words and Math (pp. 52–55)

MA.6.A.3.1

Write each phrase as a numerical or algebraic expression.

617 minus 191 $617 - 191$

d multiplied by 5 $5 \cdot d$ or $5d$

Write two phrases for the expression.

■ $a \div 5$ *a divided by 5*
          the quotient of a and 5

Write each phrase as a numerical or algebraic expression.

19. 15 plus b **20.** 2 minus k

21. the product of 6 and 5

22. the quotient of g and 9

Write two phrases for each expression.

23. $4z$ **24.** $15 + x$

25. $54 \div 6$ **26.** $\frac{m}{20}$

2-4 Translating Between Tables and Expressions (pp. 56–59)

MA.6.A.3.1

■ Write an expression for the sequence.

Position	1	2	3	4	n
Value of Term	9	18	27	36	▨

Each value of the term is 9 times its position. The expression is $9n$.

Write an expression for the sequence.

27.

Position	1	2	3	4	n
Value of Term	4	7	10	13	▨

2-5 Equations and Their Solutions (pp. 62–65)

MA.6.A.3.2

■ Determine whether the given value of the variable is a solution.

$f + 14 = 50$ for $f = 34$

$f + 14 = 50$

$34 + 14 \overset{?}{=} 50$ *Substitute 34 for f.*

$48 \neq 50$ *Add.*

34 is not a solution.

Determine whether the given value of the variable is a solution.

28. $28 + n = 39$ for $n = 11$

29. $12t = 74$ for $t = 6$

30. $y - 53 = 27$ for $y = 80$

31. $96 \div w = 32$ for $w = 3$

Study Guide: Review

2-6 **Addition Equations** (pp. 66–69)

 MA.6.A.3.2

■ Solve the equation $x + 18 = 31$.

$$
\begin{array}{lll}
x + 18 = & 31 & \text{18 is added to x.} \\
\underline{} & \underline{} & \text{Subtract 18 from both} \\
x = & 13 & \text{sides to undo the addition.}
\end{array}
$$

Solve each equation.

32. $4 + x = 10$ **33.** $n + 10 = 24$

34. $c + 71 = 100$ **35.** $y + 16 = 22$

36. $44 = p + 17$ **37.** $94 + w = 103$

38. Melinda's new HD radio will play 93 channels. This is 26 more channels than her old radio played. How many channels could she listen to with her old radio?

2-7 **Subtraction Equations** (pp. 70–72)

 MA.6.A.3.2

■ Solve the equation $c - 7 = 16$.

$$
\begin{array}{lll}
c - 7 = & 16 & \text{7 is subtracted from c.} \\
\underline{} & \underline{} & \text{Add 7 to each side to} \\
c = & 23 & \text{undo the subtraction.}
\end{array}
$$

Solve each equation.

39. $28 = k - 17$ **40.** $d - 8 = 1$

41. $p - 55 = 8$ **42.** $n - 31 = 36$

43. $3 = r - 11$ **44.** $97 = w - 47$

45. There are 14 Winter Olympics sports. This is 17 fewer than the number of Summer Olympics sports. How many Summer sports are there?

2-8 **Multiplication Equations** (pp. 73–76)

 MA.6.A.3.2

■ Solve the equation $6x = 36$.

$$
\begin{array}{ll}
6x = 36 & \text{x is multiplied by 6.} \\
\dfrac{6x}{6} = \dfrac{36}{6} & \text{Divide both sides by 6 to} \\
x = 6 & \text{undo the multiplication.}
\end{array}
$$

Solve each equation.

46. $5v = 40$ **47.** $27 = 3y$

48. $12c = 84$ **49.** $18n = 36$

50. $72 = 9s$ **51.** $11t = 110$

52. The average American eats about 30 pounds of cheese per year. The Smith family ate 120 pounds of cheese last year. How many people are in the Smith family?

2-9 **Division Equations** (pp. 77–79)

MA.6.A.3.2

■ Solve the equation $\frac{k}{4} = 8$.

$$
\begin{array}{ll}
\dfrac{k}{4} = 8 & \text{k is divided by 4.} \\
4 \cdot \dfrac{k}{4} = 4 \cdot 8 & \text{Multiply both sides by 4} \\
k = 32 & \text{to undo the division.}
\end{array}
$$

Solve each equation.

53. $\frac{r}{7} = 6$ **54.** $\frac{t}{5} = 3$

55. $6 = \frac{y}{3}$ **56.** $12 = \frac{n}{6}$

57. $\frac{z}{13} = 4$ **58.** $20 = \frac{b}{5}$

Chapter Test

Use the Distributive Property to find each product.

1. 8×13 **2.** 4×61 **3.** 7×18 **4.** 3×59

Determine if each pair of expressions is equivalent. If so, state the property shown.

5. $11 + 13 + 29 = 11 + 29 + 13$ **6.** $3 \times (4 \times 6) = (3 \times 4) + (3 \times 6)$

Evaluate each expression to find the missing values in the tables.

7.

a	a + 18
10	28
12	
14	

8.

y	y ÷ 6
18	3
30	
42	

9.

n	n ÷ 5 + 7
10	9
20	
30	

10. A van can seat 6 people. How many people can ride in 3, 4, 5, and 6 vans?

Write an expression for the missing value in each table.

11.

Packages	Rolls
1	8
2	16
3	24
p	

12.

Students	Groups
5	1
10	2
15	3
s	

Write an expression for the sequence in the table.

13.

Position	1	2	3	4	5	n
Value of Term	2	5	8	11	14	

14. There are more reptile species than amphibian species. There are 3,100 living species of amphibians. Write an expression to show how many more reptile species there are than amphibian species.

Write an algebraic expression or phrase.

15. 26 more than n **16.** g multiplied by 4   **17.** the quotient of 180 and 15

18. $(14)(16)$ **19.** $n \div 8$ **20.** $p + 11$ **21.** $s - 6$

Determine whether the given value of the variable is a solution.

22. $5d = 70$ for $d = 12$ **23.** $15 + m = 27$ for $m = 12$

Solve each equation.

24. $a + 7 = 25$ **25.** $121 = 11d$ **26.** $3 = t - 8$ **27.** $6 = \frac{k}{9}$

28. Air typically has about 4,000 bacteria per cubic meter. If your room is 30 cubic meters, about how many bacteria would there be in the air in your room?

Mastering the Standards

Cumulative Assessment, Chapters 1–2

Multiple Choice

1. Which is an algebraic expression for the product of 15 and x?

   A. $15 - x$ **C** $x + 15$

   B. $15x$ **D.** $15 \div x$

2. Max earned $560 working as a landscaper. If he worked a total of 80 hours, which expression can be used to find how much he earned each hour?

   F. $560 - 80$ **H.** $560 + 80$

   G. $560 \div 80$ **I.** $560 \cdot 80$

3. Find the expression for the table.

x	
3	9
8	19
11	25
15	33

   A. $3x$ **C.** $2x + 3$

   B. $x + 18$ **D.** $3x - 5$

4. A rectangular classroom has an area of 252 square feet. The width of the classroom is 14 feet. What is its length?

   F. 14 feet   **H.** 18 feet

   G. 16 feet   **I.** 20 feet

5. Tom drives 186 miles to his aunt's house. His average speed is 62 miles per hour. Which equation could you use to determine the time of Tom's trip?

   A. $186 = 62 + t$ **C.** $186 = 62t$

   B. $62 = 186t$ **D.** $\frac{t}{62} = 186$

6. Solve: $\frac{x}{2} = 8$

   F. 4   **H.** 10

   G. 8   **I.** 16

7. Zane biked 23 miles this week. This is 8 miles more than he biked the week before. Solve the equation $x + 8 = 23$ to find how many miles Zane biked last week.

   A. 15 miles   **C.** 31 miles

   B. 23 miles   **D.** 33 miles

8. The track team sold 215 fewer products than the soccer team. How many products did the soccer team sell?

Fund-raising Results by Team	
Team	**Products Sold**
Golf	6,536
Soccer	
Swim	6,879
Track	6,019

   F. 5,804   **H.** 6,321

   G. 6,234   **I.** 6,664

9. Which equation is an example of the Associative Property?

   A. $3 + (4 + 6) = (3 + 4) + 6$

   B. $(42 + 6) + 18 = (42 + 18) + 6$

   C. $(3 \times 20) + (3 \times 4) = 3 \times 24$

   D. $8(2 \times 6) = (8 \times 2) + (8 \times 6)$

HOT TIP! Substitute the values given in the answers into an equation to see which value makes the equation true.

10. Nicole is 15 years old. She is 3 years younger than her sister Jan. Solve the equation $j - 3 = 15$ to find Jan's age.

   F. 18 years   **H.** 12 years

   G. 17 years   **I.** 5 years

11. Which expression is equivalent to 8×92?

   A. $8 \times 90 + 8 \times 2$ **C.** $8 \times 90 + 2$

   B. $8 + (90 + 2)$ **D.** $8 \times 90 \times 2$

Gridded Response

12. Use the table to find the unknown value.

t	$11 \times t + 3$
5	58
8	▨

13. Scott spends 16 minutes in the pool treading water during swim practice. This is $\frac{1}{3}$ of his practice time. How many total minutes is Scott's swim practice?

14. A case of pencils costs $15. If the academic team spends $135 on pencils for the school tournament, how many cases of pencils did the academic team buy?

15. What is the solution to the equation $8a = 48$?

16. Cherries costs $3.50/lb at Bundle-Boy. At Lou's Fruits cherries cost $4.10/lb. Yoga spends $8.75 on cherries at Bundle-Boy. How much more money in dollars would he spend at Lou's Fruits for the same amount of cherries?

Short Response

S1. Every week Brandi runs 7 more miles than her sister Jamie.

   a. Write an expression for the number of miles that Brandi runs each week. Identify the variable.

   b. Evaluate your expression to find the number of miles Brandi runs when Jamie runs 5 miles.

S2. A vacation tour costs $450. Additional outings cost $25 each. The table shows the total cost to go on additional outings.

Outings	1	2	3	n
Total Cost ($)	475	500	525	▨

Write an expression for the cost of n outings. Use the expression to find how much it costs to go on 5 outings.

Extended Response

E1. Chrissy and Kathie are sisters. Chrissy was born on Kathie's birthday and is exactly 8 years younger. Chrissy celebrated her 16th birthday on December 8, 2005.

   a. Complete the table to show the ages of the sisters in the years 2005, 2008, and 2011.

Year	Kathie's Age	Chrissy's Age
2005	▨	▨
2008	▨	▨
2011	▨	▨

   b. Write an equation that could be used to find Kathie's age in 2011. Identify the variable in the equation.

   c. Solve the equation. Show your work. Compare your answer to the value in the table. Are the two solutions the same? Explain your answer.

Additional instruction, practice, and activities are available online, including:

- **Lesson Tuturial Videos**
- **Homework Help**
- **Animated Math**

Go to **thinkcentral.com**

Why Learn This?

Most statistics in sports are reported as decimals. In baseball, for example, a player who has 15 hits in 50 at bats would have a batting average of 0.300.

Tampa Bay Rays
Tampa

Chapter Focus
- Compare, order, and estimate decimals.
- Use common procedures to multiply and divide decimals.

Are You Ready?

Are You Ready? THINK central

Go to **thinkcentral.com**

✓ Vocabulary

Choose the best term from the list to complete each sentence.

1. The first place value to the left of the decimal point is the
   ___?___ place, and the place value two places to the
   left of the decimal point is the ___?___ place.

2. In the expression 72 ÷ 9, 72 is the ___?___, and 9 is
   the ___?___.

3. The answer to a subtraction expression is the
   _____?_____.

4. A(n) ___?___ is a mathematical statement that says
   two quantities are equivalent.

difference

dividend

divisor

equation

ones

quotient

tens

Complete these exercises to review skills you will need for this chapter.

✓ Place Value of Whole Numbers

Identify the place value of each underlined digit.

5. 1<u>5</u>2

6. <u>7</u>,903

7. <u>1</u>45,072

8. 4,8<u>9</u>3,025

9. 1<u>3</u>,796,020

10. 1<u>4</u>5,683,032

✓ Add and Subtract Whole Numbers

Find each sum or difference.

11. \$425 − \$75

12. 532 + 145

13. 160 − 82

✓ Multiply and Divide Whole Numbers

Find each product or quotient.

14. \$320 × 5

15. 125 ÷ 5

16. 54 × 3

✓ Exponents

Find each value.

17. 10^3

18. 3^6

19. 10^5

20. 4^5

21. 8^3

22. 2^7

✓ Solve One-Step Equations

Solve each equation.

23. $y + 382 = 743$

24. $n - 150 = 322$

25. $9x = 108$

Study Guide: Preview

Before

Previously, you

- compared and ordered whole numbers.
- wrote large whole numbers in standard form.
- rounded numbers to a given place value.
- used addition, subtraction, multiplication, and division of whole numbers to solve problems.

Now

You will study

- reading, writing, comparing, and ordering decimals.
- using rounding to estimate answers to problems that involve decimals.
- multiplying and dividing decimals.
- solving decimal equations.

Why?

You can use the skills learned in this chapter

- to solve problems using decimals in classes, such as science.
- to solve two-step decimal equations in higher-level math classes, such as Algebra 1.

Key Vocabulary/Vocabulario

clustering	aproximación
front-end estimation	estimación por partes

Vocabulary Connections

To become familiar with some of the vocabulary terms in the chapter, consider the following. You may refer to the chapter, the glossary, or a dictionary if you like.

1. When you estimate, you approximate the value of something. What part of a decimal do you think you are using to approximate a value when you use **front-end estimation**?

2. A *cluster* is a close grouping of similar items. When do you think **clustering** might be a good method of estimation?

Study Guide: Preview

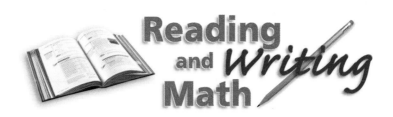

Reading and Writing Math

Writing Strategy: Keep a Math Journal

You can help improve your writing and reasoning skills by keeping a math journal. When you express your thoughts on paper, you can make sense of confusing math concepts.

You can also record your thoughts about each lesson and reflect on what you learned in class. Your journal will become a personal math reference book from which to study.

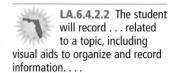

LA.6.4.2.2 The student will record . . . related to a topic, including visual aids to organize and record information. . . .

Journal Entry:
Read the entry Jaime wrote in his math journal about translating between math and words.

> Journal Entry 2   October
> Today's lesson was on translating between words and math. I understand that a math expression like 18 x 2 can be written as "18 multiplied by 2." However, I am confused which symbol to use when translating from words to math. My teacher suggested that I make a list in this journal of common terms and their symbols.
>
> | Words | Symbols |
> |---|---|
> | sum, added, plus | + |
> | difference, less than | - |
> | product, times | x or • |
> | divide, quotient | ÷ |
>
> Now I understand!
> This list will help me when I need to know which symbol goes with which word.

Try This

Begin a math journal. Make an entry every day for one week. Use the following ideas to start your journal entries. Be sure to date each entry.

- What I already know about this lesson is . . .

- The skills I used to complete this lesson were . . .

- What problems did I have? How did I deal with these problems?

- What I liked/did not like about this lesson . . .

3-1 Representing, Comparing, and Ordering Decimals

MA.6.A.5.2
Compare and order . . . decimals . . . including finding their approximate location on a number line.

The smaller the apparent magnitude of a star, the brighter the star appears when viewed from Earth. The magnitudes of some stars are listed in the table as decimal numbers.

Apparent Magnitudes of Stars	
Star	**Magnitude**
Procyon	0.38
Proxima Centauri	11.0
Wolf 359	13.5
Vega	0.03

Decimal numbers represent combinations of whole numbers and numbers between whole numbers.

Math
@ thinkcentral.com

Place value can help you understand, write, and compare decimal numbers.

Place Value

Hundreds	Tens	Ones	Tenths	Hundredths	Thousandths	Ten-Thousandths	Hundred-Thousandths
	2	3 ● 0	0	5	0	3	

EXAMPLE 1 **Reading and Writing Decimals**

Write each decimal in standard form, expanded form, and words.

A 1.05

Expanded form: 1 + 0.05
Word form: one *and* five hundredths

Reading Math

Read the decimal point as "and."

B 0.05 + 0.001 + 0.0007

Standard form: 0.0517
Word form: five hundred seventeen ten-thousandths

C sixteen and nine hundredths

Standard form: 16.09
Expanded form: 10 + 6 + 0.09

You can use place value to compare decimal numbers.

Video Lesson Tutorial Videos @ thinkcentral.com

EXAMPLE 2

Earth Science Application

Rigel and Betelgeuse are two stars in the constellation Orion. The apparent magnitude of Rigel is 0.12. The apparent magnitude of Betelgeuse is 0.50. Which star has the smaller magnitude? Which star appears brighter?

Betelgeuse

Rigel

0.⃝12   *Line up the decimal points. Start from the left and compare the digits.*

0.⃝50   *Look for the first place where the digits are different.*

1 is less than 5.
0.12 < 0.50

Rigel has a smaller apparent magnitude than Betelgeuse.
The star with the smaller magnitude appears brighter. When seen from Earth, Rigel appears brighter than Betelgeuse.

EXAMPLE 3

Comparing and Ordering Decimals

Order the decimals from least to greatest.
14.35, 14.3, 14.05

Helpful Hint

Writing zeros at the end of a decimal does not change the value of the decimal.

0.3 = 0.30 = 0.300

14.35		*Compare two of the numbers at a time.*
14.30	14.30 < 14.35	*Write 14.3 as "14.30."*
14.35		
14.05	14.05 < 14.35	*Start at the left and compare the digits.*
14.30		*Look for the first place where the*
14.05	14.05 < 14.30	*digits are different.*

Graph the numbers on a number line.

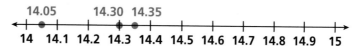

The numbers are ordered when you read the number line from left to right. The numbers in order from least to greatest are 14.05, 14.3, and 14.35.

⋆⋆⋆⋆⋆⋆⋆⋆⋆⋆⋆⋆⋆⋆⋆⋆⋆⋆⋆⋆

Think and Discuss

1. Explain why 0.5 is greater than 0.29 even though 29 is greater than 5.

2. Name the decimal with the least value: 0.29, 2.09, 2.009, 0.029

3. Name three numbers between 1.5 and 1.6.

Exercises

Homework Help

Go to <u>thinkcentral.com</u>
Exercises 1–16, 19, 23, 27, 29, 31, 37, 41

 MA.6.A.5.2

GUIDED PRACTICE

See Example **1** Write each decimal in standard form, expanded form, and words.

1. 1.98

2. ten and forty-one thousandths

3. 0.07 + 0.006 + 0.0005

4. 0.0472

See Example **2** **5. Physical Science** Osmium and iridium are precious metals. The density of osmium is 22.58 g/cm³, and the density of iridium is 22.56 g/cm³. Which metal is denser?

See Example **3** Order the decimals from least to greatest.

6. 9.5, 9.35, 9.65

7. 4.18, 4.1, 4.09

8. 12.39, 12.09, 12.92

INDEPENDENT PRACTICE

See Example **1** Write each decimal in standard form, expanded form, and words.

9. 7.0893

10. 12 + 0.2 + 0.005

11. seven and fifteen hundredths

12. 3 + 0.1 + 0.006

See Example **2** **13. Astronomy** Two meteorites landed in Mexico. The one found in Bacuberito weighed 24.3 tons, and the one found in Chupaderos weighed 26.7 tons. Which meteorite weighed more?

See Example **3** Order the decimals from least to greatest.

14. 15.25, 15.2, 15.5

15. 1.56, 1.62, 1.5

16. 6.7, 6.07, 6.23

PRACTICE AND PROBLEM SOLVING

Write each number in words.

17. 9.007

18. 5 + 0.08 + 0.004

19. 10.022

20. 4.28

21. 142.6541

22. 0.001 + 0.0007

23. 0.92755

24. 1.02

Compare. Write <, >, or =.

25. $8.04 ▮ $8.40

26. 0.907 ▮ 0.6801

27. 1.246 ▮ 1.29

28. one and fifty-two ten-thousandths ▮ 1.0052

29. ten and one hundredth ▮ 10.100

Write the value of the red digit in each number.

30. 3.026

31. 17.53703

32. 0.000598

33. 425.1055

Order the numbers from greatest to least.

34. 32.525, 32.5254, 31.6257

35. 0.34, 1.43, 4.034, 1.043, 1.424

36. 1.01, 1.1001, 1.101, 1.0001

37. 652.12, 65.213, 65.135, 61.53

○ = **WORKED-OUT SOLUTIONS**
on p. WS3

Proxima Centauri, the closest star to Earth other than the Sun, was discovered in 1913. It would take about 115,000 years for a spaceship traveling from Earth at 25,000 mi/h to reach Proxima Centauri.

NEXT EXITS

MOON	238,855 mi
SUN	92,000,000 mi
PLUTO	2,700,000,000 mi
PROXIMA CENTAURI	24,000,000,000,000 mi

Use the table for Exercises 38–44.

38. Order the stars Sirius, Luyten 726-8, and Lalande 21185 from closest to farthest from Earth.

39. Which star in the table is farthest from Earth?

40. How far in light-years is Ross 154 from Earth? Write the answer in words and expanded form.

41. List the stars that are less than 5 light-years from Earth.

42. **?** **What's the Error?** A student wrote the distance of Proxima Centauri from Earth as "four hundred and twenty-two hundredths." Explain the error. Write the correct answer.

43. **✏** **Write About It** Which star is closer to Earth, Alpha Centauri or Proxima Centauri? Explain how you can compare the distances of these stars. Then answer the question.

44. **★** **Challenge** Wolf 359 is located 7.75 light-years from Earth. If the stars in the table were listed in order from closest to farthest from Earth, between which two stars would Wolf 359 be located?

| Distance of Stars from Earth ||
Star	Distance (light-years)
Alpha Centauri	4.35
Barnard's Star	5.98
Lalande 21185	8.22
Luyten 726-8	8.43
Proxima Centauri	4.22
Ross 154	9.45
Sirius	8.65

45. Multiple Choice Which shows the numbers from least to greatest?

A. 0.32, 3.2, 0.23, 0.03

C. 3.2, 0.32, 0.23, 0.03

B. 0.03, 0.23, 0.32, 3.2

D. 0.03, 0.32, 0.23, 3.2

46. Gridded Response What number is shown on the number line?

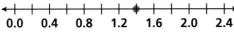

0.0   0.4   0.8   1.2   1.6   2.0   2.4

Use mental math to find each sum or product. (Lesson 2-1)

47. $14 + 20 + 6$ **48.** $6 \times 80 \times 5$ **49.** $28 + 14 + 12 + 21$ **50.** $2 \times 12 \times 10 \times 5$

Solve each equation. (Lesson 2-7)

51. $n - 52 = 71$ **52.** $30 = k - 15$ **53.** $c - 22 = 30$

3-2 Estimating Decimals

MA.6.A.5.3
Estimate the results of computations with . . . decimals . . . and judge the reasonableness of the results.

Vocabulary

clustering

front-end estimation

Billy's health class is learning about fitness and nutrition. The table shows the approximate number of calories burned by someone who weighs 90 pounds.

Activity (45 min)	Calories Burned (Approx.)
Cycling	198.45
Playing ice hockey	210.6
Rowing	324
Water skiing	194.4

When numbers are about the same value, you can use *clustering* to estimate.

Clustering means rounding the numbers to the same value.

EXAMPLE **1**   *Health Application*

Billy wants to cycle, play ice hockey, and water ski. If Billy weighs 90 pounds and spends 45 minutes doing each activity, *about* how many calories will he burn in all?

$$198.45 \longrightarrow 200$$ *The addends cluster around 200.*
$$210.6 \longrightarrow 200$$ *To estimate the total number of calories,*
$$+\,194.4 \longrightarrow +\,200$$ *round each addend to 200.*
$$\,600$$ *Add.*

Billy will burn about 600 calories.

EXAMPLE **2**   **Rounding Decimals to Estimate Sums and Differences**

Estimate by rounding to the indicated place value.

Caution!

Look at the digit to the right of the place to which you are rounding.
- If it is *5 or greater*, round *up*.
- If it is *less than 5*, round *down*.

See Skills Bank p. SB3.

A   3.92 + 6.48; ones

$$3.92 + 6.48$$ *Round to the nearest whole number.*
$$4 + 6 = 10$$ *The sum is about 10.*

B   8.6355 − 5.039; hundredths

8.6355	8.64	*Round to the hundredths.*
− 5.039	− 5.04	*Align the decimals.*
	3.60	*Subtract.*

Video **Lesson Tutorial Videos @ thinkcentral.com**

EXAMPLE 3 Using Compatible Numbers to Estimate Products and Quotients

Remember!

Compatible numbers are close to the numbers that are in the problem and are helpful when you are solving the problem mentally.

Estimate each product or quotient.

A 26.76 × 2.93

     25 × 3 = 75   *25 and 3 are compatible.*

So 26.76 × 2.93 is about 75.

B 42.64 ÷ 16.51

     45 ÷ 15 = 3   *45 and 15 are compatible.*

So 42.64 ÷ 16.51 is about 3.

You can also use *front-end estimation* to estimate with decimals. **Front-end estimation** means to use only the whole-number part of the decimal.

EXAMPLE 4 Using Front-End Estimation

Estimate a range for the sum.

9.99 + 22.89 + 8.3

Use front-end estimation.

9.99 → 9	*Add the whole numbers only.*
22.89 → 22	*The whole-number values of the decimals*
+ 8.30 → + 8	*are less than the actual numbers, so the*
at least 39	*answer is an underestimate.*

The exact answer of 9.99 + 22.89 + 8.3 is greater than 39.

You can estimate a range for the sum by adjusting the decimal part of the numbers. Round the decimals to 0.5 or 1.

0.99 → 1.00	*Add the adjusted decimal part of the numbers.*
0.89 → 1.00	*Add the whole-number estimate and this*
+ 0.30 → + 0.50	*sum.*
2.50	*The adjusted decimals are greater than the*
39.00 + 2.50 = 41.50	*actual decimals, so 41.50 is an overestimate.*

The estimated range for the sum is between 39.00 and 41.50.

Think and Discuss

1. Tell what number the following decimals cluster around: 34.5, 36.78, and 35.234.

2. Determine whether a front-end estimation without adjustment is always an overestimation or an underestimation.

MA.6.A.5.3

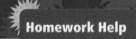 **Homework Help**
Go to thinkcentral.com
Exercises 1–21, 23, 25, 27, 29

GUIDED PRACTICE

See Example **1** **1.** Elba runs every Monday, Wednesday, and Friday. Last week she ran 3.62 miles on Monday, 3.8 miles on Wednesday, and 4.3 miles on Friday. About how many miles did she run last week?

See Example **2** **Estimate by rounding to the indicated place value.**

2. 2.746 − 0.866; tenths   **3.** 6.735 + 4.9528; ones

4. 10.8071 + 5.392; hundredths   **5.** 5.9821 − 0.48329; ten-thousandths

See Example **3** **Estimate each product or quotient.**

6. 38.92 ÷ 4.06   **7.** 14.51 × 7.89   **8.** 22.47 ÷ 3.22

See Example **4** **Estimate a range for each sum.**

9. 7.8 + 31.39 + 6.95   **10.** 14.27 + 5.4 + 21.86

INDEPENDENT PRACTICE

See Example **1** **11. Multi-Step** Before Mike's trip, the odometer in his car read 146.8 miles. He drove 167.5 miles to a friend's house and 153.9 miles to the beach. About how many miles did the odometer read when he arrived at the beach?

12. The rainfall in July, August, and September was 16.76 cm, 13.97 cm, and 15.24 cm, respectively. About how many total centimeters of rain fell during those three months?

See Example **2** **Estimate by rounding to the indicated place value.**

13. 2.0993 + 1.256; tenths   **14.** 7.504 − 2.3792; hundredths

15. 0.6271 + 4.53027; thousandths   **16.** 13.274 − 8.5590; tenths

See Example **3** **Estimate each product or quotient.**

17. 9.64 × 1.769   **18.** 11.509 ÷ 4.258   **19.** 19.03 ÷ 2.705

See Example **4** **Estimate a range for each sum.**

20. 17.563 + 4.5 + 2.31   **21.** 1.620 + 10.8 + 3.71

PRACTICE AND PROBLEM SOLVING

Estimate by rounding to the nearest whole number.

22. 8.456 + 7.903   **23.** 12.43 × 3.72   **24.** 1,576.2 − 150.50

25. Estimate the quotient of 67.55 and 3.83.

26. Estimate $84.85 divided by 17.

○ = WORKED-OUT SOLUTIONS
on p. WS3

Use the table for Exercises 27–31.

27. **Money** Round each cost in the table to the nearest cent. Write your answer using a dollar sign and decimal point.

28. About how much does it cost to phone someone in Russia and talk for 8 minutes?

(29.) About how much more does it cost to make a 12-minute call to Japan than to make an 18-minute call within the United States?

Long-Distance Costs for Callers in the United States	
Country	Cost per Minute (¢)
Venezuela	22
Russia	9.9
Japan	7.9
United States	3.7

30. Will the cost of a 30-minute call to someone within the United States be greater or less than $1.20? Explain.

31. **Multi-Step** Kim is in New York. She calls her grandmother in Venezuela and speaks for 20 minutes, then calls a friend in Japan and talks for 15 minutes, and finally calls her mother in San Francisco and talks for 30 minutes. Estimate the total cost of all her calls.

32. **Health** The recommended daily allowance (RDA) for iron is 15 mg/day for teenage girls. Julie eats a hamburger that contains 3.88 mg of iron. About how many more milligrams of iron does she need to meet the RDA?

33. **Write a Problem** Write a problem with three decimal numbers that have a total sum between 30 and 32.5.

34. **Write About It** How do you adjust a front-end estimation? Why is this done?

35. **Challenge** Place a decimal point in each number so that the sum of the numbers is between 124 and 127: 1059 + 725 + 815 + 1263.

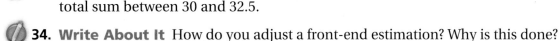

Florida Spiral Review   MA.6.A.5.3, MA.6.A.3.2, MA.6.A.5.2

36. **Multiple Choice** What is the estimated difference of 34.45 − 24.71 rounded to the nearest whole number?

   A. 11   **B.** 10   **C.** 9   **D.** 8

37. **Short Response** The average rainfall in Oklahoma City is 2.8 inches in April, 5.3 inches in May, and 4.3 inches in June. A weather forecaster predicts that the rainfall one year will double the average in April and May and half the average in June. Estimate the predicted rainfall each month to the nearest inch.

Solve each equation. (Lesson 2-6)

38. $83 + n = 157$ 39. $x + 23 = 92$ 40. $25 + c = 145$

Order the decimals from least to greatest. (Lesson 3-1)

41. 8.304, 8.009, 8.05   42. 5.62, 15.34, 1.589   43. 30.211, 30.709, 30.75

Prep for
MA.6.A.5.3
Estimate the results
of computations with . . .
decimals, . . . and judge the
reasonableness of the results.
Review of MA.5.A.2.2

At the 2004 U.S. Gymnastics Championships, Carly Patterson and Courtney Kupets tied for the All-Around title.

Carly Patterson's Preliminary Scores	
Event	**Points**
Floor exercise	9.7
Balance beam	9.7
Vault	9.3
Uneven bars	9.45

To find the total number of points, you can add all of the scores.

Carly Patterson also won a gold medal in the Women's Individual All-Around in the 2004 Olympic Games.

EXAMPLE 1 **Sports Application**

Animated Math
@ thinkcentral.com

Helpful Hint

Estimating before you add or subtract will help you check whether your answer is reasonable.

A **What was Carly Patterson's preliminary total score in the 2004 U.S. Championships?**

First estimate the sum of 9.7, 9.7, 9.3, and 9.45.

$$9.7 + 9.7 + 9.3 + 9.45$$

Estimate by rounding to the nearest whole number.

$$10 + 10 + 9 + 9 = 38$$

The total is about 38 points.

Then add.

9.70	*Align the decimal points.*
9.70	
9.30	*Use zeros as placeholders.*
+ 9.45	
38.15	*Add. Then place the decimal point.*

Since 38.15 is close to the estimate of 38, the answer is reasonable. Patterson's total preliminary score was 38.15 points.

B **How many more points did Patterson need on the uneven bars to have a perfect score of 10?**

Find the difference between 10 and 9.45.

10.00	*Align the decimal points.*
− 9.45	*Use zeros as placeholders.*
0.55	*Subtract. Then place the decimal point.*

Patterson needed another 0.55 points to have a perfect score.

Video **Lesson Tutorial Videos** @ thinkcentral.com

EXAMPLE **2** **Using Mental Math to Add and Subtract Decimals**

Find each sum or difference.

A 1.6 + 0.4

1.6 + 0.4   *Think: 0.6 + 0.4 = 1*

1.6 + 0.4 = 2

B 3 − 0.8

3 − 0.8   *Think: 0.8 + 0.2 = 1,*

3 − 0.8 = 2.2   *so 1 − 0.8 = 0.2.*

EXAMPLE **3** **Evaluating Decimal Expressions**

Evaluate $7.52 - s$ for each value of *s*.

 A $s = 2.9$

$$7.52 - s$$

$$7.52 - 2.9 \quad \textit{Substitute 2.9 for s.}$$

$$\begin{array}{r} 7.52 \\ -\ 2.90 \\ \hline 4.62 \end{array}$$

Align the decimal points.
Use a zero as a placeholder.

Subtract.
Place the decimal point.

Remember!

You can place any number of zeros at the end of a decimal number without changing its value.

B $s = 4.5367$

$$7.52 - s$$

$$7.52 - 4.5367 \quad \textit{Substitute 4.5367 for s.}$$

$$\begin{array}{r} 7.5200 \\ -\ 4.5367 \\ \hline 2.9833 \end{array}$$

Align the decimal points.
Use zeros as placeholders.

Subtract.
Place the decimal point.

Think and Discuss

1. **Show** how you would write 2.678 + 124.5 to find the sum.

2. **Tell** why it is a good idea to estimate the answer before you add and subtract.

3. **Explain** how you can use mental math to find how many more points Carly Patterson would have needed to have scored a perfect 10 on the floor exercise.

Homework Help THINK central

Go to **thinkcentral.com**
Exercises 1–29, 31, 33, 35, 37, 39, 43, 45

Prep for MA.6.A.5.3

GUIDED PRACTICE

See Example 1 · **Use the table for Exercises 1–3.**

Rea's Triathlon Training	
Sport	**Distance (mi)**
Cycling	14.25
Running	4.35
Swimming	1.6

1. How many miles in all is Rea's triathlon training?

2. How many miles did Rea run and swim in all?

3. How much farther did Rea cycle than swim?

See Example 2 · **Find each sum or difference.**

4. $2.7 + 0.3$ **5.** $6 - 0.4$ **6.** $5.2 + 2.8$ **7.** $8.9 - 4$

See Example 3 · **Evaluate $5.35 - m$ for each value of m.**

8. $m = 2.37$ **9.** $m = 1.8$ **10.** $m = 4.7612$ **11.** $m = 0.402$

INDEPENDENT PRACTICE

See Example 1 · **12. Sports** During a diving competition, Phil performed two reverse dives and two dives from a handstand position. He received the following scores: 8.765, 9.45, 9.875, and 8.025. What was Phil's total score?

13. Brad works after school at a local grocery store. How much did he earn in all for the month of October?

Brad's Earnings for October				
Week	1	2	3	4
Earnings	$123.48	$165.18	$137.80	$140.92

See Example 2 · **Find each sum or difference.**

14. $7.2 + 1.8$ **15.** $8.5 - 7$ **16.** $3.3 + 0.7$ **17.** $15.9 + 2.1$

18. $7 - 0.6$ **19.** $7.55 - 3.25$ **20.** $21.4 + 3.6$ **21.** $5 - 2.7$

See Example 3 · **Evaluate $9.67 - x$ for each value of x.**

22. $x = 1.52$ **23.** $x = 3.8$ **24.** $x = 7.21$ **25.** $x = 0.635$

26. $x = 6.9$ **27.** $x = 1.001$ **28.** $x = 8$ **29.** $x = 9.527$

PRACTICE AND PROBLEM SOLVING

Add or subtract.

30. $5.62 + 4.19$ **31.** $10.508 - 6.73$ **32.** $13.009 + 12.83$

33. Find the sum of 0.0679 and 3.75.   **34.** Subtract 3.0042 from 7.435.

35. Sports Terin Humphrey was ranked third at the 2004 U.S. Gymnastics Championships with a score of 75.45. What was the difference between her score and Courtney Kupet's and Carly Patterson's score of 76.45?

○ = WORKED-OUT SOLUTIONS
on p. WS4

Evaluate each expression.

36. $8.09 - a$ for $a = 4.5$

37. $7.03 + 33.8 + n$ for $n = 12.006$

38. $b + (5.68 - 3.007)$ for $b = 6.134$

39. $(2 \times 14) - a + 1.438$ for $a = 0.062$

40. $5^2 - w$ for $w = 3.5$

41. $100 - p$ for $p = 15.034$

42. Career A fire helmet must be sturdy enough to protect the firefighter's head from dangerous objects and extremely high temperatures while still being as light as possible. One fire helmet has a mass of 1.616 kg, and another fire helmet has a mass of 1.403 kg. What is the difference in mass?

43. Multi-Step Logan wants to buy a new bike that costs $135.00. He started with $14.83 in his savings account. Last week, he deposited $15.35 into his account. Today, he deposited $32.40. How much more money does he need to buy the bike?

44. Swimming With a time of 60.35 seconds, Martina Moracova broke Jennifer Thompson's world record time in the women's 100-meter medley. How much faster was Thompson than Moracova when, in the next heat, she reclaimed the record with a time of 59.30 seconds?

45. Sports The highest career batting average ever achieved by a professional baseball player is 0.366. Bill Bergen finished with a career 0.170 average. How much lower is Bergen's career average than the highest career average?

46. What's the Question? A cup of rice contains 0.8 mg of iron, and a cup of lima beans contains 4.4 mg of iron. If the answer is 6 mg, what is the question?

47. Write About It Why is it important to align the decimal points before adding or subtracting decimal numbers?

48. Challenge Evaluate $(5.7 + a) \times (9.75 - b)$ for $a = 2.3$ and $b = 7.25$.

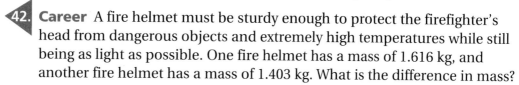

Florida Spiral Review   MA.6.A.3.2, MA.6.A.5.3

49. Multiple Choice What is the sum of 24.91 and 35.8?

A. 28.49   **B.** 59.99   **C.** 60.71   **D.** 60.99

50. Multiple Choice Lead has an atomic weight of 207.19. Mercury has an atomic weight of 200.6. How much greater is the atomic weight of lead than mercury?

F. 6.59   **G.** 7.41   **H.** 7.59   **I.** 187.13

Solve each equation. (Lesson 2-7)

51. $s - 47 = 23$ **52.** $73 = a - 78$ **53.** $823 = t - 641$

Estimate each product or quotient. (Lesson 3-2)

54. 15.72×4.08 **55.** 14.87×3.78 **56.** $53.67 \div 9.18$

Quiz for Lessons 3-1 Through 3-3

 3-1 **Representing, Comparing, and Ordering Decimals**

Write each decimal in standard form, expanded form, and words.

1. 4.012

2. ten and fifty-four thousandths

3. On Monday Jamie ran 3.54 miles. On Wednesday he ran 3.6 miles. On which day did he run farther?

Order the decimals from least to greatest.

4. 3.406, 30.08, 3.6

5. 10.10, 10.01, 101.1

6. 16.782, 16.59, 16.79

7. 62.0581, 62.148, 62.0741

8. 123.05745, 132.05628, 123.05749

Graph the numbers on a number line. Then order the decimals from least to greatest.

9. 1.4, 0.6, 1.6. 1.8

10. 3.4, 3.04, 3.44, 3.24

 3-2 **Estimating Decimals**

11. Matt drove 106.8 miles on Monday, 98.3 miles on Tuesday, and 103.5 miles on Wednesday. About how many miles did he drive in all?

Estimate.

12. $8.345 - 0.6051$; round to the hundredths

13. $16.492 - 2.613$; round to the tenths

14. 18.79×4.68

15. $71.378 \div 8.13$

16. 52.055×7.18

Estimate a range for each sum.

17. $7.42 + 13.87 + 101.2$

18. $1.79 + 3.45 + 7.92$

3-3 **Adding and Subtracting Decimals**

19. Greg's scores at four gymnastic meets were 9.65, 8.758, 9.884, and 9.500. What was his total score for all four meets?

20. Mrs. Henry buys groceries each week and uses a spreadsheet to keep track of how much she spends. How much did she spend in all for the month of December?

Grocery Spending for December				
Week	1	2	3	4
Amount Spent ($)	52.35	77.97	90.10	42.58

21. Sally walked 1.2 miles on Monday, 1.6 miles on Wednesday, and 2.1 miles on Friday. How many miles did she walk in all?

Find each sum or difference.

22. $0.47 + 0.03$

23. $8 - 0.6$

24. $2.2 + 1.8$

Focus on Problem Solving

 Solve

• **Write an equation**

Read the whole problem before you try to solve it. Sometimes you need to solve the problem in more than one step.

Read the problem. Determine the steps needed to solve the problem.

Brian buys erasers and pens for himself and 4 students in his class. The erasers cost $0.79 each, and the pens cost $2.95 each. What is the total amount that Brian spends on the erasers and pens?

Here is one way to solve the problem.

5 erasers cost	5 pens cost
5 · $0.79	5 · $2.95

$$(5 \cdot \$0.79) + (5 \cdot \$2.95)$$

 Read each problem. Decide whether you need more than one step to solve the problem. List the possible steps. Then choose an equation with which to solve the problem.

1 Joan is making some costumes. She cuts 3 pieces of fabric, each 3.5 m long. She has 5 m of fabric left. Which equation can you use to find f, the amount of fabric she had to start with?

A. $(3 \cdot 3.5) + 5 = f$

B. $3 + 3.5 + 5 = f$

C. $(5 \times 3.5) \div 3 = f$

D. $5 - (3 \cdot 3.5) = f$

2 Mario buys 4 chairs and a table. He spends $245.99 in all. If each chair costs $38.95, which equation can you use to find T, the cost of the table?

F. $4 + \$245.99 + \$38.95 = T$

G. $(4 \cdot \$38.95) + \$245.99 = T$

H. $\$245.99 - (4 \cdot \$38.95) = T$

I. $\$245.99 \div (4 \cdot \$38.95) = T$

3 Mya skis down Ego Bowl three times and down Fantastic twice. Ego Bowl is 5.85 km long, and Fantastic is 8.35 km long. Which equation can you use to estimate d, the distance Mya skis in all?

A. $(6 \cdot 3) + (8 \cdot 2) = d$

B. $(6 + 8) + (3 + 2) = d$

C. $3(6 + 8) = d$

D. $(6 \div 3) + (8 \div 2) = d$

3-4 # Multiplying Decimals

MA.6.A.1.2
Multiply . . .
decimals efficiently.
MA.6.A.1.3 Solve real-
world problems involving
multiplication . . . of . . .
decimals.
Also **MA.6.A.1.1**

Because the Moon has less mass than Earth, it has a smaller gravitational effect. An object that weighs 1 pound on Earth weighs only 0.17 pound on the Moon.

You can multiply the weight of an object on Earth by 0.17 to find its weight on the Moon.

Gravity on Earth is about six times the gravity on the surface of the Moon.

You can multiply decimals by first multiplying as you would whole numbers. Then place the decimal point by finding the total of the number of decimal places in the factors. The product will have the same number of decimal places.

E X A M P L E *Science Application*

A flag weighs 3 pounds on Earth. What is the weight of the flag on the Moon?

Multiply 3 by 0.17, since 1 pound on Earth is 0.17 pound on the Moon.

$$\begin{array}{r} 0.17 \\ \times\ \ \ 3 \\ \hline 51 \end{array}$$ *Multiply as you would with whole numbers.*

Place the decimal point by adding the number of decimal places in the numbers multiplied.

$$\begin{array}{r} 0.17 \\ \times\ \ \ 3 \\ \hline 0.51 \end{array}$$ *2 decimal places*
+ 0 decimal places
2 decimal places

A 3 lb flag on Earth weighs 0.51 lb on the Moon.

E X A M P L E **Multiplying a Decimal by a Decimal**

Find each product.

A **0.2 × 0.6**

Multiply. Then place the decimal point.

$$\begin{array}{r} 0.2 \\ \times\ 0.6 \\ \hline 0.12 \end{array}$$ *1 decimal place*
+ 1 decimal place
2 decimal places

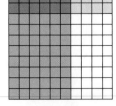

Helpful Hint

You can use a decimal grid to model multiplication of decimals.

Video **Lesson Tutorial Videos @ thinkcentral.com**

Find each product.

B **3.25 × 4.8**

$3 × 5 = 15$ *Estimate the product. Round each factor to the nearest whole number.*

Multiply. Then place the decimal point.

$$\begin{array}{r} 3.25 \\ \times\ 4.8 \\ \hline 2600 \\ 13000 \\ \hline 15.600 \end{array}$$

2 + 1 = 3 decimal places

15.600 is close to the estimate of 15. The answer is reasonable.

C **0.05 × 0.9**

$0.05 × 1 = 0.05$ *Estimate the product. 0.9 is close to 1.*

Multiply. Then place the decimal point.

$$\begin{array}{r} 0.05 \\ \times\ 0.9 \\ \hline 0.045 \end{array}$$

2 decimal places
+ 1 decimal place
3 decimal places; use a placeholder zero.

0.045 is close to the estimate of 0.05. The answer is reasonable.

EXAMPLE **3** **Evaluating Decimal Expressions**

Evaluate 3x for each value of x.

Remember!

These notations all mean multiply 3 times *x*.

$3 \cdot x$ $3x$ $3(x)$

A $x = 4.047$

$3x = 3(\mathbf{4.047})$ *Substitute 4.047 for x.*

$$\begin{array}{r} 4.047 \\ \times\ \ \ \ 3 \\ \hline 12.141 \end{array}$$

3 decimal places
+ 0 decimal places
3 decimal places

B $x = 2.95$

$3x = 3(\mathbf{2.95})$ *Substitute 2.95 for x.*

$$\begin{array}{r} 2.95 \\ \times\ \ \ \ 3 \\ \hline 8.85 \end{array}$$

2 decimal places
+ 0 decimal places
2 decimal places

Think and Discuss

1. Tell how many decimal places are in the product of 235.2 and 0.24.

2. Show how to use the Distributive Property to find 1.7 × 2.

3. Describe how the products of 0.3 × 0.5 and 3 × 5 are similar. How are they different?

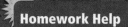
Homework Help THINK central

Go to **thinkcentral.com**
Exercises 1–28, 29, 37, 39, 45, 47, 49, 51

 MA.6.A.1.2, MA.6.A.1.1,
MA.6.A.1.3

GUIDED PRACTICE

See Example **1**

1. Each can of cat food costs $0.28. How much will 6 cans of cat food cost?

2. Jorge buys 8 baseballs for $9.29 each. How much does he spend in all?

See Example **2** **Find each product.**

3. 0.6	**4.** 0.008	**5.** 3.0	**6.** 0.12
× 0.4	× 0.5	× 0.07	× 0.6

See Example **3** **Evaluate $5x$ for each value of x.**

7. $x = 3.304$ **8.** $x = 4.58$ **9.** $x = 7.126$ **10.** $x = 1.9$

INDEPENDENT PRACTICE

See Example **1**

11. Gwenyth walks her dog each morning. If she walks 0.37 kilometers each morning, how many kilometers will she have walked in 7 days?

12. Consumer Math Apples are on sale for $0.49 per pound. What is the price for 4 pounds of apples?

See Example **2** **Find each product.**

13. 0.9	**14.** 4.5	**15.** 0.31	**16.** 1.6
× 0.03	× 0.5	× 0.7	× 0.08

17. 0.007×0.06 **18.** 0.04×3.0 **19.** 2.0×0.006 **20.** 0.005×0.003

See Example **3** **Evaluate $7x$ for each value of x.**

21. $x = 1.903$ **22.** $x = 2.461$ **23.** $x = 3.72$ **24.** $x = 4.05$

25. $x = 0.164$ **26.** $x = 5.89$ **27.** $x = 0.3702$ **28.** $x = 1.82$

PRACTICE AND PROBLEM SOLVING

Multiply.

29. 0.3×0.03 **30.** 1.4×0.21 **31.** 0.06×1.02 **32.** 8.2×4.1

33. 12.6×2.1 **34.** 3.04×0.6 **35.** 0.66×2.52 **36.** 3.08×0.7

37. $0.2 \times 0.94 \times 1.3$ **38.** $1.54 \times 3.05 \times 2.6$ **39.** $1.98 \times 0.4 \times 5.2$

40. $1.7 \times 2.41 \times 0.5$ **41.** $2.5 \times 1.52 \times 3.7$ **42.** $6.5 \times 0.15 \times 3.8$

Evaluate.

43. $6n$ for $n = 6.23$ **44.** $5t + 0.462$ for $t = 3.04$

45. $8^2 - 2b$ for $b = 0.95$ **46.** $4^3 + 5c$ for $c = 1.9$

47. $3h - 15 + h$ for $h = 5.2$ **48.** $5^2 + 6j + j$ for $j = 0.27$

○ = WORKED-OUT SOLUTIONS
on p. WS4

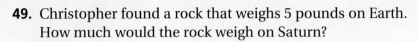

Saturn is the second-largest planet in the solar system. Saturn is covered by thick clouds. Saturn's density is very low. Suppose you weigh 180 pounds on Earth. If you were able to stand on Saturn, you would weigh only 165 pounds. To find the weight of an object on another planet, multiply its weight on Earth by the gravitational pull listed in the table.

49. Christopher found a rock that weighs 5 pounds on Earth. How much would the rock weigh on Saturn?

50. On which two planets would the weight of an object be the same?

51. **Multi-Step** An object weighs 9 pounds on Earth. How much more would this object weigh on Neptune than on Mars?

52. **Write a Problem** Use the data in the table to write a word problem that can be answered by evaluating an expression with multiplication. Solve your problem.

53. **? What's the Error?** A student said that his new baby brother, who weighs 10 pounds, would weigh 120 pounds on Neptune. What is the error? Write the correct answer.

54. **Challenge** An object weighs between 2.79 lb and 5.58 lb on Saturn. Give a range for the object's weight on Earth.

Gravitational Pull of Planets (Compared with Earth)	
Planet	Gravitational Pull
Mercury	0.38
Venus	0.91
Mars	0.38
Jupiter	2.54
Saturn	0.93
Neptune	1.2

Galileo Galilei was the first person to look at Saturn through a telescope. He thought there were groups of stars on each side of the planet, but it was later determined that he had seen Saturn's rings.

55. Multiple Choice Max uses 1.6 liters of gasoline each hour mowing lawns. How much gas does he use in 5.8 hours?

    A. 7.4 liters   **B.** 9.28 liters   **C.** 92.8 liters   **D.** 928 liters

56. Multiple Choice What is the value of $5x$ when $x = 3.2$?

    F. 16   **G.** 8.2   **H.** 1.6   **I.** 0.16

Solve each equation. (Lesson 2-9)

57. $\frac{x}{8} = 4$ **58.** $\frac{y}{12} = 5$ **59.** $3 = \frac{t}{17}$ **60.** $2 = \frac{s}{21}$

Compare. Write <, >, or =. (Lesson 3-1)

61. 0.3 ▮ 0.03   **62.** 2.185 ▮ 2.19   **63.** 1.01 ▮ 1.010   **64.** 3.45 ▮ 3.4

3-5 Dividing Decimals by Whole Numbers

MA.6.A.1.2 Multiply and divide . . . decimals efficiently. *Also* **MA.6.A.1.1, MA.6.A.1.3**

Emily and two of her friends are going to share equally the cost of making pottery for the art fair.

To find how much each person should pay for the materials, you will need to divide a decimal by a whole number.

EXAMPLE 1 **Dividing a Decimal by a Whole Number**

Find each quotient.

Remember!

Quotient
↓
$\underset{\uparrow\qquad\nwarrow}{5\overline{)0.75}}$
Divisor Dividend

For more on dividing with whole numbers, see Skills Bank page SB5.

A $0.75 \div 5$

$$
\begin{array}{r}
0.15 \\
5\overline{)0.75} \\
-5\downarrow \\
\hline
25 \\
-25 \\
\hline
0
\end{array}
$$

Place a decimal point in the quotient directly above the decimal point in the dividend.
Divide as you would with whole numbers.

B $2.52 \div 3$

$$
\begin{array}{r}
0.84 \\
3\overline{)2.52} \\
-2\,4\downarrow \\
\hline
12 \\
-12 \\
\hline
0
\end{array}
$$

Place a decimal point in the quotient directly above the decimal point in the dividend.
Divide as you would with whole numbers.

EXAMPLE 2 **Evaluating Decimal Expressions**

Evaluate $0.435 \div x$ for each given value of x.

A $x = 3$

$0.435 \div x$

$0.435 \div 3$ *Substitute 3 for x.*

$$
\begin{array}{r}
0.145 \\
3\overline{)0.435} \\
-3\downarrow \\
\hline
13 \\
-12\downarrow \\
\hline
15 \\
-15 \\
\hline
0
\end{array}
$$

Divide as you would with whole numbers.

B $x = 15$

$0.435 \div x$

$0.435 \div 15$ *Substitute 15 for x.*

$$
\begin{array}{r}
0.029 \\
15\overline{)0.435} \\
-0\downarrow \\
\hline
43 \\
-30\downarrow \\
\hline
135 \\
-135 \\
\hline
0
\end{array}
$$

Sometimes you need to use a zero as a placeholder.

15 > 4, so place a zero in the quotient and divide 15 into 43.

Video **Lesson Tutorial Videos @ thinkcentral.com**

EXAMPLE **3** *Consumer Math Application*

Emily and two of her friends are making pottery using clay, glaze, and paint. The materials cost $11.61. If they share the cost equally, how much should each person pay?

$11.61 should be divided into three equal groups.
Divide $11.61 by 3.

$$
\begin{array}{r}
3.87 \\
3{\overline{\smash{\big)}\,11.61}} \\
\underline{-9} \\
2\,6 \\
\underline{-2\,4} \\
21 \\
\underline{-21} \\
0
\end{array}
$$

Place a decimal point in the quotient directly above the decimal point in the dividend.

Divide as you would with whole numbers.

Remember!

Multiplication can "undo" division. To check your answer to a division problem, multiply the divisor by the quotient.

Check

$3.87 \times 3 = 11.61$

Each person should pay $3.87.

Think and Discuss

1. Tell how you know where to place the decimal point in the quotient.

2. Explain why you can use multiplication to check your answer to a division problem.

3-5 Exercises

MA.6.A.1.2, MA.6.A.1.1, MA.6.A.1.3

Homework Help THINK central

Go to thinkcentral.com
Exercises 1–18, 19, 21, 23

GUIDED PRACTICE

See Example **1** **Find each quotient.**

1. $1.38 \div 6$ **2.** $0.96 \div 8$ **3.** $1.75 \div 5$ **4.** $0.72 \div 4$

See Example **2** **Evaluate $0.312 \div x$ for each given value of x.**

5. $x = 4$ **6.** $x = 6$ **7.** $x = 3$ **8.** $x = 12$

See Example **3** **9. Consumer Math** Mr. Richards purchased 8 T-shirts for the volleyball team. The total cost of the T-shirts was $70.56. How much did each shirt cost?

 Lesson Tutorial Videos @ thinkcentral.com *3-5 Dividing Decimals by Whole Numbers* **113**

See Example **1**   **Find each quotient.**

10. $0.91 \div 7$ **11.** $1.32 \div 6$ **12.** $4.68 \div 9$ **13.** $0.81 \div 3$

See Example **2**   **Evaluate $0.684 \div x$ for each given value of x.**

14. $x = 3$ **15.** $x = 4$ **16.** $x = 18$ **17.** $x = 9$

See Example **3**   **18. Consumer Math** Charles, Kate, and Kim eat lunch in a restaurant. The bill is $27.12. If they share the bill equally, how much will each person pay?

PRACTICE AND PROBLEM SOLVING

Find the value of each expression.

19. $(0.49 + 0.045) \div 5$ **20.** $(4.9 - 3.125) \div 5$ **21.** $(13.28 - 7.9) \div 4$

Evaluate the expression $x \div 4$ for each value of x.

22. $x = 0.504$ **23.** $x = 0.944$ **24.** $x = 57.484$ **25.** $x = 1.648$

26. Multi-Step At the grocery store, a 6 lb bag of oranges costs $2.04. Is this more or less expensive than the price shown at the farmers' market?

27. Critical Thinking How could you use rounding to check your answer to the problem $5.58 \div 6$?

? 28. Choose a Strategy Sarah had $1.19 in coins. Jeff asked her for change for a dollar, but she did not have the correct change. What coins did she have?

29. Write About It When do you use a placeholder zero in the quotient?

30. Challenge Evaluate the expression $x \div 2$ for the following values of $x = 520$, 52, and 5.2. Try to predict the value of the same expression for $x = 0.52$.

Oranges
$0.30/lb

Farmers' Market

31. Multiple Choice What is the value of $0.98 \div x$ when $x = 2$?

A. 49   **B.** 4.9   **C.** 0.49   **D.** 0.049

32. Gridded Response Danika spent $89.24 on two pairs of shoes. Each pair of shoes cost the same amount. How much, in dollars, did each pair cost?

Solve each equation. (Lesson 2-8)

33. $3y = 18$ **34.** $15x = 90$ **35.** $4a = 92$

Multiply. (Lesson 3-4)

36. 0.2×0.8 **37.** 10.7×3.02 **38.** $1.65 \times 0.4 \times 2.8$ **39.** $9.4 \times 3.8 \times 0.15$

○ = **WORKED-OUT SOLUTIONS**
on p. WS4

3-6 Dividing by Decimals

MA.6.A.1.3 Solve real-world problems involving . . . division of . . . decimals. *Also* MA.6.A.1.1, MA.6.A.1.2, MA.6.A.5.3

Julie and her family traveled to the Grand Canyon. They stopped to refill their gas tank with 13.4 gallons of gasoline after they had driven 368.5 miles.

To find the miles that they drove per gallon, you will need to divide a decimal by a decimal.

EXAMPLE 1 — Dividing a Decimal by a Decimal

Find each quotient.

A **3.6 ÷ 1.2**

$1.2\overline{)3.6}$

Multiply the divisor by 10^1, or 10, to make it a whole number. Multiply the dividend by the same power of 10.

Think: $1.2 \times 10 = 12$ $3.6 \times 10 = 36$

Divide as with whole numbers.

$$\begin{array}{r} 3 \\ 12\overline{)36} \\ -36 \\ \hline 0 \end{array}$$

$3.6 \div 1.2 = 3$

B **42.3 ÷ 0.12**

$0.12\overline{)42.3}$

Multiply the divisor by 10^2, or 100, to make it a whole number. Multiply the dividend by the same power of 10.

Think: $0.12 \times 100 = 12$ $42.3 \times 100 = 4{,}230$

$$\begin{array}{r} 352.5 \\ 12\overline{)4230.0} \\ -36 \\ \hline 63 \\ -60 \\ \hline 30 \\ -24 \\ \hline 60 \\ -60 \\ \hline 0 \end{array}$$

Place the decimal point in the quotient. Divide as with whole numbers.

When there is a remainder, place a zero after the decimal point in the dividend and continue to divide.

$42.3 \div 0.12 = 352.5$

Helpful Hint

Multiplying the divisor and the dividend by the same number does not change the quotient.

$$\begin{array}{c} 42 \ \div \ 6 \ = 7 \\ {\scriptstyle \times 10 \downarrow} \ {\scriptstyle \times 10 \downarrow} \\ 420 \ \div \ 60 \ = 7 \end{array}$$

$$\begin{array}{c} 42 \ \div \ 6 \ = 7 \\ {\scriptstyle \times 100 \downarrow} \ {\scriptstyle \times 100 \downarrow} \\ 4{,}200 \ \div \ 600 = 7 \end{array}$$

EXAMPLE 2 **PROBLEM SOLVING APPLICATION**

After driving 368.5 miles, Julie and her family refilled the tank of their car with 13.4 gallons of gasoline. On average, how many miles did they drive per gallon of gas?

1 Understand the Problem

The **answer** will be the average number of miles per gallon.

List the **important information:**

- They drove 368.5 miles.
- They used 13.4 gallons of gas.

2 Make a Plan

Solve a simpler problem by replacing the decimals in the problem with whole numbers.

If they drove 10 miles using 2 gallons of gas, they averaged 5 miles per gallon. You need to divide miles by gallons to solve the problem.

3 Solve

First estimate the answer. You can use compatible numbers.
$$368.5 \div 13.4 \longrightarrow 360 \div 12 = 30$$

$$13.4\overline{)368.5}$$

Multiply the divisor and the dividend by 10.
Think: 13.4 × 10 = 134   368.5 × 10 = 3,685

$$
\begin{array}{r}
27.5 \\
134\overline{)3685.0} \\
-268 \\
\hline
1005 \\
-938 \\
\hline
67\,0 \\
-67\,0 \\
\hline
0
\end{array}
$$

Place the decimal point in the quotient.
Divide as with whole numbers.

Julie and her family averaged 27.5 miles per gallon.

4 Look Back

The answer is reasonable, since 27.5 is close to the estimate of 30.

Think and Discuss

1. Tell how the quotient of 48 ÷ 12 is similar to the quotient of 4.8 ÷ 1.2. How is it different?

 Lesson Tutorial Videos @ thinkcentral.com

3-6

Exercises

Homework Help THINK central

Go to **thinkcentral.com**
Exercises 1–20, 23, 27, 29, 31, 35, 37, 39

MA.6.A.1.3, MA.6.A.1.1,
MA.6.A.1.2, MA.6.A.5.3

GUIDED PRACTICE

See Example **1** **Find each quotient.**

1. $6.5 \div 1.3$　　　　**2.** $20.7 \div 0.6$　　　　**3.** $25.5 \div 1.5$

4. $5.4 \div 0.9$　　　　**5.** $13.2 \div 2.2$　　　　**6.** $63.39 \div 0.24$

See Example **2** **7.** Marcus drove 354.9 miles in 6.5 hours. On average, how many miles per hour did he drive?

8. Consumer Math Anthony spends $87.75 on shrimp. The shrimp cost $9.75 per pound. How many pounds of shrimp does Anthony buy?

INDEPENDENT PRACTICE

See Example **1** **Find each quotient.**

9. $3.6 \div 0.6$　　　**10.** $8.2 \div 0.5$　　　**11.** $18.4 \div 2.3$

12. $4.8 \div 1.2$　　　**13.** $52.2 \div 0.24$　　**14.** $32.5 \div 2.6$

15. $49.5 \div 4.5$　　**16.** $96.6 \div 0.42$　　**17.** $6.5 \div 1.3$

See Example **2** **18.** Jen spends $5.98 on ribbon. Ribbon costs $0.92 per meter. How many meters of ribbon does Jen buy?

19. Kyle's family drove 329.44 miles. Kyle calculated that the car averaged 28.4 miles per gallon of gas. How many gallons of gas did the car use?

20. Consumer Math Peter is saving $4.95 each week to buy a DVD that costs $24.75, including tax. For how many weeks will he have to save?

PRACTICE AND PROBLEM SOLVING

Divide.

21. $2.52 \div 0.4$　　　**22.** $12.586 \div 0.35$　　**23.** $0.5733 \div 0.003$

24. $10.875 \div 1.2$　　**25.** $92.37 \div 0.5$　　　**26.** $8.43 \div 0.12$

Evaluate.

27. $0.732 \div n$ for $n = 0.06$　　　**28.** $73.814 \div c$ for $c = 1.3$

29. $b \div 0.52$ for $b = 6.344$　　　**30.** $r \div 4.17$ for $r = 10.5918$

Find the value of each expression.

31. $6.35 \times 10^2 \div 0.5$　　**32.** $8.1 \times 10^2 \div 0.9$　　**33.** $4.5 \times 10^3 \div 4$

34. $20.1 \times 10^3 \div 0.1$　　**35.** $2.76 \times 10^2 \div 0.3$　　**36.** $6.2 \times 10^3 \div 8$

37. Find the value of $6.45 \times 10^6 \div 0.3$.

○ = **WORKED-OUT SOLUTIONS**
on p. WS4

38. Earth Science A planet's year is the time it takes that planet to revolve around the Sun. A Mars year is 1.88 Earth years. If you are 13 years old in Earth years, about how old would you be in Mars years?

39. History The U.S. Treasury first printed paper money in 1862. The paper money we use today is 0.0043 inch thick. Estimate the number of bills you would need to stack to make a pile that is 1 inch thick. If you stacked $20 bills, what would be the total value of the money in the pile?

Use the map for Exercises 40 and 41.

40. Multi-Step Bill drove from Washington, D.C., to Charlotte in 6.5 hours. What was his average speed in miles per hour?

41. Estimation Betty drove a truck from Richmond to Washington, D.C. It took her about 2.5 hours. Estimate the average speed she was driving.

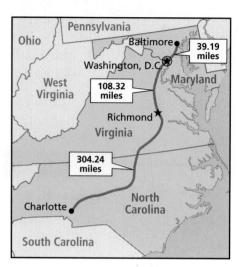

42. What's the Error? A student incorrectly answered the division problem below. Explain the error and write the correct quotient.

$$\begin{array}{r} 13.456 \\ 0.004\overline{)53.824} \end{array}$$

43. Write About It Explain how you know where to place the decimal point in the quotient when you divide by a decimal number.

44. Challenge Find the value of a in the division problem.

$$\begin{array}{r} 1.01 \\ 4a3\overline{)0417.13} \end{array}$$

45. Multiple Choice Nick bought 2.5 pounds of popcorn for $8.35. How much did he pay for each pound of popcorn?

   A. $20.88   **B.** $3.43   **C.** $3.34   **D.** $33.40

46. Extended Response In the 2006–2007 NBA season, Kevin Garnett earned a salary of $21,000,000. He played in 76 games and averaged 39.4 minutes per game. How much money did Kevin Garnett earn each minute he played? Round your answer to the nearest dollar. Explain how you solved the problem.

Translate each phrase into a numerical or algebraic expression. (Lesson 2-2)

47. 12 more than x **48.** the product of 8 and 12   **49.** a less than 15

Evaluate $4y$ for each value of y. (Lesson 3-4)

50. $y = 2.13$ **51.** $y = 4.015$ **52.** $y = 3.6$ **53.** $y = 0.78$ **54.** $y = 1.4$

3-7 Interpreting the Quotient

MA.6.A.5.3
Estimate the results of computations with . . . decimals . . . and judge the reasonableness of the results.
Also **MA.6.A.1.1, MA.6.A.1.2, MA.6.A.1.3**

In science lab, Ken learned to make slime from corn starch, water, and food coloring. He has 0.87 kg of corn starch, and the recipe for one bag of slime calls for 0.15 kg. To find the number of bags of slime Ken can make, you need to divide.

EXAMPLE Measurement Application

Remember!

To divide decimals, first write the divisor as a whole number. Multiply the divisor and dividend by the same power of ten.

Ken will use 0.87 kg of corn starch to make gift bags of slime for his friends. If each bag requires 0.15 kg of corn starch, how many bags of slime can he make?

The question asks how many whole bags of slime can be made when the corn starch is divided into groups of 0.15 kg.

$0.87 \div 0.15 = ?$
$87 \div 15 = 5.8$

Think: The quotient shows that there is not enough to make 6 bags of slime that are 0.15 kg each. There is only enough for 5 bags. The decimal part of the quotient will not be used in the answer.

Ken can make **5** gift bags of slime.

EXAMPLE Photography Application

There are 246 students in the sixth grade. If Ms. Lee buys rolls of film with 24 exposures each, how many rolls will she need to take every student's picture?

The question asks how many whole rolls are needed to take a picture of every one of the students.

$246 \div 24 = ?$

$246 \div 24 = 10.25$

Think: Ten rolls of film will not be enough to take every student's picture. Ms. Lee will need to buy another roll of film. The quotient must be rounded up to the next highest whole number.

Ms. Lee will need 11 rolls of film.

EXAMPLE 3 *Social Studies Application*

Marissa is drawing a time line of the Stone Age. She plans for 6 equal sections, two each for the Paleolithic, Mesolithic, and Neolithic periods. If she has 7.8 meters of paper, how long is each section?

The question asks exactly how long each section will be when the paper is divided into 6 sections.

7.8 ÷ 6 = 1.3   *Think: The question asks for an exact answer, so do not estimate. Use the entire quotient.*

Each section will be **1.3** meters long.

When the question asks	→ You should
How many whole groups can be made when you divide?	→ Drop the decimal part of the quotient.
How many whole groups are needed to put all items from the dividend into a group?	→ Round the quotient up to the next highest whole number.
What is the exact number when you divide?	→ Use the entire quotient as the answer.

Think and Discuss

1. Tell how you would interpret the quotient: A group of 27 students will ride in vans that carry 12 students each. How many vans are needed?

3-7 Exercises

MA.6.A.5.3, MA.6.A.1.1, MA.6.A.1.2, MA.6.A.1.3

Homework Help THINK central

Go to thinkcentral.com
Exercises 1–6, 7, 13

GUIDED PRACTICE

See Example 1
1. Kay is making beaded belts for her friends from 6.5 meters of cord. One belt uses 0.625 meter of cord. How many belts can she make?

See Example 2
2. Julius is supplying cups for a party of 136 people. If cups are sold in packs of 24, how many packs of cups will he need?

See Example 3
3. Miranda is decorating for a party. She has 13 balloons and 29.25 meters of ribbon. She wants to tie the same length of ribbon on each balloon. How long will each ribbon be?

      Lesson Tutorial Videos @ thinkcentral.com

See Example 1 **4.** There are 0.454 kg of corn starch in a container. How many 0.028 kg portions are in one container?

See Example 2 **5.** Tina needs 36 flowers for her next project. The flowers are sold in bunches of 5. How many bunches will she need?

See Example 3 **6.** Bobby's goal is to run 27 miles a week. If he runs the same distance 6 days a week, how many miles would he have to run each day?

PRACTICE AND PROBLEM SOLVING

7. Nick wants to write thank-you notes to 15 of his friends. The cards are sold in packs of 6. How many packs does Nick need to buy?

8. Multi-Step The science teacher has 7 packs of seeds and 36 students. If the students should each plant the same number of seeds, how many can each student plant?

9. Critical Thinking How do you know when to round your answer up to the next whole number?

10. Write a Problem Create a problem that is solved by interpreting the quotient.

11. Write About It Explain how a calculator shows the remainder when you divide 145 by 8.

12. Challenge Leonard wants to place a fence on both sides of a 10-meter walkway. If he puts a post at both ends and at every 2.5 meters in between, how many posts does he use?

Florida Spiral Review

MA.6.A.5.3, MA.6.A.1.2, MA.6.A.1.3, MA.6.A.3.2

13. Multiple Choice There are 375 students going on a field trip. Each bus holds 65 students. How many buses are needed for the field trip?

A. 4   **B.** 5   **C.** 6   **D.** 7

14. Multiple Choice Mrs. Neal has 127 stickers. She wants to give each of the 22 students in her class the same number of stickers. Which expression can be used to find how many stickers each student will get?

F. $127 - 22$ **G.** $127 \div 22$ **H.** $127 + 22$ **I.** 127×22

Solve for *y*. (Lessons 2-5, 2-6, 2-7)

15. $y - 23 = 40$ **16.** $14y = 168$ **17.** $36 + y = 53$ **18.** $\frac{y}{5} = 7$

Find each quotient. (Lesson 3-5, 3-6)

19. $45.5 \div 5$ **20.** $103.7 \div 2$ **21.** $35 \div 2.5$ **22.** $4.25 \div 0.25$

○ = **WORKED-OUT SOLUTIONS**
on p. WS4

3-8 Solving Decimal Equations

Preview of MA.7.A.3.3
Formulate and use different strategies to solve one-step and two-step linear equations, including equations with rational coefficients.

Felipe has earned $45.20 by mowing lawns for his neighbors. He wants to buy inline skates that cost $69.95. Write and solve an equation to find how much more money Felipe must earn to buy the skates.

Let m be the amount of money Felipe needs. $45.20 + m = $69.95

Animated Math @ thinkcentral.com

You can solve equations with decimals using inverse operations just as you solved equations with whole numbers.

$$\begin{array}{r} \$45.20 + m = \$69.95 \\ -\ \$45.20 \qquad -\ \$45.20 \\ \hline m = \$24.75 \end{array}$$

Felipe needs $24.75 more to buy the inline skates.

EXAMPLE 1 · Solving One-Step Equations with Decimals

Remember!
Use inverse operations to get the variable alone on one side of the equation.

Solve each equation. Check your answer.

A $g - 3.1 = 4.5$

$$\begin{array}{r} g - 3.1 = \quad 4.5 \\ +\ 3.1 \quad +\ 3.1 \\ \hline g = \quad 7.6 \end{array}$$

3.1 is subtracted from g.

Add 3.1 to both sides to undo the subtraction.

Check
$$g - 3.1 = 4.5$$
$$7.6 - 3.1 \overset{?}{=} 4.5$$
$$4.5 \overset{?}{=} 4.5 \checkmark$$

Substitute 7.6 for g in the equation.

7.6 is the solution.

B $3k = 8.1$

$$3k = 8.1$$
$$\frac{3k}{3} = \frac{8.1}{3}$$
$$k = 2.7$$

k is multiplied by 3.

Divide both sides by 3 to undo the multiplication.

Check
$$3k = 8.1$$
$$3(2.7) \overset{?}{=} 8.1$$
$$8.1 \overset{?}{=} 8.1 \checkmark$$

Substitute 2.7 for k in the equation.

2.7 is the solution.

Video **Lesson Tutorial Videos @ thinkcentral.com**

Solve each equation. Check your answer.

C $\dfrac{m}{5} = 1.5$

$\dfrac{m}{5} = 1.5$ *m is divided by 5.*

$\dfrac{m}{5} \cdot 5 = 1.5 \cdot 5$ *Multiply both sides by 5 to undo the division.*

$m = 7.5$

Check

$\dfrac{m}{5} = 1.5$

$\dfrac{7.5}{5} \overset{?}{=} 1.5$ *Substitute 7.5 for m in the equation.*

$1.5 \overset{?}{=} 1.5$ ✔   *7.5 is the solution.*

EXAMPLE 2   *Measurement Application*

Remember!

The area of a rectangle is its length times its width.

ℓ

$A = \ell w$

A The area of the floor in Jonah's bedroom is 28 square meters. If its length is 3.5 meters, what is the width of the bedroom?

area	=	length	·	width
28	=	3.5	·	*w*

$28 = 3.5w$ *Write the equation for the problem. Let w be the width of the room. w is multiplied by 3.5.*

$\dfrac{28}{3.5} = \dfrac{3.5w}{3.5}$ *Divide both sides by 3.5 to undo the multiplication.*

$8 = w$

The width of Jonah's bedroom is 8 meters.

B Jonah is carpeting his bedroom. The carpet costs $22.50 per square meter. What is the total cost to carpet the bedroom?

total cost = area · cost of carpet per square meter

$C = 28 \cdot 22.50$ *Let C be the total cost. Write the equation for the problem.*

$C = 630$ *Multiply.*

The cost of carpeting the bedroom is $630.

Think and Discuss

1. Explain whether the value of *m* will be less than or greater than 1 when you solve $5m = 4.5$.

2. Tell how you can check the answer in Example 2A.

Homework Help THINK central

Go to **thinkcentral.com**
Exercises 1–19, 21, 23, 25, 27, 29, 31, 33

 Preview of MA.7.A.3.3

GUIDED PRACTICE

See Example 1   Solve each equation. Check your answer.

1. $a - 2.3 = 4.8$ **2.** $6n = 8.4$ **3.** $\frac{c}{4} = 3.2$

4. $8.5 = 2.49 + x$ **5.** $\frac{d}{3.2} = 1.09$ **6.** $1.6 = m \cdot 4$

See Example 2   **7.** The length of a window is 10.5 meters, and the width is 5.75 meters. Solve the equation $a \div 10.5 = 5.75$ to find the area of the window.

8. Gretchen wants to add a wallpaper border along the top of the walls of her square room. The distance around her room is 20.4 meters.

   a. What is the length of each wall of Gretchen's room?

   b. The price of wallpaper border is $1.25 per meter. What is the total cost to add the border to her room?

INDEPENDENT PRACTICE

See Example 1   Solve each equation. Check your answer.

9. $b - 5.6 = 3.7$ **10.** $1.6 = \frac{p}{7}$ **11.** $3r = 62.4$

12. $9.5 = 5x$ **13.** $a - 4.8 = 5.9$ **14.** $\frac{n}{8} = 0.8$

15. $8 + f = 14.56$ **16.** $5.2s = 10.4$ **17.** $1.95 = z - 2.05$

See Example 2   **18. Geometry** The area of a rectangle is 65.8 square units. The length is 7 units. Solve the equation $7 \cdot w = 65.8$ to find the width of the rectangle.

19. Ken wants to fence his square garden. He will need 6.4 meters of fence to enclose all four sides of the garden.

   a. How long is each side of his garden?

   b. The price of fencing is $2.25 per meter. What is the total cost to fence Ken's garden?

PRACTICE AND PROBLEM SOLVING

Solve each equation and check your answer.

20. $9.8 = t - 42.1$ **21.** $q \div 2.6 = 9.5$ **22.** $45.36 = 5.6 \cdot m$

23. $1.3b = 5.46$ **24.** $4.93 = 0.563 + m$ **25.** $\frac{a}{5} = 2.78$

26. $w - 64.99 = 13.044$ **27.** $6.205z = 80.665$ **28.** $74.2 = 38.06 + c$

29. Geometry The shortest side of the triangle is 10 units long.

   a. What are the lengths of the other two sides of the triangle?

   b. What is the perimeter of the triangle?

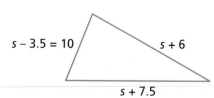

$s - 3.5 = 10$ $s + 6$ $s + 7.5$

◯ = **WORKED-OUT SOLUTIONS**
on p. WS4

The London Eye is the world's largest Ferris wheel. Use the table for Exercises 30–32.

30. Write the height of the wheel in kilometers.

31. Multi-Step There are 1,000 kilograms in a metric ton. What is the mass of the wheel in kilograms?

32. a. How many seconds does it take for the wheel to make one revolution?

b. The wheel moves at a rate of 0.26 meters per second. Use the equation $d \div 0.26 = 1,800$ to find the distance of one revolution.

33. Each capsule can hold 25 passengers. How many capsules are needed to hold 210 passengers?

Mass of wheel	1,900 metric tons
Time to revolve	30 minutes
Height of wheel	135 meters

34. In 2007, 15 standard flight adult tickets for the London Eye cost £217.50 (about $432.43). What is the cost for one ticket? Give the answer in both pounds sterling (£) and U.S. dollars.

35. What's the Error? When solving the equation $b - 12.98 = 5.03$, a student said that $b = 7.95$. Describe the error. What is the correct value for b?

36. Write About It Explain how you solve for the variable in a multiplication equation such as $2.3a = 4.6$.

37. Challenge Solve $1.45n \times 3.2 = 23.942 + 4.13$.

Florida Spiral Review
MA.6.A.1.2, MA.6.A.1.3, MA.6.A.3.1

38. Multiple Choice Solve the equation $d \div 4 = 6.7$ for d.

A. $d = 26.8$ **B.** $d = 10.7$ **C.** $d = 2.7$ **D.** $d = 1.675$

39. Multiple Choice Kelly bought 2.8 pounds of beef for $5.04. How much did she pay for each pound of beef?

F. $18.00   **G.** $7.84   **H.** $1.80   **I.** $0.18

Write each phrase as a numerical or algebraic expression. (Lesson 2-3)

40. 103 less than 739   **41.** the product of 7 and z **42.** the difference of 12 and n

Find each quotient. (Lesson 3-5)

43. $25.5 \div 5$ **44.** $44.7 \div 3$ **45.** $96.48 \div 6$ **46.** $0.0378 \div 9$

Quiz for Lessons 3-4 Through 3-8

3-4 Multiplying Decimals

Multiply.

1. 0.6×0.06 **2.** 3.8×0.002 **3.** 4.9×5.1

4. $0.7 \times 1.6 \times 0.25$ **5.** $1.2 \times 4.7 \times 6.36$ **6.** $0.3 \times 0.8 \times 0.64$

Evaluate $5x$ for each value of x.

7. $x = 1.025$ **8.** $x = 6.2$ **9.** $x = 2.64$

10. Neptune has a gravitational pull 1.2 times that of Earth. If an object weighs 15 pounds on Earth, how much would it weigh on Neptune?

3-5 Dividing Decimals by Whole Numbers

Find each quotient.

11. $17.5 \div 5$ **12.** $11.6 \div 8$ **13.** $23.4 \div 6$ **14.** $35.5 \div 5$

15. Five apples cost $4.90. How much does each apple cost?

3-6 Dividing by Decimals

Find each quotient.

16. $2.226 \div 0.42$ **17.** $13.49 \div 7.1$ **18.** $35.34 \div 6.2$ **19.** $178.64 \div 81.2$

20. Peri spent $21.89 on material to make a skirt. The material cost $3.98 per yard. How many yards did Peri buy?

3-7 Interpreting the Quotient

21. There are 352 students graduating from high school. The photographer takes one picture of each student as the student receives his or her diploma. If the photographer has 36 exposures on each roll of film, how many rolls will she have to buy to take each student's picture?

22. Alissa has 42 hotdogs for a party. There are 8 hotdog buns in a package. How many packages of hotdog buns does she need to buy so that she has a bun for every hotdog?

3-8 Solving Decimal Equations

Solve each equation.

23. $t - 6.3 = 8.9$ **24.** $4h = 20.4$ **25.** $\dfrac{p}{7} = 4.6$ **26.** $d + 2.8 = 9.5$

Ready to Go On?

Real-World CONNECTIONS

Florida Keys

Bridges in the Florida Keys The Florida Keys are a group of about 1,700 islands at the southern end of Florida. The islands are connected by 42 bridges. Some the the bridges are as short as 140 feet and some are nearly 7 miles long!

Use the map for Exercises 1–4.

1. Estimate the total length of the five bridges shown in the map.

2. List the Shark Channel, Indian Key, and Snake Creek in order from shortest to longest. Explain how you decided on the order.

3. How much longer is the Seven Mile Bridge than the Long Key Bridge?

4. The Spanish Harbor Bridge (not shown on the map) is 1.6 times as long as the Shark Channel Bridge. Find the length of the Spanish Harbor Bridge.

N
Gulf of Mexico

Snake Creek
0.04 mi

ISLAMORADA

Long Key
2.28 mi

Shark Channel
0.4 mi

Indian Key
0.47 mi

MARATHON

Seven Mile
6.79 mi

Atlantic Ocean

LOWER KEYS

KEY WEST

5. The bridges and islands that form the Florida Keys have a total distance of about 126 miles.

   a. Suppose that you drive an average speed of 52.5 miles per hour. About how long does it take to drive through the Florida Keys?

   b. Suppose that you stop to rest along the route every 45 minutes. How many stops do you make? (*Hint:* 45 minutes = 0.75 hour)

Florida Keys

Real-World Connections

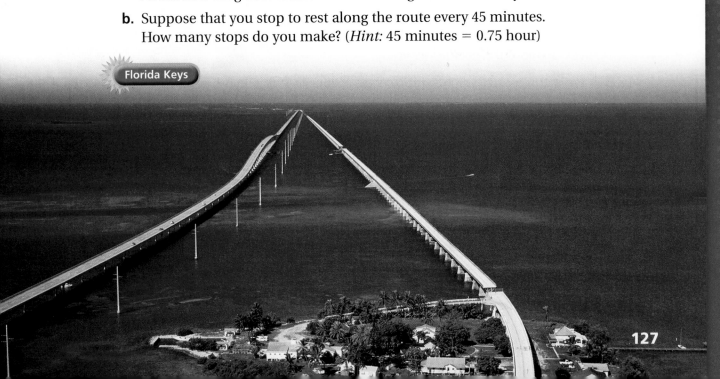

Game Time

Jumbles

Do you know what eleven plus two equals?

Use your calculator to evaluate each expression. Keep the letters under the expressions with the answers you get. Then order the answers from least to greatest, and write down the letters in that order. You will spell the answer to the riddle.

$4 - 1.893$　$0.21 \div 0.3$　$0.443 - 0.0042$　$4.509 - 3.526$　$3.14 \cdot 2.44$　$1.56 \cdot 3.678$

E　　　　**L**　　　　**E**　　　　　　**V**　　　　　**E**　　　　　**N**

$6.34 \div 2.56$　　$1.19 + 1.293$　　$8.25 \div 2.5$　　$7.4 - 2.356$

P　　　　　**L**　　　　　**U**　　　　　**S**

$0.0003 + 0.003$　　$0.3 \cdot 0.04$　　$2.17 + 3.42$

T　　　　　　**W**　　　　　**O**

Make A Buck

The object of the game is to win the most points by adding decimal numbers to make a sum close to but not over $1.00.

Most cards have a decimal number on them representing an amount of money. Others are wild cards: The person who receives a wild card decides its value.

The dealer gives each player four cards. Taking turns, players add the numbers in their hand. If the sum is less than $1.00, a player can either draw a card from the top of the deck or pass.

When each player has taken a turn or passed, the player whose sum is closest to but not over $1.00 scores a point. If players tie for the closest sum, each of those players scores a point. All cards are then discarded and four new cards are dealt to each player.

When all of the cards have been dealt, the player with the most points wins.

Games

THINK central

Go to thinkcentral.com

A complete copy of the rules and game pieces are available online.

Materials
- 2 plastic slide holders
- squares of card stock
- clear tape
- permanent marker

It's in the Bag!

PROJECT ## Project E Z 2 C Decimals

Practice reading decimals by making this see-through decimal holder.

Directions

1. Cut out about 40 small squares of colored card stock. Remove ten of the squares. On these squares, write "Ones," "Tens," "Hundreds," "Thousands," "Ten-Thousands," "Tenths," "Hundredths," "Thousandths," "Ten-Thousandths," and "Hundred-Thousandths." **Figure A**

2. On each of the remaining squares, write a number from 0 to 9.

3. Tape the two slide holders together. Using a permanent marker, draw decimal points down the middle where the holders are taped together. **Figure B**

4. Put the squares with the names of the place values in the correct slots along the top row.

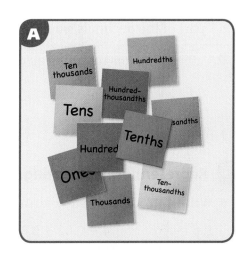

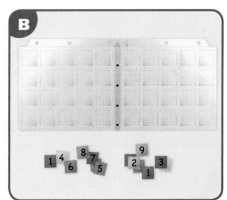

Putting the Math into Action

Put numbered squares in the remaining slots. Work with a partner to practice reading the resulting decimals. Mix up the numbered squares and repeat the process several more times, sometimes using all of the slots in a row and sometimes making shorter decimals.

Study Guide: Review

Multi–Language Glossary

THINK central

Go to thinkcentral.com

Vocabulary

clustering 98

front-end estimation 99

Complete the sentences below with vocabulary words from the list above.

1. When you estimate a sum by using only the whole-number part of the decimals, you are using ___?___.

2. ___?___ means rounding all the numbers to the same value.

EXAMPLES

EXERCISES

3-1 Representing, Comparing, and Ordering Decimals (pp. 94–97)

MA.6.A.5.2

- Write 4.025 in expanded form and words.

  Expanded form: $4 + 0.02 + 0.005$

  Word form: four and twenty-five thousandths

- Order the decimals from least to greatest.
  7.8, 7.83, 7.08

  $7.08 < 7.80 < 7.83$ *Compare the numbers.*
  7.08, 7.8, 7.83   *Then order the numbers.*

Write each in expanded form and words.

3. 5.68   **4.** 1.0076

5. 1.203   **6.** 23.005

7. 71.038   **8.** 99.9999

Order the decimals from least to greatest.

9. 1.2, 1.3, 1.12   **10.** 11.17, 11.7, 11.07

11. 0.3, 0.303, 0.033   **12.** 5.009, 5.950, 5.5

13. 101.52, 101.25, 101.025

3-2 Estimating Decimals (pp. 98–101)

MA.6.A.5.3

- Estimate.

  5.35 − 0.7904; round to tenths

    5.4   *Align the decimals.*
  −0.8   *Subtract.*
  ─────
    4.6

  ? 67 × 2.88.

  150

Estimate.

14. 8.0954 + 3.218; round to the hundredths

15. 6.8356 − 4.507; round to the tenths

16. 9.258 + 4.97; round to the ones

Estimate each product or quotient.

17. 21.19 × 4.23

18. 53.98 ÷ 5.97

19. 102.89 × 19.95

Study Guide: Review

3-3 **Adding and Subtracting Decimals** (pp. 102–105)

 Prep for MA.6.A.5.3

■ **Find the sum.**

7.62 + 0.563

$$
\begin{array}{r}
7.620 \\
+ \ 0.563 \\
\hline
8.183
\end{array}
$$

Align the decimal points. Use zeros as placeholders. Add. Place the decimal point.

Find each sum or difference.

20. $7.08 + 4.5 + 13.27$ **21.** $6 - 0.7$

22. $6.21 + 5.8 + 21.01$ **23.** $7.001 - 2.0785$

Evaluate $6.48 - s$ **for each value of s.**

24. $s = 3.9$ **25.** $s = 3.6082$

26. $s = 5.01$ **27.** $s = 0.057$

28. Rodney bought a new book for $15.75 and two new CDs for $12.99 each. How much did Rodney spend?

3-4 **Multiplying Decimals** (pp. 108–111)

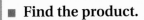 MA.6.A.1.2

■ **Find the product.**

$$
\begin{array}{r}
0.3 \\
\times \ 0.08 \\
\hline
0.024
\end{array}
$$

1 decimal place
+ 2 decimal places
3 decimal places

■ **Evaluate** $2.4x$ **for** $x = 0.124$.

$2.4x = 2.4(0.124)$ *Substitue 0.124 for x.*

$$
\begin{array}{r}
0.124 \\
\times \ 2.4 \\
\hline
0.2976
\end{array}
$$

3 decimal places
+ 1 decimal place
4 decimal places

Find each product.

29. 4×2.36 **30.** 0.5×1.73

31. 0.6×0.012 **32.** 8×3.052

33. 1.2×0.45 **34.** 9.7×1.084

35. An object on the surface of the Sun would weigh around 28 times as much as it weighs on Earth. How much would a 202.8-pound man weigh on the Sun?

Evaluate.

36. $4n$ for $n = 3.81$

37. $2.5a$ for $a = 2.05$

38. $0.2x$ for $x = 7.31$

39. $10.3n + 2.8$ for $n = 0.8$

40. $0.7x + 1.2x$ for $x = 2.5$

3-5 **Dividing Decimals by Whole Numbers** (pp. 112–114)

 MA.6.A.1.2

■ **Find the quotient.**

0.95 ÷ 5

Place a decimal point directly above the decimal point in the dividend. Then divide.

$$
\begin{array}{r}
0.19 \\
5\overline{)0.95}
\end{array}
$$

Find each quotient.

41. $6.18 \div 6$ **42.** $2.16 \div 3$

43. $34.65 \div 9$ **44.** $20.72 \div 8$

45. If four people equally share a bill for $14.56, how much should each person pay?

3-6 Dividing by Decimals (pp. 115–118)

MA.6.A.1.3

■ **Find the quotient.**

9.65 ÷ 0.5

Make the divisor a whole number.

Place the decimal point in the quotient.

$$\begin{array}{r} 19.3 \\ 5\overline{)96.5} \end{array}$$

Find each quotient.

46. $4.86 \div 0.6$ **47.** $1.85 \div 0.3$

48. $34.89 \div 9$ **49.** $62.73 \div 1.2$

50. Ana cuts some wood that is 3.75 meters long into 5 pieces of equal length. How long is each piece?

51. Julie is making bookmarks using ribbon. She has 0.84 yards of ribbon and needs 0.06 yards for each bookmark. How many bookmarks can she make?

52. Chris's garden is 13.6 feet long. He has a plant every 1.7 feet. How many plants does he have in his garden?

3-7 Interpreting the Quotient (pp. 119–121)

MA.6.A.5.3

■ **Ms. Ald needs 26 stickers for her preschool class. Stickers are sold in packs of 8. How many packs should she buy?**

$26 \div 8 = 3.25$

3.25 is between 3 and 4.

3 packs will not be enough.

Ms. Ald should buy 4 packs of stickers.

53. Billy has 3.6 liters of juice. How many 0.25 L containers can he fill?

54. There are 34 people going on a field trip. If each car holds 4 people, how many cars will they need for the field trip?

55. Mr. Paxton has 16.5 feet of twine. If he is wrapping 3 packages, how much twine can he use on each package?

56. Carla has 78 photos to put in an album. If she can place 8 photos on a page, how many pages will she need?

3-8 Solving Decimal Equations (pp. 122–125)

Prep MA.7.A.3.3

■ **Solve $4x = 20.8$.**

$4x = 20.8$ *x is multiplied by 4.*

$\dfrac{4x}{4} = \dfrac{20.8}{4}$ *Divide both sides by 4.*

$x = 5.2$

Solve each equation.

57. $a - 6.2 = 7.18$ **58.** $3y = 7.86$

59. $n + 4.09 = 6.38$ **60.** $\dfrac{p}{7} = 8.6$

61. Jasmine buys 2.25 kg of apples for $11.25. How much does 1 kg of apples cost?

Chapter Test

Order the decimals from least to greatest.

1. 12.6, 12.07, 12.67

2. 3.5, 3.25, 3.08

3. 0.10301, 0.10318, 0.10325

For 4 and 5, use the table.

4. The table shows the number of oranges produced in 5 counties in Florida in 2006. Put the numbers in order from greatest to least.

5. Estimate the total number of oranges in millions produced by Highlands and Polk Counties.

County	Oranges (millions)
DeSoto	20.03
Hardee	14.35
Hendry	14.66
Highlands	21.82
Polk	27.69

Estimate.

6. 21.35×3.18

7. $98.547 \div 4.93$

8. 11.855×8.45

Find each sum or difference.

9. $3.89 + 42.71$

10. $20.751 + 17.4$

11. $4.987 - 0.098$

12. Britney wants to exercise in a step aerobics class. The class uses the 4-inch step for 15 minutes and the 6-inch step for 15 minutes. About how many calories will she burn in all?

Step Height (in.)	Calories Burned in 15 minutes
4	67.61
6	82.2
8	96

Find each product.

13. 0.5×0.7

14. 6.12×5.9

15. 0.12×0.006

16. 1.8×2.07

17. One car tire costs $69.99. How much do 4 tires cost?

Find each quotient.

18. $0.84 \div 6$

19. $11.07 \div 9$

20. $5.85 \div 3.9$

21. $0.84 \div 0.006$

22. Marci pays $8.97 at the grocery store for 3 pounds of cherries. How much does each pound cost?

23. The school band is going to a competition. There are 165 students in the band. If each bus holds 25 students, how many buses will be needed?

Solve each equation.

24. $b - 4.7 = 2.1$

25. $5a = 4.75$

26. $\frac{y}{6} = 7.2$

27. $c + 1.9 = 26.04$

28. Marisol bought six sweaters on sale for a total of $126.24. How much did each sweater cost if they were all marked down to the same price?

Chapter Test

Test Tackler

Standardized Test Strategies

Short Response: Write Short Responses

Short-response test items require a solution to the problem and the reasoning or work used to get that solution. Short-response test items are scored according to a 2-point scoring rubric. A sample scoring rubric is provided below.

EXAMPLE 1

Short Response Coach Mott needs to order jackets for the boys' basketball team. Each jacket costs $28.75. The team has $125 from their fund-raiser to go toward the total cost of the jackets. If there are 10 players on the team, how much money will each player need to give to Coach Mott for a jacket so he can place the order? Explain.

2-point response:

Cost of one jacket: $28.75
Total cost for team jackets (10 players):
$28.75 × 10 = $287.50

Subtract the money the team already has from the total cost.
$287.50 − $125 = $162.50

Divide the remaining cost by the number of players on the team.
$162.50 ÷ 10 = $16.25

Each player needs to give Coach Mott $16.25 so he can place the order for the jackets.

1-point response:

($287.50 − $125) ÷ $10 = $16.25

He will need $16.25 from each player.

0-point response:

$16.25

Scoring Rubric

2 points: The student demonstrates a thorough understanding of mathematics concepts, responds correctly to the task, and provides clear and complete explanations when required.

1 point: The student's response is only partially correct. The student may provide a correct solution but may demonstrate a misunderstanding of the underlying mathematics, or the student may provide an incorrect solution but may have applied mathematically sound procedures.

0 points: The student provides no response at all or a completely incorrect or uninterpretable response.

The student correctly solved the problem but did not show all of his or her work or did not provide an explanation.

The student gave a correct answer but did not show any work or give an explanation.

Never leave a short-response test item blank. Showing your work and providing a reasonable explanation will result in at least some credit.

Read each test item and answer the questions that follow by using the scoring rubric below.

Item A
Short Response Write two equations that each have a solution of 12. You cannot use the same mathematical operation for both equations. Explain how to solve both equations.

Student's Answer

One equation that has a solution of 12 is $\frac{x}{6} = 2$. To solve this equation, I must undo the division by multiplying by 6 on both sides.

$$\frac{x}{6} = 2$$
$$6 \cdot \left(\frac{x}{6}\right) = 6 \cdot 2$$
$$x = 12$$

Another equation with a solution of 12 is $x - 8 = 20$.

To solve this equation, I must add the opposite of 8 to both sides.

$$\begin{aligned} x - 8 &= 20 \\ -8 &= -8 \\ \hline x &= 12 \end{aligned}$$

1. The student's answer will not receive full credit. Find the error in the student's answer.

2. Rewrite the student's answer so that it receives full credit.

Item B
Short Response June is 8 years older than her cousin Liv. Write an expression to find June's age. Identify the variable and list three possible solutions showing the ages of June and Liv.

Student's Answer

Let x = Liv's age. Since June is 8 years older, the expression $x + 8$ can be used to find June's age.

Three possible solutions for Liv and June follow:

$x = 3$, $3 + 8 = 11$; Liv: 3, June: 11
$x = 8$, $8 + 8 = 16$; Liv: 8, June: 16
$x = 11$, $11 + 8 = 19$; Liv: 11, June: 19

3. What score should the student's answer receive? Explain your reasoning.

4. What additional information, if any, should the student's answer include in order to receive full credit?

Item C
Short Response Write an equation to represent the following situation. Define the variable. Solve the problem. *Sam has two kittens. The larger kitten has a mass of 3.2 kg. The other kitten needs to gain 1.9 kg to have the same mass of the larger kitten. What is the mass of the smaller kitten?*

Student's Answer

Let x = the mass of the smaller kitten.
$x + 1.9 = 3.2$
$3.2 + 1.9 = 5.1$

5. How would you score the student's response? Explain.

6. Rewrite the response so that it receives full credit.

Mastering the Standards

Florida Test Practice

Go to thinkcentral.com

THINK central

Cumulative Assessment, Chapters 1–3

Multiple Choice

1. What number is shown on the number line?

   ```
   1.0   1.2   1.4   1.6   1.8   2.0
   ```

   A. 0.3   **C.** 1.35

   B. 1.3   **D.** 1.4

2. The weights of three backpacks are 15.8 pounds, 18.1 pounds, and 16.7 pounds. About how many pounds do the backpacks weigh all together?

   F. 30 pounds   **H.** 50 pounds

   G. 40 pounds   **I.** 60 pounds

3. For which equation is $c = 8$ NOT a solution?

   A. $\frac{c}{4} = 2$ **C.** $4c = 28$

   B. $c + 4 = 12$ **D.** $c - 5 = 3$

4. Jerah scored 15 more points than his brother Jim. Jim scored 7 points. Which expression can be used to find the number of points Jerah scored?

   F. $15 - 7$ **H.** $15 \div 7$

   G. 15×7 **I.** $15 + 7$

5. Manuel is buying 0.9 pound of nuts. How much will he pay, in dollars, if the nuts are $1.40 a pound?

   A. 0.126   **C.** 1.26

   B. 0.36   **D.** 1.36

6. The top four times in a race were 18.095 s, 18.9 s, 18.907 s, and 18.75 s. What was the winner's time?

   F. 18.095   **H.** 18.907

   G. 18.9   **I.** 18.75

7. The heights of four different plants are listed below. Which statement is supported by the data?

Plant Height (in.)				
Plant	T	S	U	W
Week 1	15.9	23.6	17.1	12.5
Week 2	21.4	27.4	22.9	16.4

   A. Plant T was the shortest during week 1.

   B. Plant S grew more than 4 inches between week 1 and week 2.

   C. Plant U grew the most between week 1 and week 2.

   D. Plant W is the tallest.

8. If $x = 0.04$ what is the value of $3.2x$?

   F. 0.128   **H.** 12.8

   G. 1.28   **I.** 128

9. Katie is making hair clips for a fund raiser. She has 6.25 yards of ribbon. Each hair clip uses 0.35 yards of ribbon. How many hair clips can Katie make?

   A. 18   **C.** 17

   B. 17.85   **D.** 0.056

10. Tomas needs 42 cups for a party. The cups are sold in packages of 5. How many packages should he buy?

    F. 10 packages   **H.** 8 packages

    G. 9 packages   **I.** 7 packages

11. Which expression is NOT equal to 2.63?

    A. $7.89 \div 3$ **C.** $13.15 \div 5$

    B. $26.3 \div 10$ **D.** $0.263 \div 100$

12. Which set of numbers is in order from least to greatest?

    F. 23.7, 23.07, 23.13, 23.89

    G. 21.4, 21.45, 21.79, 21.8

    H. 22, 22.09, 21.9, 22.1

    I. 25.4, 25.09, 25.6, 25.7

13. Megan is beginning an exercise routine. She plans to walk 1 mile on day 1 and increase her distance each day by 0.25 mile. How many miles will she be walking on day 10?

    A. 2.5 miles   **C.** 4.75 miles

    B. 3.25 miles   **D.** 6.0 miles

 Estimate your answer before solving the question. Use your estimate to check the reasonableness of your answer.

Gridded Response

14. What is the value of c in the equation $\frac{c}{6} = 3.4$?

15. Tom bought 7.4 feet of wire. The wire cost $0.85 for each foot. How much did the wire cost, in dollars?

16. Sam has 10 boxes full of computer games. Each box holds 13 games. How many games does Sam own?

17. Cindy bought 3 bunches of daisies and 4 bunches of carnations. There are 6 daisies and 10 carnations in a bunch. How many flowers does she have in all?

18. Bart and his 2 friends buy lunch. The total is $13.74. If they share the cost equally, how much, in dollars, should each person pay?

19. Daisy buys a shirt that costs $21.64 after tax. She gives the cashier $25. How much, in dollars, does she get back in change?

Short Response

S1. Kevin buys 5 steaks for $43.75. Let b equal the cost of one steak. Write and solve the equation to find the cost of one steak.

S2. Ms. Maier has 8 packs of pencils to give out to students taking a state test. Each pack has 8 pencils. There are 200 students taking the test who need pencils.

    a. How many more packs of pencils does Ms. Maier need to buy? Explain your answer and show your work.

    b. If each pack of pencils costs $0.79, how much money will Ms. Maier need to spend to buy the extra pencils? Show your work.

Extended Response

E1. Admission to the Children's Museum is listed below. Use the chart to answer the following questions.

Admission Costs ($)	
Adult	7.50
Child	5.75

    a. Write an expression to find the cost of admission for 2 adults and c children.

    b. Use your expression to find the total cost for Mr. and Mrs. Chu and their 8-year-old triplets. Show your work.

    c. If Mr. Chu pays for admission using a $50 bill, how much change does he get back? Show your work.

    d. On the Chu's next visit, Mrs. Chu plans to use a coupon and will only pay $28.50 for the family. How much will she save using the coupon?

Number Theory and Fractions

Worktext
pages 145–180

Additional instruction, practice, and activities are available online, including:
- Lesson Tutorial Videos
- Homework Help
- Animated Math

Go to **thinkcentral.com**

THINK central

Why Learn This?

Recipes often list quantities of ingredients as fractions and mixed numbers. Professional chefs must be able to work with these numbers in order to follow recipes.

Chapter Focus
- Use equivalent forms of fractions and decimals to solve problems.
- Compare and order fractions and decimals and find their approximate location on a number line.

 **Are You Ready?**

✓ Vocabulary

Choose the best term from the list to complete each sentence.

1. To find the sum of two numbers, you should ___?___.
2. Fractions are written as a ___?___ over a ___?___.
3. In the equation 4 · 3 = 12, 12 is the ___?___.
4. The ___?___ of 18 and 10 is 8.
5. The numbers 18, 27, and 72 are ___?___ of 9.

add
denominator
difference
multiples
numerator
product
quotient

Complete these exercises to review skills you will need for this chapter.

✓ Write and Read Decimals

Write each decimal in word form.

6. 0.5
7. 2.78
8. 0.125
9. 12.8
10. 125.49
11. 8.024

✓ Multiples

List the first four multiples of each number.

12. 6
13. 8
14. 5
15. 12
16. 7
17. 20
18. 14
19. 9

✓ Evaluate Expressions

Evaluate each expression for the given value of the variable.

20. $y + 4.3$ for $y = 3.2$
21. $\frac{x}{5}$ for $x = 6.4$
22. $3c$ for $c = 0.75$
23. $a + 4 \div 8$ for $a = 3.75$
24. $27.8 - d$ for $d = 9.25$
25. $2.5b$ for $b = 8.4$

✓ Factors

Find all the whole-number factors of each number.

26. 8
27. 12
28. 24
29. 30
30. 45
31. 52
32. 75
33. 150

Study Guide: Preview

Before

Previously, you

- identified a number as prime or composite.
- identified common factors of a set of whole numbers.
- generated equivalent fractions.
- compared two fractions with common denominators.

Now

You will study

- writing the prime factorization of a number.
- finding the greatest common factor (GCF) of a set of whole numbers.
- generating equivalent forms of numbers, including whole numbers, fractions, and decimals.
- comparing and ordering fractions, decimals, and whole numbers.

Why?

You can use the skills learned in this chapter

- to double or halve recipes when cooking.
- to add together fractions when determining volume in a science class.

Key Vocabulary/Vocabulario

common denominator	denominador común
equivalent fractions	fracciones equivalentes
greatest common factor (GCF)	máximo común divisor (MCD)
improper fraction	fracción impropia
mixed number	número mixto
prime factorization	factorización prima
proper fraction	fracción propia
repeating decimal	decimal repetido
terminating decimal	decimal cerrado

Vocabulary Connections

To become familiar with some of the vocabulary terms in the chapter, consider the following. You may refer to the chapter, the glossary, or a dictionary if you like.

1. The word *equivalent* means "equal in value." What do you think **equivalent fractions** are?

2. To *terminate* something means to bring it to an end. If a decimal is a **terminating decimal**, what do you think happens to it? Explain.

3. When people have something in *common*, they have something that they share. What do you think **common denominators** share?

4. If something is *improper*, it is not right. In fractions, it is *improper* to have the numerator be greater than the denominator. How would you expect an **improper fraction** to look?

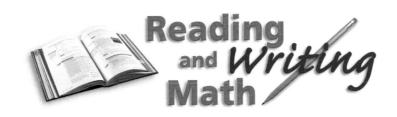 **Reading and Writing Math**

Reading Strategy: Read a Lesson for Understanding

 LA.6.4.2.2 The student will record information (e.g., observations, notes . . .) related to a topic . . .

Reading ahead will prepare you for new ideas and concepts presented in class. As you read a lesson, make notes. Write down the main points of the lesson, math terms that you do not understand, examples that need more explanation, and questions you can ask during class.

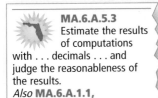 **MA.6.A.5.3** Estimate the results of computations with . . . decimals . . . and judge the reasonableness of the results.
Also **MA.6.A.1.1, MA.6.A.1.2, MA.6.A.1.3**

Identify the standard or standards of the lesson. Then skim through the lesson to get a sense of how the standards are covered.

Work through the examples and write down any questions you have.

Social Studies Application

Marissa is drawing a time line of the Stone Age. She plans for 6 equal sections, two each for the Paleolithic, Mesolithic, and Neolithic periods. If she has 7.8 meters of paper, how long is each section?

The question asks exactly how long each section will be when the paper is divided into 6 sections.

$7.8 \div 6 = 1.3$ *Think: The question asks for an exact answer, so do not estimate. Use the entire quotient.*

Each section will be **1.3** meters long.

Questions:
• *How do I know when to use an exact answer?*
• *How do I know when to round the answer up to the next whole number?*

Write down questions you have as you read the lesson.

 Try This

Read Lesson 4-1 before your next class and answer the following questions.

1. What standard does the lesson prepare you for?

2. Are there new vocabulary terms, formulas, or symbols? If so, what are they?

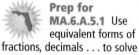

4-1 Divisibility

Prep for MA.6.A.5.1 Use equivalent forms of fractions, decimals . . . to solve problems.
Review of MA.5.A.6.1

Vocabulary

divisible

composite number

prime number

This year, 42 girls signed up to play soccer for the Junior Girls League, which has 6 teams. To find whether each team can have the same number of girls, decide if 42 is divisible by 6.

A number is **divisible** by another number if the quotient is a whole number with no remainder.

$$42 \div 6 = 7 \leftarrow \text{Quotient}$$

Since there is no remainder, 42 is divisible by 6. The Junior Girls League can have 6 teams with 7 girls each.

Animated Math
@ thinkcentral.com

Remember!

Division by 0 is undefined.

A number is divisible by...	Divisible	Not Divisible
Divisibility Rules		
2 if the last digit is even (0, 2, 4, 6, or 8).	3,978	4,975
3 if the sum of the digits is divisible by 3.	315	139
4 if the last two digits form a number divisible by 4.	8,512	7,518
5 if the last digit is 0 or 5.	14,975	10,978
6 if the number is divisible by both 2 and 3.	48	20
9 if the sum of the digits is divisible by 9.	711	93
10 if the last digit is 0.	15,990	10,536

EXAMPLE 1 **Checking Divisibility**

A **Tell whether 610 is divisible by 2, 3, 4, and 5.**

2	*The last digit, 0, is even.*	Divisible
3	*The sum of the digits is 6 + 1 + 0 = 7. 7 is not divisible by 3.*	Not divisible
4	*The last two digits form the number 10. 10 is not divisible by 4.*	Not divisible
5	*The last digit is 0.*	Divisible

So 610 is divisible by 2 and 5.

B Tell whether 387 is divisible by 6, 9, and 10.

6	The last digit, 7, is odd, so 387 is not divisible by 2.	Not divisible
9	The sum of the digits is 3 + 8 + 7 = 18. 18 is divisible by 9.	Divisible
10	The last digit is 7, not 0.	Not divisible

So 387 is divisible by 9.

Any number greater than 1 is divisible by at least two numbers—1 and the number itself. Numbers that are divisible by more than two numbers are called **composite numbers**.

A **prime number** is divisible by only the numbers 1 and itself. For example, 11 is a prime number because it is divisible by only 1 and 11. The numbers 0 and 1 are neither prime nor composite.

EXAMPLE **2** **Identifying Prime and Composite Numbers**

Tell whether each number is prime or composite.

A 45
   divisible by 1, 3, 5, 9, 15, 45
   composite

B 13
   divisible by 1, 13
   prime

C 19
   divisible by 1, 19
   prime

D 49
   divisible by 1, 7, 49
   composite

The prime numbers from 1 through 50 are highlighted below.

1	2	3	4	5	6	7	8	9	10
11	12	13	14	15	16	17	18	19	20
21	22	23	24	25	26	27	28	29	30
31	32	33	34	35	36	37	38	39	40
41	42	43	44	45	46	47	48	49	50

Think and Discuss

1. Tell which whole numbers are divisible by 1.

2. Explain how you know that 87 is a composite number.

3. Tell how the divisibility rules help you identify composite numbers.

Prep MA.6.A.5.1

Homework Help

Go to thinkcentral.com
Exercises 1–32, 33, 35, 41, 43, 45

GUIDED PRACTICE

See Example 1 Tell whether each number is divisible by 2, 3, 4, 5, 6, 9, and 10.

1. 508　　　　**2.** 432　　　　**3.** 247　　　　**4.** 189

See Example 2 Tell whether each number is prime or composite.

5. 75　　　　**6.** 17　　　　**7.** 27　　　　**8.** 63

9. 72　　　　**10.** 83　　　　**11.** 99　　　　**12.** 199

INDEPENDENT PRACTICE

See Example 1 Tell whether each number is divisible by 2, 3, 4, 5, 6, 9, and 10.

13. 741　　　　**14.** 810　　　　**15.** 675　　　　**16.** 480

17. 908　　　　**18.** 146　　　　**19.** 514　　　　**20.** 405

See Example 2 Tell whether each number is prime or composite.

21. 34　　　　**22.** 29　　　　**23.** 61　　　　**24.** 81

25. 51　　　　**26.** 23　　　　**27.** 97　　　　**28.** 93

29. 77　　　　**30.** 41　　　　**31.** 67　　　　**32.** 39

PRACTICE AND PROBLEM SOLVING

Copy and complete the table. Write *yes* if the number is divisible by the given number. Write *no* if it is not.

		2	3	4	5	6	9	10
33.	**677**	*no*	▪	▪	*no*	▪	▪	*no*
34.	**290**	*yes*	▪	▪	▪	▪	▪	▪
35.	**1,744**	▪	▪	▪	▪	▪	▪	▪
36.	**12,180**	▪	▪	▪	▪	▪	▪	▪

Tell whether each statement is true or false. Explain your answers.

37. All even numbers are divisible by 2.

38. All odd numbers are divisible by 3.

39. Some even numbers are divisible by 5.

40. All odd numbers are prime.

Replace each box with a digit that will make the number divisible by 3.

41. 74▪　　　　**42.** 8,10▪　　　　**43.** 3,▪41

44. ▪,335　　　　**45.** 67,▪11　　　　**46.** 10,0▪1

○ = WORKED-OUT SOLUTIONS
on p. WS4

47. Make a table that shows the prime numbers from 50 to 100.

48. Astronomy Earth has a diameter of 7,926 miles. Tell whether this number is divisible by 2, 3, 4, 5, 6, 9, and 10.

49. On which of the bridges in the table could a light fixture be placed every 6 meters so that the first light is at the beginning of the bridge and the last light is at the end of the bridge? Explain.

Verrazano-Narrows Bridge

Longest Bridges in the U.S.	
Name and State	**Length (m)**
Verrazano-Narrows, NY	1,298
Golden Gate, CA	1,280
Mackinac Straits, MI	1,158
George Washington, NY	1,067

50. Critical Thinking A number is between 80 and 100 and is divisible by both 5 and 6. What is the number?

51. Choose a Strategy Find the greatest four-digit number that is divisible by 1, 2, 3, and 4.

52. What's the Error? To find whether 3,463 is divisible by 4, a student added the digits. The sum, 16, is divisible by 4, so the student stated that 3,463 is divisible by 4. Explain the error.

53. Write About It If a number is divisible by both 4 and 9, by what other numbers is it divisible? Explain.

54. Challenge Find a number that is divisible by 2, 3, 4, 5, 6, and 10, but not 9.

Florida Spiral Review   MA.6.A.3.1, MA.6.A.1.2

55. Multiple Choice ___?___ numbers are divisible by more than two numbers.

   A. Whole   **B.** Prime   **C.** Equivalent   **D.** Composite

56. Short Response What is the least three-digit number that is divisible by both 5 and 9? Show your work.

Evaluate each expression for the given value of the variable. (Lesson 2-2)

57. $2x + 28$ for $x = 4$ **58.** $x + 18$ for $x = 12$ **59.** $\frac{x}{5}$ for $x = 25$

Find each quotient. (Lesson 3-6)

60. $5.4 \div 0.08$ **61.** $2.24 \div 3.2$ **62.** $13.2 \div 0.06$ **63.** $0.2835 \div 2.7$

Factors and Prime Factorization

Prep for MA.6.A.5.1 Use equivalent forms of fractions, decimals . . . to solve problems.
Review of MA.5.A.2.4

Vocabulary

factor

prime factorization

Whole numbers that are multiplied to find a product are called **factors** of that product. A number is divisible by its factors.

$$2 \cdot 3 = 6 \qquad 6 \div 3 = 2$$
$$6 \div 2 = 3$$

Factors   Product

6 is divisible by 3 and 2.

EXAMPLE 1   **Finding Factors**

Animated Math @ thinkcentral.com

List all of the factors of each number.

A 18

Begin listing factors in pairs.

$18 = 1 \cdot 18$ *1 is a factor.*

$18 = 2 \cdot 9$ *2 is a factor.*

$18 = 3 \cdot 6$ *3 is a factor.*

                 4 and 5 are not factors.

$18 = 6 \cdot 3$ *6 and 3 have already been listed, so stop here.*

   1   2   3   6   9   18   *You can draw a diagram to illustrate the factor pairs.*

The factors of 18 are 1, 2, 3, 6, 9, and 18.

B 13

$13 = 1 \cdot 13$ *Begin listing factors in pairs. 13 is not divisible by any other whole numbers.*

The factors of 13 are 1 and 13.

You can use factors to write a number in different ways.

Factorization of 12			
$1 \cdot 12$	$2 \cdot 6$	$3 \cdot 4$	$3 \cdot 2 \cdot 2$

Notice that these factors are all prime.

The **prime factorization** of a number is the number written as the product of its prime factors.

EXAMPLE 2 **Writing Prime Factorizations**

Write the prime factorization of each number.

A 36

Method 1: Use a factor tree.

Choose any two factors of 36 to begin. Keep finding factors until each branch ends at a prime factor.

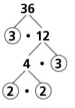

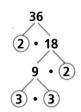

$36 = 3 \cdot 2 \cdot 2 \cdot 3$ $36 = 2 \cdot 3 \cdot 3 \cdot 2$

The prime factorization of 36 is **2 · 2 · 3 · 3, or $2^2 \cdot 3^2$**.

B 54

Method 2: Use a ladder diagram.

Choose a prime factor of 54 to begin. Keep dividing by prime factors until the quotient is 1.

```
2 | 54                      3 | 54
  3 | 27                      3 | 18
    3 | 9                       2 | 6
      3 | 3                       3 | 3
          1                           1
```

$54 = 2 \cdot 3 \cdot 3 \cdot 3$ $54 = 3 \cdot 3 \cdot 2 \cdot 3$

The prime factorization of 54 is **2 · 3 · 3 · 3, or $2 \cdot 3^3$**.

Helpful Hint

You can use exponents to write prime factorizations. Remember that an exponent tells you how many times the base is a factor.

In Example 2, notice that the prime factors may be written in a different order, but they are still the same factors. Except for changes in the order, there is only one way to write the prime factorization of a number.

Think and Discuss

1. **Tell** how you know when you have found all of the factors of a number.

2. **Tell** how you know when you have found the prime factorization of a number.

3. **Explain** the difference between factors of a number and prime factors of a number.

Homework Help

Go to **thinkcentral.com**
Exercises 1–24, 33, 35, 37, 39, 43, 45, 47

 Prep MA.6.A.5.1

GUIDED PRACTICE

See Example 1 **List all of the factors of each number.**

1. 12   **2.** 21   **3.** 52   **4.** 75

See Example 2 **Write the prime factorization of each number.**

5. 48   **6.** 20   **7.** 66   **8.** 34

INDEPENDENT PRACTICE

See Example 1 **List all of the factors of each number.**

9. 24   **10.** 37   **11.** 42   **12.** 56

13. 67   **14.** 72   **15.** 85   **16.** 92

See Example 2 **Write the prime factorization of each number.**

17. 49   **18.** 38   **19.** 76   **20.** 60

21. 81   **22.** 132   **23.** 140   **24.** 87

PRACTICE AND PROBLEM SOLVING

Write each number as a product in two different ways.

25. 34   **26.** 82   **27.** 88   **28.** 50

29. 15   **30.** 78   **31.** 94   **32.** 35

33. Sports Little League Baseball began in 1939 in Pennsylvania. When it first started, there were 45 boys on 3 teams.

     a. If the teams were equally sized, how many boys were on each team?

     b. Name another way the boys could have been divided into equally sized teams. (Remember that a baseball team must have at least 9 players.)

34. Critical Thinking Use the divisibility rules to list the factors of 171. Explain how you determined the factors.

Find the prime factorization of each number.

35. 99   **36.** 249   **37.** 284   **38.** 620

39. 840   **40.** 150   **41.** 740   **42.** 402

43. The prime factorization of 50 is $2 \cdot 5^2$. Without dividing or using a diagram, find the prime factorization of 100.

44. Geometry The area of a rectangle is the product of its length and width. Suppose the area of a rectangle is 24 in^2. What are the possible whole number measurements of its length and width?

45. Physical Science The speed of sound at sea level at 20 °C is 343 meters per second. Write the prime factorization of 343.

○ = **WORKED-OUT SOLUTIONS**
on p. WS4

Climate changes, habitat destruction, and overhunting can cause animals and plants to die in large numbers. When the entire population of a species begins to die out, the species is considered endangered.

The graph shows the number of endangered species in each category of animal.

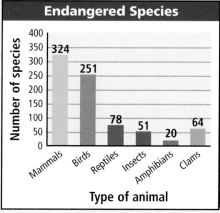

Endangered Species

46. How many species of mammals are endangered? Write this number as the product of prime factors.

47. Which category of animal has a prime number of endangered species?

48. How many species of reptiles and amphibians combined are endangered? Write the answer as the product of prime factors.

Most white tigers are found in zoos or sanctuaries for big cats. They are very rarely seen in the wild.

49. **(?) What's the Error?** When asked to write the prime factorization of the number of endangered amphibian species, a student wrote 4 × 5. Explain the error and write the correct answer.

50. **Write About It** A team of five scientists is going to study endangered insect species. The scientists want to divide the species evenly among them. Will they be able to do this? Why or why not?

51. **Challenge** Add the number of endangered mammal species to the number of endangered bird species. Find the prime factorization of this number.

Florida Spiral Review

52. **Multiple Choice** Which expression shows the prime factorization of 50?

   A. 2×5^2 **B.** 2×5^{10} **C.** 10^5 **D.** 5×10

53. **Gridded Response** What number has a prime factorization of 2 × 2 × 3 × 5?

Determine if each pair of expressions is equivalent. If so, state the property shown. (Lesson 2-1)

54. 15 × 2 × 3 and 3 × 15 × 2   55. (12 ÷ 3) ÷ 4 and 12 ÷ (3 ÷ 4)

56. 4 + 56 and 56 + 4   57. 15 × 2 and (10 × 2)(5 × 2)

58. The difference between Mary's height and Jeff's height is 7 inches. Jeff's height is 61 inches, and he is shorter than Mary. Write and solve an equation to find Mary's height in inches. (Lesson 2-7)

Greatest Common Factor

Prep for MA.6.A.5.1
Use equivalent forms of fractions, decimals . . . to solve problems.
Review of MA.5.A.6.1

Vocabulary

greatest common factor (GCF)

Factors shared by two or more whole numbers are called common factors. The largest of the common factors is called the **greatest common factor**, or **GCF**.

Factors of 24: 1, 2, 3, 4, 6, 8, 12, 24

Factors of 36: 1, 2, 3, 4, 6, 9, 12, 18, 36

Common factors: 1, 2, 3, 4, 6, (12)

The greatest common factor (GCF) of 24 and 36 is 12.

Example 1 shows three different methods for finding the GCF.

E X A M P L E **Finding the GCF**

Find the GCF of each set of numbers.

A 16 and 24
Method 1: List the factors.
factors of 16: 1, 2, 4, (8), 16   *List all the factors.*
factors of 24: 1, 2, 3, 4, 6, (8), 12, 24   *Circle the GCF.*

The GCF of 16 and 24 is 8.

B 12, 24, and 32
Method 2: Use prime factorization.
$12 = \boxed{2} \cdot \boxed{2} \cdot 3$ *Write the prime factorization of each number.*
$24 = \boxed{2} \cdot \boxed{2} \cdot 2 \cdot 3$
$32 = \boxed{2} \cdot \boxed{2} \cdot 2 \cdot 2 \cdot 2$ *Find the common prime factors.*

$2 \cdot 2 = 4$ *Find the prime factors common to all the numbers.*

The GCF of 12, 24, and 32 is 4.

C 12, 18, and 60
Method 3: Use a ladder diagram.

2	12	18	60
3	6	9	30
	2	3	10

Begin with a factor that divides into each number. Keep dividing until the three numbers have no common factors.

$2 \cdot 3 = 6$ *Find the product of the numbers you divided by.*

The GCF is 6.

EXAMPLE 2

PROBLEM SOLVING APPLICATION

There are 12 boys and 18 girls in Ms. Ruiz's science class. The students must form lab groups. Each group must have the same number of boys and the same number of girls. What is the greatest number of groups Ms. Ruiz can make if every student must be in a group?

1 Understand the Problem

The **answer** will be the *greatest* number of groups 12 boys and 18 girls can form so that each group has the same number of boys, and each group has the same number of girls.

2 Make a Plan

You can make an organized list of the possible groups.

3 Solve

There are more girls than boys in the class, so there will be more girls than boys in each group.

Boys	Girls	Groups
1	2	(B/GG) (B/GG) (B/GG) (B/GG) (B/GG) (B/GG) (B/GG) (B/GG) (B/GG) 9 boys, 18 girls: There are 3 boys not in groups. ✗
2	3	(BB/GGG) (BB/GGG) (BB/GGG) (BB/GGG) (BB/GGG) (BB/GGG) 12 boys, 18 girls: Every student is in a group. ✓

The greatest number of groups is 6.

4 Look Back

The number of groups will be a common factor of the number of boys and the number of girls. To form the largest number of groups, find the GCF of 12 and 18.

factors of 12: 1, 2, 3, 4, ⑥, 12   factors of 18: 1, 2, 3, ⑥, 9, 18

The GCF of 12 and 18 is 6.

> **Helpful Hint**
>
> If more students are put in each group, there will be fewer groups. You need the most groups possible, so put the smallest possible number of students in each team. Start with 1 boy in each group.

Think and Discuss

1. **Explain** what the GCF of two prime numbers is.

2. **Tell** what the least common factor of a group of numbers would be.

Homework Help THINK central

Go to thinkcentral.com
Exercises 1–18, 23, 25, 27, 29, 31, 35, 37

GUIDED PRACTICE

See Example 1 **Find the GCF of each set of numbers.**

1. 18 and 27

2. 32 and 72

3. 21, 42, and 56

4. 15, 30, and 60

5. 18, 24, and 36

6. 9, 36, and 81

See Example 2 **7.** Kim is making flower arrangements. She has 16 red roses and 20 pink roses. Each arrangement must have the same number of red roses and the same number of pink roses. What is the greatest number of arrangements Kim can make if every flower is used?

INDEPENDENT PRACTICE

See Example 1 **Find the GCF of each set of numbers.**

8. 10 and 35

9. 28 and 70

10. 36 and 72

11. 26, 48, and 62

12. 16, 40, and 88

13. 12, 60, and 68

14. 30, 45, and 75

15. 24, 48, and 84

16. 16, 48, and 72

See Example 2 **17.** The local recreation center held a scavenger hunt. There were 15 boys and 9 girls at the event. The group was divided into the greatest number of teams possible with the same number of boys on each team and the same number of girls on each team. How many teams were made if each person was on a team?

18. Ms. Kline makes balloon arrangements. She has 32 blue balloons, 24 yellow balloons, and 16 white balloons. Each arrangement must have the same number of each color. What is the greatest number of arrangements that Ms. Kline can make if every balloon is used?

PRACTICE AND PROBLEM SOLVING

Write the GCF of each set of numbers.

19. 60 and 84

20. 14 and 17

21. 10, 35, and 110

22. 21 and 306

23. 630 and 712

24. 16, 24, and 40

25. 75, 225, and 150

26. 42, 112, and 105

27. 12, 16, 20, and 24

28. Jared has 12 jars of grape jam, 16 jars of strawberry jam, and 24 jars of raspberry jam. He wants to place the jam into the greatest possible number of boxes so that each box has the same number of jars of each kind of jam. How many boxes does he need?

29. Pam is making fruit baskets. She has 30 apples, 24 bananas, and 12 oranges. What is the greatest number of baskets she can make if each type of fruit is distributed equally among the baskets?

30. **Critical Thinking** Write a set of three different numbers that have a GCF of 9. Explain your method.

○ = WORKED-OUT SOLUTIONS
on p. WS4

Write the GCF of each set of numbers.

31. 16, 24, 30, and 42　　**32.** 25, 90, 45, and 100　　**33.** 27, 90, 135, and 72

34. $2 \times 2 \times 3$ and 2×2　　**35.** $2 \times 3^2 \times 7$ and $2^2 \times 3$　　**36.** $3^2 \times 7$ and $2 \times 3 \times 5^2$

37. Mr. Chu is planting 4 types of flowers in his garden. He wants each row to contain the same number of each type of flower. What is the greatest number of rows Mr. Chu can plant if every bulb is used?

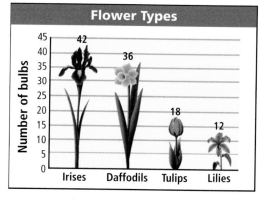
Flower Types

Number of bulbs — Irises 42, Daffodils 36, Tulips 18, Lilies 12

38. In a parade, one school band will march directly behind another school band. All rows must have the same number of students. The first band has 36 students, and the second band has 60 students. What is the greatest number of students who can be in each row?

39. Social Studies Branches of the U.S. Mint in Denver and Philadelphia make all U.S. coins for circulation. A tiny *D* or *P* on the coin tells you where the coin was minted. Suppose you have 32 *D* quarters and 36 *P* quarters. What is the greatest number of groups you can make with the same number of *D* quarters in each group and the same number of *P* quarters in each group so that every quarter is placed in a group?

40. What's the Error? Mike says if $12 = 2^2 \cdot 3$ and $24 = 2^3 \cdot 3$, then the GCF of 12 and 24 is $2 \cdot 3$, or 6. Explain Mike's error.

41. Write About It What method do you like best for finding the GCF? Why?

42. Challenge The GCF of three numbers is 9. The sum of the numbers is 90. Find the three numbers.

Florida Spiral Review

MA.6.A.3.2, MA.6.A.5.2

43. Multiple Choice For which set of numbers is 16 the GCF?

A. 16, 32, 48　　**B.** 12, 24, 32　　**C.** 24, 48, 60　　**D.** 8, 80, 100

44. Multiple Choice Mrs. Lyndon is making baskets of muffins. She has 48 lemon muffins, 120 blueberry muffins, and 112 banana nut muffins. How many baskets can Mrs. Lyndon make with each type of muffin distributed evenly?

F. 4　　**G.** 6　　**H.** 8　　**I.** 12

Solve each equation. (Lesson 2-7)

45. $c - 5 = 19$　　**46.** $37 = y - 9$　　**47.** $m - 21 = 13$　　**48.** $28 = p - 15$

Order the decimals from least to greatest. (Lesson 3-1)

49. 71.3, 70.1, 73.7, 71.03　　**50.** 149.6, 94.16, 196.1, 169.4

Quiz for Lessons 4-1 Through 4-3

4-1 Divisibility

Tell whether each number is divisible by 2, 3, 4, 5, 6, 9, and 10.

1. 708   **2.** 514   **3.** 470   **4.** 338

5. A highway loop around a city is 45 miles long. If exits are placed every 5 miles, will the exits be evenly spaced around the loop? Explain.

6. Hoover Dam is 1,244 feet across at the top. Tell whether this number is divisible by 2, 3, 4, 5, 6, 9, and 10.

Tell whether each number is prime or composite.

7. 76   **8.** 59   **9.** 69   **10.** 33

4-2 Factors and Prime Factorization

List all of the factors of each number.

11. 26   **12.** 32   **13.** 39   **14.** 84

15. Mr. Collins's bowling league has 48 members. If the league splits into teams of 12 members each, how many equally sized teams will there be?

Write the prime factorization of each number.

16. 96   **17.** 50   **18.** 104   **19.** 63

20. Scientists classify many sunflowers in the genus *Helianthus*. There are approximately 67 species of *Helianthus*. Write the prime factorization of 67.

4-3 Greatest Common Factor

Find the GCF of each set of numbers.

21. 16 and 36   **22.** 22 and 88   **23.** 65 and 91   **24.** 20, 55, and 85

25. There are 36 sixth-graders and 40 seventh-graders. What is the greatest number of teams that the students can form if each team has the same number of sixth-graders and the same number of seventh-graders and every student must be on a team?

26. There are 14 girls and 21 boys in Mrs. Sutter's gym class. To play a certain game, the students must form teams. Each team must have the same number of girls and the same number of boys. What is the greatest number of teams Mrs. Sutter can make if every student is on a team?

27. Mrs. Young, an art teacher, is organizing the art supplies. She has 76 red markers, 52 blue markers, and 80 black markers. She wants to divide the markers into boxes with the same number of red, the same number of blue, and the same number of black markers in each box. What is the greatest number of boxes she can have if every marker is placed in a box?

Focus on Problem Solving

 Understand the Problem

• Interpret unfamiliar words

You must understand the words in a problem in order to solve it. If there is a word you do not know, try to use context clues to figure out its meaning. Suppose there is a problem about red, green, blue, and chartreuse fabric. You may not know the word *chartreuse*, but you can guess that it is probably a color. To make the problem easier to understand, you could replace *chartreuse* with the name of a familiar color, such as *white*.

In some problems, the name of a person, place, or thing might be difficult to pronounce, such as *Mr. Joubert*. When you see a proper noun that you do not know how to pronounce, you can use another proper noun or a pronoun in its place. You could replace *Mr. Joubert* with *he*. You could replace *Koenisburg Street* with *K Street*.

 Copy each problem. Underline any words that you do not understand. Then replace each word with a more familiar word.

❶ Grace is making flower bouquets. She has 18 chrysanthemums and 42 roses. She wants to arrange them in groups that each have the same number of chrysanthemums and the same number of roses. What is the fewest number of flowers that Grace can have in each group? How many chrysanthemums and how many roses will be in each group?

❷ Most marbles are made from glass. The glass is liquefied in a furnace and poured. It is then cut into cylinders that are rounded off and cooled. Suppose 1,200 cooled marbles are put into packages of 8. How many packages could be made? Would there be any marbles left over?

❸ In ancient times, many civilizations used calendars that divided the year into months of 30 days. A year has 365 days. How many whole months were in these ancient calendars? Were there any days left over? If so, how many?

❹ Mrs. LeFeubre is tiling her garden walkway. It is a rectangle that is 4 feet wide and 20 feet long. Mrs. LeFeubre wants to use square tiles, and she does not want to have to cut any tiles. What is the size of the largest square tile that Mrs. LeFeubre can use?

Prep for
MA.6.A.5.1 Use
equivalent forms of
fractions . . . to solve problems.
Review of MA.4.A.6.3

Vocabulary

equivalent fractions

simplest form

Rulers often have marks for inches, $\frac{1}{2}$, $\frac{1}{4}$, and $\frac{1}{8}$ inches.

Notice that $\frac{1}{2}$ in., $\frac{2}{4}$ in., and $\frac{4}{8}$ in. all name the same length. Fractions that represent the same value are **equivalent fractions**. So $\frac{1}{2}$, $\frac{2}{4}$, and $\frac{4}{8}$ are equivalent fractions.

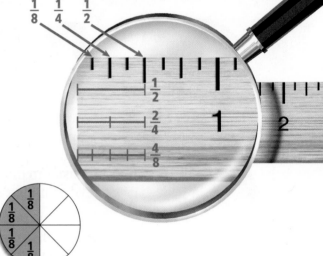

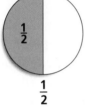 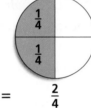

$$\frac{1}{2} = \frac{2}{4} = \frac{4}{8}$$

EXAMPLE **1** **Finding Equivalent Fractions**

Animated **Math**
@ **thinkcentral.com**

Find two equivalent fractions for $\frac{6}{8}$.

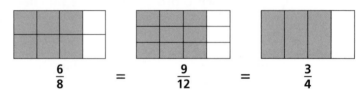

$$\frac{6}{8} = \frac{9}{12} = \frac{3}{4}$$

The same area is shaded when the rectangle is divided into 8 parts, 12 parts, and 4 parts.

So $\frac{6}{8}$, $\frac{9}{12}$, and $\frac{3}{4}$ are all equivalent fractions.

EXAMPLE **2** **Multiplying and Dividing to Find Equivalent Fractions**

Find the missing number that makes the fractions equivalent.

A $\quad \frac{2}{3} = \frac{\blacksquare}{18}$

$\frac{2 \cdot 6}{3 \cdot 6} = \frac{12}{18}$ *In the denominator, 3 is multiplied by 6 to get 18. Multiply the numerator, 2, by the same number, 6.*

So $\frac{2}{3}$ is equivalent to $\frac{12}{18}$.

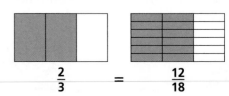

$$\frac{2}{3} = \frac{12}{18}$$

Find the missing number that makes the fractions equivalent.

B $\dfrac{70}{100} = \dfrac{7}{\blacksquare}$

$\dfrac{70 \div 10}{100 \div 10} = \dfrac{7}{10}$ *In the numerator, 70 is divided by 10 to get 7.*
Divide the denominator by the same number, 10.

So $\dfrac{70}{100}$ is equivalent to $\dfrac{7}{10}$.

$\dfrac{70}{100}$ = $\dfrac{7}{10}$

Every fraction has one equivalent fraction that is called the simplest form of the fraction. A fraction is in **simplest form** when the GCF of the numerator and the denominator is 1.

Example 3 shows two methods for writing a fraction in simplest form.

EXAMPLE **3**   **Writing Fractions in Simplest Form**

Write each fraction in simplest form.

A $\dfrac{18}{24}$

The GCF of 18 and 24 is 6, so $\dfrac{18}{24}$ is not in simplest form.

Method 1: Use the GCF.

$\dfrac{18 \div 6}{24 \div 6} = \dfrac{3}{4}$ *Divide 18 and 24 by their GCF, 6.*

Method 2: Use prime factorization.

$\dfrac{18}{24} = \dfrac{2 \cdot 3 \cdot 3}{2 \cdot 2 \cdot 2 \cdot 3} = \dfrac{3}{4}$ *Write the prime factors of 18 and 24. Simplify.*

So $\dfrac{18}{24}$ written in simplest form is $\dfrac{3}{4}$.

B $\dfrac{8}{9}$

The GCF of 8 and 9 is 1, so $\dfrac{8}{9}$ is already in simplest form.

Helpful Hint

Method 2 is useful when you know that the numerator and denominator have common factors, but you are not sure what the GCF is.

Think and Discuss

1. Explain whether a fraction is equivalent to itself.

2. Tell which of the following fractions are in simplest form: $\dfrac{9}{21}$, $\dfrac{20}{25}$, and $\dfrac{5}{13}$. Explain.

3. Explain how you know that $\dfrac{7}{16}$ is in simplest form.

Homework Help

Go to **thinkcentral.com**
Exercises 1–36, 39, 41, 45

Prep MA.6.A.5.1

GUIDED PRACTICE

See Example 1 Find two equivalent fractions for each fraction.

1. $\frac{4}{6}$ **2.** $\frac{3}{12}$ **3.** $\frac{3}{6}$ **4.** $\frac{6}{16}$

See Example 2 Find the missing numbers that make the fractions equivalent.

5. $\frac{2}{5} = \frac{10}{\square}$ **6.** $\frac{7}{21} = \frac{1}{\square}$ **7.** $\frac{3}{4} = \frac{\square}{28}$ **8.** $\frac{8}{12} = \frac{\square}{3}$

See Example 3 Write each fraction in simplest form.

9. $\frac{2}{10}$ **10.** $\frac{6}{18}$ **11.** $\frac{4}{16}$ **12.** $\frac{9}{15}$

INDEPENDENT PRACTICE

See Example 1 Find two equivalent fractions for each fraction.

13. $\frac{3}{9}$ **14.** $\frac{2}{10}$ **15.** $\frac{3}{21}$ **16.** $\frac{3}{18}$

17. $\frac{12}{15}$ **18.** $\frac{4}{10}$ **19.** $\frac{10}{12}$ **20.** $\frac{6}{10}$

See Example 2 Find the missing numbers that make the fractions equivalent.

21. $\frac{3}{7} = \frac{\square}{35}$ **22.** $\frac{6}{48} = \frac{1}{\square}$ **23.** $\frac{2}{5} = \frac{28}{\square}$ **24.** $\frac{12}{18} = \frac{\square}{3}$

25. $\frac{2}{7} = \frac{\square}{21}$ **26.** $\frac{8}{32} = \frac{\square}{4}$ **27.** $\frac{2}{7} = \frac{40}{\square}$ **28.** $\frac{3}{5} = \frac{21}{\square}$

See Example 3 Write each fraction in simplest form.

29. $\frac{2}{8}$ **30.** $\frac{10}{15}$ **31.** $\frac{6}{30}$ **32.** $\frac{6}{14}$

33. $\frac{12}{16}$ **34.** $\frac{4}{28}$ **35.** $\frac{4}{8}$ **36.** $\frac{10}{35}$

PRACTICE AND PROBLEM SOLVING

37. Multi-Step The Lady Hornets made 16 out of 24 free throw attempts during a basketball game. The Lady Tigers made 14 out of 20 attempts.

  a. Write the number of free throws made out of the number of free throws attempted by each team as a fraction. Are the fractions equivalent? Explain.

  b. If the Lady Tigers attempted one more free throw and missed, would the fractions be equivalent? Explain.

38. Critical Thinking A fraction has a numerator that is 6 less than its denominator. The fraction is equivalent to $\frac{1}{3}$. What is the fraction?

Write each fraction in simplest form. Show two ways to simplify.

39. $\frac{10}{40}$ **40.** $\frac{4}{52}$ **41.** $\frac{28}{70}$ **42.** $\frac{112}{220}$

○ = WORKED-OUT SOLUTIONS
on p. WS5

The Old City Market is a public market in Charleston, South Carolina. Local artists, craftspeople, and vendors display and sell their goods in open-sided booths.

43. You can buy food, such as southern sesame seed cookies, at $\frac{1}{10}$ of the booths. Write two equivalent fractions for $\frac{1}{10}$.

44. Handwoven sweetgrass baskets are a regional specialty. About 8 out of every 10 baskets sold are woven at the market. Write a fraction for "8 out of 10." Then write this fraction in simplest form.

45. Suppose the circle graph shows the number of each kind of craft booth at the Old City Market. For each type of booth, tell what fraction it represents of the total number of craft booths. Write these fractions in simplest form.

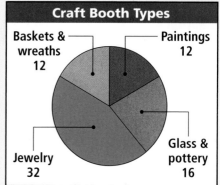

Craft Booth Types

Baskets & wreaths 12 — Paintings 12 — Glass & pottery 16 — Jewelry 32

46. Customers can buy packages of dried rice and black-eyed peas, which can be made into black-eyed pea soup. One recipe for black-eyed pea soup calls for $\frac{1}{2}$ tsp of basil. How could you measure the basil if you had only a $\frac{1}{4}$ tsp measuring spoon? What if you had only a $\frac{1}{8}$ tsp measuring spoon?

47. **Write About It** The recipe for soup also calls for $\frac{1}{4}$ tsp of pepper. How many fractions are equivalent to $\frac{1}{4}$? Explain.

48. **Challenge** Silver jewelry is a popular item at the market. Suppose there are 28 bracelets at one jeweler's booth and that $\frac{3}{7}$ of these bracelets have red stones. How many bracelets have red stones?

49. Multiple Choice Which fraction is NOT equivalent to $\frac{1}{6}$?

A. $\frac{2}{12}$ **B.** $\frac{6}{1}$ **C.** $\frac{3}{18}$ **D.** $\frac{6}{36}$

50. Multiple Choice Which denominator makes the fractions $\frac{7}{28}$ and $\frac{21}{\blacksquare}$ equivalent?

F. 3   **G.** 4   **H.** 84   **I.** 112

Solve each equation. Check your answer. (Lesson 2-9)

51. $\frac{x}{3} = 15$ **52.** $8 = \frac{h}{8}$ **53.** $\frac{w}{2} = 9$ **54.** $\frac{p}{5} = 10$

55. Reid wants to buy two CDs that cost $10.99 each. He receives an allowance of $7.50 each week. In how many weeks will Reid have enough money to buy the CDs? (Lesson 3-7)

4-5 Decimals and Fractions

The Oregon State University baseball team won the College World Series in 2006 and 2007.

 MA.6.A.5.1 Use equivalent forms of fractions, decimals . . . to solve problems.
Also **MA.6.A.5.2**

Vocabulary

mixed number

terminating decimal

repeating decimal

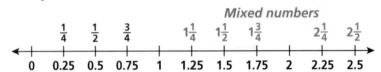
@ thinkcentral.com

Decimals and fractions can often be used to represent the same number.

For example, a baseball player's or baseball team's batting average can be represented as a fraction:

$$\frac{\text{number of hits}}{\text{number of times at bat}}$$

In 2007, the Oregon State University baseball team won its second College World Series title. During that season, the team had 659 hits and 2,297 at bats. The team's batting average was $\frac{659}{2,297}$.

$$659 \div 2,297 = 0.2868959512\ldots$$

The 2007 batting average for the Oregon State baseball team is reported as .287.

Decimals can be written as fractions or mixed numbers. A number that contains both a whole number greater than 0 and a fraction, such as $1\frac{3}{4}$, is called a **mixed number**.

Mixed numbers

| $\frac{1}{4}$ | $\frac{1}{2}$ | $\frac{3}{4}$ | | $1\frac{1}{4}$ | $1\frac{1}{2}$ | $1\frac{3}{4}$ | | $2\frac{1}{4}$ | $2\frac{1}{2}$ |

| 0 | 0.25 | 0.5 | 0.75 | 1 | 1.25 | 1.5 | 1.75 | 2 | 2.25 | 2.5 |

EXAMPLE 1 Writing Decimals as Fractions or Mixed Numbers

Write each decimal as a fraction or mixed number.

A 0.23

0.23   *Identify the place value of the digit farthest to the right.*

$\frac{23}{100}$ *The 3 is in the **hundred**ths place, so use **100** as the denominator.*

Remember!

Place Value			
Ones	Tenths	Hundredths	Thousandths

B 1.7

1.7   *Identify the place value of the digit farthest to the right.*

$1\frac{7}{10}$ *Write the whole number, 1. The 7 is in the **ten**ths place, so use **10** as the denominator.*

EXAMPLE 2 **Writing Fractions as Decimals**

Write each fraction or mixed number as a decimal.

A $\frac{3}{4}$

$$
\begin{array}{r}
0.75 \\
4\overline{)3.00} \\
-28 \\
\hline
20 \\
-20 \\
\hline
0
\end{array}
$$

Divide 3 by 4.
Add zeros after the decimal point.
The remainder is 0.

$\frac{3}{4} = 0.75$

B $5\frac{2}{3}$

$$
\begin{array}{r}
0.666 \\
3\overline{)2.000} \\
-18 \\
\hline
20 \\
-18 \\
\hline
20 \\
-18 \\
\hline
2
\end{array}
$$

Divide 2 by 3.
Add zeros after the decimal point.
The 6 repeats in the quotient.

$5\frac{2}{3} = 5.666... = 5.\overline{6}$

Writing Math

To write a repeating decimal, you can show three dots or draw a bar over the repeating part: $0.666... = 0.\overline{6}$

A **terminating decimal**, such as 0.75, has a finite number of decimal places. A **repeating decimal**, such as 0.666..., has a block of one or more digits that repeat without end.

Common Fractions and Equivalent Decimals								
$\frac{1}{5}$	$\frac{1}{4}$	$\frac{1}{3}$	$\frac{2}{5}$	$\frac{1}{2}$	$\frac{3}{5}$	$\frac{2}{3}$	$\frac{3}{4}$	$\frac{4}{5}$
0.2	0.25	$0.\overline{3}$	0.4	0.5	0.6	$0.\overline{6}$	0.75	0.8

EXAMPLE 3 **Comparing and Ordering Fractions and Decimals**

Brigitte made the following measurements: 0.5 cm, $\frac{1}{5}$ cm, and 0.37 cm. Order the measurements from least to greatest.

First rewrite the fraction as a decimal. $\frac{1}{5} = 0.2$

Order the three decimals.

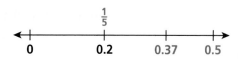

The measurements from least to greatest are $\frac{1}{5}$ cm, 0.37 cm, and 0.5 cm.

Think and Discuss

1. Tell how reading the decimal 6.9 as "six and nine tenths" helps you to write 6.9 as a mixed number.

2. Look at the decimal 0.121122111222.... If the pattern continues, is this a repeating decimal? Why or why not?

Homework Help

Go to **thinkcentral.com**
Exercises 1–33, 37, 39, 45, 49, 55, 61

MA.6.A.5.1, MA.6.A.5.2

GUIDED PRACTICE

See Example 1 **Write each decimal as a fraction or mixed number.**

1. 0.15 **2.** 1.25 **3.** 0.43 **4.** 2.6

See Example 2 **Write each fraction or mixed number as a decimal.**

5. $\frac{2}{5}$ **6.** $2\frac{7}{8}$ **7.** $\frac{1}{8}$ **8.** $4\frac{1}{10}$

See Example 3 **Order the fractions and decimals from least to greatest.**

9. $\frac{2}{3}$, 0.78, 0.21 **10.** $\frac{5}{16}$, 0.67, $\frac{1}{6}$ **11.** 0.52, $\frac{1}{9}$, 0.3

INDEPENDENT PRACTICE

See Example 1 **Write each decimal as a fraction or mixed number.**

12. 0.31 **13.** 5.71 **14.** 0.13 **15.** 3.23

16. 0.5 **17.** 2.7 **18.** 0.19 **19.** 6.3

See Example 2 **Write each fraction or mixed number as a decimal.**

20. $\frac{1}{9}$ **21.** $1\frac{3}{5}$ **22.** $\frac{8}{9}$ **23.** $3\frac{11}{40}$

24. $2\frac{5}{6}$ **25.** $\frac{3}{8}$ **26.** $4\frac{4}{5}$ **27.** $\frac{5}{8}$

See Example 3 **Order the fractions and decimals from least to greatest.**

28. 0.49, 0.82, $\frac{1}{2}$ **29.** $\frac{3}{8}$, 0.29, $\frac{1}{9}$ **30.** 0.94, $\frac{4}{5}$, 0.6

31. 0.11, $\frac{1}{10}$, 0.13 **32.** $\frac{2}{3}$, 0.42, $\frac{2}{5}$ **33.** $\frac{3}{7}$, 0.76, 0.31

PRACTICE AND PROBLEM SOLVING

Write each fraction as a decimal. Tell whether the decimal terminates or repeats.

34. $\frac{7}{9}$ **35.** $\frac{1}{6}$ **36.** $\frac{17}{20}$ **37.** $\frac{5}{12}$ **38.** $\frac{7}{8}$

39. $\frac{4}{5}$ **40.** $\frac{9}{5}$ **41.** $\frac{15}{18}$ **42.** $\frac{7}{3}$ **43.** $\frac{11}{12}$

Compare. Write < , >, or =.

44. 0.75 ▨ $\frac{3}{4}$ **45.** $\frac{5}{8}$ ▨ 0.5 **46.** 0.78 ▨ $\frac{7}{9}$ **47.** $\frac{1}{3}$ ▨ 0.35

48. $\frac{2}{5}$ ▨ 0.4 **49.** 0.75 ▨ $\frac{4}{5}$ **50.** $\frac{3}{8}$ ▨ 0.25 **51.** 0.8 ▨ $\frac{5}{6}$

52. Multi-Step Peter walked $1\frac{3}{5}$ miles on a treadmill. Sally walked 1.5 miles on the treadmill. Who walked farther? Explain.

53. Measurement There are 100 centimeters in 1 meter. Which measurement is greater: $\frac{1}{10}$ cm or 1.5 m? Write both measurements as decimals with units in centimeters. Show your work.

○ = **WORKED-OUT SOLUTIONS**
on p. WS5

Order the mixed numbers and decimals from greatest to least.

54. $9\frac{2}{3}$, 9.8, $9\frac{3}{5}$ **55.** 4.48, 3.92, $4\frac{1}{2}$ **56.** $10\frac{5}{9}$, 10.5, $10\frac{1}{5}$ **57.** 125.205, 125.25, $125\frac{1}{5}$

Sports The table shows batting averages for two baseball seasons. Use the table for Exercises 58–60.

Player	Season 1	Season 2
Pedro	0.360	$\frac{3}{10}$
Jill	0.380	$\frac{3}{8}$
Lamar	0.290	$\frac{1}{3}$
Britney	0.190	$\frac{3}{20}$

58. Which players had higher batting averages in season 1 than they had in season 2?

59. Who had the highest batting average in either season?

60. Multi-Step Whose batting average changed the most between season 1 and season 2?

61. Life Science Most people with color deficiency (often called color blindness) have trouble distinguishing shades of red and green. About 0.05 of men in the world have color deficiency. What fraction of men have color deficiency?

62. What's the Error? A student found the decimal equivalent of $\frac{7}{18}$ to be $0.\overline{38}$. Explain the error. What is the correct answer?

63. Write About It The decimal for $\frac{1}{25}$ is 0.04, and the decimal for $\frac{2}{25}$ is 0.08. Without dividing, find the decimal for $\frac{6}{25}$. Explain how you found your answer.

64. Challenge Write $\frac{1}{999}$ as a decimal.

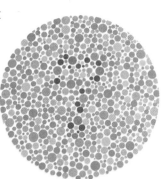

People with normal color vision will see "7" in this color-blindness test.

65. Multiple Choice Which numbers are listed from least to greatest?

A. 0.65, 0.81, $\frac{4}{5}$ **B.** 0.81, 0.65, $\frac{4}{5}$ **C.** $\frac{4}{5}$, 0.81, 0.65   **D.** 0.65, $\frac{4}{5}$, 0.81

66. Gridded Response What is $5\frac{1}{8}$ written as a decimal?

67. Naomi has p pens to divide equally among her and three friends. Write an expression to show the number of pens each person should receive. (Lesson 2-3)

Find each product. (Lesson 3-4)

68. 6.1 × 0.03   **69.** 0.8 × 0.075   **70.** 5.0 × 1.7   **71.** 30.5 × 2.6

4-6 Mixed Numbers and Improper Fractions

MA.6.A.5.1 Use equivalent forms of fractions . . . to solve problems.

Have you ever witnessed a total eclipse of the sun? It occurs when the sun's light is completely blocked out. A total eclipse is rare—only three have been visible in the continental United States since 1963.

The graph shows that the eclipse in 2017 will last $2\frac{3}{4}$ minutes. There are eleven $\frac{1}{4}$-minute sections, so $2\frac{3}{4} = \frac{11}{4}$.

Vocabulary

improper fraction

proper fraction

Reading Math

$\frac{11}{4}$ is read as "eleven-fourths."

An **improper fraction** is a fraction in which the numerator is greater than or equal to the denominator, such as $\frac{11}{4}$.

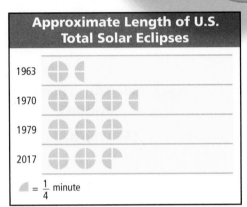

Approximate Length of U.S. Total Solar Eclipses

1963	
1970	
1979	
2017	

$\blacksquare = \frac{1}{4}$ minute

Whole numbers can be written as improper fractions. The whole number is the numerator, and the denominator is 1. For example, $7 = \frac{7}{1}$.

Animated Math
@ thinkcentral.com

When the numerator is less than the denominator, the fraction is called a **proper fraction**.

Improper and Proper Fractions		
Improper Fractions		
• Numerator equals denominator → fraction is equal to 1	$\frac{3}{3} = 1$	$\frac{102}{102} = 1$
• Numerator greater than denominator → fraction is greater than 1	$\frac{9}{5} > 1$	$\frac{13}{1} > 1$
Proper Fractions		
• Numerator less than denominator → fraction is less than 1	$\frac{2}{5} < 1$	$\frac{102}{351} < 1$

You can write an improper fraction as a mixed number.

EXAMPLE 1 *Astronomy Application*

The longest total solar eclipse in the next 200 years will take place in 2186. It will last about $\frac{15}{2}$ minutes. Write $\frac{15}{2}$ as a mixed number.

Method 1: Use a model.

Draw squares divided into half sections. Shade 15 of the half sections.

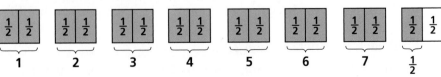

There are 7 whole squares and 1 half square, or $7\frac{1}{2}$ squares, shaded.

Method 2: Use division.

$$2\overline{)15}$$
$$\underline{-14}$$
$$1$$

Divide the numerator by the denominator.

To form the fraction part of the quotient, use the remainder as the numerator and the divisor as the denominator.

The 2186 eclipse will last about $7\frac{1}{2}$ minutes.

Mixed numbers can be written as improper fractions.

EXAMPLE 2 **Writing Mixed Numbers as Improper Fractions**

Write $2\frac{1}{5}$ as an improper fraction.

Method 1: Use a model.

You can draw a diagram to illustrate the whole and fractional parts.

There are 11 fifths, or $\frac{11}{5}$.   *Count the fifths in the diagram.*

Method 2: Use multiplication and addition.

When you are changing a mixed number to an improper fraction, spiral clockwise as shown in the picture. The order of operations will help you remember to multiply before you add.

Then add.

First multiply.

$$2\frac{1}{5} = \frac{(5 \cdot 2) + 1}{5}$$

$$= \frac{10 + 1}{5}$$

$$= \frac{11}{5}$$

Multiply the whole number by the denominator and add the numerator. Keep the same denominator.

Think and Discuss

1. Read each improper fraction: $\frac{10}{7}, \frac{25}{9}, \frac{31}{16}$.

2. Tell whether each fraction is less than 1, equal to 1, or greater than 1: $\frac{21}{21}, \frac{54}{103}, \frac{9}{11}, \frac{7}{3}$.

3. Explain why any mixed number written as a fraction will be improper.

Homework Help THINK central

Go to **thinkcentral.com**
Exercises 1–15, 19, 23, 27, 31, 35, 37, 43

MA.6.A.5.1, MA.6.A.5.2

GUIDED PRACTICE

See Example **1**
1. The fifth largest meteorite found in the United States is named the Navajo. The Navajo weighs $\frac{12}{5}$ tons. Write $\frac{12}{5}$ as a mixed number.

See Example **2** Write each mixed number as an improper fraction.

2. $1\frac{1}{4}$ **3.** $2\frac{2}{3}$ **4.** $1\frac{2}{7}$ **5.** $2\frac{2}{5}$

INDEPENDENT PRACTICE

See Example **1**
6. **Astronomy** Saturn is the sixth planet from the Sun. It takes Saturn $\frac{59}{2}$ years to revolve around the Sun. Write $\frac{59}{2}$ as a mixed number.

7. **Astronomy** Pluto has low surface gravity. A person who weighs 143 pounds on Earth weighs $\frac{43}{5}$ pounds on Pluto. Write $\frac{43}{5}$ as a mixed number.

See Example **2** Write each mixed number as an improper fraction.

8. $1\frac{3}{5}$ **9.** $2\frac{2}{9}$ **10.** $3\frac{1}{7}$ **11.** $4\frac{1}{3}$

12. $2\frac{3}{8}$ **13.** $4\frac{1}{6}$ **14.** $1\frac{4}{9}$ **15.** $3\frac{4}{5}$

PRACTICE AND PROBLEM SOLVING

Write each improper fraction as a mixed number or whole number. Tell whether your answer is a mixed number or whole number.

16. $\frac{21}{4}$ **17.** $\frac{32}{8}$ **18.** $\frac{20}{3}$ **19.** $\frac{43}{5}$

20. $\frac{108}{9}$ **21.** $\frac{87}{10}$ **22.** $\frac{98}{11}$ **23.** $\frac{105}{7}$

Write each mixed number as an improper fraction.

24. $9\frac{1}{4}$ **25.** $4\frac{9}{11}$ **26.** $11\frac{4}{9}$ **27.** $18\frac{3}{5}$

28. **Measurement** The actual dimensions of a piece of lumber called a 2-by-4 are $1\frac{1}{2}$ inches and $3\frac{1}{2}$ inches. Write these numbers as improper fractions.

Replace each shape with a number that will make the equation correct.

29. $\blacksquare\frac{2}{5} = \frac{17}{\bullet}$ **30.** $\blacksquare\frac{6}{11} = \frac{83}{\bullet}$ **31.** $\blacksquare\frac{1}{9} = \frac{118}{\bullet}$

32. $\blacksquare\frac{6}{7} = \frac{55}{\bullet}$ **33.** $\blacksquare\frac{9}{10} = \frac{29}{\bullet}$ **34.** $\blacksquare\frac{1}{3} = \frac{55}{\bullet}$

35. Daniel is a costume designer for movies and music videos. He recently purchased $\frac{256}{9}$ yards of metallic fabric for space-suit costumes. Write a mixed number to represent the number of yards of fabric Daniel purchased.

Write the improper fraction as a decimal. Then use <, >, or = to compare.

36. $\frac{7}{5}$ $\blacksquare$ 1.8   **37.** 6.875 $\blacksquare$ $\frac{55}{8}$ **38.** $\frac{27}{2}$ $\blacksquare$ 13   **39.** $\frac{20}{5}$ $\blacksquare$ 4.25

$\bigcirc$ = **WORKED-OUT SOLUTIONS**
on p. WS5

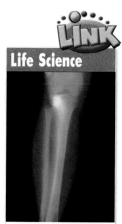
Life Science The table lists the lengths of the longest bones in the human body. Use the table for Exercises 40–42.

Longest Human Bones	
Fibula (outer lower leg)	$\frac{81}{2}$ cm
Ulna (inner lower arm)	$28\frac{1}{5}$ cm
Femur (upper leg)	$\frac{101}{2}$ cm
Humerus (upper arm)	$36\frac{1}{2}$ cm
Tibia (inner lower leg)	43 cm

40. Write the length of the ulna as an improper fraction. Then do the same for the length of the humerus.

41. Write the length of the fibula as a mixed number. Then do the same for the length of the femur.

42. Use the mixed-number form of each length. Compare the whole-number part of each length to write the bones in order from longest to shortest.

43. Social Studies The European country of Monaco, with an area of only $1\frac{4}{5}$ km², is one of the smallest countries in the world. Write $1\frac{4}{5}$ as an improper fraction.

44. For a disc to be approved by the Professional Disc Golf Association, it must not have a mass greater than $8\frac{3}{10}$ gram for each centimeter of its diameter. Write $8\frac{3}{10}$ as an improper fraction.

45. What's the Question? The lengths of Victor's three favorite movies are $\frac{11}{4}$ hours, $\frac{9}{4}$ hours, and $\frac{7}{4}$ hours. The answer is $2\frac{1}{4}$ hours. What is the question?

46. Write About It Draw models representing $\frac{4}{4}$, $\frac{5}{5}$, and $\frac{9}{9}$. Use your models to explain why a fraction whose numerator is the same as its denominator is equal to 1.

47. Challenge Write $\frac{65}{12}$ as a decimal.

Florida Spiral Review

48. Multiple Choice What is $3\frac{2}{11}$ written as an improper fraction?

A. $\frac{35}{11}$ **B.** $\frac{35}{3}$ **C.** $\frac{33}{22}$ **D.** $\frac{70}{11}$

49. Multiple Choice It takes $\frac{24}{5}$ new pencils placed end to end to be the same length as one yardstick. What is this improper fraction written as a mixed number?

F. $3\frac{4}{5}$ **G.** $4\frac{1}{4}$ **H.** $4\frac{1}{5}$ **I.** $4\frac{4}{5}$

50. Write an expression for the missing value in the table. (Lesson 2-4)

Cara's Age	8	9	10	11	a
Avery's Age	13	14	15	16	

51. Joshua spent one-fourth of his homework time studying for a math quiz. He spent 25 minutes studying for the quiz. How much time did Joshua spend on homework? (Lesson 2-9)

Comparing and Ordering Fractions

MA.6.A.5.2 Compare and order fractions ... including finding their approximate location on a number line. Also **MA.6.A.5.1**

Vocabulary

like fractions

unlike fractions

common denominator

Rachel and Hannah are making a kind of dumpling called a *potsticker*. They have $\frac{1}{2}$ cup of green onion, but the recipe requires $\frac{1}{3}$ cup.

To determine if they have enough for the recipe, they need to compare the fractions $\frac{1}{2}$ and $\frac{1}{3}$.

Potstickers

3/4 cup ground pork
1 1/2 cup chopped cabbage
1/3 cup chopped green onion
1 tablespoon minced garlic
2 tablespoons minced ginger
1/2 cup soy sauce
48 dumpling wrappers

When you are comparing fractions, first check their denominators. When fractions have the same denominator, they are called **like fractions**. For example, $\frac{1}{8}$ and $\frac{5}{8}$ are like fractions. When two fractions have different denominators, they are called **unlike fractions**. For example, $\frac{7}{10}$ and $\frac{1}{2}$ are unlike fractions.

EXAMPLE **1**

Comparing Fractions

Compare. Write <, >, or =.

Helpful Hint

When two fractions have the same denominator, the one with the larger numerator is greater.

$\frac{2}{5} < \frac{3}{5}$ $\qquad \frac{3}{8} > \frac{1}{8}$

A $\frac{1}{8}$ ▢ $\frac{5}{8}$

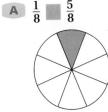 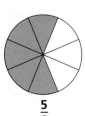

$\frac{1}{8}$ $\qquad$ $\frac{5}{8}$

Model $\frac{1}{8}$ and $\frac{5}{8}$.

From the model, $\frac{1}{8} < \frac{5}{8}$.

B $\frac{7}{10}$ ▢ $\frac{1}{2}$

$\frac{7}{10}$ $\qquad$ $\frac{1}{2}$

Model $\frac{7}{10}$ and $\frac{1}{2}$.

From the model, $\frac{7}{10} > \frac{1}{2}$.

Video **Lesson Tutorial Videos** @ thinkcentral.com

To compare unlike fractions without models, first rename the fractions so they have the same denominator. This is called finding a **common denominator**. This method can be used to compare mixed numbers as well.

EXAMPLE 2 *Cooking Application*

Rachel and Hannah have $1\frac{2}{3}$ cups of cabbage. They need $1\frac{1}{2}$ cups to make potstickers. Do they have enough for the recipe?

Compare $1\frac{2}{3}$ and $1\frac{1}{2}$.

Compare the whole-number parts of the numbers.
$1 = 1$ The whole-number parts are equal.

Compare the fractional parts. Find a common denominator by multiplying the denominators. $2 \cdot 3 = 6$

Find equivalent fractions with 6 as the denominator.

$$\frac{2}{3} = \frac{}{6} \qquad\qquad \frac{1}{2} = \frac{}{6}$$

$$\frac{2 \cdot 2}{3 \cdot 2} = \frac{4}{6} \qquad\qquad \frac{1 \cdot 3}{2 \cdot 3} = \frac{3}{6}$$

$$\frac{2}{3} = \frac{4}{6} \qquad\qquad \frac{1}{2} = \frac{3}{6}$$

Compare the like fractions. $\frac{4}{6} > \frac{3}{6}$, so $\frac{2}{3} > \frac{1}{2}$.

Therefore, $1\frac{2}{3}$ is greater than $1\frac{1}{2}$.

Since $1\frac{2}{3}$ cups is more than $1\frac{1}{2}$ cups, they have enough cabbage.

EXAMPLE 3 **Ordering Fractions**

Order $\frac{3}{7}$, $\frac{3}{4}$, and $\frac{1}{4}$ from least to greatest.

$$\frac{3 \cdot 4}{7 \cdot 4} = \frac{12}{28} \qquad \frac{3 \cdot 7}{4 \cdot 7} = \frac{21}{28} \qquad \frac{1 \cdot 7}{4 \cdot 7} = \frac{7}{28} \qquad \textit{Rename with like denominators.}$$

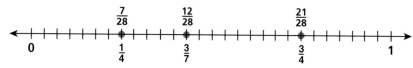

The fractions in order from least to greatest are $\frac{1}{4}$, $\frac{3}{7}$, $\frac{3}{4}$.

Remember!

Numbers increase in value as you move from left to right on a number line.

Think and Discuss

1. **Tell** whether the values of the fractions change when you rename two fractions so that they have common denominators.

2. **Explain** how to compare $\frac{2}{5}$ and $\frac{4}{5}$.

Exercises

MA.6.A.5.2, MA.6.A.5.1

GUIDED PRACTICE

See Example 1 **Compare. Write <, >, or =.**

1. $\frac{3}{5}$ ⬜ $\frac{2}{5}$

2. $\frac{1}{9}$ ⬜ $\frac{2}{9}$

3. $\frac{6}{8}$ ⬜ $\frac{3}{4}$

4. $\frac{3}{7}$ ⬜ $\frac{6}{7}$

See Example 2 5. Arsenio has $\frac{2}{3}$ cup of brown sugar. The recipe he is using requires $\frac{1}{4}$ cup of brown sugar. Does he have enough brown sugar for the recipe? Explain.

See Example 3 **Order the fractions from least to greatest.**

6. $\frac{3}{8}, \frac{1}{5}, \frac{2}{3}$

7. $\frac{1}{4}, \frac{2}{5}, \frac{1}{3}$

8. $\frac{5}{9}, \frac{1}{8}, \frac{2}{7}$

9. $\frac{1}{2}, \frac{1}{6}, \frac{2}{3}$

INDEPENDENT PRACTICE

See Example 1 **Compare. Write <, >, or =.**

10. $\frac{2}{5}$ ⬜ $\frac{4}{5}$

11. $\frac{1}{10}$ ⬜ $\frac{3}{10}$

12. $\frac{3}{4}$ ⬜ $\frac{3}{8}$

13. $\frac{5}{6}$ ⬜ $\frac{4}{6}$

14. $\frac{4}{5}$ ⬜ $\frac{5}{5}$

15. $\frac{2}{4}$ ⬜ $\frac{1}{2}$

16. $\frac{4}{8}$ ⬜ $\frac{16}{24}$

17. $\frac{11}{16}$ ⬜ $\frac{9}{16}$

See Example 2 18. Kelly needs $\frac{2}{3}$ gallon of paint to finish painting her deck. She has $\frac{5}{8}$ gallon of paint. Does she have enough paint to finish her deck? Explain.

See Example 3 **Order the fractions from least to greatest.**

19. $\frac{1}{2}, \frac{3}{5}, \frac{3}{7}$

20. $\frac{1}{6}, \frac{2}{5}, \frac{1}{4}$

21. $\frac{4}{9}, \frac{3}{8}, \frac{1}{3}$

22. $\frac{1}{4}, \frac{5}{6}, \frac{5}{9}$

23. $\frac{3}{4}, \frac{7}{10}, \frac{2}{3}$

24. $\frac{13}{18}, \frac{5}{9}, \frac{5}{6}$

25. $\frac{3}{8}, \frac{1}{4}, \frac{2}{3}$

26. $\frac{3}{10}, \frac{2}{3}, \frac{5}{11}$

PRACTICE AND PROBLEM SOLVING

Compare. Write <, >, or =.

27. $\frac{4}{15}$ ⬜ $\frac{3}{10}$

28. $\frac{7}{12}$ ⬜ $\frac{13}{30}$

29. $\frac{5}{9}$ ⬜ $\frac{4}{11}$

30. $\frac{8}{14}$ ⬜ $\frac{8}{9}$

31. $\frac{3}{5}$ ⬜ $\frac{26}{65}$

32. $\frac{3}{5}$ ⬜ $\frac{2}{21}$

33. $\frac{24}{41}$ ⬜ $\frac{2}{7}$

34. $\frac{10}{38}$ ⬜ $\frac{1}{4}$

Order the fractions from least to greatest.

35. $\frac{2}{5}, \frac{1}{2}, \frac{3}{10}$

36. $\frac{3}{4}, \frac{3}{5}, \frac{7}{10}$

37. $\frac{7}{15}, \frac{2}{3}, \frac{1}{5}$

38. $\frac{3}{4}, \frac{1}{3}, \frac{8}{15}$

39. $\frac{2}{5}, \frac{4}{9}, \frac{11}{15}$

40. $\frac{7}{12}, \frac{5}{8}, \frac{1}{2}$

41. $\frac{5}{8}, \frac{3}{4}, \frac{5}{12}$

42. $\frac{2}{3}, \frac{7}{8}, \frac{7}{15}$

43. Laura and Kim receive the same amount of allowance each week. Laura spends $\frac{3}{5}$ of it on going to the movies. Kim spends $\frac{4}{7}$ of it on a CD. Which girl spent more of her allowance? Explain.

44. Kyle operates a hot dog cart in a large city. He spends $\frac{2}{5}$ of his budget on supplies, $\frac{1}{12}$ on advertising, and $\frac{2}{25}$ on taxes and fees. Does Kyle spend more on advertising or more on taxes and fees?

○ = **WORKED-OUT SOLUTIONS**
on p. WS5

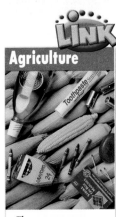

Agriculture

There are over 3,500 different uses for corn products, from ethanol fuel and industrial products to the household items you see above.

Order the numbers from least to greatest.

 45. $1\frac{2}{5}, 1\frac{1}{8}, 3\frac{4}{5}, 3, 3\frac{2}{5}$

46. $7\frac{1}{2}, 9\frac{4}{7}, 9\frac{1}{2}, 8, 8\frac{3}{4}$

47. $\frac{1}{2}, 3\frac{1}{5}, 3\frac{1}{10}, \frac{3}{4}, 3\frac{1}{15}$

48. $2\frac{1}{5}, 2\frac{5}{6}, 1\frac{1}{4}, 2, \frac{7}{8}$

49. $4\frac{3}{4}, 5, 3\frac{5}{7}, 4\frac{2}{3}, 5\frac{1}{3}$

50. $6\frac{1}{3}, 5\frac{1}{4}, 5\frac{7}{8}, 6, 5\frac{1}{2}$

51. Agriculture The table shows the fraction of the world's total corn each country produces.

World's Corn Production	
United States	$\frac{39}{100}$
China	$\frac{1}{5}$
Canada	$\frac{7}{500}$

   a. List the countries in order from the country that produces the most corn to the country that produces the least corn.

   b. Brazil produces $\frac{1}{10}$ of the world's corn. Tell whether Brazil's corn production is more than or less than Canada's corn production.

52. Multi-Step The Dixon Dragons must win at least $\frac{3}{7}$ of their remaining games to qualify for their district playoffs. If they have 15 games left and they win 7 of them, will the Dragons compete in the playoffs? Explain.

53. Critical Thinking The fraction $\frac{n}{8}$ is greater than $\frac{9}{16}$ and less than 1. Which of the following could be the value of the numerator n: 4, 5, 8, or 9? Explain your answer.

 54. Write a Problem Write a problem that involves comparing two fractions with different denominators.

 55. Write About It Compare the fractions below. What do you notice about two fractions that have the same numerator but different denominators? Which one is greater?

$\frac{1}{2}$ ▩ $\frac{1}{4}$ $\frac{2}{3}$ ▩ $\frac{2}{5}$ $\frac{3}{4}$ ▩ $\frac{3}{7}$ $\frac{4}{5}$ ▩ $\frac{4}{9}$

56. Challenge Name a fraction that would make the inequality true.

$$\frac{1}{4} > \blacksquare > \frac{1}{5}$$

Florida Spiral Review

MA.6.A.5.2, MA.6.A.3.2, MA.6.A.1.3

57. Multiple Choice Which fraction has the least value?

A. $\frac{1}{5}$ **B.** $\frac{3}{11}$ **C.** $\frac{2}{15}$ **D.** $\frac{4}{18}$

58. Extended Response Kevin is making potato soup. The recipe shows that he needs $\frac{1}{2}$ gallon of milk and 3.5 pounds of potatoes. He has $\frac{2}{5}$ gallon of milk and $\frac{21}{5}$ pounds of potatoes. Does Kevin have enough milk and potatoes to make the soup? Show your work, and explain your answer.

Solve each equation. Check your answers. (Lesson 2-6)

59. $7 + f = 35$ **60.** $81 = a + 15$ **61.** $n + 23 = 58$ **62.** $62 = 19 + x$

63. Phuong spent $22.33 on 7 pounds of mixed nuts for a party. How much would 1 pound of nuts cost? (Lesson 3-5)

Prep for MA.6.A.5.1 Use equivalent forms of fractions, decimals . . . to solve problems.
Review of MA.5.A.2.1

You can estimate the age of an oak tree by measuring around the trunk at four feet above the ground.

The distance around a young oak tree's trunk increases at a rate of approximately $\frac{1}{8}$ inch per month.

EXAMPLE **1** *Life Science Application*

Sophie plants a young oak tree in her backyard. The distance around the trunk grows at a rate of $\frac{1}{8}$ inch per month. Use pictures to model how much this distance will increase in two months, and then write your answer in simplest form.

$$\frac{1}{8} + \frac{1}{8}$$

$\frac{1}{8} + \frac{1}{8} = \frac{2}{8}$ *Add the numerators. Keep the same denominator.*

$\quad\quad = \frac{1}{4}$ *Write your answer in simplest form.*

The distance around the trunk will increase by $\frac{1}{4}$ inch.

EXAMPLE **2** **Subtracting Like Fractions and Mixed Numbers**

Subtract. Write each answer in simplest form.

A $1 - \frac{2}{3}$

$\downarrow \quad \downarrow$ *To get a common denominator, rewrite 1 as a fraction with a denominator of 3.*

$\frac{3}{3} - \frac{2}{3} = \frac{1}{3}$ *Subtract the numerators. Keep the same denominator.*

Check

   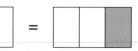

Remember!

When the numerator equals the denominator, the fraction is equal to 1.

$\frac{3}{3} = 1 \quad\quad \frac{173}{173} = 1$

Subtract. Write each answer in simplest form.

B $3\frac{7}{12} - 1\frac{1}{12}$

$3\frac{7}{12} - 1\frac{1}{12}$ *Subtract the fractions. Then subtract the whole numbers.*

$2\frac{6}{12}$

$2\frac{1}{2}$ *Write your answer in simplest form.*

Check

EXAMPLE 3   Evaluating Expressions with Fractions

Evaluate each expression for $x = \frac{3}{8}$. Write each answer in simplest form.

A $\frac{5}{8} - x$

$\frac{5}{8} - x$ *Write the expression.*

$\frac{5}{8} - \frac{3}{8} = \frac{2}{8}$ *Substitute $\frac{3}{8}$ for x and subtract the numerators. Keep the same denominator.*

$= \frac{1}{4}$ *Write your answer in simplest form.*

B $x + 1\frac{1}{8}$

$x + 1\frac{1}{8}$ *Write the expression.*

$\frac{3}{8} + 1\frac{1}{8} = 1\frac{4}{8}$ *Substitute $\frac{3}{8}$ for x. Add the fractions. Then add the whole numbers.*

$= 1\frac{1}{2}$ *Write your answer in simplest form.*

C $x + \frac{7}{8}$

$x + \frac{7}{8}$ *Write the expression.*

$\frac{3}{8} + \frac{7}{8} = \frac{10}{8}$ *Substitute $\frac{3}{8}$ for x and add the numerators. Keep the same denominator.*

$= \frac{5}{4}$ or $1\frac{1}{4}$ *Write your answer in simplest form.*

Helpful Hint

When adding a fraction to a mixed number, you can think of the fraction as having a whole number of 0.

$\frac{3}{8} = 0\frac{3}{8}$

Think and Discuss

1. **Explain** how to add or subtract like fractions.

2. **Tell** why the sum of $\frac{1}{5}$ and $\frac{3}{5}$ is not $\frac{4}{10}$. Give the correct sum.

3. **Describe** how you would add $2\frac{3}{8}$ and $1\frac{1}{8}$. How would you subtract $1\frac{1}{8}$ from $2\frac{3}{8}$?

Homepage Help

Go to thinkcentral.com
Exercises 1–18, 23, 25, 27, 31, 33, 39

GUIDED PRACTICE

See Example **1**

1. Marta is filling a bucket with water. The height of the water is increasing $\frac{1}{6}$ foot each minute. Use pictures to model how much the height of the water will change in three minutes, and then write your answer in simplest form.

See Example **2** Subtract. Write each answer in simplest form.

2. $2 - \frac{3}{5}$

3. $8 - \frac{6}{7}$

4. $4\frac{2}{3} - 1\frac{1}{3}$

5. $8\frac{7}{12} - 3\frac{5}{12}$

See Example **3** Evaluate each expression for $x = \frac{3}{10}$. Write each answer in simplest form.

6. $\frac{9}{10} - x$

7. $x + \frac{1}{10}$

8. $x + \frac{9}{10}$

9. $x - \frac{1}{10}$

INDEPENDENT PRACTICE

See Example **1**

10. Wesley drinks $\frac{2}{13}$ gallon of juice each day. Use pictures to model the number of gallons of juice Wesley drinks in 5 days, and then write your answer in simplest form.

See Example **2** Subtract. Write each answer in simplest form.

11. $1 - \frac{5}{7}$

12. $1 - \frac{3}{8}$

13. $2\frac{4}{5} - 1\frac{1}{5}$

14. $9\frac{9}{14} - 5\frac{3}{14}$

See Example **3** Evaluate each expression for $x = \frac{11}{20}$. Write each answer in simplest form.

15. $x + \frac{13}{20}$

16. $x - \frac{3}{20}$

17. $x - \frac{9}{20}$

18. $x + \frac{17}{20}$

PRACTICE AND PROBLEM SOLVING

Write each sum or difference in simplest form.

19. $\frac{1}{16} + \frac{9}{16}$

20. $\frac{15}{26} - \frac{11}{26}$

21. $\frac{10}{33} + \frac{4}{33}$

22. $1 - \frac{9}{10}$

23. $\frac{26}{75} + \frac{24}{75}$

24. $\frac{100}{999} + \frac{899}{999}$

25. $37\frac{13}{18} - 24\frac{7}{18}$

26. $\frac{1}{20} + \frac{7}{20} + \frac{3}{20}$

27. $\frac{11}{24} + \frac{1}{24} + \frac{5}{24}$

28. Lily took $\frac{5}{6}$ lb of peanuts to a baseball game. She ate $\frac{2}{6}$ lb. How many pounds of peanuts does she have left? Write the answer in simplest form.

Evaluate. Write each answer in simplest form.

29. $a + \frac{7}{18}$ for $a = \frac{1}{18}$

30. $\frac{6}{13} - j$ for $j = \frac{4}{13}$

31. $c + c$ for $c = \frac{5}{14}$

32. $m - \frac{6}{17}$ for $m = 1$

33. $8\frac{14}{15} - z$ for $z = \frac{4}{15}$

34. $13\frac{1}{24} + y$ for $y = 2\frac{5}{24}$

35. Sheila spent x hour studying on Tuesday and $\frac{1}{4}$ hour studying on Thursday. What was the total amount of time in hours Sheila spent studying if $x = \frac{2}{4}$?

○ = WORKED-OUT SOLUTIONS
on p. WS5

36. Carlos had 7 cups of chocolate chips. He used $1\frac{2}{3}$ cups to make a chocolate sauce and $3\frac{1}{3}$ cups to make cookies. How many cups of chocolate chips does Carlos have now?

37. A concert was $2\frac{1}{4}$ hr long. The first musical piece lasted $\frac{1}{4}$ hr. The intermission also lasted $\frac{1}{4}$ hr. How long was the rest of the concert?

38. A flight from Washington, D.C., stops in San Francisco and then continues to Seattle. The trip to San Francisco takes $4\frac{5}{8}$ hr. The trip to Seattle takes $1\frac{1}{8}$ hr. What is the total flight time?

Life Science Use the graph for Exercises 39–41.

Sheila performed an experiment to find the most effective plant fertilizer. She used a different fertilizer on each of 5 different plants. The heights of the plants at the end of her experiment are shown in the graph.

39. What is the combined height of plants C and E?

40. What is the difference in height between the tallest plant and the shortest plant?

? **41.** **What's the Error?** Sheila found the combined heights of plants B and E to be $1\frac{6}{24}$ feet. Explain the error and give the correct answer in simplest form.

42. **Write About It** When writing 1 as a fraction in a subtraction problem, how do you know what the numerator and denominator should be? Give an example.

43. **Challenge** Explain how you might estimate the difference between $\frac{3}{4}$ and $\frac{6}{23}$.

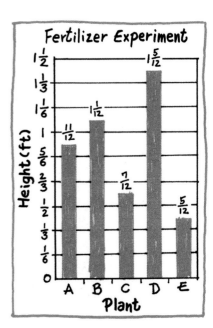

Fertilizer Experiment

44. Multiple Choice What is the solution of $x - \frac{6}{11} = \frac{5}{11}$?

A. $x = \frac{1}{22}$ **B.** $x = \frac{1}{11}$ **C.** $x = 1$ **D.** $x = 11$

45. Short Response Your friend was absent from school and asked you for help with the math assignment. Give your friend detailed instructions on how to subtract $4\frac{7}{12}$ from $13\frac{11}{12}$.

Solve each equation. Check your answers. (Lesson 2-8)

46. $9r = 99$ **47.** $225 = 5a$ **48.** $4m = 48$ **49.** $144 = 12y$

Order the fractions from least to greatest. (Lesson 4-7)

50. $\frac{3}{7}, \frac{5}{4}, \frac{2}{6}$ **51.** $\frac{2}{3}, \frac{4}{11}, \frac{5}{8}$ **52.** $\frac{3}{10}, \frac{3}{8}, \frac{1}{3}$

Prep for MA.6.A.5.3 Estimate the results of computations with fractions . . . and judge the reasonableness of the results. **Review of MA.5.A.2.3**

Members of the Nature Club went mountain biking in Shenandoah National Park, Virginia. They biked $10\frac{3}{10}$ miles on Monday.

You can estimate fractions by rounding to 0, $\frac{1}{2}$, or 1.

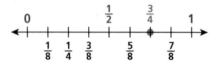

The fraction $\frac{3}{4}$ is halfway between $\frac{1}{2}$ and 1, but we usually round up. So the fraction $\frac{3}{4}$ rounds to 1.

You can round fractions by comparing the numerator and denominator.

closer to 0	closer to $\frac{1}{2}$	closer to 1
$\frac{1}{5}$ $\frac{2}{11}$ $\frac{2}{15}$	$\frac{5}{11}$ $\frac{4}{7}$ $\frac{9}{20}$	$\frac{9}{10}$ $\frac{16}{19}$ $\frac{6}{7}$
Each numerator is much less than half the denominator, so the fractions are close to 0.	Each numerator is about half the denominator, so the fractions are close to $\frac{1}{2}$.	Each numerator is about the same as the denominator, so the fractions are close to 1.

EXAMPLE 1 Estimating Fractions

Estimate each sum or difference by rounding to 0, $\frac{1}{2}$, or 1.

A $\frac{8}{9} + \frac{2}{11}$

$\frac{8}{9} + \frac{2}{11}$ *Think: $\frac{8}{9}$ rounds to 1 and $\frac{2}{11}$ rounds to 0.*

$1 + 0 = 1$

$\frac{8}{9} + \frac{2}{11}$ is about 1.

B $\frac{7}{12} - \frac{8}{15}$

$\frac{7}{12} - \frac{8}{15}$ *Think: $\frac{7}{12}$ rounds to $\frac{1}{2}$ and $\frac{8}{15}$ rounds to $\frac{1}{2}$.*

$\frac{1}{2} - \frac{1}{2} = 0$

$\frac{7}{12} - \frac{8}{15}$ is about 0.

You can also estimate by rounding mixed numbers. Compare the mixed number to the two nearest whole numbers and the nearest $\frac{1}{2}$.

Does $10\frac{3}{10}$ round to 10, $10\frac{1}{2}$, or 11?

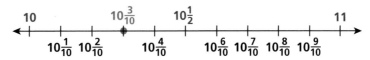

The mixed number $10\frac{3}{10}$ rounds to $10\frac{1}{2}$.

EXAMPLE **2** **Sports Application**

Nature Club's Biking Distances	
Day	Distances (mi)
Monday	$10\frac{3}{10}$
Tuesday	$9\frac{3}{4}$
Wednesday	$12\frac{1}{4}$
Thursday	$4\frac{7}{10}$

A **About how far did the Nature Club ride on Monday and Tuesday?**

$$10\frac{3}{10} + 9\frac{3}{4}$$
$$\downarrow \qquad \downarrow$$
$$10\frac{1}{2} + 10 = 20\frac{1}{2}$$

They rode about $20\frac{1}{2}$ miles.

Helpful Hint

$\frac{1}{4}$ is halfway between 0 and $\frac{1}{2}$. Round $\frac{1}{4}$ up to $\frac{1}{2}$.

B **About how much farther did the Nature Club ride on Wednesday than on Thursday?**

$$12\frac{1}{4} - 4\frac{7}{10}$$
$$\downarrow \qquad \downarrow$$
$$12\frac{1}{2} - 4\frac{1}{2} = 8$$

They rode about 8 miles farther on Wednesday than on Thursday.

C **Estimate the total distance that the Nature Club rode on Monday, Tuesday, and Wednesday.**

$$10\frac{3}{10} + 9\frac{3}{4} + 12\frac{1}{4}$$
$$\downarrow \qquad \downarrow \qquad \downarrow$$
$$10\frac{1}{2} + 10 + 12\frac{1}{2} = 33$$

They rode about 33 miles.

Think and Discuss

1. Tell whether each fraction rounds to 0, $\frac{1}{2}$, or 1: $\frac{5}{6}$, $\frac{2}{15}$, $\frac{7}{13}$.

2. Explain how to round mixed numbers to the nearest whole number.

3. Determine whether the Nature Club met their goal to ride at least 35 total miles.

Homework Help

Go to **thinkcentral.com**
Exercises 1–17, 19, 21, 23, 25, 27, 29, 33

GUIDED PRACTICE

See Example **1** Estimate each sum or difference by rounding to 0, $\frac{1}{2}$, or 1.

1. $\frac{8}{9} + \frac{1}{6}$ **2.** $\frac{11}{12} - \frac{4}{9}$ **3.** $\frac{3}{7} + \frac{1}{12}$ **4.** $\frac{6}{13} - \frac{2}{5}$

See Example **2** Use the table for Exercises 5 and 6.

5. About how far did Mark run during week 1 and week 2?

6. About how much farther did Mark run during week 2 than during week 3?

Mark's Running Distances	
Week	Distance (mi)
1	$8\frac{3}{4}$
2	$7\frac{1}{5}$
3	$5\frac{5}{6}$

INDEPENDENT PRACTICE

See Example **1** Estimate each sum or difference by rounding to 0, $\frac{1}{2}$, or 1.

7. $\frac{7}{8} - \frac{3}{8}$ **8.** $\frac{3}{10} + \frac{3}{4}$ **9.** $\frac{5}{6} - \frac{7}{8}$ **10.** $\frac{7}{10} + \frac{1}{6}$

11. $\frac{3}{4} + \frac{7}{10}$ **12.** $\frac{9}{20} - \frac{1}{6}$ **13.** $\frac{8}{9} + \frac{4}{5}$ **14.** $\frac{19}{20} + \frac{9}{10}$

See Example **2** Use the table for Exercises 15–17.

15. About how much do the meteorites in Brenham and Goose Lake weigh together?

16. About how much more does the meteorite in Willamette weigh than the meteorite in Norton County?

17. About how much do the two meteorites in Kansas weigh together?

Meteorites in the United States	
Location	Weight (tons)
Willamette, AZ	$16\frac{1}{2}$
Brenham, KS	$2\frac{3}{5}$
Goose Lake, CA	$1\frac{3}{10}$
Norton County, KS	$1\frac{1}{10}$

PRACTICE AND PROBLEM SOLVING

Estimate each sum or difference to compare. Write < or >.

18. $\frac{5}{6} + \frac{7}{9}$ ▇ 3   **19.** $2\frac{8}{15} - 1\frac{1}{11}$ ▇ 1   **20.** $1\frac{2}{21} + \frac{3}{7}$ ▇ 2

21. $1\frac{7}{13} - \frac{8}{9}$ ▇ 1   **22.** $3\frac{2}{10} + 2\frac{2}{5}$ ▇ 6   **23.** $4\frac{6}{9} - 2\frac{3}{19}$ ▇ 2

24. **Critical Thinking** Describe a situation in which it is better to round a mixed number up to the next whole number even if the fraction in the mixed number is closer to $\frac{1}{2}$ than 1.

Estimate.

25. $\frac{7}{8} + \frac{4}{7} + \frac{7}{13}$ **26.** $\frac{6}{11} + \frac{9}{17} + \frac{3}{5}$ **27.** $\frac{8}{9} + \frac{3}{4} + \frac{9}{10}$

28. $1\frac{5}{8} + 2\frac{1}{15} + 2\frac{12}{13}$ **29.** $4\frac{11}{12} + 3\frac{1}{19} + 5\frac{4}{7}$ **30.** $10\frac{1}{9} + 8\frac{5}{9} + 11\frac{13}{14}$

○ = WORKED-OUT SOLUTIONS
on p. WS5

Life Science Use an inch ruler for Exercises 31–32. Measure to the nearest $\frac{1}{4}$ inch.

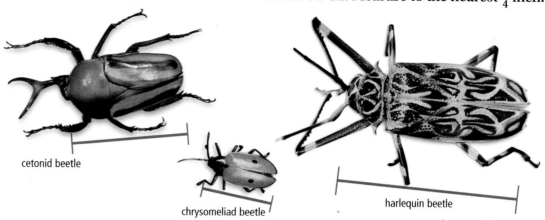

cetonid beetle

chrysomeliad beetle

harlequin beetle

31. About how much longer is the harlequin beetle than the cetonid beetle?

32. About how much longer is the harlequin beetle than the chrysomeliad beetle?

33. Use the table to estimate the total weekly snowfall.

Day	Mon	Tue	Wed	Thu	Fri	Sat	Sun
Snowfall (in.)	$3\frac{4}{7}$	$\frac{7}{8}$	0	$2\frac{1}{6}$	$\frac{2}{11}$	$1\frac{9}{20}$	$1\frac{4}{7}$

34. Write a Problem Write a problem about a trip that can be solved by estimating fractions. Exchange with a classmate and solve.

35. Write About It Explain how to estimate the sum of two mixed numbers. Give an example to explain your answer.

36. Challenge Estimate. $\left[5\frac{7}{8} - 2\frac{3}{20}\right] + 1\frac{4}{7}$

Florida Spiral Review   MA.6.A.3.1, MA.6.A.5.1

37. Multiple Choice Larry ran $3\frac{1}{3}$ miles on Monday and $5\frac{3}{4}$ miles on Tuesday. About how many miles did Larry run on Monday and Tuesday?

 A. 8   **B.** 9   **C.** 10   **D.** 11

38. Multiple Choice Marie used $2\frac{4}{5}$ cups of flour for a recipe. Linda used $1\frac{1}{4}$ cups of flour for a recipe. About how many more cups of flour did Marie use than Linda?

 F. 1   **G.** 2   **H.** 3   **I.** 4

Write an expression for the missing value in each table. (Lesson 2-3)

39.

Games Played	2	4	6	8	n
Points Scored	14	28	42	56	

40.

Month	1	3	5	7	n
Hours Worked	6	8	10	12	

41. Ricky bought a soccer ball that was on sale for $\frac{1}{5}$ off the original price. What decimal represents the discount Ricky received? (Lesson 4-5)

Ready To Go On?

SECTION 4B

Ready To Go On?

THINK central

Go to thinkcentral.com

Quiz for Lessons 4-4 Through 4-9

 **4-4** **Equivalent Fractions**

1. Mandy ate $\frac{1}{6}$ of a pizza. Write two equivalent fractions for $\frac{1}{6}$.

Write each fraction in simplest form.

2. $\frac{20}{24}$ 3. $\frac{14}{49}$ 4. $\frac{12}{28}$ 5. $\frac{34}{51}$

4-5 **Decimals and Fractions**

Write each decimal as a fraction and each fraction as a decimal.

6. 0.67   7. 0.9   8. 0.43   9. 0.6

10. $\frac{2}{5}$ 11. $\frac{1}{6}$ 12. $\frac{3}{4}$ 13. $\frac{5}{9}$

Compare. Write $<$, $>$, or $=$.

14. $\frac{7}{10}$ ■ 0.9   15. 0.4 ■ $\frac{2}{5}$ 16. $\frac{3}{5}$ ■ 0.5   17. 0.35 ■ $\frac{3}{8}$

4-6 **Mixed Numbers and Improper Fractions**

Use the table for Exercises 18–20.

18. Write the lengths of *1900* and *Empire* as mixed numbers in simplest form.

19. Write the lengths of *Fanny and Alexander* and *War and Peace* as improper fractions.

20. Write the movies in order from longest to shortest.

World's Longest Movies	
Title	**Length (h)**
1900	$\frac{318}{60}$
Empire	$\frac{480}{60}$
Fanny and Alexander	$5\frac{1}{5}$
War and Peace	$8\frac{31}{60}$

4-7 **Comparing and Ordering Fractions**

Order the fractions from least to greatest.

21. $\frac{5}{8}, \frac{1}{2}, \frac{3}{4}$ 22. $\frac{3}{4}, \frac{3}{5}, \frac{7}{10}$ 23. $\frac{1}{3}, \frac{3}{8}, \frac{1}{4}$ 24. $\frac{2}{5}, \frac{4}{9}, \frac{11}{15}$

25. Mrs. Wilson split a bag of marbles between her three sons. Ralph got $\frac{1}{10}$, Pete got $\frac{1}{2}$, and Jon got $\frac{8}{20}$. Who got the most marbles?

4-8 **Adding and Subtracting with Like Denominators**

Add or subtract. Write each answer in simplest form.

26. $1 - \frac{3}{4}$ 27. $6\frac{5}{9} + 5\frac{1}{9}$ 28. $10\frac{7}{16} - 4\frac{3}{16}$ 29. $1 + \frac{7}{8}$

4-9 **Estimating Fraction Sums and Differences**

Estimate each sum or difference.

30. $\frac{3}{4} - \frac{1}{10}$ 31. $\frac{7}{9} + \frac{7}{9}$ 32. $\frac{15}{16} - \frac{4}{5}$ 33. $3\frac{7}{8} - 1\frac{1}{10}$

Real-World CONNECTIONS

The Trailwalker Program

Florida's state forests are crisscrossed by dozens of hiking trails. The Trailwalker Program offers rewards for exploring these trails. Participants in the free program receive a patch and a certificate for hiking a minimum of ten trails.

1. Elena plans to start the Trailwalker Program by hiking the Mud Spring Trail and the Johnson Pond Trail. She wants to start with the shorter trail. Which trail should she hike first?

2. Next, Elena hikes the Sweetwater Trail. Write the length of the trail as a decimal.

3. Elena takes a photo at the beginning and end of the Sweetwater Trail and every 0.25 mile along the way. How many photos does she take?

4. In April, Elena hikes the Anderson Springs Trail and the Holly Hammock Trail. What is the total distance she hikes for the month?

Trails in Florida State Forests	
Trail Name	**Length (mi)**
Dunn's Farm	$1\frac{9}{10}$
Anderson Springs	$4\frac{3}{10}$
Mud Spring	$1\frac{7}{10}$
Holly Hammock	$2\frac{3}{10}$
Johnson Pond	$1\frac{4}{5}$
Sabal Palm	$3\frac{1}{5}$
Sweetwater	$1\frac{1}{4}$
Karick Lake	$3\frac{4}{5}$

5. In May, Elena plans to hike the Dunn's Farm Trail, the Sabal Palm Trail, and the Karick Lake Trail. Estimate the total length of these trails.

6. Elena can usually hike one mile in 20 minutes. What is the total time she should expect to spend hiking in May?

Game Time

Riddle Me This

"When you go from there to here,
you'll find I disappear.
Go from here to there, and then
you'll see me again.
What am I?"

To solve this riddle, copy the square below. If a number is divisible by 3, color that box red. Remember the divisibility rule for 3. If a number is not divisible by 3, color that box blue.

102	981	210	6,015	72
79	1,204	576	10,019	1,771
548	3,416	12,300	904	1,330
217	2,662	1,746	3,506	15,025
34,351	725	2,352	5,675	6,001

On a Roll

The object is to be the first person to fill in all the squares on your game board.

On your turn, roll a number cube and record the number rolled in any blank square on your game board. Once you have placed a number in a square, you cannot move that number. If you cannot place the number in a square, then your turn is over. The winner is the first player to complete their game board correctly.

A complete copy of the rules and game pieces are available online.

Games

THINK central

Go to **thinkcentral.com**

Materials
- tan card stock
- scissors
- reinforcements
- hole punch
- wire ring
- markers

PROJECT ## Spec-Tag-Ular Number Theory

Tags will help you keep notes about number theory and fractions on an easy-to-use reference ring.

Directions

1. Make tags by cutting ten rectangles from card stock, each approximately $2\frac{3}{4}$ inches by $1\frac{1}{2}$ inches.

2. Use scissors to clip off two corners at the end of each tag. **Figure A**

3. Punch a hole between the clipped corners of each tag. Put a reinforcement around the hole on both sides of the tag. **Figure B**

4. Hook all of the tags together on a wire ring. On one of the tags, write the number and name of the chapter. **Figure C**

Taking Note of the Math

Use the tags to record important facts about fractions. You can also write a divisibility rule from the chapter on each tag.

Multi–Language Glossary

THINK central

Go to thinkcentral.com

Vocabulary

Complete the sentences below with vocabulary words from the list above.

1. The number $\frac{11}{9}$ is an example of a(n) ___?___, and $3\frac{1}{6}$ is an example of a(n) ___?___.

2. A(n) ___?___, such as 0.3333..., has a block of one or more digits that repeat without end. A(n) ___?___, such as 0.25, has a finite number of decimal places.

3. A(n) ___?___ is divisible by only two numbers, 1 and itself. A(n) ___?___ is divisible by more than two numbers.

EXAMPLES

EXERCISES

4-1 **Divisibility** (pp. 142–145)

■ Tell whether 210 is divisible by 2, 3, 4, and 6.

2	*The last digit, 0, is even.*	Divisible
3	*The sum of the digits is divisible by 3.*	Divisible
4	*The number formed by the last two digits is not divisible by 4.*	Not divisible
6	*210 is divisible by 2 and 3.*	Divisible

■ Tell whether each number is prime or composite.

17 *only divisible by 1 and 17* prime

25 *divisible by 1, 5, and 25* composite

 Prep MA.6.A.5.1

Tell whether each number is divisible by 2, 3, 4, 5, 6, 9, and 10.

4. 118   **5.** 90

6. 342   **7.** 284

8. 170   **9.** 393

Tell whether each number is prime or composite.

10. 121   **11.** 77

12. 13   **13.** 118

14. 67   **15.** 93

16. 39   **17.** 97

18. 85   **19.** 61

4-2 Factors and Prime Factorization (pp. 146–149)

 Prep MA.6.A.5.1

■ List all of the factors of 10.

$10 = 1 \cdot 10$ $10 = 2 \cdot 5$

The factors of 10 are 1, 2, 5, and 10.

■ Write the prime factorization of 30.

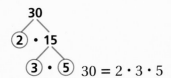

$30 = 2 \cdot 3 \cdot 5$

List all of the factors of each number.

20. 60   **21.** 72

22. 29   **23.** 56

24. 85   **25.** 71

Write the prime factorization of each number.

26. 65   **27.** 110   **28.** 81

29. 99   **30.** 77   **31.** 46

4-3 Greatest Common Factor (pp. 150–153)

Prep MA.6.A.5.1

■ Find the GCF of 35 and 50.

factors of 35: 1, ⑤, 7, 35

factors of 50: 1, 2, ⑤, 10, 25, 50

The GCF of 35 and 50 is 5.

Find the GCF of each set of numbers.

32. 36 and 60   **33.** 24 and 32

34. 50, 75, and 125   **35.** 54 and 72

36. 45, 81, and 99   **37.** 14, 35, and 63

4-4 Equivalent Fractions (pp. 156–159)

 Prep MA.6.A.5.1

■ Find an equivalent fraction for $\frac{4}{5}$.

$\frac{4}{5} = \frac{\blacksquare}{15}$ $\frac{4 \cdot 3}{5 \cdot 3} = \frac{12}{15}$

■ Write $\frac{8}{12}$ in simplest form.

$\frac{8 \div 4}{12 \div 4} = \frac{2}{3}$

Find two equivalent fractions.

38. $\frac{4}{6}$ **39.** $\frac{4}{5}$ **40.** $\frac{3}{12}$

Write each fraction in simplest form.

41. $\frac{14}{16}$ **42.** $\frac{9}{30}$ **43.** $\frac{7}{10}$

4-5 Decimals and Fractions (pp. 160–163)

 MA.6.A.5.1, MA.6.A.5.2

■ Write 1.29 as a mixed number.

$1.29 = 1\frac{29}{100}$

■ Write $\frac{3}{5}$ as a decimal.

$5\overline{)3.0}$ gives 0.6 $\frac{3}{5} = 0.6$

Write as a fraction or mixed number.

44. 0.37   **45.** 1.8   **46.** 0.4

Write as a decimal.

47. $\frac{7}{8}$ **48.** $\frac{2}{5}$ **49.** $\frac{7}{9}$

50. Olanda needs a board that is 1.4 feet long. She has two boards; one that is $1\frac{7}{16}$ feet long and another that is $1\frac{3}{8}$ feet. Is either board that Olanda has long enough? If so, which one? Explain.

Study Guide: Review

4-6 Mixed Numbers and Improper Fractions (pp. 164–167)

 MA.6.A.5.1

- Write $3\frac{5}{6}$ as an improper fraction.

$$3\frac{5}{6} = \frac{(3 \cdot 6) + 5}{6} = \frac{18 + 5}{6} = \frac{23}{6}$$

Write as an improper fraction.

51. $3\frac{7}{9}$ **52.** $2\frac{5}{12}$ **53.** $5\frac{2}{7}$

- Write $\frac{19}{4}$ as a mixed number.

Write as a mixed number.

54. $\frac{23}{6}$ **55.** $\frac{17}{5}$ **56.** $\frac{41}{8}$

$$\begin{array}{r} 4R3 \\ 4\overline{)19} \end{array} \qquad \frac{19}{4} = 4\frac{3}{4}$$

57. Lucas needs an envelope that is at least $\frac{17}{4}$ inches long. He has two envelopes; one is $4\frac{3}{4}$ inches long and the other is 4 inches long. Which envelope should Lucas use?

4-7 Comparing and Ordering Fractions (pp. 168–171)

 MA.6.A.5.2, MA.6.A.5.1

- Order from least to greatest.

$$\frac{3}{5}, \frac{2}{3}, \frac{1}{3} \qquad \textit{Rename with like denominators.}$$

$$\frac{3 \cdot 3}{5 \cdot 3} = \frac{9}{15} \qquad \frac{2 \cdot 5}{3 \cdot 5} = \frac{10}{15} \qquad \frac{1 \cdot 5}{3 \cdot 5} = \frac{5}{15}$$

$$\frac{1}{3}, \frac{3}{5}, \frac{2}{3}$$

Compare. Write <, >, or =.

58. $\frac{6}{8} \blacksquare \frac{3}{6}$ **59.** $\frac{7}{9} \blacksquare \frac{2}{3}$

60. $\frac{4}{5} \blacksquare \frac{8}{10}$ **61.** $\frac{2}{5} \blacksquare \frac{2}{3}$

Order from least to greatest.

62. $\frac{3}{8}, \frac{2}{3}, \frac{7}{8}$ **63.** $\frac{4}{6}, \frac{3}{12}, \frac{1}{3}$

64. $\frac{1}{2}, \frac{3}{8}, \frac{1}{3}$ **65.** $\frac{5}{6}, \frac{9}{10}, \frac{7}{8}$

4-8 Adding and Subtracting with Like Denominators (pp. 172–175)

 Prep MA.6.A.5.1

- Subtract $4\frac{5}{6} - 2\frac{1}{6}$. Write your answer in simplest form.

$$4\frac{5}{6} - 2\frac{1}{6} = 2\frac{4}{6} = 2\frac{2}{3}$$

Add or subtract. Write each answer in simplest form.

66. $\frac{1}{5} + \frac{4}{5}$ **67.** $1 - \frac{3}{12}$

68. $\frac{9}{10} - \frac{3}{10}$ **69.** $4\frac{2}{7} + 2\frac{3}{7}$

70. Lia painted $\frac{3}{8}$ of her bedroom. How much of the room still needs to be painted?

4-9 Estimating Fraction Sums and Differences (pp. 176–179)

 Prep MA.6.A.5.3

- Estimate $\frac{7}{8} + \frac{1}{7}$ by rounding fractions to 0, $\frac{1}{2}$, or 1.

$$\frac{7}{8} + \frac{1}{7} \qquad \textit{Think: } 1 + 0.$$

$\frac{7}{8} + \frac{1}{7}$ is about 1.

Estimate each sum or difference by rounding fractions to 0, $\frac{1}{2}$, or 1.

71. $\frac{3}{5} + \frac{3}{7}$ **72.** $\frac{6}{7} - \frac{5}{9}$

73. $4\frac{9}{10} + 6\frac{1}{5}$ **74.** $7\frac{5}{11} - 4\frac{3}{4}$

Study Guide: Review

Chapter Test

FLORIDA
CHAPTER
4

List all of the factors of each number. Then tell whether each number is prime or composite.

1. 98 **2.** 40 **3.** 45

Write the prime factorization of each number.

4. 64 **5.** 130 **6.** 49

Find the GCF of each set of numbers.

7. 24 and 108 **8.** 45, 18, and 39 **9.** 49, 77, and 84

10. Lee is making fruit salad. The recipe calls for $\frac{1}{2}$ cup shredded coconut. Lee has only a $\frac{1}{4}$ cup measuring cup. How can she measure the correct $\frac{1}{2}$ cup amount?

Write each fraction in simplest form.

11. $\frac{4}{12}$ **12.** $\frac{6}{9}$ **13.** $\frac{3}{15}$

Write each decimal as a fraction or mixed number. Write each fraction or mixed number as a decimal.

14. 0.37 **15.** 1.9 **16.** 0.92

17. $\frac{3}{8}$ **18.** $9\frac{3}{5}$ **19.** $\frac{2}{3}$

Write each mixed number as an improper fraction.

20. $4\frac{7}{8}$ **21.** $7\frac{5}{12}$ **22.** $3\frac{5}{7}$

Compare. Write <, >, or =.

23. $\frac{5}{6}$ ■ $\frac{3}{6}$ **24.** $\frac{3}{4}$ ■ $\frac{7}{8}$ **25.** $\frac{4}{5}$ ■ $\frac{7}{10}$

Order the fractions and decimals from least to greatest.

26. 2.17, 2.3, $2\frac{1}{9}$ **27.** 0.1, $\frac{3}{8}$, 0.3 **28.** 0.9, $\frac{2}{8}$, 0.35

29. If Juan answers 23 out of 25 questions correctly on his social studies test, then he will have met a personal goal. Juan's test score is 0.90. Did Juan meet his goal? Explain.

30. On Monday, it snowed $2\frac{1}{4}$ inches. On Tuesday, an additional $3\frac{3}{4}$ inches of snow fell. How much snow fell altogether on Monday and Tuesday?

Estimate each sum or difference by rounding fractions to 0, $\frac{1}{2}$, or 1.

31. $\frac{1}{8} + \frac{4}{7}$ **32.** $\frac{11}{12} - \frac{4}{9}$ **33.** $\frac{4}{5} + \frac{1}{9}$ **34.** $2\frac{9}{10} - 2\frac{1}{7}$

Chapter Test

Mastering the Standards

Florida Test Practice

Go to thinkcentral.com

Cumulative Assessment, Chapters 1–4

Multiple Choice

1. The fraction $\frac{4}{9}$ is found between which pair of fractions on a number line?

   A. $\frac{9}{18}$ and $\frac{12}{27}$ **C.** $\frac{7}{18}$ and $\frac{13}{27}$

   B. $\frac{8}{18}$ and $\frac{10}{27}$ **D.** $\frac{6}{18}$ and $\frac{11}{27}$

2. A museum store sells geode bookends in pairs. The store buys a box of the bookends for $104.00 and sells each pair for $24.99. Let b represent the number of pairs of bookends in each box. Which expression could be used to find the difference between the total sale price of all the bookends in a box and the store's cost for one box of bookends?

   F. $104.00b - 24.99$

   G. $104.00b + 24.99$

   H. $24.99b - 104.00$

   I. $24.99b + 104.00$

3. The quotient of 2.5 divided by 0.4 is equal to the sum of which two numbers?

   A. 2 and 0.5

   B. 5 and 0.75

   C. 5 and 0.8

   D. 6 and 0.25

4. A writer spends $144.75 on 5 ink cartridges. Which equation can be used to find the cost c of one ink cartridge?

   F. $5c = 144.75$

   G. $\frac{c}{144.75} = 5$

   H. $5 + c = 144.75$

   I. $144.75 - c = 5$

5. Three quarters is 0.75 of one dollar. Which fraction is equal to 0.75?

   A. $\frac{1}{3}$ **C.** $\frac{2}{5}$

   B. $\frac{3}{4}$ **D.** $\frac{1}{25}$

6. Freddy wants to buy 4 tickets to a basketball game. Prices for tickets are shown below. How much money will Freddy save if he buys 4 tickets in Section B rather than 4 tickets in Section A?

Tickets	Price
Section A	$29.95
Section B	$24.95
Section C	$17.95

   F. $5.00 **H.** $28.00

   G. $20.00 **I.** $48.00

7. Which of the following algebraic expressions is NOT equal to $5m + 2(m + 3n)$?

   A. $2(m + 3n) + 5m$

   B. $5m + 2m + 6n$

   C. $2(3n + m) + 5m$

   D. $5m + 2m + 3n$

8. Four boys each order their own small pizza. William eats $\frac{2}{3}$ of his pizza. Mike eats $\frac{2}{5}$ of his pizza. Julio eats $\frac{1}{2}$ of his pizza. Lee eats $\frac{3}{8}$ of his pizza. Who ate the least amount of pizza?

   F. Lee **H.** Julio

   G. Mike **I.** William

9. Audrey spent $\frac{14}{30}$ of June visiting her grandparents. Which of the following is the fraction $\frac{14}{30}$ NOT equal to?

A. $\frac{7}{15}$ C. $\frac{21}{45}$

B. $0.9\overline{3}$ D. $0.4\overline{6}$

10. What is the value of the expression $3.9 \div 0.4 + 6 \cdot 2.8 - 1.7$?

F. 16.35   H. 26.55

G. 24.85   I. 42.4

11. Which of the following is equivalent to 2.52?

A. $2\frac{52}{100}$ C. $\frac{52}{200}$

B. $2\frac{52}{10}$ D. $\frac{2}{52}$

 You can answer some problems without doing many calculations. Use mental math, estimation, or logical reasoning to eliminate answer choices and save time.

Gridded Response

12. Cherie earns $7.25 per hour baby-sitting. Last week she earned $50.75. This week she baby-sat for 6 hours. How much money did Cherie earn baby-sitting during these two weeks?

13. Which of the following values is the greatest?

$\frac{12}{13}$, 1.1, $\frac{8}{7}$, $1\frac{1}{9}$

14. To cater a dinner, a restaurant charges $65 per hour plus $28.89 per person. Alfredo is planning a 2-hour dinner for p persons. The expression $2 \cdot 65 + 28.89 \cdot p$ represents the total cost of dinner for p persons. What is the total cost of dinner for 24 people?

15. What is the solution to the equation $97 + x = 143$?

Short Response

S1. Stacie has $16\frac{3}{8}$ yards of material. She uses $7\frac{1}{8}$ yards for a skirt. How much material does she have left? Write your answer as a mixed number in simplest form. Then give three other equivalent answers, including one decimal.

S2. Jordan is 53 years old. She is 37 years younger than her mother. Write an equation that relates Jordan's age to her mother's age. Then solve the equation. How old is Jordan's mother? Show your work.

S3. A student multiplied 0.471 and 0.53 and got an answer greater than 1. Explain how you know that the student's answer is incorrect.

S4. Raja wants to order a window shade that is $\frac{3}{8}$ foot longer than her $3\frac{7}{8}$-foot-long window. To order online, Raja must enter the length as a decimal. What is the length she must enter? Explain.

Extended Response

E1. Mr. Peters needs to build a rectangular pig pen $14\frac{4}{5}$ meters long and $5\frac{1}{5}$ meters wide.

a. How much fencing does Mr. Peters need to buy? Show how you found your answer. Write your answer in simplest form.

b. Mr. Peters's pig pen will need 6 meters more fencing than the rectangular pig pen his neighbor is building. Write and solve an equation to find how much fencing his neighbor needs to buy. Show your work.

c. If the neighbor's pig pen is going to be 4 meters wide, how long will it be? Show your work.

Fraction Operations

Worktext
pages 181–222

Additional instruction, practice, and activities are available online, including:

- Lesson Tutorial Videos
- Homework Help
- Animated Math

Go to **thinkcentral.com**

Why Learn This?

Fractions are used to describe many things in the real world. For example, $\frac{9}{10}$ of orange juice produced in the United States is made from Florida oranges.

Orange World
Kissimmee

Chapter Focus

- Multiply and divide fractions efficiently.
- Evaluate expressions and solve real-world problems with fractions.

Are You Ready?

Are You Ready?

THINK central

Go to **thinkcentral.com**

✓ Vocabulary

Choose the best term from the list to complete each sentence.

denominator

factors

improper fraction

like fractions

multiples

numerator

proper fraction

simplest form

unlike fractions

1. The first five ___?___ of 6 are 6, 12, 18, 24, and 30. The ___?___ of 6 are 1, 2, 3, and 6.

2. Fractions with the same denominator are called ___?___.

3. A fraction is in ___?___ when the GCF of the numerator and the denominator is 1.

4. The fraction $\frac{13}{9}$ is a(n) ___?___ because the ___?___ is greater than the ___?___.

Complete these exercises to review skills you will need for this chapter.

✓ Simplify Fractions

Write each fraction in simplest form.

5. $\frac{6}{10}$ 6. $\frac{5}{15}$ 7. $\frac{14}{8}$ 8. $\frac{8}{12}$

9. $\frac{10}{100}$ 10. $\frac{12}{144}$ 11. $\frac{33}{121}$ 12. $\frac{15}{17}$

✓ Write a Mixed Number as an Improper Fraction

Write each mixed number as an improper fraction.

13. $1\frac{1}{8}$ 14. $2\frac{3}{4}$ 15. $2\frac{4}{5}$ 16. $1\frac{7}{9}$

17. $3\frac{1}{5}$ 18. $5\frac{2}{3}$ 19. $4\frac{4}{7}$ 20. $3\frac{11}{12}$

✓ Add and Subtract Like Fractions

Add or subtract. Write each answer in simplest form.

21. $\frac{5}{8} + \frac{1}{8}$ 22. $\frac{3}{7} + \frac{5}{7}$ 23. $\frac{9}{10} - \frac{3}{10}$ 24. $\frac{5}{9} - \frac{2}{9}$

25. $\frac{1}{2} + \frac{1}{2}$ 26. $\frac{7}{12} - \frac{5}{12}$ 27. $\frac{3}{5} + \frac{4}{5}$ 28. $\frac{4}{15} - \frac{1}{15}$

✓ Multiplication Facts

Multiply.

29. 8×11 30. 7×8 31. 4×12 32. 12×7

33. 10×13 34. 9×7 35. 6×8 36. 11×12

Before

Previously, you

- modeled addition and subtraction of fractions with like denominators.

- estimated sums and differences of whole numbers.

- wrote equivalent fractions.

Now

You will study

- adding and subtracting fractions and mixed numbers with unlike denominators.

- multiplying and dividing fractions and mixed numbers.

- solving equations with fractions.

Why?

You can use the skills learned in this chapter

- to solve measurement problems that involve fractions and mixed numbers.

- to convert measurements from one unit to another.

Key Vocabulary/Vocabulario

least common denominator (LCD)	mínimo común denominador (MCD)
least common multiple (LCM)	mínimo común múltiplo (MCM)
reciprocal	recíproco

Vocabulary Connections

To become familiar with some of the vocabulary terms in the chapter, consider the following. You may refer to the chapter, the glossary, or a dictionary if you like.

1. The word *reciprocal* means "inversely related or opposite." What do you think the **reciprocal** of a fraction will look like?

2. When people have something in *common,* they have something that they share. What do you think two numbers with a common multiple share? What do you think the **least common multiple** of two numbers is?

3. Fractions with the same denominator have a common denominator. What do you think the **least common denominator** of two fractions is?

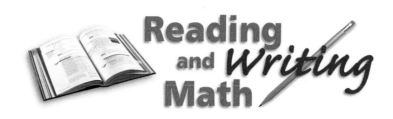 

Reading and Writing Math

Study Strategy: Make Flash Cards

Create flash cards to help you learn a sequence of steps, vocabulary, math symbols, formulas, or mathematical rules. Study your flash cards often.

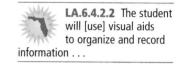 **LA.6.4.2.2** The student will [use] visual aids to organize and record information . . .

Use these suggestions to make flash cards.

- Label each card with the lesson number so you can look back at your textbook when studying.

- Write the name of the formula, term, or rule on one side of the card, and the meaning or an example on the other side of the card.

- Write definitions using your own words.

From Lesson 4-8

Life Science Application

Sophie plants a young oak tree in her backyard. The distance around the trunk grows at a rate of $\frac{1}{8}$ inch per month. Use pictures to model how much this distance will increase in two months, then write your answer in simplest form.

$\frac{1}{8} + \frac{1}{8}$

$\frac{1}{8} + \frac{1}{8} = \frac{2}{8}$ *Add the numerators. Keep the same denominator.*

$\qquad = \frac{1}{4}$ *Write your answer in simplest form.*

The distance around the trunk will increase by $\frac{1}{4}$ inch.

Sample Flash Card

Lesson 4-8
Pages 202–205

Adding and Subtracting
Fractions with
Like Denominators

$\frac{1}{8} + \frac{1}{8}$

Keep the denominators.	$\frac{1}{8} + \frac{1}{8} = \frac{}{8}$
Add the numerators.	$\frac{1}{8} + \frac{1}{8} = \frac{2}{8}$
Write in simplest form.	$\frac{1}{4}$

Front   **Back**

Try This

1. Use Lesson 4-6 to make flash cards for the rules for writing mixed numbers as improper fractions.

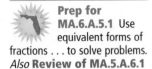

5-1 > Least Common Multiple

Prep for MA.6.A.5.1 Use equivalent forms of fractions . . . to solve problems. *Also* **Review of MA.5.A.6.1**

Vocabulary

least common multiple (LCM)

After games in Lydia's basketball league, one player's family brings snacks for both teams to share. This week Lydia's family will provide juice boxes and granola bars for 24 players.

You can make a model to help you find the least number of juice and granola packs Lydia's family should buy. Use colored counters, drawings, or pictures to illustrate the problem.

EXAMPLE 1 *Consumer Application*

Remember!

A multiple of a number is the product of the number and any nonzero whole number.

Juice comes in packs of 6, and granola bars in packs of 8. If there are 24 players, what is the least number of packs needed so that each player has a drink and granola bar and there are none left over?

Draw juice boxes in groups of 6. Draw granola bars in groups of 8. Stop when you have drawn the same number of each.

There are 24 juice boxes and 24 granola bars.

Lydia's family should buy 4 packs of juice and 3 packs of granola bars.

The smallest number that is a multiple of two or more numbers is the **least common multiple (LCM)**. In Example 1, the LCM of 6 and 8 is 24.

Video **Lesson Tutorial Videos @ thinkcentral.com**

EXAMPLE 2 **Using Multiples to Find the LCM**

Find the least common multiple (LCM).

Method 1: Use a number line.

A **6 and 9**

Use a number line to skip count by 6 and 9.

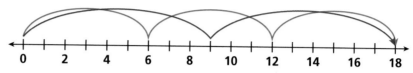

The least common multiple (LCM) of 6 and 9 is 18.

Method 2: Use a list.

B **3, 5, and 6**

3: 3, 6, 9, 12, 15, 18, 21, 24, 27, 30, 33, . . .

5: 5, 10, 15, 20, 25, 30, 35, . . .

6: 6, 12, 18, 24, 30, 36, . . .

List multiples of 3, 5, and 6.

Find the smallest number that is in all the lists.

LCM: 30

Method 3: Use prime factorization.

> **Remember!**
>
> The prime factorization of a number is the number written as a product of its prime factors.

C **8 and 12**

$8 = 2 \cdot 2 \cdot 2$

$12 = 2 \cdot 2 \cdot 3$

$2 \cdot 2 \cdot 2 \cdot 3$

$2 \cdot 2 \cdot 2 \cdot 3 = 24$

Write the prime factorization of each number. Line up the common factors.

To find the LCM, multiply one number from each column.

LCM: 24

D **12, 10, and 15**

$12 = 2^2 \cdot 3$

$10 = 2 \cdot 5$

$15 = 3 \cdot 5$

$2^2 \cdot 3 \cdot 5$

$2^2 \cdot 3 \cdot 5 = 60$

Write the prime factorization of each number in exponential form.

To find the LCM, multiply each prime factor once with the greatest exponent used in any of the prime factorizations.

LCM: 60

Think and Discuss

1. Explain why you cannot find a greatest common multiple for a group of numbers.

2. Tell whether the LCM of a set of numbers can ever be smaller than any of the numbers in the set.

Homework Help  THINK central

Go to thinkcentral.com
Exercises 1–30, 31, 35, 37

Prep MA.6.A.5.1

GUIDED PRACTICE

See Example **1**   **1.** Pencils are sold in packs of 12, and erasers in packs of 9. Mr. Joplin wants to give each of 36 students a pencil and an eraser. What is the least number of packs he should buy so there are none left over?

See Example **2**   **Find the least common multiple (LCM).**

2. 3 and 5   **3.** 4 and 9   **4.** 2, 3, and 6   **5.** 2, 4, and 5

6. 4 and 12   **7.** 6 and 16   **8.** 4, 6, and 8   **9.** 2, 5, and 8

10. 6 and 10   **11.** 21 and 63   **12.** 3, 5, and 9   **13.** 5, 6, and 25

INDEPENDENT PRACTICE

See Example **1**   **14.** String-cheese sticks are sold in packs of 10, and celery sticks in packs of 15. Ms. Sobrino wants to give each of 30 students one string-cheese stick and one celery stick. What is the least number of packs she should buy so there are none left over?

See Example **2**   **Find the least common multiple (LCM).**

15. 2 and 8   **16.** 3 and 7   **17.** 4 and 10   **18.** 3 and 9

19. 3, 6, and 9   **20.** 4, 8, and 10   **21.** 4, 6, and 12   **22.** 4, 6, and 7

23. 3, 8, and 12   **24.** 3, 7, and 10   **25.** 2, 6, and 11   **26.** 2, 3, 6, and 9

27. 2, 4, 5, and 6   **28.** 10 and 11   **29.** 4, 5, and 7   **30.** 2, 3, 6, and 8

PRACTICE AND PROBLEM SOLVING

31. What is the LCM of 6 and 12?   **32.** What is the LCM of 5 and 11?

33. The diagram at right is a Venn diagram. The numbers in the red circle are multiples of 4. The numbers in the blue circle are multiples of 6. The numbers in the purple section are multiples of both 4 and 6.

Find the missing numbers in the Venn diagram.

a. a two-digit multiple of 4 that is not a multiple of 6

b. a two-digit multiple of 6 that is not a multiple of 4

c. the LCM of 4 and 6

d. a three-digit common multiple of 4 and 6

Find a pair of numbers that has the given characteristics.

34. The LCM of the two numbers is 26. One number is even and one is odd.

35. The LCM of the two numbers is 48. The sum of the numbers is 28.

36. The LCM of the two numbers is 60. The difference of the two numbers is 3.

○ = WORKED-OUT SOLUTIONS on p. WS5

37. During its grand opening weekend, a restaurant offered the specials shown in order to attract new customers.

GRAND OPENING SPECIALS

Every 8th customer: FREE APPETIZER!

Every 12th customer: FREE BEVERAGE!

Every 15th customer: FREE DESSERT!

    a. Which customer was the first to receive all three free items?

    b. Which customer was the first to receive a free appetizer and frozen yogurt?

    c. If the restaurant served 500 customers that weekend, how many of those customers received all three free items?

38. Choose a Strategy Sophia gave $\frac{1}{2}$ of her semi-precious-rock collection to her son. She gave $\frac{1}{2}$ of what she had left to her grandson. Then she gave $\frac{1}{2}$ of what she had left to her great-grandson. She kept 10 rocks for herself. How many rocks did she have in the beginning?

    A. 40   **B.** 80   **C.** 100   **D.** 160

39. Write About It Explain the steps you can use to find the LCM of two numbers. Choose two numbers to show an example of your method.

40. Challenge Find the LCM of each pair of numbers.

    a. 4 and 6   **b.** 8 and 9   **c.** 5 and 7   **d.** 8 and 10

When is the LCM of two numbers equal to the product of the two numbers?

Florida Spiral Review   **MA.6.A.3.2, MA.6.A.1.2, MA.6.A.5.2**

41. Multiple Choice Cheese cubes are sold in packs of 60. Crackers are sold in packs of 12. To make 60 snacks of 2 cheese cubes and 1 cracker, what is the least number of packs of each type needed?

    A. 2 cheese, 1 cracker   **C.** 2 cheese, 2 cracker

    B. 2 cheese, 5 cracker   **D.** 5 cheese, 2 cracker

42. Multiple Choice What is the least common multiple of 5 and 8?

    F. 40   **G.** 20   **H.** 80   **I.** 60

Determine whether the given value of the variable is a solution. (Lesson 2-5)

43. $p + 16 = 34$ for $p = 12$ **44.** $25 - d = 6$ for $d = 19$ **45.** $7n = 42$ for $n = 6$

Multiply. (Lesson 3-4)

46. 0.3×0.1 **47.** 0.16×0.5 **48.** 1.2×0.2 **49.** 0.7×9

Compare. Write <, >, or =. (Lesson 4-7)

50. $\frac{2}{9}$ ▨ $\frac{2}{13}$ **51.** $\frac{10}{11}$ ▨ $\frac{100}{110}$ **52.** $5\frac{2}{7}$ ▨ $3\frac{5}{7}$

Adding and Subtracting with Unlike Denominators

Prep for MA.6.A.5.1 Use equivalent forms of fractions . . . to solve problems. *Also* **Review of MA.5.A.2.2**

Vocabulary

least common denominator (LCD)

Remember!

Fractions that represent the same value are equivalent.

The Pacific Ocean covers $\frac{1}{3}$ of Earth's surface. The Atlantic Ocean covers $\frac{1}{5}$ of Earth's surface. To find the fraction of Earth's surface that is covered by both oceans, you can add $\frac{1}{3}$ and $\frac{1}{5}$, which are unlike fractions.

To add or subtract unlike fractions, first rewrite them as equivalent fractions with a common denominator.

EXAMPLE 1 *Social Studies Application*

What fraction of Earth's surface is covered by the Atlantic and Pacific Oceans? Add $\frac{1}{3}$ and $\frac{1}{5}$.

$$\begin{array}{r} \frac{1}{3} \\ + \frac{1}{5} \\ \hline \end{array}$$

Find a common denominator for 3 and 5: $3 \times 5 = 15$.

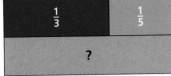

$\frac{1}{3} \rightarrow \frac{5}{15}$

Write equivalent fractions with 15 as the common denominator.

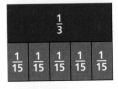

$+ \frac{1}{5} \rightarrow \frac{3}{15}$

$\frac{8}{15}$

Add the numerators. Keep the common denominator.

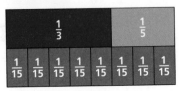

The Pacific and Atlantic Oceans cover $\frac{8}{15}$ of Earth's surface.

You can use *any* common denominator or the *least common denominator* to add and subtract unlike fractions. The **least common denominator (LCD)** is the least common multiple of the denominators.

Video **Lesson Tutorial Videos @ thinkcentral.com**

EXAMPLE 2 | **Adding and Subtracting Unlike Fractions**

Add or subtract. Write each answer in simplest form.

Method 1: Multiply the denominators.

A $\dfrac{9}{10} - \dfrac{7}{8}$

$\dfrac{9}{10} - \dfrac{7}{8}$ *Multiply the denominators. $10 \cdot 8 = 80$*

$\dfrac{72}{80} - \dfrac{70}{80}$ *Write equivalent fractions with a common denominator.*

$\dfrac{2}{80}$ *Subtract.*

$\dfrac{1}{40}$ *Write the answer in simplest form.*

Method 2: Use the LCD.

B $\dfrac{9}{10} - \dfrac{7}{8}$ *Multiples of 10: 10, 20, 30, 40, . . .*

$\dfrac{9}{10} - \dfrac{7}{8}$ *Multiples of 8: 8, 16, 24, 32, 40, . . . The LCD is 40.*

$\dfrac{36}{40} - \dfrac{35}{40}$ *Write equivalent fractions with a common denominator.*

$\dfrac{1}{40}$ *Subtract.*

Method 3: Use mental math.

C $\dfrac{5}{12} + \dfrac{1}{6}$

$\dfrac{5}{12} + \dfrac{1}{6}$ *Think: 12 is a multiple of 6, so the LCD is 12.*

$\dfrac{5}{12} + \dfrac{2}{12}$ *Rewrite $\frac{1}{6}$ with a denominator of 12.*

$\dfrac{7}{12}$ *Add.*

D $\dfrac{1}{3} - \dfrac{2}{9}$

$\dfrac{1}{3} - \dfrac{2}{9}$ *Think: 9 is a multiple of 3, so the LCD is 9.*

$\dfrac{3}{9} - \dfrac{2}{9}$ *Rewrite $\frac{1}{3}$ with a denominator of 9.*

$\dfrac{1}{9}$ *Subtract.*

Think and Discuss

1. **Explain** an advantage of using the least common denominator (LCD) when adding unlike fractions.

2. **Tell** when the least common denominator (LCD) of two fractions is the product of their denominators.

3. **Explain** how you can use mental math to subtract $\frac{1}{12}$ from $\frac{3}{4}$.

Exercises

Homework Help THINK central

Go to **thinkcentral.com**
Exercises 1-15, 17, 19, 25, 31, 37, 39, 41

Prep MA.6.A.5.1

GUIDED PRACTICE

See Example 1

1. A trailer hauling wood weighs $\frac{2}{3}$ ton. The trailer weighs $\frac{1}{4}$ ton without the wood. What is the weight of the wood?

See Example 2

Add or subtract. Write each answer in simplest form.

2. $\frac{1}{3} + \frac{1}{9}$ **3.** $\frac{7}{10} - \frac{2}{5}$ **4.** $\frac{2}{3} - \frac{2}{5}$ **5.** $\frac{1}{2} + \frac{3}{7}$

INDEPENDENT PRACTICE

See Example 1

6. Social Studies Approximately $\frac{1}{5}$ of the world's population lives in China. The people of India make up about $\frac{1}{6}$ of the world's population. What fraction of the world's people live in either China or India?

7. Cedric is making an Italian dish using a recipe that calls for $\frac{2}{3}$ cup of grated mozarella cheese. If Cedric has grated $\frac{1}{2}$ cup of mozarella cheese, how much more does he need to grate?

See Example 2

Add or subtract. Write each answer in simplest form.

8. $\frac{3}{4} - \frac{1}{2}$ **9.** $\frac{1}{6} + \frac{5}{12}$ **10.** $\frac{5}{6} - \frac{3}{4}$ **11.** $\frac{1}{5} + \frac{1}{4}$

12. $\frac{7}{10} + \frac{1}{8}$ **13.** $\frac{1}{3} + \frac{4}{5}$ **14.** $\frac{8}{9} - \frac{2}{3}$ **15.** $\frac{5}{8} + \frac{1}{2}$

PRACTICE AND PROBLEM SOLVING

Find each sum or difference. Write your answer in simplest form.

16. $\frac{3}{10} + \frac{1}{2}$ **17.** $\frac{4}{5} - \frac{1}{3}$ **18.** $\frac{5}{8} - \frac{1}{6}$ **19.** $\frac{1}{6} + \frac{2}{9}$

20. $\frac{2}{7} + \frac{2}{5}$ **21.** $\frac{7}{12} - \frac{1}{4}$ **22.** $\frac{7}{8} - \frac{2}{3}$ **23.** $\frac{2}{11} + \frac{2}{3}$

Evaluate each expression for $b = \frac{1}{2}$. Write your answer in simplest form.

24. $b + \frac{1}{3}$ **25.** $\frac{8}{9} - b$ **26.** $b - \frac{2}{11}$ **27.** $\frac{7}{10} - b$

28. $\frac{2}{7} + b$ **29.** $b + b$ **30.** $b - b$ **31.** $b + \frac{5}{8}$

Evaluate. Write each answer in simplest form.

32. $\frac{1}{3} + \frac{1}{9} + \frac{1}{3}$ **33.** $\frac{9}{10} - \frac{2}{10} - \frac{1}{5}$ **34.** $\frac{1}{2} + \frac{1}{4} - \frac{1}{8}$ **35.** $\frac{3}{7} + \frac{1}{14} + \frac{2}{28}$

36. $\frac{5}{6} - \frac{2}{3} + \frac{7}{12}$ **37.** $\frac{2}{3} + \frac{1}{4} - \frac{1}{6}$ **38.** $\frac{2}{9} + \frac{1}{6} + \frac{1}{3}$ **39.** $\frac{1}{2} - \frac{1}{4} + \frac{5}{8}$

40. Bailey spent $\frac{2}{3}$ of his monthly allowance at the movies and $\frac{1}{5}$ of it on baseball cards. What fraction of Bailey's allowance is left?

41. Multi-Step Betty is making punch for a party. She needs a total of $\frac{9}{10}$ gallon of water to add to fruit juice. In one container she has $\frac{1}{3}$ gallon water, and in another she has $\frac{2}{5}$ gallon. How much more water does she need?

○ = **WORKED-OUT SOLUTIONS**
on p. WS5

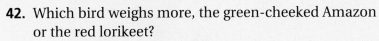

Life Science LINK

The red lorikeet, galah cockatoo, and green-cheeked Amazon are three very colorful birds. The African grey parrot is known for its ability to mimic sounds it hears. In fact, one African grey named Prudle had a vocabulary of almost 1,000 words.

42. Which bird weighs more, the green-cheeked Amazon or the red lorikeet?

43. What is the difference in weights between the green-cheeked Amazon and the red lorikeet?

44. Does the red lorikeet weigh more or less than $\frac{1}{2}$ lb? Explain.

45. **?** **What's the Error?** A student found the difference in weight between the African grey parrot and the galah cockatoo to be 1 lb. Explain the error. Then find the correct difference between the weights of these birds.

46. **Write About It** Explain how you find the difference in weight between the galah cockatoo and green-cheeked Amazon.

47. **Challenge** Find the average weight of the birds.

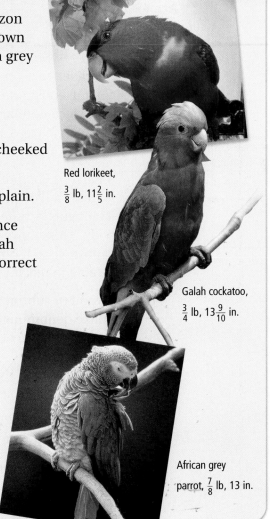

Red lorikeet, $\frac{3}{8}$ lb, $11\frac{2}{5}$ in.

Galah cockatoo, $\frac{3}{4}$ lb, $13\frac{9}{10}$ in.

African grey parrot, $\frac{7}{8}$ lb, 13 in.

Green-cheeked Amazon, $\frac{3}{5}$ lb, $13\frac{1}{5}$ in.

Florida Spiral Review

MA.6.A.3.2, MA.6.A.1.2

48. Multiple Choice One apple weighs $\frac{1}{4}$ lb and another apple weighs $\frac{3}{16}$ lb. Find the difference in their weights.

    A. $\frac{1}{16}$ lb   **B.** $\frac{1}{6}$ lb   **C.** $\frac{1}{4}$ lb   **D.** $\frac{7}{16}$ lb

49. Short Response Wanda walked $\frac{7}{24}$ mile more than Lori. Lori walked $\frac{5}{6}$ mile less than Jack. Wanda walked $\frac{3}{8}$ mile. How many miles did Jack walk? Give your answer in simplest form. Explain how you solved the problem.

Solve each equation. (Lesson 2-6)

50. $8 + m = 11$ **51.** $17 = d + 11$ **52.** $a + 5 = 21$ **53.** $19 = 12 + f$

Divide. (Lesson 3-5)

54. $1.40 \div 2$ **55.** $3.3 \div 3$ **56.** $0.85 \div 5$ **57.** $0.375 \div 3$

Chameleons can change color at any time to camouflage themselves. They live high in trees and are seldom seen on the ground.

A Parsons chameleon, which is the largest kind of chameleon, can extend its tongue $1\frac{1}{2}$ times the length of its body. This allows the chameleon to capture food it otherwise would not be able to reach.

To add or subtract mixed numbers with unlike denominators, you must first find a common denominator for the fractions.

The chameleon is the only animal capable of moving each eye independently of the other. A chameleon can turn its eyes about 360°.

EXAMPLE **1** **Adding and Subtracting Mixed Numbers**

Find each sum or difference. Write the answer in simplest form.

A $2\frac{3}{4} + 1\frac{1}{6}$

$3 + 1 = 4$

$2\frac{3}{4} \longrightarrow 2\frac{18}{24}$

$+ 1\frac{1}{6} \longrightarrow + 1\frac{4}{24}$

$\overline{\qquad 3\frac{22}{24} = 3\frac{11}{12}}$

Estimate the sum. Round each fraction to the nearest whole number.
Multiply the denominators. 4 · 6 = 24
Write equivalent fractions with a common denominator of 24.
Add the fractions and then the whole numbers, and simplify.

$3\frac{11}{12}$ is close to the estimate of 4. The answer is reasonable.

B $4\frac{5}{6} - 2\frac{2}{9}$

$5 - 2 = 3$

$4\frac{5}{6} \longrightarrow 4\frac{15}{18}$

$- 2\frac{2}{9} \longrightarrow - 2\frac{4}{18}$

$\overline{\qquad 2\frac{11}{18}}$

Estimate the difference.
The LCD of 6 and 9 is 18.
Write equivalent fractions with a common denominator of 18.
Subtract the fractions and then the whole numbers.

$2\frac{11}{18}$ is close to the estimate of 3. The answer is reasonable.

Video **Lesson Tutorial Videos @ thinkcentral.com**

Find each sum or difference. Write the answer in simplest form.

C $8\frac{2}{5} - 6\frac{3}{10}$

$8 - 6 = 2$ *Estimate the difference.*

Think: 10 is a multiple of 5, so 10 is the LCD.

$$8\frac{2}{5} \longrightarrow 8\frac{4}{10}$$

Write equivalent fractions with a common denominator of 10.

$$-6\frac{3}{10} \longrightarrow -6\frac{3}{10}$$

$$2\frac{1}{10}$$

Subtract the fractions and then the whole numbers.

$2\frac{1}{10}$ is close to the estimate of 2. The answer is reasonable.

EXAMPLE 2 *Life Science Application*

The length of a Parsons chameleon's body is $23\frac{1}{2}$ inches. The chameleon can extend its tongue $35\frac{1}{4}$ inches. What is the total length of its body and its tongue?

Add $23\frac{1}{2}$ and $35\frac{1}{4}$.

$$23\frac{1}{2} \longrightarrow 23\frac{2}{4}$$

Find a common denominator. Write equivalent fractions with the LCD, 4, as the denominator.

$$+35\frac{1}{4} \longrightarrow +35\frac{1}{4}$$

Add the fractions and then the whole numbers.

$$58\frac{3}{4}$$

The total length of the chameleon's body and tongue is $58\frac{3}{4}$ inches.

Helpful Hint

You can use mental math to find an LCD. *Think:* 4 is a multiple of 2 and 4.

Think and Discuss

1. **Tell** what mistake was made when subtracting $2\frac{1}{2}$ from $5\frac{3}{5}$ gave the following result: $5\frac{3}{5} - 2\frac{1}{2} = 3\frac{2}{3}$. Then find the correct answer.

2. **Explain** why you first find equivalent fractions when adding $1\frac{1}{5}$ and $1\frac{1}{2}$.

3. **Tell** how you know that $5\frac{1}{2} - 3\frac{1}{4}$ is more than 2.

Homework Help THINK central

Go to **thinkcentral.com**
Exercises 1-14, 21, 23, 27, 31, 33, 37, 45

Prep MA.6.A.5.1

GUIDED PRACTICE

See Example **1** Find each sum or difference. Write the answer in simplest form.

1. $7\frac{1}{12} + 3\frac{1}{3}$ **2.** $2\frac{1}{6} + 2\frac{3}{8}$ **3.** $8\frac{5}{6} - 2\frac{3}{4}$ **4.** $6\frac{6}{7} - 1\frac{1}{2}$

See Example **2** **5. Life Science** A sea turtle traveled $7\frac{3}{4}$ hours in two days. It traveled $3\frac{1}{2}$ hours on the first day. How many hours did it travel on the second day?

INDEPENDENT PRACTICE

See Example **1** Find each sum or difference. Write the answer in simplest form.

6. $3\frac{9}{10} - 1\frac{2}{5}$ **7.** $2\frac{1}{6} + 4\frac{5}{12}$ **8.** $5\frac{9}{11} + 5\frac{1}{3}$ **9.** $9\frac{3}{4} - 3\frac{1}{2}$

10. $6\frac{3}{10} + 3\frac{2}{5}$ **11.** $10\frac{2}{3} - 2\frac{1}{12}$ **12.** $14\frac{3}{4} - 6\frac{5}{12}$ **13.** $19\frac{1}{10} + 10\frac{1}{2}$

See Example **2** **14. School** The drama club rehearsed $1\frac{3}{4}$ hours Friday and $3\frac{1}{6}$ hours Saturday. How many total hours did the students rehearse?

PRACTICE AND PROBLEM SOLVING

Add or subtract. Write each answer in simplest form.

15. $15\frac{5}{6} + 18\frac{2}{3}$ **16.** $17\frac{1}{6} + 12\frac{1}{4}$ **17.** $23\frac{9}{10} - 20\frac{3}{9}$ **18.** $32\frac{5}{7} - 13\frac{2}{5}$

19. $28\frac{11}{12} - 8\frac{5}{9}$ **20.** $12\frac{2}{11} + 20\frac{2}{3}$ **21.** $36\frac{5}{8} - 24\frac{5}{12}$ **22.** $48\frac{9}{11} + 2\frac{1}{4}$

23. Measurement Kyle's backpack weighs $14\frac{7}{20}$ lb. Kirsten's backpack weighs $12\frac{1}{4}$ lb.

a. How much do the backpacks weigh together?

b. How much more does Kyle's backpack weigh than Kirsten's backpack?

c. Kyle takes his $3\frac{1}{4}$ lb math book out of his backpack. How much does his backpack weigh now?

Add or subtract. Write each answer as a fraction in simplest form.

24. $0.3 + \frac{2}{5}$ **25.** $\frac{4}{5} + 0.9$ **26.** $5\frac{4}{5} - 3.2$ **27.** $14\frac{1}{4} + 9.5$

28. $6.3 + \frac{4}{5}$ **29.** $23\frac{3}{4} - 10.5$ **30.** $18.9 - 6\frac{1}{2}$ **31.** $21.8 - 3\frac{3}{5}$

32. A wheelbarrow can hold $52\frac{1}{2}$ lb. Five rocks that weigh $9\frac{5}{8}$ lb, $12\frac{1}{6}$ lb, $9\frac{1}{4}$ lb, $11\frac{1}{8}$ lb, and $10\frac{1}{2}$ lb are to be loaded into the wheelbarrow. Can the wheelbarrow hold all five rocks? Explain.

33. The route Jo usually takes to work is $4\frac{2}{5}$ mi. After heavy rains, when that road is flooded, she must take a different route that is $4\frac{9}{10}$ mi. How much longer is Jo's alternate route?

34. Multi-Step Mr. Hansley used $1\frac{2}{3}$ c of flour to make muffins and $4\frac{1}{2}$ c to make bread. If he has $3\frac{5}{6}$ c left, how much flour did Mr. Hansley have before making the muffins and bread?

○ = WORKED-OUT SOLUTIONS
on p. WS5

Evaluate each expression for $n = 2\frac{1}{3}$. Write your answer in simplest form.

35. $2\frac{2}{3} + n$ **36.** $5 - \left(1\frac{2}{3} + n\right)$ **37.** $n - 1\frac{1}{4}$ **38.** $5 - n$

39. $n + 5\frac{7}{9}$ **40.** $6 + \left(3\frac{4}{9} + n\right)$ **41.** $2\frac{1}{3} - n$ **42.** $3 + \left(2\frac{3}{4} - n\right)$

43. Life Science Elephants can communicate through low-frequency infrasonic rumbles. Such sounds can travel from $\frac{1}{8}$ km to $9\frac{1}{2}$ km. Find the difference between these two distances.

Use the drawing for Exercises 44–47.

44. Sarah is a landscape architect designing a garden. Based on her drawing, how much longer is the south side of the building than the west side?

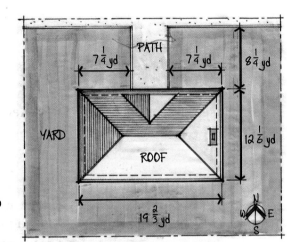

45. Sarah needs to determine how many azalea bushes she can plant along both sides of the path. What is the sum of the lengths of the two sides of the path?

46. How wide is the path?

47. What's the Question? The answer is $63\frac{2}{3}$ yd. What is the question?

48. Write About It Explain how you would use the sum of $\frac{2}{5}$ and $\frac{1}{3}$ to find the sum of $10\frac{2}{5}$ and $6\frac{1}{3}$.

49. Challenge Find each missing numerator.

a. $3\frac{x}{9} + 4\frac{2}{9} = 7\frac{7}{9}$ **b.** $1\frac{3}{10} + 9\frac{x}{2} = 10\frac{4}{5}$

Florida Spiral Review

MA.6.A.1.2, MA.6.A.5.1

50. Multiple Choice Which expression does NOT have a sum of $6\frac{3}{10}$?

A. $1\frac{1}{20} + 5\frac{1}{4}$ **B.** $3\frac{1}{5} + 3\frac{1}{10}$ **C.** $3\frac{2}{5} + 3\frac{1}{5}$ **D.** $4\frac{3}{20} + 2\frac{3}{20}$

51. Multiple Choice A bumblebee bat is $1\frac{1}{5}$ inches in length. A thread snake is $4\frac{1}{4}$ inches in length. How much longer is a thread snake than a bumblebee bat?

F. $3\frac{1}{4}$ inches **G.** $3\frac{1}{5}$ inches **H.** $3\frac{1}{10}$ inches **I.** $3\frac{1}{20}$ inches

Find each quotient. (Lesson 3-6)

52. $2.5 \div 0.5$ **53.** $2.56 \div 1.6$ **54.** $1.17 \div 0.9$ **55.** $1.495 \div 0.65$

Write each decimal as a fraction or mixed number. (Lesson 4-5)

56. 0.35 **57.** 1.5 **58.** 0.7 **59.** 1.4

Regrouping to Subtract Mixed Numbers

Prep for MA.6.A.5.1
Use equivalent forms of fractions . . . to solve problems. *Also* **Review of MA.5.A.2.2**

Jimmy and his mother planted a tree when it was $1\frac{3}{4}$ ft tall. Now the tree is $2\frac{1}{4}$ ft tall. How much has the tree grown since it was planted?

The difference in the heights can be represented by the expression $2\frac{1}{4} - 1\frac{3}{4}$.

You will need to regroup $2\frac{1}{4}$ because the fraction in $1\frac{3}{4}$ is greater than $\frac{1}{4}$.

Divide *one whole* of $2\frac{1}{4}$ into fourths.

1	1	$\frac{1}{4}$

1	$\frac{1}{4}$	$\frac{1}{4}$	$\frac{1}{4}$	$\frac{1}{4}$	$\frac{1}{4}$

Regroup $2\frac{1}{4}$ as $1\frac{5}{4}$.

1	$\frac{1}{4}$	$\frac{1}{4}$	$\frac{1}{4}$	$\frac{1}{4}$	$\frac{1}{4}$

Remove $1\frac{3}{4}$.

$$2\frac{1}{4} \rightarrow 1\frac{5}{4}$$
$$-1\frac{3}{4} \rightarrow -1\frac{3}{4}$$
$$\frac{2}{4} = \frac{1}{2}$$

The tree has grown $\frac{1}{2}$ ft since it was planted.

EXAMPLE **1** **Regrouping Mixed Numbers**

Subtract. Write each answer in simplest form.

A $6\frac{5}{12} - 2\frac{7}{12}$

$6 - 3 = 3$

$$6\frac{5}{12} \longrightarrow 5\frac{17}{12}$$
$$-2\frac{7}{12} \longrightarrow -2\frac{7}{12}$$
$$3\frac{10}{12}$$
$$= 3\frac{5}{6}$$

Estimate the difference.

Regroup $6\frac{5}{12}$ as $5 + 1\frac{5}{12} = 5 + \frac{12}{12} + \frac{5}{12}$.

Subtract the fractions and then the whole numbers.

Write the answer in simplest form.

$3\frac{5}{6}$ is close to the estimate of 3. The answer is reasonable.

Video **Lesson Tutorial Videos** @ thinkcentral.com

Subtract. Write each answer in simplest form.

B $8 - 5\frac{3}{4}$

$8 - 6 = 2$ *Estimate the difference.*

$$8 \longrightarrow 7\frac{4}{4}$$
$$- 5\frac{3}{4} \longrightarrow - 5\frac{3}{4}$$
$$\overline{\hspace{2cm}} \qquad \overline{2\frac{1}{4}}$$

Write 8 as a mixed number with a denominator of 4. Regroup 8 as $7 + \frac{4}{4}$.

Subtract the fractions and then the whole numbers.

$2\frac{1}{4}$ is close to the estimate of 2. The answer is reasonable.

EXAMPLE **Measurement Application**

Dave is re-covering an old couch and cushions. He determines that he needs 17 yards of fabric for the job.

A Dave has $1\frac{2}{3}$ yards of fabric. How many more yards does he need?

$$17 \longrightarrow 16\frac{3}{3}$$
$$- 1\frac{2}{3} \longrightarrow - 1\frac{2}{3}$$
$$\overline{\hspace{2cm}} \qquad \overline{15\frac{1}{3}}$$

Write 17 as a mixed number with a denominator of 3. Regroup 17 as $16 + \frac{3}{3}$.

Subtract the fractions and then the whole numbers.

Dave needs another $15\frac{1}{3}$ yards of material.

B If Dave uses $9\frac{5}{6}$ yards of fabric to cover the couch frame, how much of the 17 yards will he have left?

$$17 \longrightarrow 16\frac{6}{6}$$
$$- 9\frac{5}{6} \longrightarrow - 9\frac{5}{6}$$
$$\overline{\hspace{2cm}} \qquad \overline{7\frac{1}{6}}$$

Write 17 as a mixed number with a denominator of 6. Regroup 17 as $16 + \frac{6}{6}$.

Subtract the fractions and then the whole numbers.

Dave will have $7\frac{1}{6}$ yards of material left.

Think and Discuss

1. **Explain** why you regroup 2 as $1\frac{8}{8}$ instead of $1\frac{3}{3}$ when you find $2 - 1\frac{3}{8}$.

2. **Give an example** of a subtraction expression in which you would need to regroup the first mixed number to subtract.

3. **Explain** whether you would need to regroup to simplify the expression $7\frac{7}{8} - 2\frac{5}{8} - 1\frac{3}{8}$.

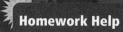

Homework Help THINK central

Go to **thinkcentral.com**
Exercises 1-15, 19, 23, 25, 27, 37, 39, 41

 Prep MA.6.A.5.1

GUIDED PRACTICE

See Example 1 **Subtract. Write each answer in simplest form.**

1. $2\frac{1}{2} - 1\frac{3}{4}$ **2.** $8\frac{2}{9} - 2\frac{7}{9}$ **3.** $3\frac{2}{6} - 1\frac{2}{3}$ **4.** $7\frac{1}{4} - 4\frac{11}{12}$

See Example 2 **5.** Mr. Jones purchased a 4-pound bag of flour. He used $1\frac{2}{5}$ pounds of flour to make bread. How many pounds of flour are left?

INDEPENDENT PRACTICE

See Example 1 **Subtract. Write each answer in simplest form.**

6. $6\frac{3}{11} - 3\frac{10}{11}$ **7.** $9\frac{2}{5} - 5\frac{3}{5}$ **8.** $4\frac{3}{10} - 3\frac{3}{5}$ **9.** $10\frac{1}{2} - 2\frac{5}{8}$

10. $11\frac{1}{4} - 9\frac{3}{8}$ **11.** $7\frac{5}{9} - 2\frac{5}{6}$ **12.** $6 - 2\frac{2}{3}$ **13.** $5\frac{3}{10} - 3\frac{1}{2}$

See Example 2 **14. Measurement** A standard piece of notebook paper has a length of 11 inches and a width of $8\frac{1}{2}$ inches. What is the difference between these two measures?

15. Chad opened a 10-pound bag of birdseed to refill his feeders. He used $3\frac{1}{3}$ pounds to fill them. How many pounds of birdseed were left?

PRACTICE AND PROBLEM SOLVING

Find each difference. Write the answer in simplest form.

16. $8 - 6\frac{4}{7}$ **17.** $13\frac{1}{9} - 11\frac{2}{3}$ **18.** $10\frac{3}{4} - 6\frac{1}{2}$ **19.** $13 - 4\frac{2}{11}$

20. $15\frac{2}{5} - 12\frac{3}{4}$ **21.** $17\frac{5}{9} - 6\frac{1}{3}$ **22.** $18\frac{1}{4} - 14\frac{3}{8}$ **23.** $20\frac{1}{6} - 7\frac{4}{9}$

24. Economics A single share of stock in a company cost $\$23\frac{2}{5}$ on Monday. By Tuesday, the cost of a share in the company had fallen to $\$19\frac{1}{5}$. By how much did the price of a share fall?

25. Jasmine is $62\frac{1}{2}$ inches tall. Her brother, Antoine, is $69\frac{3}{4}$ inches tall. What is the difference, in inches, in their heights?

Simplify each expression. Write the answer in simplest form.

26. $4\frac{2}{3} + 5\frac{1}{3} - 7\frac{1}{8}$ **27.** $12\frac{5}{9} - 6\frac{2}{3} + 1\frac{4}{9}$ **28.** $7\frac{7}{8} - 4\frac{1}{8} + 1\frac{1}{4}$

29. $7\frac{4}{11} - 2\frac{8}{11} - \frac{10}{11}$ **30.** $8\frac{1}{3} - 5\frac{8}{9} + 8\frac{1}{2}$ **31.** $5\frac{2}{7} - 2\frac{1}{14} + 8\frac{5}{14}$

32. Multi-Step Octavio used a brand new 6-hour tape to record some television shows. He recorded a movie that is $1\frac{1}{2}$ hours long and a cooking show that is $1\frac{1}{4}$ hours long. How much time is left on the tape?

○ = **WORKED-OUT SOLUTIONS**
on p. WS5

Evaluate each expression for $a = 6\frac{2}{3}$, $b = 8\frac{1}{2}$, and $c = 1\frac{3}{4}$. Write the answer in simplest form.

33. $a - c$ **34.** $b - c$ **35.** $b - a$ **36.** $10 - b$

37. $b - (a + c)$ **38.** $c + (b - a)$ **39.** $(a + b) - c$ **40.** $(10 - c) - a$

Use the table for Exercises 41–44.

41. Gustavo is working at a gift wrap center. He has 2 yd^2 of wrapping paper to wrap a small box. How much wrapping paper will be left after he wraps the gift?

42. Gustavo must now wrap two extra-large boxes. If he has 6 yd^2 of wrapping paper, how much more wrapping paper will he need to wrap the two gifts?

43. To wrap a large box, Gustavo used $\frac{3}{4}$ yd^2 less wrapping paper than the amount listed in the table. How many square yards did he use to wrap the gift?

Gustavo's Gift Wrap Table

Gift Size	Paper Needed (yd^2)
Small	$\frac{11}{12}$
Medium	$1\frac{5}{9}$
Large	$2\frac{2}{3}$
X-large	$3\frac{1}{9}$

44. What's the Error? Gustavo calculated the difference between the amount needed to wrap an extra-large box and the amount needed to wrap a medium box to be $2\frac{4}{9}$ yd^2. Explain his error and find the correct answer.

45. Write About It Explain why you write equivalent fractions before you regroup them. Explain why you do not regroup them first.

46. Challenge Fill in the box with a mixed number that makes the inequality true.

$$12\frac{1}{2} - 8\frac{3}{4} > 10 - \boxed{}$$

Florida Spiral Review MA.6.A.3.1, MA.6.A.1.2

47. Multiple Choice Find the difference of $5 - \frac{4}{9}$.

A. $5\frac{5}{9}$ **B.** $5\frac{1}{9}$ **C.** $4\frac{5}{9}$ **D.** $4\frac{1}{9}$

48. Gridded Response Tami worked 4 hours on Saturday at the city pool. She spent $1\frac{3}{4}$ hours cleaning the pool and the remaining time working as a lifeguard. How many hours did Tami spend working as a lifeguard?

49. Write an expression for the sequence in the table. (Lesson 2-4)

Position	1	2	3	4	n
Value of Term	4	6	8	10	

Find each product. (Lesson 3-4)

50. 0.45×1.2 **51.** 3.4×0.09 **52.** 0.6×1.1 **53.** 5.5×0.7

Quiz for Lessons 5-1 Through 5-4

5-1 Least Common Multiple

1. Markers are sold in packs of 8, and crayons are sold in packs of 16. If there are 32 students in Mrs. Reading's art class, what is the least number of packs needed so that each student can have one marker and one crayon and none will be left over?

2. Cans of soup are sold in packs of 24, and packets of crackers are sold in groups of 4. If there are 120 people to be fed and each will get one can of soup and one packet of crackers, what is the least number of packs needed to feed everyone such that no crackers or soup are left over?

Find the least common multiple (LCM).

3. 4 and 6   4. 2 and 15   5. 3, 5, and 9   6. 4, 6, and 10

5-2 Adding and Subtracting with Unlike Denominators

Add or subtract. Write each answer in simplest form.

7. $\frac{5}{7} - \frac{3}{14}$ 8. $\frac{7}{8} + \frac{1}{24}$ 9. $\frac{8}{9} - \frac{1}{10}$ 10. $\frac{1}{6} + \frac{1}{2}$

11. Alexia needs to add $\frac{2}{3}$ cup of sugar for the recipe she is making. She has added $\frac{1}{2}$ cup already. How much more sugar does she need to add?

12. Brad ran $\frac{5}{6}$ mile on Monday and $\frac{5}{8}$ mile on Tuesday. How much farther did Brad run on Monday?

5-3 Adding and Subtracting Mixed Numbers

Find each sum or difference. Write each answer in simplest form.

13. $2\frac{9}{13} - 1\frac{1}{26}$ 14. $9\frac{5}{10} + 11\frac{4}{5}$ 15. $7\frac{8}{9} - 1\frac{1}{18}$ 16. $2\frac{4}{5} + 1\frac{1}{10}$

17. Lizann bought a piece of fabric $2\frac{2}{3}$ yards long. She returned to the store later and purchased another piece of fabric $1\frac{1}{4}$ yards long. What is the total length of the fabric Lizann bought?

18. Andy has a picture frame with a photo opening that measures $1\frac{3}{4}$ inches in width and $2\frac{1}{2}$ inches in length. How much longer is the length than the width?

5-4 Regrouping to Subtract Mixed Numbers

Subtract. Write each answer in simplest form.

19. $2\frac{1}{13} - 1\frac{1}{26}$ 20. $7\frac{1}{3} - 5\frac{7}{9}$ 21. $3\frac{3}{10} - 1\frac{4}{5}$ 22. $10\frac{1}{2} - 5\frac{2}{3}$

23. Mary Ann buys $4\frac{2}{5}$ pounds of bananas. She uses $1\frac{1}{2}$ pounds making banana bread. How many pounds of bananas does she have left?

Focus on Problem Solving

Solve

- **Choose the operation: multiplication or division**

Read the whole problem before you try to solve it. Determine what action is taking place in the problem. Then decide whether you need to multiply or divide in order to solve the problem.

If you are asked to combine equal groups, you need to multiply. If you are asked to share something equally or to separate something into equal groups, you need to divide.

Action	Operation	
Combining equal groups	Multiplication	
Sharing things equally or separating into equal groups	Division	

Read each problem, and determine the action taking place. Choose an operation to solve the problem. Then solve, and write the answer in simplest form.

1 Jason picked 30 cups of raspberries. He put them in giant freezer bags with 5 cups in each bag. How many bags does he have?

2 When the cranberry flowers start to open in June, cranberry growers usually bring in about $2\frac{1}{2}$ beehives per acre of cranberries to pollinate the flowers. A grower has 36 acres of cranberries. About how many beehives does she need?

3 A recipe that makes 3 cranberry banana loaves calls for 4 cups of cranberries. Linh wants to make only 1 loaf. How many cups of cranberries does she need?

4 Clay wants to double a recipe for blueberry muffins that calls for 1 cup of blueberries. How many blueberries will he need?

Focus on Problem Solving **211**

Multiplying Fractions by Whole Numbers

MA.6.A.1.2
Multiply and divide fractions . . . efficiently.
Also **MA.6.A.1.3**

Recall that multiplication by a whole number can be represented as repeated addition. For example, $4 \cdot 5 = 5 + 5 + 5 + 5$. You can multiply a whole number by a fraction using the same method.

$$3 \cdot \frac{1}{4} = \frac{1}{4} + \frac{1}{4} + \frac{1}{4} = \frac{3}{4}$$

 **Math**
@ thinkcentral.com

There is another way to multiply with fractions. Remember that a whole number can be written as an improper fraction with 1 in the denominator. So $3 = \frac{3}{1}$.

$$\frac{3}{1} \cdot \frac{1}{4} = \frac{3 \cdot 1}{1 \cdot 4} = \frac{3}{4}$$ ⟵ Multiply numerators.
⟵ Multiply denominators.

Notice that when you multiply a proper fraction and a number greater than 1, the product is between the factors.

EXAMPLE **Multiplying Fractions and Whole Numbers**

Multiply. Write each answer in simplest form.

Method 1: Use repeated addition.

A $5 \cdot \frac{1}{8}$

$5 \cdot \frac{1}{8} = \frac{1}{8} + \frac{1}{8} + \frac{1}{8} + \frac{1}{8} + \frac{1}{8}$ *Write $5 \cdot \frac{1}{8}$ as addition. Add the numerators.*

$= \frac{5}{8}$

B $3 \cdot \frac{1}{9}$

$3 \cdot \frac{1}{9} = \frac{1}{9} + \frac{1}{9} + \frac{1}{9}$ *Write $3 \cdot \frac{1}{9}$ as addition. Add the numerators.*

$= \frac{3}{9}$

$= \frac{1}{3}$ *Write your answer in simplest form.*

Method 2: Multiply.

C $4 \cdot \frac{7}{8}$

$\frac{4}{1} \cdot \frac{7}{8} = \frac{28}{8}$ *Multiply.*

$= \frac{7}{2} \text{ or } 3\frac{1}{2}$ *Write your answer in simplest form.*

    Video **Lesson Tutorial Videos** @ thinkcentral.com

EXAMPLE **2** **Evaluating Fraction Expressions**

Evaluate **6x** for each value of x. Write each answer in simplest form.

A $x = \frac{1}{8}$

$6x$	*Write the expression.*
$6 \cdot \frac{1}{8}$	*Substitute $\frac{1}{8}$ for x.*
$\frac{6}{1} \cdot \frac{1}{8} = \frac{6}{8}$	*Multiply.*
$= \frac{3}{4}$	*Write your answer in simplest form.*

B $x = \frac{2}{3}$

$6x$	*Write the expression.*
$6 \cdot \frac{2}{3}$	*Substitute $\frac{2}{3}$ for x.*
$\frac{6}{1} \cdot \frac{2}{3} = \frac{12}{3}$	*Multiply.*
$= \frac{4}{1}$	
$= 4$	

Remember!

$\frac{12}{3}$ means $12 \div 3$.

Sometimes the denominator of an improper fraction will divide into the numerator without a remainder, as in Example 2B. When this happens, the improper fraction is equivalent to a whole number, not a mixed number.

$$\frac{12}{3} = 4$$

EXAMPLE **3** *Social Studies Application*

Any proposed amendment to the U.S. Constitution must be ratified, or approved, by $\frac{3}{4}$ of the states. When the 13th Amendment abolishing slavery was proposed in 1865, there were 36 states. How many states needed to ratify this amendment in order for it to pass?

To find $\frac{3}{4}$ of 36, multiply.

$$\frac{3}{4} \cdot 36 = \frac{3}{4} \cdot \frac{36}{1}$$
$$= \frac{108}{4}$$
$$= 27$$

Divide 108 by 4 and write your answer in simplest form.

For the 13th Amendment to pass, 27 states had to ratify it.

Think and Discuss

1. Describe a model you could use to show the product of $4 \cdot \frac{1}{5}$.

2. Choose the expression that is correctly multiplied.

$$2 \cdot \frac{3}{7} = \frac{6}{7} \qquad 2 \cdot \frac{3}{7} = \frac{6}{14}$$

3. Explain how you know without actually multiplying that $\frac{5}{8} \cdot 16$ is greater than 8.

Homework Help

Go to **thinkcentral.com**
Exercises 1-30, 33, 35, 37, 43, 45, 47, 51

MA.6.A.1.2, MA.6.A.1.3

GUIDED PRACTICE

See Example **1** Multiply. Write each answer in simplest form.

1. $8 \cdot \frac{1}{9}$ **2.** $2 \cdot \frac{1}{5}$ **3.** $12 \cdot \frac{1}{4}$ **4.** $7 \cdot \frac{4}{9}$

5. $3 \cdot \frac{1}{7}$ **6.** $4 \cdot \frac{2}{11}$ **7.** $8 \cdot \frac{3}{4}$ **8.** $18 \cdot \frac{1}{3}$

See Example **2** Evaluate $12x$ for each value of x. Write each answer in simplest form.

9. $x = \frac{2}{3}$ **10.** $x = \frac{1}{2}$ **11.** $x = \frac{3}{4}$ **12.** $x = \frac{5}{6}$

See Example **3** **13.** The school Community Service Club has 45 members. Of these 45 members, $\frac{3}{5}$ are boys. How many boys are members of the Community Service Club?

INDEPENDENT PRACTICE

See Example **1** Multiply. Write each answer in simplest form.

14. $4 \cdot \frac{1}{10}$ **15.** $6 \cdot \frac{1}{8}$ **16.** $3 \cdot \frac{1}{12}$ **17.** $2 \cdot \frac{2}{5}$

18. $6 \cdot \frac{10}{11}$ **19.** $2 \cdot \frac{3}{11}$ **20.** $15 \cdot \frac{2}{15}$ **21.** $20 \cdot \frac{1}{2}$

See Example **2** Evaluate $8x$ for each value of x. Write each answer in simplest form.

22. $x = \frac{1}{2}$ **23.** $x = \frac{3}{4}$ **24.** $x = \frac{1}{8}$ **25.** $x = \frac{1}{4}$

26. $x = \frac{2}{5}$ **27.** $x = \frac{5}{7}$ **28.** $x = \frac{7}{8}$ **29.** $x = \frac{4}{9}$

See Example **3** **30.** **School** Kiesha spent 120 minutes completing her homework last night. Of those minutes, $\frac{1}{6}$ were spent on Spanish. How many minutes did Kiesha spend on her Spanish homework?

PRACTICE AND PROBLEM SOLVING

Evaluate each expression. Write each answer in simplest form.

31. $12b$ for $b = \frac{7}{12}$ **32.** $20m$ for $m = \frac{1}{20}$ **33.** $33z$ for $z = \frac{5}{11}$

34. $\frac{2}{3}y$ for $y = 18$ **35.** $\frac{1}{4}x$ for $x = 20$ **36.** $\frac{3}{5}a$ for $a = 30$

37. $\frac{4}{5}c$ for $c = 12$ **38.** $14x$ for $x = \frac{3}{8}$ **39.** $\frac{9}{10}n$ for $n = 50$

Compare. Write <, >, or =.

40. $9 \cdot \frac{1}{16}$ ▆ $\frac{1}{2}$ **41.** $15 \cdot \frac{2}{5}$ ▆ 5 **42.** $\frac{8}{13}$ ▆ $4 \cdot \frac{2}{13}$

43. $3 \cdot \frac{2}{9}$ ▆ $\frac{2}{3}$ **44.** $6 \cdot \frac{4}{15}$ ▆ $\frac{11}{24}$ **45.** 5 ▆ $12 \cdot \frac{3}{4}$

46. $3 \cdot \frac{1}{7}$ ▆ $3 \cdot \frac{1}{5}$ **47.** $7 \cdot \frac{3}{4}$ ▆ $6 \cdot \frac{3}{7}$ **48.** $2 \cdot \frac{5}{6}$ ▆ $6 \cdot \frac{2}{5}$

49. Denise spent $55 shopping. Of that $55, she spent $\frac{3}{5}$ on a pair of shoes. How much money did Denise spend on the pair of shoes?

○ = WORKED-OUT SOLUTIONS
on p. WS6

GENERAL SHERMAN

The General Sherman, a giant sequoia tree in California's Sequoia National Park, is one of the largest trees in the world at 275 ft tall.

California also has some of the nation's tallest grand firs, ponderosa pines, and sugar pines. The table shows how the heights of these trees compare with the height of the General Sherman. For example, the grand fir is $\frac{23}{25}$ the height of the General Sherman.

50. Find the heights of the trees in the table. Write your answers in simplest form.

51. The world's tallest bluegum eucalyptus tree is $\frac{3}{5}$ the height of the General Sherman tree. How tall is this bluegum eucalyptus?

52. **? What's the Question?** Joshua trees can grow to be 40 ft tall. The answer is $\frac{8}{55}$. What is the question?

53. **✐ Write About It** Find $\frac{1}{5}$ the height of the General Sherman. Then divide the height of the General Sherman by 5. What do you notice? Why does this make sense?

54. **★ Challenge** The world's tallest incense cedar tree is 152 ft tall. What is $\frac{1}{5}$ of $\frac{1}{2}$ of $\frac{1}{4}$ of 152?

Tree Heights Compared with the General Sherman	
Tallest Grand Fir	$\frac{23}{25}$
Tallest Ponderosa Pine	$\frac{41}{50}$
Tallest Sugar Pine	$\frac{21}{25}$

Source: The Top 10 of Everything 2000

Florida Spiral Review   MA.6.A.1.2, MA.6.A.1.3, MA.6.A.3.1

55. Multiple Choice A recipe uses $\frac{1}{3}$ cup of sugar. Daniela doubled the recipe. How much sugar did she use?

A. $\frac{1}{4}$ cup   **B.** $\frac{1}{3}$ cup   **C.** $\frac{2}{3}$ cup   **D.** $\frac{3}{4}$ cup

56. Extended Response Mario bought $\frac{1}{5}$ pound of turkey. Rose bought four times as much turkey as Mario. And Celia bought 2 times as much as Rose. How many pounds of turkey did Rose buy? How many pounds did Celia buy? How much more did Celia buy than Mario? Show your work.

Write each phrase as a numerical or algebraic expression. (Lesson 2-3)

57. w less than 75   **58.** the product of n and 16   **59.** the quotient of p and 7

60. Jennifer has 50 oz of formula to make bottles for her twin babies. Each bottle needs to have 6.5 oz of formula. How many bottles can Jennifer make? (Lesson 3-7)

MA.6.A.1.2
Multiply and divide fractions . . . efficiently.
Also **MA.6.A.1.3**

On average, people spend $\frac{1}{3}$ of their lives asleep. About $\frac{1}{4}$ of the time they sleep, they dream. What fraction of a lifetime does a person typically spend dreaming?

One way to find $\frac{1}{4}$ of $\frac{1}{3}$ is to make a model.

$$\frac{1}{4} \cdot \frac{1}{3} = \frac{1}{12}$$

Your brain keeps working even when you're asleep. It makes sure that you keep breathing and that your heart keeps beating.

Notice that there is 1 section where the shading overlaps, and the product of the numerators is 1. Notice that there are 12 sections in the model, and the product of the denominators is 12. You can use these observations to write a rule for multiplying fractions.

$$\frac{1}{4} \cdot \frac{1}{3} = \frac{1 \cdot 1}{4 \cdot 3}$$ ⟵ *Multiply the numerators.*
  ⟵ *Multiply the denominators.*

$$= \frac{1}{12}$$ *The answer is in simplest form.*

A person typically spends $\frac{1}{12}$ of his or her lifetime dreaming.

EXAMPLE 1 **Multiplying Fractions**

Multiply. Write each answer in simplest form.

Helpful Hint

Notice that when you multiply two proper fractions, the product is less than either factor.

A $\frac{1}{3} \cdot \frac{3}{5}$

$$\frac{1}{3} \cdot \frac{3}{5} = \frac{1 \cdot 3}{3 \cdot 5}$$ *Multiply numerators. Multiply denominators.*

$$= \frac{3}{15}$$ *The GCF of 3 and 15 is 3.*

$$= \frac{1}{5}$$ *The answer is in simplest form.*

B $\frac{6}{7} \cdot \frac{2}{3}$

$$\frac{\overset{2}{\cancel{6}}}{7} \cdot \frac{2}{\underset{1}{\cancel{3}}} = \frac{2}{7} \cdot \frac{2}{1}$$ *Use the GCF to simplify the fractions before multiplying. The GCF of 6 and 3 is 3.*

$$= \frac{2 \cdot 2}{7 \cdot 1}$$ *Multiply numerators. Multiply denominators.*

$$= \frac{4}{7}$$ *The answer is in simplest form.*

Video **Lesson Tutorial Videos** @ **thinkcentral.com**

Multiply. Write each answer in simplest form.

C $\dfrac{3}{8} \cdot \dfrac{2}{9}$

$\dfrac{3}{8} \cdot \dfrac{2}{9} = \dfrac{3 \cdot 2}{8 \cdot 9}$ *Multiply numerators. Multiply denominators.*

$= \dfrac{6}{72}$ *The GCF of 6 and 72 is 6.*

$= \dfrac{1}{12}$ *The answer is in simplest form.*

EXAMPLE 2   **Evaluating Fraction Expressions**

Evaluate the expression $a \cdot \dfrac{1}{3}$ for each value of a. Write the answer in simplest form.

A $a = \dfrac{5}{8}$ $a \cdot \dfrac{1}{3}$

$\dfrac{5}{8} \cdot \dfrac{1}{3}$ *Substitute $\dfrac{5}{8}$ for a.*

$\dfrac{5 \cdot 1}{8 \cdot 3}$ *Multiply.*

$\dfrac{5}{24}$ *The answer is in simplest form.*

> **Helpful Hint**
>
> You can look for a common factor in a numerator and a denominator to determine whether you can simplify before multiplying.

B $a = \dfrac{9}{10}$ $a \cdot \dfrac{1}{3}$

$\dfrac{9}{10} \cdot \dfrac{1}{3}$ *Substitute $\dfrac{9}{10}$ for a.*

$\dfrac{\overset{3}{\cancel{9}}}{10} \cdot \dfrac{1}{\underset{1}{\cancel{3}}}$ *Use the GCF to simplify.*

$\dfrac{3 \cdot 1}{10 \cdot 1}$ *Multiply.*

$\dfrac{3}{10}$ *The answer is in simplest form.*

C $a = \dfrac{3}{4}$ $a \cdot \dfrac{1}{3}$

$\dfrac{3}{4} \cdot \dfrac{1}{3}$ *Substitute $\dfrac{3}{4}$ for a.*

$\dfrac{3 \cdot 1}{4 \cdot 3}$ *Multiply numerators. Multiply denominators.*

$\dfrac{3}{12}$ *The GCF of 3 and 12 is 3.*

$\dfrac{1}{4}$ *The answer is in simplest form.*

Think and Discuss

1. **Determine** whether the product of two proper fractions is greater than or less than each factor.

2. **Name** the missing denominator in the equation $\dfrac{1}{\blacksquare} \cdot \dfrac{2}{3} = \dfrac{2}{21}$.

3. **Tell** how to find the product of $\dfrac{4}{12} \cdot \dfrac{6}{10}$ in two different ways.

GUIDED PRACTICE

See Example **1** **Multiply. Write each answer in simplest form.**

1. $\frac{1}{2} \cdot \frac{1}{3}$ **2.** $\frac{2}{5} \cdot \frac{1}{4}$ **3.** $\frac{4}{7} \cdot \frac{3}{4}$ **4.** $\frac{5}{6} \cdot \frac{3}{5}$

See Example **2** **Evaluate the expression $b \cdot \frac{1}{5}$ for each value of b. Write the answer in simplest form.**

5. $b = \frac{2}{3}$ **6.** $b = \frac{5}{8}$ **7.** $b = \frac{1}{4}$ **8.** $b = \frac{3}{5}$

INDEPENDENT PRACTICE

See Example **1** **Multiply. Write each answer in simplest form.**

9. $\frac{1}{3} \cdot \frac{2}{7}$ **10.** $\frac{1}{3} \cdot \frac{1}{5}$ **11.** $\frac{5}{6} \cdot \frac{2}{3}$ **12.** $\frac{1}{3} \cdot \frac{6}{7}$

13. $\frac{3}{10} \cdot \frac{5}{6}$ **14.** $\frac{7}{9} \cdot \frac{3}{5}$ **15.** $\frac{1}{2} \cdot \frac{10}{11}$ **16.** $\frac{3}{5} \cdot \frac{3}{4}$

See Example **2** **Evaluate the expression $x \cdot \frac{1}{6}$ for each value of x. Write the answer in simplest form.**

17. $x = \frac{4}{5}$ **18.** $x = \frac{6}{7}$ **19.** $x = \frac{3}{4}$ **20.** $x = \frac{5}{6}$

21. $x = \frac{8}{9}$ **22.** $x = \frac{9}{10}$ **23.** $x = \frac{5}{8}$ **24.** $x = \frac{3}{8}$

PRACTICE AND PROBLEM SOLVING

Find each product. Simplify the answer.

25. $\frac{3}{5} \cdot \frac{4}{9}$ **26.** $\frac{5}{12} \cdot \frac{9}{10}$ **27.** $\frac{2}{5} \cdot \frac{2}{7} \cdot \frac{5}{8}$ **28.** $\frac{2}{7} \cdot \frac{1}{8}$

29. $\frac{6}{7} \cdot \frac{9}{10}$ **30.** $\frac{4}{9} \cdot \frac{2}{3}$ **31.** $\frac{1}{2} \cdot \frac{2}{5} \cdot \frac{9}{11}$ **32.** $\frac{1}{12} \cdot \frac{3}{7}$

33. A walnut muffin recipe calls for $\frac{3}{4}$ cup walnuts. Mrs. Hooper wants to make $\frac{1}{3}$ of the recipe. What fraction of a cup of walnuts will she need?

34. Jim spent $\frac{5}{6}$ of an hour doing chores. He spent $\frac{2}{5}$ of that time washing dishes. What fraction of an hour did he spend washing dishes?

Compare. Write <, >, or =.

35. $\frac{2}{3} \cdot \frac{1}{4} \ \blacksquare \ \frac{1}{3} \cdot \frac{3}{4}$ **36.** $\frac{3}{5} \cdot \frac{3}{4} \ \blacksquare \ \frac{1}{2} \cdot \frac{9}{10}$ **37.** $\frac{5}{6} \cdot \frac{2}{3} \ \blacksquare \ \frac{1}{3} \cdot \frac{2}{3}$

38. $\frac{5}{8} \cdot \frac{1}{4} \ \blacksquare \ \frac{2}{9} \cdot \frac{1}{7}$ **39.** $\frac{2}{5} \cdot \frac{1}{10} \ \blacksquare \ \frac{3}{5} \cdot \frac{2}{3}$ **40.** $\frac{1}{2} \cdot \frac{4}{5} \ \blacksquare \ \frac{10}{20} \cdot \frac{16}{20}$

41. A multiplying number machine uses a rule to change one fraction into another fraction. The machine changed $\frac{1}{2}$ into $\frac{1}{8}$, $\frac{1}{5}$ into $\frac{1}{20}$, and $\frac{5}{7}$ into $\frac{5}{28}$.

   a. What is the rule?

   b. Into what fraction will the machine change $\frac{1}{3}$?

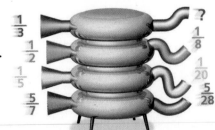

○ = **WORKED-OUT SOLUTIONS**
on p. WS6

42. Alex exercised for $\frac{3}{4}$ hour. He lifted weights for $\frac{1}{5}$ of that time. What fraction of an hour did he spend lifting weights?

43. **Life Science** A bat can eat half its weight in insects in one night. If a bat weighing $\frac{3}{4}$ lb eats half its weight in insects, how much do the insects weigh?

44. **Multi-Step** Once, 20 million bison roamed the United States. Now, there are only $\frac{1}{40}$ of that number of bison. Of those, only $\frac{1}{25}$ roam in the wild. The number of American bison currently roaming in the wild is what fraction of 20 million? How many bison is that?

45. The seating plan shows Oak School's theater. The front section has $\frac{3}{4}$ of the seats, and the rear section has $\frac{1}{4}$ of the seats. The school has reserved $\frac{1}{2}$ of the seats in the front section for students.

  a. What fraction of the seating is reserved for students?

  b. The theater has 960 seats. How many seats are reserved for students?

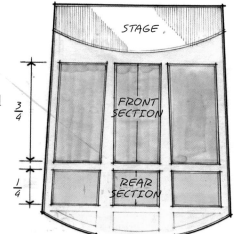

46. **Write a Problem** Use the seating plan to write a problem in which you need to multiply two fractions. Then solve the problem.

47. **Write About It** Explain how you can use the GCF before multiplying so that the product of two fractions is in simplest form.

48. **Challenge** Simplify the expression.

$$\frac{(2+6)}{5} \cdot \frac{1}{4} \cdot 6$$

Florida Spiral Review   MA.6.A.1.2, MA.6.A.3.2, MA.6.A.5.3

49. Multiple Choice Which shows the product of $\frac{4}{5}$ and $\frac{3}{5}$ in simplest form?

  A. $1\frac{2}{5}$ **B.** $1\frac{1}{3}$ **C.** $\frac{3}{5}$ **D.** $\frac{12}{25}$

50. Multiple Choice Julie spent $\frac{1}{3}$ of her birthday money on new clothes. She spent $\frac{3}{10}$ of that money on shoes. What fraction of her birthday money did Julie spend on shoes?

  F. $\frac{1}{30}$ **G.** $\frac{1}{10}$ **H.** $\frac{2}{15}$ **I.** $\frac{3}{13}$

Solve each equation. (Lesson 2-7)

51. $15n = 45$ **52.** $7t = 147$ **53.** $6a = 78$ **54.** $12b = 216$

Estimate each product or quotient. (Lesson 3-2)

55. 0.49×3.9 **56.** $11.85 \div 4.211$ **57.** $14.75 \div 2.76$ **58.** 6.89×3.02

5-7 Multiplying Mixed Numbers

MA.6.A.1.2
Multiply and divide fractions . . . efficiently.
Also **MA.6.A.1.3**

Janice and Carla are making homemade pasta from a recipe that calls for $1\frac{1}{2}$ cups of flour. They want to make $\frac{1}{3}$ of the recipe.

You can find $\frac{1}{3}$ of $1\frac{1}{2}$, or multiply $\frac{1}{3}$ by $1\frac{1}{2}$, to find how much flour Janice and Carla need.

EXAMPLE 1 **Multiplying Fractions and Mixed Numbers**

Multiply. Write each answer in simplest form.

Animated Math
@ thinkcentral.com

Remember!

To write a mixed number as an improper fraction, start with the denominator, multiply by the whole number, and add the numerator. Use the same denominator.

$1\frac{1}{5} = \frac{1 \cdot 5 + 1}{5} = \frac{6}{5}$

A $\frac{1}{3} \cdot 1\frac{1}{2}$

$\frac{1}{3} \cdot \frac{3}{2}$ *Write $1\frac{1}{2}$ as an improper fraction. $1\frac{1}{2} = \frac{3}{2}$*

$\frac{1 \cdot 3}{3 \cdot 2}$ *Multiply numerators. Multiply denominators.*

$\frac{3}{6}$

$\frac{1}{2}$ *Write the answer in simplest form.*

B $1\frac{1}{5} \cdot \frac{2}{3}$

$\frac{6}{5} \cdot \frac{2}{3}$ *Write $1\frac{1}{5}$ as an improper fraction. $1\frac{1}{5} = \frac{6}{5}$*

$\frac{6 \cdot 2}{5 \cdot 3}$ *Multiply numerators. Multiply denominators.*

$\frac{12}{15}$

$\frac{4}{5}$ *Write the answer in simplest form.*

C $\frac{3}{4} \cdot 2\frac{1}{3}$

$\frac{3}{4} \cdot \frac{7}{3}$ *Write $2\frac{1}{3}$ as an improper fraction. $2\frac{1}{3} = \frac{7}{3}$*

$\frac{\overset{1}{\cancel{3}}}{4} \cdot \frac{7}{\underset{1}{\cancel{3}}}$ *Use the GCF to simplify before multiplying.*

$\frac{1 \cdot 7}{4 \cdot 1}$

$\frac{7}{4} = 1\frac{3}{4}$ *You can write the answer as a mixed number.*

Video **Lesson Tutorial Videos @ thinkcentral.com**

EXAMPLE 2 Multiplying Mixed Numbers

Find each product. Write the answer in simplest form.

A $2\frac{1}{2} \cdot 1\frac{1}{3}$

$\frac{5}{2} \cdot \frac{4}{3}$ *Write the mixed numbers as improper fractions. $2\frac{1}{2} = \frac{5}{2}$ $1\frac{1}{3} = \frac{4}{3}$*

$\frac{5 \cdot 4}{2 \cdot 3}$ *Multiply numerators.*
Multiply denominators.

$\frac{20}{6}$

$3\frac{2}{6}$ *Write the improper fraction as a mixed number.*

$3\frac{1}{3}$ *Simplify.*

B $1\frac{1}{4} \cdot 1\frac{1}{3}$

$\frac{5}{4} \cdot \frac{4}{3}$ *Write the mixed numbers as improper fractions. $1\frac{1}{4} = \frac{5}{4}$ $1\frac{1}{3} = \frac{4}{3}$*

$\frac{5}{4} \cdot \frac{\overset{1}{4}}{3}$ *Use the GCF to simplify before multiplying.*
$\underset{1}{}$

$\frac{5 \cdot 1}{1 \cdot 3}$ *Multiply numerators. Multiply denominators.*

$\frac{5}{3}$

$1\frac{2}{3}$ *Write the answer as a mixed number.*

C $5 \cdot 3\frac{2}{11}$

$5 \cdot 3\frac{2}{11}$

$5 \cdot \left(3 + \frac{2}{11}\right)$

$(5 \cdot 3) + \left(5 \cdot \frac{2}{11}\right)$ *Use the Distributive Property.*

$(5 \cdot 3) + \left(\frac{5}{1} \cdot \frac{2}{11}\right)$

$15 + \frac{10}{11}$ *Multiply.*

$15\frac{10}{11}$ *Add.*

Think and Discuss

1. Tell how you multiply a mixed number by a mixed number.

2. Explain two ways you would multiply a mixed number by a whole number.

3. Explain whether the product of a proper fraction and a mixed number is less than, between, or greater than the two factors.

Homework Help
Go to **thinkcentral.com**
Exercises 1–28, 31, 35, 37, 49, 51

 MA.6.A.1.2, MA.6.A.3.2

GUIDED PRACTICE

See Example **1** Multiply. Write each answer in simplest form.

1. $1\frac{1}{4} \cdot \frac{2}{3}$

2. $2\frac{2}{3} \cdot \frac{1}{4}$

3. $\frac{3}{7} \cdot 1\frac{5}{6}$

4. $1\frac{1}{3} \cdot \frac{6}{7}$

5. $\frac{2}{3} \cdot 1\frac{3}{10}$

6. $2\frac{6}{11} \cdot \frac{2}{7}$

See Example **2** Find each product. Write the answer in simplest form.

7. $1\frac{5}{6} \cdot 1\frac{1}{8}$

8. $2\frac{2}{5} \cdot 1\frac{1}{12}$

9. $4 \cdot 5\frac{3}{7}$

10. $2\frac{3}{4} \cdot 1\frac{5}{6}$

11. $2\frac{3}{8} \cdot 5\frac{1}{5}$

12. $10\frac{1}{2} \cdot 1\frac{1}{4}$

INDEPENDENT PRACTICE

See Example **1** Multiply. Write each answer in simplest form.

13. $1\frac{1}{4} \cdot \frac{3}{4}$

14. $\frac{4}{7} \cdot 1\frac{1}{4}$

15. $1\frac{1}{6} \cdot \frac{2}{5}$

16. $2\frac{1}{6} \cdot \frac{3}{7}$

17. $\frac{5}{9} \cdot 1\frac{9}{10}$

18. $2\frac{2}{9} \cdot \frac{3}{5}$

19. $1\frac{3}{10} \cdot \frac{5}{7}$

20. $\frac{3}{4} \cdot 1\frac{2}{5}$

See Example **2** Find each product. Write the answer in simplest form.

21. $1\frac{1}{3} \cdot 1\frac{5}{7}$

22. $1\frac{2}{3} \cdot 2\frac{3}{10}$

23. $4 \cdot 3\frac{7}{8}$

24. $6 \cdot 2\frac{1}{3}$

25. $5 \cdot 4\frac{7}{10}$

26. $2\frac{2}{3} \cdot 3\frac{5}{8}$

27. $1\frac{1}{2} \cdot 2\frac{2}{5}$

28. $3\frac{5}{6} \cdot 2\frac{3}{4}$

PRACTICE AND PROBLEM SOLVING

Write each product in simplest form.

29. $1\frac{2}{3} \cdot \frac{2}{9}$

30. $3\frac{1}{3} \cdot \frac{7}{10}$

31. $2 \cdot \frac{5}{8}$

32. $2\frac{8}{11} \cdot \frac{3}{10}$

33. $\frac{3}{8} \cdot \frac{4}{9}$

34. $2\frac{1}{12} \cdot 1\frac{3}{5}$

35. $3\frac{3}{10} \cdot 4\frac{1}{6}$

36. $2\frac{1}{4} \cdot 1\frac{2}{9}$

37. $2 \cdot \frac{4}{5} \cdot 1\frac{2}{3}$

38. $3\frac{5}{6} \cdot \frac{9}{10} \cdot 4\frac{2}{3}$

39. $1\frac{7}{8} \cdot 2\frac{1}{3} \cdot 4$

40. $1\frac{2}{7} \cdot 3 \cdot 2\frac{5}{8}$

41. Multi-Step Jared used $1\frac{2}{5}$ bags of soil for his garden. He is digging another garden that will need $\frac{1}{5}$ as much soil as the original. How much will he use total?

42. Milo is making $1\frac{1}{2}$ batches of muffins. If one batch calls for $1\frac{3}{4}$ cups flour, how much flour will he need?

43. Critical Thinking Is the product of two mixed numbers less than, between, or greater than the two factors?

Evaluate each expression.

44. $\frac{1}{2} \cdot c$ for $c = 4\frac{2}{5}$

45. $1\frac{5}{7} \cdot x$ for $x = \frac{5}{6}$

46. $1\frac{3}{4} \cdot b$ for $b = 1\frac{1}{7}$

47. $1\frac{5}{9} \cdot n$ for $n = 18$

48. $2\frac{5}{9} \cdot t$ for $t = 4$

49. $3\frac{3}{4} \cdot p$ for $p = \frac{1}{2}$

50. $\frac{4}{5} \cdot m$ for $m = 2\frac{2}{3}$

51. $6y$ for $y = 3\frac{5}{8}$

52. $2\frac{3}{5} \cdot c$ for $c = 1\frac{1}{5}$

○ = WORKED-OUT SOLUTIONS
on p. WS6

Muffins probably started out as a form of cake, or possibly as a variety of cornbread. Early muffins didn't have nearly as much variety as is available today.

Use the recipe for Exercises 53–57.

53. How much flour and baking powder would you need if you doubled the recipe?

54. How much baking powder is needed for half of the recipe?

55. Raquel is baking muffins for a bake sale at school. She plans on multiplying the recipe by $3\frac{1}{2}$.

  a. How much flour will she need?

  b. How much sugar will she need?

  c. How much salt will she need?

56. Each muffin contains $22\frac{1}{5}$ grams of carbohydrates. How many grams of carbohydrates are contained in 12 muffins?

57. ⭐ **Challenge** What is the smallest number by which you could multiply the entire recipe so that the amount of each ingredient would be a whole number?

Fresh Fruit Muffins

1 3/4 cups all-purpose flour
1/3 cup granulated sugar
2 1/2 teaspoons baking powder
1/2 teaspoon salt
3/4 cup milk
1 egg
1/3 cup butter, melted
1 cup fresh fruit

In a large bowl, whisk together dry ingredients. Add milk, egg, and butter, and mix until ingredients are moistened – do not over-beat. Stir in fruit and pour into greased muffin cups. Bake at 400°F for 20-25 minutes, or until tops spring back when lightly touched. Makes 12 muffins.

Florida Spiral Review   MA.6.A.1.2, MA.6.A.3.2

58. Multiple Choice A chef uses $2\frac{1}{4}$ cups of water for a recipe. The chef doubled the recipe. How much water did the chef use?

  A. 4 cups   **B.** $4\frac{1}{4}$ cups   **C.** $4\frac{1}{2}$ cups   **D.** $4\frac{3}{4}$ cups

59. Gridded Response Keith ate $\frac{1}{3}$ pound of grapes last week. Jamal ate five times as many grapes as Keith last week. How many pounds of grapes did Jamal eat?

60. Short Response Josh is training to run in a half-marathon. So far this week, he has run $6\frac{3}{8}$ miles on each of three days. What is the total distance Josh has run this week?

Solve each equation. (Lesson 2-8)

61. $7a = 35$ **62.** $63 = 9d$ **63.** $11g = 121$ **64.** $85 = 17p$

Multiply. Write each answer in simplest form. (Lesson 5-5)

65. $5 \times \frac{1}{10}$ **66.** $21 \times \frac{1}{3}$ **67.** $\frac{2}{7} \times 14$ **68.** $\frac{5}{12} \times 2$

5-8 Dividing Fractions and Mixed Numbers

MA.6.A.1.2 Multiply and divide fractions . . . efficiently. *Also* **MA.6.A.1.3**

Curtis is making sushi rolls. First, he will place a sheet of seaweed, called *nori*, on the sushi rolling mat. Then, he will use the mat to roll up rice, cucumber, avocado, and crabmeat. Finally, he will slice the roll into smaller pieces.

Vocabulary

reciprocal

multiplicative inverse

Curtis has 2 cups of rice and will use $\frac{1}{3}$ cup for each sushi roll. How many sushi rolls can he make?

Think: How many $\frac{1}{3}$ pieces equal 2 wholes?

There are six $\frac{1}{3}$ pieces in 2 wholes, so Curtis can make 6 sushi rolls.

Reciprocals can help you divide by fractions. Two numbers are **reciprocals** or *multiplicative inverses*, if their product is 1.

Multiplicative Inverse Property	
Words	**Numbers**
The product of a nonzero number and its reciprocal, or **multiplicative inverse**, is 1.	$\frac{3}{4} \cdot \frac{4}{3} = 1$

EXAMPLE **1** **Finding Reciprocals**

Find the reciprocal.

A $\frac{1}{5}$

$\frac{1}{5} \cdot \blacksquare = 1$ *Think: $\frac{1}{5}$ of what number is 1?*

$\frac{1}{5} \cdot 5 = 1$ $\frac{1}{5}$ *of $\frac{5}{1}$ is 1.*

The reciprocal of $\frac{1}{5}$ is 5.

B $2\frac{1}{3}$

$\frac{7}{3} \cdot \blacksquare = 1$ *Write $2\frac{1}{3}$ as $\frac{7}{3}$.*

$\frac{7}{3} \cdot \frac{3}{7} = \frac{21}{21} = 1$ $\frac{7}{3}$ *of $\frac{3}{7}$ is 1.*

The reciprocal of $\frac{7}{3}$ is $\frac{3}{7}$.

Video **Lesson Tutorial Videos @ thinkcentral.com**

Look at the relationship between the fractions $\frac{3}{4}$ and $\frac{4}{3}$. If you switch the numerator and denominator of a fraction, you will find its reciprocal. Dividing by a number is the same as multiplying by its reciprocal.

$$24 \div 4 = 6 \qquad 24 \cdot \frac{1}{4} = 6$$

EXAMPLE **2** **Using Reciprocals to Divide Fractions and Mixed Numbers**

Divide. Write each answer in simplest form.

A $\frac{4}{5} \div 5$

$$\frac{4}{5} \div 5 = \frac{4}{5} \cdot \frac{1}{5}$$ *Rewrite as multiplication using the reciprocal of 5, $\frac{1}{5}$.*

$$= \frac{4 \cdot 1}{5 \cdot 5}$$ *Multiply by the reciprocal.*

$$= \frac{4}{25}$$ *The answer is in simplest form.*

B $\frac{3}{4} \div \frac{1}{2}$

$$\frac{3}{4} \div \frac{1}{2} = \frac{3}{4} \cdot \frac{2}{1}$$ *Rewrite as multiplication using the reciprocal of $\frac{1}{2}$, $\frac{2}{1}$.*

$$= \frac{3 \cdot \overset{1}{2}}{\underset{2}{4} \cdot 1}$$ *Simplify before multiplying.*

$$= \frac{3}{2}$$ *Multiply.*

$$= 1\frac{1}{2}$$ *You can write the answer as a mixed number.*

C $2\frac{2}{3} \div 1\frac{1}{6}$

$$2\frac{2}{3} \div 1\frac{1}{6} = \frac{8}{3} \div \frac{7}{6}$$ *Write the mixed numbers as improper fractions. $2\frac{2}{3} = \frac{8}{3}$ and $1\frac{1}{6} = \frac{7}{6}$*

$$= \frac{8}{3} \cdot \frac{6}{7}$$ *Rewrite as multiplication.*

$$= \frac{8 \cdot \overset{2}{6}}{\underset{1}{3} \cdot 7}$$ *Simplify before multiplying.*

$$= \frac{16}{7}$$ *Multiply.*

$$= 2\frac{2}{7}$$ *You can write the answer as a mixed number.*

Caution!

When you divide by a proper fraction, the quotient will be greater than the dividend. For example, since there are 8 halves in 4, $4 \div \frac{1}{2} = 8$.

Think and Discuss

1. Explain how you can use mental math to find the value of n in the equation $\frac{5}{8} \cdot n = 1$.

2. Explain how to find the reciprocal of $3\frac{6}{11}$.

Homework Help

Go to **thinkcentral.com**
Exercises 1-35, 37, 39, 43, 45, 49, 55, 61

GUIDED PRACTICE

See Example **1**   Find the reciprocal.

1. $\frac{2}{7}$ **2.** $\frac{5}{9}$ **3.** $\frac{1}{9}$ **4.** $\frac{3}{11}$ **5.** $2\frac{3}{5}$

See Example **2**   Divide. Write each answer in simplest form.

6. $\frac{5}{6} \div 3$ **7.** $2\frac{1}{7} \div 1\frac{1}{4}$ **8.** $\frac{5}{12} \div 5$ **9.** $1\frac{5}{8} \div \frac{3}{4}$

10. $\frac{2}{3} \div \frac{1}{6}$ **11.** $\frac{3}{10} \div 1\frac{2}{3}$ **12.** $\frac{4}{7} \div 1\frac{1}{7}$ **13.** $4 \div \frac{7}{8}$

INDEPENDENT PRACTICE

See Example **1**   Find the reciprocal.

14. $\frac{7}{8}$ **15.** $\frac{1}{10}$ **16.** $\frac{3}{8}$ **17.** $\frac{11}{12}$ **18.** $2\frac{5}{8}$

19. $\frac{8}{11}$ **20.** $\frac{5}{6}$ **21.** $\frac{6}{7}$ **22.** $\frac{2}{9}$ **23.** $5\frac{1}{4}$

See Example **2**   Divide. Write each answer in simplest form.

24. $\frac{7}{8} \div 4$ **25.** $2\frac{3}{8} \div 1\frac{3}{4}$ **26.** $\frac{8}{9} \div 12$ **27.** $9 \div \frac{3}{4}$

28. $3\frac{5}{6} \div 1\frac{5}{9}$ **29.** $\frac{9}{10} \div 3$ **30.** $2\frac{4}{5} \div 1\frac{5}{7}$ **31.** $3\frac{1}{5} \div 1\frac{2}{7}$

32. $\frac{5}{8} \div \frac{1}{2}$ **33.** $1\frac{1}{2} \div 2\frac{1}{4}$ **34.** $\frac{7}{12} \div 2\frac{5}{8}$ **35.** $\frac{1}{8} \div 5$

PRACTICE AND PROBLEM SOLVING

Multiply or divide. Write each answer in simplest form.

36. $2\frac{3}{4} \div 2\frac{1}{5}$ **37.** $4\frac{4}{5} \div 2\frac{6}{7}$ **38.** $\frac{3}{8} \cdot \frac{5}{12}$

39. $6 \cdot \frac{7}{9}$ **40.** $3\frac{1}{7} \div 5$ **41.** $\frac{9}{14} \cdot \frac{1}{6}$

42. At Lina's restaurant, one serving of chili is $1\frac{1}{2}$ cups. The chef makes 48 cups of chili each night. How many servings of chili are in 48 cups?

(43.) Rhula bought 12 lb of raisins. She packed them into freezer bags so that each bag weighs $\frac{3}{4}$ lb. How many freezer bags did she pack?

Decide whether the fractions in each pair are reciprocals. If not, write the reciprocal of each fraction.

44. $\frac{1}{2}, 2$ **45.** $\frac{3}{8}, \frac{16}{6}$ **46.** $\frac{7}{9}, \frac{21}{27}$ **47.** $\frac{5}{6}, \frac{12}{10}$

48. $1\frac{1}{2}, \frac{2}{3}$ **49.** $\frac{2}{5}, \frac{4}{25}$ **50.** $\frac{3}{7}, 2\frac{1}{3}$ **51.** $5, \frac{5}{1}$

52. Lisa had some wood that was $12\frac{1}{2}$ feet long. She cut it into 5 pieces that are equal in length. How long is each piece of wood?

53. Critical Thinking How can you recognize the reciprocal of a fraction?

○ = **WORKED-OUT SOLUTIONS**
on p. WS6

Multiply or divide. Write each answer in simplest form.

54. $\frac{11}{12} \cdot \frac{9}{10} \div 1\frac{1}{4}$

55. $2\frac{3}{4} \cdot 1\frac{2}{3} \div 5$

56. $1\frac{1}{2} \div \frac{3}{4} \cdot \frac{2}{5}$

57. $\frac{3}{4} \cdot \left(\frac{5}{7} \div \frac{1}{2}\right)$

58. $4\frac{2}{3} \div \left(6 \cdot \frac{3}{5}\right)$

59. $5\frac{1}{5} \cdot \left(3\frac{2}{5} \cdot 2\frac{1}{3}\right)$

Life Science The bar graph shows the lengths of some species of snakes found in the United States. Use the bar graph for Exercises 60–62.

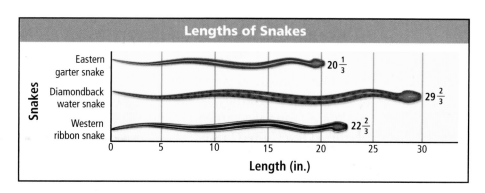

60. Is the length of the eastern garter snake greater than or less than $\frac{1}{2}$ yd? Explain.

61. What is the average length of all the snakes?

62. Jim measured the length of a rough green snake. It was $27\frac{1}{3}$ in. long. What would the average length of the snakes be if Jim's measure of a rough green snake were added?

63. What's the Error? A student said the reciprocal of $6\frac{2}{3}$ is $6\frac{3}{2}$. Explain the error. Then write the correct reciprocal.

64. Write About It Explain how to divide fractions to find $\frac{3}{4} \div 2\frac{1}{3}$.

65. Challenge Evaluate the expression $\frac{(6-3)}{4} \div \frac{1}{8} \cdot 5$.

Florida Spiral Review   MA.6.A.1.2

66. Multiple Choice A piece of wood was 12 feet long. Gene cut the wood into pieces $\frac{2}{3}$ foot long. How many pieces did Gene have?

A. 4   **B.** 8   **C.** 16   **D.** 18

67. Multiple Choice Which product is NOT equal to 1?

F. $\frac{2}{3} \cdot \frac{3}{2}$ **G.** $8 \cdot \frac{1}{8}$ **H.** $\frac{1}{9} \cdot \frac{9}{3}$ **I.** $\frac{2}{13} \cdot \frac{13}{2}$

Find the number of decimal places in each product. Then multiply. (Lesson 3-4)

68. 2.4×1.8

69. 19×0.5

70. 7.04×2.3

71. 0.4×0.1

Find each product. (Lesson 5-7)

72. $2\frac{2}{3} \cdot \frac{1}{8}$

73. $\frac{1}{4} \cdot 3\frac{1}{2}$

74. $1\frac{1}{4} \cdot 1\frac{2}{5}$

75. $2\frac{1}{5} \cdot 2\frac{2}{3}$

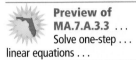

Preview of MA.7.A.3.3 . . . Solve one-step . . . linear equations . . .

Sugarcane is the main source of the sugar we use to sweeten our foods. It grows in tropical areas, such as Costa Rica and Brazil.

In one year, the average person in Costa Rica consumes $24\frac{1}{4}$ lb less sugar than the average person in the United States consumes.

EXAMPLE 1 **Solving Equations by Adding and Subtracting**

Solve each equation. Write the solution in simplest form.

@ thinkcentral.com

A $x + 6\frac{2}{3} = 11$

$$x + 6\frac{2}{3} = 11$$
$$\underline{-6\frac{2}{3} \quad\quad -6\frac{2}{3}}$$

Subtract $6\frac{2}{3}$ from both sides to undo the addition.

$$x = 10\frac{3}{3} - 6\frac{2}{3}$$

Regroup 11 as $10\frac{3}{3}$.

$$x = 4\frac{1}{3}$$

Subtract.

B $2\frac{1}{4} = x - 3\frac{1}{2}$

$$2\frac{1}{4} = x - 3\frac{1}{2}$$
$$\underline{+3\frac{1}{2} \quad\quad +3\frac{1}{2}}$$

Add $3\frac{1}{2}$ to both sides to undo the subtraction.

$$2\frac{1}{4} + 3\frac{2}{4} = x$$

Find a common denominator. $3\frac{1}{2} = 3\frac{2}{4}$

$$5\frac{3}{4} = x$$

Add.

C $5\frac{3}{5} = m + \frac{7}{10}$

$$5\frac{3}{5} = m + \frac{7}{10}$$
$$\underline{-\frac{7}{10} \quad\quad -\frac{7}{10}}$$

Subtract $\frac{7}{10}$ from both sides to undo the addition.

$$5\frac{6}{10} - \frac{7}{10} = m$$

Find a common denominator. $5\frac{3}{5} = 5\frac{6}{10}$

$$4\frac{16}{10} - \frac{7}{10} = m$$

Regroup $5\frac{6}{10}$ as $4\frac{10}{10} + \frac{6}{10}$.

$$4\frac{9}{10} = m$$

Subtract.

Video **Lesson Tutorial Videos @ thinkcentral.com**

Solve each equation. Write the solution in simplest form.

D $w - \frac{1}{2} = 2\frac{3}{4}$

$$w - \frac{1}{2} = 2\frac{3}{4}$$

$$\underline{\;\; + \frac{1}{2} \quad + \frac{1}{2}\;\;}$$ *Add $\frac{1}{2}$ to both sides to undo the subtraction.*

$$w = 2\frac{3}{4} + \frac{1}{2}$$

$$w = 2\frac{3}{4} + \frac{2}{4}$$ *Find a common denominator. $\frac{1}{2} = \frac{2}{4}$*

$$w = 2\frac{5}{4}$$ *Add.*

$$w = 3\frac{1}{4}$$ *Regroup: $2\frac{5}{4} = 2 + 1\frac{1}{4}$*

EXAMPLE 2 *Social Studies Application*

Costa Rica

On average, a person in Costa Rica consumes $132\frac{1}{4}$ lb of sugar per year. If the average person in Costa Rica consumes $24\frac{1}{4}$ lb less than the average person in the U.S., what is the average sugar consumption per year by a person in the U.S.?

$$u - 24\frac{1}{4} = 132\frac{1}{4}$$ *Let u represent the average amount of sugar consumed in the U.S.*

$$\underline{\;\; +24\frac{1}{4} \quad +24\frac{1}{4}\;\;}$$ *Add $24\frac{1}{4}$ to both sides to undo the subtraction.*

$$u = 156\frac{2}{4} = 156\frac{1}{2}$$ *Simplify.*

Check

$$u - 24\frac{1}{4} = 132\frac{1}{4}$$

$$156\frac{1}{2} - 24\frac{1}{4} \stackrel{?}{=} 132\frac{1}{4}$$ *Substitute $156\frac{1}{2}$ for u.*

$$156\frac{2}{4} - 24\frac{1}{4} \stackrel{?}{=} 132\frac{1}{4}$$ *Find a common denominator.*

$$132\frac{1}{4} \stackrel{?}{=} 132\frac{1}{4} ✔$$ *$156\frac{1}{2}$ is the solution.*

On average, a person in the U.S. consumes $156\frac{1}{2}$ lb of sugar per year.

Think and Discuss

1. **Explain** how regrouping a mixed number when subtracting is similar to regrouping when subtracting whole numbers.

2. **Give an example** of an addition equation with a solution that is a fraction between 3 and 4.

Preview MA.7.A.3.3

Homework Help THINK central

Go to thinkcentral.com
Exercises 1-15, 17, 21, 23, 25, 27, 29, 31

GUIDED PRACTICE

See Example 1 Solve each equation. Write the solution in simplest form.

1. $x + 2\frac{1}{2} = 7$

2. $3\frac{1}{3} = x - 5\frac{1}{9}$

3. $9\frac{3}{4} = x + 4\frac{1}{8}$

4. $x + 1\frac{1}{5} = 5\frac{3}{10}$

5. $3\frac{2}{5} + x = 7\frac{1}{2}$

6. $8\frac{7}{10} = x - 4\frac{1}{4}$

See Example 2 **7.** A tailor increased the length of a robe by $2\frac{1}{4}$ inches. The new length of the robe is 60 inches. What was the original length?

INDEPENDENT PRACTICE

See Example 1 Solve each equation. Write the solution in simplest form.

8. $x - 4\frac{3}{4} = 1\frac{1}{12}$

9. $x + 5\frac{3}{8} = 9$

10. $3\frac{1}{2} = 1\frac{3}{10} + x$

11. $4\frac{2}{3} = x - \frac{1}{6}$

12. $6\frac{3}{4} + x = 9\frac{1}{8}$

13. $x - 3\frac{7}{9} = 5$

See Example 2 **14.** Robert is taking a movie-making class in school. He edited his short video and cut $3\frac{2}{5}$ minutes. The new length of the video is $12\frac{1}{10}$ minutes. How long was his video before he cut it?

15. An extension for a table increased its length by $2\frac{1}{2}$ feet. The new length of the table is $8\frac{3}{4}$ feet. What was the original length?

PRACTICE AND PROBLEM SOLVING

Find the solution to each equation. Check your answers.

16. $y + 8\frac{2}{4} = 10$

17. $p - 1\frac{2}{5} = 3\frac{7}{10}$

18. $6\frac{2}{3} + n = 7\frac{5}{6}$

19. $5\frac{3}{5} = s - 2\frac{3}{10}$

20. $k - 8\frac{1}{4} = 1\frac{1}{3}$

21. $\frac{23}{24} = c + \frac{5}{8}$

22. The difference between Cristina's and Erin's heights is $\frac{1}{2}$ foot. Erin's height is $4\frac{1}{4}$ feet, and she is shorter than Cristina. How tall is Cristina?

23. **Measurement** Lori used $2\frac{5}{8}$ ounces of shampoo to wash her dog. When she was finished, the bottle contained $13\frac{3}{8}$ ounces of shampoo. How many ounces of shampoo were in the bottle before Lori washed her dog?

24. **Sports** Jack decreased his best time in the 400-meter race by $1\frac{3}{10}$ seconds. His new best time is $52\frac{3}{5}$ seconds. What was Jack's old time in the 400-meter race?

25. **Crafts** Juan makes bracelets to sell at his mother's gift shop. He alternates between green and blue beads.

What is the length of the green bead?

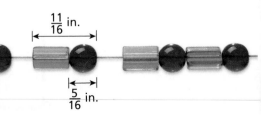

$\frac{11}{16}$ in.

$\frac{5}{16}$ in.

○ = WORKED-OUT SOLUTIONS on p. WS6

Find the solution to each equation. Check your answers.

26. $m + 4 = 6\frac{3}{8} - 1\frac{1}{4}$ **27.** $3\frac{2}{9} - 1\frac{1}{3} = p - 5\frac{1}{2}$ **28.** $q - 4\frac{1}{4} = 1\frac{1}{6} + 1\frac{1}{2}$

29. $a + 5\frac{1}{4} + 2\frac{1}{2} = 13\frac{1}{6}$ **30.** $11\frac{2}{7} = w + 3\frac{1}{2} - 1\frac{1}{7}$ **31.** $9 - 5\frac{7}{8} = x - 1\frac{1}{8}$

32. Music A string quartet is performing Antonio Vivaldi's *The Four Seasons*. The concert is scheduled to last 45 minutes.

  a. After playing "Spring," "Summer," and "Autumn," how much time will be left in the concert?

  b. Is the concert long enough to play the four movements and another piece that is $6\frac{1}{2}$ minutes long? Explain.

33. Write a Problem Use the pictograph to write a subtraction problem with two mixed numbers.

34. Choose a Strategy How can you draw a line that is 5 inches long using only one sheet of $8\frac{1}{2}$ in. × 11 in. notebook paper?

35. Write About It Explain how you know whether to add a number to or subtract a number from both sides of an equation in order to solve the equation.

36. Challenge Use the numbers 1, 2, 3, 4, 5, and 6 to write a subtraction problem with two mixed numbers that have a difference of $4\frac{13}{20}$.

Florida Spiral Review   MA.6.A.3.2, MA.6.A.1.2

37. Multiple Choice Solve $4\frac{1}{2} + x = 6\frac{1}{6}$ for x.

  A. $x = 1\frac{1}{4}$ **B.** $x = 1\frac{2}{3}$ **C.** $x = 2\frac{1}{4}$ **D.** $x = 2\frac{2}{3}$

38. Multiple Choice Ambra's hair was $7\frac{2}{3}$ inches long. After she got her hair cut, the length of her hair was $5\frac{4}{5}$ inches. How many inches of hair were cut?

  F. $1\frac{13}{15}$ **G.** $2\frac{2}{5}$ **H.** $2\frac{2}{3}$ **I.** $2\frac{13}{15}$

Solve each equation. (Lesson 2-9)

39. $\frac{b}{6} = 3$ **40.** $8 = \frac{y}{7}$ **41.** $12 = \frac{s}{12}$ **42.** $\frac{h}{5} = 16$

Multiply. Write each answer in simplest form. (Lesson 5-6)

43. $\frac{1}{3} \cdot \frac{6}{7}$ **44.** $\frac{2}{5} \cdot \frac{15}{16}$ **45.** $\frac{1}{2} \cdot \frac{2}{5}$ **46.** $\frac{3}{5} \cdot \frac{4}{9}$

Solving Fraction Equations: Multiplication and Division

Preview of MA.7.A.3.3 ... Solve one-step ... linear equations ...

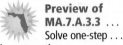

Josef is building a fish pond for koi in his backyard. He makes the width of the pond $\frac{2}{3}$ of the length. The width of the pond is 14 feet. You can use the equation $\frac{2}{3}\ell = 14$ to find the length of the pond.

Small koi in a backyard pond usually grow 2 to 4 inches per year.

EXAMPLE 1 Solving Equations by Multiplying and Dividing

Solve each equation. Write the answer in simplest form.

Animated Math @ thinkcentral.com

Remember!

Dividing by a number is the same as multiplying by its reciprocal.

A $\frac{2}{3}\ell = 14$

$$\frac{2}{3}\ell = 14$$

$$\frac{2}{3}\ell \div \frac{2}{3} = 14 \div \frac{2}{3} \qquad \textit{Divide both sides of the equation by } \frac{2}{3}.$$

$$\frac{2}{3}\ell \cdot \frac{3}{2} = 14 \cdot \frac{3}{2} \qquad \textit{Multiply by } \frac{3}{2}, \textit{ the reciprocal of } \frac{2}{3}.$$

$$\ell = 14 \cdot \frac{3}{2}$$

$$\ell = \frac{14 \cdot 3}{1 \cdot 2}$$

$$\ell = \frac{42}{2}, \text{ or } 21$$

B $2x = \frac{1}{3}$

$$2x = \frac{1}{3}$$

$$\frac{2}{1}x \cdot \frac{1}{2} = \frac{1}{3} \cdot \frac{1}{2} \qquad \textit{Multiply both sides by the reciprocal of 2.}$$

$$x = \frac{1 \cdot 1}{3 \cdot 2}$$

$$x = \frac{1}{6} \qquad \textit{The answer is in simplest form.}$$

C $\frac{5}{6}x = 4$

$$\frac{5}{6}x = 4$$

$$\frac{5}{6}x \div \frac{5}{6} = \frac{4}{1} \div \frac{5}{6} \qquad \textit{Divide both sides by } \frac{5}{6}.$$

$$\frac{5}{6}x \cdot \frac{6}{5} = \frac{4}{1} \cdot \frac{6}{5} \qquad \textit{Multiply by the reciprocal of } \frac{5}{6}.$$

$$x = \frac{24}{5}, \text{ or } 4\frac{4}{5}$$

Video Lesson Tutorial Videos @ thinkcentral.com

EXAMPLE 2

PROBLEM SOLVING APPLICATION

Dexter makes dog biscuits for the animal shelter. He makes $\frac{3}{4}$ of a recipe and uses 15 cups of powdered milk. How many cups of powdered milk are in the recipe?

1 Understand the Problem

The **answer** will be the number of cups of powdered milk in the recipe.

List the **important information:**

- He makes $\frac{3}{4}$ of the recipe.

- He uses 15 cups of powdered milk.

2 Make a Plan

You can write and solve an equation. Let x represent the number of cups in the recipe.

He uses 15 cups, which is three-fourths of the amount in the recipe. $15 = \frac{3}{4}x$

3 Solve

$$15 = \frac{3}{4}x$$

$$15 \cdot \frac{4}{3} = \frac{3}{4}x \cdot \frac{4}{3}$$ *Multiply both sides by $\frac{4}{3}$, the reciprocal of $\frac{3}{4}$.*

$$\frac{\overset{5}{\cancel{15}}}{1} \cdot \frac{4}{\underset{1}{\cancel{3}}} = x$$ *Simplify. Then multiply.*

$$20 = x$$

There are 20 cups of powdered milk in the recipe.

4 Look Back

Check $15 = \frac{3}{4}x$

$$15 \overset{?}{=} \frac{3}{4}(20)$$ *Substitute 20 for x.*

$$15 \overset{?}{=} \frac{\overset{15}{\cancel{60}}}{\underset{1}{\cancel{4}}}$$ *Multiply and simplify.*

$$15 \overset{?}{=} 15 \checkmark$$ *20 is the solution.*

Pets

No more than $\frac{1}{10}$ of a dog's diet should consist of treats and biscuits.

Think and Discuss

1. **Explain** whether $\frac{2}{3}x = 4$ is the same as $\frac{2}{3} = 4x$.

2. **Tell** how you know which numbers to divide by in the following equations: $\frac{2}{3}x = 4$ and $\frac{4}{5} = 8x$.

Homework Help THINK central

Go to thinkcentral.com
Exercises 1-15, 17, 21, 27, 29, 31, 33

Preview MA.7.A.3.3

GUIDED PRACTICE

See Example 1 — Solve each equation. Write the answer in simplest form.

1. $\frac{3}{4}z = 12$ **2.** $4n = \frac{3}{5}$ **3.** $\frac{2}{3}x = 5$ **4.** $2c = \frac{9}{10}$

See Example 2 — **5. School** In PE class, $\frac{3}{8}$ of the students want to play volleyball. If 9 students want to play volleyball, how many students are in the class?

INDEPENDENT PRACTICE

See Example 1 — Solve each equation. Write the answer in simplest form.

6. $3t = \frac{2}{7}$ **7.** $\frac{1}{3}x = 3$ **8.** $\frac{3}{5}r = 9$ **9.** $8t = \frac{4}{5}$

10. $\frac{4}{5}a = 1$ **11.** $\frac{y}{4} = 5$ **12.** $2b = \frac{6}{7}$ **13.** $\frac{7}{9}j = 10$

See Example 2 — **14.** Jason uses 2 cans of paint to paint $\frac{1}{2}$ of his room. How many cans of paint will he use to paint the whole room?

15. Cassandra baby-sits for $\frac{4}{5}$ of an hour and earns \$8. What is her hourly rate?

PRACTICE AND PROBLEM SOLVING

Solve each equation. Write the answer in simplest form.

16. $m = \frac{3}{8} \cdot 4$ **17.** $\frac{3}{5}y = 6$ **18.** $4z = \frac{7}{10}$ **19.** $t = \frac{4}{5} \cdot 20$

20. $\frac{3}{5}a = \frac{3}{5}$ **21.** $\frac{1}{6}b = 2\frac{1}{3}$ **22.** $5c = \frac{2}{3} \div \frac{2}{3}$ **23.** $\frac{3}{4}x = 7$

24. $\frac{1}{2} = \frac{w}{4}$ **25.** $8 = \frac{2}{3}n$ **26.** $\frac{1}{4} \cdot \frac{1}{2} = 4d$ **27.** $2y = \frac{4}{5} \div \frac{3}{5}$

Write each equation. Then solve, and check the solution.

28. A number n is divided by 4 and the quotient is $\frac{1}{2}$.

29. A number n is multiplied by $1\frac{1}{2}$ and the product is 9.

30. A recipe for a loaf of bread calls for $\frac{3}{4}$ cup of oatmeal.

    a. How much oatmeal do you need if you make half the recipe?

    b. How much oatmeal do you need if you double the recipe?

31. Entertainment Connie rode the roller coaster at the amusement park. After 3 minutes, the ride was $\frac{3}{4}$ complete. How long did the entire ride take?

32. Zac moved $\frac{1}{5}$ of the things from his old bedroom to his new dorm room in $32\frac{1}{2}$ minutes. How long will it take in minutes for him to move all of his things to his new dorm room?

33. A dress pattern requires $3\frac{1}{8}$ yards of fabric. Jody wants to make matching dresses for the girls in her sewing club so she purchased $34\frac{3}{8}$ yards of fabric. How many dresses can Jody make using this pattern?

○ = WORKED-OUT SOLUTIONS
on p. WS6

34. Multi-Step Alder cut 3 pieces of fabric from a roll. Each piece of fabric she cut is $1\frac{1}{2}$ yd long. She has 2 yards of fabric left on the roll. How much fabric was on the roll before she cut it?

35. Life Science Sasha's book report is about animals in Madagascar. She writes 10 pages, which represents $\frac{1}{3}$ of her report, about lemurs. How many more pages does Sasha have to write to complete her book report?

36. Critical Thinking How can you tell, without solving the equation $\frac{1}{2}x = 4\frac{7}{8}$, that x is greater that $4\frac{7}{8}$?

Use the circle graph for Exercises 37 and 38.

37. The circle graph shows the results of a survey of people who were asked to choose their favorite kind of bagel.

 a. One hundred people chose plain bagels as their favorite kind of bagel. How many people were surveyed in all?

 b. One-fifth of the people who chose sesame bagels also chose plain cream cheese as their favorite spread. How many people chose plain cream cheese? (*Hint*: Use the answer to part **a** to help you solve this problem.)

Favorite Bagels

$\frac{1}{4}$ Sesame

$\frac{1}{2}$ Plain

$\frac{1}{8}$ Poppy

$\frac{1}{8}$ Raisin

38. What's the Question? If the answer is 25 people, what is the question?

39. Write About It Explain how to solve $\frac{3}{5}x = 4$.

40. Challenge Solve $2\frac{3}{4}n = \frac{11}{12}$.

---

41. Multiple Choice Solve $\frac{3}{10}x = 9$.

 A. $x = 15$　　　　**B.** $x = 30$　　　　**C.** $x = 60$　　　　**D.** $x = 90$

42. Multiple Choice Which of the following is a solution to $4x = \frac{3}{4}$?

 F. $x = \frac{3}{16}$　　　　**G.** $x = \frac{3}{4}$　　　　**H.** $x = 3$　　　　**I.** $x = 5\frac{1}{3}$

43. Gridded Response What value of y is a solution to $\frac{4}{5}y = 28$?

Write each improper fraction as a mixed number. (Lesson 4-6)

44. $\frac{11}{3}$　　　　**45.** $\frac{15}{4}$　　　　**46.** $\frac{22}{5}$　　　　**47.** $\frac{13}{2}$

Divide. Write each answer in simplest form. (Lesson 5-8)

48. $\frac{2}{3} \div \frac{1}{3}$　　　　**49.** $\frac{9}{10} \div \frac{3}{4}$　　　　**50.** $2\frac{3}{8} \div \frac{1}{4}$　　　　**51.** $1\frac{1}{4} \div 2\frac{1}{3}$

 **Ready To Go On?**

SECTION 5B

 **Ready To Go On?** THINK central

Go to thinkcentral.com

Quiz for Lessons 5-5 Through 5-10

✓ **5-5** Multiplying Fractions by Whole Numbers

1. Michelle ordered 5 lb of fruit for a family picnic. Of that fruit, $\frac{1}{3}$ was watermelon. How much of the fruit was watermelon?

2. Philip has 35 comic books. Of those comics, $\frac{2}{10}$ take place in space. How many of Philip's comic books take place in space?

✓ **5-6** Multiplying Fractions

Multiply. Write each answer in simplest form.

3. $\frac{2}{7} \cdot \frac{3}{4}$

4. $\frac{3}{5} \cdot \frac{2}{3}$

5. $\frac{7}{12} \cdot \frac{4}{5}$

✓ **5-7** Multiplying Mixed Numbers

Multiply. Write each answer in simplest form.

6. $\frac{1}{4} \cdot 2\frac{1}{3}$

7. $1\frac{1}{6} \cdot \frac{2}{3}$

8. $\frac{7}{8} \cdot 2\frac{2}{3}$

9. $2\frac{1}{4} \cdot 1\frac{1}{6}$

10. $1\frac{2}{3} \cdot 2\frac{1}{5}$

11. $3 \cdot 4\frac{2}{7}$

✓ **5-8** Dividing Fractions and Mixed Numbers

Find the reciprocal.

12. $\frac{2}{7}$

13. $\frac{5}{12}$

14. $\frac{3}{5}$

Divide. Write each answer in simplest form.

15. $\frac{3}{5} \div 4$

16. $1\frac{3}{10} \div 3\frac{1}{4}$

17. $1\frac{1}{5} \div 2\frac{1}{3}$

✓ **5-9** Solving Fraction Equations: Addition and Subtraction

Solve each equation. Write the solution in simplest form.

18. $t + 2\frac{5}{8} = 9$

19. $5\frac{1}{6} = x - \frac{7}{8}$

20. $g + \frac{1}{4} = 2\frac{9}{10}$

21. $a + \frac{3}{5} = 1\frac{7}{10}$

22. Bryn bought $5\frac{1}{8}$ yards of material. She used $3\frac{7}{9}$ yards to make a dress. How much material does she have left?

✓ **5-10** Solving Fraction Equations: Multiplication and Division

Solve each equation.

23. $\frac{2}{3}y = 10$

24. $6p = \frac{3}{4}$

25. $\frac{2}{3}x = 9$

26. Michael has a black cat and a gray kitten. The black cat weighs 12 pounds. The gray kitten weighs $\frac{3}{5}$ the weight of the black cat. How much does the gray kitten weigh?

Ready to Go On?

Real-World CONNECTIONS

Citrus Fruits   Have you ever enjoyed a glass of orange juice or grapefruit juice with breakfast? There is a good chance that the juice you drank came from fruit grown in Florida. More than $\frac{4}{5}$ of the nation's supply of citrus fruits is produced in Florida.

1. Anne makes a Florida Sunshine Shake by first combining the orange juice and grapefruit juice. How many total cups of juice does she have?

2. After making the shake, Anne pours $6\frac{1}{3}$ fluid ounces into a glass. How many fluid ounces remain in the blender?

3. Kendra has a different recipe for a citrus shake. Her recipe calls for $\frac{2}{3}$ of the amount of grapefruit juice that is in the Florida Sunshine Shake recipe. How much grapefruit juice is in Kendra's recipe?

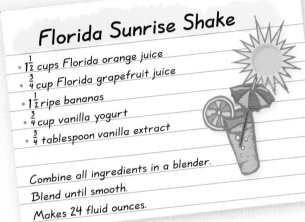

Florida Sunrise Shake

- $1\frac{1}{2}$ cups Florida orange juice
- $\frac{3}{4}$ cup Florida grapefruit juice
- $1\frac{1}{2}$ ripe bananas
- $\frac{3}{4}$ cup vanilla yogurt
- $\frac{3}{4}$ tablespoon vanilla extract

Combine all ingredients in a blender.
Blend until smooth.
Makes 24 fluid ounces.

4. Miguel makes a large batch of Florida Sunshine Shake by multiplying all of the amounts in the recipe by $1\frac{1}{2}$. Does Miguel need more or less than 1 cup of vanilla yogurt? Explain.

5. How many fluid ounces of shake does Miguel make?

6. Miguel divides his shake into 5 equal servings. How many fluid ounces are in each serving?

Game Time

Fraction Riddles

1 What is the value of one-half of two-thirds of three-fourths of four-fifths of five-sixths of six-sevenths of seven-eighths of eight-ninths of nine-tenths of one thousand?

2 What is the next fraction in the sequence below?

$$\frac{1}{12}, \frac{1}{6}, \frac{1}{4}, \frac{1}{3}, \cdots$$

3 I am a three-digit number. My hundreds digit is one-third of my tens digit. My tens digit is one-third of my ones digit. What number am I?

4 A *splorg* costs three-fourths of a dollar plus three-fourths of a *splorg*. How much does a *splorg* cost?

5 How many cubic inches of dirt are in a hole that measures $\frac{1}{3}$ feet by $\frac{1}{4}$ feet by $\frac{1}{2}$ feet?

Fraction Bingo

The object is to be the first player to cover five squares in a row horizontally, vertically, or diagonally.

One person is the caller. On each of the caller's cards, there is an expression containing fractions. When the caller draws a card, he or she reads the expression aloud for the players.

The players must find the value of the expression. If a square on the player's card has that value or a fraction equivalent to that value, they cover the square.

The first player to cover five squares in a row is the winner. Take turns being the caller. A variation can be played in which the winner is the first person to cover all their squares.

Games

Go to **thinkcentral.com**

THINK central

A complete copy of the rules and game pieces are available online.

Materials
- file folder
- scissors
- white paper
- hole punch
- chenille stem
- surveyor's flagging tape
- tape

PROJECT ## Flipping over Fractions

Make a flip-flop book to take notes and work sample problems related to fraction operations.

Directions

1 Cut the folder in half from the fold to the edge. Then cut out a flip-flop shape, with the "toe" of the flip-flop along the folded edge. **Figure A**

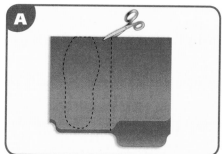

2 Cut about ten flip-flop shapes out of the white paper. They should be slightly smaller than the flip-flop you cut out of the file folder.

3 Put the white flip-flops inside the file-folder flip-flop. Punch a hole at the top through all the layers. Also punch holes at the sides of the flip-flip cover. These side holes should go through only the cover. **Figure B**

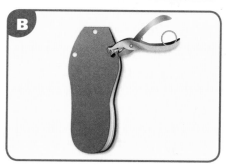

4 Insert the chenille stem into the hole at the top, make a loop, and trim. Insert the surveyor's flagging tape through the loop, and insert the ends into the holes at the sides of the flip-flop. Tape the surveyor's flagging tape to the back of the cover to hold it in place. **Figure C**

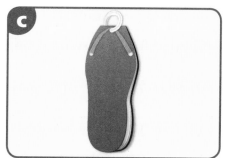

Taking Note of the Math

Write the chapter number and title on the flip-flop. Then use the inside pages to work problems from the chapter. Choose problems that will help you remember the most important concepts.

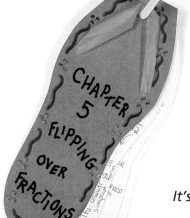

Study Guide: Review

Vocabulary

least common denominator (LCD) 198

least common multiple (LCM) 194

reciprocal 224

multiplicative inverse 224

Complete the sentences below with vocabulary words from the list above.

1. Two numbers are ___?___ if their product is 1.

2. The ___?___ is the smallest number that is a common multiple of two or more denominators.

EXAMPLES

EXERCISES

5-1 **Least Common Multiple** (pp. 194–197)

 Prep MA.6.A.5.1

■ Find the least common multiple (LCM) of 4, 6, and 8.

4: 4, 8, 12, 16, 20, 24, 28, . . .
6: 6, 12, 18, 24, 30, . . .
8: 8, 16, 24, 32, . . .
LCM: 24

Find the least common multiple (LCM).

3. 3, 5, and 10

4. 6, 8, and 16

5. 3, 9, and 27

6. 4, 12, and 30

7. 25 and 45

8. 12, 22, and 30

5-2 **Adding and Subtracting with Unlike Denominators** (pp. 198–201)

 Prep MA.6.A.5.1

■ Add. Write the answer in simplest form.

$\frac{7}{9} + \frac{2}{3}$

$\frac{7}{9} + \frac{2}{3}$ *Write equivalent fractions. Add.*

$\frac{7}{9} + \frac{6}{9} = \frac{13}{9} = 1\frac{4}{9}$

Add or subtract. Write each answer in simplest form.

9. $\frac{1}{5} + \frac{5}{8}$

10. $\frac{1}{6} + \frac{7}{12}$

11. $\frac{13}{15} - \frac{4}{5}$

12. $\frac{7}{8} - \frac{2}{3}$

5-3 **Adding and Subtracting Mixed Numbers** (pp. 202–205)

 Prep MA.6.A.5.1

■ Find the difference. Write the answer in simplest form.

$5\frac{5}{8} - 3\frac{1}{6}$

$5\frac{15}{24} - 3\frac{4}{24}$ *Write equivalent fractions.*

$2\frac{11}{24}$ *Subtract.*

Find each sum or difference. Write the answer in simplest form.

13. $1\frac{3}{10} + 3\frac{2}{5}$

14. $4\frac{5}{9} - 1\frac{1}{2}$

15. Angela had $\frac{7}{10}$ gallon of paint. She used $\frac{1}{3}$ gallon for a project. How much paint did she have left?

5-4 Regrouping to Subtract Mixed Numbers (pp. 206–209)

 Prep MA.6.A.5.1

■ Subtract. Write the answer in simplest form.

$4\frac{7}{10} - 2\frac{9}{10}$

$3\frac{17}{10} - 2\frac{9}{10}$ *Regroup $4\frac{7}{10}$. Subtract.*

$1\frac{8}{10}$

$1\frac{4}{5}$

Subtract. Write each answer in simplest form.

16. $7\frac{2}{9} - 3\frac{5}{9}$ **17.** $3\frac{1}{5} - 1\frac{7}{10}$

18. $8\frac{7}{12} - 2\frac{11}{12}$ **19.** $5\frac{3}{8} - 2\frac{3}{4}$

20. $11\frac{6}{7} - 4\frac{13}{14}$ **21.** $10 - 8\frac{7}{8}$

22. Linda needs 8 ft of ribbon to decorate gifts. She has $3\frac{1}{4}$ ft of ribbon. How many more feet does Linda need?

5-5 Multiplying Fractions by Whole Numbers (pp. 212–215)

 MA.6.A.1.2, MA.6.A.1.3

■ Multiply $3 \cdot \frac{3}{5}$. Write your answer in simplest form.

$3 \cdot \frac{3}{5} = \frac{3}{5} + \frac{3}{5} + \frac{3}{5} = \frac{9}{5}$ or $1\frac{4}{5}$

Multiply. Write each answer in simplest form.

23. $5 \cdot \frac{1}{7}$ **24.** $2 \cdot \frac{3}{8}$ **25.** $3 \cdot \frac{6}{7}$

26. $4 \cdot \frac{5}{8}$ **27.** $6 \cdot \frac{1}{2}$ **28.** $2 \cdot \frac{3}{5}$

29. There are 105 members of the high school band. Of these members, $\frac{1}{5}$ play percussion instruments. How many members play percussion?

5-6 Multiplying Fractions (pp. 216–219)

 MA.6.A.1.2, MA.6.A.1.3

■ Multiply. Write the answer in simplest form.

$\frac{3}{4} \cdot \frac{1}{3}$ *Multiply. Then simplify.*

$\frac{3 \cdot 1}{4 \cdot 3} = \frac{3}{12} = \frac{1}{4}$

Multiply. Write each answer in simplest form.

30. $\frac{5}{6} \cdot \frac{2}{5}$ **31.** $\frac{5}{7} \cdot \frac{3}{4}$ **32.** $\frac{4}{5} \cdot \frac{1}{8}$

33. $\frac{7}{10} \cdot \frac{2}{5}$ **34.** $\frac{1}{9} \cdot \frac{5}{9}$ **35.** $\frac{1}{4} \cdot \frac{6}{7}$

36. Andrew's hockey team won $\frac{4}{5}$ of their games. Andrew scored in $\frac{2}{3}$ of the games his team won. In what fraction of his team's games did Andrew score?

5-7 Multiplying Mixed Numbers (pp. 220–223)

 MA.6.A.1.2, MA.6.A.1.3

■ Multiply. Write the answer in simplest form.

$\frac{2}{5} \cdot 1\frac{2}{3} = \frac{2}{5} \cdot \frac{5}{3} = \frac{10}{15} = \frac{2}{3}$

Multiply. Write each answer in simplest form.

37. $\frac{2}{5} \cdot 2\frac{1}{4}$ **38.** $\frac{3}{4} \cdot 1\frac{2}{3}$ **39.** $3\frac{1}{3} \cdot \frac{3}{5}$

40. $1\frac{1}{3} \cdot \frac{1}{4}$ **41.** $2\frac{2}{5} \cdot 1\frac{1}{2}$ **42.** $2\frac{3}{4} \cdot 2\frac{1}{3}$

Study Guide: Review

5-8 **Dividing Fractions and Mixed Numbers** (pp. 224–227)

 MA.6.A.1.2, MA.6.A.1.3

■ **Divide. Write the answer in simplest form.**

$$\frac{3}{4} \div 6 = \frac{3 \cdot 1}{4 \cdot 6} = \frac{3}{24} = \frac{1}{8}$$

Divide. Write each answer in simplest form.

43. $\frac{4}{7} \div 3$ **44.** $\frac{3}{10} \div 2$ **45.** $1\frac{1}{3} \div 2\frac{2}{5}$

46. Beverly needs to measure $2\frac{2}{3}$ cups of bread crumbs. She has a $\frac{1}{3}$ cup measuring scoop. How many times must she fill the $\frac{1}{3}$ cup measuring scoop to get $2\frac{2}{3}$ cups of bread crumbs?

5-9 **Solving Fraction Equations: Addition and Subtraction** (pp. 228–231)

Preview MA.7.A.3.3

■ **Solve $n + 2\frac{5}{7} = 8$. Write the solution in simplest form.**

$$n + 2\frac{5}{7} - 2\frac{5}{7} = 8 - 2\frac{5}{7}$$
$$n = 8 - 2\frac{5}{7}$$
$$n = 7\frac{7}{7} - 2\frac{5}{7}$$
$$n = 5\frac{2}{7}$$

Solve each equation. Write the solution in simplest form.

47. $x - 12\frac{3}{4} = 17\frac{2}{5}$ **48.** $t + 6\frac{11}{12} = 21\frac{5}{6}$

49. $3\frac{2}{3} = m - 1\frac{3}{4}$ **50.** $5\frac{2}{3} = p + 2\frac{2}{9}$

51. $y - 1\frac{2}{3} = 3\frac{4}{5}$ **52.** $4\frac{2}{5} + j = 7\frac{7}{10}$

53. Abigail is walking to her grandparents' house. If she has walked $1\frac{1}{3}$ miles and her grandparents live 3 miles away, how much farther does Abigail have to walk?

5-10 **Solving Fraction Equations: Multiplication and Division** (pp. 232–235)

 Preview MA.7.A.3.3

■ **Solve the equation.**

$$\frac{4}{5}n = 12$$
$$\frac{4}{5}n \div \frac{4}{5} = 12 \div \frac{4}{5} \quad \textit{Divide both sides by } \frac{4}{5}.$$
$$\frac{4}{5}n \cdot \frac{5}{4} = 12 \cdot \frac{5}{4} \quad \textit{Multiply by the reciprocal.}$$
$$n = \frac{60}{4} = 15$$

Solve each equation.

54. $4a = \frac{1}{2}$ **55.** $\frac{3}{4}b = 1\frac{1}{2}$

56. $\frac{2}{7}m = 5$ **57.** $6g = \frac{4}{5}$

58. $\frac{5}{6}r = 9$ **59.** $\frac{s}{8} = 6\frac{1}{4}$

60. $6p = \frac{2}{3}$ **61.** $\frac{8}{9}j = 1\frac{5}{8}$

62. Marcus is $66\frac{2}{3}$ inches tall. If Marcus is $\frac{5}{6}$ as tall as his father, how tall is Marcus's father?

Find the least common multiple (LCM).

1. 10 and 15 **2.** 4, 6, and 18 **3.** 9, 10, and 12 **4.** 6, 15, and 20

Add or subtract. Write the answer in simplest form.

5. $4\frac{1}{9} - 2\frac{4}{9}$ **6.** $1\frac{7}{10} + 3\frac{3}{4}$ **7.** $\frac{2}{3} - \frac{3}{8}$ **8.** $2\frac{1}{3} - \frac{5}{6}$

9. $4 + 2\frac{2}{7}$ **10.** $\frac{1}{12} + \frac{5}{6}$ **11.** $\frac{3}{8} + \frac{3}{4}$ **12.** $\frac{5}{6} - \frac{2}{3}$

13. On Saturday, Cecelia ran $3\frac{3}{7}$ miles. On Sunday, she ran $4\frac{5}{6}$ miles. How much farther did Cecelia run on Sunday than on Saturday?

14. Michael studied social studies for $\frac{3}{4}$ of an hour, Spanish for $1\frac{1}{2}$ hours, and math for $1\frac{1}{4}$ hours. How many hours did Michael spend studying all three subjects?

15. Quincy needs $6\frac{1}{3}$ feet of rope to tie down the things he is hauling in his truck. He finds a 9 foot long rope in his garage. How much extra rope does Quincy have?

Find the reciprocal.

16. $\frac{3}{5}$ **17.** $\frac{7}{11}$ **18.** $\frac{5}{9}$ **19.** $\frac{1}{8}$

Multiply or divide. Write the answer in simplest form.

20. $\frac{3}{7} \cdot \frac{4}{9}$ **21.** $1\frac{3}{8} \cdot \frac{6}{11}$ **22.** $2\frac{1}{4} \cdot 2\frac{2}{3}$ **23.** $\frac{7}{8} \div 2$

24. $3\frac{1}{3} \div 1\frac{5}{12}$ **25.** $\frac{4}{5} \cdot 1\frac{1}{3}$ **26.** $3\frac{1}{8} \div 1\frac{1}{4}$ **27.** $\frac{3}{8} \cdot \frac{2}{3}$

Evaluate the expression $n \cdot \frac{1}{4}$ for each value of n. Write the answer in simplest form.

28. $n = \frac{7}{8}$ **29.** $n = \frac{2}{5}$ **30.** $n = \frac{8}{9}$ **31.** $n = \frac{4}{11}$

32. Twenty-four students tried out for the cheerleading squad. Only $\frac{5}{6}$ of the students will be chosen. How many students will be chosen for the squad?

33. A recipe for granola bars require $1\frac{1}{2}$ cups of flour. How much flour is needed to make a triple batch of granola bars?

Solve each equation. Write the solution in simplest form.

34. $3r = \frac{9}{10}$ **35.** $n + 3\frac{1}{6} = 12$ **36.** $5\frac{5}{6} = x - 3\frac{1}{4}$

37. $\frac{2}{5}t = 9$ **38.** $\frac{4}{5}m = 7$ **39.** $y - 15\frac{3}{5} = 2\frac{1}{3}$

40. Jessica purchased a bag of cat food. She feeds her cat 1 cup of cat food each day. After 7 days, she has fed her cat $\frac{2}{3}$ of the food in the bag. How many cups of food were in the bag of cat food when Jessica bought it?

Test Tackler

Standardized Test Strategies

Test Tackler

Gridded Response: Write Gridded Responses

When responding to a test item that has an answer grid, you must fill out the grid correctly, or the item will be marked as incorrect.

EXAMPLE 1

Gridded Response: Simplify the expression $(8 \times 3) - 5 \times (6 - 3)$.

$(8 \times 3) - 5 \times (6 - 3)$

$24 - 5 \times 3$ *Perform operations within parentheses.*

$24 - 15$ *Multiply.*

9 *Subtract.*

The expression simplifies to 9.

- Use a pencil to write your answer in the answer boxes at the top of the grid.

- The answer can be entered starting in the far left column, or in the far right column, but not in the middle.

- Write only one digit in each box. Do not leave a blank box in the middle of an answer.

- Shade the correct bubble below your written digit.

EXAMPLE 2

Gridded Response: Evaluate $2\frac{1}{4} + 1\frac{1}{4} + 3\frac{3}{4}$.

$2\frac{1}{4} + 1\frac{1}{4} + 3\frac{3}{4}$

$6\frac{5}{4}$ *Add the fractions and then add the whole numbers.*

$6\frac{5}{4} = 6 + 1\frac{1}{4} = 7\frac{1}{4}$ or 7.25 or $\frac{29}{4}$ *Simplify.*

- You cannot fill in mixed numbers. You must fill in the answer as an improper fraction or a decimal.

- Use a pencil to write your answer in the answer boxes at the top of the grid.

- Write only one digit or symbol in each box. On some grids, the fraction bar and the decimal point have a special box. If so, write your fraction or decimal around it correctly. Do not leave a blank box in the middle of an answer.

- Shade the correct bubble below your written digit.

When filling out a grid be sure to use a pencil and completely fill in the bubbles directly below each digit or symbol you wrote.

Read each sample and then answer the questions that follow.

Sample A
A student divided two fractions and got $\frac{4}{25}$ as a result. Then the student filled in the grid as shown.

1. What error did the student make when filling in the grid?

2. Explain how to fill in the answer correctly.

Sample B
A student added two mixed numbers and got $2\frac{9}{10}$ as a result. Then the student converted the answer to a decimal and filled in the grid as shown.

3. What error did the student make when filling in the grid?

4. Explain how to fill in the answer correctly.

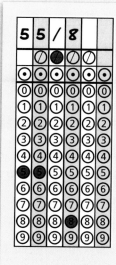

Sample C
A student correctly simplified the expression $6\frac{7}{8} + 1\frac{3}{8} - 2\frac{5}{8}$. Then the student filled in the grid as shown.

5. What answer does the grid show?

6. Explain why you cannot grid a mixed number.

7. Write the answer $5\frac{5}{8}$ in two forms that could be entered in the grid correctly.

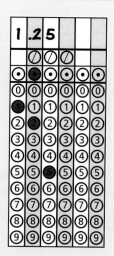

Sample D
A student wrote the standard form of the decimal one and twenty-five hundredths and then filled in the grid as shown.

8. What error did the student make when filling in the grid?

9. Explain how to fill in the answer correctly.

Mastering the Standards

Cumulative Assessment, Chapters 1–5

Multiple Choice

1. Which number is less than $\frac{3}{4}$?

A. $\frac{2}{3}$ **C.** $\frac{5}{6}$

B. $\frac{4}{5}$ **D.** $\frac{9}{10}$

2. Each rabbit listed in the table is expected to gain 0.46 pound over the next month. At the end of the month, which rabbit will weigh closest to 8 pounds?

Rabbit	Weight (lb)
Hopper	7.41
Jumper	7.65
Bouncer	7.05
Bob	7.25

F. Hopper

G. Jumper

H. Bouncer

I. Bob

3. Russell Avenue is 3 times as long as Boyd Street. Russell Avenue is 16.8 miles long. Which equation can you solve to find the length of Boyd Street?

A. $3b = 16.8$

B. $16.8b = 3$

C. $b = 3 + 16.8$

D. $16.8 - b = 3$

4. What is the best estimate of $5x$ when $x = 4\frac{7}{8}$?

F. $4\frac{7}{8}$ **H.** 20

G. 5 **I.** 25

5. Which fraction is closest to $2\frac{1}{2}$ on a number line?

A. $2\frac{1}{3}$ **C.** $2\frac{3}{8}$

B. $2\frac{1}{4}$ **D.** $2\frac{5}{6}$

6. Leah ordered 24 helium-filled balloons for a party. Of the balloons, $\frac{3}{8}$ are red. How many of the balloons are NOT red?

F. 9 balloons **H.** 15 balloons

G. 12 balloons **I.** 21 balloons

7. Let d represent the number of dogs that Max walks in 1 day. Max walks the same number of dogs each day. Which expression shows the number of dogs Max walks in 7 days?

A. $7 + d$ **C.** $7d$

B. $d - 7$ **D.** $\frac{d}{7}$

8. Charlie ate $\frac{5}{8}$ of a pizza. The only mushrooms on the pizza were on $\frac{1}{5}$ of what Charlie ate. How much of the pizza was covered with mushrooms?

F. $\frac{1}{8}$ pizza

G. $\frac{5}{13}$ pizza

H. $\frac{1}{5}$ pizza

I. $3\frac{1}{8}$ pizzas

9. Which of the following sets of decimals is ordered from least to greatest?

A. 3.8, 3.89, 3.08, 3.9

B. 3.89, 3.8, 3.9, 3.08

C. 3.08, 3.89, 3.8, 3.9

D. 3.08, 3.8, 3.89, 3.9

10. Which of the following correctly shows the use of the Distributive Property to find the product of 64 and 8?

  F. $64 \times 8 = (8 \times 60) + (8 \times 4)$

  G. $64 \times 8 = 8 \times 64$

  H. $64 \times 8 = 8 + (60 + 4)$

  I. $64 \times 8 = (8 \times 4) \times 60$

11. Emmanuel has $4\frac{1}{4}$ pounds of strawberries. He divides the strawberries into 3 groups that weigh the same amount. What is the total weight of 2 of those groups?

  A. $1\frac{5}{12}$ pounds

  B. $2\frac{5}{6}$ pounds

  C. $3\frac{1}{6}$ pounds

  D. $4\frac{1}{4}$ pounds

 Underline key words given in the test question so you know for certain what the question is asking.

Gridded Response

12. What is the value of $2x + 9$ when $x = 3^2 \div (5 - 2)$?

13. Juliana bought a pair of sneakers at $12 off the original price. The sale price was $23. What was the original price, in dollars, of the sneakers?

14. What is the reciprocal of $6\frac{1}{7}$?

15. One serving of cottage cheese is $\frac{1}{2}$ cup. A large container contains 8 cups of cottage cheese. How many servings of cottage cheese are in 2 large containers?

16. What decimal is equivalent to $\frac{3}{5}$?

Short Response

S1. Jane is building a tank for her pet snake. The tank's length should be two-thirds of the snake's length, and the tank's width should be half the snake's length. Jane's snake is $121\frac{1}{2}$ feet long. Explain how to find the dimensions of the tank.

S2. The area of a rectangle is the product of its length and width. Marco's garden has 4 plots like the one shown below. Explain how to find the total area of the plots in Marco's garden.

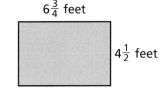

Extended Response

E1. Garrett attends a summer day camp for 6 hours each day. The circle graph below shows what fraction of each day he spends doing different activities.

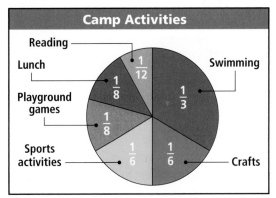

  a. How long does Garrett spend doing each activity? Write the activities in order from longest to shortest.

  b. Sports activities and playground games are all held on the camp fields. What fraction of the camp day does Garrett spend on the fields? Write your answer in simplest form.

  c. Garret spends half of sports activities time playing soccer. How many hours does Garret spend playing soccer during a 5-day week at day camp?

CHAPTER 6

Collecting and Displaying Data

Worktext
pages 223–256

Additional instruction, practice, and activities are available online, including:
- Lesson Tutorial Videos
- Homework Help
- Animated Math

THINK central

Go to thinkcentral.com

Why Learn This?

The Blue Angels are the flight demonstration squadron of the U.S. Navy. They have performed maneuvers at altitudes ranging from 50 feet to 15,000 feet, at speeds ranging from 120 miles per hour to 700 miles per hour.

Pensacola, Florida

Chapter Focus
- Use mean, median, mode, and range to summarize data sets.
- Make and interpret a variety of graphs.

Are You Ready?

Are You Ready? **THINK** central

Go to thinkcentral.com

✓ Vocabulary

Choose the best term from the list to complete each sentence.

1. The answer to an addition problem is called the ___?___.

2. The ___?___ of the 6 in 5,672 is hundreds.

3. When you move ___?___, you move left or right.
When you move ___?___, you move up or down.

horizontally

place value

quotients

sum

vertically

Complete these exercises to review skills you will need for this chapter.

✓ Place Value of Whole Numbers

Write the digit in the tens place of each number.

4. 718   **5.** 989   **6.** 55   **7.** 7,709

✓ Compare and Order Whole Numbers

Order the numbers from least to greatest.

8. 40, 32, 51, 78, 26, 43, 27   **9.** 132, 150, 218, 176, 166

10. 92, 91, 84, 92, 87, 90   **11.** 23, 19, 33, 27, 31, 31, 28, 18

Find the greatest number in each set.

12. 452, 426, 502, 467, 530, 512   **13.** 711, 765, 723, 778, 704, 781

14. 143, 122, 125, 137, 140, 118, 139   **15.** 1,053; 1,106; 1,043; 1,210; 1,039; 1,122

✓ Write Fractions as Decimals

Write each fraction as a decimal.

16. $\frac{1}{4}$ **17.** $\frac{5}{8}$ **18.** $\frac{1}{6}$ **19.** $\frac{2}{5}$

20. $\frac{5}{6}$ **21.** $\frac{1}{2}$ **22.** $\frac{3}{4}$ **23.** $\frac{9}{11}$

✓ Locate Points on a Number Line

Name the point on the number line that corresponds to each given value.

24. 5   **25.** 12   **26.** 8   **27.** 1

Study Guide: Preview

Before

Previously, you

- described characteristics of data such as the shape of the data and the middle number.
- graphed a given set of data using an appropriate graphical representation.
- used tables of related number pairs to make line graphs.

Now

You will study

- using mean, median, mode, and range to describe data.
- solving problems by collecting, organizing, and displaying data.
- drawing and comparing different graphical representations of the same data.

Why?

You can use the skills learned in this chapter

- to recognize misuses of graphical information and evaluate conclusions based on data analysis.
- to display data correctly for projects in social studies and science.

Key Vocabulary/Vocabulario

bar graph	gráfica de barras
coordinate grid	cuadrícula de coordenadas
line graph	gráfica lineal
mean	media
median	mediana
mode	moda
ordered pair	par ordenado
outlier	valor extremo
range	rango (en estadística)
stem-and-leaf plot	diagrama de tallo y hojas

Vocabulary Connections

To become familiar with some of the vocabulary terms in the chapter, consider the following. You may refer to the chapter, the glossary, or a dictionary if you like.

1. The *median* of a highway divides the highway into two equal sections. For a set of numerical data, what do you think the **median** represents?

2. A *bar* can be a straight stripe or band. What do you think a **bar graph** uses to display data?

3. A *grid* is a network of uniformly spaced horizontal and perpendicular lines. What do you think a **coordinate grid** looks like?

4. *Ordered* means "to be arranged." The word *pair* can mean "two things designed for use together." What do you think an **ordered pair** is made up of?

5. A *range* can mean the distance between possible extremes. If you are looking for the **range** of a set of numbers, what do you think you are looking for?

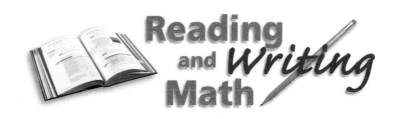

Reading Strategy: Read and Interpret Graphics

Figures, diagrams, charts, and graphs are used to illustrate data. Knowing how to understand these visual aids will help you learn the important facts and details of a problem.

LA.6.4.2.2 The student will . . . organize and record information . . .

Chart

Gustavo's Gift Wrap Table	
Gift Size	Paper Needed (yd²)
Small	$\frac{11}{12}$
Medium	$1\frac{5}{9}$
Large	$2\frac{2}{3}$
X-large	$3\frac{1}{9}$

Read and understand each column head and each row head.

- **Title:** Gustavo's Gift Wrap Table
- **Gift Size:** Small, Medium, Large, and X-large
- **Paper Needed (yd²):** Tells how much paper is needed to wrap the given gift size.

Graph

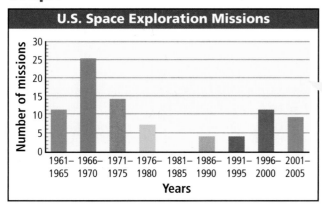

The titles of the graph describe what information is being graphed. Read the label on each axis.

- **Title:** U.S. Space Exploration Missions
- **x-axis:** Years (given as 5-year intervals)
- **y-axis:** Number of missions

Try This

Look up each exercise in your textbook and answer the following questions.

1. Lesson 5-9, Exercise 32: What type of graph is shown? How many minutes long is "Winter"? Explain.

2. Lesson 5-10, Exercise 37: What is the title of the circle graph? What types of bagels are listed?

Collecting and Displaying Data **251**

Mean, Median, Mode, and Range

MA.6.S.6.1 Determine the measures of central tendency and variability . . .

Players on a volleyball team measured how high they could jump. The results in inches are recorded in the table.

13	23	21	20	21	24	18

Vocabulary

mean

median

mode

range

One way to describe this data set is to find the *mean*. The **mean** is the sum of all the items divided by the number of items in the set. Sometimes the mean is also called the *average*. The mean of this set of data is the average height that the volleyball team could jump.

EXAMPLE 1 Finding the Mean of a Data Set

Find the mean of each data set.

A

Heights of Vertical Jumps (in.)						
13	23	21	20	21	24	18

$13 + 23 + 21 + 20 + 21 + 24 + 18 = 140$ *Add all values.*
$140 \div 7 = 20$ *Divide the sum by the number of items.*

The mean is 20 inches.

B

Numbers of Pets Owned				
2	4	1	1	2

$2 + 4 + 1 + 1 + 2 = 10$ *Add all values.*
$10 \div 5 = 2$ *Divide the sum by the number of items.*

The mean is 2. The average number of pets that these five people own is 2.

Check

Use counters to make stacks that match the data.

| 2 | 4 | 1 | 1 | 2 |

Move the chips so that each stack has the same number.

Each stack has 2 counters. The mean is 2.

Some other descriptions of a set of data are called the *median, mode,* and *range.*

- The **median** is the middle value when the data are in numerical order, or the mean of the two middle values if there are an even number of items.

- The **mode** is the value or values that occur most often. There may be more than one mode for a data set. If no value is repeated in the set, the data set has no mode.

- The **range** is the difference between the least and greatest values in the set.

E X A M P L E **2** **Finding the Mean, Median, Mode, and Range of a Data Set**

Find the mean, median, mode, and range of each data set.

NFL Career Touchdowns			
Marcus Allen	145	Franco Harris	100
Jim Brown	126	Walter Payton	125

mean: $\dfrac{145 + 126 + 100 + 125}{4}$ *Add all values. Divide the sum by the number of items.*

$= 124$

Write the data in numerical order: 100, 125, 126, 145

median: 100, (125, 126) 145   *There are an even number of items, so find the mean of the two middle values.*

$\dfrac{125 + 126}{2} = 125.5$

mode: none   *No value occurs most often.*

range: $145 - 100 = 45$ *Subtract least value from greatest value.*

The mean is 124 touchdowns; the median is 125.5 touchdowns; there is no mode; and the range is 45 touchdowns.

Think and Discuss

1. **Describe** what you can say about the values in a data set if the set has a small range.

2. **Tell** how many modes are in the following data set. Explain your answer. 15, 12, 13, 15, 12, 11

3. **Describe** how adding 20 inches to the data set in Example 1A would affect the mean.

Homework Help THINK central

Go to thinkcentral.com
Exercises 1–5, 7, 9, 11, 13, 15

GUIDED PRACTICE

See Example **1** Find the mean of the data set.

1.

Number of Petals	13	24	35	18	15	27

See Example **2** Find the mean, median, mode, and range of the data set.

2.

Heights of Students (in.)	51	67	63	52	49	48	48

INDEPENDENT PRACTICE

See Example **1** Find the mean of the data set.

3.

Numbers of Books Read	6	4	10	5	6	8

See Example **2** Find the mean, median, mode, and range of each data set.

4.

Ages of Students (yr)	14	16	15	17	16	12

5.

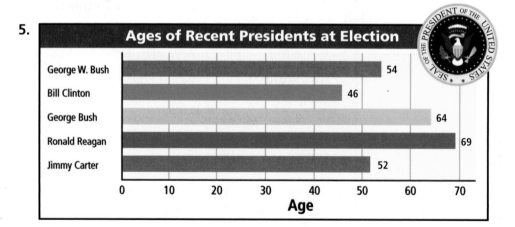

Ages of Recent Presidents at Election

George W. Bush — 54
Bill Clinton — 46
George Bush — 64
Ronald Reagan — 69
Jimmy Carter — 52

PRACTICE AND PROBLEM SOLVING

6. Frank has 3 nickels, 5 dimes, and 2 quarters. Find the range, mean, median, and mode of the values of Frank's coins.

7. **Education** For the six New England states, the mean scores on the math section of the SAT one year were as follows: Connecticut, 509; Maine, 500; Massachusetts, 513; New Hampshire, 519; Rhode Island, 500; and Vermont, 508. Create a table using this data. Then find the range, mean, median, and mode.

8. **Critical Thinking** Gina spent $4, $5, $7, $7, and $6 over the past 5 days buying lunch. Is the mean, median, mode, or range the most useful way to describe this data set? Explain.

○ = **WORKED-OUT SOLUTIONS**
on p. WS6

Find each missing value.

9. 3, 5, 7, 9, ▊; mean: 7

10. 15, 17, ▊, 28, 30; mean: 23

11. 10, 9, ▊, 4, 8, 8, 4, 7; mode: 4

12. 7, 2, ▊, 15, 20, 8, 14, 29; median: 13

13. 50, 100, 75, 60, ▊, 25, 105, 40; median: 65

14. 14, 8, 17, 21, ▊, 11, 3, 13; range: 20

15. Critical Thinking Find the set of 5 items of data that has a range of 9, a mean of 11, a median of 12, and a mode of 15.

? **16. What's the Error?** Joey says that the mean of the set of data is 23.5. Describe Joey's error.

Numbers of Flowers in Bouquets	25	20	21	22	25	25

? **17. What's the Question?** On an exam, three students scored 75, four students scored 82, three students scored 88, four students scored 93, and one student scored 99. If the answer is 88, what is the question?

18. Challenge In the Super Bowls from 2002 to 2007, the winning team won by a mean of $9\frac{5}{6}$ points. By how many points did the New England Patriots win in 2002?

Year	Super Bowl Champion	Points Won By
2007	Indianapolis Colts	12
2006	Pittsburgh Steelers	11
2005	New England Patriots	3
2004	New England Patriots	3
2003	Tampa Bay Buccaneers	27
2002	New England Patriots	▊

19. Choose a Strategy A data set consists of the positive integers 1 through n. Find an expression for the median of the data. (Hint: Find the median for various values of n and look for a pattern.)

Florida Spiral Review

MA.6.S.6.1, MA.6.A.5.1, MA.6.A.5.3

20. Multiple Choice Over 5 days, Pedro jogged 6.5 miles, 5 miles, 2 miles, 2 miles, and 4.5 miles. Find the mean distance that Pedro jogged.

A. 2 miles   **B.** 3.5 miles   **C.** 4 miles   **D.** 4.75 miles

21. Gridded Response The mean of 12, 15, 20 and x is 18. Find the value of x.

Estimate each product or quotient. (Lesson 3-2)

22. 6.11×9.83

23. $43.77 \div 11.03$

24. 3.92×5.88

25. Some friends order 3 large pizzas. A large pizza has 8 slices. The leftover slices from each pizza are as follows: 1 slice, 3 slices, and 1 slice. Write a mixed fraction to describe how much of the pizzas were eaten. (Lesson 4-6)

6-2 Additional Data and Outliers

MA.6.S.6.2 Select and analyze the measures of central tendency . . .

The mean, median, and mode may change when you add data to a data set.

USA's Shani Davis at the 2007 ISU World Single Distances Speed Skating Championships.

EXAMPLE 1 *Sports Application*

Vocabulary
outlier

A Find the mean, median, and mode of the data in the table.

U.S. Winter Olympic Medals Won								
Year	2006	2002	1998	1994	1992	1988	1984	1980
Medals	25	34	13	13	11	6	8	12

mean = 15.25   mode = 13   median = 12.5

B The United States also won 10 medals in 1976 and 8 medals in 1972. Add this data to the data in the table and find the mean, median, and mode.

mean = 14   *The mean decreased by 1.25.*
modes = 8, 13   *There is an additional mode.*
median = 11.5   *The median decreased by 1.*

 Math @ thinkcentral.com

An **outlier** is a value in a set that is very different from the other values.

EXAMPLE 2 *Social Studies Application*

In 2001, 64-year-old Sherman Bull became the oldest American to reach the top of Mount Everest. Other climbers to reach the summit that day were 33, 31, 31, 32, 33, and 28 years old. Find the mean, median, and mode without and with Bull's age, and explain the changes.

Data without Bull's age: mean ≈ 31.3   modes = 31, 33   median = 31.5

Data with Bull's age: mean = 36   modes = 31, 33   median = 32

When you add Bull's age, the mean increases by 4.7, the modes stay the same, and the median increases by 0.5. The mean is the most affected by the outlier.

Helpful Hint

In Example 2, Sherman Bull's age is an outlier because he is much older than the others in the group.

Sometimes one or two data values can greatly affect the mean, median, or mode. When one of these values is affected like this, you should choose a different value to best describe the data set.

EXAMPLE **3**   **Describing a Data Set**

The Seawells are shopping for a DVD player. They found ten DVD players with the following prices:

$175, $180, $130, $150, $180, $500, $160, $180, $150, $160

What are the mean, median, and mode of this data set? Which one best describes the data set?

mean:

$$\frac{175 + 180 + 130 + 150 + 180 + 500 + 160 + 180 + 150 + 160}{10} = \frac{1965}{10}$$
$$= 196.50$$

The mean is $196.50.

Most of the DVD players cost less than $200, so the mean does not describe the data set best.

median:

130, 150, 150, 160, 160, 175, 180, 180, 180, 500

$$\frac{160 + 175}{2} = 167.50$$

The median is $167.50.

The median best describes the data set because a majority of the data is clustered around the value $167.50.

mode:

The value $180 occurs 3 times, more than any other value. The mode is $180.

The mode represents only 3 of the 10 values. The mode does not describe the entire data set.

Some data sets, such as {red, blue, red}, do not contain numbers. In this case, the only way to describe the data set is with the mode.

Think and Discuss

1. Explain how an outlier with a large value will affect the mean of a data set. What is the effect of a small outlier value?

2. Explain why the mean would not be a good description of the following high temperatures that occurred over 7 days: 72°F, 73°F, 70°F, 68°F, 70°F, 71°F, and 39°F.

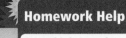

Homework Help THINK central

Go to thinkcentral.com
Exercises 1–6, 7, 13

GUIDED PRACTICE

See Example **1**

1. **Sports** The graph shows how many times some countries have won the Davis Cup in tennis from 1900 to 2000.

   a. Find the mean, median, and mode of the data.

   b. The United States won 31 Davis Cups between 1900 and 2000. Add this number to the data in the graph and find the mean, median, and mode.

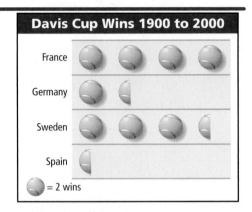

Davis Cup Wins 1900 to 2000

France
Germany
Sweden
Spain

= 2 wins

See Example **2**

2. In 1998, 77-year-old John Glenn became the oldest person to travel into space. Other astronauts traveling on that same mission were 43, 37, 38, 46, 35, and 42 years old. Find the mean, median, and mode of all their ages with and without Glenn's age, and explain the changes.

See Example **3**

3. Kate read books that were 240, 450, 180, 160, 195, 170, 240, and 165 pages long. What are the mean, median, and mode of this data set? Which one best describes the data set?

INDEPENDENT PRACTICE

See Example **1**

4. **History** The table shows the ages of the 10 youngest signers of the Declaration of Independence.

   a. Find the mean, median, and mode of the data.

   b. Benjamin Franklin was 70 years old when he signed the Declaration of Independence. Add his age to the data in the table and find the mean, median, and mode.

Ages of 10 Youngest Signers of Declaration of Independence						
Age	26	29	30	31	33	34
Number Of Signers	//	/	/	/	///	//

See Example **2**

5. **Geography** The map shows the population densities of several states along the Atlantic coast. Find the mean, median, and mode of the data with and without Maine's population density, and explain the changes.

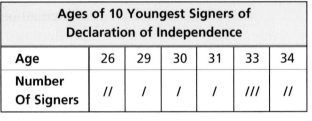

Population Density (people per square mile)

Maine 41
Massachusetts 810
New Jersey 1,138
Rhode Island 1,003
Connecticut 702

See Example **3**

6. The passengers in a van are 16, 19, 17, 18, 15, 14, 32, 32, and 41 years old. What are the mean, median, and mode of this data set? Which one best describes the data set?

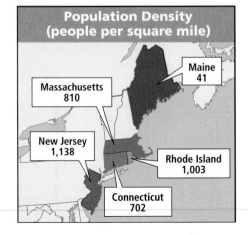

= WORKED-OUT SOLUTIONS
on p. WS7

On September 13, 1922, the temperature in El Azizia, Libya, reached 136 °F, the record high for the planet. (*Source: The World Almanac and Book of Facts*)

7. What are the mean, median, and mode of the highest recorded temperatures on each continent?

8. a. Which temperature is an outlier?

   b. What are the mean, median, and mode of the temperatures if the outlier is not included?

Continent	Highest Temperature (°F)
Africa	136
Antarctica	59
Asia	129
Australia	128
Europe	122
North America	134
South America	120

Erg Murzuq Dunes in the Libyan Desert

9. **? What's the Error?** A student stated that the median temperature would rise to 120.6 °F if a new record high of 75 °F were recorded in Antarctica. Explain the error. How would the median temperature actually be affected if a high of 75 °F were recorded in Antarctica?

10. **✐ Write About It** Is the data in the table best described by the mean, median, or mode? Explain.

11. **☆ Challenge** Suppose a new high temperature were recorded in Europe, and the new mean temperature became 120 °F. What is Europe's new high temperature?

Florida Spiral Review

12. Multiple Choice Which value will change the most when 5 is added to the data set 0, 1, 4, 0, 3, 4, 2, and 1?

  A. Range   **B.** Median   **C.** Mode   **D.** Mean

13. Gridded Response The table shows the speeds, in miles per hour, of certain animals. What is the mean speed when the outlier is removed?

Animal	House cat	Rabbit	Cheetah	Reindeer	Zebra	Elk	Elephant
Speed (mi/h)	30	35	70	32	40	45	25

Solve each equation. Check your answers. (Lesson 2-6)

14. $32 = v + 13$ **15.** $x + 19 = 50$ **16.** $47 + t = 101$

17. Find the median, mode, and range of the animal speeds in Exercise 13. (Lesson 6-1)

Quiz for Lessons 6-1 Through 6-2

6-1 Mean, Median, Mode, and Range

Find the mean, median, mode, and range of each data set.

1.

Distance (mi)					
5	6	4	7	3	5

2.

Test Scores				
78	80	85	92	90

3.

Ages of Students (yr)							
11	13	12	12	12	13	9	14

4.

Number of Pages in Each Book						
145	119	156	158	125	128	135

6-2 Additional Data and Outliers

5. The table shows the number of people who attended each monthly meeting from January to May.

Number of People Attending				
Jan	Feb	Mar	Apr	May
27	26	32	30	30

   a. Find the mean, median, and mode of the attendances.

   b. In June, 39 people attended the meeting, and in July, 26 people attended the meeting. Add this data to the table and find the mean, median, and mode with the new data.

6. The four states with the longest coastlines are Alaska, Florida, California, and Hawaii. Alaska's coastline is 6,640 miles. Florida's coastline is 1,350 miles. California's coastline is 840 miles, and Hawaii's coastline is 750 miles. Find the mean, median, and mode of the lengths with and without Alaska's, and explain the changes.

7. The daily snowfall amounts for the first ten days of December are listed below.

   2 in., 5 in., 0 in., 0 in., 15 in., 1 in., 0 in., 3 in., 1 in., 4 in.

   What are the mean, median, and mode of this data set? Which one best describes the data set?

8. The following is true about the data set for Mr. Pho's astronomy quiz:
   - There were 10 quizzes.
   - The mean score was 90.
   - The range of the scores was 38.
   - There was one outlier.

   a. A few students got a score of 100. What was the least quiz score?

   b. Find the outlier. Explain.

   c. Find the sum of the 10 quiz scores. Explain.

Ready to Go On?

Focus on Problem Solving

 Make a Plan

LA.6.4.2.2 The student will . . . (organize) information . . .

• **Prioritize and sequence information**

Some problems give you a lot of information. Read the entire problem carefully to be sure you understand all of the facts. You may need to read it over several times, perhaps aloud so that you can hear yourself say the words.

Then decide which information is most important (prioritize). Is there any information that is absolutely necessary to solve the problem? This information is important.

Finally, put the information in order (sequence). Use comparison words like *before, after, longer, shorter,* and so on to help you. Write the sequence down before you try to solve the problem.

Read the problems below and answer the questions that follow.

1 The portable MP3 player appeared 300 years after the piano. The tape recorder was invented in 1898. Thomas Edison invented the phonograph 21 years before the tape recorder and 122 years before the portable MP3 player. What is the date of each invention?

a. Which invention's date can you use to find the dates of all the others?

b. Can you solve the problem without this date? Explain.

c. List the inventions in order from earliest invention to latest invention.

2 Jon recorded the heights of his family members. There are 4 people in Jon's family, including Jon. Jon's mother is 2 inches taller than Jon's father. Jon is 56 inches tall. Jon's sister is 4 inches taller than Jon and 5 inches shorter than Jon's father. What are the heights of Jon and his family members?

a. Whose height can you use to find the heights of all the others?

b. Can you solve the problem without this height? Explain.

c. List Jon's family members in order from shortest to tallest.

?

1898

?

?

6-3 Bar Graphs

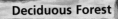

Deciduous Forest

Tundra

Rain Forest

Savannah

MA.6.S.6.1
Determine the measures of central tendency and variability . . .

A biome is a large region characterized by a specific climate. There are ten land biomes on Earth. Some are pictured at right. Each gets a different amount of rainfall.

A *bar graph* can be used to display and compare data about rainfall. A **bar graph** displays data with vertical or horizontal bars.

Vocabulary

bar graph

double-bar graph

EXAMPLE 1 Reading a Bar Graph

Use the bar graph to answer each question.

A **Which biome in the graph has the most rainfall?**

Find the highest bar.

The rain forest has the most rainfall.

B **Approximate the range of the rainfall data for the biomes.**

Subtract the shortest bar from the tallest bar. Estimate each height.
150 – 20 = 130

The range of the rainfall data is approximately 130 inches.

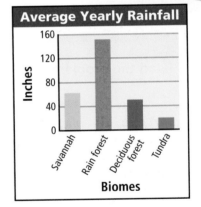

EXAMPLE 2 Making a Bar Graph

Use the given data to make a bar graph.

Coal Reserves (billion metric tons)		
Asia	Europe	Africa
695	404	66

Step 1: Find an appropriate scale and interval. The scale must include all of the data values. The interval separates the scale into equal parts.

Step 2: Use the data to determine the lengths of the bars. Draw bars of equal width. The bars cannot touch.

Step 3: Title the graph and label the axes.

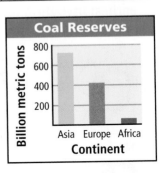

Video Lesson Tutorial Videos @ thinkcentral.com

A **double-bar graph** shows two sets of related data.

EXAMPLE 3

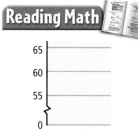

PROBLEM SOLVING APPLICATION

Make a double-bar graph to compare the data in the table.

Life Expectancies in Atlantic South America				
	Brazil	**Argentina**	**Uruguay**	**Paraguay**
Male (yr)	59	71	73	70
Female (yr)	69	79	79	74

1. Understand the Problem

You are asked to use a graph to compare the data given in the table. You will need to use all of the information given.

2. Make a Plan

You can make a double-bar graph to display the two sets of data.

3. Solve

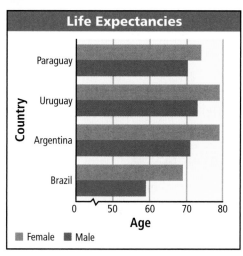

Determine appropriate scales for both sets of data.

Use the data to determine the lengths of the bars. Draw bars of equal width. Bars should be in pairs. Use a different color for male ages and female ages. Title the graph and label both axes.

Include a key to show what each bar represents.

4. Look Back

You could make two separate graphs, one of male ages and one of female ages. However, it is easier to compare the two data sets when they are on the same graph.

Reading Math

65
60
55
0

This symbol means there is a break in the scale. Some intervals were left out because they were not needed for the graph.

Think and Discuss

1. Give comparisons you can make by looking at a bar graph.

2. Describe the kind of data you would display in a bar graph.

3. Tell why the graph in Example 3 needs a key.

Homework Help

Go to thinkcentral.com
Exercises 1–8, 9, 11

GUIDED PRACTICE

See Example **1** **Use the bar graph to answer each question.**

1. Which color was the least common among the cars in the parking lot?

2. Which colors appeared more than ten times?

See Example **2** 3. Use the given data to make a bar graph. What is the mean of the data?

Students in Mr. Jones's History Classes			
Period 1	28	Period 6	22
Period 2	27	Period 7	7

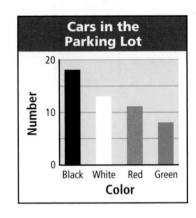

See Example **3** 4. Make a double-bar graph to compare the data in the table.

Movie Preferences of Men and Women Polled at the Mall						
	Comedy	Action	Sci-Fi	Horror	Drama	Other
Men	16	27	16	23	12	6
Women	21	14	8	18	30	9

INDEPENDENT PRACTICE

See Example **1** **Use the bar graph to answer each question.**

5. Which fruit was liked the best?

6. Which fruits were liked by equal numbers of people?

See Example **2** 7. Use the given data to make a bar graph.

Days with Rainfall			
January	14	March	16
February	12	April	23

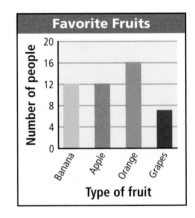

See Example **3** 8. Make a double-bar graph to compare the data in the table.

Heart Rates Before and After Exercise (beats per minute)						
	Jason	Jamal	Ray	Tonya	Peter	Brenda
Before	60	62	61	65	64	65
After	131	140	128	140	135	120

Social Studies Use the bar graph for Exercises 9–12.

9. What is the range of the land area of the continents?

10. What is the mode of the land area of the continents?

11. What is the mean of the land area of the continents?

12. What is the median of the land area of the continents?

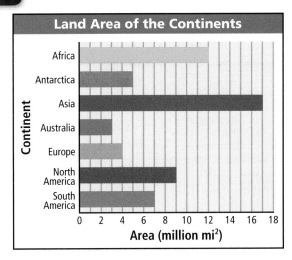

Land Area of the Continents

13. The basketball coach divided the team into two practice squads, the Blue Squad and the Green Squad. The table shows the scores from 6 weeks of practice games.

    a. Draw a double bar graph.

    b. Find the mean score and range for each squad.

    c. Which squad would you pick to play in an upcoming tournament? Explain your reasoning.

 14. **Write About It** Explain how you would make a bar graph of the five most populated cities in the United States.

 15. **Challenge** Create a bar graph displaying the number of A's, B's, C's, D's, and F's in Ms. Walker's class if the grades were the following: 81, 87, 80, 75, 77, 98, 52, 78, 75, 82, 74, 95, 76, 52, 76, 53, 86, 77, 90, 83, 96, 83, 74, 67, 90, 65, 69, 93, 68, and 76.

Scores of Practice Games		
	Blue	**Green**
Week 1	62	40
Week 2	40	44
Week 3	42	44
Week 4	54	48
Week 5	36	52
Week 6	50	56

Grading System	
A	90–100
B	80–89
C	70–79
D	60–69
F	0–59

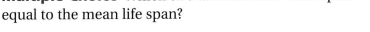

Florida Spiral Review

MA.6.S.6.1, MA.6.A.1.2

Use the bar graph for Exercises 16 and 17.

16. **Multiple Choice** What is the range of the life spans?

    A. 5 yr   **B.** 10 yr   **C.** 15 yr   **D.** 20 yr

17. **Multiple Choice** Which two animals have a life span equal to the mean life span?

    F. Lion and horse   **G.** Squirrel and cow   **H.** Horse and squirrel   **I.** Lion and cow

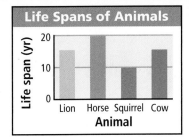

Life Spans of Animals

Compare. Write <, >, or =. (Lessons 5-5 and 5-6)

18. $\frac{2}{3} \cdot \frac{1}{2}$ ▧ $\frac{2}{3} \cdot \frac{1}{3}$

19. $3\frac{1}{2} \cdot \frac{1}{3}$ ▧ $2\frac{1}{2} \cdot \frac{3}{4}$

20. $\frac{7}{10} \cdot 4$ ▧ $5\frac{3}{5} \cdot \frac{1}{2}$

○ = WORKED-OUT SOLUTIONS
on p. WS7

Review of
MA.5.S.7.2
Differentiate . . .
discrete data . . . and represent
those using graphs . . .

Vocabulary

frequency

frequency table

line plot

Your fingerprints are unlike anyone else's. Even identical twins have slightly different fingerprint patterns.

All fingerprints have one of three patterns: whorl, loop, or arch.

The **frequency** of a discrete data value is the number of times it occurs.

A **frequency table** lists items together according to the frequency of the items.

Loop

Whorl

Arch

EXAMPLE 1

Using Tally Marks to Make a Frequency Table

Each student in Mrs. Choe's class recorded their fingerprint pattern. Which type is most common in Mrs. Choe's class?

| whorl | loop | loop | loop | loop | arch | loop |
| whorl | arch | loop | arch | loop | arch | whorl |

Make a table to show each type of fingerprint.

Step 1: For each fingerprint, make a tally mark in the appropriate row.

Step 2: Count the number of tally marks for each pattern. This is the frequency.

Reading Math

A group of four tally marks with a line through it means five.

卅 = 5

卅 卅 = 10

Fingerprint Patterns		
Pattern	**Tallies**	**Frequency**
Whorl	///	3
Arch	////	4
Loop	卅 //	7

The loop pattern is the most common in Mrs. Choe's class.

A **line plot** uses a number line and *x*'s or other symbols to show frequencies of values.

EXAMPLE 2

Making a Line Plot

Students in Mr. Lee's class each ran several miles in a week. Make a line plot of the data.

Step 1: Draw a number line.

Step 2: For each student, use an *x* on the number line to represent how many miles he or she ran.

Number of Miles Run
8 3 5 6 7 8 5 5 3 6 10 7 5

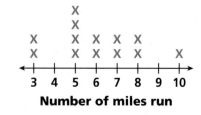

Number of miles run

Video **Lesson Tutorial Videos** @ **thinkcentral.com**

EXAMPLE **3** **Making a Frequency Table with Intervals**

Use the data in the table to make a frequency table with intervals.

Number of Representatives per State in the U.S. House of Representatives												
7	1	6	4	52	6	6	1	1	23	11	2	2
20	10	5	4	6	7	2	8	10	16	8	5	9
1	3	2	2	13	3	31	12	1	19	6	5	21
2	6	1	9	30	3	1	11	9	3	9		

Step 1: Choose equal intervals.

Step 2: Find the number of data values in each interval. Write these numbers in the "Frequency" row.

Number of Representatives per State in the U.S. House of Representatives									
Number	0–5	6–11	12–17	18–23	24–29	30–35	36–41	42–47	48–53
Frequency	22	18	3	4	0	2	0	0	1

This table shows that 22 states have between 0 and 5 representatives, 18 states have between 6 and 11 representatives, and so on.

Think and Discuss

1. Explain how you can use the second table in Example 3 to find the interval that contains the median.

 **6-4** **Exercises**

 Review of MA.5.S.7.2

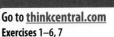 **Homework Help** THINK central
Go to thinkcentral.com
Exercises 1–6, 7

 **GUIDED PRACTICE**

See Example **1** 1. The final grades in Mr. Cho's physics class were B, A, C, A, B, C, B, A, B, D, and B. Make a frequency table for the data. What is the mode?

See Example **2** 2. Make a line plot of the data.

Length of Each U.S. Presidency (yr)												
8	4	8	8	8	4	8	4	0	4	4	1	3	4	4	4	4	8	4	0	4
4	4	4	4	8	4	8	2	6	4	12	8	8	2	6	5	3	4	8	4	8

See Example **3** 3. Use the data in the table in Exercise 2 to make a frequency table with intervals.

6-4 Line Plots, Frequency Tables, and Histograms **267**

See Example 1

4. Survey your classmates about the type of pets they own. Make a frequency table of the data. Determine the mode.

See Example 2

5. Make a line plot of the data.

Number of Olympic Medals Won by 27 Countries													
8	88	59	12	11	57	38	17	14	28	28	26	25	23
18	8	29	34	14	17	13	13	58	12	97	10	9	

See Example 3

6. Use the data in the table in Exercise 5 to make a frequency table with intervals.

PRACTICE AND PROBLEM SOLVING

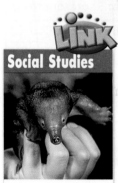

Social Studies

Echidnas are egg-laying mammals found only in Australia and New Guinea. A baby echidna is called a puggle.

7. Social Studies The map shows the populations of Australia's states and territories. Use the data to make a frequency table with intervals.

8. Multi-Step Gather data on the number of pairs of shoes your classmates own. Make two line plots of the data, one for the boys and one for the girls. Compare the data.

Northern Territory 187,100
Queensland 3,401,200
New South Wales 6,274,400
AUSTRALIA
Australian Capital Territory 309,800
Western Australia 1,798,100
South Australia 1,479,800
Victoria 4,605,100
Tasmania 473,500

9. Critical Thinking Can a frequency table have intervals of 0–5, 5–10, and 10–15? Why or why not?

10. Challenge Can you find the mean, median, and mode price using this frequency table? If so, find them. If not, explain why not.

Cost of Video Game Rentals at Different Stores				
Price	$2.00–$2.99	$3.00–$3.99	$4.00–$4.99	$5.00–$5.99
Frequency	5	12	8	5

Florida Spiral Review

MA.6.S.6.1, MA.6.A.5.2

Use the line plot to answer Exercises 11 and 12.

11. Gridded Response Find the mean number of goals.

12. Multiple Choice Which two measures are equal?

    A. mean and median   **C.** mode and median

    B. median and mean   **D.** mean and range

Goals Scored

Order the numbers from least to greatest. (Lessons 3-1 and 4-7)

13. $\frac{2}{3}$, 0.6, $\frac{5}{6}$ **14.** 0.82, $\frac{17}{20}$, $\frac{4}{5}$ **15.** $\frac{13}{16}$, $\frac{5}{8}$, 0.16

○ = WORKED-OUT SOLUTIONS
on p. WS7

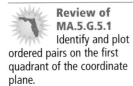

6-5 Ordered Pairs

San Diego, CA. Image courtesy of spaceimaging.com.

Review of MA.5.G.5.1 Identify and plot ordered pairs on the first quadrant of the coordinate plane.

Vocabulary

coordinate grid

ordered pair

Animated Math @ thinkcentral.com

Cities, towns, and neighborhoods are often laid out on a grid. This makes it easier to map and find locations.

A **coordinate grid** is formed by horizontal and vertical lines and is used to locate points.

Each point on a coordinate grid can be located by using an **ordered pair** of numbers, such as (4, 6). The starting point is (0, 0).

- The first number tells how far to move horizontally from (0, 0).
- The second number tells how far to move vertically.

EXAMPLE **1** **Identifying Ordered Pairs**

Name the ordered pair for each location.

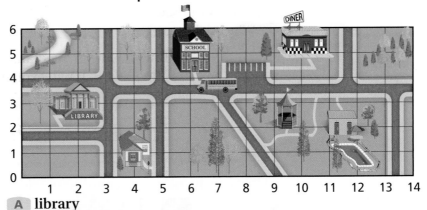

A library

Start at (0, 0). Move right 2 units and then up 3 units.

The library is located at (2, 3).

B school

Start at (0, 0). Move right 6 units and then up 5 units.

The school is located at (6, 5).

C pool

Start at (0, 0). Move right 12 units and up 1 unit.

The pool is located at (12, 1).

EXAMPLE 2 Graphing Ordered Pairs

Graph and label each point on a coordinate grid.

A $Q\left(4\frac{1}{2}, 6\right)$

Start at (0, 0).
Move right $4\frac{1}{2}$ units.
Move up 6 units.

B $S(0, 4)$

Start at (0, 0).
Move right 0 units.
Move up 4 units.

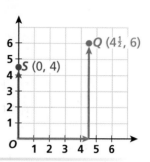

Think and Discuss

1. Tell what point is the starting location when you are graphing on a coordinate grid.

2. Describe how to graph $(2\frac{1}{2}, 8)$ on a coordinate grid.

6-5 Exercises

Review MA.5.G.5.1

Homebook Help THINK central

Go to thinkcentral.com
Exercises 1–22, 23, 25, 27, 29, 31, 33

GUIDED PRACTICE

See Example **1** Name the ordered pair for each location.

1. school   **2.** store

3. hospital   **4.** mall

5. office   **6.** hotel

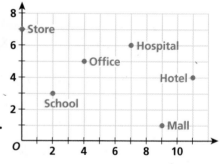

See Example **2** Graph and label each point on a coordinate grid.

7. $T\left(3\frac{1}{2}, 4\right)$ **8.** $S(2, 8)$

9. $U(5, 5)$ **10.** $V\left(4\frac{1}{2}, 1\right)$

INDEPENDENT PRACTICE

See Example **1** Name the ordered pair for each location.

11. diner   **12.** library

13. store   **14.** bank

15. theater   **16.** town hall

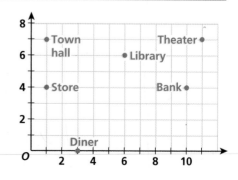

See Example 2 **Graph and label each point on a coordinate grid.**

17. $P\left(5\frac{1}{2}, 1\right)$ **18.** $R(2, 4)$ **19.** $Q\left(3\frac{1}{2}, 2\right)$

20. $V(6, 5)$ **21.** $X\left(1\frac{1}{2}, 3\right)$ **22.** $Y(7, 4)$

PRACTICE AND PROBLEM SOLVING

Use the coordinate grid for Exercises 23–35.
Name the point found at each location.

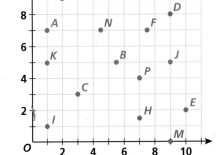

23. $(1, 7)$ **24.** $\left(5, 9\frac{1}{2}\right)$ **25.** $(3, 3)$

26. $\left(4\frac{1}{2}, 7\right)$ **27.** $(7, 4)$ **28.** $\left(7\frac{1}{2}, 7\right)$

Give the ordered pair for each point.

29. D **30.** H **31.** K

32. Q **33.** M **34.** B

35. Multi-Step The coordinates of points B, J, and M in the coordinate grid above form three of the corners of a rectangle. What are the coordinates of the fourth corner? Explain how you found your answer.

36. Write About It Explain the difference between the points $(3, 2)$ and $(2, 3)$.

37. What's the Question? If the answer is "Start at $(0, 0)$ and move 3 units to the right," what is the question?

38. Challenge Locate and graph points that can be connected to form your initials. What are the ordered pairs for these points?

Florida Spiral Review

MA.6.A.1.2, MA.6.A.3.1

Use the coordinate grid for Exercises 39 and 40.

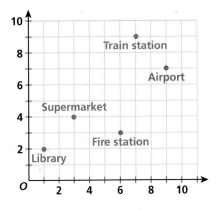

39. Multiple Choice At which ordered pair is the airport located?

   A. $(7, 9)$ **B.** $(3, 4)$ **C.** $(6, 3)$ **D.** $(9, 7)$

40. Multiple Choice Which location is at $(1, 2)$?

   F. Airport   **H.** Supermarket

   G. Library   **I.** Train station

Evaluate $4k$ for each value of k. (Lesson 3-4)

41. $k = 3.62$ **42.** $k = 6.401$ **43.** $k = 2.6$ **44.** $k = 5.019$

Find each product. Write each answer in simplest form. (Lesson 5-6)

45. $\frac{2}{3} \cdot \frac{1}{5}$ **46.** $\frac{3}{7} \cdot \frac{1}{4}$ **47.** $\frac{2}{9} \cdot \frac{3}{8}$ **48.** $\frac{1}{4} \cdot \frac{6}{7}$

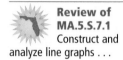

Review of MA.5.S.7.1 Construct and analyze line graphs . . .

The first permanent English settlement in the New World was founded in 1607. It contained 104 colonists. Population increased quickly as more and more immigrants left Europe for North America.

ARRIVAL AT JAMESTOWN.

© The Granger Collection, New York

Vocabulary

line graph

double-line graph

The table shows the estimated population of English American colonies from 1650 to 1700.

Population of American Colonies				
Year	1650	1670	1690	1700
Population	50,400	111,900	210,400	250,900

Data that shows change over time is best displayed in a *line graph*. A **line graph** displays a set of data using line segments.

EXAMPLE **1** **Making a Line Graph**

Use the data in the table above to make a line graph.

Caution!

Because time passes whether or not the population changes, time is *independent* of population. Always put the independent quantity on the horizontal axis.

Step 1: Place *year* on the horizontal axis and *population* on the vertical axis. Label the axes.

Step 2: Determine an appropriate scale and interval for each axis.

Step 3: Mark a point for each data value. Connect the points with straight lines.

Step 4: Title the graph.

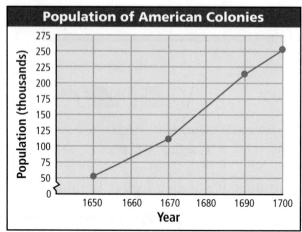

EXAMPLE 2 · **Reading a Line Graph**

Use the line graph to answer each question.

A · In which year did mountain bikes cost the least? 2004

B · About how much did mountain bikes cost in 2006? about $300

C · Did mountain bike prices increase or decrease from 2004 through 2008? They increased.

Line graphs that display two sets of data are called **double-line graphs**.

EXAMPLE 3 · **Making a Double-Line Graph**

Use the data in the table to make a double-line graph.

United States Trade (Billions of $)						
	1980	1985	1990	1995	2000	2005
Export	272	289	535	794	1,071	1,289
Import	291	411	616	890	1,450	1,997

Helpful Hint

Use different colors of lines to connect the export and import values so you will easily be able to tell the data apart.

Step 1: Determine an appropriate scale and interval.

Step 2: Mark a point for each export value and connect the points.

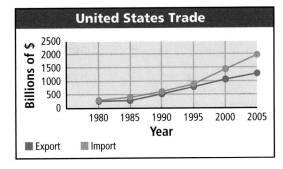

Step 3: Mark a point for each import value and connect the points.

Step 4: Title the graph and label both axes. Include a key.

Think and Discuss

1. **Explain** when it would be helpful to use a line graph instead of a bar graph to display data.

2. **Describe** how you might use a line graph to make predictions.

3. **Tell** why the graph in Example 3 needs a key.

Homework Help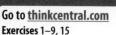

Go to thinkcentral.com
Exercises 1–9, 15

GUIDED PRACTICE

See Example **1**

1. Use the data in the table to make a line graph.

School Enrollment				
Year	2005	2006	2007	2008
Students	2,000	2,500	2,750	3,500

See Example **2**

Use the line graph to answer each question.

2. In which year did the most students participate in the science fair?

3. About how many students participated in 2007?

4. Did the number of students increase or decrease from 2005 to 2006?

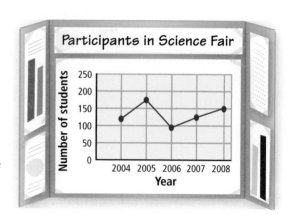

See Example **3**

5. Use the data in the table to make a double-line graph.

	January	February	March	April	May
Stock A	$10	$12	$20	$25	$22
Stock B	$8	$8	$12	$20	$30

INDEPENDENT PRACTICE

See Example **1**

6. Use the data in the table to make a line graph.

Winning Times in the Iditarod Trail Sled Dog Race								
Year	2000	2001	2002	2003	2004	2005	2006	2007
Time (hr)	217	236	215	232	228	235	227	222

See Example **2**

Use the line graph to answer each question.

7. About how many people used the Internet in the United States in 2004?

8. When was the number of Internet users about 205 million?

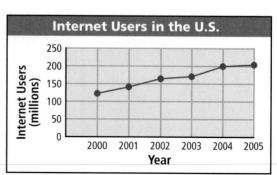

○ = **WORKED-OUT SOLUTIONS**
on p. WS7

9. Use the data in the table to make a double-line graph.

Soccer Team's Total Fund-Raising Sales						
Day	0	1	2	3	4	5
Team A	$0	$100	$225	$300	$370	$450
Team B	$0	$50	$100	$150	$200	$250

PRACTICE AND PROBLEM SOLVING

Use the double-line graph for 10 and 11.

10. Life Science Estimate the difference in the dogs' weights in March.

11. Life Science One of Dion's dogs is a Great Dane, and the other is a Jack Russell Terrier. Which dog is probably the Great Dane? Justify your answer.

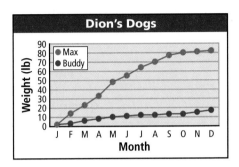

12. Life Science The table shows the weights in pounds for Sara Beth's two pets. Use the data to make a double-line graph.

	Jan	Feb	Mar	Apr	May	Jun	Jul	Aug	Sep	Oct	Nov	Dec
Ginger	3	9	15	21	24	25	26	25	26	27	26	28
Toto	4	8	13	17	24	26	27	29	25	26	28	28

13. Write About It You have a bowl of soup for lunch. Draw a line graph that could represent the changes in the soup's temperature during lunch. Explain.

14. Challenge Describe a situation that this graph could represent.

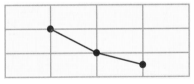

Life Science

Larger dogs usually have shorter life spans than smaller dogs. Great Danes live an average of 8.4 years, and Jack Russell terriers live an average of 13.6 years.

Florida Spiral Review   MA.6.S.6.2, MA.6.A.3.2, MA.6.A.1.3

15. Multiple Choice Tom has scores of 70, 80, 80, and 90 on his first four quizzes. What score can Tom get on his next quiz so that his mean quiz score does not change?

A. 70   **B.** 75   **C.** 80   **D.** 85

16. Short Response Use the graph from Exercises 10 and 11. How do the ranges of the weight data for the dogs compare? Explain.

Solve each equation. (Lesson 2-8)

17. $5s = 90$ **18.** $4g = 128$ **19.** $8m = 120$ **20.** $17a = 544$

21. Will takes a written exam with 80 questions. Exactly $\frac{2}{5}$ of the questions are multiple choice. How many of the questions are multiple choice? (Lesson 5-5)

Misleading Graphs

Preview of MA.8.S.3.1
Select, organize and construct appropriate data displays . . . and make conjectures about possible relationships.

Data can be displayed in many different ways. Sometimes people who make graphs choose to display data in a misleading way.

This bar graph was created by a group of students who believe their school should increase support of the football team. How could this bar graph be misleading?

Animated Math
@ thinkcentral.com

At a glance, you might conclude that about three times as many students prefer football to basketball. But if you look at the values of the bars, you can see that only 20 students chose football over basketball.

EXAMPLE 1 **Misleading Bar Graphs**

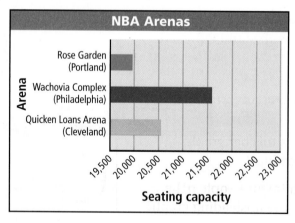

A **Why is this bar graph misleading?**

Because the lower part of the horizontal scale is missing, the differences in seating capacities are exaggerated.

B **What might people believe from the misleading graph?**

People might believe that the Wachovia Complex holds 2–4 times as many people as Quicken Loans Arena and the Rose Garden. In reality, the Wachovia Complex holds only one to two thousand more people than the other two arenas.

EXAMPLE 2 **Misleading Line Graphs**

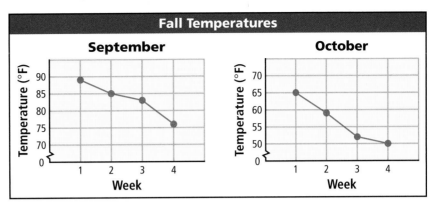

Fall Temperatures

Why are these line graphs misleading?

If you look at the scale for each graph, you will notice that the September graph goes from 75 °F to 90 °F and the October graph goes from 50 °F to 65 °F.

Think and Discuss

1. **Give an example** of a situation in which you think someone would intentionally try to make a graph misleading.

2. **Tell** how you could change the graphs in Example 2 so they are not misleading.

6-7 Exercises

Prev. MA.8.S.3.1

Homework Help THINK central

Go to thinkcentral.com
Exercises 1–8, 9

GUIDED PRACTICE

See Example 1

1. Why is this bar graph misleading?

2. What might people believe from the misleading graph?

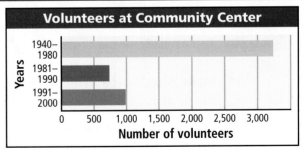

Volunteers at Community Center

See Example 2

3. Why is this line graph misleading?

4. What might people believe from the misleading graph?

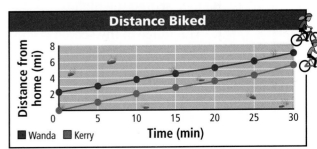

Distance Biked

See Example **1** **5.** Why is this bar graph misleading?

6. What might people believe from the misleading graph?

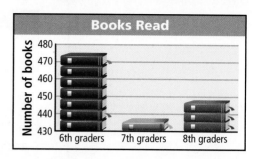

See Example **2** **7.** Why is this line graph misleading?

8. What might people believe from the misleading graph?

PRACTICE AND PROBLEM SOLVING

9. **Critical Thinking** A survey about teeth-whitening products stated that 1,007 people chose strips, 995 people chose paste, and 998 chose paint. Make two bar graphs, each showing that either strips or paint is significantly more effective than the other two products.

10. The table shows the average high temperatures in Atlanta for six months of one year. How could a misleading line graph make the range of the temperatures seem less than it actually is? Justify your answer.

Month	Jan	Mar	May	Jul	Sep	Nov
Temp. (°F)	54	63	81	88	83	62

Florida Spiral Review

MA.6.S.6.2, MA.6.S.6.1, MA.6.A.3.2

11. **Multiple Choice** Which statement is supported by the information in the bar graph?

A. Damon scored twice as high as Kyle on the test.

B. Kyle scored the highest on the test.

C. The range of the scores is about 95.

D. Brent's score represents the median score.

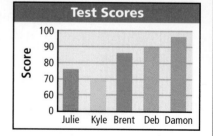

Solve each equation. (Lessons 2-6, 2-7, 2-8)

12. $x + 13 = 26$ **13.** $13x = 26$ **14.** $x - 13 = 26$

○ = **WORKED-OUT SOLUTIONS**
on p. WS7

Stem-and-Leaf Plots

Preview of MA.7.S.6.2
Construct and analyze . . . stem-and-leaf plots . . .

A **stem-and-leaf plot** shows data arranged by place value. You can use a stem-and-leaf plot when you want to display data in an organized way that allows you to see each value.

Bryan Berg holds the Guinness World Record for cardstacking. The Explorer Scouts had a competition to see who could build the highest card tower. The table shows the number of levels reached by each scout.

Vocabulary
stem-and-leaf plot

Number of Card-Tower Levels

12	23	31	50	14	17	25	44	51	20
23	18	35	15	19	15	23	42	21	13

EXAMPLE 1

Creating Stem-and-Leaf Plots

Use the data in the table above to make a stem-and-leaf plot.

Step 1: Group the data by tens digits.

Step 2: Order the data from least to greatest.

Step 3: List the tens digits of the data in order from least to greatest. Write these in the "stems" column.

12 13 14 15 15 17 18 19
20 21 23 23 23 25
31 35
42 44
50 51

Helpful Hint

To write 42 in a stem-and-leaf plot, write each digit in a separate column.

4 | 2
Stem   Leaf

Step 4: For each tens digit, record the ones digits of each data value in order from least to greatest. Write these in the "leaves" column.

Step 5: Title the graph and add a key.

Number of Card Tower Levels

Stems	Leaves
1	2 3 4 5 5 7 8 9
2	0 1 3 3 3 5
3	1 5
4	2 4
5	0 1

Key: 1|5 means 15

 Lesson Tutorial Videos @ thinkcentral.com

EXAMPLE 2

Reading Stem-and-Leaf Plots

Find the least value, greatest value, mean, median, mode, and range of the data.

Stems	Leaves
5	8
6	8 9
7	2 4 8
8	0 4 5 6 8
9	0 0 2 3 6 7 8
10	
11	7

Key: 5|8 means 58

Caution!

If a stem has no leaves, there are no data points with that stem. In the stem-and-leaf plot in Example 2, there are no data values between 100 and 109.

The least stem and least leaf give the least value, 58.

The greatest stem and greatest leaf give the greatest value, 117.

Use the data values to find the mean.
$(58 + \ldots + 117) \div 19 = 85$

The median is the middle value in the table, 86.

To find the mode, look for the number that occurs most often in a row of leaves. Then identify its stem. The mode is 90.

The range is the difference between the greatest and least value.
$117 - 58 = 59$

Think and Discuss

1. Describe how to show 25 on a stem-and-leaf plot.

Homework Help

 THINK central

Go to **thinkcentral.com**
Exercises 1–14, 15, 17

 6-8

Exercises

Preview MA.7.S.6.2

GUIDED PRACTICE

See Example 1

1. Use the data in the table to make a stem-and-leaf plot.

Daily High Temperatures (°F)	45	56	40	39	37	48	51

See Example 2

Find each value of the data.

2. smallest value   **3.** largest value

4. mean   **5.** median

6. mode   **7.** range

Stems	Leaves
1	0 2
2	
3	2
4	1 4

Key: 1|0 means 10

INDEPENDENT PRACTICE

See Example 1

8. Use the data in the table to make a stem-and-leaf plot.

Heights of Plants (cm)	30	12	27	28	15	47	37	28	40	20

Find each value of the data.

9. least value   10. greatest value

11. mean   12. median

13. mode   14. range

Stems	Leaves
4	1 2 2
5	1 3
6	7 8

Key: 4|1 means 41

PRACTICE AND PROBLEM SOLVING

For Exercises 15 and 16, write the letter of the stem-and-leaf plot described.

A.

Stems	Leaves
1	0 3 4
2	0 0 1 1 1 3
3	4 5 9
4	8

Key: 1|0 means 10

B.

Stems	Leaves
1	6
2	2 3
3	0 1 4
4	1 4 8

Key: 1|6 means 16

C.

Stems	Leaves
1	4
2	
3	6
4	3 6 8

Key: 1|4 means 14

15. The data set has a mode of 21.   **16.** The data set has a median of 31.

Use the table for Exercises 17 and 18.

17. Karla recorded the number of cars with only one passenger that came through a toll booth each day. Use Karla's data to make a stem-and-leaf plot.

Cars with Only One Passenger					
82	103	95	125	88	94
89	92	94	99	87	80
109	101	100	83	124	81

? 18. What's the Error? Karla's classmate looked at the stem-and-leaf plot and said that the mean number of cars with only one passenger is 4. Explain Karla's classmate's error. What is the correct mean?

★ 19. Challenge Josh is the second youngest of 4 teenage boys, all 2 years apart in age. Josh's mother is 3 times as old as Josh is, and she is 24 years younger than her father. Make a stem-and-leaf plot to show the ages of Josh, his brothers, his mother, and his grandfather.

Florida Spiral Review

MA.6.A.3.2, MA.6.A.1.3

20. Multiple Choice What is the value of 1|2 in the stem-and-leaf plot?

A. 12   **C.** 100,002

B. 1,200   **D.** 100,200

Key: 1|1 means 1,100

Stems	Leaves
1	0 1 2 3
2	7 9 9 9

21. Gridded Response What is the median of the data in Exercise 20?

Solve each equation. Check your answers. (Lesson 2-9)

22. $\dfrac{h}{12} = 4$ **23.** $3 = \dfrac{x}{5}$ **24.** $\dfrac{p}{4} = \dfrac{3}{8}$

25. Alice buys $3\frac{3}{4}$ lb of turkey and $2\frac{1}{2}$ lb of roast beef. She plans to make sandwiches with $\frac{1}{4}$ lb of meat in each one. How many can she make? (Lesson 5-7)

Quiz for Lessons 6-3 Through 6-8

✓ **6-3** **Bar Graphs**

The students in Ms. Bain's class voted on their favorite fruit juice. Use the bar graph to answer each question.

1. How many more students prefer orange juice than prefer grape juice?

2. How many students in all voted?

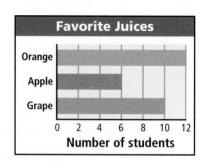

✓ **6-4** **Line Plots and Frequency Tables**

Shoppers leaving Midtown Mall were each asked to give their age. Use the line plot to answer each question.

3. What are the range and mode of the data?

4. How many of the shoppers surveyed were older than 20?

5. Find the median of the data. Suppose an additional shopper was included in the data. How would this affect the median of the data? Explain.

Shoppers at Midtown Mall

```
                            X
         X              X       X
         X              X   X   X
     X   X      X   X   X   X   X
  +--+---+---+---+---+---+---+---+-->
    15  16  17  18  19  20  21  22
```

Ages of shoppers

✓ **6-5** **Ordered Pairs**

Graph and label each point on a coordinate grid.

6. $A\,(4, 5)$

7. $B\left(0, 3\frac{1}{2}\right)$

✓ **6-6** **Line Graphs**

8. Use the data in the table to make a line graph.

Graphicworks	
Year	Numbers of Employees
2003	852
2004	1,098
2005	1,150
2006	1,150

✓ **6-7** **Misleading Graphs**

9. Bob drew a line graph of the Graphicworks data. For the vertical scale representing the number of employees, he used these intervals: 0; 800; 1,000; and 1,500. Explain why his graph is misleading.

✓ **6-8** **Stem-and-Leaf Plots**

10. Use the data in the line plot in problems 3 and 4 to make a stem-and-leaf plot.

Real-World CONNECTIONS

Pensacola

Florida's Rainiest City Florida may be known as the Sunshine State, but it also has some very rainy locations. For example, Pensacola receives about 65 inches of rain per year. That makes it the rainiest city in Florida and the second rainiest city in the country.

1. The table shows the annual rainfall in Pensacola from 2000 to 2007. Make a bar graph of the data.

2. What is the mode of the data? Explain how you can find the mode by looking at the bar graph.

3. Find the mean number of inches of rain per year.

4. Find the median number of inches of rain per year.

5. Which year's rainfall is an outlier?

6. Find the mean, median, and mode of the data set without the outlier and describe any changes.

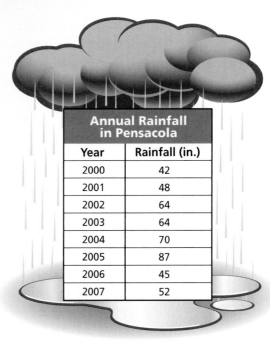

Annual Rainfall in Pensacola	
Year	Rainfall (in.)
2000	42
2001	48
2002	64
2003	64
2004	70
2005	87
2006	45
2007	52

Real-World Connections

Game Time

A Thousand Words

Did you ever hear the saying "A picture is worth a thousand words"?
A graph can be worth a thousand words too!

Each of the graphs below tells a story about a student's trip to school.
Read each story and think about what each graph is showing. Can you
match each graph with its story?

Kyla:
I rode my bike to
school at a steady pace.
I had to stop and wait
for the light to change at
two intersections.

Tom:
I walked to my bus stop
and waited there for the
bus. After I boarded the
bus, it was driven straight
to school.

Megan:
On my way to school, I
stopped at my friend's
house. She wasn't ready
yet, so I waited for her.
Then we walked to school.

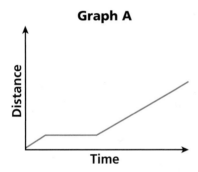

Graph A

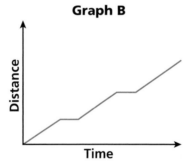

Graph B

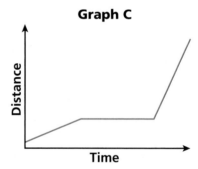

Graph C

Spinnermeania

Round 1: On your turn, spin the spinner four
times and record the results. After everyone has
had a turn, find the mean, median, and mode
of your results. For every category in which you
have the highest number, you get one point. If
there is a tie in a category, each player with that
number gets a point. If your data set has more
than one mode, use the greatest one.

Spin five times in round 2, eight times
in round 3, ten times in round 4, and
twelve times in round 5. The player with
the highest score at the end of five rounds
is the winner.

Games

Go to **thinkcentral.com**

THINK central

A complete copy of the rules and game pieces are available online.

Materials
- 2 pieces of card stock
- 6 sandwich-size zipper bags
- clear packaging tape
- graph paper
- scissors

It's in the Bag!

PROJECT **Graphing According to Me**

Create different types of graphs and make a zippered accordion book to hold them all.

Directions

❶ Place one piece of card stock that is $6\frac{1}{2}$ inches by 7 inches next to one of the bags. The opening of the bag should be at the top, and there should be a small space between the card stock and the bag. Tape the card stock and bag together on the front and back sides. **Figure A**

❷ Lay another bag down next to the first, keeping a small space between them. Tape them together, front and back. **Figure B**

❸ Continue with the rest of the bags. At the end of the chain, tape a second piece of card stock that is $6\frac{1}{2}$ inches by 7 inches to the last bag. **Figure C**

❹ Fold the bags accordion-style, back and forth, with the two card stock covers on the front and back.

❺ Cut out squares of graph paper so they will fit in the bags.

Taking Note of the Math

Write the number and title of the chapter on the cover. On each piece of graph paper, draw and label an example of one type of graph from the chapter. Store the graphs in the bags.

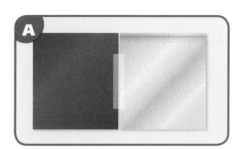

A

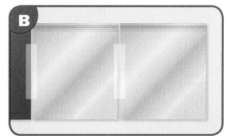

B

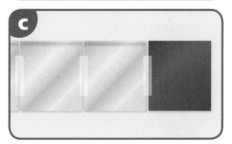

C

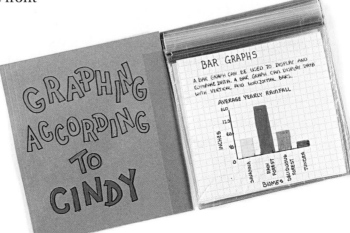

Study Guide: Review

Multi–Language Glossary
Go to thinkcentral.com
THINK central

Vocabulary

bar graph 262	frequency table 266	mode 253
coordinate grid 269	line graph 272	ordered pair 269
double-bar graph 263	line plot 266	outlier 256
double-line graph 273	mean 252	range 253
frequency 266	median 253	stem-and-leaf plot 279

Complete the sentences below with vocabulary words from the list above.

1. A(n) ___?___ uses a number line and *x*'s or other symbols to show frequencies of values.

2. A point can be located by using a(n) ___?___ of numbers such as (3, 5).

3. In a data set, the ___?___ is the value or values that occur most often.

EXAMPLES

EXERCISES

 MA.6.S.6.1

6-1 Mean, Median, Mode, and Range (pp. 252–255)

■ Find the mean, median, mode, and range. 7, 8, 12, 10, 8

mean: $7 + 8 + 8 + 10 + 12 = 45$

$45 \div 5 = 9$

median: 8

mode: 8

range: $12 - 7 = 5$

Find the mean, median, mode, and range.

4.
Hours Worked Each Week						
32	39	39	38	36	39	36

5.
Amount Saved Each Month ($)							
50	120	75	30	40	50	35	100

  MA.6.S.6.2

6-2 Additional Data and Outliers (pp. 256–259)

■ Find the mean, median, and mode with and without the outlier.

10, 4, 7, 8, 34, 7, 7, 12, 5, 8   *The outlier is 34.*

With: **mean** = 10.2,
        median = 7.5,
        mode = 7

Without: **mean** ≈ 7.555,
        median = 7,
        mode = 7

Find the mean, median, and mode of each data set with and without the outlier.

6. 12, 11, 9, 38, 10, 8, 12

7. 34, 12, 32, 45, 32

8. 16, 12, 15, 52, 10, 13

6-3 Bar Graphs (pp. 262–265)

■ **Which grades have more than 200 students?** 6th grade and 8th grade

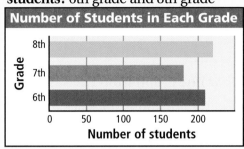

Number of Students in Each Grade

MA.6.S.6.1

Use the bar graph at left for Exercise 9.

9. Which grade has the most students?

10. Use the data to make a bar graph.

Test	Math	English	History	Science
Grade	95	85	90	80

11. Find the mean, median, and mode of the test score data in Exercise 10.

6-4 Line Plots and Frequency Tables (pp. 266–269)

Rev. of MA.5.S.7.2

■ **Make a frequency table with intervals.**

Ages of people at Irene's birthday party:
37, 39, 18, 15, 13

Ages of People at Irene's Birthday Party				
Ages	13–19	20–26	27–33	34–40
Frequency	3	0	0	2

12. Make a frequency table with intervals.

Points Scored					
6	4	5	4	7	10

13. Find the median of the data from Exercise 12.

14. Suppose another data value is included with the table in Exercise 12. If the mode does not change, what was the new data value?

6-5 Ordered Pairs (pp. 269–271)

Rev. of MA.5.G.5.1

■ **Name the ordered pairs shown.**

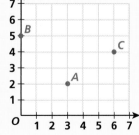

A is at (3, 2).
B is at (0, 5).
C is at (6, 4).

Name the ordered pair for each location.

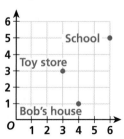

15. Bob's house

16. toy store

17. school

18. Fatima's house is located at the ordered pair (5, 1). Does Fatima live closer to Bob or the toy store? Justify your answer.

Study Guide: Review

6-6 Line Graphs (pp. 272–275)

■ **Use the temperature data to make a line graph.**

Day 1: 32°F; Day 2: 36°F; Day 3: 38°F; Day 4: 40°F; Day 5: 36°F

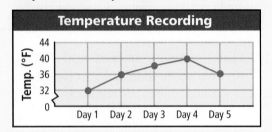

Rev. of MA.5.S.7.1

19. Use the bookstore sales data to make a line graph.

Jan: $425; Feb: $320; Mar: $450; Apr: $530

Use your line graph from Exercise 19.

20. When were bookstore sales the greatest?

21. Describe the trend in bookstore sales over the four months.

6-7 Misleading Graphs (pp. 276–279)

■ **Why is this graph misleading?**

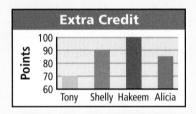

The lower part of the scale is missing, because it starts at 60 points. It appears as though Shelly has 3 times the extra points as Tony.

 Rev. of MA.5.S.7.2

22. Explain why this graph is misleading.

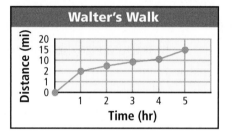

6-8 Stem-and-Leaf Plots (pp. 280–282)

■ **Make a stem-and-leaf plot of the following test scores.**
80, 75, 92, 88, 86, 85, 94, 77

Stems	Leaves
7	5 7
8	0 5 6 8
9	2 4

Key: 8|0 means 80

 Prev. of MA.7.S.6.2

23. Make a stem-and-leaf plot of the following basketball scores.

22, 26, 34, 46, 20, 44, 40, 28

24. List the least value, greatest value, mean, median, mode, and range of the data from Exercise 23.

25. The basketball team makes the playoffs. Add the data values 30 and 34 to the data from Exercise 23. Find the new median and mode.

Study Guide: Review

Chapter Test

FLORIDA

CHAPTER

6

1. Use the data about sound to make a bar graph.

   The loudness of a sound is measured by the size of its vibrations. The unit of measurement is the decibel (dB). A soft whisper is 30 dB. Conversation is 60 dB. A loud shout is 100 dB. The pain threshold for humans is 130 dB. An airplane takeoff at 100 ft is 140 dB.

Use the bar graph for Exercises 2–4.

2. Find the mean, median, mode, and range of the rainfall amounts.

3. Which month had the lowest average rainfall?

4. Does the data have an outlier? Justify your answer.

5. The table shows the number of strawberries picked by customers at a pick-your-own strawberry patch. Organize the data in a line plot.

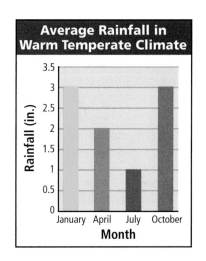

Number of Strawberries Picked							
28	33	35	27	35	28	35	29
30	27	30	35	28	27	31	32

Name the ordered pair for each point on the grid.

6. *A*   7. *B*   8. *C*   9. *D*

10. *E*   11. *F*   12. *G*   13. *H*

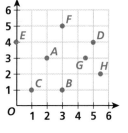

Graph and label each point on a coordinate grid.

14. $T(3, 4)$ 15. $M\left(\frac{1}{2}, 6\right)$ 16. $P(5, 1)$ 17. $S\left(3\frac{1}{2}, 2\right)$ 18. $N(0, 5)$

19. Make a stem-and-leaf plot of the push-up data. Use your stem-and-leaf plot to find the mean, median, and mode of the data.

Number of Push-ups Performed						
35	33	25	45	52	21	18
41	27	35	40	53	24	38

20. The table shows the population of a small town over several years.

    a. Find the yearly mean population from 2002 to 2005.

    b. Make a line graph for the data.

Year	2002	2003	2004	2005
Population	852	977	1,125	1,206

Chapter Test

Mastering the Standards

Cumulative Assessment, Chapters 1–6

Multiple Choice

1. The ages of the volunteers who work at a local food bank are shown. What is the median of this set of data?

Stems	Leaves
1	6
2	2 3
3	0 1 4
4	1 4 8

Key: 1|6 means 16

A. 31   **C.** 41

B. 32.1   **D.** 48

2. Toni took four quizzes in her science class. Three of the quiz scores were 79, 92, and 85. If the range of her quiz scores is 13, which could be the other quiz score?

F. 68   **H.** 78

G. 88   **I.** 98

3. Harrison spends $5\frac{1}{2}$ hours per week working in his yard. He spends $1\frac{1}{6}$ hours pulling weeds and $\frac{1}{2}$ of the remaining time mowing the lawn. How much time does Harrison spend mowing the lawn?

A. $1\frac{1}{6}$ hours   **C.** $2\frac{1}{3}$ hours

B. $2\frac{1}{6}$ hours   **D.** $4\frac{1}{3}$ hours

4. What is the product of $\frac{2}{3}$ and $\frac{9}{10}$?

F. $\frac{4}{5}$ **H.** $\frac{11}{30}$

G. $\frac{3}{5}$ **I.** $\frac{20}{27}$

5. Jamie is making a fruit salad. She needs $2\frac{1}{4}$ cups of crushed pineapple, $3\frac{3}{4}$ cups of sliced apples, $1\frac{1}{3}$ cups of mandarin oranges, and $2\frac{2}{3}$ cups of red grapes. How many cups total of fruit does she need for the fruit salad?

A. 6 cups   **C.** 10 cups

B. 8 cups   **D.** 12 cups

6. The line plot shows the ages of the number of participants in a science fair. Which of the following statements is NOT supported by the line plot?

Ages of Science Fair Participants

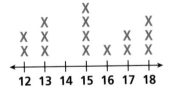

F. The range is 6.

G. The mean age of the participants in the science fair is about 15.1.

H. The mode of the ages of the participants in the science fair is 16.

I. The median age of the participants in the science fair is 15.

7. What is the mode of the following data? 17, 13, 14, 13, 21, 18, 16, 19

A. 13   **C.** 16.5

B. 16   **D.** 16.375

8. Bananas are sold for $0.69 per pound. Philippe buys 3 pounds of bananas to make smoothies. How much does he pay for the bananas?

F. $1.89   **H.** $2.07

G. $1.97   **I.** $2.10

9. Which equation has a solution of 8?

A. $2x = 18$ **C.** $x + 6 = 24$

B. $x - 4 = 12$ **D.** $\frac{x}{4} = 2$

Read graphs and diagrams carefully. Look at the labels for important information.

Gridded Response

Use the following data set for items 10 through 13.

4, 13, 7, 26, 6, 7, 3, 4, 2, 8, 10, 9

10. Which number in the data set is an outlier?

11. What is the mean of the data set?

12. Remove the outlier from the data set. What is the median of the new data set?

13. The data set has two modes. What is the product of the modes?

14. The coach of the football team orders 9 large pizzas for his players. He knows that each player is capable of eating $\frac{3}{4}$ of one pizza. Simplify the expression $9 \div \frac{3}{4}$ to determine how many players are on the team.

15. Miguel has a piece of lumber that is 48.6 centimeters long. He wants to cut it into 3 pieces of equal length. How long, in centimeters, will each piece be?

16. What integer represents the best estimate for the product 6.1×9.8?

17. Write $4\frac{3}{8}$ as a decimal.

Short Response

S1. The prices of eight blenders are shown below. What measure of central tendency would you use to describe the data? Explain your choice.

$18.00 $22.00 $19.75 $24.50
$21.00 $79.00 $17.75 $24.50

S2. The ages of the members of Springfield bowling league are shown below.

21, 23, 26, 32, 32, 35, 39, 40, 43, 51, 55, 55, 55

a. Find the range, mean, median, and mode of the data.

b. How does adding 82, 18, and 42 to the data change the range, mean, median, and mode?

Extended Response

E1. The high temperature on Monday was 54°F. On Tuesday, it was 62°F. On Wednesday, it was 65°F. On Thursday, it was 60°F. On Friday, it was 62°F.

a. Organize this data in a table. Find the range, mean, median, and mode of the data.

b. Which graph would be more appropriate to show the data—a bar graph or a line graph? Explain.

c. Make a graph of the data.

CHAPTER 7

Proportional Relationships

Worktext
pages 257–322

Additional instruction, practice, and activities are available online, including:
- Lesson Tutorial Videos
- Homework Help
- Animated Math

THINK central

Go to **thinkcentral.com**

Why Learn This?

Sand-castle sculptors say that the perfect mixture for making a sand castle is 8 parts dry sand to 1 part water. This can be written as the ratio $\frac{8 \text{ parts dry sand}}{1 \text{ part water}}$.

South Beach
Miami

Chapter Focus
- Use reasoning about multiplication and division to solve ratio and rate problems.
- Interpret and compare ratios and rates.

Are You Ready?

Are You Ready? THINK central

Go to thinkcentral.com

✓ Vocabulary

Choose the best term from the list to complete each sentence.

1. A(n) ___?___ is a three-sided polygon, and a(n) ___?___ is a four-sided polygon.

2. A(n) ___?___ is used to name a part of a whole.

3. When two numbers have the same value, they are said to be ___?___.

4. When writing 0.25 as a fraction, 25 is the ___?___ and 100 is the ___?___.

angle

denominator

equivalent

fraction

numerator

pentagon

quadrilateral

triangle

Complete these exercises to review skills you will need for this chapter.

✓ Simplify Fractions

Write each fraction in simplest form.

5. $\frac{6}{10}$

6. $\frac{9}{12}$

7. $\frac{8}{6}$

✓ Write Equivalent Fractions

Write three equivalent fractions for each given fraction.

8. $\frac{4}{16}$

9. $\frac{5}{10}$

10. $\frac{5}{6}$

✓ Compare Fractions

Compare. Write >, <, or =.

11. $\frac{3}{10}$ ▨ $\frac{2}{5}$

12. $1\frac{3}{4}$ ▨ $1\frac{5}{7}$

13. $\frac{5}{8}$ ▨ $\frac{1}{2}$

14. $2\frac{11}{12}$ ▨ $\frac{35}{12}$

✓ Write Fractions as Decimals

Write each fraction as a decimal.

15. $\frac{1}{2}$

16. $\frac{7}{20}$

17. $\frac{2}{25}$

18. $\frac{3}{25}$

✓ Multiply Decimals

Multiply.

19. $0.42 \cdot 10$

20. $0.3 \cdot 52$

21. $20.5 \cdot 0.25$

22. $6.75 \cdot 0.40$

23. $9.8 \cdot 0.2$

24. $0.8 \cdot 7.4$

25. $0.52 \cdot 0.64$

26. $0.75 \cdot 8.9$

Before

Previously, you

- used fractions to represent situations involving division.
- generated equivalent fractions and decimals.
- used multiplication and division to find equivalent fractions.

Now

You will study

- using ratios to describe proportional situations.
- representing ratios and percents with concrete models, fractions, and decimals.
- using multiplication and division to solve problems involving equivalent ratios and rates.
- using ratios to make predictions in proportional situations.

Why?

You can use the skills learned in this chapter

- to find discounts and sales tax on retail items at stores.
- to know how much of a tip to leave at restaurants.

Key Vocabulary/Vocabulario

corresponding angles	ángulos correspondientes (en polígonos)
equivalent ratios	razones equivalentes
indirect measurement	medición indirecta
percent	porcentaje
proportion	proporción
rate	tasa
ratio	razón
scale drawing	dibujo a escala
similar	semejantes
unit rate	tasa unitaria

Vocabulary Connections

To become familiar with some of the vocabulary terms in the chapter, consider the following. You may refer to the chapter, the glossary, or a dictionary if you like.

1. *Equivalent* can mean "equal in value." How do you think **equivalent ratios** are related?

2. *Indirect* means "not direct." Do you think you will use a ruler to find an **indirect measurement**?

3. *Percent* comes from *per* and the Latin word *centum*, meaning "hundred." What do you think **percent** means?

4. *Ratio* can mean "the relationship in quantity, amount, or size between two things." How many numbers do you think a **ratio** will have?

5. A *scale* shows the relationship in size between two or more things. If you are making a **scale drawing** of a room, what do you think you would include on the drawing to show the room's actual size?

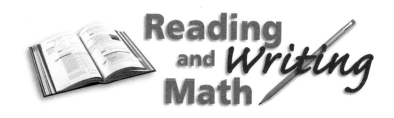 Reading and Writing Math

Writing Strategy: Write a Convincing Explanation

You will see the Write About It icons throughout the book. These icons show exercises that require you to write a convincing explanation.

A convincing explanation should include

- a restatement of the question or problem.

- a complete solution to the problem.

- any work, definitions, diagrams, or charts needed to answer the problem.

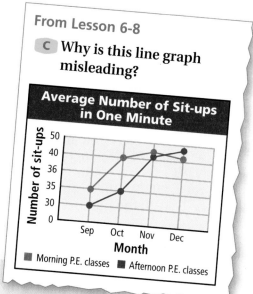

From Lesson 6-8

C Why is this line graph misleading?

Average Number of Sit-ups in One Minute

■ Morning P.E. classes ■ Afternoon P.E. classes

Step 1 **Restate the question.**
The graph is misleading because the scale does not have equal intervals.

Step 2 **Provide a complete solution to the problem with facts and an explanation.**
For example, an increase from 35 sit-ups to 40 sit-ups appears greater than an increase from 30 sit-ups to 35 sit-ups. By reading the scale, you know that this is incorrect. Therefore, the graph is misleading.

Try This

Use your textbook.

1. Write a convincing explanation to explain why there are two modes in the data set 4, 6, 1, 0, 4, 8, 9, 0.

2. Look at one of your previous Write About It exercises. Does your answer follow the method outlined above? If so, label the items that should be included. If not, rewrite the explanation.

Reading and Writing Math

7-1 Ratios and Rates

MA.6.A.2.2
Interpret and compare ratios and rates.

For a time, a local symphony orchestra was made up of 95 musicians.

Violins	29	Violas	12
Cellos	10	Basses	9
Flutes	5	Trumpets	3
Double reeds	8	Percussion	5
Clarinets	4	Harp	1
Horns	6	Trombones	3

Vocabulary

ratio

equivalent ratios

rate

unit rate

You can compare the different groups by using ratios. A **ratio** is a comparison of two quantities using division.

For example, you can use a ratio to compare the number of violins with the number of violas. This ratio can be written in three ways.

Reading Math

Read the ratio $\frac{29}{12}$ as "twenty-nine to twelve."

$$Terms \begin{cases} \frac{29}{12} \qquad 29 \text{ to } 12 \qquad 29{:}12 \end{cases}$$

Notice that the ratio of **violins** to **violas**, $\frac{29}{12}$, is different from the ratio of **violas** to **violins**, $\frac{12}{29}$. The order of the terms is important.

Ratios can be written to compare a part to a part, a part to the whole, or the whole to a part.

EXAMPLE 1 **Writing Ratios**

Use the table above to write each ratio.

A **flutes to clarinets**

$\frac{5}{4}$ *or*   5 to 4   *or*   5:4   *Part to part*

B **trumpets to total instruments**

$\frac{3}{95}$ *or*   3 to 95   *or*   3:95   *Part to whole*

C **total instruments to basses**

$\frac{95}{9}$ *or*   95 to 9   *or*   95:9   *Whole to part*

Equivalent ratios are ratios that name the same comparison. You can find an equivalent ratio by multiplying or dividing both terms of a ratio by the same number.

   Video **Lesson Tutorial Videos** @ thinkcentral.com

EXAMPLE 2

Writing Equivalent Ratios

Write three equivalent ratios to compare the number of stars with the number of moons in the pattern.

$$\frac{\text{number of stars}}{\text{number of moons}} = \frac{4}{6}$$ *There are 4 stars and 6 moons.*

$$\frac{4}{6} = \frac{4 \div 2}{6 \div 2} = \frac{2}{3}$$ *There are 2 stars for every 3 moons.*

$$\frac{4}{6} = \frac{4 \cdot 2}{6 \cdot 2} = \frac{8}{12}$$ *If you double the pattern, there will be 8 stars and 12 moons.*

So $\frac{4}{6}$, $\frac{2}{3}$, and $\frac{8}{12}$ are equivalent ratios.

Animated Math
@ thinkcentral.com

A **rate** is a ratio that compares two quantities that have different units of measure.

Suppose a 2-liter bottle of soda costs $1.98.

$$\text{rate} = \frac{\text{price}}{\text{number of liters}} = \frac{\$1.98}{2 \text{ liters}}$$ $1.98 for 2 liters

When the comparison is to one unit, the rate is called a **unit rate**.

Divide both terms by the second term to find the unit rate.

$$\text{unit rate} = \frac{\$1.98}{2} = \frac{\$1.98 \div 2}{2 \div 2} = \frac{\$0.99}{1}$$ $0.99 for 1 liter

When the prices of two or more items are compared, the item with the lowest unit rate is the best deal.

EXAMPLE 3   *Consumer Math Application*

A 2-liter bottle of soda costs $2.02. A 3-liter bottle of the same soda costs $2.79. Which is the better deal?

2-liter bottle		3-liter bottle	
$\frac{\$2.02}{2 \text{ liters}}$	*Write the rate.*	$\frac{\$2.79}{3 \text{ liters}}$	*Write the rate.*
$\frac{\$2.02 \div 2}{2 \text{ liters} \div 2}$	*Divide both terms by 2.*	$\frac{\$2.79 \div 3}{3 \text{ liters} \div 3}$	*Divide both terms by 3.*
$\frac{\$1.01}{1 \text{ liter}}$	*$1.01 for 1 liter*	$\frac{\$0.93}{1 \text{ liter}}$	*$0.93 for 1 liter*

The 3-liter bottle is the better deal.

Think and Discuss

1. Explain why the ratio 2:5 is different from the ratio 5:2.

2. Tell whether the ratios $\frac{4}{5}$ and $\frac{16}{25}$ are equivalent. If they are not, give a ratio that is equivalent to $\frac{4}{5}$.

Exercises

Homework Help
Go to thinkcentral.com
Exercises 1–11, 13, 15, 17, 19, 27

MA.6.A.2.2

GUIDED PRACTICE

See Example 1 | **Use the table to write each ratio.**

1. music programs to art programs

2. arcade games to entire collection

3. entire collection to educational games

Jacqueline's Software Collection	
Educational games	16
Word processing	2
Art programs	10
Arcade games	10
Music programs	3

See Example 2 | **4.** Write three equivalent ratios to compare the number of red hearts in the picture with the total number of hearts.

See Example 3 | **5. Consumer Math** An 8-ounce bag of sunflower seeds costs $1.68. A 4-ounce bag of sunflower seeds costs $0.88. Which is the better deal?

INDEPENDENT PRACTICE

See Example 1 | **Use the table to write each ratio.**

6. Redbirds to Blue Socks

7. right-handed Blue Socks to left-handed Blue Socks

8. left-handed Redbirds to total Redbirds

	Redbirds	Blue Socks
Left-Handed Batters	8	3
Right-Handed Batters	11	19

See Example 2 | **9.** Write three equivalent ratios to compare the number of stars in the picture with the number of stripes.

See Example 3 | **10.** Gina charges $28 for 3 hours of swimming lessons. Hector charges $18 for 2 hours of swimming lessons. Which instructor offers a better deal?

11. Consumer Math A 12-pound bag of dog food costs $12.36. A 15-pound bag of dog food costs $15.30. Which is the better deal?

PRACTICE AND PROBLEM SOLVING

Write each ratio two different ways.

12. 10 to 7   **13.** $\frac{24}{11}$ **14.** 4 to 30   **15.** $\frac{7}{10}$

16. 16 to 20   **17.** $\frac{5}{9}$ **18.** 50 to 79   **19.** 100 to 101

20. A florist can create 16 bouquets during an 8-hour work day. How many bouquets can the florist create per hour?

○ = **WORKED-OUT SOLUTIONS**
on p. WS7

Use the diagram of an oxygen atom and a boron atom for Exercises 21–24. Find each ratio. Then give two equivalent ratios.

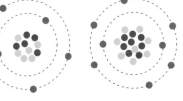

21. oxygen protons to boron protons

22. boron neutrons to boron protons

23. boron electrons to oxygen electrons

24. oxygen electrons to oxygen protons

Boron   Oxygen

25. A lifeguard received 16 hours of first aid training and 8 hours of cardiopulmonary resuscitation (CPR) training. Write the ratio of hours of CPR training to hours of first aid training.

26. **Critical Thinking** Cassandra has three pictures on her desk. The pictures measure 4 in. long by 6 in. wide, 24 mm long by 36 mm wide, and 6 cm long by 7 cm wide. Which photos have a length-to-width ratio equivalent to 2:3?

27. **Multi-Step** On which day did Alfonso run faster?

Day	Distance (m)	Time (min)
Monday	1,020	6
Wednesday	1,554	9

28. **Earth Science** Water rushes over Niagara Falls at the rate of 180 million cubic feet every 30 minutes. How much water goes over the falls in 1 minute?

29. **What's the Question?** The ratio of total students in Mr. Avalon's class to students in the class who have a blue backpack is 3 to 1. The answer is 1:2. What is the question?

30. **Write About It** How are equivalent ratios like equivalent fractions?

31. **Challenge** There are 36 performers in a dance recital. The ratio of men to women is 2:7. How many men are in the dance recital?

32. **Multiple Choice** Which ratio is equivalent to $\frac{1}{20}$?

  A. 9:180   **B.** 180 to 9   **C.** 4 to 100   **D.** 100:4

33. **Short Response** A 24-ounce box of raisins costs $4.56. A 15-ounce box of raisins costs $3.15. Which is the better deal? Explain.

Order the fractions and decimals from least to greatest. (Lesson 4-5)

34. $\frac{2}{3}, \frac{2}{5}, 0.35$ 35. $0.45, \frac{4}{9}, 0.4$ 36. $\frac{1}{6}, \frac{1}{9}, 0.18$

Evaluate 5x for each value of x. Write each answer in simplest form. (Lesson 5-5)

37. $x = \frac{1}{4}$ 38. $x = \frac{2}{3}$ 39. $x = \frac{1}{5}$ 40. $x = \frac{3}{10}$

Ratio and Rate Problems

MA.6.A.2.1
Use reasoning about multiplication and division to solve ratio and rate problems.
Also **MA.6.A.2.2**

Mrs. Kennedy's students are painting a mural. They mixed 3 cans of yellow paint and 2 cans of blue paint to make green paint. To make more of the same shade of green paint, the students will need to mix yellow paint and blue paint in the same ratio.

You can create equivalent ratios and rates by multiplying or dividing the numerator and denominator by the same number.

EXAMPLE 1 **Finding Equivalent Ratios and Rates**

Use a table to find three equivalent ratios or rates.

Helpful Hint

Multiplying the ratio in Example 1A by 2, 3, and 4 will give you three equivalent ratios, but there are many other equivalent ratios that are correct.

A Green paint was made by mixing 3 cans of yellow paint and 2 cans of blue paint.

	Original Ratio	$3 \cdot 2$	$3 \cdot 3$	$3 \cdot 4$
Cans of yellow	3	6	9	12
Cans of blue	2	4	6	8
		$2 \cdot 2$	$2 \cdot 3$	$2 \cdot 4$

The ratios 3 to 2, 6 to 4, 9 to 6, and 12 to 8 are equivalent.

B Geneva drove to see her grandmother at a rate of $\frac{480 \text{ miles}}{8 \text{ hours}}$.

	Original ratio	$480 \div 2$	$480 \div 4$	$480 \div 8$
Miles	480	240	120	60
Hours	8	4	2	1
		$8 \div 2$	$8 \div 4$	$8 \div 8$

The rates $\frac{480 \text{ miles}}{8 \text{ hours}}$, $\frac{240 \text{ miles}}{4 \text{ hours}}$, $\frac{120 \text{ miles}}{2 \text{ hours}}$, and $\frac{60 \text{ miles}}{1 \text{ hour}}$ are equivalent.

Video **Lesson Tutorial Videos @ thinkcentral.com**

Equivalent ratios or rates can be used to make comparisons.

EXAMPLE **2** **Comparing Rates**

Lena can type 52 words per minute. Which person types at the same rate as Lena?

Find rates equivalent to $\frac{52 \text{ words}}{1 \text{ min}}$.

Student	Rate
Mike	$\frac{212 \text{ words}}{4 \text{ min}}$
Marcia	$\frac{156 \text{ words}}{3 \text{ min}}$
Pat	$\frac{255 \text{ words}}{5 \text{ min}}$

Original Rate $52 \cdot 2$ $52 \cdot 3$ $52 \cdot 4$ $52 \cdot 5$

Words	52	104	**156**	208	260
Minutes	1	2	3	4	5

$1 \cdot 2$ $1 \cdot 3$ $1 \cdot 4$ $1 \cdot 5$

Marcia's rate of $\frac{156 \text{ words}}{3 \text{ min}}$ is equivalent to Lena's rate, so Marcia and Lena type at the same rate.

EXAMPLE **3** *Entertainment Application*

A group of 10 friends is in line to see a movie. It costs $15 for 3 people to see a movie. How much will the group pay?

Find the unit rate.

$\frac{15 \text{ dollars} \div 3}{3 \text{ people} \div 3}$ *Divide both terms by 3.*

$\frac{5 \text{ dollars}}{1 \text{ person}}$

Multiply the unit rate by 10 to find the rate for 10 people.

$\frac{5 \text{ dollars} \cdot 10}{1 \text{ person} \cdot 10} = 50 \text{ dollars}/10 \text{ people}$

A group of 10 friends will pay $50.

Think and Discuss

1. Explain how you can be sure that all the ratios you have written are correct when you have multiplied or divided a ratio to find equivalent ratios.

2. Explain how you can be sure that you have written the numerator and denominator in the correct order when rewriting ratios that have colons as fractions.

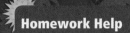
Homework Help
THiNK central
Go to **thinkcentral.com**
Exercises 1–18, 21, 23, 29

GUIDED PRACTICE

See Example 1 **Use a table to find three equivalent ratios or rates.**

1. $\frac{2}{7}$

2. 7 to 12

3. 96:48

4. $\frac{69 \text{ miles}}{3 \text{ gallons}}$

5. $\frac{\$120}{8 \text{ hours}}$

6. $\frac{9}{4}$

7. $\frac{\$0.15}{1 \text{ ounce}}$

8. 25:26

See Example 2 **9.** Marta's car gets $\frac{78 \text{ miles}}{3 \text{ gallons}}$. Beth's car gets $\frac{52 \text{ miles}}{2 \text{ gallons}}$, and Erik's car gets $\frac{32 \text{ miles}}{1 \text{ gallon}}$. Which driver gets the same miles per gallon as Marta?

See Example 3 **10. Sports** Leo runs 4 laps around a track in 20 minutes. How long will it take Leo to run 7 laps?

INDEPENDENT PRACTICE

See Example 1 **Use a table to find three equivalent ratios or rates.**

11. $\frac{200 \text{ meters}}{2 \text{ minutes}}$

12. 8 to 15

13. $\frac{12}{4}$

14. 6 to 7

15. $\frac{13}{20}$

16. 11:25

17. $\frac{\$2400}{1 \text{ month}}$

18. $\frac{51}{75}$

See Example 2 **19.** Donnette's heart rate while exercising is $\frac{128 \text{ beats}}{1 \text{ minute}}$. Nate's heart rate is $\frac{272 \text{ beats}}{2 \text{ minutes}}$, and Leslin's heart rate is $\frac{384 \text{ beats}}{3 \text{ minutes}}$. Whose heart rate is the same as Donnette's?

See Example 3 **20.** Lee Middle School orders 15 textbooks for every 12 students. How many textbooks should the school order for 72 students?

PRACTICE AND PROBLEM SOLVING

21. Biology Brown bats vary in length from 3 to 6 inches and have wing spans from 8 to 16 inches. Write a ratio in simplest form of a bat's wing span to the bat's body length.

22. Buy-A-Lot Market has tomatoes on sale. The table shows some sale prices. How much will a restaurant owner pay for 25 pounds of tomatoes?

Amount (lb)	30	20	15	10	5
Cost ($)	11.70	7.80	5.85	3.90	1.95

Complete each table to find the missing values in the ratios.

23.

6	12	18	■
5	10	■	20

24.

96	48	24	■
48	24	■	6

○ = **WORKED-OUT SOLUTIONS**
on p. WS8

History

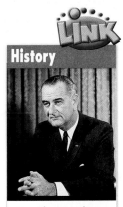

President Lyndon Baines Johnson, often referred to as LBJ, was born in Stillwater, Texas, in 1908. President Johnson had no vice president from November 1963 to January 1965.

Multiply and divide each ratio to find two equivalent ratios.

25. 36:48　　　**26.** $\frac{4}{60}$　　　**27.** $\frac{128}{48}$　　　**28.** 15:100

29. **Multi-Step** Lyndon Johnson was elected president in 1964. The ratio of the number of votes he received to the number of votes that Barry Goldwater received was about 19:12. About how many votes were cast for both candiates?

Candidates	Number of Votes
Lyndon Johnson	43,121,085
Barry Goldwater	

30. **What's the Error?** A student said that 3:4 is equivalent to 9:16 and 18:64. What did the student do wrong? Correct the ratios so they are equivalent.

31. **Write About It** If Daniel drives the same distance each day, will he be able to complete a 4,500-mile trip in 2 weeks? Explain how you solved the problem.

Days	Distance (mi)
3	1,020
5	1,700
9	3,060

32. **Challenge** The table shows the regular and sale prices of CDs at Bargain Blast. How much money will you save if you buy 10 CDs on sale?

Number of CDs	Regular Price ($)	Sale Price ($)
2	17.00	14.40
3	25.50	21.60
6	51.00	43.20

Florida Spiral Review

MA.6.A.2.1, MA.6.S.6.1

33. **Multiple Choice** Which ratio is NOT equivalent to 3 to 7?

A. 9:21　　　**B.** 36:77　　　**C.** 45:105　　　**D.** 54:126

34. **Short Response** The table shows the distances traveled and the numbers of gallons of gas used on four automobile trips. Predict the number of gallons of gas that would be used for a trip of 483 miles.

Distance (mi)	552	414	276	138
Gas Used (gal)	24	18	12	6

35. In 2005, the heights of the world's tallest buildings were 509, 452, 452, 442, 421, and 415 meters. Find the mean, median, mode, and range of the data set. (Lesson 6-1)

36. Javier saved $65, $82, $58, $74, $65, and $72 each month from his part-time job for six months. The next month he worked full-time and saved $285. Find the mean, median, and mode of the amounts saved with and without the full-time savings. (Lesson 6-2)

MA.6.A.2.2
. . . Compare ratios and rates.
Also MA.6.A.3.2

Have you ever heard water called H_2O? H_2O is the scientific formula for water. One molecule of water contains two hydrogen atoms (H_2) and one oxygen atom (O). No matter how many molecules of water you have, hydrogen and oxygen will always be in the ratio 2 to 1.

"Remember everybody this is planet Earth So whatever you do, don't drink the water"

© Cartoon Stock

Vocabulary

proportion

Water Molecules	1	2	3	4
Hydrogen atoms / Oxygen atoms	$\frac{2}{1}$	$\frac{4}{2}$	$\frac{6}{3}$	$\frac{8}{4}$

Reading Math

Read the proportion $\frac{2}{1} = \frac{4}{2}$ as "two is to one as four is to two."

Notice that $\frac{2}{1}$, $\frac{4}{2}$, $\frac{6}{3}$, and $\frac{8}{4}$ are equivalent ratios.

A **proportion** is an equation that shows two equivalent ratios.

$$\frac{2}{1} = \frac{4}{2} \qquad \frac{4}{2} = \frac{8}{4} \qquad \frac{2}{1} = \frac{6}{3}$$

EXAMPLE **1** **Using Equivalent Ratios to Solve Proportions**

Maricel spent $20 to buy 4 medium pizzas. What is the cost for 12 medium pizzas?

$\dfrac{\$20}{4} = \dfrac{x}{12}$ *Write a proportion that compares total cost to number of pizzas.*

$\dfrac{\$20}{4} = \dfrac{x}{12}$ *Think: 4 × 3 = 12 and $20 × 3 = x.*

$\times 3$

$x = \$20 \times 3 = \$60$

The cost for 12 medium pizzas is $60.

Check

Find the unit rate: $\dfrac{\$20}{4 \text{ pizzas}} = \dfrac{\$5}{1 \text{ pizza}}$. Make a table of equivalent rates:

Original Rate 5×3 5×6 5×12

		↓	↓	↓
Cost ($)	5	15	30	60
Pizzas	1	3	6	12

The cost of 12 pizzas was $60.

In the proportion $\dfrac{\$20}{4} = \dfrac{\$60}{12}$, 4 × $60 and $20 × 12 are cross products. Notice that 4 × $60 = $240 and $20 × 12 = $240. When two ratios form a proportion, the cross products are equal.

Video **Lesson Tutorial Videos @ thinkcentral.com**

CROSS PRODUCTS

Cross products in proportions are equal.

$8 \cdot 2 = 4 \cdot 4$	$5 \cdot 9 = 3 \cdot 15$	$6 \cdot 3 = 9 \cdot 2$	$7 \cdot 2 = 14 \cdot 1$
$16 = 16$	$45 = 45$	$18 = 18$	$14 = 14$

E X A M P L E **2** **Using Cross Products to Solve Proportions**

Find the missing value in the proportion $\frac{3}{4} = \frac{n}{16}$.

     Find the cross products.

$4 \cdot n = 3 \cdot 16$ *The cross products are equal.*

$4n = 48$ *n is multiplied by 4.*

$\frac{4n}{4} = \frac{48}{4}$ *Divide both sides by 4 to undo the multiplication.*

$n = 12$

E X A M P L E **3** *Measurement Application*

The label from a bottle of pet vitamins shows recommended dosages. What dosage would you give an adult dog that weighs 15 lb?

Pet Vitamins
- **Adult dogs:**
  1 tsp per 20 lb body weight
- **Puppies, pregnant dogs, or nursing dogs:**
  1 tsp per 10 lb body weight
- **Cats:**
  1 tsp per 12 lb body weight

$\frac{1 \text{ tsp}}{20 \text{ lb}} = \frac{v}{15 \text{ lb}}$ *Let v be the amount of vitamins for a 15 lb dog.*

     Write a proportion.

$20 \cdot v = 1 \cdot 15$ *The cross products are equal.*

$20v = 15$ *v is multiplied by 20.*

$\frac{20v}{20} = \frac{15}{20}$ *Divide both sides by 20 to undo the multiplication.*

$v = \frac{3}{4} \text{ tsp}$ *Write your answer in simplest form.*

You should give $\frac{3}{4}$ tsp of vitamins to a 15 lb dog.

> **Caution!**
>
> In a proportion, the units must be in the same order in both ratios.
>
> $\frac{\text{tsp}}{\text{lb}} = \frac{\text{tsp}}{\text{lb}}$
>
> or $\frac{\text{lb}}{\text{tsp}} = \frac{\text{lb}}{\text{tsp}}$

Think and Discuss

1. Tell whether $\frac{7}{8} = \frac{4}{14}$ is a proportion. How do you know?

2. Give an example of a proportion. Tell how you know that it is a proportion.

MA.6.A.2.2, MA.6.A.3.2

GUIDED PRACTICE

See Example **1**   1. Colin bought 3 vintage T-shirts for $45. How much would Colin pay for 6 vintage T-shirts?

2. Amanda purchased 2 movie tickets for $14. How many movie tickets can Amanda buy with $42?

See Example **2**   **Find the missing value in each proportion.**

3. $\frac{12}{9} = \frac{n}{3}$ 4. $\frac{t}{5} = \frac{28}{20}$ 5. $\frac{1}{c} = \frac{6}{12}$ 6. $\frac{6}{7} = \frac{30}{b}$

See Example **3**   7. Ursula is entering a bicycle race for charity. Her mother pledges $0.75 for every 0.5 mile she bikes. If Ursula bikes 17.5 miles, how much will her mother donate?

INDEPENDENT PRACTICE

See Example **1**   8. Zed buys a sports magazine each month for 3 months and spends $18. How much will Zed spend if he buys the same sports magazine every month for 12 months?

9. Morgan bought 3 pounds of cheese for a party platter for $27. How many pounds of the same cheese can Morgan buy with $54?

See Example **2**   **Find the missing value in each proportion.**

10. $\frac{3}{2} = \frac{24}{d}$ 11. $\frac{p}{40} = \frac{3}{8}$ 12. $\frac{6}{14} = \frac{x}{7}$ 13. $\frac{5}{p} = \frac{7}{77}$

See Example **3**   14. According to Ty's study guidelines, how many minutes of science reading should he do if his science class is 90 minutes long?

Ty's Study Guidelines	
Class	**Reading Time**
Literature	35 minutes for every 50 minutes of class time
Science	20 minutes for every 60 minutes of class time
History	30 minutes for every 55 minutes of class time

PRACTICE AND PROBLEM SOLVING

Find the value of p in each proportion.

15. $\frac{18}{6} = \frac{6}{p}$ 16. $\frac{4}{p} = \frac{48}{60}$ 17. $\frac{p}{10} = \frac{15}{50}$ 18. $\frac{3}{5} = \frac{12}{p}$

19. $\frac{21}{15} = \frac{p}{5}$ 20. $\frac{3}{6} = \frac{p}{8}$ 21. $\frac{15}{5} = \frac{9}{p}$ 22. $\frac{6}{p} = \frac{4}{28}$

23. **Patterns** The first term in a sequence is $\frac{7}{2}$. The second term of the sequence is proportional to the first term and has a denominator of 6. What is the second term?

○ = WORKED-OUT SOLUTIONS
on p. WS8

The value of the U.S. dollar as compared to the values of currencies from other countries changes every day. The graph shows recent values of various currencies compared to the U.S. dollar. Use the graph for Exercises 24–28.

24. What is the value of 9.72 European euros in U.S. dollars?

25. Multi-Step Tamara converts 100 U.S. dollars to euros. She spends 55 euros while vacationing in Europe. How much does she have left in U.S. dollars?

26. **?** **What's the Error?** A student set up the proportion $\frac{1}{7.52} = \frac{x}{30}$ to determine the value of 30 U.S. dollars in China. Why is this proportion incorrect? Write the correct proportion, and find the missing value.

27. **Write About It** Which is worth more: five U.S. dollars or five Canadian dollars? Why?

28. **Challenge** A dime is worth about how many Mexican pesos?

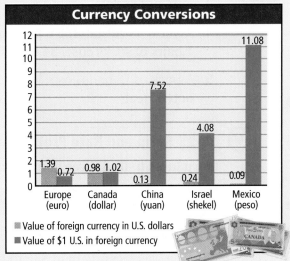

Currency Conversions

- Value of foreign currency in U.S. dollars
- Value of $1 U.S. in foreign currency

Europe (euro): 1.39, 0.72
Canada (dollar): 0.98, 1.02
China (yuan): 7.52, 0.13
Israel (shekel): 4.08, 0.24
Mexico (peso): 11.08, 0.09

Florida Spiral Review

MA.6.A.2.1, MA.6.A.2.2, MA.6.A.5.2

29. Multiple Choice A recipe calls for 4 cups of sugar and 16 cups of water. If the recipe is reduced, how many cups of water should be used with 1 cup of sugar?

    A. 0.25 cups   **B.** 1.6 cups   **C.** 4 cups   **D.** 16 cups

30. Multiple Choice Li mixes 3 units of red paint with 8 units of white paint to get pink. How many units of red paint should she mix with 12 units of white paint to get the same pink shade?

    F. $2\frac{3}{4}$ **G.** 3   **H.** $3\frac{1}{4}$ **I.** $4\frac{1}{2}$

Compare. Write <, >, or =. (Lesson 4-7)

31. $\frac{4}{7}$ ■ $\frac{7}{10}$ **32.** $\frac{3}{5}$ ■ $\frac{14}{15}$ **33.** $\frac{9}{27}$ ■ $\frac{6}{18}$ **34.** $\frac{45}{18}$ ■ $\frac{18}{9}$

Write each ratio two different ways. (Lesson 7-1)

35. 4:9   **36.** eight to eleven   **37.** $\frac{6}{13}$ **38.** 7:5

Quiz for Lessons 7-1 Through 7-3

7-1 Ratios and Rates

Use the table to write each ratio.

1. classical CDs to rock CDs

2. country to total CDs

3. pop and rock to total CDs

Types of CDs in Mark's Music Collection			
Classical	4	Jazz	3
Country	9	Pop	14
Dance	8	Rock	10

4. A package containing 6 pairs of socks costs $6.89. A package containing 4 pairs of socks costs $4.64. Which is the better deal?

5. A pack of 12 pens costs $5.52. A pack of 8 pens costs $3.92. Which is the better deal?

7-2 Ratio and Rate Problems

Use a table to find three equivalent ratios or rates.

6. $\frac{21}{30}$

7. 15:6

8. 3 to 101

9. $\frac{20 \text{ students}}{1 \text{ teacher}}$

10. $\frac{4 \text{ quarts}}{1 \text{ gallon}}$

11. $\frac{\$39.96}{4 \text{ CDs}}$

12. Meg was recently paid $35 to babysit for 5 hours. Carla was paid $30 to babysit for 6 hours, and Shayna was paid $28 to babysit for 4 hours. Who was paid at the same rate as Meg?

13. The Westview Middle School Band serves pizza to students after band concerts. They order 10 pizzas for 50 students. How many pizzas should they order for 175 students?

14. Daniel bought 3 concert tickets for a total of $255. How much would 8 concert tickets cost?

7-3 Proportions

Find the missing value in each proportion.

15. $\frac{1}{4} = \frac{n}{12}$

16. $\frac{3}{n} = \frac{15}{25}$

17. $\frac{n}{4} = \frac{18}{6}$

18. $\frac{10}{4} = \frac{5}{n}$

19. $\frac{5}{4} = \frac{n}{12}$

20. $\frac{2}{9} = \frac{4}{n}$

21. $\frac{6}{10} = \frac{n}{5}$

22. $\frac{7}{8} = \frac{21}{n}$

23. To make 2 quarts of punch, Jenny adds 16 grams of powdered juice mix to 2 quarts of water. How much mix does Jenny need to make 3 quarts of punch?

Focus on Problem Solving

 Make a Plan

MA.6.A.5.3 Estimate the results of computations with . . . decimals . . .

• **Estimate or find an exact answer**

Sometimes an estimate is all you need to solve a problem, and sometimes you need to find an exact answer.

One way to decide whether you can estimate is to see if you can rewrite the problem using the words *at most, at least,* or *about.* For example, suppose Laura has $30. Then she could spend *at most* $30. She would not have to spend *exactly* $30. Or, if you know it takes 15 minutes to get to school, you must leave your house *at least* (not exactly) 15 minutes before school starts.

 Read the problems below. Decide whether you can estimate or whether you must find the exact answer. How do you know?

1 Alex is a radio station disc jockey. He is making a list of songs that should last no longer than 30 minutes total when played in a row. His list of songs and their playing times are given in the table. Does Alex have the right amount of music?

Song Title	Length (min)
Color Me Blue	4.5
Hittin' the Road	7.2
Stand Up, Shout	2.6
Top Dog	3.6
Kelso Blues	4.3
Smile on Me	5.7
A Long Time Ago	6.4

2 For every 10 minutes of music, Alex has to play 1.5 minutes of commercials. If Alex plays the songs on the list, how much time does he need to allow for commercials?

3 If Alex must play the songs on the list and the commercials in 30 minutes, how much music time does he need to cut to allow for commercials?

7-4 Percents

MA.6.A.5.1
Use equivalent forms of fractions, decimals, and percents to solve problems.

Vocabulary
percent

Most states charge sales tax on items you purchase. Sales tax is a percent of the item's price. A **percent** is a ratio of a number to 100.

You can remember that *percent* means "per hundred." For example, 8% means "8 per hundred," or "8 out of 100."

$160

If a sales tax rate is 8%, the following statements are true:

At a sales tax rate of 8%, the tax on this wakeskate would be $12.80.

- For every $1.00 you spend, you pay $0.08 in sales tax.

- For every $10.00 you spend, you pay $0.80 in sales tax.

- For every $100 you spend, you pay $8 in sales tax.

Because *percent* means "per hundred," 100% means "100 out of 100." This is why 100% is often used to mean "all" or "the whole thing."

EXAMPLE **1** **Modeling Percents**

Animated Math
@ thinkcentral.com

Use a 10-by-10-square grid to model 8%.

A 10-by-10-square grid has 100 squares.

8% means "8 out of 100," or $\frac{8}{100}$.

Shade 8 squares out of 100 squares.

EXAMPLE **2** **Writing Percents as Fractions**

Write 40% as a fraction in simplest form.

$40\% = \frac{40}{100}$ *Write the percent as a fraction with a denominator of 100.*

$\frac{40 \div 20}{100 \div 20} = \frac{2}{5}$ *Write the fraction in simplest form.*

Written as a fraction, 40% is $\frac{2}{5}$.

EXAMPLE 3 *Life Science Application*

Up to 55% of the heat lost by your body can be lost through your head. Write 55% as a fraction in simplest form.

$55\% = \dfrac{55}{100}$ *Write the percent as a fraction with a denominator of 100.*

$\dfrac{55 \div 5}{100 \div 5} = \dfrac{11}{20}$ *Write the fraction in simplest form.*

Written as a fraction, 55% is $\dfrac{11}{20}$.

EXAMPLE 4 **Writing Percents as Decimals**

Write 24% as a decimal.

$24\% = \dfrac{24}{100}$ *Write the percent as a fraction with a denominator of 100.*

Write the fraction as a decimal.

$$
\begin{array}{r}
0.24 \\
100\,\overline{)24.00} \\
-\underline{200} \\
400 \\
-\underline{400} \\
0
\end{array}
$$

Written as a decimal, 24% is 0.24.

Remember!

To divide by 100, move the decimal point two places to the left.

$24 \div 100 = 0.24$

EXAMPLE 5 *Earth Science Application*

The water frozen in glaciers makes up almost 75% of the world's fresh water supply. Write 75% as a decimal.

$75\% = \dfrac{75}{100}$ *Write the percent as a fraction with a denominator of 100.*

$75 \div 100 = 0.75$ *Write the fraction as a decimal.*

Written as a decimal, 75% is 0.75.

Think and Discuss

1. **Give an example** of a situation in which you have seen percents.

2. **Explain** how to write a percent as a fraction.

3. **Write** 100% as a decimal and as a fraction.

 MA.6.A.5.1

GUIDED PRACTICE

See Example 1 **Use a 10-by-10-square grid to model each percent.**

    1. 45%   **2.** 3%   **3.** 61%

See Example 2 **Write each percent as a fraction in simplest form.**

    4. 25%   **5.** 80%   **6.** 54%

See Example 3 **7. Social Studies** Belize is a country in Central America. Of the land in Belize, 92% is made up of forests and woodlands. Write 92% as a fraction in simplest form.

See Example 4 **Write each percent as a decimal.**

    8. 72%   **9.** 4%   **10.** 90%

See Example 5 **11.** About 64% of the runways at airports in the United States are not paved. Write 64% as a decimal.

INDEPENDENT PRACTICE

See Example 1 **Use a 10-by-10-square grid to model each percent.**

    12. 14%   **13.** 98%   **14.** 36%   **15.** 28%

See Example 2 **Write each percent as a fraction in simplest form.**

    16. 20%   **17.** 75%   **18.** 11%   **19.** 72%

    20. 5%   **21.** 64%   **22.** 31%   **23.** 85%

See Example 3 **24.** Nikki must answer 80% of the questions on her final exam correctly to pass her class. Write 80% as a fraction in simplest form.

See Example 4 **Write each percent as a decimal.**

    25. 44%   **26.** 13%   **27.** 29%   **28.** 51%

    29. 60%   **30.** 92%   **31.** 7%   **32.** 87%

See Example 5 **33.** Brett was absent 2% of the school year. Write 2% as a decimal.

PRACTICE AND PROBLEM SOLVING

Write each percent as a fraction in simplest form and as a decimal.

    34. 23%   **35.** 1%   **36.** 49%   **37.** 70%   **38.** 10%

    39. 37%   **40.** 85%   **41.** 8%   **42.** 63%   **43.** 75%

    44. 94%   **45.** 100%   **46.** 0%   **47.** 52%   **48.** 12%

49. Model 15%, 52%, 71%, and 100% using different 10-by-10 grids. Then write each percent as a fraction in simplest form.

○ = WORKED-OUT SOLUTIONS
on p. WS8

Music LINK

The circle graph shows the percent of radio stations around the world that play each type of music listed. Use the graph for Exercises 50–57.

50. What fraction of the radio stations play easy listening music? Write this fraction in simplest form.

51. Use a 10-by-10-square grid to model the percent of radio stations that play country music. Then write this percent as a decimal.

52. Which type of music makes up $\frac{1}{20}$ of the graph?

53. Someone reading the graph said, "More than $\frac{1}{10}$ of the radio stations play top 40 music." Do you agree with this statement? Why or why not?

54. Suppose you converted all of the percents in the graph to decimals and added them. Without actually doing this, tell what the sum would be. Explain.

55. ✏️ **Write a Problem** Write a question about the circle graph that involves changing a percent to a fraction. Then answer your question.

56. ✏️ **Write About It** How does the percent of radio stations that play Spanish music compare with the fraction $\frac{1}{6}$? Explain.

57. ⭐ **Challenge** Name a fraction that is greater than the percent of radio stations that play Spanish music but less than the percent of radio stations that play urban/rap music.

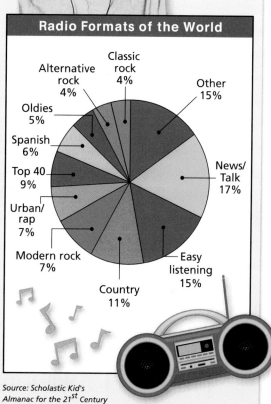

Radio Formats of the World

Classic rock 4%
Alternative rock 4%
Other 15%
Oldies 5%
Spanish 6%
News/Talk 17%
Top 40 9%
Urban/rap 7%
Modern rock 7%
Easy listening 15%
Country 11%

Source: Scholastic Kid's Almanac for the 21st Century

---

58. Multiple Choice Which decimal is equivalent to 85%?

   A. 85.0   **B.** 8.5   **C.** 0.85   **D.** 0.085

59. Multiple Choice Which term describes a number compared to 100?

   F. Rate   **G.** Ratio   **H.** Percent   **I.** Proportion

Solve each equation. (Lesson 2-8)

60. $4x = 28$ **61.** $5x = 35$ **62.** $24 = 6x$

63. Mowers R Us charges $45 to mow a lawn 3 times. Grass Cutters charges $50 to mow a lawn 4 times. Which is the better deal? (Lesson 7-1)

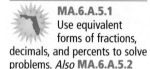

MA.6.A.5.1
Use equivalent forms of fractions, decimals, and percents to solve problems. *Also* **MA.6.A.5.2**

Percents, decimals, and fractions appear in newspapers, on television, and on the Internet. To fully understand the data you see in your everyday life, you should be able to change from one number form to another.

In Lesson 7-4, you learned how to write a percent as a fraction or as a decimal. You can also express decimals and fractions as percents.

$$\frac{1}{2} = 0.5 = 50\%$$

EXAMPLE **1** **Writing Decimals as Percents**

Animated **Math**
@ **thinkcentral.com**

Write each decimal as a percent.

Method 1: Use place value.

A **0.3**

$$0.3 = \frac{3}{10}$$ *Write the decimal as a fraction.*

$$\frac{3 \cdot 10}{10 \cdot 10} = \frac{30}{100}$$ *Write an equivalent fraction with 100 as the denominator.*

$$\frac{30}{100} = 30\%$$ *Write the numerator with a percent symbol.*

B **0.43**

$$0.43 = \frac{43}{100}$$ *Write the decimal as a fraction.*

$$\frac{43}{100} = 43\%$$ *Write the numerator with a percent symbol.*

Method 2: Multiply by 100.

C **0.7431**

0.7431 · 100   *Multiply by 100.*

74.31%   *Add the percent symbol.*

D **0.023**

0.023 · 100   *Multiply by 100.*

2.3%   *Add the percent symbol.*

Video **Lesson Tutorial Videos** @ thinkcentral.com

E X A M P L E **2** **Writing Fractions as Percents**

Write each fraction as a percent.

Method 1: Write an equivalent fraction with a denominator of 100.

A $\dfrac{4}{5}$

$\dfrac{4 \cdot 20}{5 \cdot 20} = \dfrac{80}{100}$ *Write an equivalent fraction with a denominator of 100.*

$\dfrac{80}{100} = 80\%$ *Write the numerator with a percent symbol.*

Method 2: Use division to write the fraction as a decimal.

B $\dfrac{3}{8}$

$$\begin{array}{r} 0.375 \\ 8\overline{)3.000} \end{array}$$ *Divide the numerator by the denominator.*

$0.375 = 37.5\%$ *Multiply by 100 by moving the decimal point right two places. Add the percent symbol.*

> **Helpful Hint**
>
> When the denominator is a factor of 100, it is often easier to use method 1. When the denominator is not a factor of 100, it is usually easier to use method 2.

E X A M P L E **3** *Earth Science Application*

About $\dfrac{39}{50}$ of Earth's atmosphere is made up of nitrogen. About what percent of the atmosphere is nitrogen?

$\dfrac{39}{50}$

$\dfrac{39 \cdot 2}{50 \cdot 2} = \dfrac{78}{100}$ *Write an equivalent fraction with a denominator of 100.*

$\dfrac{78}{100} = 78\%$ *Write the numerator with a percent symbol.*

About 78% of Earth's atmosphere is made up of nitrogen.

The number line below shows common equivalent fractions, decimals, and percents.

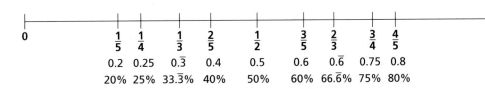

Think and Discuss

1. Tell which method you prefer for converting decimals to percents—using equivalent fractions or multiplying by 100. Why?

2. Give two different ways to write three-tenths.

3. Explain how to write fractions as percents using two different methods.

MA.6.A.5.1, MA.6.A.5.2

GUIDED PRACTICE

See Example **1**   Write each decimal as a percent.

     1. 0.39   **2.** 0.125   **3.** 0.8   **4.** 0.112

See Example **2**   Write each fraction as a percent.

     5. $\frac{11}{25}$ **6.** $\frac{7}{8}$ **7.** $\frac{7}{10}$ **8.** $\frac{1}{2}$ **9.** $\frac{9}{15}$

See Example **3**   **10.** Patti spent $\frac{3}{4}$ of her allowance on a new backpack. What percent of her allowance did she spend?

INDEPENDENT PRACTICE

See Example **1**   Write each decimal as a percent.

     11. 0.6   **12.** 0.55   **13.** 0.34   **14.** 0.308   **15.** 0.62

See Example **2**   Write each fraction as a percent.

     16. $\frac{3}{5}$ **17.** $\frac{3}{10}$ **18.** $\frac{24}{25}$ **19.** $\frac{9}{20}$ **20.** $\frac{17}{20}$

     21. $\frac{1}{8}$ **22.** $\frac{11}{16}$ **23.** $\frac{37}{50}$ **24.** $\frac{2}{5}$ **25.** $\frac{18}{45}$

See Example **3**   **26.** About $\frac{1}{125}$ of the people in the United States have the last name *Johnson.* What percent of people in the United States have this last name?

PRACTICE AND PROBLEM SOLVING

Write each decimal as a percent and a fraction.

27. 0.04   **28.** 0.32   **29.** 0.45   **30.** 0.59   **31.** 0.01

32. 0.81   **33.** 0.6   **34.** 0.39   **35.** 0.14   **36.** 0.62

Write each fraction as a percent and as a decimal. Round to the nearest hundredth, if necessary.

37. $\frac{4}{5}$ **38.** $\frac{1}{3}$ **39.** $\frac{5}{6}$ **40.** $\frac{7}{12}$ **41.** $\frac{17}{50}$

42. $\frac{2}{30}$ **43.** $\frac{1}{25}$ **44.** $\frac{8}{11}$ **45.** $\frac{4}{15}$ **46.** $\frac{22}{35}$

Compare. Write <, >, or =.

47. 70% ▨ $\frac{3}{4}$ **48.** $\frac{5}{8}$ ▨ 6.25%   **49.** 0.2 ▨ $\frac{1}{5}$ **50.** 1.25 ▨ $\frac{1}{8}$

51. 0.7 ▨ 7%   **52.** $\frac{9}{10}$ ▨ 0.3   **53.** 37% ▨ $\frac{3}{7}$ **54.** $\frac{17}{20}$ ▨ 0.85

55. Language Arts The longest word in all of Shakespeare's plays is *honorificabilitudinitatibus.* About what percent of the letters in this word are vowels? About what percent of the letters are consonants?

○ = WORKED-OUT SOLUTIONS
on p. WS8

Order the numbers from least to greatest.

56. $45\%, \frac{21}{50}, 0.43, 89\%$ **57.** $\frac{7}{8}, 90\%, 0.098$ **58.** $0.7, 26\%, \frac{1}{4}, 34\%$

59. $38\%, \frac{7}{25}, 0.21$ **60.** $\frac{9}{20}, 14\%, 0.125, 24\%$ **61.** $0.605, 17\%, \frac{5}{9}$

62. Entertainment A record-company official estimates that 3 out of every 100 albums released become hits. What percent of albums do not become hits?

63. Multi-Step About 97 million households in the United States have at least one television. Use the table below to answer the questions that follow.

Television in the United States	
Fraction of households with at least one television	$\frac{49}{50}$
Percent of households with three televisions	38%
Fraction of television owners with basic cable	$\frac{2}{3}$

a. About what percent of television owners have basic cable?

b. Write a decimal to express the percent of television owners who have three televisions.

64. What's the Question? Out of 25 students, 12 prefer to take their test on Monday, and 5 prefer to take their test on Tuesday. The answer is 32%. What is the question?

65. Write About It Explain why 0.8 is equal to 80% and not 8%.

66. Challenge The dimensions of a rectangle are 0.5 yard and 24% of a yard. What is the area of the rectangle? Write your answer as a fraction in simplest form.

Florida Spiral Review   MA.6.A.5.1, MA.6.A.1.2, MA.6.A.2.1

67. Multiple Choice Which expression is NOT equal to half of n?

A. $0.5n$ **B.** $\frac{n}{2}$ **C.** $n \div 2$ **D.** 5% of n

68. Multiple Choice Approximately $\frac{2}{3}$ of U.S. homeowners own a cell phone. About what percent of homeowners do NOT own a cell phone?

F. 0.67%   **G.** 2.3%   **H.** 33.3%   **I.** 66.7%

Multiply. Write each answer in simplest form. (Lesson 5-6)

69. $\frac{4}{5} \cdot \frac{5}{12}$ **70.** $\frac{2}{9} \cdot \frac{3}{8}$ **71.** $\frac{7}{10} \cdot \frac{5}{14}$ **72.** $\frac{8}{21} \cdot \frac{7}{8}$

Complete each table to find the missing ratios. (Lesson 7-2)

73.

3	6	9	
4	8		16

74.

5	10		20
6	12	18	

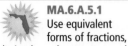

7-6 Percent Problems

MA.6.A.5.1
Use equivalent forms of fractions, decimals, and percents to solve problems. *Also* **MA.6.A.5.3**

The frozen-yogurt stand in the mall sells 420 frozen-yogurt cups per day, on average. Forty-five percent of the frozen-yogurt cups are sold to teenagers. On average, how many frozen-yogurt cups are sold to teenagers each day?

To answer this question, you will need to find 45% of 420.

To find the percent one number is of another, use this proportion:

$$\frac{\%}{100} = \frac{is}{of}$$

Because you are looking for **45% of 420**, 45 replaces the **percent sign** and 420 replaces "**of.**" The first denominator, 100, always stays the same. The "is" part is what you have been asked to find.

EXAMPLE **1** *Consumer Math Application*

@ **thinkcentral.com**

How many frozen-yogurt cups are sold to teenagers each day?

First estimate your answer. Think: $45\% = \frac{45}{100}$, which is close to $\frac{50}{100}$, or $\frac{1}{2}$. So about $\frac{1}{2}$ of the 420 yogurt cups are sold to teenagers.

$\frac{1}{2} \cdot 420 = 210$ ⟵ *This is the estimate.*

Now solve:

$\frac{45}{100} = \frac{y}{420}$	*Let y represent the number of yogurt cups sold to teenagers.*
$100 \cdot y = 45 \cdot 420$	*The cross products are equal.*
$100y = 18,900$	*y is multiplied by 100.*
$\frac{100y}{100} = \frac{18,900}{100}$	*Divide both sides of the equation by 100 to undo the multiplication.*
$y = 189$	

Since 189 is close to your estimate of 210, 189 is a reasonable answer. About 189 yogurt cups per day are sold to teenagers.

Helpful Hint

Think: "45 out of 100 is how many out of 420?"

Video **Lesson Tutorial Videos** @ **thinkcentral.com**

EXAMPLE 2

EXAMPLE **2**   *Technology Application*

Heather is downloading a file from the Internet. So far, she has downloaded 75% of the file. If 30 minutes have passed since she started, how long will it take her to download the rest of the file?

$$\frac{\%}{100} = \frac{is}{of}$$

$$\frac{75}{100} = \frac{30}{m}$$ *75% of the file has downloaded, so 30 minutes* ***is*** *75%* ***of*** *the total time needed.*

$100 \cdot 30 = 75 \cdot m$ *The cross products are equal.*

$3{,}000 = 75m$ *m is multiplied by 75.*

$$\frac{3{,}000}{75} = \frac{75m}{75}$$ *Divide both sides by 75 to undo the multiplication.*

$40 = m$

The time needed to download the entire file is 40 min. So far, the file has been downloading for 30 min. Because $40 - 30 = 10$, the remainder of the file will be downloaded in 10 min.

Instead of using proportions, you can also multiply to find a percent of a number.

EXAMPLE **3**   **Multiplying to Find a Percent of a Number**

Find 20% of 150.

$20\% = 0.20$ *Write the percent as a decimal.*

$0.20 \cdot 150$ *Multiply using the decimal.*

$\quad 30$

So 30 is 20% of 150.

Check

Use a model to check the answer.

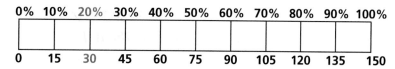

0%	10%	20%	30%	40%	50%	60%	70%	80%	90%	100%
0	15	30	45	60	75	90	105	120	135	150

Think and Discuss

1. Explain why you must subtract 30 from 40 in Example 2.

2. Give an example of a time when you would need to find a percent of a number.

GUIDED PRACTICE

See Example 1

1. Members of the drama club sold T-shirts for their upcoming musical. Of the 80 T-shirts sold, 55% were size medium. How many of the T-shirts sold were size medium?

See Example 2

2. Loni has read 25% of a book. If she has been reading for 5 hours, how many more hours will it take her to complete the book?

See Example 3

3. Find 12% of 56.   **4.** Find 65% of 240.   **5.** Find 2% of 20.

6. Find 85% of 115.   **7.** Find 70% of 54.   **8.** Find 85% of 355.

INDEPENDENT PRACTICE

See Example 1

9. Tamara collects porcelain dolls. Of the 24 dolls that she has, 25% have blond hair. How many of her dolls have blond hair?

10. Mr. Green has a garden. Of the 40 seeds he planted, 35% were vegetable seeds. How many vegetable seeds did he plant?

See Example 2

11. Kevin has mowed 40% of the lawn. If he has been mowing for 20 minutes, how long will it take him to mow the rest of the lawn?

12. Maggie ordered a painting. She paid 30% of the total cost when she ordered it, and she will pay the remaining amount when it is delivered. If she has paid $15, how much more does she owe?

See Example 3

13. Find 22% of 130.   **14.** Find 78% of 350.   **15.** Find 28% of 65.

16. Find 9% of 50.   **17.** Find 45% of 210.   **18.** Find 54% of 602.

PRACTICE AND PROBLEM SOLVING

Find the percent of each number.

19. 6% of 38   **20.** 20% of 182   **21.** 13% of 40

22. 32% of 205   **23.** 14% of 88   **24.** 98% of 105

25. 78% of 52   **26.** 31% of 345   **27.** 62% of 50

28. 10% of 50   **29.** 1.5% of 800   **30.** 0.3% of 9

31. **Geometry** The width of a rectangular room is 75% of the length of the room. The room is 12 feet long.

   a. How wide is the room?

   b. The area of a rectangle is the product of the length and the width. What is the area of the room?

32. **Multi-Step** Marissa is shopping and finds a sales rack with items that are 25% off. If Marissa likes a shirt on the rack that originally cost $15, how much will she pay for the shirt before tax?

○ = WORKED-OUT SOLUTIONS
on p. WS8

33. **Chemistry** Glucose is a type of sugar. A glucose molecule is composed of 24 atoms. Hydrogen atoms make up 50% of the molecule, carbon atoms make up 25% of the molecule, and oxygen atoms make up the other 25%. How many of each atom are in a molecule of glucose?

34. **Technology** Students were asked in a school survey about how they use their computers. The circle graph shows the results.

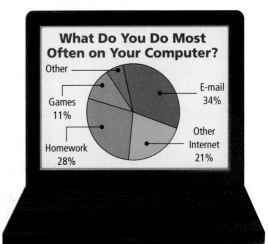

What Do You Do Most Often on Your Computer?

Other
E-mail 34%
Games 11%
Other Internet 21%
Homework 28%

a. If there are 850 students in the school, how many spend most of their computer time using e-mail?

b. Fifty-one students selected "other." What percent of the school population does this represent?

c. Which choices were selected by more than 200 students?

d. How many more students chose Internet than chose playing games?

35. **What's the Error?** To find 80% of 130, a student set up the proportion $\frac{80}{100} = \frac{130}{x}$. Explain the error. Write the correct proportion, and find the missing value.

36. **Write About It** Suppose you were asked to find 48% of 300 and your answer was 6.25. Would your answer be reasonable? How do you know? What is the correct answer?

37. **Challenge** Mrs. Peterson makes ceramic figurines. She recently made 25 figurines. Of those figurines, 16 are animals. What percent of the figurines are NOT animals?

Florida Spiral Review

MA.6.A.5.1

38. **Multiple Choice** Which of the following amounts is greatest?

A. 45% of 200   B. 50% of 150   C. 60% of 190   D. 100% of 110

39. **Short Response** If Sara orders 8 sports magazines and 12 health magazines on sale, how much will she save compared to the regular price? Explain.

Magazine Type	Original Price	Sale
Sports	8 for $60	Save 60%
Health	12 for $72	Save 30%

Write each decimal as a fraction or mixed number. (Lesson 4-5)

40. 0.25   **41.** 0.78   **42.** 1.4   **43.** 0.99   **44.** 5.36

45. About $\frac{7}{8}$ of the flowers in Monica's garden are snapdragons. What percent of the flowers in the garden are snapdragons? (Lesson 7-5)

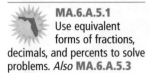

7-7 Applying Percents

MA.6.A.5.1
Use equivalent
forms of fractions,
decimals, and percents to solve
problems. *Also* MA.6.A.5.3

Vocabulary

discount

tip

sales tax

Percents show up often in daily
life. Think of examples that you have
seen of percents—sales at stores,
tips in restaurants, and sales tax on
purchases. You can estimate
percents such as these to find
amounts of money.

"Yogi always said '90% of the game is
half mental' ... I think it's more
like 95%."

© Cartoon Stock

Common Uses of Percents	
Discounts	A **discount** is an amount that is subtracted from the regular price of an item. discount = price · discount rate total cost = price − discount
Tips	A **tip** is an amount added to a bill for service. tip = bill · tip rate total cost = bill + tip
Sales tax	**Sales tax** is an amount added to the price of an item. sales tax = price · sales tax rate total cost = price + sales tax

EXAMPLE 1 Finding Discounts

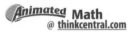 **Math**
@ thinkcentral.com

Remember!

To multiply by 0.10,
move the decimal
point one place left.

**A music store sign reads "10% off the regular price." If Nichole
wants to buy a CD whose regular price is $14.99, about how
much will she pay for her CD after the discount?**

Step 1: First round $14.99 to $15.

Step 2: Find 10% of $15 by multiplying 0.10 · $15. (*Hint:* Moving the
decimal point one place left is a shortcut.)

$$10\% \text{ of } 15 = 0.10 \cdot \$15 = \$1.50$$

The approximate discount is $1.50. Subtract this amount from $15.00
to estimate the cost of the CD.

$$\$15.00 - \$1.50 = \$13.50$$

Nichole will pay about $13.50 for the CD.

Video **Lesson Tutorial Videos @ thinkcentral.com**

When estimating percents, use percents that you can calculate mentally.

- You can find 10% of a number by moving the decimal point one place to the left.
- You can find 1% of a number by moving the decimal point two places to the left.
- You can find 5% of a number by finding one-half of 10% of the number.

EXAMPLE **2** **Finding Tips**

Leslie's lunch bill is $13.95. She wants to leave a tip that is 15% of the bill. About how much should her tip be?

Step 1: First round $13.95 to $14.

Step 2: Think: 15% = 10% + 5%

10% of $14 = 0.10 · $14 = $1.40

Step 3: 5% = 10% ÷ 2

= $1.40 ÷ 2 = $0.70

Step 4: 15% = 10% + 5%

= $1.40 + $0.70 = $2.10

Leslie should leave about $2.10 as a tip.

EXAMPLE **3** **Finding Sales Tax**

Marc is buying a scooter for $79.65. The sales tax rate is 6%. About how much will the total cost of the scooter be?

Step 1: First round $79.65 to $80.

Step 2: Think: 6% = 6 · 1%

1% of $80 = 0.01 · $80 = $0.80

Step 3: 6% = 6 · 1%

= 6 · $0.80 = $4.80

The approximate sales tax is $4.80. Add this amount to $80 to estimate the total cost of the scooter.

$80 + $4.80 = $84.80

Marc will pay about $84.80 for the scooter.

Think and Discuss

1. Tell when it would be useful to estimate the percent of a number.

2. Explain how to estimate to find the sales tax of an item.

 Homework Help THINK central

Go to **thinkcentral.com**
Exercises 1–9, 13, 19

 MA.6.A.5.1, MA.6.A.5.3

GUIDED PRACTICE

See Example **1**
1. Norine wants to buy a beaded necklace that is on sale for 10% off the marked price. If the marked price is $8.49, about how much will the necklace cost after the discount?

See Example **2**
2. Alice and Wagner ordered a pizza to be delivered. The total bill was $12.15. They want to give the delivery person a tip that is 20% of the bill. About how much should the tip be?

See Example **3**
3. A bicycle sells for $139.75. The sales tax rate is 8%. About how much will the total cost of the bicycle be?

INDEPENDENT PRACTICE

See Example **1**
4. Peter has a coupon for 15% off the price of any item in a sporting goods store. He wants to buy a pair of sneakers that are priced at $36.99. About how much will the sneakers cost after the discount?

5. All DVDs are discounted 25% off the original price. The DVD that Marissa wants to buy was originally priced at $24.98. About how much will the DVD cost after the discount?

See Example **2**
6. Michael's breakfast bill came to $7.65. He wants to leave a tip that is 15% of the bill. About how much should he leave for the tip?

7. Betty and her family went out for dinner. Their bill was $73.82. Betty's parents left a tip that was 15% of the bill. About how much was the tip that they left?

See Example **3**
8. A computer game costs $36.85. The sales tax rate is 6%. About how much will the total cost be for this computer game?

9. Irene is buying party supplies. The cost of her supplies is $52.75. The sales tax rate is 5%. About how much will the total cost of her party supplies be?

PRACTICE AND PROBLEM SOLVING

10. **Multi-Step** Lenny, Robert, and Katrina went out for lunch. The items they ordered are listed on the receipt, and the sales tax rate was 7%. They want to leave a tip equal to 15% of the total bill. Is $3.60 a reasonable amount for their tip? Explain.

**** Thank you ****	
Chicken Sandwich - 1	$5.95
Hamburger - 1	$4.75
Roast Beef Sandwich - 1	$7.35
Milk - 2	$2.40
Iced Tea - 1	$1.89

11. Jackie has $32.50 to buy a new pair of jeans. The pair she likes costs $38 but is marked "20% off ticketed price." The sales tax rate is 5%. Does Jackie have enough money to buy the jeans? Explain.

○ = WORKED-OUT SOLUTIONS
on p. WS8

12. Evan buys a bike that is on sale for 20% off the original price of $95. His brother Kyle buys the same bike at a different store on sale for 15% off the original price of $90. Who paid more? Explain.

13. **Multi-Step** An electronics store is going out of business. The sign on the door reads "All items on sale for 60% off the ticketed price." A computer has a ticketed price of $649, and a printer has a ticketed price of $199. What is the total cost of both items after the discount?

14. **Social Studies** Use the table.

   a. A shirt costs $18.95. Will the shirt cost more after sales tax in Georgia or in Kentucky? About how much more?

   b. A video game in North Carolina costs $59.75. The same video game in New York costs $60. After sales tax, in which state will the video game cost less? How much less?

State	Sales Tax Rate
Georgia	4%
Kentucky	6%
New York	4%
North Carolina	4.25%

15. **What's the Error?** The original price of an item was $48.65. The item was discounted 40%. A customer calculated the price after the discount to be $19.46. What's the error? Give the correct price after the discount.

16. **Write About It** Discuss the difference between a discount, sales tax, and a tip, in relation to the total cost. How does each affect the total cost? Give examples of situations in which each one is used.

17. **Challenge** Suppose a jacket is discounted 50% off the original price and then discounted an additional 20%. Is this the same as discounting the jacket 70% off the original price? Explain.

Florida Spiral Review   MA.6.A.5.1, MA.6.A.3.2

18. **Multiple Choice** Electric City is offering a 20% discount on all radios. Pedro would like to buy a radio that was originally priced at $36.50. What is the total cost after the discount?

   A. $7.30   B. $16.50   C. $29.20   D. $36.70

19. **Extended Response** Ann is researching the price of a CD. At Music Place, the CD that Ann wants was originally priced at $15.96 but is discounted 25%. At Awesome Sound, the CD was originally priced at $12.99 but is discounted 10%. What is the sale price of each CD? Which is the better deal? Explain.

Determine whether the given value of the variable is a solution. (Lesson 2-5)

20. $2x + 3 = 10$ for $x = 4$ 21. $5(b - 3) = 25$ for $b = 8$ 22. $18 = 3a - 9$ for $a = 3$

Find 20% of each number. (Lesson 7-6)

23. 15   24. 50   25. 65   26. 200   27. 3,000

Preview of MA.7.A.1.3 Solve problems involving similar figures.

Matching sides of two or more polygons are called **corresponding sides**, and matching angles are called **corresponding angles**.

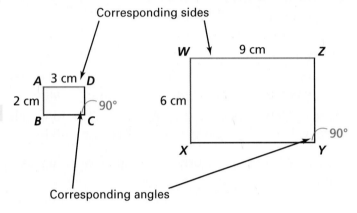

Corresponding sides

Corresponding angles

Vocabulary

corresponding sides

corresponding angles

similar

Similar figures have the same shape but not necessarily the same size.

Animated Math @ thinkcentral.com

SIMILAR FIGURES

Two figures are similar if

- the measures of the corresponding angles are equal.

- the ratios of the lengths of the corresponding sides are proportional.

In the rectangles above, one proportion is $\frac{AB}{WX} = \frac{AD}{WZ}$, or $\frac{2}{6} = \frac{3}{9}$.

EXAMPLE 1 **Finding Missing Measures in Similar Figures**

The two triangles are similar. Find the missing length x and the measure of $\angle A$.

$\frac{8}{12} = \frac{6}{x}$ *Write a proportion using corresponding side lengths.*

$12 \cdot 6 = 8 \cdot x$ *The cross products are equal.*

$72 = 8x$ *x is multiplied by 8.*

$\frac{72}{8} = \frac{8x}{8}$ *Divide both sides by 8 to undo the multiplication.*

$9 \text{ cm} = x$

Angle A corresponds to angle B, and the measure of $\angle B = 37°$. The measure of $\angle A = 37°$.

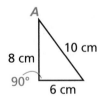

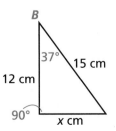

Video **Lesson Tutorial Videos @ thinkcentral.com**

EXAMPLE **2** **PROBLEM SOLVING APPLICATION**

PROBLEM
SOLVING

Children at the Ice Cream Stand was painted by American artist William H. Johnson. This reduction is similar to the actual painting. The height of the actual painting is 32 cm. To the nearest centimeter, what is the width of the actual painting?

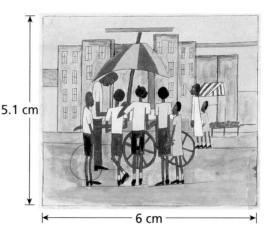

5.1 cm

6 cm

1 Understand the Problem

The **answer** will be the width of the actual painting.

List the **important information:**

- The actual painting and the reduction above are similar.
- The reduced painting is 5.1 cm tall and 6 cm wide.
- The actual painting is 32 cm tall.

Reduced

5.1

6

2 Make a Plan

Draw a diagram to represent the situation.
Use the corresponding sides to write a proportion.

Actual

32

w

3 Solve

$$\frac{5.1 \text{ cm}}{32 \text{ cm}} = \frac{6 \text{ cm}}{w \text{ cm}}$$ *Write a proportion.*

$32 \cdot 6 = 5.1 \cdot w$ *The cross products are equal.*

$192 = 5.1w$ *w is multiplied by 5.1.*

$$\frac{192}{5.1} = \frac{5.1}{5.1}$$ *Divide both sides by 5.1 to undo the multiplication.*

$38 \approx w$ *Round to the nearest centimeter.*

Remember!

The symbol ≈ means "is approximately equal to."

The width of the actual painting is about 38 cm.

4 Look Back

Estimate to check your answer. The ratio of the heights is about 5:30, or 1:6. The ratio of the widths is about 6:36, or 1:6. Since these ratios are equal, 38 cm is a reasonable answer.

Think and Discuss

1. Name two items in your classroom that appear to be similar figures.

2. Explain whether all squares are similar.

Exercises

Prev. of MA.7.A.1.3

GUIDED PRACTICE

See Example **1**

1. The two triangles are similar. Find the missing length x and the measure of $\angle G$.

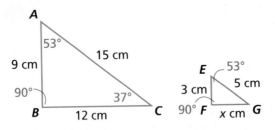

See Example **2**

2. Pat's school photo package includes one large photo and several smaller photos. The large photo is similar to the photo at right. If the height of the large photo is 10 in., what is its width?

INDEPENDENT PRACTICE

See Example **1**

3. The two triangles are similar. Find the missing length n and the measure of $\angle M$.

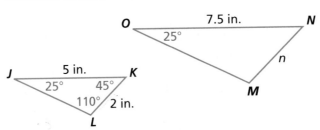

See Example **2**

4. LeJuan swims in a pool that is similar to an Olympic-sized pool. LeJuan's pool is 30 m long by 8 m wide. The length of an Olympic-sized pool is 50 m. To the nearest meter, what is the width of an Olympic-sized pool?

PRACTICE AND PROBLEM SOLVING

Name the corresponding sides and angles for each pair of similar figures.

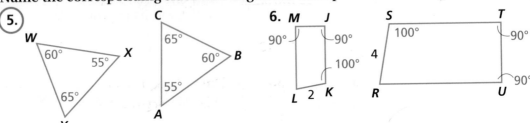

7. Critical Thinking The ratio of the lengths of two similar paintings is $\frac{100}{32}$. If the length of one painting is 100 cm, is the length of the other less than or greater than 100 cm? Explain.

○ = WORKED-OUT SOLUTIONS
on p. WS8

The figures in each pair are similar. Find the unknown measures.

8.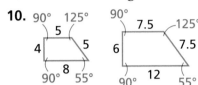

9.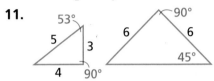

Tell whether the figures in each pair are similar. Explain your answers.

10.
90° 125°
5
4   5
8
90° 55°

90°
7.5 125°
6   7.5
12
90° 55°

11.
53°
5   3
4 90°

90°
6   6
45°

12. Graphic Art Lenny sketches designs for billboards. The sketch and the billboard are similar. If the height of the billboard is 30 ft, what is the width to the nearest foot of the billboard?

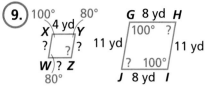

1.5 in.

2.5 in.

13. What's the Error? A student drew two rectangles with dimensions 10 in. by 9 in. and 5 in. by 3 in. The student said that the rectangles are similar. What's the error?

14. Write About It Are all triangles that have one 90° angle similar? Explain your answer.

15. Challenge Draw two similar rectangles whose sides are in a ratio of 5:2.

Florida Spiral Review   MA.6.A.3.5, MA.6.A.2.2

16. Multiple Choice The triangles are similar. Find the missing angle measure.

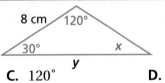

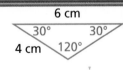

A. 30°   **B.** 60°   **C.** 120°   **D.** 180°

17. Multiple Choice Use the similar triangles in Exercise 16. Find the missing length y.

F. 4 cm   **G.** 12 cm   **H.** 18 cm   **I.** 24 cm

Identify the property that is illustrated by each equation. (Lesson 2-1)

18. $3 + (4 + 5) = (3 + 4) + 5$ **19.** $19(24) = 19(20) + 19(4)$ **20.** $(2)(13) = (13)(2)$

Find the value of n in each proportion. (Lesson 7-3)

21. $\frac{n}{7} = \frac{30}{42}$ **22.** $\frac{4}{n} = \frac{16}{8}$ **23.** $\frac{1}{9} = \frac{n}{6.3}$

Preview of MA.7.A.1.6
Apply proportionality to measurement in multiple contexts . . .

Vocabulary

indirect measurement

The Statue of Liberty has been standing in New York Harbor since 1876. How could you measure the height of the statue?

One way to find a height that you cannot measure directly is to use similar figures and proportions. This method is called **indirect measurement**.

Suppose that on a sunny day, the statue cast a shadow that was 610 feet long. A 6-foot-tall person standing by the statue cast a 12-foot-long shadow.

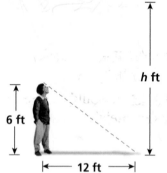

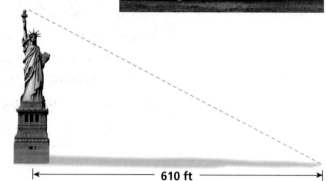

Both the person and the statue form 90° angles with the ground, and their shadows are cast at the same angle. This means we can form two similar triangles and use proportions to find the missing height.

EXAMPLE **1** **Using Indirect Measurement**

 Math
@ **thinkcentral.com**

Use the similar triangles above to find the height of the Statue of Liberty.

$$\frac{6}{h} = \frac{12}{610}$$ *Write a proportion using corresponding sides.*

$$12 \cdot h = 6 \cdot 610$$ *The cross products are equal.*

$$12h = 3{,}660$$ *h is multiplied by 12.*

$$\frac{12h}{12} = \frac{3{,}660}{12}$$ *Divide both sides by 12 to undo the multiplication.*

$$h = 305$$

The Statue of Liberty is about 305 feet tall.

EXAMPLE 2 **Measurement Application**

A lighthouse casts a shadow that is 36 m long when a meterstick casts a shadow that is 3 m long. How tall is the lighthouse?

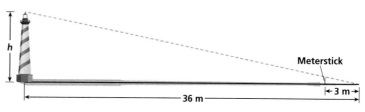

Measurement

The Cape Hatteras lighthouse, located on Hatteras Island, North Carolina, is the tallest lighthouse in America at 225 ft tall. You can climb the 268 steps to the top for a magnificent view of the Atlantic.

$$\frac{h}{1} = \frac{36}{3}$$ *Write a proportion using corresponding sides.*

$1 \cdot 36 = 3 \cdot h$ *The cross products are equal.*

$36 = 3h$ *h is multiplied by 3.*

$$\frac{36}{3} = \frac{3h}{3}$$ *Divide both sides by 3 to undo the multiplication.*

$12 = h$

The lighthouse is 12 m tall.

Think and Discuss

1. Name two items for which it would make sense to use indirect measurement to find their heights.

2. Name two items for which it would **not** make sense to use indirect measurement to find their heights.

7-9 Exercises

Prev. of MA.7.A.1.6

Homework Help **THINK**central

Go to **thinkcentral.com**
Exercises 1–4, 5, 7

GUIDED PRACTICE

See Example 1

1. Use the similar triangles to find the height of the flagpole.

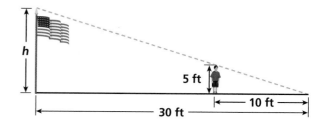

See Example 2

2. A tree casts a shadow that is 26 ft long. At the same time, a 3-foot-tall sunflower casts a shadow that is 4 ft long. How tall is the tree?

See Example **1**   **3.** Use the similar triangles to find the height of the lamppost.

See Example **2**   **4.** The Eiffel Tower casts a shadow that is 328 feet long. A 6-foot-tall person standing by the tower casts a 2-foot-long shadow. How tall is the Eiffel Tower?

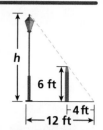

PRACTICE AND PROBLEM SOLVING

Find the unknown heights.

5.

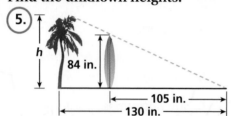

84 in.
105 in.
130 in.

6.

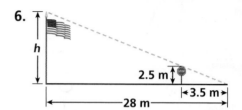

2.5 m
3.5 m
28 m

7. A statue casts a shadow that is 360 m long. At the same time, a person who is 2 m tall casts a shadow that is 6 m long. How tall is the statue?

 8. Write About It How are indirect measurements useful?

9. Challenge A 5.5-foot-tall girl stands so that her shadow lines up with the shadow of a telephone pole. The tip of her shadow is even with the tip of the pole's shadow. If the length of the pole's shadow is 40 feet and the girl is standing 27.5 feet away from the pole, how tall is the telephone pole?

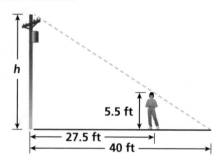

h
5.5 ft
27.5 ft
40 ft

Florida Spiral Review   MA.6.A.5.3, MA.6.A.5.2

10. Multiple Choice An 18-foot-tall telephone pole casts a shadow that is 28.8 feet long. At the same time, a woman casts a shadow that is 8.8 feet long. How tall is the woman?

A. 4.4 feet   **B.** 5.5 feet   **C.** 14.08 feet   **D.** 158.4 feet

11. Gridded Response A 4-foot-tall girl casts a shadow that is 7.2 feet long. A nearby tree casts a shadow that is 25.56 feet long. How tall, in feet, is the tree?

Estimate by rounding to the indicated place value. (Lesson 3-2)

12. $4.325 - 1.895$; tenths   **13.** $5.121 - 0.1568$; tenths   **14.** $7.592 + 9.675$; hundredths

Compare. Write <, >, or =. (Lesson 7-5)

15. $\frac{1}{3}$ ▢ 0.3 **16.** 56% ▢ $\frac{5}{6}$ **17.** $\frac{11}{20}$ ▢ 50% **18.** 0.6 ▢ $\frac{3}{5}$

○ = **WORKED-OUT SOLUTIONS**
on p. WS9

Preview of MA.7.A.1.6 Apply proportionality to measurement in multiple contexts, including scale drawings . . .

Vocabulary

scale drawing

scale

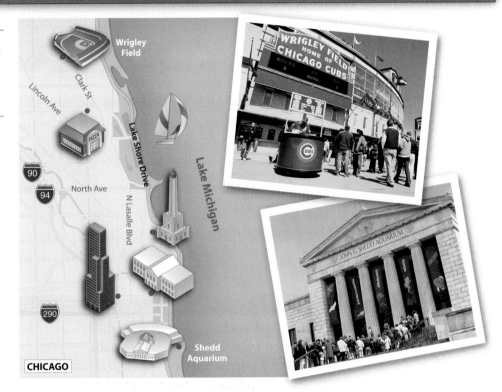

The map of Chicago shown above is a *scale drawing*. A **scale drawing** is a drawing of a real object that is proportionally smaller or larger than the real object. In other words, measurements on a scale drawing are in proportion to the measurements of the real object.

Animated Math
@ thinkcentral.com

A **scale** is a ratio between two sets of measurements. In the map above, the scale is 1 in:2 mi. This ratio means that 1 inch on the map represents 2 miles in Chicago.

EXAMPLE **1** **Finding Actual Distances**

On the map, the distance between Wrigley Field and the Shedd Aquarium is approximately 3.3 inches. What is the actual distance?

Helpful Hint

In Example 1, think "1 inch is 2 miles, so 3.3 inches is how many miles?" This approach will help you set up proportions in similar problems.

$$\frac{1 \text{ in.}}{2 \text{ mi}} = \frac{3.3 \text{ in.}}{x \text{ mi}}$$ *Write a proportion using the scale. Let x be the actual number of miles from Wrigley Field to the Shedd Aquarium.*

$$2 \cdot 3.3 = 1 \cdot x$$ *The cross products are equal.*

$$6.6 = x$$ *Identify Property of Multiplication*

The actual distance from Wrigley Field to the Shedd Aquarium is approximately 6.6 miles.

EXAMPLE 2 *Astronomy Application*

What is the actual distance from Mercury to Earth?

Mercury and Earth are about 3 inches apart on the drawing.

$$\frac{1 \text{ in.}}{30 \text{ million km}} = \frac{3 \text{ in.}}{x \text{ million km}}$$

Write a proportion. Let x be the actual distance from Mercury to Earth. The cross products are equal.

$$30 \cdot 3 = 1 \cdot x$$
$$90 = x$$

The actual distance from Mercury to Earth is about 90 million km.

Think and Discuss

1. Suppose that you are making a scale drawing of your classroom with a scale of 1 inch:3 feet. What will the length of one wall of the room be on your drawing?

7-10 Exercises

Prev. of MA.7.A.1.6

Homework Help THINK central
Go to thinkcentral.com
Exercises 1–6, 7, 11

GUIDED PRACTICE

See Example 1

1. On the map, the distance between the post office and the fountain is 6 cm. What is the actual distance?

Scale 1 cm:50 ft — Post Office

See Example 2 **Use a ruler for Exercises 2 and 3.**

2. What is the actual length of the car?

3. The actual height of the car is 1.6 meters. Is the car's height in the drawing correct?

Scale: 1 cm:0.8 m

See Example **1**   **4.** On the map of California, Los Angeles is 1.25 inches from Malibu. Find the actual distance from Los Angeles to Malibu.

Scale: 1 in:20 mi

See Example **2**   **5.** Riverside, California, is 50 miles from Los Angeles. On the map, how far should Riverside be from Los Angeles?

PRACTICE AND PROBLEM SOLVING

6. Suppose you are asked to make a scale drawing of a room. The room has four walls. The lengths of the walls are as follows: north wall, 8 ft; west wall, 12 ft; south wall, 20 ft; slanted east wall, 17 ft. The scale for the drawing is 1 in:4 ft.

   a. Use the actual lengths of the walls to find the lengths in the drawing.

   b. Sketch the room and label each wall. What shape does the room resemble?

   c. Mark a 2.5 ft wide window on the west wall, and a 3.5 ft wide door on the south wall. Give the width of each on the scale drawing.

7. **Hobbies** A popular scale used in model trains is called HO. The scale for HO is 1 ft:87 ft. If a model train is 3 feet long, how long is the actual train?

8. **Life Science** A paramecium is a one-celled organism. The scale drawing at right is larger than an actual paramecium. Use a ruler and find the actual length of the paramecium.

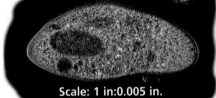
Scale: 1 in:0.005 in.

9. **Write About It** Explain how to find the actual distance between two cities if you know the distance on a map and the scale of the map.

10. **Multiple Choice** The distance between towns A and C on a map is 13 centimeters. What is the actual distance between towns B and C?

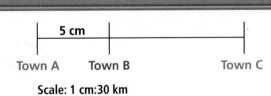
Town A   Town B   Town C
Scale: 1 cm:30 km

   A. 0.27 kilometers   **B.** 150 kilometers   **C.** 240 kilometers   **D.** 390 kilometers

11. **Gridded Response** Tanya has a 1 in:32 in. scale model car. The length of the model car is 2 inches. What is the actual length of the car?

Find the missing value in each proportion. (Lesson 7-3)

12. $\frac{9}{15} = \frac{x}{5}$ **13.** $\frac{b}{20} = \frac{3}{15}$ **14.** $\frac{1}{7} = \frac{6}{k}$ **15.** $\frac{8}{3} = \frac{a}{9}$ **16.** $\frac{p}{4} = \frac{11}{44}$

○ = **WORKED-OUT SOLUTIONS**
     on p. WS9

Quiz for Lessons 7-4 Through 7-10

✓ **7-4** **Percents**

Write each percent as a fraction in simplest form and a decimal.

1. 60% **2.** 15% **3.** 75% **4.** 34%

✓ **7-5** **Percents, Decimals, and Fractions**

Write each fraction or decimal as a percent.

5. $\frac{9}{20}$ **6.** $\frac{21}{50}$ **7.** 0.9 **8.** 0.02

✓ **7-6** **Percent Problems**

Find the percent of each number.

9. 40% of 80 **10.** 5% of 30 **11.** 30% of 98

12. 15% of 220 **13.** 5% of 72 **14.** 4% of 12,000

✓ **7-7** **Applying Percents**

15. Max and Dan order a pizza. The total bill is $11.60. If they give the delivery person a tip that is 20% of the bill, how much is the tip?

16. Mia wants to buy a poster that is 10% off the marked price. If the marked price is $15.99, about how much will the poster cost with the discount?

✓ **7-8** **Similar Figures**

17. The two triangles are similar. Find the missing length *n* and the measure of ∠*R*.

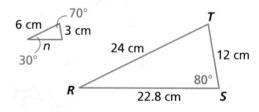

✓ **7-9** **Indirect Measurement**

18. A tree casts a shadow that is 18 feet long. At the same time, a 5-foot-tall person casts a shadow that is 3.6 feet long. How tall is the tree?

✓ **7-10** **Scale Drawings and Maps**

Use the scale drawing and a metric ruler to answer each question.

19. What is the actual length of the kitchen?

20. What are the actual length and width of bedroom 1?

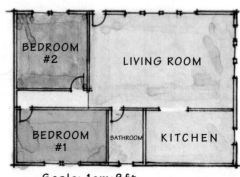

Scale: 1cm:8ft

Real-World CONNECTIONS

Sarasota

The Ringling Circus Museum The Ringling Circus Museum in Sarasota, Florida tells the story of the American circus. The museum features the Howard Brothers Circus Model, a miniature circus consisting of more than 35,000 objects.

The table gives data on the Howard Brothers Circus Model. Use the table for Exercises 1–3.

1. What is the ratio of wagons to circus tents?

2. The model includes miniature townspeople. The ratio of townspeople to performers is 25:13. How many townspeople are there?

3. A menagerie is a part of a circus where visitors can view exotic animals. In the Howard Brothers Circus Model, there are 211 animals in the menagerie. Estimate the percent of the model's animals that are in the menagerie. Explain how you made the estimate.

The Howard Brothers Circus Model	
Object	Number in Circus Model
Circus Tents	8
Wagons	152
Performers	1,300
Animals	800
Folding Chairs	7,000

4. The complete model is made up of about 35,000 pieces. What percent of the model is made up of folding chairs? Write this percent as a decimal and as a fraction in simplest form.

5. The height of a radio tower in the model is about 6% of the tower's actual height. The actual radio tower is 48 ft tall. How tall is the tower in the model? Round to the nearest foot.

Real-World Connections

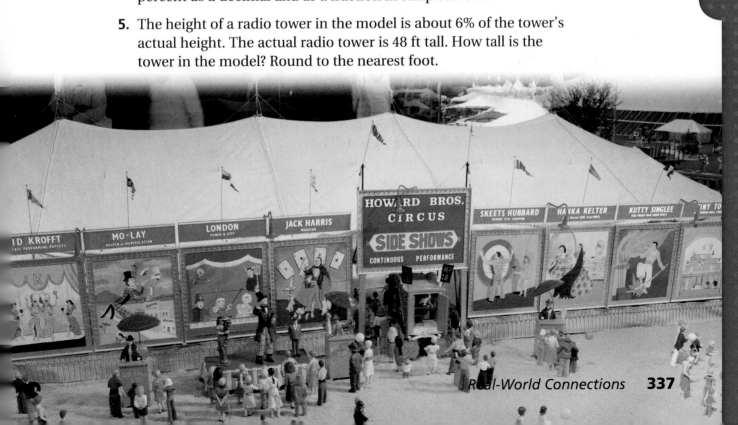

The Golden Rectangle

Which rectangle do you find most visually pleasing?

Did you choose rectangle 3? If so, you agree with artists and architects throughout history. Rectangle 3 is a golden rectangle. Golden rectangles are said to be the most pleasing to the human eye.

In a golden rectangle, the ratio of the length of the longer side to the length of the shorter side is approximately equal to 1.6. In other words,

$$\frac{\text{length of longer side}}{\text{length of shorter side}} \approx \frac{1.6}{1}$$

Measure the length and width of each rectangle below. Which could be golden rectangles? Are they the most pleasing to your eye?

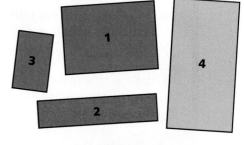

Triple Play

Number of players: 3–5

Deal five cards to each player. Place the remaining cards in a pile facedown. At any time, you may remove *triples* from your hand. A *triple* is a fraction card, a decimal card, and a percent card that are all equivalent.

On your turn, ask any other player for a specific card. For example, if you have the $\frac{3}{5}$ card, you might ask another player if he or she has the 60% card. If so, he or she must give it to you, and you repeat your turn. If not, take the top card from the deck, and your turn is over.

The first player to get rid of his or her cards is the winner.

Games

THiNK central

Go to <u>thinkcentral.com</u>

A complete copy of the rules and game pieces are available online.

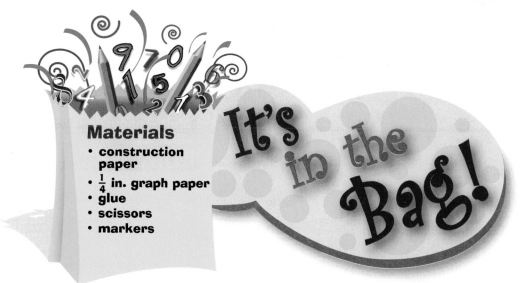

Materials
- construction paper
- $\frac{1}{4}$ in. graph paper
- glue
- scissors
- markers

PROJECT **Double-Door Fractions, Decimals, and Percents**

Open the door to fractions, decimals, and percents by making this handy converter.

Directions

1 Cut the construction paper to $6\frac{1}{2}$ inches by $8\frac{1}{2}$ inches. Fold it in half lengthwise and then unfold it. Fold the top and bottom edges to the middle crease to make a double door. **Figure A**

2 Cut a strip of graph paper that is 2 inches wide by $8\frac{1}{2}$ inches long. Make a percent number line along the middle of the strip. Include 0%, 5%, 10%, and so on, up to 100%. **Figure B**

3 Cut two 1-by-$8\frac{1}{2}$-inch strips of graph paper. On one strip, make a fraction number line that includes $\frac{0}{20}$, $\frac{1}{20}$, and so on, up to $\frac{20}{20}$. Write the fractions in simplest form. On the other strip, make a decimal number line that includes 0.0, 0.05, 0.1, and so on, up to 1. **Figure C**

4 Glue the percent number line along the center fold of the construction paper. **Figure D**

5 Close the double doors. Glue the remaining number lines to the outside of the doors, making sure the number lines match up.

Putting the Math into Action

Team up with a classmate. Use your double-door converters to quiz each other on equivalent fractions, decimals, and percents.

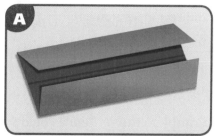

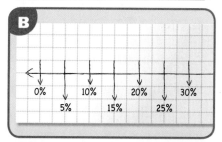

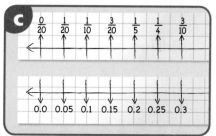

Study Guide: Review

Multi–Language Glossary
Go to thinkcentral.com

Vocabulary

Complete the sentences below with vocabulary words from the list above.

1. A(n) ____?____ is an amount subtracted from the regular price of an item.

2. A ____?____ is a ratio of a number to 100.

3. In similar figures, ____?____ have the same measure.

EXAMPLES

EXERCISES

7-1 Ratios and Rates (pp. 296–299)

 MA.6.A.2.2

■ Write the ratio of hearts to diamonds.

♥ ♥ ♥ ♥

♦ ♦ ♦ ♦ ♦ ♦ ♦ ♦ $\frac{\text{hearts}}{\text{diamonds}} = \frac{4}{8}$

4. Write three equivalent ratios for 4:8.

5. Which is the better deal—an 8 oz package of pretzels for $1.92 or a 12 oz package of pretzels for $2.64?

7-2 Ratio and Rate Problems (pp. 300–303)

 MA.6.A.2.1, MA.6.A.2.2

■ Use a table to find three ratios equivalent to 6:7.

6	12	18	24
7	14	21	28

Multiply the numerator and denominator by 2, 3, and 4.

The ratios 6:7, 12:14, 18:21, and 24:28 are equivalent.

Use a table to find three equivalent ratios.

6. $\frac{3}{10}$ 7. 5 to 21   8. 15:7

9. The table below shows the cost of canoeing for different-sized groups. Predict how much a group of 9 will pay.

Number in Group	2	4	8	10
Cost ($)	10.50	21	42	52.50

7-3 Proportions (pp. 304–307)

MA.6.A.2.2, MA.6.A.3.2

■ Find the value of n in $\frac{5}{6} = \frac{n}{12}$.

$6 \cdot n = 5 \cdot 12$ *Cross products are equal.*

$\frac{6n}{6} = \frac{60}{6}$ *Divide both sides by 6.*

$n = 10$

Find the value of n in each proportion.

10. $\frac{3}{5} = \frac{n}{15}$ **11.** $\frac{1}{n} = \frac{3}{9}$

12. $\frac{7}{8} = \frac{n}{16}$ **13.** $\frac{n}{4} = \frac{8}{16}$

14. A fruit salad recipe calls for 2 cups of bananas for every 3 cups of apples. If Shannon is using 9 cups of apples to make fruit salad for a party, how many cups of bananas does she need?

7-4 Percents (pp. 310–313)

MA.6.A.5.1

■ Write 48% as a fraction in simplest form.

$48\% = \frac{48}{100}$ $\frac{48 \div 4}{100 \div 4} = \frac{12}{25}$

■ Write 16% as a decimal.

$16\% = \frac{16}{100}$ $16 \div 100 = 0.16$

Write each as a fraction in simplest form.

15. 75%   **16.** 6%   **17.** 30%

Write each percent as a decimal.

18. 8%   **19.** 65%   **20.** 20%

7-5 Percents, Decimals, and Fractions (pp. 314–317)

MA.6.A.5.1, MA.6.A.5.2

■ Write 0.365 as a percent.

$0.365 = 36.5\%$ *Multiply by 100.*

■ Write $\frac{3}{5}$ as a percent.

$\frac{3 \cdot 20}{5 \cdot 20} = \frac{60}{100} = 60\%$

Write each decimal or fraction as a percent.

21. 0.896   **22.** 0.70   **23.** 0.057

24. 0.12   **25.** $\frac{7}{10}$ **26.** $\frac{3}{12}$

27. $\frac{7}{8}$ **28.** $\frac{4}{5}$ **29.** $\frac{1}{16}$

30. Water constitutes approximately $\frac{13}{20}$ of the body of an average adult male. About what percent of the average adult male body is made of water?

7-6 Percent Problems (pp. 318–321)

MA.6.A.5.1, MA.6.A.5.3

■ Find 30% of 85.

$30\% = 0.30$ *Write 30% as a decimal.*

$0.30 \cdot 85 = 25.5$ *Multiply.*

31. Find 25% of 48.

32. Find 33% of 18.

33. A total of 325 tickets were sold for the school concert, and 36% of these were sold to students. How many tickets were sold to students?

34. When paying for his lunch, Archie decides to leave a 15% tip. How much should he leave if his lunch totaled $11.90?

Study Guide: Review

7-7 Applying Percents (pp. 322–325)

MA.6.A.5.1, MA.6.A.5.3

■ A DVD costs $24.98. The sales tax is 5%. About how much is the tax?

Step 1: Round $24.98 to $25.

Step 2: $5\% = 5 \cdot 1\%$

1% of $25 = 0.01 \cdot \$25 = \$0.25$

Step 3: $5\% = 5 \cdot 1\%$

$= 5 \cdot \$0.25 = \$1.25$

The tax is about $1.25.

35. A sweater is marked 40% off the original price. The original price was $31.75. About how much is the sweater after the discount?

36. Barry and his friends went out for lunch. The bill was $28.68. About how much should they leave for a 15% tip?

37. Ana is purchasing a book for $17.89. The sales tax rate is 6%. About how much will she pay in sales tax?

7-8 Similar Figures (pp. 326–329)

Prev. MA.7.A.1.3

■ The triangles are similar. Find *b*.

 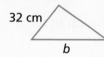

1 cm / 2 cm

32 cm / b

$\frac{1}{32} = \frac{2}{b}$ *Write a proportion.*

$32 \cdot 2 = 1 \cdot b$ *Cross products are equal.*

$64 \text{ cm} = b$

38. The shapes are similar. Find *n* and the measure of $\angle A$.

6 in.

22 in.

A

3 in.

n

7-9 Indirect Measurement (pp. 330–332)

Prev. MA.7.A.1.6

■ A tree casts a 12 ft shadow when a 6 ft man casts a 4 ft shadow. How tall is the tree?

$\frac{h}{6} = \frac{12}{4}$ *Write a proportion.*

$6 \cdot 12 = 4 \cdot h$ *The cross products are equal.*

$\frac{72}{4} = \frac{4h}{4}$ *Divide both sides by 4.*

$18 = h$ The tree is 18 ft tall.

39. Find the height of the building.

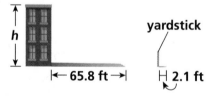

h

yardstick

← 65.8 ft →

2.1 ft

7-10 Scale Drawings and Maps (pp. 333–335)

Prev. MA.7.A.1.6

■ Find the actual distance from *A* to *B*.

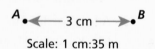

A ← 3 cm → B

Scale: 1 cm:35 m

$\frac{1 \text{ cm}}{35 \text{ m}} = \frac{3 \text{ cm}}{x \text{ m}}$ *Write a proportion.*

$35 \cdot 3 = 1 \cdot x$ *Cross products are equal.*

$105 = x$

The actual distance is 105 m.

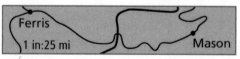

Ferris

1 in:25 mi

Mason

40. Find the actual distance from Ferris to Mason.

41. Renfield is 75 mi from Mason. About how far apart should Renfield and Mason be on the map?

Chapter Test

Use the table to write each ratio.

1. three equivalent ratios to compare dramas to documentaries

2. documentaries to total videos

3. Which is a better deal—5 videos for $29.50 or 3 videos for $17.25?

Types of Videos in Richard's Collection			
Comedy	5	Cartoon	7
Drama	6	Exercise	3
Music	3	Documentary	2

4. Jenny can swim 8 laps in 6 minutes. Myka can swim 12 laps in 8 minutes. Cheryl can swim 16 laps in 12 minutes. Who swims laps at the same rate as Jenny?

Find the value of n in each proportion.

5. $\frac{5}{6} = \frac{n}{24}$

6. $\frac{8}{n} = \frac{12}{3}$

7. $\frac{n}{10} = \frac{3}{6}$

8. $\frac{3}{9} = \frac{4}{n}$

9. A cocoa recipe calls for 4 tbsp cocoa mix to make an 8 oz serving. How many tbsp of cocoa mix are needed to make a 15 oz serving?

Write each percent as a fraction in simplest form and as a decimal.

10. 66%

11. 90%

12. 5%

13. 18%

Write each decimal or fraction as a percent.

14. 0.546

15. 0.092

16. $\frac{14}{25}$

17. $\frac{1}{8}$

Find each percent.

18. 55% of 218

19. 30% of 310

20. 25% of 78

21. A bookstore sells paperback books at 20% off the listed price. If Brandy wants to buy a paperback book whose listed price is $12.95, about how much will she pay for the book after the discount?

22. Two picture frames are similar. The width of the first frame is 3 in., and its length is 5 in. The width of the second frame is 5 in. What is the length of the second frame?

23. A 3-foot-tall mailbox casts a shadow that is 1.8 feet long. At the same time, a nearby street lamp casts a shadow that is 12 feet long. How tall is the street lamp?

Use the scale drawing for Problems 24 and 25.

24. The length of the court in the drawing is 6 cm. How long is the actual court?

25. The free-throw line is always 15 feet from the backboard. Is the distance between the backboard and the free-throw line correct in the drawing? Explain.

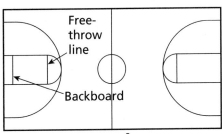

Scale: 1 cm : $15\frac{2}{3}$ ft

Test Tackler

Standardized Test Strategies

Extended Response: Write Extended Responses

When you answer an extended-response test item, you need to explain your reasoning clearly. Extended-response items are scored using a 4-point scoring rubric like the one shown below.

EXAMPLE

Extended Response Amber tracks her math test scores. Her goal is to have a 92% average. Her 10 test scores are 94, 76, 90, 98, 91, 93, 88, 90, 89, and 85. Find the range, mean, median, and mode of the data set. If her lowest score is dropped, will she meet her goal? Explain your answer.

Here is an example of a 4-point response according to the scoring rubric at right.

Scoring Rubric

4 Points = The student demonstrates a thorough understanding of mathematics concepts, responds correctly to the task, and provides clear and complete explanations.

3 Points = The student demonstrates an understanding of mathematics concepts, and the response is essentially correct, but the work shows minor flaws.

2 Points = The student demonstrates only a partial understanding of the concepts and/or procedures embodied in the task. The approach or solution may be correct.

1 Point = The student demonstrates a very limited understanding of the concepts and/or procedures embodied in the task. The response exhibits many flaws or is incomplete.

0 Points = The student provides no response at all or a completely incorrect or uninterpretable response.

4-point response:

Range: $98 - 76 = 22$
The range is 22.
Mean:
$$\frac{94 + 76 + 90 + 98 + 91 + 93 + 88 + 90 + 89 + 85}{10} = \frac{894}{10} = 89.4$$

The mean is 89.4.

Median: There are an even number of values in this set. The two middle numbers are 90 and 90. The median is 90.

Mode: The value that occurs most often is 90. The mode is 90.

When the lowest score, 76, is dropped, the average is
$$\frac{894 - 76}{9} = \frac{818}{9} = 90.9.$$ This value is less than 92. Even if the lowest score is dropped, Amber will not meet her goal.

The student correctly calculates and shows how to find the range, mean, median, and mode of this data set.

The student correctly answers the questions and shows how the answer is calculated.

Once you have answered an extended-response test item, double-check to make sure that you answered all of the different parts.

Read each test item and use the scoring rubric to answer the questions that follow.

Item A
Extended Response Write an expression for the missing value in the table. Justify your expression. Use your expression to find the value of the term when the position number is 100.

Position	Value of Term
1	4
2	7
3	10
4	13
5	16
n	

1. What needs to be included in a response that would receive 4 points?

2. Write a response that would receive full credit.

Item B
Extended Response An online games website offers a 3-game package for $19.50. Another online games site offers a 5-game package for $33.75. Which package is the better deal? Justify your answer.

Kim wrote this response:

$$\frac{\$19.50}{3 \text{ games}} = \frac{\$6.50}{1 \text{ game}} \qquad \frac{\$33.75}{5 \text{ games}} = \frac{\$6.75}{1 \text{ game}}$$
The 3-game package is a better deal.

3. Score Kim's response. Explain your scoring decision.

4. Rewrite Kim's response so that it receives full credit.

Item C
Extended Response Look at the graph. Why is this graph misleading? Explain your answer. What might someone believe from this graph? What changes would you make to the graph so it is not misleading?

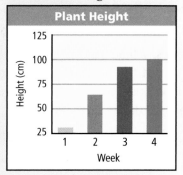

5. What needs to be included in a response that would receive 4 points?

6. Write a response that would receive full credit.

Item D
Extended Response The ages of the employees at a discount store are shown below. Find the mean, median, and mode of the data set. Which one bests describes the data set? Explain your answer.

68	32	16	23	21
17	28	20	39	38
21	22	17	23	37

7. Should the response shown receive a score of 4 points? Why or why not?

The mean is 28.
The modes are 17 and 23.
The median is 22.
The best descriptor is the mode because there is more than one.

8. Correct or add any information, if necessary, for the response to receive full credit.

Mastering the Standards

Cumulative Assessment, Chapters 1–7

Multiple Choice

1. Janet has a flower garden with 6 rose bushes, 7 lilac bushes, and 5 azaleas. Which of the following shows the ratio of lilac bushes to the total number of plants in Janet's garden?

   A. 7:11

   B. 7:18

   C. 11:18

   D. 18:5

2. Which decimal is closest to 7%?

   F. 0.005

   G. 0.007

   H. 0.05

   I. 7

3. Carina rode her exercise bike 30 minutes on Monday, 45 minutes on Tuesday, 30 minutes on Wednesday, 60 minutes on Thursday, and 50 minutes on Friday. What is the mean amount of time that Carina rode her bike in these 5 days?

   A. 30 minutes

   B. 43 minutes

   C. 45 minutes

   D. 215 minutes

4. Flora wrote the ratio $\frac{n}{6}$ to compare the number of black tiles to white tiles in the pattern below. What is the value of n?

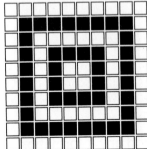

   F. 1

   G. 2

   H. 3

   I. 4

5. The numerator of the fraction $\frac{n}{6}$ is a whole number. The fraction has a value greater than 30% but less than 50%. What is the value of n?

   A. 1

   B. 2

   C. 3

   D. 5

6. The ratio of cats to dogs at a pet care center is $\frac{2}{3}$. The total number of cats and dogs at the center is 50. How many cats are at the center?

   F. 2

   G. 15

   H. 20

   I. 30

7. Esperanza has a puppy that weighs $3\frac{1}{4}$ pounds. In 3 months, the puppy should weigh 3 times as much as it weighs now. How much weight should the puppy gain in the next 3 months?

   A. $6\frac{1}{2}$ pounds

   B. $6\frac{3}{4}$ pounds

   C. $8\frac{1}{4}$ pounds

   D. $9\frac{3}{4}$ pounds

8. The Cook family's bill for dinner is $46.37. They want to leave a 15% tip. Which is the best estimate for the Cooks' total bill plus tip?

   F. $6.75

   G. $6.90

   H. $52.90

   I. $60.00

9. Deion bought 24 ounces of trail mix for $6.24. What is the unit price for the trail mix?

   A. $0.26 per ounce

   B. $3.85 per ounce

   C. $4.16 per ounce

   D. $6.24 per ounce

10. Sabrina is training as a long-distance runner. Her coach recorded how far she had run at various times.

Time (min)	5	25	40	45
Distance (km)	1.2	6	9.6	10.8

At what rate is Sabrina running?

F. 0.24 kilometer per minute

G. 1.2 kilometers per minute

H. 4.17 kilometers per minute

I. 4.8 kilometers per minute

Estimate your answer before solving the problem. You can often use your estimate to eliminate some of the answer choices.

Gridded Response

11. The ratio of red roses to white roses in a bouquet is $\frac{5}{2}$. There are 6 white roses. How many total roses are in the bouquet?

12. Jerry has 25 video games. Of those, 4 games are driving or racing games. What percent of Jerry's games are driving or racing games?

13. Rylee has a collection of music boxes. Of the 36 music boxes she owns, 25% of them have parts that move when the music plays. How many of her music boxes have moving parts?

14. Nadia makes $29 per day working part time at a coffee shop. She recently received a 3% raise. How much in dollars will she make per day with her raise?

15. Ms. Chavez is ordering art supplies. She orders enough pencils for every student to have one and then adds 20% more for extras. If she has 210 students, how many pencils does she order?

Short Response

S1. A jar contains blue marbles, red marbles, and white marbles. Of those marbles, $\frac{1}{4}$ are blue marbles and $\frac{1}{5}$ are red marbles. The remainder of the marbles are white marbles.

   a. What percent of the marbles are blue? What percent are red? What percent are white?

   b. There are 560 marbles in the jar. How many of each color are there?

S2. Chrissy is shopping for T-shirts for the pep club. Package A is 10 shirts for $15.50. Package B is 15 shirts for $20.50. Package C is 20 shirts for $25.50. Find the unit price for each package. Which T-shirt package is the best deal? Explain your reasoning and show your work.

S3. A computer is marked 30% off the original price. The computer originally cost $685. Find the amount of the discount and the sale price of the computer.

Extended Response

E1. The regular price of a pair of jeans is $32. One weekend the store has a sale, and everything in the store is priced at a 25% discount.

   a. How much money can you save by buying the jeans on sale?

   b. What is the sale price of the jeans? Show your work.

   c. At the end of the sale, the store manager asks an employee to put the jeans back to the original price. To do this, the employee adds 25% to the sale price. Explain whether you agree with the employee's method.

Measurement and Geometry

Additional instruction, practice, and activities are available online, including:
- Lesson Tutorial Videos
- Homework Help
- Animated Math

Go to **thinkcentral.com**

Why Learn This?

Measurements can help us describe objects. For example, the Bok Singing Tower is 205-feet tall and is surrounded by a 15-foot moat that serves as a Koi pond.

Bok Singing Tower
Lake Wales

Chapter Focus
- Use ratios to solve problems involving customary and metric units.
- Use formulas to solve problems involving perimeter and circumference.

Are You Ready?

Are You Ready? THINK central

Go to thinkcentral.com

✓ Vocabulary

Choose the best term from the list to complete each sentence.

capacity
length
proportion
ratio
rectangle
temperature
weight

1. If you find how heavy an object is, you are finding the __?__.

2. A __?__ is a comparison of two quantities using division.

3. If you find the amount a container can hold when filled, you are finding the __?__ of the container.

4. A __?__ is an equation that shows two equivalent ratios.

5. A parallelogram with four right angles is a __?__.

Complete these exercises to review skills you will need for this chapter.

✓ Write and Read Decimals

Write each decimal in standard form.

6. 12 and 4 tenths   7. 150 and 18 hundredths   8. 1 thousand, 60 and 5 tenths

✓ Simplify Fractions

Write each fraction in simplest form.

9. $\frac{8}{12}$ 10. $\frac{4}{20}$ 11. $\frac{6}{8}$ 12. $\frac{8}{16}$

✓ Write Ratios

Write each ratio three different ways.

13. Hearts to rectangles

14. Rectangles to circles

15. Triangles to squares

16. Hexagons to triangles

✓ Solve Proportions

Solve for n.

17. $\frac{2}{n} = \frac{4}{10}$ 18. $\frac{3}{8} = \frac{6}{n}$ 19. $\frac{n}{7} = \frac{8}{14}$ 20. $\frac{5}{9} = \frac{n}{18}$

Study Guide: Preview

Before

Previously, you

- performed simple conversions within the metric system.

- classified polygons according to their sides.

Now

You will study

- converting measures within the same measurement system.

- solving problems involving perimeter.

- describing the relationship between the radius, diameter, and circumference of a circle.

Why?

You can use the skills learned in this chapter

- to understand the relationship between the perimeter and the area of a polygon.

- to determine how much fencing to buy to enclose an animal pen or garden.

Key Vocabulary/Vocabulario

center of a circle	centro de un círculo
circle	círculo
circumference	circunferencia
customary system	sistema usual de medidas
diameter	diámetro
metric system	sistema métrico
perimeter	perímetro
pi	*pi*
radius	radio

Vocabulary Connections

To become familiar with some of the vocabulary terms in the chapter, consider the following. You may refer to the chapter, the glossary, or a dictionary if you like.

1. The word *perimeter* has the prefix *peri-*, which means "all around or surrounding," and the root *meter,* which is the basic unit of length in the metric system. What do you think the **perimeter** of a figure is?

2. The word *circumference* has the prefix *circum-*, which means "around." What do you think you will measure if you find the **circumference** of a circle?

3. The word *radius* is related to the word *radiate,* which means to move outward in all directions from the center. What do you think the **radius** of a circle is?

4. The word *diameter* has the prefix *dia-*, which means "across." What do you think you will measure if you find the **diameter** of a circle?

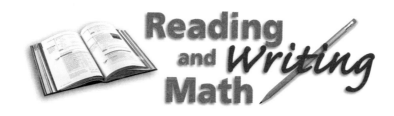

Study Strategy: Use Multiple Representations

Math concepts can be explained using multiple representations. As you study, pay attention to any tables, lists, graphs, diagrams, symbols, and words used to describe a concept.

From Lesson 5-5

In this example, the procedure for multiplying fractions by whole numbers is explained using words, diagrams, and examples.

Example

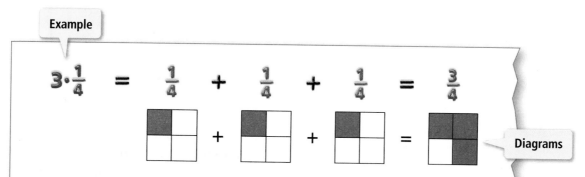

Diagrams

There is another way to multiply with fractions. Remember that a whole number can be written as an improper fraction with 1 in the denominator. So $3 = \frac{3}{1}$.

$$\frac{3}{1} \cdot \frac{1}{4} = \frac{3 \cdot 1}{1 \cdot 4} = \frac{3}{4} \quad \longleftarrow \text{Multiply numerators.}$$
$$\longleftarrow \text{Multiply denominators.}$$

Words

Try This

1. Show how to divide 2 by $\frac{1}{3}$ using a diagram. What is the quotient?

2. Review your notes from the previous chapter. Which representations did you use to explain proportions? Which representation do you prefer? Why?

Reading and Writing Math

Prep for MA.6.A.2.2
Interpret and compare ratios and rates.
Review of MA.5.G.5.3

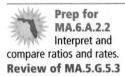

If you do not have an instrument, such as a ruler, scale, or measuring cup, you can estimate the length, weight, and capacity of an object by using a benchmark.

The **customary system** is the measurement system often used in the United States. It includes units of measurement for length, weight, and capacity.

Vocabulary

customary system

Customary Units of Length		
Unit	**Abbreviation**	**Benchmark**
Inch	in.	Width of your thumb
Foot	ft	Distance from your elbow to your wrist
Yard	yd	Width of a classroom door
Mile	mi	Four times around a track

EXAMPLE 1 Choosing Appropriate Units of Length

What unit of measure provides the best estimate? Explain.

A A table is about 4 ___?___ long.
A table is about 4 ft long.

Think: The length of a table is about 4 times the distance from your elbow to your wrist.

B A ceiling is about 3 ___?___ high.
A ceiling is about 3 yd high.

Think: The height of a ceiling is about 3 times the width of a classroom door.

Customary Units of Weight		
Unit	**Abbreviation**	**Benchmark**
Ounce	oz	A slice of bread
Pound	lb	A loaf of bread
Ton	T	A small car

EXAMPLE 2 Choosing Appropriate Units of Weight

What unit of measure provides the best estimate? Explain.

A A female elephant can weigh up to 4 ___?___.

Think: An elephant has a weight of about 4 small cars.

A female elephant can weigh up to 4 T.

What unit of measure provides the best estimate? Explain.

B **A remote control weighs about 5 ___?___.**

Think: A remote control has a weight of about 5 slices of bread.

A remote control weighs about 5 oz.

Capacity deals with volume, or the amount a container can hold.

Customary Units of Capacity		
Unit	**Abbreviation**	**Benchmark**
Fluid Ounce	fl oz	A spoonful
Cup	c	A glass of juice
Pint	pt	A small bottle of salad dressing
Quart	qt	A small container of paint
Gallon	gal	A large container of milk

EXAMPLE 3 **Choosing Appropriate Units of Capacity**

What unit of measure provides the best estimate? Explain.

A bathtub holds about 50 ___?___ of water.

Think: A bathtub holds about 50 large containers of milk.

A bathtub holds about 50 gal of water.

Inch rulers are usually separated into sixteenths of an inch.

EXAMPLE 4 **Finding Measurements**

Helpful Hint

All measurements are approximate. Their precision depends on the tools being used and on how the tools are used.

Use a ruler to measure the length of the golf tee to the nearest half, fourth, or eighth inch.

The golf tee is between $3\frac{1}{4}$ in. and $3\frac{3}{8}$ in. It is closer to $3\frac{1}{4}$ in.

The length of the golf tee is about $3\frac{1}{4}$ in.

Think and Discuss

1. **Give an example** of when you might need to estimate the weight of an object.

2. **Give an example** of when you might need to estimate the capacity of a container.

Homework Help

Go to thinkcentral.com
Exercises 1–8, 9, 11, 13, 21

 Prep MA.6.A.2.2

GUIDED PRACTICE

See Example 1   **What unit of measure provides the best estimate? Explain.**

1. A pencil is about 7 ___?___ long.

See Example 2   **2.** A tube of toothpaste weighs about 8 ___?___.

See Example 3   **3.** A swimming pool holds about 20,000 ___?___ of water.

See Example 4   **4.** Use a ruler to measure the length of the key to the nearest half, fourth, or eighth inch.

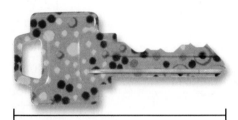

INDEPENDENT PRACTICE

See Example 1   **What unit of measure provides the best estimate? Explain.**

5. The distance from New York City to Boston is about 200 ___?___.

See Example 2   **6.** A small dog weighs about 12 ___?___.

See Example 3   **7.** A pot for cooking soup holds about 10 ___?___ of water.

See Example 4   **8.** Use a ruler to measure the length of the green bean to the nearest half, fourth, or eighth inch.

PRACTICE AND PROBLEM SOLVING

Which unit of measure would you use for each? Justify your answer.

9. the height of a flagpole   **10.** the width of a CD case

11. the capacity of a car's gas tank   **12.** the capacity of a baby's bottle

13. the weight of an egg   **14.** the weight of a chair

Use benchmarks to estimate each measure.

15. the width of your math textbook   **16.** the width of an armchair

17. the capacity of a flower pot   **18.** the weight of an alarm clock

19. Critical Thinking When would you choose to measure to the nearest eighth inch rather than the nearest fourth inch?

○ = WORKED-OUT SOLUTIONS
on p. WS9

Find the weight of each object to the nearest half, fourth, or eighth of a pound.

20.

21.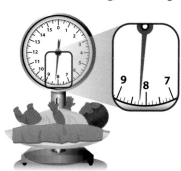

22. **History** The early Saxon kings of England wore a sash around their waist that they used as a benchmark for measuring length. The name of the sash eventually became the name of one of the customary units of length. What unit of length did the sash represent: the inch, foot, yard, or mile? Explain.

Find how much liquid is in each container to the nearest half, fourth, or eighth of a cup or quart.

23.

24.

 25. **Write a Problem** Write a problem that can be answered using a pen as a benchmark.

 26. **Write About It** Make up your own personal benchmarks for an inch, a cup, and a pound.

27. **Challenge** Look up the words *rod, peck,* and *dram* in a dictionary. Tell what each one is and what it is used to measure.

Florida Spiral Review

MA.6.A.1.2, MA.6.S.6.1

28. **Multiple Choice** Which is the best estimate for the width of a classroom?

    A. 30 inches   **B.** 30 feet   **C.** 30 yards   **D.** 30 miles

29. **Multiple Choice** Madison needs to buy a turkey to feed 12 people. What weight turkey should she buy?

    F. 16 pounds   **G.** 16 ounces   **H.** 16 cups   **I.** 16 tons

Multiply. Write each answer in simplest form. (Lessons 5-5, 5-6)

30. $\frac{7}{8} \cdot \frac{4}{5}$ **31.** $21 \cdot \frac{3}{7}$ **32.** $\frac{3}{16} \cdot \frac{4}{9}$ **33.** $6 \cdot \frac{1}{8}$

Find the mean, median, and mode of each data set. (Lesson 6-1)

34. 72, 67, 80, 73, 75, 53   **35.** 14, 5, 16, 21, 5, 30, 7

Understanding Metric Units of Measure

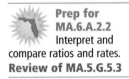
Prep for MA.6.A.2.2 Interpret and compare ratios and rates.
Review of MA.5.G.5.3

The **metric system** of measurement is used almost everywhere in the world. Its advantage over the customary system is that all metric units are related by the decimal system.

The shortest Olympic track race is 100 meters. Use the length of your classroom as a benchmark. A classroom is about 10 meters long, so a 100-meter race is about the length of 10 classrooms.

Vocabulary

metric system

Animated Math
@ thinkcentral.com

Metric Units of Length			
Unit	**Abbreviation**	**Relation to a Meter**	**Benchmark**
Millimeter	mm	0.001 m	Thickness of a dime
Centimeter	cm	0.01 m	Width of a fingernail
Decimeter	dm	0.1 m	Width of a CD case
Meter	m	1 m	Width of a single bed
Kilometer	km	1,000 m	Distance around a city block

EXAMPLE 1   **Choosing Appropriate Units of Length**

What unit of measure provides the best estimate? Explain.

A **A TV remote control is about 19 ___?___ long.**   *Think: A TV remote control is about 19 times the width of a fingernail.*

A TV remote control is about 19 cm long.

B **A school auditorium is about 40 ___?___ long.**   *Think: An auditorium is about 40 times the width of a single bed.*

A school auditorium is about 40 m long.

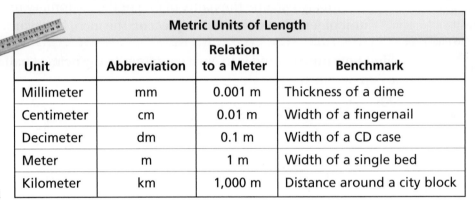

Metric Units of Mass			
Unit	**Abbreviation**	**Relation to a Gram**	**Benchmark**
Milligram	mg	0.001 g	Very small insect
Gram	g	1 g	Paper clip
Kilogram	kg	1,000 g	Textbook

EXAMPLE **2** **Choosing Appropriate Units of Mass**

What unit of measure provides the best estimate? Explain.

A sandwich has a mass of
about 400 ___?___.

Think: A sandwich has a mass of about 400 paper clips.

A sandwich has a mass of about 400 g.

Metric Units of Capacity			
Unit	Abbreviation	Relation to a Liter	Benchmark
Milliliter	mL	0.001 L	Drop of water
Liter	L	1 L	Water pitcher

EXAMPLE **3** **Choosing Appropriate Units of Capacity**

What unit of measure provides the best estimate? Explain.

A bucket has a capacity of
about 10 ___?___.

Think: A bucket has a capacity of about 10 water pitchers.

A bucket has a capacity of about 10 L.

EXAMPLE **4** **Finding Measurements**

Use a ruler to measure the length of the barrette to the nearest centimeter.

The barrette is between 6 and 7 cm. It is closer to 7 cm than 6 cm.

The length of the barrette is about 7 cm.

Think and Discuss

1. Explain how you would estimate the length of the board in your classroom using the barrette in Example 4 as a benchmark.

Homework Help **THINK** central

Go to **thinkcentral.com**
Exercises 1–10, 11, 13, 15, 17

GUIDED PRACTICE

See Example **1** **What unit of measure provides the best estimate? Explain.**

    1. The height of a doorknob from the floor is about 1 ___?___.

See Example **2** **2.** A greeting card has a mass of about 28 ___?___.

See Example **3** **3.** A kitchen sink holds about 20 ___?___ of water.

    4. A bowl holds about 350 ___?___ of soup.

See Example **4** **5.** Use a ruler to measure the length of the party favor to the nearest centimeter.

INDEPENDENT PRACTICE

See Example **1** **What unit of measure provides the best estimate? Explain.**

    6. The width of a desk is about 10 ___?___.

See Example **2** **7.** The mass of a packet of sugar is about 3 ___?___.

See Example **3** **8.** A washing machine holds about 50 ___?___ of water.

    9. A cooking pot holds about 1.5 ___?___.

See Example **4** **10.** Use a ruler to measure the length of the feather to the nearest centimeter.

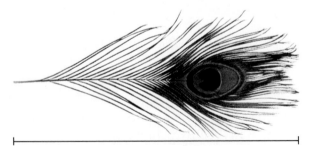

PRACTICE AND PROBLEM SOLVING

    11. Estimation Felipe is estimating the length of his baseball bat using a benchmark. He gets an estimate of about 10 ___?___. Which benchmark was Felipe most likely using: the width of his fist, the length of his foot, the distance from his elbow to his fingertip, or the length of his baseball cap?

Which unit of measure would you use for each? Justify your answer.

12. the length of a movie screen   **13.** the length of a walk around a campus

14. the mass of a single flower   **15.** the mass of a CD case

16. the capacity of a jug   **17.** the capacity of a thimble

18. Multi-Step A shipment of DVD players contains 8 cartons. Each carton has 6 players in it. A single player has a mass of 1.5 kg. All the players can be unpacked and placed on a shelf in the stockroom. A sign above the shelf reads "Maximum mass 80 __?__." What is the missing unit of measure on the sign above the shelf?

19. Physics The mass of an empty balloon is 4.5 g. A filled balloon has a mass of 5.3 g. Find the mass of the air in the balloon. Does air have mass? Explain.

20. What's the Error? Ellis made a travel brochure for his social studies project. He wrote that the common highway speed in Canada is 8,000 km per hour. What error did Ellis make?

21. Write About It Tell which metric units of measure you would use to measure the dimensions of a shoebox and estimate the mass of the box when it contains a pair of shoes.

22. Challenge Jermaine is trying to limit the amount of fat in his diet to 50 g per day. At breakfast, Jermaine has one serving of milk, two servings of peanut butter, and a serving of apple, which has almost no fat. If his lunch and dinner contain the same amount of fat as his breakfast, is Jermaine likely to meet his goal for the day? Explain.

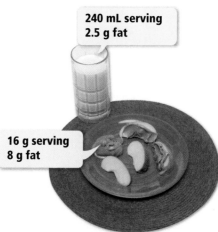

240 mL serving
2.5 g fat

16 g serving
8 g fat

Florida Spiral Review

MA.6.A.3.2, MA.6.A.2.1

23. Multiple Choice Which unit could NOT reasonably be used to measure something involving a home aquarium?

A. A liter   **B.** A meter   **C.** A kilometer   **D.** A kilogram

24. Short Response What metric unit of measure provides the best estimate of the width of a bedroom window? Justify your answer.

Solve each equation. (Lesson 2-9)

25. $\frac{y}{6} = 12$ **26.** $39 = \frac{m}{3}$ **27.** $\frac{r}{5} = 7$ **28.** $5 = \frac{f}{11}$

29. Christopher bought four pounds of apples for $1.96. What is the unit rate? (Lesson 7-1)

Converting Customary Units

MA.6.A.2.1 Use reasoning about multiplication and division to solve ratio and rate problems. **MA.6.A.2.2** Interpret . . . ratios and rates. *Also* **MA.6.A.3.6**

Jacques Freitag is the first athlete to win gold medals at the International Association of Athletic Federations (IAAF) Youth, Junior, and Senior Championships. His personal best in the high jump is over 93 inches. How many feet is this?

You can use the information in the table below to convert one customary unit to another.

Common Customary Measurements		
Length	**Weight**	**Capacity**
1 foot = 12 inches	1 pound = 16 ounces	1 cup = 8 fluid ounces
1 yard = 36 inches	1 ton = 2,000 pounds	1 pint = 2 cups
1 yard = 3 feet		1 quart = 2 pints
1 mile = 5,280 feet		1 quart = 4 cups
1 mile = 1,760 yards		1 gallon = 4 quarts
		1 gallon = 16 cups
		1 gallon = 128 fluid ounces

 Math @ thinkcentral.com

To convert one unit of measure to another, you can multiply by a conversion factor. A conversion factor is a rate in which the two quantities are equal but use different units, such as $\frac{1\text{ ft}}{12\text{ in.}}$.

EXAMPLE 1 **Using a Conversion Factor**

Convert.

A 93 in. = ▊ ft

Set up a conversion factor.

$$93 \text{ in.} \times \frac{1\text{ ft}}{12\text{ in.}} = 7.75 \text{ ft}$$

Think: inches to feet. 1 ft = 12 in., so use the rate $\frac{1\text{ ft}}{12\text{ in.}}$. Multiply 93 in. by the conversion factor. Cancel the common unit, in.

93 in. = 7.75 ft

B 2 lb = ▊ oz

Set up a conversion factor.

$$2 \text{ lb} \times \frac{16\text{ oz}}{1\text{ lb}} = 32 \text{ oz}$$

Think: pounds to ounces. 16 oz = 1 lb, so use the rate $\frac{16\text{ oz}}{1\text{ lb}}$. Multiply 2 lb by the conversion factor. Cancel the common unit, lb.

2 lb = 32 oz

Caution!

In the conversion factor, write the unit you are converting *to* in the numerator and the unit you are converting *from* in the denominator.

Video **Lesson Tutorial Videos @ thinkcentral.com**

Another way to convert units is to use proportions.

EXAMPLE **2**

Remember!

A proportion shows that two ratios are equivalent. Use a conversion factor for one of the ratios. See p. 304.

Converting Units of Measure by Using Proportions

Convert 48 quarts to gallons.

$$\frac{4 \text{ qt}}{1 \text{ gal}} = \frac{48 \text{ qt}}{x \text{ gal}}$$ *1 gallon = 4 quarts. Write a proportion. Use a variable for the value you are trying to find.*

$4 \cdot x = 1 \cdot 48$ *The cross products are equal.*

$4x = 48$ *Divide both sides by 4 to undo the multiplication.*

$x = 12$

$48 \text{ qt} = 12 \text{ gal}$

EXAMPLE **3**

PROBLEM
SOLVING

PROBLEM SOLVING APPLICATION

The Washington Monument is about 185 yards tall. This height is almost equal to the length of two football fields. About how many feet tall is the Washington Monument?

 Understand the Problem

The **answer** will be the height of the Washington Monument in feet.

List the **important information:**

• The height of the Washington Monument is about 185 yards.

 Make a Plan

Make a table to show the number of feet in 1, 2, and 3 yards. Then find the number of feet in *n* yards.

3 Solve

Yards	Feet
1	3
2	6
3	9
n	3*n*

Look for a pattern.

1 · 3 = 3

2 · 3 = 6

3 · 3 = 9

n · 3 = 3n

$185 \cdot 3 = 555$, so the Washington Monument is about 555 feet tall.

 Look Back

Round 185 to 200, and then multiply by 3: $200 \cdot 3 = 600$.

The answer is reasonable because 555 is close to 600.

Think and Discuss

1. Explain how to set up a proportion to convert miles to yards.

MA.6.A.2.1, MA.6.A.2.2, MA.6.A.3.6

GUIDED PRACTICE

See Example **1** Convert.

1. 9 ft = ■ in.   **2.** 10 pt = ■ qt   **3.** 14,000 lb = ■ T

4. 5 yd = ■ ft   **5.** 24 fl oz = ■ c   **6.** 4 lb = ■ oz

See Example **2** **7.** 32 qt = ■ gal   **8.** 9 lb = ■ oz   **9.** 36 in. = ■ ft

10. 2 yd = ■ in.   **11.** 11 qt = ■ pt   **12.** 6 T = ■ lb

See Example **3** **13. Biology** An adult male of average size normally has about 6 quarts of blood in his body. Approximately how many cups of blood does the average adult male have in his body?

INDEPENDENT PRACTICE

See Example **1** Convert.

14. 96 oz = ■ lb   **15.** 6 c = ■ fl oz   **16.** 3 mi = ■ ft

17. 4,000 lb = ■ T   **18.** 6 lb = ■ oz   **19.** 3,520 yd = ■ mi

See Example **2** **20.** 27 ft = ■ yd   **21.** 3 T = ■ lb   **22.** 16 qt = ■ gal

23. 48 oz = ■ lb   **24.** 3 yd = ■ in.   **25.** 10 pt = ■ c

See Example **3** **26. Architecture** The steel used to make the Statue of Liberty weighs about 125 tons. About how many pounds of steel were used to make the Statue of Liberty?

PRACTICE AND PROBLEM SOLVING

Compare. Use <, >, or =.

27. 18 ft ■ 220 in.   **28.** 24 lb ■ 388 oz   **29.** $\frac{1}{2}$ pt ■ 1 c

30. 2 mi ■ 10,000 ft   **31.** 12 pt ■ 3 gal   **32.** 72 ft ■ 24 yd

33. 9 c ■ 72 fl oz   **34.** 30 yd ■ 93 ft   **35.** 145 in. ■ 4 yd

36. Linda cut off $1\frac{1}{2}$ feet of her hair to donate to an organization that makes wigs. How many inches of hair did Linda cut off?

37. Geography Lake Superior is about 1,302 feet deep at its deepest point. What is this depth in yards?

38. Multi-Step A company produces 3 tons of cereal each week. How many 12-ounce cereal boxes can be filled each week?

39. Sports The width of a singles tennis court is 27 feet.

   a. How many yards wide is a singles tennis court?

   b. How many inches wide is a singles tennis court?

○ = WORKED-OUT SOLUTIONS
on p. WS9

Art

Long-Term Parking is 65 feet tall and stands in front of a parking lot in Paris.

Convert.

40. 108 in. = ▊ ft = ▊ yd

41. 10,560 ft = ▊ yd = ▊ mi

42. 12 qt = ▊ c = ▊ fl oz

43. 2 gal = ▊ qt = ▊ pt

44. **Art** In Paris, the sculpture *Long-Term Parking*, created by Armand Fernandez, contains 60 cars embedded in 3.5 million pounds of concrete. How many tons of concrete is this?

45. **Multi-Step** If a half-gallon of milk sells for $1.60, what is the cost of a fluid ounce of milk? Round your answer to the nearest cent.

46. **Critical Thinking** Make a table to convert ounces to pounds. Write an expression for the number of pounds in *n* ounces. Then write an expression for the number of ounces in *n* pounds.

47. **Multi-Step** If you drink 14 quarts of water per week, on average, how many pints do you drink per day?

48. **What's the Error?** Sari said that she walked a total of 8,800 feet in a 5-mile walk-a-thon. Explain Sari's error.

49. **Write About It** Explain how to compare a length given in inches to a length given in feet.

50. **Challenge** In 1942, there were 15,000 troops on the ship *Queen Mary*. Each soldier was given 2 quarts of fresh water for the entire journey.

    a. How many gallons of fresh water did the soldiers have in all?

    b. **Estimation** If the journey took 5 days, about how many fluid ounces of fresh water should a soldier have rationed himself each day?

51. **Multiple Choice** Which of the following amounts is NOT equivalent to 1 gallon?

    A. 64 fluid ounces   **B.** 16 cups   **C.** 8 pints   **D.** 4 quarts

52. **Multiple Choice** The world's largest ice cream sundae weighed about 55,000 pounds. How many tons did it weigh?

    F. 2.7 tons   **G.** 27.5 tons   **H.** 275 tons   **I.** 2,750 tons

Solve each equation. (Lessons 2-6, 2-7)

53. $6 + x = 15$ **54.** $y - 17 = 29$ **55.** $43 = 26 + d$ **56.** $32 = w - 8$

Find each product. (Lesson 3-4)

57. 7.3×0.8 **58.** 10×2.15 **59.** 0.05×0.12 **60.** 6.6×1.4

61. Seven out of 91 students are unable to go on the school field trip. To the nearest tenth, about what percent of the students is this? (Lesson 7-5)

Converting Metric Units

 MA.6.A.2.1 Use reasoning about multiplication and division to solve ratio and rate problems. **MA.6.A.2.2** Interpret . . . ratios and rates.

The first Tour de France was in 1903 and was 2,428 km long. It had only 6 stages. Compare that to the 2005 Tour de France, which had 21 stages and covered 3,607 km.

During the 2005 Tour de France, Lance Armstrong was the stage winner from Tours to Blois, which has a distance of 67.5 km. How many meters is this distance?

In the metric system, the value of each place is 10 times greater than the value of the place to its right. When you convert one unit of measure to another, you can multiply or divide by a power of 10.

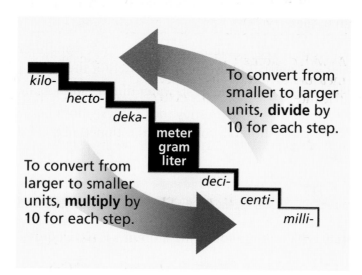

EXAMPLE 1 *Sports Application*

Helpful Hint

To multiply by a power of 10, move the decimal to the right; to divide by a power of 10, move the decimal to the left.

During the 2005 Tour de France, Lance Armstrong was the stage winner from Tours to Blois, which has a distance of 67.5 km. How many meters is this distance?

67.5 km = ▊ m

Think: Kilometer to meter is going from a bigger unit to a smaller unit. A meter is 3 places to the right of a kilometer in the chart, so 10 · 10 · 10 or 10^3 = 1,000.

67.5 km = (67.5 · 1,000) m

1 km = 1,000 m. You are converting a bigger unit to a smaller unit, so multiply by 1,000.

67.5 km = 67,500 m

Move the decimal point 3 places to the right.

Video **Lesson Tutorial Videos @ thinkcentral.com**

EXAMPLE 2 **Using Powers of Ten to Convert Metric Units of Measure**

Convert.

Caution! ///////

Make sure you are multiplying or dividing by the correct power of ten.

A The width of a book is about 22 cm. 22 cm = ■ mm

22 cm = (22 · 10) mm   *1 cm = 10 mm, bigger unit to smaller unit, so multiply by 10.*

22 cm = 220 mm   *Move the decimal point 1 place right.*

B A water bottle holds about 400 mL. 400 mL = ■ L

400 mL = (400 ÷ 1,000) L   *1,000 mL = 1 L, smaller unit to bigger unit, so divide by 1,000.*

400 mL = 0.4 L   *Move the decimal point 3 places left.*

Metric Measurements		
Distance	**Mass**	**Capacity**
1 km = 1,000 m	1 kg = 1,000 g	1 L = 1,000 mL
1 m = 100 cm	1 g = 1,000 mg	
1 cm = 10 mm		

As with customary measurements, you can convert one metric unit of measure to another by using a conversion factor or by using a proportion. The rate $\frac{100\ cm}{1\ m}$ can be used to convert meters to centimeters.

EXAMPLE 3 **Converting Metric Units of Measure**

Convert.

A Method 1: Use a conversion factor.

11 m = ■ cm   *Think: 100 cm = 1 m, so use the rate $\frac{100\ cm}{1\ m}$.*

11 m × $\frac{100\ cm}{1\ m}$ = 1,100 cm   *Multiply 11 m by the conversion factor. Cancel the common unit, m.*

11 m = 1,100 cm

B Method 2: Use a proportion.

190 mL = ■ L

$\frac{190\ mL}{x\ L} = \frac{1,000\ mL}{1\ L}$ *1 L = 1,000 mL. Write a proportion.*

$1,000x = 190$ *The cross products are equal. Divide both sides by 1,000 to undo the multiplication.*

$x = 0.19\ L$

Think and Discuss

1. Explain how you know that $\frac{100\ cm}{1\ m}$ is a unit rate.

Exercises

MA.6.A.2.1, MA.6.A.2.2

Homework Help

Go to **thinkcentral.com**
Exercises 1–22, 23, 25, 27, 29, 31, 33, 35

GUIDED PRACTICE

See Example ① **1.** The length of a school hallway is 115 meters. How many kilometers long is the hallway?

See Example ② **Convert.**

2. The diameter of a ceiling fan is about 95 cm. 95 cm = ⬛ m

3. A rock has a mass of about 852 g. 852 g = ⬛ kg

4. A vase holds about 1.25 L of water. 1.25 L = ⬛ mL

5. A sheet of paper has a mass of about 3.5 g. 3.5 g = ⬛ mg

See Example ③ **6.** 3 kg = ⬛ g **7.** 4.4 L = ⬛ mL **8.** 1 kg = ⬛ mg

9. 50 mm = ⬛ m **10.** 21 km = ⬛ cm **11.** 6 mL = ⬛ L

INDEPENDENT PRACTICE

See Example ① **12.** A juice container holds 300 milliliters. How many liters of juice are in the container?

See Example ② **Convert.**

13. A teacup holds about 110 mL. 110 mL = ⬛ L

14. The distance around a school is about 825 m. 825 m = ⬛ km

15. A chair has a mass of about 22.5 kg. 22.5 kg = ⬛ g

16. A gas tank holds about 85 L. 85 L = ⬛ mL

See Example ③ **17.** 2,460 m = ⬛ km **18.** 842 mm = ⬛ cm **19.** 9,680 mg = ⬛ g

20. 25 cm = ⬛ mm **21.** 782 g = ⬛ kg **22.** 1.2 km = ⬛ m

PRACTICE AND PROBLEM SOLVING

23. **Multi-Step** There are 28 L of soup in a pot. Marshall serves 400 mL in each bowl. If he fills 16 bowls, how much soup is left in the pot? Write your answer two ways: as a number of liters and as a number of milliliters.

24. **Multi-Step** Joanie wants to frame a rectangular picture that is 1.7 m by 0.9 m. Joanie has 500 cm of wood to use for a frame. Does Joanie have enough wood to frame the picture? Justify your answer.

Convert.

25. $\dfrac{23{,}850 \text{ cm}}{x \text{ km}} = \dfrac{100{,}000 \text{ cm}}{1 \text{ km}}$

26. $\dfrac{350 \text{ L}}{x \text{ mL}} = \dfrac{1 \text{ L}}{1{,}000 \text{ mL}}$

27. $7 \text{ km} \cdot \dfrac{1{,}000 \text{ m}}{1 \text{ km}} = ⬛ \text{ m}$

28. $9.5 \text{ L} \cdot \dfrac{1{,}000 \text{ mL}}{1 \text{ L}} = ⬛ \text{ mL}$

○ = **WORKED-OUT SOLUTIONS**
on p. WS9

Compare. Use <, >, or =.

29. 1,000 mm ▧ 1 m **30.** 5.2 kg ▧ 60 g **31.** 3 L ▧ 6,000 mL

32. 2 g ▧ 20,000 mg **33.** 0.0065 m ▧ 6.5 mm **34.** 0.1 km ▧ 10 mm

35. Multi-Step The St. Louis Gateway Arch in Missouri is about 19,200 centimeters tall. The San Jacinto Monument, outside of Houston, Texas, is about 174 m tall. Which structure is taller? by how much? Give your answer in meters.

St. Louis Gateway Arch   San Jacinto Monument

36. Critical Thinking A *nanometer* is equal to one-billionth of a meter. How many nanometers are there in 2.5 meters?

37. What's the Error? Edgar wanted to know the mass of a package of cereal in kilograms. The label on the box says 672 g. Edgar said that the mass is 672,000 kg. Explain Edgar's error, and give the correct answer.

38. Write About It Amy ran a 1,000-meter race. Explain how to find the number of centimeters in 1,000 meters.

39. Challenge The lemonade cooler at the class picnic holds 12.5 liters. One liter is approximately equal to 0.26 gallons. Each plastic cup holds 7.5 fluid ounces. Estimate the number of cups that can be filled from the cooler.

Florida Spiral Review

MA.6.A.5.2, MA.6.A.1.3

40. Multiple Choice Complete the statement with the most reasonable metric unit. A snail might crawl at a rate of about 0.01 ___?___ per hour.

A. millimeter **B.** meter **C.** milliliter **D.** kilometer

41. Extended Response Liza, Toni, and Kim collected some shells at the beach. The masses of the shells were 29 g, 52 g, 18 g, 103 g, 154 g, and 96 g. What was the combined mass of the shells in kilograms? in milligrams? What is the difference in kilograms between the shells?

Compare. Write <, >, or =. (Lesson 4-7)

42. $\frac{5}{8}$ ▧ $\frac{3}{4}$ **43.** $\frac{11}{12}$ ▧ $\frac{4}{5}$ **44.** $\frac{1}{7}$ ▧ $\frac{2}{11}$ **45.** $\frac{7}{9}$ ▧ $\frac{21}{27}$

46. Freddy is making hamburgers for a family picnic. Each hamburger patty weighs $\frac{1}{4}$ pound. How many hamburgers can Freddy make with 8 pounds of ground beef? (Lesson 5-8)

Convert. (Lesson 8-3)

47. 21 ft = ▧ yd **48.** 3 qt = ▧ fl oz **49.** 2.5 T = ▧ lb

Time and Temperature

MA.6.A.2.1 Use reasoning about multiplication and division to solve ratio and rate problems. *Also* **MA.6.A.2.2, MA.6.A.3.4**

Jamie took a tour of London on a double-decker bus. The tour started at 11:45 A.M. and ended at 3:15 P.M. Jamie was on the bus for 3 hours 30 minutes.

You can use the information in the table below to convert one unit of time to another.

Time	
1 year (yr) = 365 days	1 day = 24 hours (h)
1 year = 12 months (mo)	1 hour = 60 minutes (min)
1 year = 52 weeks	1 minute = 60 seconds (s)
1 week = 7 days	

EXAMPLE 1 **Converting Time**

Convert.

A 1 min 45 s = ▮ s

1 minute 45 seconds

60 seconds + 45 seconds   *Think: 1 minute = 60 seconds.*

105 seconds

1 min 45 s = 105 s

B 450 min = ▮ h

$450 \text{ min} \cdot \frac{1 \text{ h}}{60 \text{ min}} = \frac{450}{60} \text{ h}$ *Think: 1 hour = 60 minutes,*
so use the rate $\frac{1 \text{ h}}{60 \text{ min}}$.

$450 \text{ min} = 7\frac{1}{2} \text{ h}$ *Write $\frac{450}{60}$ as a mixed number.*

C 6 weeks = ▮ h

$6 \text{ weeks} \cdot \frac{7 \text{ days}}{1 \text{ week}} \cdot \frac{24 \text{ h}}{1 \text{ day}} = 1{,}008 \text{ h}$ *Think: 1 week = 7 days*
and 1 day = 24 hours.

6 weeks = 1,008 h

The time between the start of an activity and the end of an activity is called the *elapsed time*.

EXAMPLE 2 **Finding Elapsed Time**

A Jamie's flight to London was scheduled to arrive at 9:10 A.M. It was 4 hours 25 minutes late. When did it arrive?

Scheduled time: 9:10 A.M.   *Think: 4 hours after 9:10 A.M. is*
Arrival time: 1:35 P.M.   *1:10 P.M. 25 minutes after 1:10 P.M. is*
                                   1:35 P.M.
The flight arrived at 1:35 P.M.

B Jamie's friend Tina joined her in London. Tina's flight arrived at 2:30 P.M. The flight was 3 hours 15 minutes long. At what time did Tina's plane depart?

Arrival time: 2:30 P.M.   *Think: 3 hours before 2:30 P.M. is 11:30 A.M.*
Departure: 11:15 A.M.   *15 minutes before 11:30 A.M. is 11:15 A.M.*

The plane departed at 11:15 A.M.

Celsius and Fahrenheit are two scales used to measure temperature. You can use the formulas below to convert temperature.

Temperature Conversions	
To convert Celsius to Fahrenheit: $F = \frac{9}{5}C + 32.$	To convert Fahrenheit to Celsius: $C = \frac{5}{9}(F - 32).$

EXAMPLE 3 **Estimating Temperature**

Remember!

Dividing by 2 is the same as multiplying by $\frac{1}{2}$.
See p. 225.

Estimate the temperature.

A 20 °C is about ▓ °F.

$F = \frac{9}{5} \cdot C + 32$ *Use the formula.*

Round $\frac{9}{5}$ to 2, and 32 to 30.

$F \approx 2 \cdot 20 + 30$ *Use the order*
                              of operations.
$F \approx 40 + 30$

$F \approx 70$

20 °C is about 70 °F.

B 50 °F is about ▓ °C.

$C = \frac{5}{9}(F - 32)$ *Use the formula.*

Round $\frac{5}{9}$ to $\frac{1}{2}$, and 32 to 30.

$C \approx \frac{1}{2}(50 - 30)$ *Use the order*
                                   of operations.
$C \approx \frac{1}{2}(20)$

$C \approx 10$

50 °F is about 10 °C.

Think and Discuss

1. **Explain** how to find the number of minutes in a week.

2. **Explain** how to find the elapsed time between 7:45 A.M. and 10:30 P.M. if you know the elapsed time between 7:45 A.M. and 10:30 A.M.

8-5

Exercises

MA.6.A.2.1, MA.6.A.2.2,
MA.6.A.3.4

Homework Help

Go to **thinkcentral.com**
Exercises 1–22, 23, 25, 27, 29

GUIDED PRACTICE

See Example 1 **Convert.**

1. 20 min = ☐ s

2. 98 days = ☐ weeks

3. 30 mo = ☐ yr

4. 3 min 25 s = ☐ s

5. 8 h = ☐ min

6. 4,320 min = ☐ days

See Example 2 **7.** A movie starts at 11:50 A.M. and runs for 2 hours 25 minutes. At what time does the movie end?

8. Nick drove to visit some friends. If he arrived at 1:30 P.M. and took 4 hours 10 minutes to get there, at what time did Nick start out?

See Example 3 **Estimate the temperature.**

9. 12 °C is about ☐ °F.

10. 78 °F is about ☐ °C.

11. 15 °C is about ☐ °F.

INDEPENDENT PRACTICE

See Example 1 **Convert.**

12. 2 h 25 min = ☐ min

13. 96 h = ☐ days

14. 1 yr 6 mo = ☐ mo

15. 7,200 s = ☐ h

16. 5 weeks 1 day = ☐ days

17. 4,368 h = ☐ weeks

See Example 2 **18.** A bus arrived at its destination at 2:15 P.M. If the trip took 3 hours 50 minutes, at what time did the bus depart?

19. Multi-Step The school play lasts 1 hour 25 minutes, and there is a 15-minute intermission. The play started at 10:30 A.M. When will it end?

See Example 3 **Estimate the temperature.**

20. 56 °F is about ☐ °C.

21. 84 °C is about ☐ °F.

22. 75 °F is about ☐ °C.

PRACTICE AND PROBLEM SOLVING

Compare. Use <, >, or =.

23. 21 h ☐ $\frac{5}{6}$ day

24. 2 yr ☐ 104 weeks

25. 80,000 s ☐ 1 day

26. Patterns The sequence below shows the times that a radio station gives a traffic report. When will the radio station give the next traffic report?
11:18 A.M., 11:30 A.M., 11:42 A.M., 11:54 A.M., …

For Exercises 27 and 28, use the table.

27. Which bus from Miami to Orlando would you take to spend the least amount of time on the bus? the greatest amount of time on the bus?

28. Bus 490 was delayed in traffic for 1 hour 15 minutes. At what time did the bus finally arrive?

Miami to Orlando Schedule		
Bus	**Depart**	**Arrive**
460	8:00 A.M.	2:45 P.M.
470	10:50 A.M.	5:45 P.M.
480	1:00 P.M.	7:40 P.M.
490	4:30 P.M.	11:20 P.M.

○ = WORKED-OUT SOLUTIONS
on p. WS9

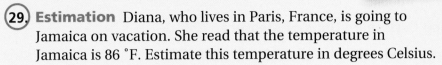

The United States and Jamaica are the only two countries in the world that use the Fahrenheit scale for daily temperature readings. All the other countries in the world use the Celsius scale.

29. Estimation Diana, who lives in Paris, France, is going to Jamaica on vacation. She read that the temperature in Jamaica is 86 °F. Estimate this temperature in degrees Celsius.

30. Multi-Step The table shows the average monthly temperatures from April to July in degrees Fahrenheit for New York City and in degrees Celsius for London. In which months is the average monthly temperature in New York City higher than it is in London?

Average Monthly Temperatures		
Month	New York City (°F)	London (°C)
April	50	10
May	61	13
June	70	16
July	76	19

31. Bobby's trip from Paris, Texas, to Paris, France, should have taken $10\frac{1}{2}$ hours, but it was 3 hours 20 minutes longer. About how long was his trip?

32. ? What's the Error? David read in a travel book that the average temperature in Dublin in July is 15 °C. He estimated the temperature in degrees Fahrenheit by adding 30 to the Celsius temperature and then multiplying by 2. What did David do wrong?

33. Write About It Explain how to find the elapsed time between two given times.

34. Challenge Below is a list of the daily high temperatures in Glasgow, Scotland, for one week. What was the mean high temperature in degrees Fahrenheit? 7 °C, 12 °C, 9 °C, 10 °C, 14 °C, 10 °C, 8 °C

35. Multiple Choice Which measure is NOT equivalent to the others?

    A. 8 hours   **B.** 480 minutes   **C.** 28,000 seconds   **D.** $\frac{1}{3}$ day

36. Multiple Choice If a person's temperature is about 100 °F, the person has a fever. Approximately what is this temperature in degrees Celsius?

    F. 38 °C   **G.** 56 °C   **H.** 68 °C   **I.** 72 °C

Compare. Write <, >, or =. (Lesson 3-1)

37. 9.17 ▩ 9.107   **38.** 3.456 ▩ 3.65   **39.** 0.051 ▩ 0.052   **40.** 12.5 ▩ 12.50

Convert. (Lesson 8-4)

41. 16 m = ▩ cm   **42.** 84 g = ▩ kg   **43.** 0.51 L = ▩ mL

Quiz for Lessons 8-1 Through 8-5

✓ **8-1** **Understanding Customary Units of Measure**

What unit of measure provides the best estimate? Explain.

1. A fishbowl can hold about 2 ___?___ of water.

2. A Columbian mammoth, which was about the same size as an elephant, lived in Mexico about 1.5 million years ago. A mammoth weighed about 10 ___?___ .

✓ **8-2** **Understanding Metric Units of Measure**

What unit of measure provides the best estimate? Explain.

3. A cat has a mass of about 3 ___?___ .

4. The length of an airport runway is about 3 ___?___ .

Measure the length of each line segment to the nearest centimeter.

5. ●━━━━━━━●   **6.** ●━━━━━━━━━━●

✓ **8-3** **Converting Customary Units**

Use the table for Exercises 7 and 8.

7. Convert Ty's length to feet and inches.

8. How many ounces does Ty weigh?

Baby Ty Rodriguez	
Birth Date	July 8, 2005, 11:50 P.M.
Weight	9 lb 8 oz
Length	$21\frac{1}{2}$ in.

✓ **8-4** **Converting Metric Units**

Convert.

9. 8 m = ▨ cm   **10.** 12 kg = ▨ g   **11.** 2,000 mL = ▨ L

✓ **8-5** **Time and Temperature**

Convert.

12. 5 min 32 s = ▨ s   **13.** 3 days = ▨ min   **14.** 24 mo = ▨ yr   **15.** 330 s = ▨ h

Estimate the temperature.

16. 30 °C is about ▨ °F.   **17.** 80 °F is about ▨ °C.   **18.** 54 °F is about ▨ °C.

19. What is the elapsed time between 8:45 P.M. and 12:15 A.M.?

20. A train scheduled to arrive at 10:35 A.M. was delayed 3 hours 20 minutes. What time did it arrive?

Focus on Problem Solving

 Look Back
 • **Check that the question is answered.**

Sometimes a problem requires you to go through a series of steps to find the answer. When you read a question, ask yourself what information you need to find in order to answer it. After you have solved the problem, reread the question to make sure you have answered it completely.

 Read each problem and determine whether the given solution answers the question in the problem. If not, provide the correct answer.

1 The giant house spider has a leg span of 70 millimeters. The western black widow has a leg span of 4 centimeters. How many centimeters longer is the leg span of the giant house spider?
Solution: 3 centimeters

2 A recipe for fruit punch calls for 8 fluid ounces of pineapple juice. Daryl pours the required amount of pineapple juice into a bowl that holds 1 gallon. How many additional fluid ounces of liquid can the bowl hold?
Solution: 120 fluid ounces

3 The distance from Belleville to Cedar Falls is twice the distance from Appleton to Belleville. The distance from Cedar Falls to Donner is twice the distance from Belleville to Cedar Falls. What is the distance from Belleville to Donner?

```
     2 km
  ●────●────●──────────●
Appleton Belleville Cedar Falls   Donner
```

Solution: 8 kilometers

4 The 1939 film *Gone with the Wind* had a running time of 3 hours 50 minutes. The film was usually shown with one 15-minute intermission. An afternoon showing of the film started at 2:30 P.M. At what time did the film end?
Solution: 4 hr 5 min

5 A typical chicken egg weighs 2 ounces. A typical ostrich egg weighs 3 pounds. How many times greater is the weight of the ostrich egg than the chicken egg?
Solution: 48 ounces

8-6 Perimeter

MA.6.A.3.4 Solve problems given a formula.
Also MA.6.A.5.3, MA.6.G.4.2

One of the largest jigsaw puzzles ever assembled depicted a painting titled *Portrait of a Young Venetian* by Albrecht Dürer. The puzzle was 20 meters long and 15 meters wide.

The **perimeter** of a figure is the distance around it. To find the perimeter of the puzzle, you can add the lengths of the sides.

Vocabulary

perimeter

$20 + 15 + 20 + 15 = 70$

The perimeter of the puzzle was 70 meters.

EXAMPLE 1

Animated Math
@ thinkcentral.com

Finding the Perimeter of a Polygon

Find the perimeter of the figure.

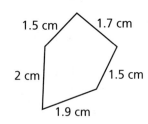

$2 + 2 + 2 + 2 + 2 = 10$
Estimate the perimeter.
$1.5 + 1.7 + 1.5 + 1.9 + 2 = 8.6$
Add all the side lengths.
The perimeter is 8.6 cm. Your estimate shows that this is reasonable.

PERIMETER OF A RECTANGLE

The opposite sides of a rectangle are equal in length. Find the perimeter of a rectangle by using the formula, in which ℓ is the length and w is the width.

$P = 2\ell + 2w$

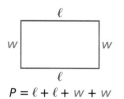

$P = \ell + \ell + w + w$

EXAMPLE 2

Using a Formula to Find Perimeter

Find the perimeter *P* of the frame.

$P = 2\ell + 2w$
$P = (2 \cdot 3) + (2 \cdot 2)$ *Substitute 3 for ℓ and 2 for w.*

$P = 6 + 4$ *Multiply.*
$P = 10$ *Add.*

The perimeter is 10 feet.

Video **Lesson Tutorial Videos** @ thinkcentral.com

A **What is the length of side *a* if the perimeter equals 105 m?**

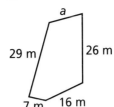

P = sum of side lengths

$105 = a + 26 + 16 + 7 + 29$ *Use the values you know.*

$105 = a + 78$ *Add the known lengths.*

$105 - 78 = a + 78 - 78$ *Subtract 78 from both sides.*

$27 = a$

Side *a* is 27 m long.

B **What is the perimeter of the polygon?**

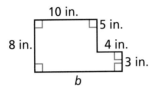

First find the unknown side length.

Find the sides opposite side b.

The length of side b = 10 + 4.

Side *b* is 14 in. long.

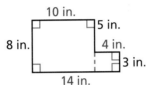

Find the perimeter.

$P = 14 + 8 + 10 + 5 + 4 + 3$

$P = 44$

The perimeter of the polygon is 44 in.

C **The width of a rectangle is 12 cm. What is the perimeter of the rectangle if the length is 3 times the width?**

$\ell = 3w$ *Find the length.*

$\ell = (3 \cdot 12)$ *Substitute 12 for w.*

$\ell = 36$ *Multiply.*

The length is 36 cm.

$P = 2\ell + 2w$ *Use the formula for the perimeter of a rectangle.*

$P = 2(36) + 2(12)$ *Substitute 36 and 12.*

$P = 72 + 24$ *Multiply.*

$P = 96$ *Add.*

The perimeter of the rectangle is 96 cm.

Think and Discuss

1. Explain how to find the perimeter of a regular pentagon if you know the length of one side.

2. Tell what formula you can use to find the perimeter of a square.

Homewok Help
Go to **thinkcentral.com**
Exercises 1–12, 13, 15, 17, 19

 MA.6.A.3.4, MA.6.G.4.2

GUIDED PRACTICE

See Example ① **Find the perimeter of each figure.**

1.
0.5 in.   0.5 in.

0.5 in.   0.5 in.

2.
7 m   9 m
12 m

See Example ② **Find the perimeter _P_ of each rectangle.**

3.
12 m
8 m

4.
|← 7.3 in. →|
4 in.

See Example ③ **5.** What is the length of side _b_ if the perimeter equals 21 yd?

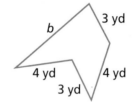
_b_   3 yd

4 yd   4 yd
3 yd

INDEPENDENT PRACTICE

See Example ① **Find the perimeter of each figure.**

6.
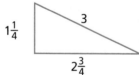
$1\frac{1}{4}$ 3

$2\frac{3}{4}$

7. regular octagon

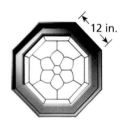
12 in.

See Example ② **Find the perimeter _P_ of each rectangle.**

8.
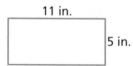
11 in.
5 in.

9.
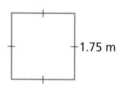
1.75 m

10.
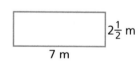
$2\frac{1}{2}$ m
7 m

See Example ③ **11.** What is the perimeter of the polygon?

6 m   5 m
_b_
4 m
 11 m

12. The width of a rectangle is 15 ft. What is the perimeter of the rectangle if the length is 5 ft longer than the width?

Use the figure *ACDEFG* for Exercises 13–15.

13. What is the length of side *FE*?

14. If the perimeter of rectangle *BCDE* is 34 in., what is the length of side *BC*?

15. Use your answers from Exercises 13 and 14 to find the perimeter of figure *ACDEFG*.

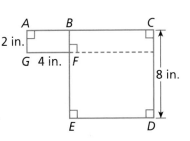

Find the perimeter of each figure.

16. a triangle with side lengths 6 in., 8 in., and 10 in.

17. a regular pentagon with side length $\frac{2}{5}$ km

18. a regular dodecagon (12-sided figure) with side length 3 m

19. Sports The diagram shows one-half of a badminton court.

   a. What are the dimensions of the whole court?

   b. What is the perimeter of the whole court?

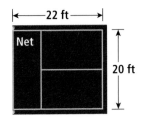

20. What's the Error? A student found the perimeter of a 10-inch-by-13-inch rectangle to be 23 inches. Explain the student's error. Then find the correct perimeter.

21. Write About It Explain how to find the unknown length of a side of a triangle that has a perimeter of 24 yd and two sides that measure 6 yd and 8 yd.

22. Challenge The perimeter of a regular octagon is 20 m. What is the length of one side of the octagon?

23. Multiple Choice What is the perimeter of the figure?

   A. 17 cm   **C.** 21 cm

   B. 19 cm   **D.** 25 cm

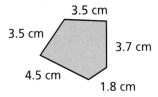

24. Multiple Choice The width of a rectangle is 16 m. What is the perimeter of the rectangle if the length is 2 times the width?

   F. 16 m   **G.** 32 m   **H.** 64 m   **I.** 96 m

25. Philip's score on a 35-question language arts test was 80%. How many questions did Philip answer correctly? (Lesson 7-6)

Estimate the temperature. (Lesson 8-5)
26. 23 °C is about ▢ °F.   **27.** 350 °F is about ▢ °C.   **28.** 49 °C is about ▢ °F.

○ = **WORKED-OUT SOLUTIONS**
   on p. WS9

8-7 Circles and Circumference

MA.6.G.4.1
Understand the concept of π, know common estimates of π (3.14; 22/7) and use these values to estimate and calculate the circumference . . . of circles.
Also **MA.6.A.3.4**

The shape of a drum is a *circle*. A **circle** is the set of all points in a plane that are the same distance from a given point, called the **center**.

Like a polygon, a circle is a plane figure. But a circle is not a polygon because it is not made of line segments.

Vocabulary

circle

center

chord

diameter

radius (radii)

circumference

pi

Chord A line segment that has both endpoints on the circle.

Center

Diameter A chord that passes through the center of the circle. Diameters are the longest chords in a circle.

Radius (plural radii) A line segment with one endpoint at the center of the circle and the other endpoint on the circle.

The length of the diameter is twice the length of the radius.

EXAMPLE 1 **Naming Parts of a Circle**

Name the circle, two chords, a diameter, and three radii.

A circle is named by its center, so this is circle O.
$\overline{AB}$ and $\overline{DE}$ are chords.
$\overline{AB}$ is a diameter.
$\overline{OA}$, $\overline{OB}$, and $\overline{OC}$ are radii.

The distance around a circle is called the **circumference**.

The ratio of the circumference to the diameter, $\frac{C}{d}$, is the same for any circle. This ratio is represented by the Greek letter π, which is read " **pi** ."

$$\frac{C}{d} = \pi$$

The decimal representation of *pi* starts with 3.14159265 . . . and goes on forever without repeating. Most people approximate π using either 3.14 or $\frac{22}{7}$. To make multiplying by *pi* easier, you can round π to 3.

The formula for the circumference of a circle is $C = \pi d$, or $C = 2\pi r$.

Circumference of a Circle	
Words	**Formula**
The circumference of any circle is equal to π times the diameter, or 2π times the radius.	$C = \pi d$ or $C = 2\pi r$

EXAMPLE 2 **Architecture Application**

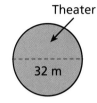
Theater

32 m

An architect is making a plan for a new circular theater. Estimate the circumference of the theater by rounding π to 3.

$C = \pi d$ *Use the formula.*

$C \approx 3 \cdot 32$ *Replace π with 3 and d with 32.*

$C \approx 96$

The circumference of the theater is about 96 meters.

EXAMPLE 3 **Using the Formula for the Circumference of a Circle**

Find each missing value to the nearest hundredth. Use 3.14 for π.

A
8 ft

$d = 8$ ft; $C = ?$

$C = \pi d$ *Write the formula.*

$C \approx 3.14 \cdot 8$ *Replace π with 3.14 and d with 8.*

$C \approx 25.12$ ft

B
3 cm

$r = 3$ cm; $C = ?$

$C = 2\pi r$ *Write the formula.*

$C \approx 2 \cdot 3.14 \cdot 3$ *Replace π with 3.14 and r with 3.*

$C \approx 18.84$ cm

C $C = 37.68$ in.; $d = ?$

$C = \pi d$ *Write the formula.*

$37.68 \approx 3.14d$ *Replace C with 37.68, and π with 3.14.*

$\dfrac{37.68}{3.14} \approx \dfrac{3.14d}{3.14}$ *Divide both sides by 3.14.*

12.00 in. $\approx d$

Think and Discuss

1. Explain how to find the radius in Example 3C.

2. Tell whether rounding *pi* to 3 in Example 3B will result in an overestimation or an underestimation.

3. Explain why $\frac{22}{7}$ is a good estimate of *pi*.

Homework Help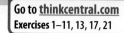

Go to thinkcentral.com
Exercises 1–11, 13, 17, 21

MA.6.G.4.1, MA.6.A.3.4

GUIDED PRACTICE

See Example **1**
1. Point *G* is the center of the circle. Name the circle, two chords, a diameter, and three radii.

See Example **2**
A builder is putting in a circular window. Estimate the circumference by rounding π to 3.

2. What is the circumference if the diameter is 8 feet?

3. What is the circumference if the radius is 2 feet?

window

See Example **3**
Find each missing value to the nearest hundredth. Use 3.14 for π.

4. *C* = ?

d = 10 mm

5. *C* = ?

r = 2 in.

INDEPENDENT PRACTICE

See Example **1**
6. Point *P* is the center of the circle. Name the circle, two chords, a diameter, and three radii.

See Example **2**
A gardener is digging a circular pond and planting a circular herb garden around it. Estimate the circumference by rounding π to 3.

7. If the diameter of the pond is 5 yards, what is its circumference?

8. If the radius of the garden is 7 yards, what is its circumference?

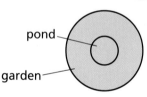
pond
garden

See Example **3**
Find each missing value to the nearest hundredth. Use 3.14 for π.

9. *C* = ?

d = 1.5 m

10. *C* = ?
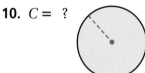
r = 0.8 cm

11. *d* = ?
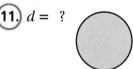
C = 1.57 in.

PRACTICE AND PROBLEM SOLVING

Fill in the blanks. Use 3.14 for π and round to the nearest hundredth.

12. If *r* = 7 m, then *d* = ___?___, and *C* = ___?___.

13. If *d* = 11.5 ft, then *r* = ___?___, and *C* = ___?___.

14. If *C* = 7.065 cm, then *d* = ___?___, and *r* = ___?___.

15. If *C* = 16.956 in., then *d* = ___?___, and *r* = ___?___.

○ = WORKED-OUT SOLUTIONS
on p. WS10

History

Performers like Thea Ulrich have learned to twirl multiple Hula Hoops around their bodies. The world record for most Hula Hoops kept in revolution is 100!

16. Measurement Draw a circle. Name the center P and make the radius 2 inches long.

    a. Draw the diameter $\overline{AB}$ and give its length.

    b. Find the circumference. Use 3.14 for π. Round your answer to the nearest hundredth.

17. History The first Hula Hoop® was introduced in 1958. What is the circumference of a Hula Hoop with a 3-foot diameter? Use 3.14 for π.

Use the cylinders for Exercises 18 and 19.

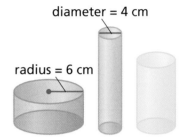
diameter = 4 cm

radius = 6 cm

18. Estimation About how many times greater is the circumference of the purple cylinder than the circumference of the blue cylinder?

19. Choose a Strategy If the circumference of the top of the yellow cylinder is 22.5 centimeters, which method can you use to find the radius?

    A. Divide 22.5 by π.

    B. Multiply 22.5 by π.

    C. Divide 22.5 by π and then divide the quotient by 2.

    D. Multiply 22.5 by π and then multiply the product by 2.

 20. Write About It The circumference of a circle is 3.14 meters. Explain how you can find the diameter and radius of the circle.

21. Challenge An Olympic outdoor archery target is made up of 10 equally spaced concentric circles. *Concentric* means that the center of each of the circles is the same. If the diameter of the biggest ring on the target is 122 centimeters and the diameter of the bullseye is 12.2 centimeters, what is the diameter of the fourth ring from the inside?

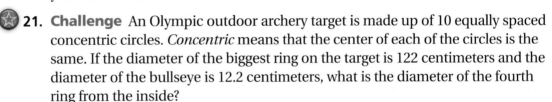

Florida Spiral Review

MA.6.A.5.2, MA.6.A.5.1

22. Multiple Choice A mini-DVD has a radius of 4 centimeters. Which formula can you use to find the circumference of the mini-DVD?

  A. $C = 4\pi$ **B.** $C = 8\pi$ **C.** $C = 16\pi$ **D.** $C = 2 \cdot 2 \cdot \pi \cdot 8$

23. Short Response The wheels on Ryan's bike are each about 2 feet in diameter. If Ryan rides his bike for 1 mile, about how many times will each wheel rotate? Use 3 for π.

Order the fractions from greatest to least. (Lesson 4-7)

24. $\frac{1}{2}, \frac{3}{8}, \frac{5}{8}$ **25.** $\frac{3}{4}, \frac{10}{12}, \frac{1}{12}$ **26.** $\frac{3}{10}, \frac{3}{5}, \frac{7}{10}$ **27.** $\frac{7}{16}, \frac{3}{4}, \frac{5}{8}$

Write each percent as a decimal. (Lesson 7-4)

28. 50%   **29.** 5%   **30.** 85%   **31.** 100%   **32.** 15%

8-7 Circles and Circumference   **381**

Quiz for Lessons 8-6 Through 8-7

☑ **8-6** Perimeter

Find the perimeter of each figure.

1.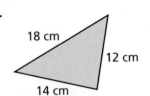

18 cm
12 cm
14 cm

2.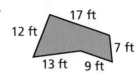

17 ft
12 ft
7 ft
13 ft   9 ft

3.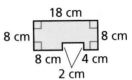

18 cm
8 cm   8 cm
8 cm   4 cm
2 cm

4.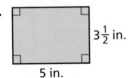

$3\frac{1}{2}$ in.
5 in.

5.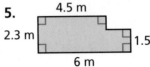

4.5 m
2.3 m
1.5 m
6 m

6.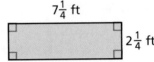

$7\frac{1}{4}$ ft
$2\frac{1}{4}$ ft

7. A rectangle has a perimeter of 18 feet. The length of the rectangle is 6 feet. What is the width of the rectangle?

☑ **8-7** Circles and Circumference

Name the circle, a chord, and two radii, and then find the circumference for each circle. Use 3.14 for π and round to the nearest hundredth.

8.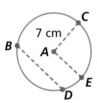

7 cm
B
A
C
E
D

9.

G
D
3 in.
H

10.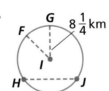

G
F $8\frac{1}{4}$ km
I
H   J

11.

J   M
K
42 cm
L

12. An architect is making a plan for a new circular playground. Estimate the circumference of the playground by rounding π to 3.

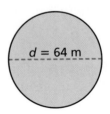

d = 64 m

Find each unknown value. Use 3.14 for π.

13. $r = 9$ in.; $C = $ ____?____   14. $d = 20$ m; $C = $ ____?____   15. $C = 37.68$ ft; $d = $ ____?____

Real-World CONNECTIONS

St. Petersburg

Tropicana Field Tropicana Field® in St. Petersburg is the home of baseball's Tampa Bay Rays. With a capacity of more than 35,000, the domed stadium is also a popular venue for other sports, including hockey, basketball, and figure skating.

1. The stadium features a tank with 30 stingrays that fans can feed during baseball games. The tank holds 40,000 quarts of water. What is the capacity of the tank in gallons?

2. The entrance to Tropicana Field has a ceramic mural whose length is 10,800 inches. A fan claims that the mural is more than 1,000 feet long. Do you agree or disagree? Why?

3. The stadium has several rectangular video boards. The dimensions of the video boards are shown in the table. Find the missing values.

Tropicana Field Video Boards			
Size	Length (ft)	Width (ft)	Perimeter (ft)
Large	64	35	
Small	50		120

4. Tropicana Field is a circle with a diameter of 700 feet. What is the radius and circumference of the stadium? Use 3.14 for π.

5. For a special event, a crew installs strings of lights around the outside of the stadium. The lights are available in strings that are each 50 feet long. What is the minimum number of strings that the crew needs?

Game Time

Logic Puzzle

Each day from Monday through Friday, Mayuri, Naomi, Brett, Thomas, and Angela took turns picking a restaurant for lunch. They ate at restaurants that serve either Chinese food, hamburgers, pizza, seafood, or tacos. Use the clues below to determine which student picked the restaurant on each day and which restaurant the student picked.

① Angela skipped Friday's lunch to play in a basketball game.

② Brett picked the restaurant on Wednesday.

③ The students ate tacos on Friday.

④ Naomi is allergic to seafood and volunteered to pick the first restaurant.

⑤ Thomas picked a hamburger restaurant on the day before another student chose a pizza restaurant.

You can use a chart like the one below to help you solve this puzzle. Place an *O* in a square for something that is true and an *X* in a square for something that cannot be true. Remember that when you place an *O* in a square, you can put *X*'s in the rest of the squares in that row and column. The information from the first two clues has been entered for you.

		Student					Restaurant				
		Mayuri	Naomi	Brett	Thomas	Angela	Seafood	Pizza	Hamburger	Chinese	Tacos
Day	Monday			X							
	Tuesday			X							
	Wednesday	X	X	O	X	X					
	Thursday			X							
	Friday			X		X					
Restaurant	Seafood										
	Pizza										
	Hamburgers										
	Chinese										
	Tacos										

A copy of a blank logic puzzle chart is available online.

Games

Go to **thinkcentral.com**

THINK central

Materials
- **Magnetic strip**
- **construction paper**
- **glue**
- **scissors**
- **6 paint chips**
- **small metal box**

PROJECT ## Perfectly Packaged Perimeters

This metal box stores magnetic vocabulary tiles and small squares that you can use to create a variety of shapes.

Directions

1 Glue construction paper onto the magnetic strip.

2 Write vocabulary words from this chapter on the magnetic strip. Then cut the words apart to form magnetic vocabulary tiles. **Figure A**

3 Cut the paint chips into smaller squares, each approximately $1\frac{1}{4}$ inches by $1\frac{1}{4}$ inches.

4 Glue a small piece of construction paper onto the lid of the metal box. Label it with the number and title of the chapter. **Figure B**

5 Store the vocabulary tiles and the small squares in the metal box.

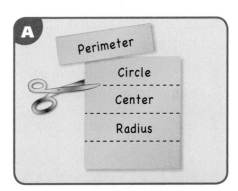

Putting the Math into Action

Place the vocabulary tiles on the outside of the box or on another metal surface to review key terms from the chapter. Arrange the small squares to form shapes with various perimeters. What is the greatest perimeter you can make?

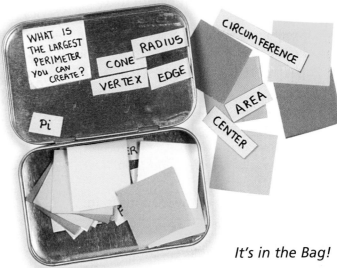

Study Guide: Review

Multi–Language Glossary

THINK central

Go to thinkcentral.com

Vocabulary

Complete the sentences below with vocabulary words from the list above.

1. The distance around a polygon is called the ___?___ , and the distance around a circle is called the ___?___.

2. A line segment that passes through the center of a circle and has both endpoints on the circle is a ___?___.

3. The ___?___ is the measurement system often used in the United States.

EXAMPLES

EXERCISES

8-1 **Understanding Customary Units of Measure** (pp. 352–355)

 **Prep MA.6.A.2.2**

■ **What unit of measure provides the best estimate? Explain.**

A desk is about 3 ___?___ long.
Think: The length of a desk is about 3 times the distance from your elbow to your wrist.
A desk is about 3 ft long.

■ **Measure the length of the arrow to the nearest half, fourth, or eighth inch.**

The arrow is between $1\frac{1}{4}$ and $1\frac{3}{8}$ in. It is closer to $1\frac{3}{8}$.
The length of the arrow is about $1\frac{3}{8}$ in.

What unit of measure provides the best estimate? Explain.

4. A crayon is about 5 ___?___ long.

5. The distance from Denver, CO, to Dallas, TX, is about 800 ___?___.

6. A bunch of bananas weighs about 2 ___?___.

7. An eyedropper holds about 1 ___?___ of liquid.

8. Measure the length of the arrow to the nearest half, fourth, or eighth inch.

8-2 Understanding Metric Units of Measure (pp. 356–359)

 **Prep MA.6.A.2.2**

- **What unit of measure provides the best estimate? Explain.**

  A sofa is about 3 ___?___ long.

  Think: The length of a sofa is about 3 times the width of a single bed.

  A sofa is about 3 m long.

- **Measure the length of the arrow to the nearest centimeter.**

  The arrow is between 2 and 3 cm. It is closer to 2 cm.

  The length of the arrow is about 2 cm.

What unit of measure provides the best estimate? Explain.

9. A paper clip is about 32 ___?___ long.

10. A grain of rice has a mass of about 5 ___?___.

11. A laptop computer has a mass of about 2 ___?___.

12. A large pitcher has a capacity of about 2 ___?___.

13. Measure the length of the arrow to the nearest centimeter.

8-3 Converting Customary Units (pp. 360–363)

MA.6.A.2.1, MA.6.A.2.2, MA.6.A.3.6

- **Convert 5 yards to feet.**

  Set up a conversion factor.

  $5 \text{ yd} \times \dfrac{3 \text{ ft}}{1 \text{ yd}}$

  Think: yards to feet. 3 ft = 1 yd, so use the rate $\dfrac{3 \text{ ft}}{1 \text{ yd}}$. Multiply 5 yd by the conversion factor. Cancel the common unit, yd.

  5 yd = 15 ft

Convert.

14. 3 mi to feet

15. 18 ft to yards

16. 3 qt to cups

17. 48 c to gallons

18. 128 oz to pounds

19. 8,000 lb to tons

20. $\dfrac{64 \text{ oz}}{x \text{ lb}} = \dfrac{16 \text{ oz}}{1 \text{ lb}}$

21. $\dfrac{12 \text{ ft}}{x \text{ in.}} = \dfrac{1 \text{ ft}}{12 \text{ in.}}$

22. $\dfrac{8 \text{ pt}}{x \text{ qt}} = \dfrac{2 \text{ pt}}{1 \text{ qt}}$

23. $\dfrac{3 \text{ ft}}{1 \text{ yd}} = \dfrac{x \text{ ft}}{33 \text{ yd}}$

24. The Golden Gate Bridge, in San Francisco, has a tower height of 750 ft. How many yards tall is this?

8-4 Converting Metric Units (pp. 364–367)

MA.6.A.2.1, MA.6.A.2.2

- **Convert.**

  29 cm = m

  $29 \text{ cm} \cdot \dfrac{1 \text{ m}}{100 \text{ cm}}$

  Think: 1 m = 100 cm, so use the rate $\dfrac{1 \text{ m}}{100 \text{ cm}}$. Multiply 29 by the conversion factor. Cancel the common unit, cm.

  29 cm = 0.29 m

Convert.

25. 3.2 L = mL

26. 7 mL = ▮ L

27. 342 m = ▮ km

28. 42 g = ▮ kg

29. 51 mm = ▮ m

30. 71 km = ▮ m

31. The heaviest pumpkin ever grown had a mass of 681.296 kg. How many grams is this?

8-5 Time and Temperature (pp. 368–371)

MA.6.A.2.1, MA.6.A.2.2, MA.6.A.3.4

- **Convert.**

  14 hours = ▨ minutes

  $14 \cancel{h} \cdot \dfrac{60 \text{ min}}{1 \cancel{h}}$ *1 h = 60 min, so use the rate $\frac{60 \text{ min}}{1 \text{ h}}$.*

  14 hours = 840 minutes

Convert.

32. 3,600 seconds = ▨ hours

33. 990 minutes = ▨ seconds

34. 15 weeks = ▨ days

35. Ariel arrived in Boston at 2:33 P.M. after a 2 hour 23 minute bus trip. At what time did Ariel's bus depart?

- **Estimate the temperature.**

  78 °F is about ▨ °C.

  $C = \frac{5}{9}(F - 32)$ *Round $\frac{5}{9}$ to $\frac{1}{2}$ and 32 to 30.*

  $C \approx \frac{1}{2}(78 - 30)$

  $C \approx \frac{1}{2}(48)$

  $C \approx 24$

  78 °F is about 24 °C.

Estimate the temperature.

36. 41 °F is about ▨ °C.

37. 32 °C is about ▨ °F.

38. 122 °F is about ▨ °C.

8-6 Perimeter (pp. 374–377)

MA.6.A.3.4, MA.6.G.4.2

- **Find the perimeter of the figure.**

  Add all the side lengths.

  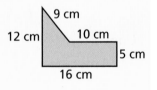

  $P = 9 + 10 + 5 + 16 + 12 = 52$
  The perimeter is 52 cm.

Find the perimeter of each figure.

39.

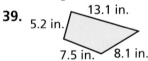

13.1 in.
5.2 in.
7.5 in.   8.1 in.

40.

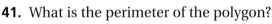

$3\frac{1}{2}$ cm

$1\frac{1}{2}$ cm

41. What is the perimeter of the polygon?

4 ft   1 ft
3 ft   1 ft   3 ft
        1 ft
          n

8-7 Circles and Circumference (pp. 378–381)

MA.6.G.4.1, MA.6.G.4.2

- **Find the circumference of the circle. Use 3.14 for π.**

  $C = \pi d$

  $C \approx 3.14 \cdot 6$

  $C \approx 18.84$ cm

  $d = 6$ cm

Find each missing value. Use 3.14 for π.

42. $d = 10$ ft; $C = \underline{\ ?\ }$ **43.** $C = 28.26$ m; $d = \underline{\ ?\ }$

44. $r = 8$ cm; $C = \underline{\ ?\ }$ **45.** $C = 69.08$ ft; $r = \underline{\ ?\ }$

Measure the length of each line segment to the nearest half, fourth, or eighth inch.

1. •———————•

2. •————————————————•

What metric unit of measure provides the best estimate? Explain.

3. A flower pot can hold about 1 __?__ of water.

4. A baby bird has a mass of about 15 __?__.

5. The length of a cricket is about 3 __?__ long.

Use the table for Problems 6–8.

6. If Darian was moved to the nursery at 2:25 P.M., how long was he in the hospital room?

7. Convert Darian's weight to ounces.

8. How long was Darian in inches?

Baby Darian Cole	
Birth Date	May 1, 2005, 11:45 A.M.
Weight	7 lb
Length	1 ft 8 in.

9. Jerry lives 2.9 kilometers from his school. How many total meters does Jerry walk to and from school each day?

Estimate the temperature.

10. 48 °C is about ▮ °F.

11. 70 °F is about ▮ °C.

Find the perimeter of each figure.

12.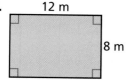
12 m / 8 m

13.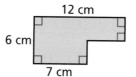
12 cm / 6 cm / 7 cm

14.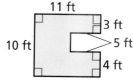
11 ft / 3 ft / 5 ft / 10 ft / 4 ft

Name the circle, a chord, and two radii, and then find the circumference for each circle. Use 3.14 for π.

15.
$2\frac{1}{2}$ m

16.
10 in.

17.
9 cm

Find each missing value. Use 3.14 for π.

18. $r = 4$ cm; $C =$ __?__

19. $d = 10$ ft; $C =$ __?__

20. $C = 37.68$ ft; $d =$ __?__

21. A gardener is digging a rose garden. Estimate the circumference of the rose garden by rounding π to 3.

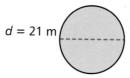
$d = 21$ m

Mastering the Standards

Cumulative Assessment, Chapters 1–8

Multiple Choice

1. Which value is best represented by the letter *B* on the number line below?

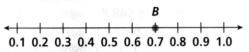

B

0.1 0.2 0.3 0.4 0.5 0.6 0.7 0.8 0.9 1.0

  A. 0.07   **C.** 7%

  B. $\frac{77}{11}$ **D.** $\frac{7}{10}$

2. Circle *S* has a radius of 3 inches. Circle *T* has a radius of 9 inches. What is $\dfrac{\text{Circumference of Circle } S}{\text{Circumference of Circle } T}$?

  F. $\frac{1}{3}$ **H.** $\frac{\pi}{3}$

  G. $\frac{1}{2}$ **I.** $\frac{\pi}{2}$

3. Savannah multiplied a whole number greater than 1 by a positive fraction less than 1. Which of the following describes the product?

  A. equal to 1

  B. less than the fraction

  C. less than the whole number

  D. greater than the whole number

4. In 2002, the U.S. Census reported that 37.4 million Latinos were living in the United States. Approximately 3.2 million of these Latinos were from Puerto Rico. What percent of the Latino population in 2002 came from Puerto Rico?

  F. 0.086%   **H.** 8.6%

  G. 0.86%   **I.** 86%

5. The length of each side of a square garden plot is 3*w* meters. The perimeter of the plot is 30 meters. What is the value of *w*?

  A. $w = 2.5$ **C.** $w = 5$

  B. $w = 3.\overline{3}$ **D.** $w = 10$

6. An online survey by Kids' Money asked children to share how much money they receive for an allowance. The results from 6- to 12-year-olds are shown below. If the survey asked the same number of children at each age, what is the average allowance for children between the ages of 8 and 12?

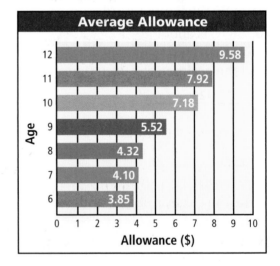

Average Allowance

  F. $6.06   **H.** $7.18

  G. $6.90   **I.** $8.49

7. Shelly has a bookshelf that is $48\frac{3}{4}$ inches long. If Shelly's textbooks are each $3\frac{1}{2}$ inches wide, how many books can Shelly fit on a shelf?

  A. 15 books   **C.** 13 books

  B. 14 books   **D.** 12 books

Mastering the Standards

8. The median price of six dresses is $66. Five of the prices are $49, $72, $75, $49, and $60. Which of the following CANNOT be the price of the sixth dress?

F. $94   **H.** $72

G. $73   **I.** $56

9. The ratio of boys to girls on a soccer team is $\frac{4}{1}$. There are 15 children on the soccer team. How many team members are girls?

A. 3   **C.** 8

B. 5   **D.** 12

 When using a conversion factor, write the unit you are converting to in the numerator and the unit you are converting from in the denominator.

Gridded Response

10. In 1912, a reticulated python was found to be 10.7 meters long. How many centimeters long was this snake?

11. Patrick and Colin played two sets of tennis. The first set lasted $1\frac{1}{4}$ hours. The second set lasted $1\frac{2}{3}$ hours. How many minutes longer was the second set than the first set?

12. Abby has a piece of ribbon that is $3\frac{1}{2}$ feet long. She cuts off a piece that is $1\frac{1}{4}$ feet long. How many $\frac{1}{4}$-foot pieces can Abby make from the remaining piece of ribbon?

13. Samuel bought apples that cost $2.45 per pound. He spent a total of $6.86 on the apples. How many pounds of apples did he buy?

14. Jessie is $1\frac{1}{2}$ times taller than her sister. If her sister is 4 feet tall, how many inches taller is Jessie than her sister?

Short Response

S1. Gene and Janice's gas tanks are empty. It cost Gene $74.27 to fill up his 25.7-gallon gas tank. At another gas station, Janice filled up her 13.8-gallon tank and paid $39.60. Who paid the most for a gallon of gas? Justify your answer.

S2. Jacob, Kelly, Renee, and Terrance ate lunch at a restaurant. The total amount of the bill was $48.80. Jacob paid $\frac{1}{4}$ of the bill, Kelly paid 20% of the bill, Renee paid $14.00, and Terrance paid the rest of the bill. How much money did each person pay for lunch? Who paid the most?

S3. A regulation football field is a rectangle that is 160 feet wide and 360 feet long. These dimensions include the end zones.

a. What is the perimeter of a regulation football field in yards? Show your work.

b. A football field has two end zones of equal length at the end of each side of the playing field. If the playing field is 100 yards long, how many inches long is one end zone? Show your work.

Extended Response

E1. Teresa is planning to build a stone border around a large walnut tree. The stones are 6 inches long.

a. How many stones will Teresa need if she creates a square border that is 8 feet long on a side? Show your work.

b. How many stones will Teresa need if she creates a circular border that has an 8-foot diameter? Use $\frac{22}{7}$ for π. Show your work.

c. If the stones cost $2.69 each, how much money will Teresa save if she builds a circular border instead of a square border? Justify your answer.

Measurement: Area and Volume

Worktext
pages 375–426

Additional instruction, practice, and
activities are available online, including:

- Lesson Tutorial Videos
- Homework Help
- Animated Math

THINK central

Go to **thinkcentral.com**

Why Learn This?

The panoramic window at the Florida
Aquarium allows for spectacular views
of the coral reef and its inhabitants. The
acrylic window is a rectangular prism
that is 42 feet wide, 14 feet tall, and
1 foot thick.

The Florida Aquarium
Tampa

Chapter Focus
- Solve problems that involve
  lengths, areas, and volumes.
- Use fractions and decimals to
  solve measurement problems.

Are You Ready?

Are You Ready?
Go to thinkcentral.com

✓ Vocabulary

Choose the best term from the list to complete each sentence.

1. A(n) ___?___ is a quadrilateral with opposite sides that are parallel and congruent.

2. Some customary units of length are ___?___ and ___?___. Some metric units of length are ___?___ and ___?___.

3. A(n) ___?___ is a quadrilateral with side lengths that are all congruent and four right angles.

4. A(n) ___?___ is a polygon with six sides.

centimeters
cube
feet
hexagon
inches
liters
meters
parallelogram
square
trapezoid

Complete these exercises to review skills you will need for this chapter.

✓ Add and Multiply Whole Numbers, Fractions, and Decimals

Find each sum or product.

5. $1.5 + 2.4 + 3.6 + 2.5$

6. $2 \cdot 3.5 \cdot 4$

7. $\frac{22}{7} \cdot 21$

8. $\frac{1}{2} \cdot 5 \cdot 4$

9. $3.2 \cdot 5.6$

10. $\frac{1}{2} \cdot 10 \cdot 3$

11. $(2 \cdot 5) + (6 \cdot 8)$

12. $2(3.5) + 2(1.5)$

13. $9(20 + 7)$

✓ Measure with Metric Units

Use a centimeter ruler to measure each line to the nearest centimeter.

14.

15. ——————————

✓ Identify Polygons

Name each polygon. Determine whether it appears to be regular or not regular.

16.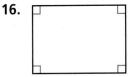

17.
2 cm

18.
2 cm   3 cm

Study Guide: Preview

Before

Previously, you

- selected appropriate units to measure perimeter, area, and volume.
- classified polygons.
- identified three-dimensional figures.

Now

You will study

- solving problems involving area.
- identifying, drawing, and building three-dimensional figures.
- finding the area of circles and composite figures.
- finding the volume of prisms and cylinders.

Why?

You can use the skills learned in this chapter

- to find the volume of pyramids, cones, and spheres.
- to find the surface area of spheres.

Key Vocabulary/Vocabulario

area	área
base	base (de un polígono o figura tridimensional)
cylinder	cilindro
edge	arista
face	cara
polyhedron	poliedro
pyramid	pirámide
surface area	área total
vertex	vértice
volume	volumen

Vocabulary Connections

To become familiar with some of the vocabulary terms in the chapter, consider the following. You may refer to the chapter, the glossary, or a dictionary if you like.

1. The word *cylinder* comes from the Greek *kylindein,* meaning "to roll." What do you think the three-dimensional shape of a **cylinder** can do? What shape base do you expect it to have?

2. The word *polyhedron* comes from the Greek *polys,* meaning "many" and *hedra,* meaning "base." What do you think **polyhedrons** are made up of?

3. The Egyptian pyramids are huge stone structures whose outside walls, in the form of four triangles, meet in a point at the top. What shapes do you think make up a **pyramid**?

4. The word *vertex* can mean "highest point." Where do you think you can find one **vertex** of a three-dimensional figure?

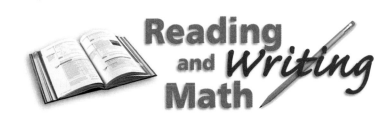 Reading and Writing Math

Reading Strategy: Learn Math Vocabulary

LA.6.1.6.5 The student will relate new vocabulary to familiar words.

Many new math terms fill the pages of your textbook. By learning these new terms and their meanings when they are introduced, you will be able to apply this knowledge to different concepts throughout your math classes.

Some ways that may help you learn vocabulary include the following:

- Try to find the meaning of the new term by its context.
- Use the prefix or suffix to figure out the meaning of the term.
- Relate the new term to familiar everyday words or situations.

Vocabulary Word	Definition	Study Tip
Origin	The point (0, 0) where the *x*-axis and *y*-axis intersect on the coordinate plane	The word begins with an "O" which can remind you that the coordinates of the origin are (0, 0).
Quadrants	The *x*- and *y*- axis divide the coordinate plane into four regions. Each region is called a quadrant.	The prefix *quad* means "four." A *quadrilateral* is a four-sided figure, for example.
Coordinate	One of the numbers of an ordered pair that locate a point on a coordinate graph	*Think: x* coordinates with *y*.

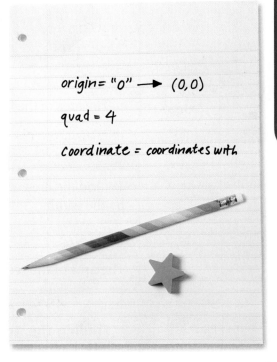

origin = "o" → (0,0)

quad = 4

coordinate = coordinates with

Try This

Complete the table as you work through the chapter to help you learn the vocabulary words.

	Vocabulary Word	Definition	Study Tip
1.	Area		
2.			
3.			

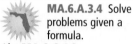

MA.6.A.3.4 Solve problems given a formula.
Also **MA.6.G.4.2**

When colonists settled the land that would become the United States, ownership boundaries were sometimes natural landmarks such as rivers, trees, and hills. Landowners who wanted to know the size of their property needed to estimate the area of their land.

Vocabulary
area

The **area** of a figure is the amount of surface it covers. We measure area in square units.

EXAMPLE 1 **Estimating the Area of an Irregular Figure**

Estimate the area of the figure.

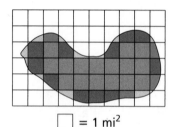

☐ = 1 mi²

Count full squares: 16 red squares.

Count almost-full squares: 11 blue squares.

Count squares that are about half-full:
4 green squares ≈ 2 full squares.

Do not count almost empty yellow squares.

Add. 16 + 11 + 2 = 29

The area of the figure is about 29 mi².

AREA OF A RECTANGLE

To find the area of a rectangle, multiply the length by the width.

$$A = \ell w$$
$$A = 4 \cdot 3 = 12$$

The area of the rectangle is 12 square units.

EXAMPLE 2 **Finding the Area of a Rectangle**

Find the area of the rectangle.

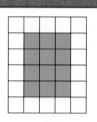

13 m
8 m

$A = \ell w$	*Write the formula.*
$A = 13 \cdot 8$	*Substitute 13 for ℓ and 8 for w.*
$A = 104$	*Multiply.*

The area is 104 m².

You can use the formula for the area of a rectangle to write a formula for the area of a parallelogram. Imagine cutting off the triangle drawn in the parallelogram and sliding it to the right to form a rectangle.

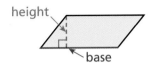

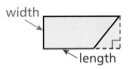

The area of a parallelogram = *bh*.   The area of a rectangle = *ℓw*.

The **base** of the parallelogram is the **length** of the rectangle.
The **height** of the parallelogram is the **width** of the rectangle.

EXAMPLE 3   **Finding the Area of a Parallelogram**

Find the area of the parallelogram.

$3\frac{1}{2}$ in.

$2\frac{1}{3}$ in.

$A = bh$	*Write the formula.*
$A = 2\frac{1}{3} \cdot 3\frac{1}{2}$	*Substitute $2\frac{1}{3}$ for b and $3\frac{1}{2}$ for h.*
$A = \frac{7}{3} \cdot \frac{7}{2}$	*Multiply.*
$A = \frac{49}{6}$, or $8\frac{1}{6}$	*The area is $8\frac{1}{6}$ in².*

EXAMPLE 4   **Recreation Application**

A rectangular park is made up of a rectangular spring-fed pool and a limestone picnic ground that surrounds it. The rectangular park is 30 yd by 25 yd, and the pool is 10 yd by 4 yd. What is the area of the limestone picnic ground?

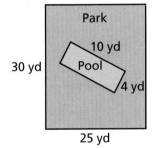

To find the area of the picnic ground, subtract the area of the pool from the area of the park.

park area	−	pool area	=	picnic ground area	
$(30 \cdot 25)$	−	$(10 \cdot 4)$	=	n	*Substitute for ℓ and w in $A = \ell w$.*
750	−	40	=	710	*Use the order of operations.*

The area of the limestone picnic ground is 710 yd².

Think and Discuss

1. Explain how the area of a rectangle can be found using the formula for the area of a parallelogram.

2. Give a formula for the area of a square.

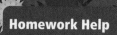
Homework Help THINK central

Go to thinkcentral.com
Exercises 1–20, 25

MA.6.A.3.4

GUIDED PRACTICE

See Example **1** **Estimate the area of each figure.**

1.

2.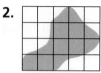

3.

See Example **2** **Find the area of each rectangle.**

4.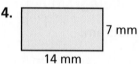
7 mm
14 mm

5.
13 in.
7.7 in.

6.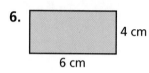
4 cm
6 cm

See Example **3** **Find the area of each parallelogram.**

7.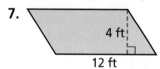
4 ft
12 ft

8. $2\frac{1}{3}$ cm
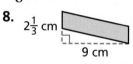
9 cm

9.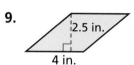
2.5 in.
4 in.

See Example **4** **10.** Mindy is designing a rectangular fountain in a courtyard. The rest of the courtyard will be covered with stone. The rectangular courtyard is 12 ft by 15 ft. What is the area of the courtyard that will be covered with stone?

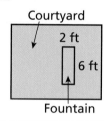
Courtyard
2 ft
6 ft
Fountain

INDEPENDENT PRACTICE

See Example **1** **Estimate the area of each figure.**

11.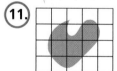

12.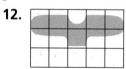

13.

See Example **2** **Find the area of each rectangle.**

14.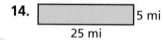
5 mi
25 mi

15.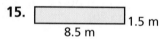
1.5 m
8.5 m

16.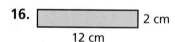
2 cm
12 cm

See Example **3** **Find the area of each parallelogram.**

17.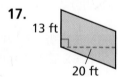
13 ft
20 ft

18.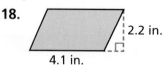
2.2 in.
4.1 in.

19.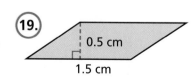
0.5 cm
1.5 cm

See Example **4** **20.** Bob is planting in a rectangular container. In the center of the container, he places a smaller rectangular tub with mint. The tub is 8 in. by 3 in. He plants flowers around the tub. What is the area of the container planted with flowers?

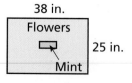
38 in.
Flowers
25 in.
Mint

○ = **WORKED-OUT SOLUTIONS**
on p. WS10

Iceland has many active volcanoes and frequent earthquakes. There are more hot springs in Iceland than in any other country in the world.

Use the map for Exercises 21 and 22.

21. **Choose a Strategy** One square on the map represents 1,700 km². Which is a reasonable estimate for the area of Iceland?

    A. Less than 65,000 km²
    B. Between 90,000 and 105,000 km²
    C. Between 120,000 and 135,000 km²
    D. Greater than 150,000 km²

22. **Estimation** About 10% of the area of Iceland is covered with glaciers. Estimate the area covered by glaciers.

23. **Write About It** The House is Iceland's oldest building. When it was built in 1765, the builders measured length in *ells*. The base of the House is 14 ells wide and 20 ells long. Explain how to find the area in ells of the House.

24. **Challenge** The length of one ell varied from country to country. In England, one ell was equal to $1\frac{1}{4}$ yd. Suppose the House were measured in English ells. Find the area in yards of the House.

Florida Spiral Review   MA.6.A.3.4, MA.6.A.1.2, MA.6.A.3.2

14 ft

25. **Multiple Choice** A small square is inside a larger square. The larger square is 14 feet long. The smaller square is 2 feet long. What is the area of the shaded region?

□ 2 ft

    A. 52 ft²   **B.** 192 ft²   **C.** 196 ft²   **D.** 200 ft²

26. **Multiple Choice** Find the area of a rectangle with length 3 in. and width 12 in.

    F. 9 in²   **G.** 18 in²   **H.** 36 in²   **I.** 144 in²

27. A tree casts a shadow that is 14 feet long. The shadow is twice the length of the tree. How tall is the tree? (Lesson 2-8)

Divide. Write each answer in simplest form. (Lesson 5-8)

28. $2\frac{2}{3} \div \frac{1}{2}$ 29. $3\frac{1}{2} \div 1\frac{1}{3}$ 30. $4 \div \frac{5}{6}$ 31. $\frac{9}{10} \div 3$

Area of Triangles and Trapezoids

MA.6.A.3.4 Solve problems given a formula.
Also **MA.6.G.4.2, MA.6.G.4.3**

The Flatiron Building in New York City was built in 1902. Many people consider it to be New York's first skyscraper. The foundation of the building is shaped like a triangle. You can find the area of the triangle to find how much land the building occupies.

You can divide any parallelogram into two congruent triangles. The area of each triangle is half the area of the parallelogram.

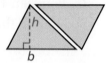

AREA OF A TRIANGLE

The area A of a triangle is half the product of its base b and its height h.

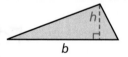

$$A = \tfrac{1}{2}bh$$

When the legs of a triangle meet at a 90° angle, the lengths of the legs can be used as the base and height.

EXAMPLE **1**   **Finding the Area of a Triangle**

Find the area of each triangle.

Reading Math

An altitude of a triangle is a perpendicular segment from one vertex to the line containing the opposite side. The length of the altitude is the height.

A
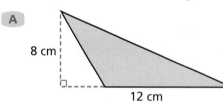

8 cm
12 cm

$A = \tfrac{1}{2}bh$ *Write the formula.*
$A = \tfrac{1}{2}(12 \cdot 8)$ *Substitute 12 for b.*
  Substitute 8 for h.
$A = \tfrac{1}{2}(96)$ *Multiply.*
$A = 48$

The area is 48 cm².

B
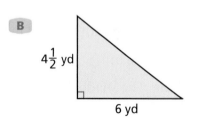

$4\tfrac{1}{2}$ yd
6 yd

$A = \tfrac{1}{2}bh$ *Write the formula.*
$A = \tfrac{1}{2}\left(6 \cdot 4\tfrac{1}{2}\right)$ *Substitute 6 for b.*
  Substitute $4\tfrac{1}{2}$ for h.
$A = \tfrac{1}{2}(27)$ *Multiply.*
$A = 13\tfrac{1}{2}$

The area is $13\tfrac{1}{2}$ yd².

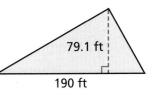

E X A M P L E **2** **Architecture Application**

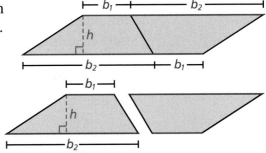

The diagram shows the outline of the foundation of the Flatiron Building. What is the area of the foundation?

$A = \frac{1}{2}bh$ *Write the formula.*

$A = \frac{1}{2}(190 \cdot 79.1)$ *Substitute 190 for b. Substitute 79.1 for h.*

$A = \frac{1}{2}(15,029) = 7,514.5$ *Multiply.*

The area of the foundation is 7,514.5 ft².

You can divide a parallelogram into two congruent trapezoids. The area of each trapezoid is half the area of the parallelogram.

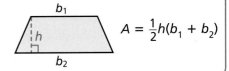

AREA OF A TRAPEZOID

The area *A* of a trapezoid is half the product of its height *h* and the sum of its bases b_1 and b_2.

$A = \frac{1}{2}h(b_1 + b_2)$

E X A M P L E **3** **Finding the Area of a Trapezoid**

Find the area of the trapezoid.

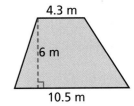

$A = \frac{1}{2}h(b_1 + b_2)$ *Write the formula.*

$A = \frac{1}{2}(6)(4.3 + 10.5)$ *Substitute 6 for h, 4.3 for b_1, and 10.5 for b_2.*

$A = \frac{1}{2}(6)(14.8) = 44.4$ *Multiply.*

The area is 44.4 m².

Think and Discuss

1. Explain how the areas of a triangle and a parallelogram with the same base and height are related.

2. Explain whether this is correct: To find the area of a trapezoid, multiply the height by the top base and the height by the bottom base. Then add the two numbers together and divide the sum by 2.

Exercises

MA.6.A.3.4

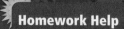 Homework Help
 THINK central
Go to thinkcentral.com
Exercises 1–15, 17, 19, 21

GUIDED PRACTICE

See Example **1** Find the area of each triangle.

1.

2 yd
3 yd

2.

11 cm
6 cm

3.
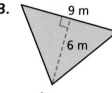
9 m
6 m

See Example **2** **4.** Harry plans to paint the triangular portion of the side of his house. How many square feet does he need to paint?

8 ft
20 ft

See Example **3** Find the area of each trapezoid.

5.
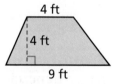
4 ft
4 ft
9 ft

6.
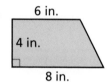
6 in.
4 in.
8 in.

7.
15 cm
8 cm
7 cm

INDEPENDENT PRACTICE

See Example **1** Find the area of each triangle.

8.

8 m
9.25 m

9.
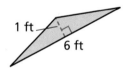
1 ft
6 ft

10.
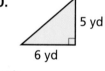
5 yd
6 yd

See Example **2** **11.** Sean is making pennants for the school football team. How many square inches of felt does he use for one pennant?

8 in.
18 in.

12. Erin has a triangular garden plot that is 5 meters long and 3 meters tall. What is the area of the plot?

See Example **3** Find the area of each trapezoid.

13.
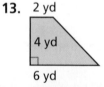
2 yd
4 yd
6 yd

14.

16 in.
12 in.
21 in.

15.
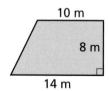
10 m
8 m
14 m

PRACTICE AND PROBLEM SOLVING

16. The water in a drainage canal is 4 feet deep. What is the area of a cross section of the water in the ditch, which is shaped like a trapezoid?

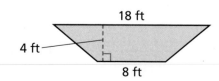
18 ft
4 ft
8 ft

Social Studies

Nevada has many ghost towns scattered around the state. Many were once boom-towns built during the gold and silver mining rush.

For Exercises 17–21, find the area of each figure.

17.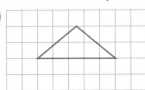

18.

19.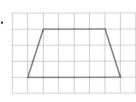

20. triangle: $b = 2\frac{1}{2}$ in.; $h = 1\frac{3}{4}$ in. **21.** trapezoid: $b_1 = 18$ m; $b_2 = 27$ m; $h = 15.4$ m

22. Social Studies The shape of the state of Nevada is similar to a trapezoid with the measurements shown. Estimate the area of the state in square miles.

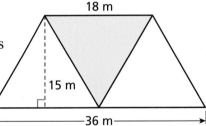

320 mi

198 mi

490 mi

23. Critical Thinking The areas and heights of a triangle and a rectangle are the same. How do the lengths of their bases compare?

Find the missing measurement for each figure.

24. Area = 16 in²

3 in.

h

5 in.

25. Area = 5 cm²

2 cm

b

26. Area = 18 m²

h

6 m

27. Write a Problem Write a problem about a trapezoid with bases 12 ft and 18 ft and height 10 ft.

28. Write About It Two triangles have the same base length. The height of one triangle is half the height of the other. How do the areas of the triangles compare?

29. Challenge Find the area of the unshaded portion of the trapezoid.

18 m

15 m

36 m

30. Multiple Choice A building sign in the shape of a trapezoid has the measurements shown. Which expression can be used to find the area of the sign?

10 ft

11 ft

18 ft

A. $\frac{1}{2}(11)(10 + 18)$ **B.** $\frac{1}{2}(18)(10)$ **C.** $\frac{1}{2}(11)(10)(18)$ **D.** $(11)(10 + 18)$

31. Gridded Response Find the area, in square centimeters, of a right triangle with legs measuring 14 cm and 25 cm.

Multiply. Write each answer in simplest form. (Lesson 5-5)

32. $3 \cdot \frac{2}{7}$ **33.** $4 \cdot \frac{3}{5}$ **34.** $12 \cdot \frac{9}{10}$ **35.** $15 \cdot \frac{1}{2}$

36. Zeb earned $24,000 last year. This year, his salary increased by 5%. How much will he earn? (Lesson 7-6)

9-3 Area of Circles

MA.6.G.4.1
. . . Estimate and
calculate . . . the
area of circles.
Also MA.6.A.3.4

In medieval times, circular shields were usually made from wood that was covered with leather or steel. The amount of leather or steel needed to cover a shield depended upon the shield's area.

AREA OF A CIRCLE

The area of a circle is equal to π times the radius squared.

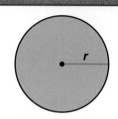

$$A = \pi r^2$$

You can estimate the area of a circle by using 3 to approximate the value of π.

EXAMPLE 1 **Estimating the Area of a Circle**

Estimate the area of each circle. Use 3 to approximate π.

A

6 in.

$A = \pi r^2$	*Write the formula for the area.*
$A \approx 3 \cdot 6^2$	*Replace π with 3 and r with 6.*
$A \approx 3 \cdot 36$	*Use the order of operations.*
$A \approx 108\ \text{in}^2$	*Multiply.*

B

50.4 m

$A = \pi r^2$	*Write the formula for the area.*
$r = d \div 2$	*The length of the radius is half the*
$r = 50.4 \div 2$	*length of the diameter.*
$r = 25.2$	*Divide.*
$r \approx 25$	*Round 25.2 to 25.*
$A \approx 3 \cdot 25^2$	*Replace π with 3 and r with 25.*
$A \approx 3 \cdot 625$	*Use the order of operations.*
$A \approx 1,875\ \text{m}^2$	*Multiply.*

EXAMPLE 2 **Using the Formula for the Area of a Circle**

Find the area of each circle. Use $\frac{22}{7}$ for π.

A

14 in.

$A = \pi r^2$ *Write the formula for the area.*

$r = d \div 2$ *The length of the radius is half*

$r = 14 \div 2$ *the length of the diameter.*

$r = 7$ *Divide.*

$A \approx \frac{22}{7} \cdot 7^2$ *Replace π with $\frac{22}{7}$ and r with 7.*

$A \approx \frac{22}{\cancel{7}_1} \cdot \overset{7}{\cancel{49}}$ *Use the GCF to simplify.*

$A \approx 154 \text{ in}^2$ *Multiply.*

B

21 cm

$A = \pi r^2$ *Write the formula for the area.*

$A \approx \frac{22}{7} \cdot 21^2$ *Replace π with $\frac{22}{7}$ and r with 21.*

$A \approx \frac{22}{7} \cdot 441$ *Use the order of operations.*

$A \approx \frac{9702}{7}$ *Multiply.*

$A \approx 1386 \text{ cm}^2$ *Divide.*

EXAMPLE 3 *History Application*

Animated Math
@ thinkcentral.com

A circular shield has a diameter of 20 inches. Find the area of the steel needed to cover one side of the shield. Use 3.14 for π.

20 in.

$A = \pi r^2$ *Write the formula for the area.*

$r = d \div 2$ *The length of the radius is half*

$r = 20 \div 2$ *the length of the diameter.*

$r = 10$ *Divide.*

$A \approx 3.14 \cdot 10^2$ *Replace π with 3.14 and r with 10.*

$A \approx 3.14 \cdot 100$ *Use the order of operations.*

$A \approx 314 \text{ in}^2$ *Multiply.*

Check Use 3 as an estimate for π. The area, πr^2, is approximately $3 \cdot 10^2 = 3 \cdot 100 = 300$, so the answer is reasonable.

Think and Discuss

1. **Describe** how you could estimate the area of a circle whose radius is 1 cm.

2. **Explain** why the area of a circle with a radius of 5 ft must be greater than 75 ft^2.

3. **Tell** how you can check that your answer is reasonable after you have calculated the area of a circle.

Homework Help

Go to **thinkcentral.com**
Exercises 1–14, 15, 17, 19

GUIDED PRACTICE

See Example ① **Estimate the area of each circle. Use 3 to approximate π.**

1.
4 ft

2.
8.1 in.

3.
18.2 in.

See Example ② **Find the area of each circle. Use $\frac{22}{7}$ for π.**

4.
7 ft

5.
28 cm

6.
3.5 m

See Example ③ **7. Architecture** A circular window has a diameter of 4 ft. Find the area of the glass needed to fill the window. Use 3.14 for π.

INDEPENDENT PRACTICE

See Example ① **Estimate the area of each circle. Use 3 to approximate π.**

8.
12 m

9.
32.4 in.

10.
6.1 m

See Example ② **Find the area of each circle. Use $\frac{22}{7}$ for π.**

11.
7 yd

12.
77 cm

13.
56 ft

See Example ③ **14. Cooking** A pizza recipe calls for the dough to be rolled out to form a circle with a diameter of 18 in. Find the area of the dough when it is rolled out. Use 3.14 for π.

PRACTICE AND PROBLEM SOLVING

Find the area and circumference of each circle. Use 3.14 for π and round to the nearest hundredth.

15.
5.7 cm

16.
63 ft

17.
14.9 in.

○ = **WORKED-OUT SOLUTIONS**
on p. WS10

Earth Science

Scientists estimate that the asteroid that struck Earth to form Meteor Crater was about 80 ft in diameter.

18. **Sports** The diameter of the circle that a shot-putter stands in is 7 ft. What is the area of the circle? Use $\frac{22}{7}$ for π.

19. **Earth Science** Meteor Crater in central Arizona was formed when an asteroid struck Earth between 20,000 and 50,000 years ago. The circular crater has a diameter of 1.2 km. Find the area of the crater to the nearest hundredth. Use 3.14 for π.

20. **Multi-Step** A restaurant makes pizzas with 6 in. diameters and 12 in. diameters.

   a. Estimate the difference between the areas of the two sizes of pizzas. (Use 3.14 for π. Round to the nearest whole number.)

   b. Is the area of the 12 in. pizza about twice the area of the 6 in. pizza? Explain.

21. **Critical Thinking** The area of a circular garden plot is 30 ft². Explain why the diameter of the plot must be greater than 6 ft.

22. **What's the Error?** A student estimated the area of the purple circle as shown. Explain the student's error.

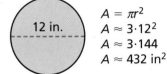

12 in.

$A = \pi r^2$
$A \approx 3 \cdot 12^2$
$A \approx 3 \cdot 144$
$A \approx 432 \text{ in}^2$

23. **Write About It** Describe a step-by-step process you can use to estimate the area of a circle.

24. **Challenge** What is the area of the shaded part of the figure? Use 3.14 for π. Round the answer to the nearest hundredth.

←— 2 m —→

Florida Spiral Review   MA.6.A.1.2, MA.6.A.3.4, MA.6.G.4.1

25. **Multiple Choice** Jerome knows the radius of a baking pan. He needs to estimate the pan's area. Which formula can Jerome use to estimate the area?

   A. $A = 3r$ **C.** $A = 3r^2$

   B. $A = \frac{r^2}{2}$ **D.** $A = (3r)^2$

26. **Gridded Response** Find the area, in square inches, of a circle with a diameter of 10 in. Use 3.14 for π.

Multiply. Write each answer in simplest form. (Lesson 5-6)

27. $\frac{3}{8} \cdot \frac{4}{9}$ 28. $\frac{7}{10} \cdot \frac{3}{14}$ 29. $\frac{8}{9} \cdot \frac{5}{16}$ 30. $\frac{6}{15} \cdot \frac{10}{21}$

31. The ratio of boys to girls in Nigel's history class is 4:5. The ratio of boys to girls in Tanya's biology class is 3:5. Does this mean that Nigel's class has more boys than Tanya's class? Explain. (Lesson 7-2)

Area of Composite Figures

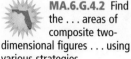

MA.6.G.4.2 Find the . . . areas of composite two-dimensional figures . . . using various strategies.
Also **MA.6.A.3.4**

To determine how many bricks are needed for a patio, you must first find the area of the patio. The patio may be made up of two or more simple shapes.

You can often divide a composite figure into simple shapes. Then add the areas of the simple shapes to find the area of the composite figure.

EXAMPLE **1** **Finding the Area of Composite Figures by Adding**

Find the shaded area. Round to the nearest tenth, if necessary.

A

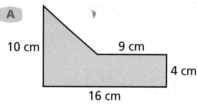

Divide the figure into a triangle and a rectangle.

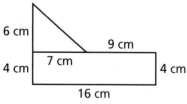

area of triangle:
$A = \frac{1}{2}bh = \frac{1}{2}(7)(6) = 21$ cm^2

area of rectangle:
$A = bh = 16(4) = 64$ cm^2

Add the area of the triangle and the area of the rectangle.

total area:
$A = 21 + 64 = 85$ cm^2

B

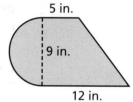

Divide the figure into a semicircle and a trapezoid.

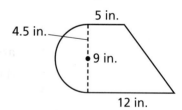

area of semicircle:
$A = \frac{1}{2}\pi r^2 = \frac{1}{2}\pi(4.5)^2$
$\approx \frac{1}{2}(3.14)(20.25) \approx 31.8$ in^2

area of trapezoid:
$A = \frac{1}{2}h(b_1 + b_2) = \frac{1}{2}(9)(5 + 12)$
$= \frac{1}{2}(9)(17) = 76.5$ in^2

Add the area of the semicircle and the area of the trapezoid.

total area:
$A \approx 31.8 + 76.5 = 108.3$ in^2

You can sometimes find the area of a composite figure by subtracting.

EXAMPLE **2** **Finding the Area of Composite Figures by Subtracting**

Find the shaded area.

Subtract the area of the triangle from the area of the rectangle.

area of rectangle:
$A = bh = 14(6) = 84$ m^2

area of triangle:
$A = \frac{1}{2}bh = \frac{1}{2}(5)(4) = 10$ m^2

shaded area:
$A = 84 - 10 = 74$ m^2

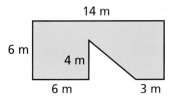

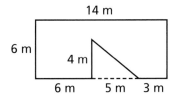

EXAMPLE **3** *Landscaping Application*

An architect is planning a brick patio for a restaurant as shown in the figure. What is the area of the patio? Round to the nearest tenth.

To find the area, divide the composite figure into a trapezoid, a rectangle, and a semicircle.

area of trapezoid:
$A = \frac{1}{2}h(b_1 + b_2) = \frac{1}{2}(8)(24 + 30)$
$= \frac{1}{2}(8)(54) = 216$ ft^2

area of rectangle:
$A = bh = 12(8) = 96$ ft^2

area of semicircle:
$A = \frac{1}{2}\pi r^2 = \frac{1}{2}\pi(6)^2 \approx \frac{1}{2}(3.14)(36) \approx 56.5$ ft^2

area of patio:
$A \approx 216 + 96 + 56.5 = 368.5$ ft^2

The area of the patio is approximately 368.5 ft^2.

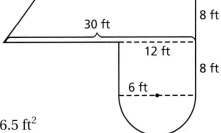

Think and Discuss

1. Describe a different way to divide the figure in Example 1A.

2. Explain how you can find the area of a trapezoid using composite figures.

Exercises

MA.6.G.4.2

GUIDED PRACTICE

See Example 1   **Find the shaded area. Round to the nearest tenth, if necessary.**

1.
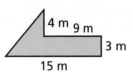

2.
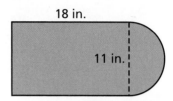

See Example 2   **3.**
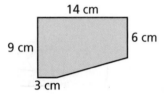

4.
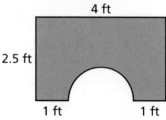

See Example 3   **5. Hobbies** Catherine makes hearts out of fabric by sewing two semicircles onto a triangle as shown. How much fabric is needed to make each heart? Round to the nearest tenth.

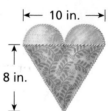

INDEPENDENT PRACTICE

See Example 1   **Find the shaded area. Round to the nearest tenth, if necessary.**

6.
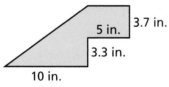

7.
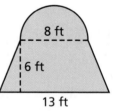

See Example 2   **8.**
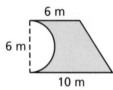

9.
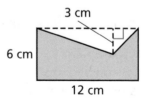

See Example 3   **10.** Derrick takes a rectangular piece of paper and cuts four congruent triangles from the corners as shown. Find the area of the remaining piece of paper.

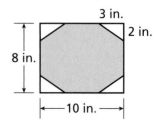

◯ = **WORKED-OUT SOLUTIONS**
on p. WS10

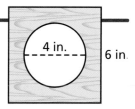

11. A carpenter cuts out a circle from a square piece of wood as shown. What is the area of the remaining piece of wood? Round to the nearest tenth.

12. **Multi-Step** The Wilson family is putting new wall-to-wall carpet in their living room. The figure shows the dimensions of the room. Carpeting costs $12 per square yard. How much will it cost to carpet the room?

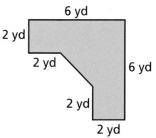

13. **Reasoning** The purple figure has an area of 100 in². What is the value of x?

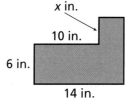

 14. **Write a Problem** Draw a figure that can be divided into a rectangle and a triangle. Label the lengths of the sides. Explain how you can find the area of the figure. Then find the area.

 15. **Write About It** Describe two different ways to find the area of the yellow figure. Do both methods give the same result?

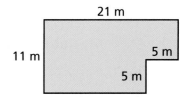

16. **Challenge** Find the area of the blue figure.

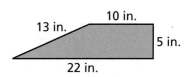

Florida Spiral Review   MA.6.G.4.2, MA.6.A.5.2, MA.6.G.4.1

17. **Multiple Choice** A right triangle is removed from a rectangle as shown. Find the area of the shaded figure.

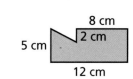

   A. 52 cm²   **B.** 56 cm²   **C.** 64 cm²   **D.** 72 cm²

18. **Multiple Choice** The figure shows a plan for a flower bed. Which of the following is the best estimate for the area of the flower bed?

   F. 40 ft²   **G.** 46 ft²   **H.** 52 ft²   **I.** 88 ft²

19. Four friends share two pizzas. Tom eats 37.5% of all the pizza. Nadia eats half of one pizza. Fred eats $\frac{5}{16}$ of all the pizza. Marie eats the rest of the pizza. Order the friends from who eats the least to the most pizza. (Lesson 7-5)

20. A circle has a circumference of 10π cm. What is its radius? (Lesson 8-7)

Quiz for Lessons 9-1 Through 9-4

9-1 Area of Rectangles and Parallelograms

Find the area of each figure.

1.

41 cm

62 cm

2.

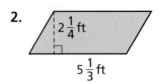

$2\frac{1}{4}$ ft

$5\frac{1}{3}$ ft

3.

6.8 in.

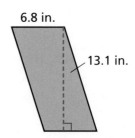

13.1 in.

4. Mark is making a rectangular vegetable garden in his backyard. The rest of the backyard is covered with gravel. What is the area of the backyard that is covered with gravel?

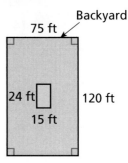

Backyard

75 ft

24 ft   120 ft

15 ft

9-2 Area of Triangles and Trapezoids

Find the area of each figure.

5.

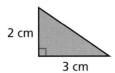

2 cm

3 cm

6.

4.5 ft

3 ft

7.5 ft

7.

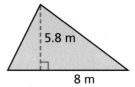

5.8 m

8 m

9-3 Area of Circles

Find the area of each circle. Use 3.14 for π. Round to the nearest hundredth.

8.

C

7 cm

A

E

9.

G

D

3 in.

H

10.

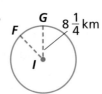

G

F $8\frac{1}{4}$ km

I

11.

J   M

K

42 cm

L

9-4 Area of Composite Figures

12. Find the area of the polygon.

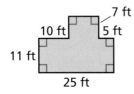

7 ft

10 ft   5 ft

11 ft

25 ft

13. Using the approximate dimensions, estimate the area of the state of Oklahoma.

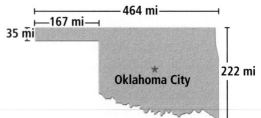

464 mi

167 mi

35 mi

222 mi

Oklahoma City

Focus on Problem Solving

 Solve

• **Choose the operation**

 LA.6.4.2.2 The student will record information . . . including visual aids . . .

Read the whole problem before you try to solve it. Determine what action is taking place in the problem. Then decide whether you need to add, subtract, multiply, or divide in order to solve the problem.

Action	Operation
Combining or putting together	Add
Removing or taking away Comparing or finding the difference	Subtract
Combining equal groups	Multiply
Sharing equally or separating into equal groups	Divide

 Read each problem and determine the action taking place. Choose an operation, and then solve the problem.

1 There are 3 lily ponds in the botanical gardens. They are identical in size and shape. The total area of the ponds is 165 ft². What is the area of each lily pond?

2 The greenhouse is made up of 6 rectangular rooms with an area of 4,800 ft² each. What is the total area of the greenhouse?

3 A shady area with 17 different varieties of magnolia trees, which bloom from March to June, surrounds the plaza in Magnolia Park. In the center of the plaza, there is a circular bed of shrubs as shown in the chart. If the total area of the park is 625 ft², what is the area of the plaza?

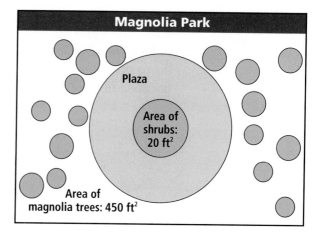

9-5 Three-Dimensional Figures

Review of MA.5.G.3.1 Analyze and compare the properties . . . of three dimensional solids (polyhedra) . . . *Also* **Prep for MA.6.G.4.3**

Vocabulary

polyhedron

face   edge

vertex

prism

base

cylinder

pyramid

cone

sphere

A **polyhedron** is a three-dimensional object with flat surfaces, called **faces**, that are polygons.

When two faces of a three-dimensional figure share a side, they form an **edge**. A point at which three or more edges meet is a **vertex** (plural: *vertices*).

A cube is formed by 6 square faces. It has 8 vertices and 12 edges. The polyhedrons in the photo each have 5 faces, 6 vertices, and 9 edges. Shapes like these are used to refract light, creating a spectrum of colors.

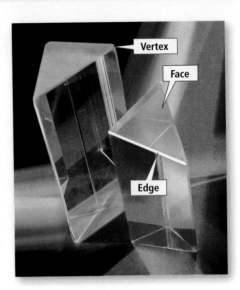

EXAMPLE 1 **Identifying Faces, Edges, and Vertices**

Animated Math @ thinkcentral.com

Identify the number of faces, edges, and vertices on each three-dimensional figure.

A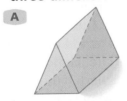

5 faces
9 edges
6 vertices

B

6 faces
12 edges
8 vertices

A **prism** is a polyhedron with two congruent, parallel **bases**, and other faces that are all parallelograms. A prism is named for the shape of its bases. A **cylinder** also has two congruent, parallel bases, but bases of a cylinder are circular. A cylinder is not a polyhedron because not every surface is a polygon.

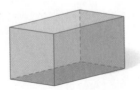

Rectangular prism

Hexagonal prism

Cylinder

A **pyramid** has one polygon-shaped base and three or more triangular faces that share a vertex. A pyramid is named for the shape of its base. A **cone** has a circular base and a curved surface that comes to a point. A **sphere** has no base and one curved surface. All points on the surface are the same distance from a point called the center of the sphere.

Square pyramid   **Triangular pyramid**   **Cone**   **Sphere**

EXAMPLE 2   **Naming Three-Dimensional Figures**

Name each three-dimensional figure represented by each object.

A

All the faces are flat and are squares.
The figure is a polyhedron.
There are two congruent, parallel bases, so the figure is a prism.
The bases are squares.
The figure is a cube.

B

There is a curved surface.
The figure is not a polyhedron.
There is a flat, circular base.
The curved surface comes to a point.
The figure represents a cone.

C

All the faces are flat and are polygons.
The figure is a polyhedron.
It has one base and the other faces are triangles that meet at a point, so the figure is a pyramid.
The base is a square.
The figure is a square pyramid.

Think and Discuss

1. **Compare** a pyramid and a prism.
2. **Compare** a cone and a pyramid.

Homework Help
Go to thinkcentral.com
Exercises 1–12, 13, 15, 17, 19, 21, 23, 25

 Review of MA.5.G.3.1

GUIDED PRACTICE

See Example 1 — Identify the number of faces, edges, and vertices on each three-dimensional figure.

1.

2.

3.

See Example 2 — Name each three-dimensional figure represented by each object.

4.

5.

6.

INDEPENDENT PRACTICE

See Example 1 — Identify the number of faces, edges, and vertices on each three-dimensional figure.

7.

8.

9.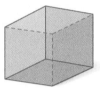

See Example 2 — Name each three-dimensional figure represented by each object.

10.

11.

12.

PRACTICE AND PROBLEM SOLVING

Name each figure and tell whether it is a polyhedron.

13.

14.

15.

Write the letter of all the figures that match each description.

16. prism

17. has triangular faces

18. has 6 faces

19. has 5 vertices

A

B

C

D

○ = **WORKED-OUT SOLUTIONS**
on p. WS10

Write *true* or *false* for each statement. If *false*, explain why.

20. A cone does not have a flat surface.

21. The bases of a cylinder are congruent.

22. All pyramids have five or more vertices.

23. All of the edges of a cube are congruent.

24. Architecture Name the three-dimensional figure represented by each building.

a.    b.    c.

25. Critical Thinking Li makes candles with her mother. She made a candle in the shape of a pyramid that had 9 faces. How many sides did the base of the candle have? Name the polyhedron formed by the candle.

26. What's the Error? A student says that any polyhedron can be named if the number of faces it has is known. What is the student's error?

27. Write About It How are a cone and cylinder alike? How are they different?

28. Challenge A square pyramid is cut in half, and the cut is made parallel to the base of the pyramid. What are the shapes of the faces of the bottom half of the pyramid?

29. Multiple Choice Which figure has the greatest number of faces?

   A. Cone   **B.** Cube   **C.** Octagonal prism   **D.** Triangular prism

30. Multiple Choice Which figure has a circular base?

   F. Cube   **G.** Cylinder   **H.** Square pyramid   **I.** Triangular prism

31. By what property are $3 \times (4 \times 7)$ and $(3 \times 4) \times 7$ equivalent? (Lesson 2-1)

32. Dirk delivered some packages over three weeks. The range of the data for the number of packages delivered per week is 33. The least number of packages delivered is 18 less than the median. If the median is 50, what is the mean? (Lesson 6-1)

33. Lucy can type 50 words per minute. She is typing a manuscript that has about 500 words per page. How many pages can Lucy type in 4 hours? (Lesson 8-5)

Volume of Prisms

MA.6.G.4.3
Determine a missing dimension of a . . . prism given its . . . volume . . . or volume given the dimensions.
Also **MA.6.A.3.4**

Vocabulary

volume

 **Math**
@ **thinkcentral.com**

Volume is the number of cubic units needed to fill a space.

You need 10, or 5 · 2, centimeter cubes to cover the bottom of this rectangular prism.

You need 3 layers of 10 cubes each to fill the prism. It takes 30, or 5 · 2 · 3, cubes.

Volume is expressed in cubic units, so the volume of the prism is 5 cm · 2 cm · 3 cm = 30 cubic centimeters, or 30 cm³.

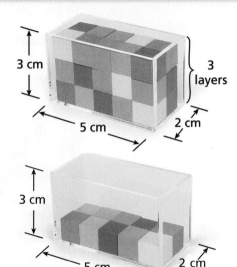

E X A M P L E ⟨1⟩ **Finding the Volume of a Rectangular Prism**

Find the volume of the rectangular prism.

20 in.
36 in. 80 in.

$V = \ell wh$ *Write the formula.*
$V = 80 \cdot 36 \cdot 20$ *$\ell = 80; w = 36; h = 20$*
$V = 57{,}600 \text{ in}^3$ *Multiply.*

To find the volume of any prism, you can use the formula $V = Bh$, where B is the area of the base, and h is the prism's height.

E X A M P L E ⟨2⟩ **Finding the Volume of a Triangular Prism**

Find the volume of each triangular prism.

Ⓐ

2.8 m   5 m
4.2 m

$V = Bh$ *Write the formula.*
$V = \left(\frac{1}{2} \cdot 2.8 \cdot 4.2\right) \cdot 5$ *$B = \frac{1}{2} \cdot 2.8 \cdot 4.2; h = 5$*
$V = 29.4 \text{ m}^3$ *Multiply.*

Caution!

The bases of a prism are always two congruent, parallel polygons.

Ⓑ

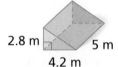
4.3 ft
9 ft   8.2 ft

$V = Bh$ *Write the formula.*
$V = \left(\frac{1}{2} \cdot 8.2 \cdot 4.3\right) \cdot 9$ *$B = \frac{1}{2} \cdot 8.2 \cdot 4.3; h = 9$*
$V = 158.67 \text{ ft}^3$ *Multiply.*

EXAMPLE  3 **PROBLEM SOLVING APPLICATION**

A toy maker ships 12 alphabet blocks in a box. What are the possible dimensions for a box of the alphabet blocks?

1. Understand the Problem

The **answer** will be all possible dimensions for a box of 12 cubic blocks.

List the **important information:**

- There are 12 blocks in a box.
- The blocks are cubic, or square prisms.

2. Make a Plan

You can make models using cubes to find the possible dimensions for a box of 12 blocks.

3. Solve

Make different arrangements of 12 cubes.

$12 \times 1 \times 1$

$4 \times 3 \times 1$

$6 \times 2 \times 1$

$3 \times 2 \times 2$

The possible dimensions for a box of 12 alphabet blocks are the following: $12 \times 1 \times 1$, $4 \times 3 \times 1$, $6 \times 2 \times 1$, and $3 \times 2 \times 2$.

4. Look Back

Notice that each dimension is a factor of 12. Also, the product of the dimensions (length · width · height) is 12, showing that the volume of each case is 12 cubes.

Think and Discuss

1. **Explain** how to find the height of a rectangular prism if you know its length, width, and volume.

2. **Describe** the difference between the units used to measure perimeter, area, and volume.

Homework Help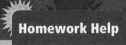

Go to **thinkcentral.com**
Exercises 1–14, 15, 17, 19, 21, 23

GUIDED PRACTICE

See Example 1   Find the volume of each rectangular prism.

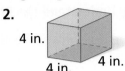

1. 2 cm, 9 cm, 9 cm

2. 4 in., 4 in., 4 in.

3. 1 ft, 2 ft, 5 ft

See Example 2   Find the volume of each triangular prism.

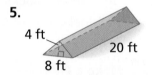 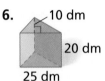

4. 6 m, 9 m, 13 m

5. 4 ft, 8 ft, 20 ft

6. 10 dm, 20 dm, 25 dm

See Example 3   **7.** A toy company packs 10 cubic boxes of toys in a case. What are the possible dimensions for a case of toys?

INDEPENDENT PRACTICE

See Example 1   Find the volume of each rectangular prism.

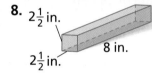

8. $2\frac{1}{2}$ in., 8 in., $2\frac{1}{2}$ in.

9. 3.2 in., 3.2 in., 7.75 in.

10. 12 ft, 12 ft, 2 ft

See Example 2   Find the volume of each triangular prism.

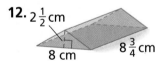

11. 3 m, 9 m, 4 m

12. $2\frac{1}{2}$ cm, 8 cm, $8\frac{3}{4}$ cm

13. 4.5 ft, 3.75 ft, 8.5 ft

See Example 3   **14.** A printing company packs 18 cubic boxes of business cards in a larger shipping box. What are the possible dimensions for the shipping box?

PRACTICE AND PROBLEM SOLVING

Find the volume of each figure.

 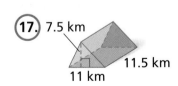

15. 8 in., 6 in., 10 in.

16. 3.5 cm, 3.5 cm, 7.25 cm

17. 7.5 km, 11 km, 11.5 km

Find the missing measurement for each rectangular prism.

18. $\ell = \underline{\ \ ?\ \ }$; $w = 25$ m; $h = 4$ m; $V = 300$ m³

19. $\ell = 9$ ft; $w = \underline{\ \ ?\ \ }$; $h = 5$ ft; $V = 900$ ft³

20. $B = 9.28$ in.; $h = \underline{\ \ ?\ \ }$; $V = 55.68$ in/3

○ = **WORKED-OUT SOLUTIONS**
on p. WS10

The density of a substance is a measure of its mass per unit of volume. The density of a particular substance is always the same. The formula for density D is the mass m of a substance divided by its volume V, or $D = \frac{m}{V}$. Density is often expressed in g/cm³.

21. Find the volume of each substance in the table.

22. Calculate the density of each substance.

23. Water has a density of 1 g/cm³. A substance whose density is less than that of water will float. Which of the substances in the table will float in water?

24. A fresh egg has a density of approximately 1.2 g/cm³. A spoiled egg has a density of about 0.9 g/cm³. How can you tell whether an egg is fresh without cracking it open?

25. **Multi-Step** Alicia has a solid rectangular prism of a substance she believes is gold. The dimensions of the prism are 2 cm by 1 cm by 2 cm, and the mass is 20.08 g. Is the substance that Alicia has gold? Explain.

26. 🖊 **Write About It** In a science lab, you are given a prism of copper. You determine that its dimensions are 4 cm, 2 cm, and 6 cm. Without using a balance, how can you determine its mass? Explain your answer.

27. ⭐ **Challenge** A solid rectangular prism of silver has a mass of 84 g. What are some possible dimensions of the prism?

Rectangular Prisms				
Substance	Length (cm)	Width (cm)	Height (cm)	Mass (g)
Copper	2	1	5	89.6
Gold	$\frac{2}{3}$	$\frac{3}{4}$	2	19.32
Iron pyrite	0.25	2	7	17.57
Pine	10	10	3	120
Silver	2.5	4	2	210

28. **Multiple Choice** A rectangular prism has a volume of 1,080 ft³. The height of the prism is 8 ft, and the width is 9 ft. What is the length of the prism?

    A. 15 ft　　　　**B.** 120 ft　　　　**C.** 135 ft　　　　**D.** 77,760 ft

29. **Gridded Response** The dimensions of a rectangular prism are 4.3 inches, 12 inches, and 1.5 inches. What is the volume, in cubic inches, of the prism?

30. Ronnie needs 4.2 meters of rope to make a rope swing. How many rope swings can he make with 50 meters of rope? (Lesson 3-7)

31. A medium pizza has a diameter of 14 inches. It is cut into 6 equal slices. Estimate the area of 3 slices. Use $\frac{22}{7}$ for π. (Lesson 9-3)

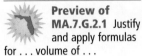

Preview of MA.7.G.2.1 Justify and apply formulas for ... volume of ... cylinders ...

Thomas Edison invented the first phonograph in 1877. The main part of this phonograph was a cylinder with a 4-inch diameter and a height of $3\frac{3}{8}$ inches.

To find the volume of a cylinder, you can use the same method as you did for prisms: Multiply the area of the base by the height.

volume of a cylinder = area of base × height

The area of the circular base is πr^2, so the formula is $V = Bh = \pi r^2 h$.

Animated Math
@ thinkcentral.com

EXAMPLE 1 **Finding the Volume of a Cylinder**

Find the volume *V* of each cylinder to the nearest cubic unit.

A

4 in.
15 in.

$V = \pi r^2 h$ *Write the formula.*

$V \approx 3.14 \times 4^2 \times 15$ *Replace π with 3.14, r with 4, and h with 15.*

$V \approx 753.6$ *Multiply.*

The volume is about 754 in³.

B

6 ft
18 ft

6 ft ÷ 2 = 3 ft   *Find the radius.*

$V = \pi r^2 h$ *Write the formula.*

$V \approx 3.14 \times 3^2 \times 18$ *Replace π with 3.14, r with 3, and h with 18.*

$V \approx 508.68$ *Multiply.*

The volume is about 509 ft³.

C

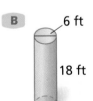

$r = \frac{h}{6} + 1$
$h = 24$ cm

$r = \frac{h}{6} + 1$ *Find the radius.*

$r = \frac{24}{6} + 1 = 5$ *Substitute 24 for h.*

$V = \pi r^2 h$ *Write the formula.*

$V \approx 3.14 \times 5^2 \times 24$ *Replace π with 3.14, r with 5, and h with 24.*

$V \approx 1,884$ *Multiply.*

The volume is about 1,884 cm³.

EXAMPLE 2 *Music Application*

The cylinder in Edison's first phonograph had a 4 in. diameter and a height of about 3 in. The standard phonograph manufactured 21 years later had a 2 in. diameter and a height of 4 in. Estimate the volume of each cylinder to the nearest cubic inch.

Remember!

The value of π can be approximated as 3.14 or $\frac{22}{7}$.

A Edison's first phonograph

4 in. ÷ 2 = 2 in.	*Find the radius.*
$V = \pi r^2 h$	*Write the formula.*
$V \approx 3.14 \times 2^2 \times 3$	*Replace π with 3.14, r with 2, and h with 3.*
$V \approx 37.68$	*Multiply.*

The volume of Edison's first phonograph was about 38 in³.

B Edison's standard phonograph

2 in. ÷ 2 = 1 in.	*Find the radius.*
$V = \pi r^2 h$	*Write the formula.*
$V \approx \frac{22}{7} \times 1^2 \times 4$	*Replace π with $\frac{22}{7}$, r with 1, and h with 4.*
$V \approx \frac{88}{7} = 12\frac{4}{7}$	*Multiply.*

The volume of the standard phonograph was about 13 in³.

EXAMPLE 3 **Comparing Volumes of Cylinders**

Find which cylinder has the greater volume.

Cylinder 1: $V = \pi r^2 h$
$V \approx 3.14 \times 6^2 \times 12$
$V \approx 1{,}356.48 \text{ cm}^3$

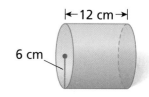

Cylinder 2: $V = \pi r^2 h$
$V \approx 3.14 \times 4^2 \times 16$
$V \approx 803.84 \text{ cm}^3$

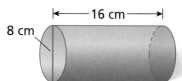

Cylinder 1 has the greater volume because 1,356.48 cm³ > 803.84 cm³.

Think and Discuss

1. **Explain** how the formula for the volume of a cylinder is similar to the formula for the volume of a rectangular prism.

2. **Explain** which parts of a cylinder are represented by πr^2 and h in the formula $V = \pi r^2 h$.

Homework Help

Go to thinkcentral.com
Exercises 1–10, 11, 13, 15, 17, 19, 21, 23

GUIDED PRACTICE

See Example **1** Find the volume *V* of each cylinder to the nearest cubic unit.

1. 4 m 15 m

2. 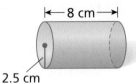 ←8 cm→ 2.5 cm

3. 10 in.  10 in.

See Example **2** **4.** A cylindrical bucket with a diameter of 4 inches is filled with rainwater to a height of 2.5 inches. Estimate the volume of the rainwater to the nearest cubic inch.

See Example **3** **5.** Find which cylinder, A or B, has the greater volume.

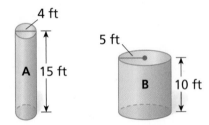
4 ft
A 15 ft
5 ft
B 10 ft

INDEPENDENT PRACTICE

See Example **1** Find the volume *V* of each cylinder to the nearest cubic unit.

6.  ←28 cm→ 14 cm

7.  4 ft 25 ft

8. 5 cm 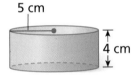 4 cm

See Example **2** **9.** Wooden dowels are solid cylinders of wood. One dowel has a radius of 1 cm, and another dowel has a radius of 3 cm. Both dowels have a height of 10 cm. Estimate the volume of each dowel to the nearest cubic centimeter.

See Example **3** **10.** Find which cylinder, X or Y, has the greater volume.

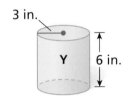
3 in.
Y 6 in.
6 in.
X 3 in.

PRACTICE AND PROBLEM SOLVING

Find the volume of each cylinder to the nearest cubic unit.

11. 2.8 in. 5.6 in.

12. 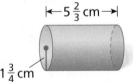 ←$5\frac{2}{3}$ cm→ $1\frac{3}{4}$ cm

13. 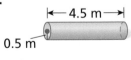 ←4.5 m→ 0.5 m

Find the volume of each cylinder using the information given.

14. $r = 6$ cm; $h = 6$ cm   **15.** $d = 4$ in.; $h = 8$ in.   **16.** $r = 2$ m; $h = 5$ m

17. $r = 7.5$ ft; $h = 11.25$ ft   **18.** $d = 12\frac{1}{4}$ yd; $h = 5\frac{3}{5}$ yd **19.** $d = 20$ mm; $h = 40$ mm

○ = **WORKED-OUT SOLUTIONS**
on p. WS11

Multi-Step Find the volume of each shaded cylinder to the nearest cubic unit.

20.

8 m
3 m
9 m

21.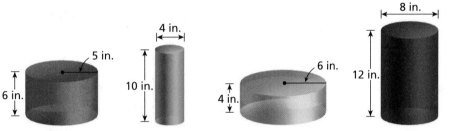

14 ft
10 ft
3 ft

22.

28 in.
7 in.
10 in.

23. **Measurement** Could this blue can hold 200 cm³ of juice? How do you know?

5 cm
10 cm

24. **Science** A scientist filled a cylindrical beaker with 942 mm³ of a chemical solution. The area of the base of the cylinder is 78.5 mm². What is the height of the solution?

25. **Choose a Strategy** Fran, Gene, Helen, and Ira have cylinders with different volumes. Gene's cylinder holds more than Fran's. Ira's cylinder holds more than Helen's, but less than Fran's. Whose cylinder has the largest volume? What color cylinder does each person have?

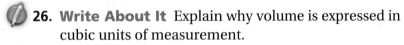

5 in.
6 in.

4 in.
10 in.

6 in.
4 in.

8 in.
12 in.

26. **Write About It** Explain why volume is expressed in cubic units of measurement.

27. **Challenge** Find the volume of the space inside of the cube but outside of the cylinder.

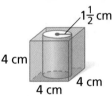

1½ cm
4 cm
4 cm
4 cm

28. **Multiple Choice** Find the volume of a cylinder with a height of $2\frac{1}{3}$ feet and a radius of $1\frac{1}{2}$ feet.

   A. 19.75 ft³   **B.** 16.5 ft³   **C.** 11 ft³   **D.** 5.5 ft³

29. **Short Response** Chicken noodle soup is sold in a can that is 11 cm tall and has a radius of 2.5 cm. Tomato soup is sold in a can that is 7.5 cm tall and has a radius of 4 cm. Find the volume of both cans. Which can holds more soup?

Solve each equation. Check your answers. (Lesson 2-7)

30. $x - 4 = 36$ 31. $12 = 17 - w$ 32. $80 = m - 47$

Estimate each product or quotient. (Lesson 3-2)

33. $9.08 \div 2.96$ 34. $83.67 \div 21.1$ 35. 5.12×7.88

Surface Area

Preview of MA.7.G.2.1 Justify and apply formulas for surface area of . . . prisms, pyramids, cylinders . . .

The amount of wrapping paper needed to cover a present depends on the surface area of the present.

The **surface area** of a three-dimensional figure is the sum of the areas of its surfaces. To help you see all the surfaces of a three-dimensional figure, you can use a *net*. A **net** is the pattern made when the surface of a three-dimensional figure is laid out flat showing each face of the figure.

Vocabulary

surface area

net

EXAMPLE **1** **Finding the Surface Area of a Prism**

Animated Math
@ thinkcentral.com

Find the surface area *S* of each prism.

A **Method 1: Use a net.**

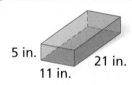

Draw a net to help you see each face of the prism.

Use the formula $A = \ell w$ to find the area of each face.

A: $A = 11 \times 5 = 55$
B: $A = 21 \times 11 = 231$
C: $A = 21 \times 5 = 105$
D: $A = 21 \times 11 = 231$
E: $A = 21 \times 5 = 105$
F: $A = 11 \times 5 = 55$

$S = 55 + 231 + 105 + 231 + 105 + 55 = 782$ *Add the areas of each face.*

The surface area is 782 in².

B **Method 2: Use a three-dimensional drawing.**

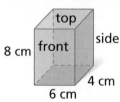

Find the area of the front, top, and side, and multiply each by 2 to include the opposite faces.

Front: $6 \times 8 = 48 \longrightarrow 48 \times 2 = 96$
Top: $6 \times 4 = 24 \longrightarrow 24 \times 2 = 48$
Side: $4 \times 8 = 32 \longrightarrow 32 \times 2 = 64$

$S = 96 + 48 + 64 = 208$ *Add the areas of the faces.*

The surface area is 208 cm².

The surface area of a pyramid equals the sum of the area of the base and the areas of the triangular faces. To find the surface area of a pyramid, think of its net.

EXAMPLE 2 **Finding the Surface Area of a Pyramid**

Find the surface area S of the pyramid.

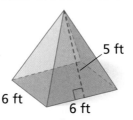

S = area of square + 4 × (area of triangular face)

$S = s^2 + 4 \times \left(\frac{1}{2}bh\right)$

$S = 6^2 + 4 \times \left(\frac{1}{2} \times 6 \times 5\right)$ *Substitute.*

$S = 36 + 4 \times 15$

$S = 36 + 60$

$S = 96$

The surface area is 96 ft^2.

The surface area of a cylinder equals the sum of the area of its bases and the area of its curved surface.

EXAMPLE 3 **Finding the Surface Area of a Cylinder**

Find the surface area S of the cylinder. Use 3.14 for π, and round to the nearest hundredth.

Helpful Hint

To find the area of the curved surface of a cylinder, multiply its height by the circumference of the base.

S = area of curved surface + 2 × (area of each base)

$S = h \times (2\pi r) + 2 \times (\pi r^2)$

$S = 5 \times (2 \times \pi \times 2) + 2 \times (\pi \times 2^2)$ *Substitute.*

$S = 5 \times 4\pi + 2 \times 4\pi$

$S \approx 5 \times 4(3.14) + 2 \times 4(3.14)$ *Use 3.14 for π.*

$S \approx 5 \times 12.56 + 2 \times 12.56$

$S \approx 62.8 + 25.12$

$S \approx 87.92$

The surface area is about 87.92 ft^2.

Think and Discuss

1. **Describe** how to find the surface area of a pentagonal prism.

2. **Tell** how to find the surface area of a cube if you know the area of one face.

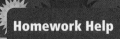

Preview of MA.7.G.2.1

GUIDED PRACTICE

See Example ① Find the surface area S of each prism.

1. 5 in. 3 in. 4 in.

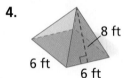

2. 4 m 8 m 2 m

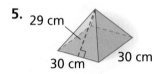

3. 2 cm 6 cm 2 cm

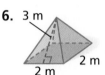

See Example ② Find the surface area S of each pyramid.

4. 8 ft 6 ft 6 ft

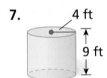

5. 29 cm 30 cm 30 cm

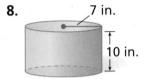

6. 3 m 2 m 2 m

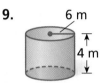

See Example ③ Find the surface area S of each cylinder. Use 3.14 for π, and round to the nearest hundredth.

7. 4 ft 9 ft

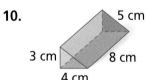

8. 7 in. 10 in.

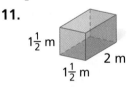

9. 6 m 4 m

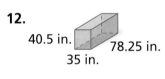

INDEPENDENT PRACTICE

See Example ① Find the surface area S of each prism.

10. 5 cm 3 cm 8 cm 4 cm

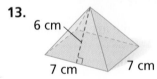

11. $1\frac{1}{2}$ m 2 m $1\frac{1}{2}$ m

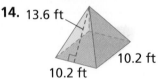

12. 40.5 in. 78.25 in. 35 in.

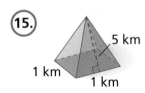

See Example ② Find the surface area S of each pyramid.

13. 6 cm 7 cm 7 cm

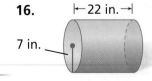

14. 13.6 ft 10.2 ft 10.2 ft

15. 5 km 1 km 1 km

See Example ③ Find the surface area S of each cylinder. Use 3.14 for π, and round to the nearest hundredth.

16. ⊢ 22 in. ⊣ 7 in.

17. 7.8 m 6.75 m

18. $1\frac{3}{4}$ in. $9\frac{3}{4}$ in.

○ = **WORKED-OUT SOLUTIONS**
on p. WS11

Architecture

I. M. Pei is the architect of the pyramid-shaped addition to the Louvre in Paris, France.

19. You are designing a container for oatmeal. Your first design is a rectangular prism with a height of 12 in., a width of 8 in., and a depth of 3 in.
   a. What is the surface area of the package?
   b. You redesign the package as a cylinder with the same surface area as the prism from part **a**. If the radius of the cylinder is 2 in., what is the height of the cylinder? Round to the nearest tenth of an inch.

20. **Architecture** The entrance to the Louvre Museum is a glass-paned square pyramid. The width of the base is 34.2 m, and the height of the triangular sides is 27 m. What is the surface area of the glass?

Estimation Estimate the surface area of each figure.

21.

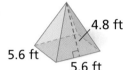

4.8 ft
5.6 ft
5.6 ft

22. 3 m

7 m

23.

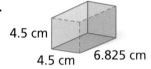

4.5 cm
4.5 cm   6.825 cm

24. **What's the Question?** The surface area of a cube is 150 cm². The answer is 5 cm. What is the question?

25. **Write About It** How is finding the surface area of a rectangular pyramid different from finding the surface area of a triangular prism?

26. **Challenge** This cube is made of 27 smaller cubes whose sides measure 1 in.
   a. What is the surface area of the large cube?
   b. Remove one small cube from each of the eight corners of the larger cube. What is the surface area of the solid formed?

Florida Spiral Review

MA.6.A.1.2, MA.6.A.3.2

27. **Multiple Choice** Find the surface area of a cube with a side length of 9.4 yd.

   A. 56.4 yd²
   B. 88.36 yd²
   C. 338.4 yd²
   D. 530.16 yd²

28. **Gridded Response** Find the surface area, in square meters, of a cylinder with a radius of 7 m and a height of 6 m. Use 3.14 for π and round to the nearest hundredth.

Solve each equation. (Lesson 2-6)

29. $12 + y = 23$
    30. $38 + y = 80$
    31. $y + 76 = 230$

Find each product. Write the answer in simplest form. (Lesson 5-7)

32. $2\frac{2}{3} \cdot \frac{1}{4}$
    33. $5\frac{1}{2} \cdot \frac{3}{5}$
    34. $1\frac{2}{3} \cdot 5\frac{1}{2}$
    35. $3\frac{5}{8} \cdot 4\frac{5}{6}$

Quiz for Lessons 9-5 Through 9-8

 9-5 **Three-Dimensional Figures**

Identify the number of faces, edges, and vertices on each figure. Then name the figure and tell whether it is a polyhedron.

1.

2.

3.

 9-6 **Volume of Prisms**

Find the volume of each prism.

4.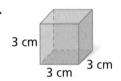
3 cm
3 cm   3 cm

5.
4 ft
11 ft
3 ft

6.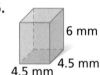
6 mm
4.5 mm
4.5 mm

7. The base of a triangular prism has an area of 4 km². The prism has a volume of 20 km³. Find the height of the prism.

 9-7 **Volume of Cylinders**

Find the volume V of each cylinder to the nearest cubic unit. Use 3.14 for π.

8.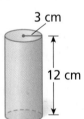
3 cm
12 cm

9.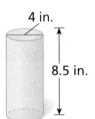
4 in.
8.5 in.

10.
5.5 ft
12.5 ft

11. Which cylinder has the greater volume?

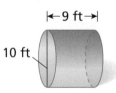
|←9 ft→|
10 ft

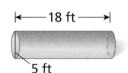
|← 18 ft →|
5 ft

 9-8 **Surface Area**

Find the surface area S of each figure. Use 3.14 for π, and round to the nearest hundredth.

12.
8 m
4 m   5 m

13.
5 ft
3 ft   3 ft

14.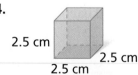
2.5 cm
2.5 cm
2.5 cm

Real-World CONNECTIONS

Merritt Island

The Kennedy Space Center   The Kennedy Space Center, on Merritt Island, is the launch site for NASA's Space Shuttle missions. The center's visitor complex features two IMAX theaters, a rocket garden, and a ride that simulates a shuttle launch.

1. The figure shows the center's conference facility. It consists of five meeting rooms that can be combined into one large room. What is the total area of the meeting rooms?

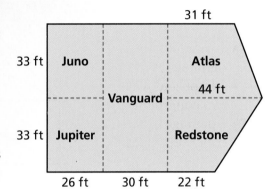

31 ft

33 ft Juno   Atlas

Vanguard   44 ft

33 ft Jupiter   Redstone

26 ft   30 ft   22 ft

2. The Vehicle Assembly Building is the largest one-story building in the world. The building is a rectangular prism that is 716 ft long and 518 ft wide. Its volume is 194,716,200 ft^3. What is the height of the building?

3. The center's Visitor Complex includes a play dome for children. The dome's floor is a circle with a diameter of 75 ft. What is the area of the dome's floor? Use 3.14 for π and round to the nearest square foot.

4. At Space Shuttle Plaza, guests see a space shuttle's external fuel tank. The tank is approximately cylindrical with a length of 154 ft and a diameter of 28 ft. A brochure states that the tank's volume is about 10,000 ft^3. Do you agree? Why or why not?

Real-World Connections

Game Time

Polygon Hide-and-Seek

Use the figure to name each polygon described.

1. an obtuse scalene triangle
2. a right isosceles triangle
3. a parallelogram with no right angles
4. a trapezoid with two congruent sides
5. a pentagon with three congruent sides

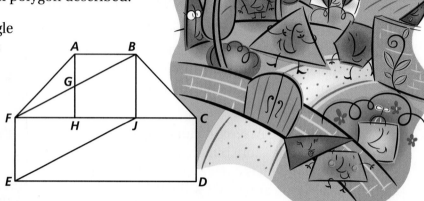

Poly-Cross Puzzle

You will use the names of the figures below to complete a crossword puzzle.

A copy of the crossword puzzle is available online.

Games

THINK central

Go to thinkcentral.com

ACROSS

1.

2.

3.

4.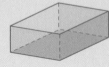

5.

6.

DOWN

1.

7.

8.

Materials
- colored file folder
- scissors
- 8 library pockets
- glue stick
- index cards
- black construction paper
- markers
- tag
- string

It's in the Bag!

PROJECT **Area and Volume Suitcase**

Carry your notes with you as you travel through Chapter 9.

Directions

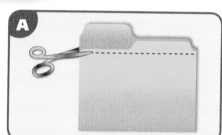

1. Cut the tabs off a colored file folder to form a rectangular folder with straight sides. **Figure A**

2. Open the folder. Glue library pockets inside the folder so that there are four on each side. Place an index card in each pocket. **Figure B**

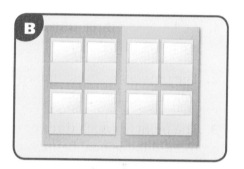

3. Cut out "handles" from the construction paper. Glue these to the folder as shown. **Figure C**

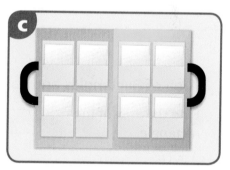

4. Use a piece of string to attach a tag to one of the handles. Write your name and the name of your class on the tag. Write the name and number of the chapter on the front of the folder.

Taking Note of the Math

Write the names of the chapter's lessons on the library pockets. Then take notes on each lesson on the appropriate index card.

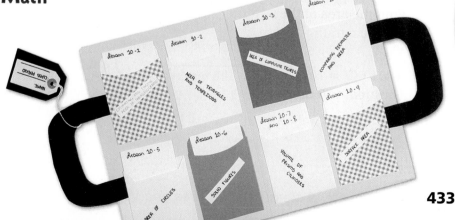

Study Guide: Review

Vocabulary

area	....	396
base	....	414
cone	....	415
cylinder	....	414
edge	....	414
face	....	414
net	....	426

polyhedron	....	414
prism	....	414
pyramid	....	415
sphere	....	415
surface area	....	426
vertex	....	414
volume	....	418

Complete the sentences below with vocabulary words from the list above.

1. A ___?___ is a three-dimensional object with flat faces that are polygons.

2. The number of cubic units needed to fill a space is called ___?___.

3. The point at which three or more edges meet on a three-dimensional figure is called a ___?___ .

EXAMPLES

EXERCISES

9-1 **Area of Rectangles and Parallelograms** (pp. 396–399)

MA.6.A.3.4, MA.6.G.4.2

Find the area of the rectangle.

4 ft ⬜ 15 ft

$A = \ell w$
$A = 15 \cdot 4 = 60$
The area is 60 ft^2

n **Find the area of the parallelogram.**

7 mm
10 mm

$A = bh$
$A = 10 \cdot 7 = 70$
The area is 70 mm^2.

Find the area of each rectangle.

4.

3 ft
6 ft

5. 1 m
7 m

Find the area of each parallelogram.

6.
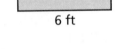
4 in.
3 in.

7. 2 in.
6 in.

9-2 **Area of Triangles and Trapezoids** (pp. 400–403)   MA.6.A.3.4, MA.6.G.4.2, MA.6.G.4.3

n **Find the area of the trapezoid.**

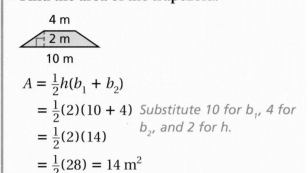

$A = \frac{1}{2}h(b_1 + b_2)$

$= \frac{1}{2}(2)(10 + 4)$ *Substitute 10 for b_1, 4 for b_2, and 2 for h.*

$= \frac{1}{2}(2)(14)$

$= \frac{1}{2}(28) = 14 \text{ m}^2$

Find the area of each triangle.

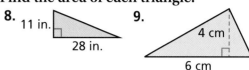

8.   **9.**

Find the area of each trapezoid.

10.   **11.**

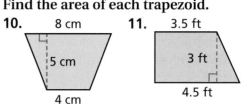

9-3 **Area of Circles** (pp. 404–407)   MA.6.G.4.1, MA.6.A.3.4

n **Find the area of the circle. Use 3.14 for π.**

$A = \pi r^2$
$r = \frac{1}{2}d$
$\quad = \frac{1}{2} \cdot 6 = 3$
$A \approx 3.14 \cdot 3^2$
$A \approx 3.14 \cdot 9 \approx 28.26 \text{ cm}^2$

$d = 6 \text{ cm}$

Find the area of each circle. Use 3.14 for π.

12. $d = 10 \text{ ft}$ **13.** $r = 8 \text{ cm}$

14. $d = 4 \text{ m}$ **15.** $r = 6 \text{ ft}$

16. A circular window has a diameter of 14 ft. Find the area of the glass needed to fill the window. Use $\frac{22}{7}$ for π.

9-4 **Area of Composite Figures** (pp. 408–411)   MA.6.G.4.2, MA.6.A.3.4

n **Find the shaded area.**

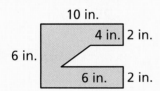

area of a rectangle:
$A = bh = 10(6) = 60 \text{ in}^2$
area of trapezoid:
$A = \frac{1}{2}h(b_1 + b_2) = \frac{1}{2}(2)(4 + 6) = 10 \text{ in}^2$
total area:
$A = (60 - 10) = 50 \text{ in}^2$

Find the shaded area. Round to the nearest tenth, if necessary.

17.

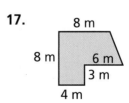

18.

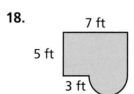

19.

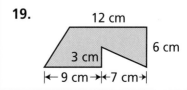

Study Guide: Review

Study Guide: Review

9-5 Three-Dimensional Figures (pp. 414–417)

 Review of MA.5.G.3.1

n Identify the number of faces, edges, and vertices on the solid figure. Then name the solid.

5 faces; 9 edges; 6 vertices
There are two congruent parallel bases, so the figure is a prism. The bases are triangles.
The solid is a triangular prism.

Identify the number of faces, edges, and vertices on each solid figure. Then name the solid.

20.

21.

9-6 Volume of Prisms (pp. 418–421)

 MA.6.G.4.3, MA.6.A.3.4

n Find the volume of the rectangular prism.

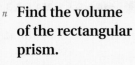

$V = \ell wh$
$V = 48 \cdot 12 \cdot 23$
$V = 13{,}248 \text{ in}^3$
The volume is 13,248 in³.

Find the volume of each prism.

22.
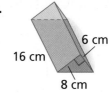

23.

9-7 Volume of Cylinders (pp. 422–425)

 Preview of MA.7.G.2.1

n Find the volume *V* of the cylinder to the nearest cubic unit.

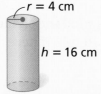
r = 4 cm
h = 16 cm

$V \approx 3.14 \cdot 4^2 \cdot 16$
$V \approx 803.84 \text{ cm}^3$
The volume is about 804 cm³.

Find the volume *V* of each cylinder to the nearest cubic unit.

24.   *h* = 12.5 m
r = 3 m

25. *r* = 7 ft
h = 15 ft

9-8 Surface Area (pp. 426–429)

 Preview of MA.7.G.2.1

n Find the surface area *S* of the cylinder.

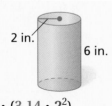
2 in.
6 in.

$S = h \cdot (2\pi r) + 2 \cdot (\pi r^2)$
$S \approx 6 \cdot (2 \cdot 3.14 \cdot 2) + 2 \cdot (3.14 \cdot 2^2)$
$S \approx 100.48 \text{ in}^2$
The surface area is about 100.48 in².

Find the surface area *S* of each solid.

26.
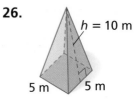
h = 10 m
5 m   5 m

27.

2 cm
3 cm
9 cm

Find the area of each figure.

1.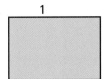
1

2.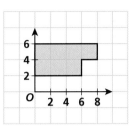

3.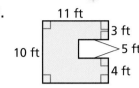

4. A track is formed from semicircles at the shorter ends of a 70-foot by 350-foot rectangle. Estimate the area enclosed by the racetrack. Use 3 for π.

5. A patio is in the shape of a trapezoid. What is the area of the patio?

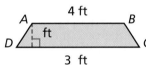

Find the area of each circle. Use 3.14 for π. Round to the nearest hundredth.

6.

7.

8.

Identify the number of faces, edges, and vertices on each three-dimensional figure. Then name the figure and tell whether it is a polyhedron.

9.

10.

11.

Find the volume V of each three-dimensional figure.

12.
4

13.

14.

15. A cinderblock is in the shape of a rectangular prism. Two of its dimensions are 8 inches. The volume of the cinder block is 1,024 cubic inches. Find the missing dimension.

Find the surface area S of each three-dimensional figure.

16.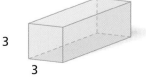

17.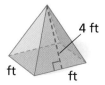

18.

Test Tackler

Any Question Type: Use a Diagram

Diagrams are a helpful tool. If a diagram is included in a test item, study it closely as it may contain useful information. Sometimes it is helpful to draw your own diagram.

EXAMPLE 1

Multiple Choice A small circle is inside a large circle. The diameter of the small circle is 10 feet. If the circumference of the large circle is 4 times greater than the circumference of the small circle, what is the radius of the large circle? (Round *pi* to 3.)

A. 20 ft   **B.** 30 ft   **C.** 40 ft   **D.** 120 ft

Draw a diagram to help you visualize the problem.
Draw two circles and label them with all the information given in the problem.

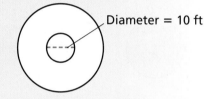

The circumference of the small circle is about 30 feet. The circumference of the large circle is about 120 feet. Divide by 2π. $120 \div (3 \cdot 2) = 20$, so the radius is about 20 feet.

Choice A is correct.

EXAMPLE 2

Short Response $\triangle ABC$ is similar to $\triangle FDE$. Find the missing length.

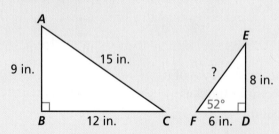

These triangles do not look similar and are not drawn to scale, but the information in the problem says that they are.

Set up a proportion to find the missing length and solve for *x*. $\frac{x}{6} = \frac{15}{9}$

The unknown side length is 10 in.

Test Tackler

Read each test item and answer the questions that follow.

Item A

Multiple Choice The temperature at the ski lodge was 21°F at 9:00 P.M. At sunrise, the temperature was 34°F. How many degrees did the temperature rise overnight?

- **A.** 54 °F
- **B.** 25 °F
- **C.** 13 °F
- **D.** 4 °F

1. What information will help you solve the problem?

2. Sketch a diagram to help you solve this problem. Be sure to label the diagram with all of the information you know.

Item B

Short Answer Prove that the two rectangles below are similar. Explain your reasoning.

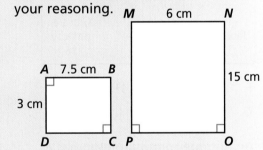

3. What information can you get from the diagram to help you prove that the figures are similar?

4. Do you think the drawings accurately illustrate the given information? If not, why?

5. What is the length of $\overline{DC}$?

Item C

Gridded Response The longest side of a triangle is 14.4 centimeters. Its shortest side is 5.9 centimeters shorter than the longest side. If the perimeter of the triangle is 35.2 centimeters, what is the length of the third side?

6. How do you determine the perimeter of a triangle?

7. Sketch a diagram of the triangle. Explain how sketching the diagram can help you answer the problem.

8. Tell how you would fill in your response to this test item on a grid.

Item D

Multiple Choice What is the area of the composite figure? Use 3.14 for π.

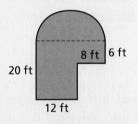

- **F.** 288 square feet
- **G.** 369 square feet
- **H.** 445 square feet
- **I.** 602 square feet

9. How can you break the composite figure into simple shapes? How will this help find the area?

10. What does the answer in choice **F** represent?

11. Explain which answer choice is correct.

Test Tackler

Mastering the Standards

Cumulative Assessment, Chapters 1–9

Multiple Choice

1. What is the perimeter of the figure?

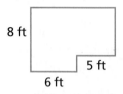

8 ft

5 ft

6 ft

A. 30 feet **C.** 48 feet

B. 38 feet **D.** 88 feet

2. A square prism has a height of 12 inches and a volume of 192 cubic inches. What is the length of a side of the base of the prism?

F. 4 inches **H.** 16 inches

G. 8 inches **I.** 25 inches

3. The volume of a pyramid is given by the formula $V = \frac{1}{3}Bh$, where B is the area of the base and h is the height. What is the area of the base of a pyramid with a height of 40 centimeters and a volume of 360 cubic centimeters?

A. 3 square centimeters

B. 9 square centimeters

C. 27 square centimeters

D. 33 square centimeters

4. Justin has 3 cups of sugar in a canister. He uses $\frac{1}{3}$ cup of sugar in a cookie recipe. He uses $\frac{3}{4}$ of what is remaining in the canister to make a pitcher of lemonade. How much sugar is left?

F. $\frac{2}{3}$ cup **H.** $1\frac{11}{12}$ cups

G. 1 cup **I.** 2 cups

5. The diameter of a circle is 14 meters. Which measure is the best estimate for the area of the circle?

A. 42 m² **C.** 114 m²

B. 49 m² **D.** 147 m²

6. The circle graph shows how many different types of booths will be at a craft fair. To the nearest whole number, what percent of the booths will be selling jewelry?

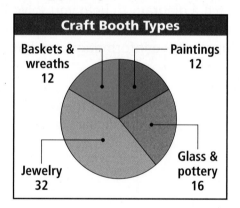

Craft Booth Types

Baskets & wreaths 12

Paintings 12

Jewelry 32

Glass & pottery 16

F. 80% **H.** 44%

G. 55% **I.** 33%

7. An antique round tabletop has a diameter of 3 feet. What is the area of the tabletop? Use 3.14 for π. Round to the nearest tenth.

A. 7.1 square feet **C.** 18.8 square feet

B. 9.4 square feet **D.** 28.3 square feet

8. The scale on a map is 1 in:50 mi. If Cincinnati, Ohio, is about 300 miles from Chicago, Illinois, about how far apart are the two cities on the map?

F. 5 inches **H.** 7 inches

G. 6 inches **I.** 8 inches

Mastering the Standards

9. In March of 2005, Steve Fossett became the first man to complete a solo nonstop flight around the world. He did not even stop to refuel. The 36,818-kilometer voyage took 67 hours and 2 minutes. How many kilometers did he travel per minute? Round to the nearest kilometer.

A. 5 km/min   **C.** 23 km/min

B. 9 km/min   **D.** 26 km/min

 Pay attention to the units used in problems. If the units used in a problem do not match the units used in the answer choices, you will need to convert from one unit to another.

Gridded Response

The table shows the number of people who attended the Super Bowl from 1967 to 1971. Use the table for items 10 and 11.

Superbowl Attendance					
Year	1967	1968	1969	1970	1971
Number of People	61,946	75,546	75,389	80,562	79,204

10. What was the mean attendance? Round to the nearest whole number.

11. Determine the range for Super Bowl attendance from 1967 to 1971.

12. The area of a triangle is 57.12 square centimeters. If the height of the triangle is 8.4 centimeters, how many centimeters long is the base?

13. Solve the equation $\frac{2}{7}k = \frac{1}{6}$ for k.

14. Marcia is buying a watermelon. Its mass is 2.89 kilograms. How many grams are in 2.89 kilograms?

Short Response

S1. The diagram for a blade from a ceiling fan is shown.

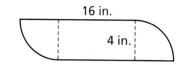

a. Describe how the composite figure can be divided into simple shapes.

b. Find the area of the ceiling fan blade. Use 3.14 for π.

S2. Sylvie and her friends each pay the same price to see a movie. It costs a total of $31 when Sylvie brings 3 friends. How much will it cost if she brings 5 friends?

S3. Carole has a piece of fabric that is 2 yards long. She wants to cut the fabric into 2.4-inch strips. Let s equal the number of fabric strips she can make. Write and solve an equation to find how many 2.4-inch strips Carole can cut from the piece of fabric.

Extended Response

E1. There are 3 pools in Marcie's neighborhood where she can go swimming. The dimensions are listed below. Pool 2 is a circular pool. The width is its diameter.

Pool	Length (ft)	Depth (ft)	Width (ft)
1	25	5	8
2	–	6	9
3	15	4	9

a. Find the volume of pool 1 and pool 3. Which pool has the greatest volume? Show your work.

b. What is the circumference of pool 2?

c. Samantha's pool has the same volume as pool 1. However, her pool is in the shape of a cube. What are the dimensions of Samantha's pool?

Functions, Equations, and Inequalities

Additional instruction, practice, and activities are available online, including:

 THINK central

• Lesson Tutorial Videos
• Homework Help
• Animated Math

Go to <u>thinkcentral.com</u>

Why Learn This?

In mathematics, a function shows how different values are related. For fireworks like these over Miami, you can use a function to show how the length of a fuse is related to the length of time before a shell explodes.

Miami

Chapter Focus
• Construct and analyze tables, graphs, and equations to describe linear functions.

• Write, solve, and graph linear equations and inequalities.

Are You Ready?

Are You Ready? THINK central

Go to thinkcentral.com

✓ Vocabulary

Choose the best term from the list to complete each sentence.

1. ___?___ operations undo each other.

2. A(n) ___?___ is a mathematical statement that two quantities are equivalent.

3. A(n) ___?___ is a ratio that compares two quantities measured in different units.

4. A(n) ___?___ of numbers is used to locate a point on a coordinate plane.

equation

ordered pair

expression

rate

inverse

Complete these exercises to review skills you will need for this chapter.

✓ Words for Operations

Write the operation and algebraic expression for each word expression.

5. the product of 3 and t
6. 9 less than z
7. the quotient of d and 17

8. 28 more than g
9. 101 times k
10. 43 minus x

✓ Inverse Operations

Use the inverse operation to solve each equation.

11. $x + 12 = 31$
12. $8n = 104$
13. $56 \div p = 8$
14. $t - 14 = 33$

15. $a - 82 = 7$
16. $\frac{s}{6} = 5$
17. $b + 22 = 93$
18. $15 = 3n$

✓ Graph Ordered Pairs

Use the coordinate plane. Write the ordered pair for each point.

19. A
20. B
21. C

22. D
23. E
24. F

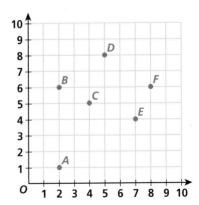

Study Guide: Preview

Before

Previously, you

- created and analyzed different types of graphs.

- graphed ordered pairs on the coordinate plane.

- solved algebraic equations by using inverse operations.

Now

You will study

- special relationships between variables called functions.

- graphing functions on the coordinate plane.

- solving two-step equations.

- solving one- and two-step inequalities.

Why?

You can use the skills learned in this chapter

- to find the total cost of items or services that charge by the number of units purchased.

- to analyze data and make predictions about linear functions in math and science courses.

Key Vocabulary/Vocabulario

function	función
inequality	desígualdad
input	entrada
linear equation	ecuación lineal
output	salida

Vocabulary Connections

To become familiar with some of the vocabulary terms in the chapter, consider the following. You may refer to the chapter, the glossary, or a dictionary if you like.

1. The prefix *in-* means "not." If two numbers are part of an **inequality**, how do you think they are related to each other?

2. The words *in* and *out* are used all the time. Certain numbers in math are **inputs**, and others are **outputs**. What do you think the difference is?

3. The word *linear* is a form of the word *line*. What do you think a picture of a **linear equation** would look like if you drew it on a coordinate plane?

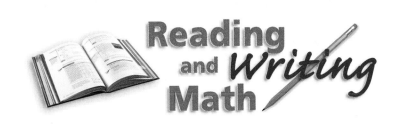

Writing Strategy:
Write a Convincing Argument

Being able to write a convincing argument about a math concept proves that you have a solid understanding of the concept.

A good argument should include

- an answer.
- support to prove the statement (including examples if necessary).
- a summary statement.

> **From Lesson 9-4**
>
> **14. Reasoning** The green figure has an area of 100 in². What is the value of x?

Step 1 **Answer statement:**
The value of x is 4.

Step 2 **Support:**
Divide the figure into two rectangles and label the dimensions you know.

The dimensions of rectangle A are 6 in. and 10 in., so the area of rectangle A is 60 in².

Since the total area of the figure is 100 in² and the area of rectangle A is 60 in², the area of rectangle B must be 40 in².

area of rectangle B = 4 × height

40 = 4 × height

The height of rectangle B must be 10 in. since 40 = 4 × 10.

height of rectangle B = 6 + x

$$10 = 6 + x$$
$$\underline{-6 = -6}$$ *Subtract 6 from both sides.*
$$4 = x$$

Step 3 **Summary Statement:**
Since $(10)(6) + (4)(6 + 4) = 100$, the value of x is 4.

Try This

Write a convincing argument to show whether or not a rectangle with whole-number dimensions can have an area of 15 m² and a perimeter of 15 m.

Reading and Writing Math

10-1 Tables and Functions

MA.6.A.3.6
Construct and analyze tables . . . and equations to describe linear functions . . . using both common language and algebraic notation.
Also **MA.6.A.3.2**

Vocabulary

function

input

output

A baseball pitch thrown too high, low, or wide is considered outside the strike zone. A pitcher threw a ball 4 inches too low. How far in centimeters was the ball outside the strike zone? Make a table to show how the number of centimeters increases as the number of inches increases.

Inches	Centimeters
1	2.54
2	5.08
3	7.62
4	10.16

+1 ... +2.54 (between each row)

The number of centimeters is 2.54 times the number of inches. Let *x* represent the number of inches and *y* represent the number of centimeters. Then the equation $y = 2.54x$ relates centimeters to inches.

A **function** is a rule that relates two quantities so that each **input** value corresponds exactly to one **output** value.

Input 2 → Rule $y = 2.54x$ → Output 5.08

Input 4 → Rule $y = 2.54x$ → Output 10.16

When the input is 4 in., the output is 10.16 cm. So the ball was 10.16 centimeters outside the strike zone.

You can use a function table to show some of the values for a function.

EXAMPLE 1 **Writing Equations from Function Tables**

Write an equation for a function that gives the values in the table. Use the equation to find the value of *y* for the indicated value of *x*.

x	3	4	5	6	7	10
y	8	11	14	17	20	▪

y is 1 less than 3 times *x*.   *Compare x and y to find a pattern.*

$y = 3x - 1$ *Use the pattern to write an equation.*

$y = 3(10) - 1$ *Substitute 10 for x.*

$y = 29$ *Use your rule to find y when x = 10.*

You can write equations for functions that are described in words.

EXAMPLE **2**

Translating Words into Math

Write an equation for the function. Tell what each variable you use represents.

The length of a rectangle is 5 times its width.

ℓ = length of rectangle   *Choose variables for the equation.*

w = width of rectangle

$\ell = 5w$ *Write an equation.*

EXAMPLE **3**

PROBLEM SOLVING APPLICATION

Car washers tracked the number of cars they washed and the total amount of money they earned. They charged the same price for each car they washed. They earned $60 for 20 cars, $66 for 22 cars, and $81 for 27 cars. Write an equation for the function.

1 Understand the Problem

The **answer** will be an equation that describes the relationship between the number of cars washed and the money earned.

2 Make a Plan

You can make a table to display the data.

3 Solve

Let c be the number of cars. Let m be the amount of money earned.

c	20	22	27
m	60	66	81

m is equal to 3 times c.   *Compare c and m.*

$m = 3c$ *Write an equation.*

4 Look Back

Substitute the c and m values in the table to check that they are solutions of the equation $m = 3c$.

$m = 3c$ (20, 60) $m = 3c$ (22, 66) $m = 3c$ (27, 81)

$60 \overset{?}{=} 3 \cdot 20$ $66 \overset{?}{=} 3 \cdot 22$ $81 \overset{?}{=} 3 \cdot 27$

$60 \overset{?}{=} 60$ ✔ $66 \overset{?}{=} 66$ ✔ $81 \overset{?}{=} 81$ ✔

Think and Discuss

1. Explain how you find the y-value when the x-value is 20 for the function $y = 5x$.

Homework Help THINK central

Go to **thinkcentral.com**
Exercises 1–9, 11, 13, 15, 17

MA.6.A.3.6

GUIDED PRACTICE

See Example 1 Write an equation for a function that gives the values in each table. Use the equation to find the value of *y* for the indicated value of *x*.

1.

x	1	2	3	6	9
y	7	8	9	12	▓

2.

x	3	4	5	6	10
y	16	21	26	31	▓

See Example 2 Write an equation for the function. Tell what each variable you use represents.

3. Jen is 6 years younger than her brother.

See Example 3 **4.** Brenda sells mini-muffin baskets. She charges a set price per dozen muffins. The cost of a basket with 2 dozen is $4, with 3 dozen is $6, and with 5 dozen is $10. Write an equation for the function.

INDEPENDENT PRACTICE

See Example 1 Write an equation for a function that gives the values in each table. Use the equation to find the value of *y* for the indicated value of *x*.

5.

x	0	1	2	5	7
y	0	4	8	20	▓

6.

x	4	5	6	7	12
y	0	2	4	6	▓

See Example 2 Write an equation for the function. Tell what each variable you use represents.

7. The cost of a case of bottled juices is $2 less than the cost of twelve individual bottles.

8. The population of New York is twice as large as the population of Michigan.

See Example 3 **9.** Oliver is playing a video game. He earns the same number of points for each prize he captures. He earned 1,050 points for 7 prizes, 1,500 points for 10 prizes, and 2,850 points for 19 prizes. Write an equation for the function.

PRACTICE AND PROBLEM SOLVING

Write an equation for a function that gives the values in each table, and then find the missing terms.

10.

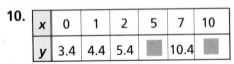

x	0	1	2	5	7	10
y	3.4	4.4	5.4	▓	10.4	▓

11.

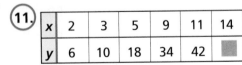

x	2	3	5	9	11	14
y	6	10	18	34	42	▓

12.

x	20	24	28	32	36	40
y	5	6	7	▓	9	10

13.

x	1	3	5	8	11	15
y	1	▓	9	▓	21	29

14. Multi-Step The height of a triangle is 5 centimeters more than twice the length of its base. Write an equation relating the height of the triangle to the length of its base. Find the height when the base is 20 centimeters long.

○ = **WORKED-OUT SOLUTIONS**
on p. WS11

Write an equation for each function. Define the variables that you use.

15.

THE NUMERATORS

$125.00 plus $55 per hour

16.

FRED'S Taxi Company

$2.50 plus $0.90 per mile

17. **Multi-Step** Georgia earns $7 per hour at a part-time job. Write an equation relating the number of hours she works to the amount of money she earns. Find how much Georgia earns by working 9 hours.

Use the table for Exercises 18–20.

18. **Graphic Design** Margo is designing a Web page displaying rectangles. The relationship between the width and the length is the same for all the rectangles. Use the table to write an equation relating the width of a rectangle to its length. Find the length of a rectangle that has a width of 250 pixels.

Width (pixels)	Length (pixels)
30	95
40	125
50	155
60	185

19. **What's the Error?** Margo predicted that the length of a rectangle with a width of 100 pixels would be 310 pixels. Explain the error she made. Then find the correct length.

20. **Write About It** Explain how to write an equation for the data in the table.

21. **Challenge** Write an equation that would give the same y-values as $y = 2x + 1$ for $x = 0, 1, 2, 3$.

22. **Multiple Choice** Sunny Lawn Care charges $25 per visit plus $2 per square foot. Which equation models this situation?

    A. $y = x + 2$ **B.** $y = x + 25$ **C.** $y = 25x + 2$ **D.** $y = 2x + 25$

23. **Multiple Choice** Which is an equation for the function that gives the values in the table?

x	3	4	5	6	7
y	8	11	14	17	20

    F. $y = 2x + 2$ **H.** $y = 2x + 6$

    G. $y = 3x - 1$ **I.** $y = 3x + 1$

Find each quotient. (Lesson 3-6)

24. $4.08 \div 1.2$ 25. $1.65 \div 1.5$ 26. $4 \div 2.5$ 27. $0.36 \div 0.9$

Find the volume of each rectangular prism using the information given. (Lesson 9-6)

28. $l = 6$ cm; $w = 6.4$ cm, $h = 6.1$ cm   29. $l = 2$ ft; $w = 3.5$ ft, $h = 4.25$ ft

MA.6.A.3.6
Construct and analyze tables, graphs, and equations to describe linear functions . . . using . . . algebraic notation.
Also **MA.6.A.3.2**

Vocabulary
linear equation

Chris is ordering art supplies online. Each canvas costs $16, and the shipping and handling charge is $6 for the whole order.

The total cost y depends on the number of canvasses x. This function is described by the equation $y = 16x + 6$.

To find solutions of an equation with two variables, first choose a replacement value for one variable and then find the value of the other variable.

EXAMPLE 1 **Finding Solutions of Equations with Two Variables**

Use the given *x*-values to write solutions of the equation $y = 16x + 6$ as ordered pairs.

Make a function table by using the given values for x to find values for y.

x	16x + 6	y
1	16(1) + 6	22
2	16(2) + 6	38
3	16(3) + 6	54
4	16(4) + 6	70

Write these solutions as ordered pairs.

(x, y)
$(1, 22)$
$(2, 38)$
$(3, 54)$
$(4, 70)$

Check if an ordered pair is a solution of an equation by putting the x and y values into the equation to see if they make it a true statement.

EXAMPLE 2 **Checking Solutions of Equations with Two Variables**

Determine whether the ordered pair is a solution of the given equation.

$(8, 16); y = 2x$

$y = 2x$ *Write the equation.*
$16 \stackrel{?}{=} 2(8)$ *Substitute 8 for x and 16 for y.*
$16 \stackrel{?}{=} 16 ✔$

So $(8, 16)$ is a solution of $y = 2x$.

You can also graph the solutions of an equation on a coordinate plane. When you graph the ordered pairs of some functions, they form a straight line. The equations that express these functions are called **linear equations** .

EXAMPLE 3 **Reading Solutions on Graphs**

Use the graph of the linear function to find the value of *y* for the given value of *x*.

$x = 1$

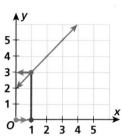

Start at the origin and move 1 unit right.

Move up until you reach the graph. Move left to find the y-value on the y-axis.

When $x = 1$, $y = 3$. The ordered pair is $(1, 3)$.

EXAMPLE 4 **Graphing Linear Functions**

Graph the function described by the equation.

$y = 2x + 1$

Make a function table. Substitute different values for x.

Write the solutions as ordered pairs.

x	2x + 1	y
0	2(0) + 1	1
1	2(1) + 1	3
2	2(2) + 1	5

(x, y)
$(0, 1)$
$(1, 3)$
$(2, 5)$

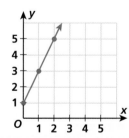

Graph the ordered pairs on a coordinate plane. Draw a line through the points to represent all the values of x you could have chosen and the corresponding values of y.

Think and Discuss

1. Explain why the points in Example 4 are not the only points on the graph. Name two points that you did not plot.

2. Tell whether the equation $y = 10x - 5$ describes a linear function.

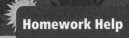
Homework Help

Go to thinkcentral.com
Exercises 1–24, 27, 29, 31

MA.6.A.3.6

GUIDED PRACTICE

See Example **1** Use the given *x*-values to write solutions of each equation as ordered pairs.

1. $y = 6x + 2$ for $x = 1, 2, 3, 4$
2. $y = 2x$ for $x = 1, 2, 3, 4$

See Example **2** Determine whether each ordered pair is a solution of the given equation.

3. $(2, 12); y = 4x$
4. $(5, 9); y = 2x - 1$

See Example **3** Use the graph of the linear function to find the value of *y* for each given value of *x*.

5. $x = 1$
6. $x = 0$
7. $x = 3$

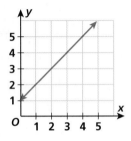

See Example **4** Graph the function described by each equation.

8. $y = x + 3$
9. $y = 3x - 1$
10. $y = 2x + 3$

INDEPENDENT PRACTICE

See Example **1** Use the given *x*-values to write solutions of each equation as ordered pairs.

11. $y = 4x - 1$ for $x = 1, 2, 3, 4$
12. $y = 5x - 5$ for $x = 1, 2, 3, 4$

See Example **2** Determine whether each ordered pair is a solution of the given equation.

13. $(3, 10); y = 6x - 8$
14. $(8, 1); y = 7x - 15$

See Example **3** Use the graph of the linear function to find the value of *y* for each given value of *x*.

15. $x = 2$
16. $x = 1$
17. $x = 0$
18. $x = 3$

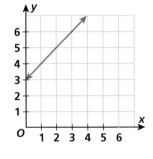

See Example **4** Graph the function described by each equation.

19. $y = 4x + 1$
20. $y = x + 2$
21. $y = x - 2$
22. $y = 2x - 4$
23. $y = 3x - 2$
24. $y = x$

PRACTICE AND PROBLEM SOLVING

Complete each table, and then use the table to graph the function.

25. $y = x - 5$

x	5	6	7	8
y				

26. $y = 3x - 6$

x	2	3	4	5
y				

(27.) Which of the ordered pairs below is not a solution of $y = 4x + 9$?
$(1, 14), (0, 9), (3, 21), (2, 17)$

○ = **WORKED-OUT SOLUTIONS**
on p. WS11

Temperature can be expressed using different scales. The Kelvin scale is divided into units called kelvins, and the Celsius scale is divided into degrees Celsius.

The table shows several temperatures recorded in degrees Celsius and their equivalent measures in kelvins.

28. Write an equation for a function that gives the values in the table. Define the variables that you use.

29. Graph the function described by your equation.

Equivalent Temperatures	
Celsius (°C)	Kelvin (K)
0	273
50	323
100	373

30. Use your graph to find the value of y when x is 0.

31. Use your equation to find the equivalent Kelvin temperature for 20 °C.

32. Use your equation to find the equivalent Celsius temperature for 310 kelvins.

33. **? What's the Question?** The answer is 75 °C. What is the question?

34. **Write About It** Explain how to use your equation to determine whether 75 °C is equivalent to 345 kelvins. Tell whether the temperatures are equivalent.

35. **Challenge** How many ordered-pair solutions exist for the equation you wrote in Exercise 28?

Temperatures of volcanic lava can range from 700 °C to 1,200 °C. This photo shows lava at Mount Etna in Italy.

Florida Spiral Review

MA.6.A.3.6, MA.6.A.3.2, MA.6.S.6.1

36. Multiple Choice Which of the ordered pairs is NOT a solution of $y = 5x - 10$?

A. (5, 20)   **B.** (3, 5)   **C.** (4, 10)   **D.** (2, 0)

37. Multiple Choice The equation $y = 12x$ shows the number of inches y in x feet. Which ordered pair is on the graph of the equation?

F. (2, 12)   **G.** (1, 13)   **H.** (4, 48)   **I.** (12, 1)

Solve each equation. Check your answers. (Lessons 2-6 through 2–9)

38. $\frac{y}{10} = 12$ **39.** $p + 5 = 24$ **40.** $j - 3 = 15$ **41.** $5m = 20$

Find the mean of each data set. (Lesson 6-1)

42. 0, 5, 2, 3, 7, 1   **43.** 6, 6, 6, 6, 6, 6, 6, 6, 6   **44.** 2, 3, 4, 5, 6, 7, 8, 1, 9

Quiz for Lessons 10-1 Through 10-2

 10-1 **Tables and Functions**

Write an equation for a function that gives the values in each table. Use the equation to find the value of *y* for each indicated value of *x*.

1.

x	2	3	4	5	8
y	7	9	11	13	

2.

x	1	4	5	6	8
y		18	23	28	38

For Problems 3–6, write an equation for the function. Tell what each variable you use represents.

3. The number of plates is 5 less than 3 times the number of cups.

4. The time Rodney spends running is 10 minutes more than twice the time he spends stretching.

5. The height of a triangle is twice the length of its base.

6. A store manager tracked T-shirt sales. The store charges the same price for each T-shirt. On Monday, 5 shirts were sold for a total of $60. On Tuesday, 8 shirts were sold for a total of $96. On Wednesday, 11 shirts were sold for a total of $132. Write an equation for the function.

10-2 **Graphing Functions**

Use the given *x*-values to write solutions of each equation as ordered pairs.

7. $y = 4x + 6$ for $x = 1, 2, 3, 4$

8. $y = 10x - 7$ for $x = 2, 3, 4, 5$

9. $y = 50 - 2x$ for $x = 5, 6, 7, 8$

10. $y = 20x - 12$ for $x = 2, 4, 6, 8$

Use the graph of the linear function at right to find the value of *y* for each given value of *x*.

11. $x = 3$

12. $x = 0$

13. $x = 1$

14. $x = 2$

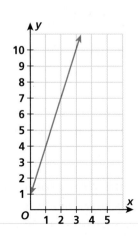

Graph the function described by each equation.

15. $y = x + 5$

16. $y = 3x + 2$

17. $y = 2x$

Focus on Problem Solving

Make a Plan

- **Choose a problem-solving strategy**

The following strategies can help you solve problems.

- Use a Venn Diagram
- Draw a Diagram
- Make a Model
- Guess and Test
- Work Backward
- Find a Pattern
- Make a Table
- Solve a Simpler Problem
- Use Logical Reasoning
- Make an Organized List

Tell which strategy from the list above you would use to solve each problem. Explain your choice. Then solve the problem.

1 The temperature on a summer day is 86 °F at 8:00 A.M., 88 °F at 9:00 A.M., and 90 °F at 10:00 A.M. The temperature continues to change by the same amount each hour. What is the temperature at 2:00 P.M.?

2 Caleb lives in one of the states listed in the table. His home is at an elevation of 300 feet. There is a park in his state at an elevation of 150 feet. Which state does Caleb live in?

State	Lowest Elevation (ft)	Highest Elevation (ft)
West Virginia	240	4,861
Florida	0	345
Tennessee	178	6,643

3 On a map of Nadia's town, the library is located at (2, 4), the museum is located at (1, 1), city hall is located at (3, 2), and the aquarium is located at (4, 2). She wants to organize a field trip to the two buildings that are closest to each other. Which two buildings should she choose?

4 Ethan arranged 4 flower vases in a row. The roses are first. The daisies are between the lilies and the orchid. The orchid is not last. In what order did Ethan arrange the flower vases?

Solving Two-Step Equations

MA.6.A.3.3 Works backward with two-step function rules to undo expressions. *Also* **MA.6.A.3.2**

Derrick has saved $40 for go-cart racing. The cost of a racing license is $16, and the cost of each race is $6. To find out how many races he can afford, Derrick can solve a *two-step equation*.

Solving two-step equations is similar to solving one-step equations as done in Chapter 2. To solve two-step equations, use two inverse operations to isolate the variable.

EXAMPLE 1 **Solving Two-Step Equations**

Solve each equation.

Helpful Hint

Undo operations in the reverse of the Order of Operations. First undo addition or subtraction. Then undo multiplication or division.

A $5x + 8 = 43$

$$5x + 8 = 43$$
$$\underline{ - 8 \quad - 8}$$ *Subtract 8 from both sides to undo the addition.*
$$5x \quad\; = 35$$

$$\frac{5x}{5} = \frac{35}{5}$$ *Divide both sides by 5 to undo the multiplication.*

$$x = 7$$

Check $5x + 8 = 43$

$$5(7) + 8 \overset{?}{=} 43$$ *Substitute 7 for x in the equation.*
$$35 + 8 \overset{?}{=} 43$$
$$43 \overset{?}{=} 43 \; ✔$$ *7 is the solution.*

B $\dfrac{x}{9} - 4 = 10$

$$\frac{x}{9} - 4 = 10$$
$$\underline{\phantom{\frac{x}{9}} + 4 \quad + 4}$$ *Add 4 to both sides to undo the subtraction.*
$$\frac{x}{9} \quad\;\; = 14$$

$$9 \cdot \frac{x}{9} = 9 \cdot 14$$ *Multiply both sides by 9 to undo the division.*

$$x = 126$$

Check $\dfrac{x}{9} - 4 = 10$

$$\frac{126}{9} - 4 \overset{?}{=} 10$$ *Substitute 126 for x in the equation.*
$$14 - 4 \overset{?}{=} 10$$
$$10 \overset{?}{=} 10 \; ✔$$ *126 is the solution.*

Video **Lesson Tutorial Videos**

C $\frac{x+7}{2} = 30$

$2 \cdot \frac{x+7}{2} = 2 \cdot 30$ *Multiply both sides by 2 to undo the division.*

$x + 7 = 60$

$\underline{-7 \quad -7}$ *Subtract 7 from both sides to undo the addition.*

$x = 53$

Check $\frac{x+7}{2} = 30$

$\frac{53+7}{2} \overset{?}{=} 30$ *Substitute 53 for x in the equation.*

$\frac{60}{2} \overset{?}{=} 30$

$30 \overset{?}{=} 30 \checkmark$ *30 is the solution.*

E X A M P L E 2   *Consumer Economics Application*

Derrick has saved \$40 for go-cart racing. The cost of a racing license is \$16, and the cost of each race is \$6. How many races can Derrick afford?

A Write a two-step equation to represent the situation.

Let x represent the number of races Derrick can afford.

cost of a race times the number of races	+	cost of license	=	total cost
$6x$	+	16	=	40

The equation $6x + 16 = 40$ represents the situation.

B Solve the equation.

$6x + 16 = 40$

$\underline{-16 \quad -16}$ *Subtract 16 from both sides.*

$6x = 24$ *Simplify.*

$\frac{6x}{6} = \frac{24}{6}$ *Divide both sides by 6.*

$x = 4$

Derrick can afford 4 races.

Check $6x + 16 = 40$

$6(4) + 16 \overset{?}{=} 40$ *Substitute 4 for x in the equation.*

$24 + 16 \overset{?}{=} 40$

$40 \overset{?}{=} 40 \checkmark$ *4 is the solution.*

EXAMPLE 3 **Working Backward with Function Rules**

The rule for a certain function is to multiply the input by 4 and subtract 3. Find the input value when the output is 33.

The function rule is

4	times	input	minus	3	equals	output
4	×	x	−	3	=	y

$4x - 3 = 33$ *Use the function rule and the given output value to write an equation.*

$$\underline{\quad +3 \qquad +3 \quad}$$ *Add 3 to both sides to undo the subtraction.*

$$4x \quad = \quad 36$$

$$\frac{4x}{4} = \frac{36}{4}$$ *Divide both sides by 4 to undo the multiplication.*

$$x = 9$$

The input value is 9.

Check Substitute the input value into the rule.

$4(9) - 3 = 36 - 3 = 39$ ✔

Think and Discuss

1. Give an example of a two-step equation that could be solved by subtracting first and then multiplying.

2. Make a conjecture about how to solve an equation with more than two steps, such as $\frac{3x + 7}{5} = 11$.

10-3 Exercises

 MA.6.A.3.2, MA.6.A.3.3

Homework Help THINK central
Go to **thinkcentral.com**
Exercises 1–17, 19, 23

GUIDED PRACTICE

See Example 1   **Solve each equation.**

1. $2x + 6 = 22$ **2.** $\frac{x}{7} - 4 = 2$ **3.** $7x - 11 = 38$

See Example 2   **4.** Zach's plant is 12 cm tall. If the plant continues to grow 3 cm each week, after how many weeks will the plant be 33 cm tall?

    a. Let x represent the number of weeks. Write a two-step equation to represent the situation.

    b. Solve the equation.

See Example 3   **5.** The rule for a certain function is to divide a number by 4 and then add 2. Find the input value when the output is 7.

See Example 1 **Solve each equation.**

6. $8x + 17 = 57$ **7.** $11x - 8 = 58$ **8.** $13 + 3x = 22$

9. $16 + \frac{x}{3} = 18$ **10.** $10 + \frac{x}{2} = 19$ **11.** $\frac{x}{7} - 4 = 6$

12. $6x - 19 = 5$ **13.** $2x - 17 = 7$ **14.** $18 + 5x = 43$

See Example 2 **15.** Rachel has budgeted $180 for the debate club party. She has purchased refreshments for $84. She would also like to hire a magician. For how many hours can Rachel pay a magician?

MAIN EVENT ENTERTAINERS

Clown $24 per hour

Juggler $21 per hour

Magician $32 per hour

  a. Let x represent the number of hours. Write a two-step equation to represent the situation.

  b. Solve the equation.

See Example 3 **16.** The rule for a certain function is to multiply a number by 3 and then subtract 8. Find the input value when the output is 4.

17. The rule for a certain function is to add 9 to a number and then multiply by 6. Find the input value when the output is 72.

18. Forrest paid a total of $7 for 3 tacos and an iced tea that cost $1. What was the cost of each taco?

19. Gracey purchased 6 tickets to a concert and paid a service charge of $16. She paid a total of $118. What was the cost of each ticket?

20. José paid $45 to rent a canoe. The cost for renting the canoe was $12 per hour and José used a coupon for $15 off the total cost. How many hours did he rent the canoe?

21. The table shows input and output values for a function.

Input, x	1	2	5	7	9	
Output, y	5	6	9	11	13	15

  a. Use the data in the table to write an equation for the function.

  b. Use your equation and the table to find the missing input value.

22. The table shows input and output values for a function.

Input, x	0	1	3	6		10
Output, y	2	4	8	14	16	22

  a. Use the data in the table to write an equation for the function.

  b. Use your equation and the table to find the missing input value.

○ = **WORKED-OUT SOLUTIONS**
on p. WS11

Write and solve an equation for each problem.

Marine Life

Elephant seals can hold their breath for more than 80 minutes and can dive to depths of almost 5,000 feet as they search for food.

23. Three less than four times a number is twenty-five.

24. Ten less than the quotient of a number and three is eight.

25. One more than five times a number is forty-one.

26. Three subtracted from the product of eight and a number is ninety-three.

27. Twelve more than the quotient of a number and nine is twenty.

28. Marine Life An elephant seal weighed 64 pounds at birth. Two weeks later the seal weighed 288 pounds. About how much weight did the seal gain each day?

   a. Let w represent the number of pounds gained each day. Write a two-step equation to represent the situation.

   b. Solve the equation.

Solve each equation.

29. $\frac{x}{4} + 8 = 13$

30. $7x - 5 = 23$

31. $2x + 7 = 9$

32. $30 = \frac{x+1}{4}$

33. $4x - 20 = 4$

34. $\frac{x+14}{5} = 4$

35. Write About It Write a two-step equation that can be solved using addition and division.

36. What's the Error? A student solved the equation $\frac{x}{4} + 2 = 10$ as shown at right. Explain the error the student made. What is the correct answer?

$$\frac{x}{4} + 2 = 10$$
$$\frac{x}{4} = 8$$
$$x = 2$$

37. Challenge Solve the equation $\frac{4x+20}{8} = -1$.

---

38. Multiple Choice Which equation does NOT have a solution of $x = 5$?

   A. $2x + 15 = 25$ **B.** $3x - 12 = 3$ **C.** $\frac{x}{5} + 11 = 16$ **D.** $\frac{x}{5} + 11 = 12$

39. Gridded Response Solve the equation $7x - 19 = 44$. What is the value of x?

Order the fractions and decimals from least to greatest. (Lesson 4-4)

40. $0.3, \frac{2}{5}, \frac{1}{3}$ **41.** $\frac{4}{3}, 1.1, 0.95$ **42.** $0.99, \frac{9}{10}, \frac{10}{11}$ **43.** $0.5, 0.35, \frac{3}{5}$

Write an equation for a function that gives the values in the table. Use the equation to find the value of y for the indicated value of x. (Lesson 10-1)

44.

x	0	1	2	3	4
y	2	3	4	5	■

45.

x	1	2	3	4	5
y	3	6	9	12	■

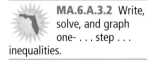
Solving Inequalities

MA.6.A.3.2 Write, solve, and graph one-...step... inequalities.

An **inequality** is a statement that two quantities are not equal. The quantities are compared by using one of the following symbols:

$< \quad > \quad \leq \quad \geq \quad \neq$

An inequality may contain a variable, as in $x > 3$. A **solution of an inequality** is any value of the variable that makes the statement true.

Vocabulary

inequality

solution of an inequality

x	$x > 3$	Solution?
0	$0 \overset{?}{>} 3$	No; 0 is **not** greater than 3, so 0 is not a solution.
3	$3 \overset{?}{>} 3$	No; 3 is **not** greater than 3, so 3 is not a solution.
4.5	$4.5 \overset{?}{>} 3$	Yes; 4.5 is greater than 3, so 4.5 is a solution.
12	$12 \overset{?}{>} 3$	Yes; 12 is greater than 3, so 12 is a solution.

The table shows that an inequality may have more than one solution. You can use a number line to show all of the solutions of an inequality.

This graph shows that any number greater than 3 is a solution of the inequality. The empty circle means that 3 is not a solution. A solid circle would indicate that 3 is a solution.

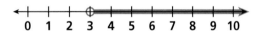

EXAMPLE 1 **Graphing Inequalities**

Graph the solutions of each inequality on a number line.

A $w \leq 7$

Draw a solid circle at the endpoint of 7 to show that 7 is a solution. Shade to the left to show that values less than 7 are also solutions.

B $z > 2$

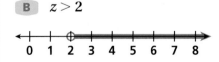

Draw an empty circle at the endpoint of 2 to show that 2 is not a solution. Shade to the right to show that values greater than 2 are solutions.

You can solve inequalities that contain addition and subtraction in the same way you solved equations.

EXAMPLE **2** **Solving Inequalities with Addition or Subtraction**

Solve and graph each inequality.

A $y + 7 < 9$

$$\begin{array}{rl} y + 7 < & 9 \\ -7 & -7 \\ \hline y < & 2 \end{array}$$

7 is added to y.
Subtract 7 from both sides of the inequality to undo the addition.

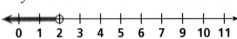

The empty circle at 2 shows that 2 is not a solution.

> **Helpful Hint**
>
> In Example 2B, the inequality $7 \le n$ can be rewritten as $n \ge 7$ to make it easier to graph the solution.

B $4 \le n - 3$

$$\begin{array}{rl} 4 \le & n - 3 \\ +3 & +3 \\ \hline 7 \le & n \end{array}$$

3 is subtracted from n.
Add 3 to both sides of the inequality to undo the subtraction.

The solid circle at 7 shows that 7 is a solution.

Solving inequalities that contain multiplication and division of positive numbers is similar to solving equations. However, there are special rules for negative numbers, which you will learn in future math courses.

EXAMPLE **3** **Solving Inequalities with Multiplication or Division**

Solve and graph each inequality.

A $\frac{x}{6} > 2$

$$\frac{x}{6} > 2$$

x is divided by 6.

$$6 \cdot \frac{x}{6} > 6 \cdot 2$$

Multiply both sides of the inequality by 6 to undo the division.

$$x > 12$$

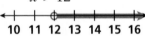

The empty circle at 12 shows that 12 is not a solution.

B $5p \le 45$

$$5p \le 45$$

p is multiplied by 5.

$$\frac{5p}{5} \le \frac{45}{5}$$

Divide both sides of the inequality by 5 to undo the multiplication.

$$p \le 9$$

The solid circle at 9 shows that 9 is a solution.

EXAMPLE 4 *Community Application*

Members of the student council are collecting food donations for a local homeless shelter this month. Their goal is to collect at least 500 pounds of food. After three weeks, they have collected 367 pounds of food. How much more must the students collect to reach their goal?

A Write an inequality to represent the situation.

Let x represent the amount the students still need to collect.

amount collected	plus	amount still needed	is at least	500
367	+	x	≥	500

The inequality $367 + x \geq 500$ represents the situation.

B Solve the inequality.

$$367 + x \geq 500$$
$$-367 \qquad -367$$

Subtract 367 from both sides to undo the addition.

$$x \geq 133$$

The students need to collect at least 133 more pounds of food to meet their goal.

Check Substitute values to test the reasonableness of your answer. Check the endpoint, a value less than the endpoint, and a value greater than the endpoint.

$367 + x \geq 500$	$367 + x \geq 500$	$367 + x \geq 500$
$367 + 100 \overset{?}{\geq} 500$	$367 + 133 \overset{?}{\geq} 500$	$367 + 200 \overset{?}{\geq} 500$
$467 \not\geq 500$	$500 \overset{?}{\geq} 500$	$567 \overset{?}{\geq} 500$

The solution appears to work for values greater than or equal to 133, so the answer is reasonable.

Think and Discuss

1. Tell how you could check your solution to an inequality.

2. Explain why it is necessary to use an empty circle to graph solutions of inequalities that contain < or >.

3. Explain why you need to check more than one value when checking the solution of an inequality for reasonableness.

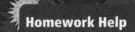

 MA.6.A.3.2

GUIDED PRACTICE

See Example **1** Graph the solutions of each inequality on a number line.

1. $w \geq 0$ **2.** $x > 5$ **3.** $z \geq 9$

See Example **2** Solve and graph each inequality.

4. $y - 5 \geq 0$ **5.** $x + 4 < 10$ **6.** $s + 2 \leq 10$

See Example **3** **7.** $3t \leq 27$ **8.** $4x < 16$ **9.** $\dfrac{d}{6} \geq 1$

See Example **4** **10.** Dana needs to make at least 400 greeting cards to sell at a craft fair. She has already made 288 cards. How many more cards does Dana still need to make?

     a. Let x represent the number of cards Dana still needs to make. Write an inequality to represent the situation.

     b. Solve the inequality.

INDEPENDENT PRACTICE

See Example **1** Graph the solutions of each inequality on a number line.

11. $n \geq 5$ **12.** $y < 10$ **13.** $q \leq 7$

See Example **2** Solve and graph each inequality.

14. $x + 2 > 4$ **15.** $y + 3 \leq 4$ **16.** $b + 1 > 5$

17. $g - 6 \geq 4$ **18.** $f - 5 \leq 2$ **19.** $w + 3 < 8$

See Example **3** **20.** $7t < 42$ **21.** $\dfrac{x}{9} < 1$ **22.** $\dfrac{y}{6} \geq 1$

23. $3a \leq 9$ **24.** $4h < 20$ **25.** $\dfrac{r}{2} \geq 4$

See Example **4** **26.** Antonio wants to earn at least \$41,000 this year. So far, he has earned \$34,000. How much more does Antonio need to earn to meet his goal?

     a. Let x represent the amount Antonio still needs to earn. Write an inequality to represent the situation.

     b. Solve the inequality.

PRACTICE AND PROBLEM SOLVING

Use the Web page for Exercises 27–29.

27. Write an inequality to represent the number of rides at the park.

28. John bought 8 water toys. Write an inequality representing how much John paid in total.

29. Sylvia bought a summer pass. Write and solve an inequality to find the cost of each visit to the water park.

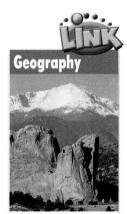
30. Social Studies The U.S. Constitution says that "No Person shall be a Representative who shall not have attained to the age of twenty five Years." Let a represent the age of any United States Representative. Write an inequality relating a to the minimum age of a United States Representative.

Write an inequality for each sentence. Then graph the solutions of your inequality on a number line.

31. c is less than or equal to two.

32. p is greater than 11.

33. 2 times r is less than 14.

34. s plus 2 is greater than or equal to 5.

35. Fishing At some lakes, people who fish must throw back any trout that is less than 10 inches long. Write an inequality that represents the lengths of trout that may be kept.

36. Geography Mt. McKinley is the highest point in the United States, with an elevation of 20,320 ft. Let a represent the elevation of any other U.S. location. Write an inequality relating a to Mt. McKinley's elevation.

37. Critical Thinking Explain why you should graph the solutions of an inequality instead of listing them.

38. What's the Error? A student graphed $x > 1$ as shown. What did the student do wrong? Draw the correct graph.

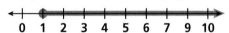

39. Write About It Describe a situation that can be represented by an inequality. Write and graph the inequality.

40. Challenge A compound inequality combines two inequalities. To solve a compound inequality, write two separate inequalities and solve each inequality separately. Solve the inequality $12 < x + 2 \leq 21$.

Florida Spiral Review

MA.6.A.3.2, MA.6.S.6.1, MA.6.A.2.1

41. Multiple Choice Which value is part of the solution to the inequality $4x > 16$?

A. $x = 0$ **B.** $x = 2$ **C.** $x = 4$ **D.** $x = 8$

42. Short Response Explain how the solution of $x + 3 = 10$ differs from the solution of $x + 3 > 10$.

Use the bar graph for Exercises 43 and 44. (Lessons 6-1 and 6-3)

43. What is the mode of the data?

44. What is the median of the ages?

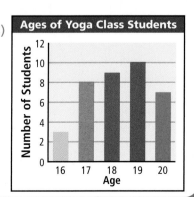

Convert. (Lesson 8-3)

45. 27 ft = ▨ yd

46. 15 qt = ▨ pt

47. 13 lb = ▨ oz

48. 23 c = ▨ qt

○ = **WORKED-OUT SOLUTIONS**
on p. WS11

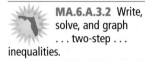

10-5 Solving Two-Step Inequalities

MA.6.A.3.2 Write, solve, and graph . . . two-step . . . inequalities.

Joseph wants to determine the lowest score he can earn on an exam to ensure that he gets an A in the class. He could write and solve a two-step inequality to find what score is needed.

To solve a two-step inequality, use inverse operations to "undo" the operations in the inequality one at a time.

EXAMPLE **1** **Solving Two-Step Inequalities**

Solve and graph each inequality.

Remember!

Undo operations in the opposite order they were applied. In Example 1A, undo addition and then undo multiplication.

A $5x + 7 \leq 62$

$$
\begin{aligned}
5x + 7 &\leq 62 \\
\underline{-7 \quad -7}& \\
5x &\leq 55
\end{aligned}
$$

Subtract 7 from both sides of the inequality to undo the addition.

$$\frac{5x}{5} \leq \frac{55}{5}$$

Divide both sides by 5 to undo the multiplication.

$$x \leq 11$$

Place a solid circle at 11, and then shade to the left.

```
◄──┼──┼──┼──┼──┼──┼──┼──┼──●──┼──┼──►
   3  4  5  6  7  8  9  10 11 12 13
```

Check $5x + 7 \leq 62$

$5(10) + 7 \overset{?}{\leq} 62$ Substitute a value less than 11 for x.

$50 + 7 \overset{?}{\leq} 62$

$57 \leq 62$ ✔   The check supports your answer.

B $\dfrac{r}{2} - 6 > 10$

$$
\begin{aligned}
\frac{r}{2} - 6 &> 10 \\
\underline{+6 \quad +6}& \\
\frac{r}{2} &> 16
\end{aligned}
$$

Add 6 to both sides of the inequality to undo the subtraction.

$$2 \cdot \frac{r}{2} > 2 \cdot 16$$

Multiply both sides by 2 to undo the division.

$$r > 32$$

Place an empty circle at 32, and then shade to the right.

```
◄──┼──┼──○──┼──┼──┼──┼──┼──┼──┼──►
  30 31 32 33 34 35 36 37 38 39 40
```

EXAMPLE **2** **PROBLEM SOLVING APPLICATION**

PROBLEM SOLVING

Joseph's scores on the first three exams in math class were 87, 96, and 98. What score can Joseph earn on the fourth exam to ensure an average of at least 90?

1 **Understand the Problem**

The **answer** will be the fourth exam score.

List the **important information:**

- The first three exam scores were 87, 96, and 98.

- The average needs to be at least 90.

2 **Make a Plan**

Write and solve an inequality. Let x equal the unknown exam score. The average of the exam scores must be greater than or equal to 90.

The sum of the scores	divided by	the number of exams	must be greater than or equal to	90
$(87 + 96 + 98 + x)$	$\div$	4	$\geq$	90

3 **Solve**

$$\frac{87 + 96 + 98 + x}{4} \geq 90 \qquad \text{\textit{Write an inequality.}}$$

$$\frac{281 + x}{4} \geq 90 \qquad \text{\textit{Simplify the numerator.}}$$

$$4 \cdot \frac{281 + x}{4} \geq 4 \cdot 90 \qquad \text{\textit{Multiply both sides of the inequality}}$$
$$281 + x \geq 360 \qquad \text{\textit{by 4 to undo the division.}}$$

$$\underline{ -281 \qquad -281} \qquad \text{\textit{Subtract 281 from both sides to}}$$
$$x \geq 79 \qquad \text{\textit{undo the addition.}}$$

Joseph must earn a 79 or greater on the fourth exam to have an average of at least 90.

4 **Look Back**

Make a table. Substitute values to test the inequality.

70	$\frac{87 + 96 + 98 + 70}{4} \not\geq 90$	85	$\frac{87 + 96 + 98 + 85}{4} \geq 90$
75	$\frac{87 + 96 + 98 + 75}{4} \not\geq 90$	90	$\frac{87 + 96 + 98 + 90}{4} \geq 90$

Think and Discuss

1. Describe the steps used to solve the inequality $\frac{x + 3}{5} \leq 6$.

2. Make a conjecture about how you would solve the inequality $\frac{w + 7}{3} \leq w - 5$.

Homework Help THINK central

Go to **thinkcentral.com**
Exercises 1–38, 39, 41, 45

 MA.6.A.3.2

GUIDED PRACTICE

See Example ① **Solve and graph each inequality.**

1. $2x - 9 \geq 3$
2. $5x + 16 > 41$
3. $9x + 17 \geq 44$
4. $10x - 12 < 28$
5. $\dfrac{x + 14}{10} \geq 2$
6. $\dfrac{x + 7}{3} > 4$
7. $\dfrac{x}{4} + 7 \leq 8$
8. $\dfrac{x + 2}{4} < 1$
9. $\dfrac{x}{5} + 12 > 15$
10. $3x - 7 > 2$
11. $\dfrac{x}{2} + 3 \leq 4$
12. $6x + 3 < 9$
13. $8x + 5 < 29$
14. $4x + 11 \leq 19$
15. $\dfrac{x}{3} - 1 < 0$
16. $\dfrac{x}{2} + 6 \geq 10$
17. $\dfrac{x}{3} + 10 < 12$
18. $\dfrac{x}{2} - 2 \geq 1$

See Example ② 19. A car salesman earns $700 per month plus a commission of 5% of his total sales. The salesman needs a monthly income of at least $2,800. Write and solve an inequality to find how much the salesman must sell each month.

INDEPENDENT PRACTICE

See Example ① **Solve and graph each inequality.**

20. $6x + 13 > 31$
21. $9x + 5 < 59$
22. $1 + \dfrac{x}{8} < 2$
23. $\dfrac{x}{2} + 16 \geq 17$
24. $7x - 4 \leq 17$
25. $5 + 3x \leq 29$
26. $\dfrac{x}{5} + 1 \geq 2$
27. $12 + \dfrac{x}{2} > 17$
28. $24x + 16 \leq 64$
29. $11x - 12 \geq 32$
30. $5x - 14 > 21$
31. $3x + 21 \leq 27$
32. $\dfrac{x + 8}{6} > 2$
33. $\dfrac{x}{9} + 6 \geq 6$
34. $\dfrac{x + 7}{2} \leq 6$
35. $\dfrac{x}{2} + 17 > 22$
36. $7x - 15 \geq 62$
37. $\dfrac{x + 9}{5} < 2$

See Example ② 38. Stephanie and Melinda are driving from Cleveland to Cincinnati. So far, they have traveled 80 miles. How fast must Stephanie and Melinda drive in order to cover the remaining distance in no more than 4 hours?

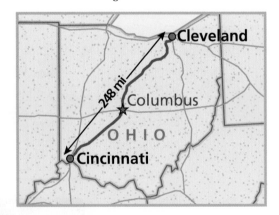

PRACTICE AND PROBLEM SOLVING

39. **Consumer Math** Peter has a budget of $120 for the Math club celebration. He wants to buy $15 worth of drinks and some pizza. Each pizza costs $12. Write and solve an inequality to determine the number of pizzas Peter can buy.

○ = WORKED-OUT SOLUTIONS
on p. WS11

Write and solve a two-step inequality for each sentence. Then graph your solution on a number line.

40. Three times a number, decreased by five, is greater than seven.

41. A number divided by two, increased by four, is less than six.

42. Two times a number, increased by one, is less than or equal to eleven.

43. The difference of a number and two, divided by three, is greater than or equal to one.

44. Travel Sarah needs at least $650 for a trip to Canada. She has already saved $186 for the trip. If she earns $8 per hour, how many hours must she work to afford her trip?

Solve each inequality. Graph the solutions on a number line.

45. $3g - 2 \le 4$

46. $5 + 4z > 17$

47. $\frac{x + 5}{3} < 4$

48. $2 \le 4n - 6$

49. $\frac{y - 5}{10} < 3$

50. $5h - 4 \ge 6$

51. Theater A theater company is trying to raise at least $6,000 for new costumes and set-construction equipment. So far, they have received $4,875 in donations. If tickets to the annual Spring Revue cost $25 each, how many tickets must the company sell to reach its goal?

52. What's the Error? A student solved the inequality as shown. What did the student do wrong? Write the correct solution.

$$2x + 5 > 17$$
$$\underline{ -5 \quad -5}$$
$$2x > 12$$
$$\frac{2x}{2} > \frac{12}{2}$$
$$x < 6$$

53. Write About It Compare the steps you would follow to solve an inequality to the steps you would follow to solve an equation.

54. Challenge What is the least whole-number solution of $2x - 3.5 > 17.7$?

55. Multiple Choice Which value is NOT a solution of $3x - 10 \ge 20$?

A. 8   **B.** 10   **C.** 12   **D.** 18

56. Short Response Explain the steps you would follow to solve and graph the inequality $5x - 12 > 13$.

Find the percent of each number. (Lesson 7-6)

57. 12% of 50   **58.** 4% of 98   **59.** 30% of 128   **60.** 20% of 20

Find the area of a rectangle with the given dimensions. (Lesson 9-1)

61. length: 5 m
width: 1.2 m

62. length: 2 cm
width: 17.3 cm

63. length: 15 ft
width: 7.5 ft

64. length: 7 in.
width: 8.25 in.

Quiz for Lessons 10-3 Through 10-5

✓ **10-3** **Solving Two-Step Equations**

Solve each equation.

1. $3x + 10 = 40$

2. $\dfrac{y + 5}{12} = 20$

3. $22z - 13 = 163$

4. $\dfrac{a}{5} + 3 = 7$

5. $14b + 9 = 149$

6. $\dfrac{c}{7} - 8 = 9$

7. $9d - 2 = 70$

8. $\dfrac{g - 24}{18} = 1$

9. $15h + 20 = 185$

10. Susan's parents are planning her birthday at a bowling alley. The bowling alley charges a $25 flat fee plus $3.50 for each child at the party. How many children, including Susan, can attend the party for a total cost of $60?

11. The rule for a certain function is to subtract 3 from a number and then multiply by 5. Find the input value when the output is 35.

✓ **10-4** **Solving Inequalities**

Solve and graph each inequality.

12. $s - 21 \geq 30$

13. $4 + k < 12$

14. $m + 1 < 18$

15. $\dfrac{n}{29} \leq 5$

16. $14p < 266$

17. $30q \leq 270$

18. $26r > 26$

19. $15j \geq 45$

20. $\dfrac{t}{12} \geq 7$

21. The Brazelton Middle School band is washing cars to raise money for an end-of-year trip. If the band members charge $7 per car, how many cars must they wash to raise at least $210?

✓ **10-5** **Solving Two-Step Inequalities**

Solve and graph each inequality.

22. $\dfrac{u}{8} + 12 < 20$

23. $16v - 13 \leq 179$

24. $8w + 10 < 18$

25. $16x - 29 \leq 243$

26. $\dfrac{y - 12}{14} \leq 0$

27. $\dfrac{x}{7} - 9 > 5$

28. $\dfrac{a - 5}{3} \geq 2$

29. $4b + 8 > 28$

30. $c - 6 > 18$

31. Ricardo is training to compete in a triathlon. This week, he ran 18 miles on Monday and 10 miles on Wednesday. How far must he run on Friday to average at least 15 miles for each of the three days?

Interstate 95 Interstate 95 is the main highway along Florida's Atlantic coast. Spanning nearly 400 miles of the state, the route begins in Miami, runs north to Jacksonville, and then continues to the Florida-Georgia border.

Kayla is driving north on Interstate 95. She gets on the highway at Fort Lauderdale, which is 25 miles north of Miami. The table shows the time Kayla drives and her distance from Miami.

Time in hours (x)	0	1	2	3	4
Distance from Miami in miles (y)	25	85	145	205	▨

1. Describe any patterns that you see in the table.

2. Write an equation for a function that gives the values in the table.

3. Use the equation to find the missing value of y in the table.

4. Graph the function described by the table.

5. The Georgia state line is about 385 miles from Miami. Write and solve an equation to find out how long it takes Kayla to reach the Georgia state line.

6. Explain how you can use your graph to find out how long it takes Kayla to reach the Georgia state line.

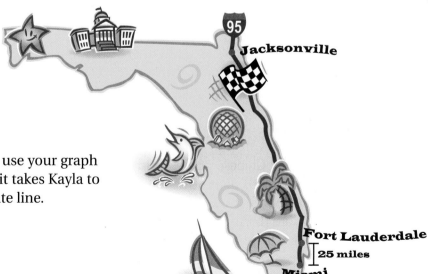

Real-World Connections

Game Time

Try Angles

Solve each equation below. Then use the values of the variables to decode the answer to the question.

$47 = 2a + 33$

$2n + 3 = 6$

$\dfrac{b}{4} = 7$

$7o + 3 = 24$

$3 + 4c = 43$

$\dfrac{p}{9} + 5 = 11$

$3d + 12 = 15$

$\dfrac{q}{11} + 13 = 16$

$3e = 72$

$\dfrac{r}{4} - 3 = 2$

$\dfrac{f + 10}{3} = 6$

$4s - 7 = 1$

$\dfrac{g}{3} + 4 = 7$

$2t + 13 = 21$

$h - 7 = 11$

$\dfrac{u}{2} - 13 = 1$

$\dfrac{i + 2}{5} = 3$

$8v + 11 = 107$

$\dfrac{j + 5}{8} = 2$

$6w - 19 = 11$

$\dfrac{7 + k}{5} = 20$

$4x + 7 = 9$

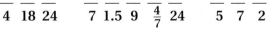

$7l + 5 = 9$

$3y - 15 = 3$

$8m + 7 = 127$

$\dfrac{z}{10} + 1 = 11$

Why did the angle make straight A's?

$\overline{\rule{1em}{0pt}}\ \overline{\rule{1em}{0pt}}\ \overline{\rule{1em}{0pt}}$ $\overline{\rule{1em}{0pt}}\ \overline{\rule{1em}{0pt}}\ \overline{\rule{1em}{0pt}}\ \overline{\rule{1em}{0pt}}\ \overline{\rule{1em}{0pt}}$ $\overline{\rule{1em}{0pt}}\ \overline{\rule{1em}{0pt}}\ \overline{\rule{1em}{0pt}}$ $\overline{\rule{1em}{0pt}}\ \overline{\rule{1em}{0pt}}\ \overline{\rule{1em}{0pt}}\ \overline{\rule{1em}{0pt}}\ \overline{\rule{1em}{0pt}}$ $\overline{\rule{1em}{0pt}}\ \overline{\rule{1em}{0pt}}\ \overline{\rule{1em}{0pt}}\ \overline{\rule{1em}{0pt}}\ \overline{\rule{1em}{0pt}}.$

4 18 24   7 1.5 9 $\frac{4}{7}$ 24   5 7 2   7 $\frac{4}{7}$ 5 7 6 2   20 13 9 18 4

24 Points

This traditional Chinese game is played using a deck of 52 cards numbered 1–13, with four of each number. The cards are shuffled, and four cards are placed face up in the center. The winner is the first player who comes up with an expression that equals 24, using each of the numbers on the four cards once.

Games

Go to **thinkcentral.com**

THINK central

Complete rules and a set of game cards are available online.

Materials
- magazine
- glue
- scissors
- index cards

It's in the Bag!

PROJECT Picture Envelopes

Make these picture-perfect envelopes in which to store your notes on the lessons of this chapter.

Directions

❶ Flip through a magazine and carefully tear out six pages with full-page pictures that you like.

❷ Lay one of the pages in front of you with the picture face down. Fold the page into thirds as shown, and then unfold the page. **Figure A**

❸ Fold the sides in, about 1 inch, and then unfold. Cut away the four rectangles at the corners of the page. **Figure B**

❹ Fold in the two middle flaps. Then fold up the bottom and glue it onto the flaps. **Figure C**

❺ Cut the corners of the top section at an angle to make a flap. **Figure D**

❻ Repeat the steps to make five more envelopes. Label them so that there is one for each lesson of the chapter.

Taking Note of the Math

Use index cards to take notes on the lessons of the chapter. Store the cards in the appropriate envelopes.

A

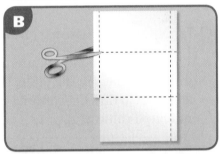

B

C

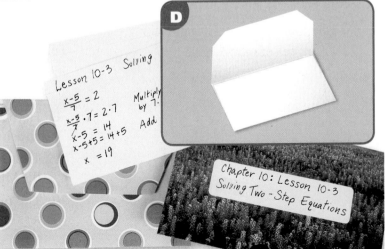

D

473

Multi–Language Glossary

THINK central

Go to thinkcentral.com

Vocabulary

Complete the sentences below with vocabulary words from the list above.

1. A(n) __?__ is a statement that two values are not equal.

2. The graph of a(n) __?__ is a straight line.

3. A(n) __?__ shows relationships between quantities.

EXAMPLES

Study Guide: Review

10-1 **Tables and Functions** (pp. 446–449)

■ Write an equation for a function that gives the values in the table. Use the equation to find the value of y for the indicated value of x.

x	2	3	4	5	6	12
y	5	8	11	14	17	■

y is 3 times x minus 1. *Find a pattern.*

$y = 3x - 1$ *Write an equation.*

$y = 3(12) - 1$ *Substitute 12 for x.*

$y = 36 - 1 = 35$

■ Write an equation for the function. Tell what each variable you use represents.

Angela has 3 more pets than Julio.

a = number of pets Angela has

j = number of pets Julio has

$a = j + 3$

EXERCISES

 MA.6.A.3.6, MA.6.A.3.2

Write an equation for a function that gives the values in each table. Use the equation to find the value of y for each indicated value of x.

4.

x	2	3	4	5	6	8
y	6	8	10	12	14	■

5.

x	5	6	7	8	9	14
y	0	1	2	3	4	■

6.

x	1	2	3	4	5	10
y	7	9	11	13	15	■

Write an equation to describe the function. Tell what each variable you use represents.

7. The length of a rectangle is 4 times its width.

8. Hunter is 2 years younger than his cousin Blake.

9. Thomas has 3 times as many songs on his MP3 player than Cynthia does.

10. The number of penguins at the zoo is 3 less than 7 times the number of giraffes.

10-2 Graphing Functions (pp. 450–453)

■ Determine whether the ordered pair (2, 7) is a solution of the equation $y = 3x + 1$.

$y = 3x + 1$

$7 \overset{?}{=} 3(2) + 1$

$7 \overset{?}{=} 7$

So, (2, 7) is a solution of $y = 3x + 1$.

■ Graph the function described by the equation $y = 3x + 4$.

Make a table.   *Write as ordered pairs.*

x	3x + 4	y
0	3(0) + 4	4
1	3(1) + 4	7
2	3(2) + 4	10

(x, y)

(0, 0)

(1, 7)

(2, 10)

Graph the ordered pairs on a coordinate plane.

MA.6.A.3.6, MA.6.A.3.2

Use the given x-values to write solutions of each equation as ordered pairs.

11. $y = 2x + 5$ for $x = 1, 2, 3, 4$

12. $y = x + 7$ for $x = 1, 2, 3, 4$

Determine whether each ordered pair is a solution of the given equation.

13. $(3, 12); y = 5x - 3$

14. $(6, 14); y = x + 7$

Graph the function described by each equation.

15. $y = x + 1$ **16.** $y = 3x$

17. $y = 2x + 1$ **18.** $y = 4x - 1$

19. $y = 2 + 3x$ **20.** $y = 8 - x$

10-3 Solving Two-Step Equations (pp. 456–460)

Solve each equation.

■ $3x + 5 = 23$

$3x + 5 = 23$

$\quad\, -5 \;\; -5$ *Subtract 5 from both sides to undo the addition.*

$\dfrac{3x}{3} = \dfrac{18}{3}$ *Divide both sides by 3 to undo the multiplication.*

$x = 6$

■ $\dfrac{y}{7} - 2 = 11$

$\dfrac{y}{7} - 2 = 11$

$\quad\, +2 \;\; +2$ *Add 2 to both sides to undo the subtraction.*

$\dfrac{y}{7} = 13$

$\dfrac{y}{7} \cdot 7 = 13 \cdot 7$ *Multiply both sides by 7 to undo the division.*

$y = 91$

MA.6.A.3.2, MA.6.A.3.3

Solve each equation.

21. $6z - 1 = 59$ **22.** $12a - 7 = 29$

23. $2b + 1 = 5$ **24.** $\dfrac{b}{5} - 11 = 4$

25. $\dfrac{c + 5}{11} = 55$ **26.** $6d - 3 = 9$

27. $2h - 9 = 7$ **28.** $\dfrac{j}{7} - 11 = 5$

29. Joseph earns $40 per night delivering pizza, plus $3 for each pizza he delivers. How many pizzas must Joseph deliver in order to earn $124 in one night?

30. The rule for a certain function is to multiply a number by 5 and then add 2. Find the input value when the output is 52.

10-4 **Solving Inequalities** (pp. 461–465)

MA.6.A.3.2

Solve and graph each inequality.

- $k - 5 > 2$

$$k - 5 > 2$$
$$\underline{+5 \quad +5}$$ *Add 5 to both sides to undo the subtraction.*
$$k \qquad > 7$$

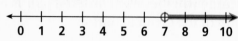

- $\dfrac{m}{3} \geq 2$

$$\dfrac{m}{3} \geq 2$$
$$3 \cdot \dfrac{m}{3} \geq 3 \cdot 2$$ *Multiply both sides by 3 to undo the division.*
$$m \geq 6$$

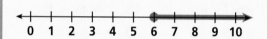

Solve and graph each inequality.

31. $\dfrac{n}{6} > 5$ **32.** $10p \leq 10$

33. $s + 3 \geq 8$ **34.** $r - 2 > 12$

35. $\dfrac{q}{6} \leq 10$ **36.** $u - 7 < 4$

37. $5t \leq 45$ **38.** $v + 5 > 9$

39. $\dfrac{w}{2} > 2$ **40.** $x + 6 > 9$

41. For his art class, Manny must do at least 8 projects per semester. If Manny has completed 5 projects so far this semester, how many more projects must he complete before the semester ends?

42. The debate club is selling tickets to a lecture. The auditorium can hold at most 520 people. So far, 133 tickets have been sold. How many more tickets can be sold?

10-5 **Solving Two-Step Inequalities** (pp. 466–469)

MA.6.A.3.2

Solve and graph each inequality.

- $9y - 4 > 14$

$$9y - 4 > 14$$
$$\underline{+4 \quad +4}$$ *Add 4 to both sides to undo the subtraction.*
$$\dfrac{9y}{9} \qquad > \dfrac{18}{9}$$ *Divide both sides by 9 to undo the multiplication.*
$$y \qquad > 2$$

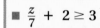

- $\dfrac{z}{7} + 2 \geq 3$

$$\dfrac{z}{7} + 2 \geq 3$$
$$\underline{-2 \quad -2}$$ *Subtract 2 from both sides to undo the addition.*
$$\dfrac{z}{7} \qquad \geq 1$$

$$7 \cdot \dfrac{z}{7} \geq 7 \cdot 1$$ *Multiply both sides by 7 to undo the division.*
$$z \geq 7$$

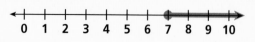

Solve and graph each inequality.

43. $3a - 1 < 23$ **44.** $\dfrac{b}{4} - 11 \leq 5$

45. $\dfrac{c}{11} - 1 \geq 7$ **46.** $11d + 3 < 36$

47. $8g + 1 > 97$ **48.** $\dfrac{h}{4} + 4 \geq 11$

49. $\dfrac{j}{11} - 3 \leq 4$ **50.** $7k + 12 < 75$

51. Masey must average at least 87 on two quizzes before she can move on to the next skill level. Masey got a 90 on her first quiz. What score must she get on her second quiz in order to advance?

52. Billy wants to walk at least 28 miles this week. On Monday, he walked 8 miles. How many miles does he need to walk on each of the 4 remaining days in order to reach his goal?

Chapter Test

Write an equation for a function that gives the values in each table. Use the equation to find the value of y for each indicated value of x.

1.

x	2	3	4	5	6	7
y	▓	8	11	14	17	20

2.

x	1	2	3	4	5	9
y	8	10	12	14	16	▓

Write an equation for the function. Tell what each variable you use represents.

3. The number of buttons on the jacket is 4 more than the number of zippers.

4. The length of a parallelogram is 2 in. more than twice the height.

Determine whether each ordered pair is a solution to the given equation.

5. $(1, 6)$; $y = 2x + 3$

6. $(3, 4)$; $y = x + 1$

7. $(2, 0)$; $y = 3x - 1$

Use the given x-values to write solutions of each equation as ordered pairs. Then graph the function described by each equation.

8. $y = 5x - 3$ for $x = 1, 2, 3, 4$

9. $y = 2x - 3$ for $x = 2, 3, 4, 5$

10. $y = 3x - 1$ for $x = 1, 2, 3, 4$

11. $y = 4x$ for $x = 0, 1, 2, 3$

Solve each equation.

12. $\frac{x}{12} - 15 = 39$

13. $\frac{y}{7} - 12 = 2$

14. $7z + 1 = 15$

15. A new one-year membership at Foster Golf Club costs $400. A registration fee of $100 is paid up front, and the rest is paid monthly. How much do new members pay each month?

16. The rule for a certain function is to subtract 1 from a number and then divide by 3. Find the input value when the output is 9.

17. The rule for a certain function is to divide a number by 2 and then add 1. Find the input value when the output is 13.

Solve and graph each inequality.

18. $15a < 150$

19. $\frac{b}{6} \geq 4$

20. $c + 6 \geq 11$

21. $d - 10 > 175$

22. $\frac{j}{15} + 6 > 6$

23. $2k - 15 \geq 3$

24. $6m + 1 \leq 121$

25. $\frac{n}{2} - 5 < 11$

26. The youth volleyball team must win at least 13 games to qualify for a tournament at the end of the year. So far this season, the team has won 7 games. How many more games must the team win to be eligible for the tournament?

27. Rudy has $8. Bagels cost $1 each, and a small container of cream cheese costs $2. At most, how many bagels can Rudy buy if he also buys one small container of cream cheese?

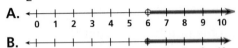
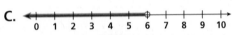

Cumulative Assessment, Chapters 1–10

Multiple Choice

1. Which number line shows the solution to $\frac{g}{2} + 6 \leq 9$?

   A.
   B.
   C.
   D.

2. Marcus surveyed people to find out how many siblings they had. People who responded to the survey had 0, 2, 4, 3, 1, 1, 2, 11, 3, and 3 siblings. What is the range of the data set?

   F. 1

   G. 2.5

   H. 3

   I. 11

3. Carla is selling some of her paintings to raise money for a new bike that costs $700. She has already raised $185. If the paintings sell for $35 each, at least how many paintings must Carla sell to have enough money to buy the bike?

   A. 6 paintings

   B. 9 paintings

   C. 15 paintings

   D. 20 paintings

4. What is the solution of the equation $\frac{r}{3} - 7 = 17$?

   F. $r = 8$

   G. $r = 27$

   H. $r = 30$

   I. $r = 72$

5. Which solution makes $5x - 11 < 34$ true?

   A. $x = 4$

   B. $x = 9$

   C. $x = 45$

   D. $x = 115$

6. Which equation describes the function shown in the table?

x	1	2	3	6	10
y	0	1	2	5	9

   F. $y = x + 1$

   G. $y = x - 1$

   H. $y = 2x$

   I. $y = 2x - 1$

7. A landscaper is planning a circular garden. The garden will have a radius of 4 meters. What will be the circumference of the garden, to the nearest tenth? Use 3.14 for π.

   A. 50.2 m

   B. 25.1 m

   C. 12.6 m

   D. 100.4 m

8. Which table matches the function $y = 5x - 2$?

   F.
x	1	2	3	4	5
y	5	10	15	20	25

   G.
x	1	2	5	6	8
y	3	8	23	28	38

   H.
x	3	4	6	8	10
y	1	3	7	11	15

   I.
x	0	2	3	6	7
y	2	12	17	32	37

9. Which point is NOT on the graph of the equation $y = 5x + 3$?

   A. (1, 8)

   B. (0, 3)

   C. (13, 2)

   D. (3, 18)

10. What is an equation for a function that gives the values in the table, and what is the missing value?

x	1	2	3	6	7
y	4	7	10		22

F. $y = x + 3$; 9   **H.** $y = 3x + 1$; 16

G. $y = x + 3$; 13   **I.** $y = 3x + 1$; 19

11. Jacques collects stamps. Currently he has 124 stamps. If Jacques collects 4 stamps a week, in how many weeks will he have 200 stamps in his collection?

A. 19 weeks   **C.** 50 weeks

B. 31 weeks   **D.** 81 weeks

12. Shaun wants to raise $350 for his favorite charity. For each mile he runs this month, his sponsors will donate $1. Shaun has already raised $210. If he plans to run 16 more times this month, at least how many miles should he run each time to reach his goal?

F. 2.5 miles   **H.** 13.125 miles

G. 8.75 miles   **I.** 21.875 miles

Gridded Response

13. In the last 5 days, a bank teller helped the following numbers of customers: 81, 96, 134, 142, and 99. To the nearest whole number, what is the mean number of customers the bank teller helped?

14. How many square feet does the figure cover?

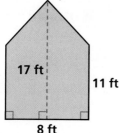

17 ft

11 ft

8 ft

15. What value of x is a solution of $\frac{x-2}{13} = 4$?

16. The rule for a certain function is to add 2 to a number and then multiply by 4. What is the input value when the output value is 36?

Short Response

S1. A new ice cream shop polled several people about their favorite ice cream flavors. The graph below shows the results.

Favorite Ice Cream Flavor

Strawberry 5%

Mint Chocolate Chip 15%

Vanilla 35%

Cookies and Cream 15%

Chocolate 30%

a. If 165 people chose mint chocolate chip as their favorite flavor, how many people chose cookies and cream?

b. What is the total number of people represented in the graph? Explain how you found your answer.

S2. A circle has a radius of 9 feet. Tom wants to draw a square with a perimeter that is larger than the circumference of the circle. How long should each side of the square be? Use 3.14 for π. Explain how you found your answer.

Extended Response

E1. It cost Raylene $118 to make 25 scarves. She wants to sell the scarves for a profit of at least $100.

a. Write and solve an inequality to find how much Raylene should charge for each scarf. Show your work.

b. Raylene decides to keep 5 scarves to give as gifts. How much should she charge for each remaining scarf to earn at least $100 in profit?

c. How much more will each scarf cost if Raylene keeps five, rather than selling all 25?

Additional instruction, practice, and activities are available online, including:

- Lesson Tutorial Videos
- Homework Help
- Animated Math

THINK central

Go to **thinkcentral.com**

Why Learn This?

Integers are useful in finding and comparing distances both above and below ground level, such as what you encounter in caves and the countryside surrounding them.

Florida Caverns State Park
Marianna

Chapter Focus
- Use negative numbers in everyday contexts.
- Add, subtract, multiply, and divide integers.

Are You Ready?

Are You Ready? THINK central
Go to thinkcentral.com

✓ Vocabulary

Choose the best term from the list to complete each sentence.

1. When you ___?___ a numerical expression, you find its value.

2. ___?___ are the set of numbers 0, 1, 2, 3, 4, ...

3. A(n) ___?___ is an exact location in space.

4. A(n) ___?___ is a mathematical statement that two quantities are equal.

equation

evaluate

exponents

less than

point

whole numbers

Complete these exercises to review skills you will need for this chapter.

✓ Compare Whole Numbers

Write <, >, or = to compare the numbers.

5. 9 ▮ 2   6. 4 ▮ 5   7. 8 ▮ 1   8. 1,076 ▮ 1,074

9. 412 ▮ 214   10. 3 ▮ 3   11. 502 ▮ 520   12. 9,123 ▮ 9,001

✓ Whole-Number Operations

Add, subtract, multiply, or divide.

13. $7 + 6$ 14. $15 - 8$ 15. $6 \cdot 7$ 16. $25 \div 5$

17. $129 + 30$ 18. $32 - 25$ 19. $119 \cdot 5$ 20. $156 \div 6$

✓ Solve One-Step Equations

Solve each equation.

21. $4t = 32$ 22. $b - 4 = 12$ 23. $24 = 6r$

24. $3x = 72$ 25. $8 = 4a$ 26. $m + 3 = 63$

✓ Graph Ordered Pairs

Graph each ordered pair.

27. $(1, 3)$ 28. $(0, 5)$ 29. $(3, 2)$ 30. $(4, 0)$

31. $(6, 4)$ 32. $(2, 5)$ 33. $(0, 1)$ 34. $(1, 0)$

Study Guide: Preview

Before

Previously, you

- graphed and located ordered pairs of whole numbers on a coordinate plane.

- graphed a given set of data.

- used equations to represent real-life situations.

Now

You will study

- using integers to represent real-life situations.

- graphing and locating ordered pairs on four quadrants of a coordinate plane.

Why?

You can use the skills learned in this chapter

- to solve multi-step equations with integers and positive and negative fractions and decimals.

Key Vocabulary/Vocabulario

absolute value	valor absoluto
coordinates	coordenadas
Identity Property	Propiedad de identidad
integer	entero
opposites	opuestos
origin	origen
quadrants	cuadrante

Vocabulary Connections

To become familiar with some of the vocabulary terms in the chapter, consider the following. You may refer to the chapter, the glossary, or a dictionary if you like.

1. The word *opposite* can mean "across from." Where do you think **opposites** will lie on a number line?

2. The word *origin* can mean "the point at which something begins." At what coordinates do you think the **origin** is?

3. The word *quadrant* comes from the Latin *quattuor,* meaning "four." How many **quadrants** do you think a coordinate plane has?

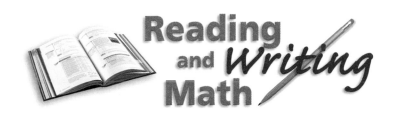 

Reading and Writing Math

Study Strategy: Prepare for Your Final Exam

In your math class, you use skills that you have learned throughout the year, so most final exams cover material from the beginning of the course.

A timeline and checklist like the one shown can help you study for the final exam in an organized way.

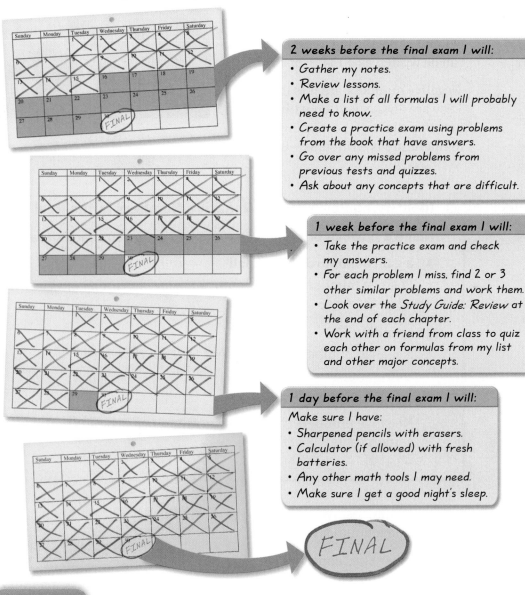

2 weeks before the final exam I will:
- Gather my notes.
- Review lessons.
- Make a list of all formulas I will probably need to know.
- Create a practice exam using problems from the book that have answers.
- Go over any missed problems from previous tests and quizzes.
- Ask about any concepts that are difficult.

1 week before the final exam I will:
- Take the practice exam and check my answers.
- For each problem I miss, find 2 or 3 other similar problems and work them.
- Look over the *Study Guide: Review* at the end of each chapter.
- Work with a friend from class to quiz each other on formulas from my list and other major concepts.

1 day before the final exam I will:

Make sure I have:
- Sharpened pencils with erasers.
- Calculator (if allowed) with fresh batteries.
- Any other math tools I may need.
- Make sure I get a good night's sleep.

FINAL

Try This

1. Create a timeline and checklist of your own to help you prepare for your final exam.

Reading and Writing Math

Integers and Absolute Value

Preview of MA.7.A.3.1 Use and justify the rules for . . . finding the absolute value of integers.

The highest temperature recorded in the United States is 134 °F, in Death Valley, California. The lowest recorded temperature is 80° below 0 °F, in Prospect Creek, Alaska.

Positive numbers are greater than 0. They may be written with a positive sign (+), but they are usually written without it. So, the highest temperature can be written as +134 °F or 134 °F.

Negative numbers are less than 0. They are always written with a negative sign (−). So, the lowest temperature is written as −80 °F.

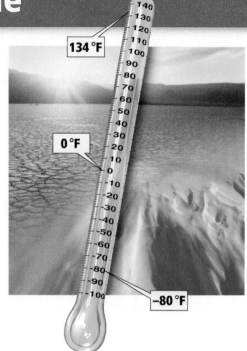

134 °F

0 °F

−80 °F

Vocabulary

positive number

negative number

opposites

integer

absolute value

EXAMPLE 1 **Identifying Positive and Negative Numbers in the Real World**

Name a positive or negative number to represent each situation.

A a gain of 20 yards in football

Positive numbers can represent *gains* or *increases*.

+20

B spending $75

Negative numbers can represent *losses* or *decreases*.

−75

C 10 feet below sea level

Negative numbers can represent values *below* or *less than* a certain value.

−10

You can graph positive and negative numbers on a number line.

On a number line, **opposites** are the same distance from 0 but on different sides of 0. Zero is its own opposite.

Integers are the set of all whole numbers and their opposites.

Remember!

The set of whole numbers includes zero and the counting numbers. {0, 1, 2, 3, 4, ...}

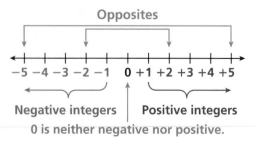

Opposites

−5 −4 −3 −2 −1 0 +1 +2 +3 +4 +5

Negative integers   Positive integers

0 is neither negative nor positive.

Video Lesson Tutorial Videos @ thinkcentral.com

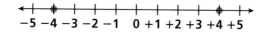

EXAMPLE 2 Graphing Integers

Graph each integer and its opposite on a number line.

A −4

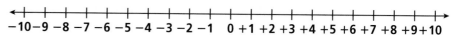

+4 is the same distance from 0 as −4.

B 3

−3 is the same distance from 0 as 3.

C 0

Zero is its own opposite.

The **absolute value** of an integer is its distance from 0 on a number line. The symbol for absolute value is | |.

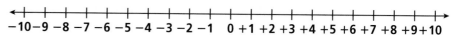

Reading Math

Read | 3 | as "the absolute value of 3."

Read | −3 | as "the absolute value of negative 3."

$|-3| = 3$ $|3| = 3$

- Absolute values are never negative.
- Opposite integers have the same absolute value.
- $|0| = 0$

EXAMPLE 3 Finding Absolute Value

Use the number line to find the absolute value of each integer.

A $|5|$

5   *5 is 5 units from 0, so $|5| = 5$.*

B $|-7|$

7   *−7 is 7 units from 0, so $|-7| = 7$.*

Think and Discuss

1. Tell whether −3.2 is an integer. Why or why not?

2. Give the opposite of 14. Then give the opposite of −11.

3. Name all the integers with an absolute value of 12.

Homework Help
Go to **thinkcentral.com**
Exercises 1–23, 29, 31, 33

 Preview MA.7.A.3.1

GUIDED PRACTICE

See Example **1** **Name a positive or negative number to represent each situation.**
  1. an increase of 5 points **2.** a loss of 15 yards

See Example **2** **Graph each integer and its opposite on a number line.**
  3. −2 **4.** 1 **5.** −6 **6.** 9

See Example **3** **Use the number line to find the absolute value of each integer.**

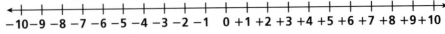

  7. |−10| **8.** |6| **9.** |3| **10.** |−5|

INDEPENDENT PRACTICE

See Example **1** **Name a positive or negative number to represent each situation.**
  11. earning $50 **12.** 20° below zero
  13. 7 feet above sea level **14.** a decrease of 39 points

See Example **2** **Graph each integer and its opposite on a number line.**
  15. −5 **16.** 6 **17.** 2 **18.** −3 **19.** 9

See Example **3** **Use the number line to find the absolute value of each integer.**

```
←─┼──┼──┼──┼──┼──┼──┼──┼──┼──┼──┼──┼──┼──┼──┼──┼──┼──┼──┼──┼─→
  −10−9 −8 −7 −6 −5 −4 −3 −2 −1  0 +1 +2 +3 +4 +5 +6 +7 +8 +9 +10
```

  20. |10| **21.** |−1| **22.** |−8| **23.** |2|

PRACTICE AND PROBLEM SOLVING

Write a situation that each integer could represent.
  24. +49 **25.** −83 **26.** −7 **27.** +15 **28.** −2

Write the opposite of each integer.
  29. −92 **30.** +75 **31.** −25 **32.** +1,001 **33.** 0

Write the absolute value of each integer.
  34. |−27| **35.** |105| **36.** |18| **37.** |−55| **38.** |−1,000|

39. Astronomy Use the table to graph the average surface temperatures of the given planets on a number line.

Planet	Earth	Mars	Jupiter
Average Surface Temperature (°C)	15	−65	−110

40. A certain stock dropped 3 points in the stock market. Another stock gained 5 points. Write an integer to represent each stock's gain or loss.

○ = **WORKED-OUT SOLUTIONS**
on p. WS12

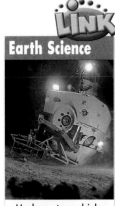

41. Sports When the Mountain Lions football team returned the kickoff, they gained 45 yards. Write an integer to represent this situation.

42. Earth Science The Mariana Trench is the deepest part of the Pacific Ocean, reaching a depth of 10,924 meters. Write the depth in meters of the Mariana Trench as an integer.

43. Earth Science From June 21 to December 21, most of the United States loses 1 to 2 minutes of daylight each day. But on December 21, most of the country begins to gain 1 to 2 minutes of daylight each day. What integer could you write for a gain of 2 minutes? a loss of 2 minutes?

44. Match each temperature with the correct point on the thermometer.

a. $-10\,°F$ b. $5\,°F$ c. $10\,°F$

d. $-2\,°F$ e. $-9\,°F$ f. $7\,°F$

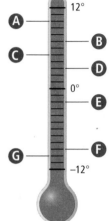

45. Which situation is least likely to be represented by -8?

A. a temperature drop of 8 °F

B. a depth of 8 meters

C. a growth of 8 centimeters

D. a time 8 years ago

46. Write A Problem Write a problem about the temperature rising and dropping. Start with the temperature labeled G on the thermometer. Then write an expression to represent the situation.

47. Write About It Is -0.5 an integer? Explain.

48. Challenge What are the opposites of the integers 3 units away from -8? Justify your answer.

Florida Spiral Review

MA.6.A.1.3, MA.6.A.5.3

49. Multiple Choice Which situation could the integer -50 represent?

A. An increase of $50 in a bank account

B. The temperature on a warm spring day

C. The distance driven on the way to the beach

D. A decrease of 50 employees

50. Multiple Choice Which expression can represent *200 years ago*?

F. -200 G. $200x$ H. 200 I. $x - 200$

Estimate by rounding to the indicated place value. (Lesson 3-2)

51. $1.892 - 0.243$; tenths   **52.** $13.4132 + 0.513$; tenths   **53.** $11.4307 - 5.2164$; thousandths

54. Marie-Claire is painting a bedroom wall that measures $9\frac{3}{4}$ feet by $11\frac{3}{4}$ feet. If a gallon of paint covers about 150 square feet, will one gallon of paint be enough to cover the wall? Justify your answer. (Lesson 5-7)

Comparing and Ordering Integers

Preview of MA.7.A.3.1 Use and justify the rules for . . . finding the absolute value of integers.

The table shows three golfers' scores from a golf tournament.

Player	Score
David Berganio	+6
Sergio Garcia	−16
Tiger Woods	−4

In golf, the player with the lowest score wins the game. You can compare integers to find the winner of the tournament.

Sergio Garcia

EXAMPLE 1 **Comparing Integers**

Use the number line to compare each pair of integers. Write < or >.

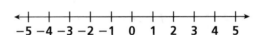

Remember!

Numbers on a number line increase in value as you move from left to right.

A −4 ☐ 2

−4 < 2   *−4 is to the left of 2 on the number line.*

B −3 ☐ −5

−3 > −5   *−3 is to the right of −5 on the number line.*

C 0 ☐ −4

0 > −4   *0 is to the right of −4 on the number line.*

EXAMPLE 2 **Ordering Integers**

Order the integers in each set from least to greatest.

A 4, −2, 1

Graph the integers on the same number line.

Then read the numbers from left to right: −2, 1, 4.

Video **Lesson Tutorial Videos @ thinkcentral.com**

Order the integers in each set from least to greatest.

B −2, 0, 2, −5

Graph the integers on the same number line.

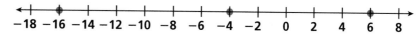

Then read the numbers from left to right: −5, −2, 0, 2.

EXAMPLE 3 **PROBLEM SOLVING APPLICATION**

At a golf tournament, David Berganio scored +6, Sergio Garcia scored −16, and Tiger Woods scored −4. One of these three players was the winner of the tournament. Who won the tournament?

1 Understand the Problem

The **answer** will be the player with the *lowest* score.
List the **important information:**

• David Berganio scored +6.
• Sergio Garcia scored −16.
• Tiger Woods scored −4.

2 Make a Plan

You can draw a diagram to order the scores from least to greatest.

3 Solve

Draw a number line and graph each player's score on it.

Sergio Garcia's score, –16, is farthest to the left, so it is the lowest score. Sergio Garcia won this tournament.

4 Look Back

Negative integers are always less than positive integers, so David Berganio cannot be the winner. Since Sergio Garcia's score of −16 is less than Tiger Woods's score of −4, Sergio Garcia won.

Sports

In golf, *par* is the standard number of strokes needed to hit the ball into the hole. A score of −12 means "12 strokes under par." A score of +2 means "2 strokes over par."

Think and Discuss

1. Tell which is greater, a negative or a positive integer. Explain.

2. Tell which is greater, 0 or a negative integer. Explain.

3. Explain how to tell which of two negative integers is greater.

Homework Help

Go to **thinkcentral.com**
Exercises 1–18, 21, 23, 25, 29, 31, 33, 35

 Preview MA.7.A.3.1

GUIDED PRACTICE

See Example **1** Use the number line to compare each pair of integers. Write < or >.

$$\overset{\longleftarrow}{\underset{-5\ -4\ -3\ -2\ -1\ \ 0\ \ 1\ \ 2\ \ 3\ \ 4\ \ 5}{+\ +\ +\ +\ +\ +\ +\ +\ +\ +\ +}}\overset{\longrightarrow}{}$$

1. -4 ▢ -5 **2.** -2 ▢ 0 **3.** -1 ▢ 3

See Example **2** Order the integers in each set from least to greatest.

4. $9, 0, -2$ **5.** $7, -4, 3, -5$ **6.** $8, -6, -1, 10$

See Example **3** **7.** Use the table.

   a. At what time was the temperature the lowest?

   b. What was the highest temperature?

Time	Temperature (°F)
10:00 P.M.	1
Midnight	−4
3:30 A.M.	−6
6:00 A.M.	1

INDEPENDENT PRACTICE

See Example **1** Use the number line to compare each pair of integers. Write < or >.

$$\overset{\longleftarrow}{\underset{-5\ -4\ -3\ -2\ -1\ \ 0\ \ 1\ \ 2\ \ 3\ \ 4\ \ 5}{+\ +\ +\ +\ +\ +\ +\ +\ +\ +\ +}}\overset{\longrightarrow}{}$$

8. 0 ▢ 2 **9.** 4 ▢ -4 **10.** -3 ▢ -1 **11.** -5 ▢ 2

See Example **2** Order the integers in each set from least to greatest.

12. $11, -6, -3$ **13.** $15, -8, 7$ **14.** $5, -12, 0, 1$

15. $-9, 13, -1, -16$ **16.** $24, -6, 7, -10, 4$ **17.** $22, 0, -19, 8, -3$

See Example **3** **18.** **Geography** Use the table, which shows the depths of the world's three largest oceans.

   a. Which ocean is the deepest?

   b. Which oceans are less than 35,000 feet deep?

Ocean	Depth (ft)
Pacific	−36,200
Atlantic	−30,246
Indian	−24,442

PRACTICE AND PROBLEM SOLVING

Compare. Write < or >.

19. -30 ▢ 25 **20.** 0 ▢ -49 **21.** -16 ▢ -51 **22.** -17 ▢ 17

23. -64 ▢ -15 **24.** 77 ▢ 300 **25.** -28 ▢ 1 **26.** 25 ▢ -30

Order the integers in each set from least to greatest.

27. $-39, 14, 21$ **28.** $-18, -9, -31$ **29.** $0, -26, 43, -12$

30. $15, -25, -4, 31$ **31.** $-67, 82, -73, -10, 20$ **32.** $42, -27, 69, -50, 38$

○ = WORKED-OUT SOLUTIONS
on p. WS12

33. Which set of integers is written in order from greatest to least?

A. $0, -4, -3, -1$ **C.** $9, -9, -10, -15$

B. $2, -4, 8, -16$ **D.** $-8, -7, -6, -5$

34. Earth Science The normal high temperature in January for Barrow, Alaska, is $-7\,°F$. The normal high temperature in January for Los Angeles is $68\,°F$. Compare the two temperatures using $<$ or $>$.

35. Geography The table shows elevations for several natural features. Write the features in order from the least elevation to the greatest elevation.

Elevations of Natural Features	
Mt. Everest	29,022 ft
Mt. Rainier	14,410 ft
Kilimanjaro	19,000 ft
San Augustin Cave	−2,189 ft
Dead Sea	−1,296 ft

36. What's the Error? Your classmate says that $0 < -91$. Explain why this is incorrect.

37. Write About It Explain how you would order from least to greatest three numbers that include a positive number, a negative number, and zero.

38. Challenge There is a missing integer from the list below. The missing integer is both the median and the mode. What is the integer? (*Hint:* There could be more than one correct answer.) $2, -10, 7, -7, 5, -5$

39. Multiple Choice Which set of integers is written in order from greatest to least?

A. $-3, -9, -6$ **B.** $-3, 2, 5$ **C.** $2, -1, -3$ **D.** $4, 10, 12$

40. Short Response The table shows the elevations relative to sea level of several cities. Order the cities from the least elevation to the greatest elevation.

City	Boston	Cincinnati	Death Valley	Salt Lake City	San Antonio
Elevation (ft)	16	483	−282	4,226	807

Find each missing value to the nearest hundredth. Use 3.14 for π. (Lesson 8-7)

41. If $d = 15.2$ ft, then $r = \underline{\quad?\quad}$, and $C \approx \underline{\quad?\quad}$.

Find the missing measurement for the rectangular prism. (Lesson 9-6)

42. $\ell = 4.2$ m; $w = \underline{\quad?\quad}$; $h = 2$ m; $V = 15.12$ m^3

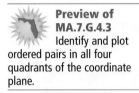

11-3 The Coordinate Plane

Preview of MA.7.G.4.3
Identify and plot ordered pairs in all four quadrants of the coordinate plane.

A **coordinate plane** is formed by two number lines in a plane that intersect at right angles. The point of intersection is the zero on each number line.

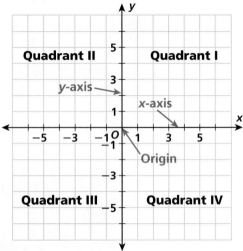

- The two number lines are called the **axes**.

- The horizontal axis is called the ***x*-axis**.

- The vertical axis is called the ***y*-axis**.

- The two axes divide the coordinate plane into four **quadrants**.

- The point where the axes intersect is called the **origin**.

Vocabulary

coordinate plane

axes

x-axis

y-axis

quadrants

origin

coordinates

x-coordinate

y-coordinate

EXAMPLE 1 Identifying Quadrants

Name the quadrant where each point is located.

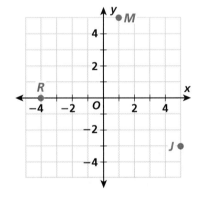

A *M*
  Quadrant I

B *J*
  Quadrant IV

C *R*
  x-axis
  no quadrant

Helpful Hint

Points on the axes are not in any quadrant.

An ordered pair gives the location of a point on a coordinate plane. The first number tells how far to move right (positive) or left (negative) from the origin. The second number tells how far to move up (positive) or down (negative).

The numbers in an ordered pair are called **coordinates**. The first number is called the ***x*-coordinate**. The second number is called the ***y*-coordinate**.

The ordered pair for the origin is (0, 0).

Video Lesson Tutorial Videos @ thinkcentral.com

Locating Points on a Coordinate Plane

Give the coordinates of each point.

A K

From the origin, K is 1 unit right and 4 units up.

$(1, 4)$

B T

From the origin, T is 2 units left on the x-axis.

$(-2, 0)$

C W

From the origin, W is 3 units left and 4 units down.

$(-3, -4)$

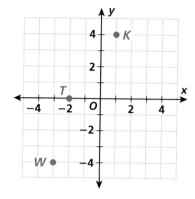

EXAMPLE **Graphing Points on a Coordinate Plane**

Graph each point on a coordinate plane.

A $P(-3, -2)$

From the origin, move 3 units left and 2 units down.

B $R(0, 4)$

From the origin, move 4 units up.

C $M(3, -4)$

From the origin, move 3 units right and 4 units down.

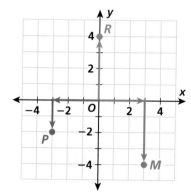

Think and Discuss

1. Tell which number in an ordered pair indicates how far to move left or right from the origin and which number indicates how far to move up or down.

2. Describe how graphing the point (5, 4) is similar to graphing the point (5, −4). How is it different?

3. Tell why it is important to start at the origin when you are graphing points.

Homework Help
Go to **thinkcentral.com**
Exercises 1–27, 31, 33, 35, 37, 45, 47, 49

Preview MA.7.G.4.3

GUIDED PRACTICE

Use the coordinate plane for Exercises 1–6.

See Example **1** Name the quadrant where each point is located.

1. T **2.** U **3.** B

See Example **2** Give the coordinates of each point.

4. A **5.** B **6.** U

See Example **3** Graph each point on a coordinate plane.

7. $E(4, 2)$ **8.** $F(-1, -4)$ **9.** $G(0, 2)$

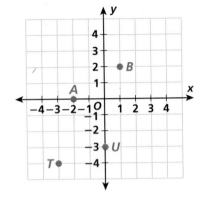

INDEPENDENT PRACTICE

Use the coordinate plane for Exercises 10–21.

See Example **1** Name the quadrant where each point is located.

10. Q **11.** X **12.** H

13. Y **14.** Z **15.** P

See Example **2** Give the coordinates of each point.

16. P **17.** R **18.** Y

19. T **20.** H **21.** Q

See Example **3** Graph each point on a coordinate plane.

22. $L(0, 3)$ **23.** $M(3, -3)$ **24.** $S(2, 0)$

25. $V(-4, 3)$ **26.** $N(-2, -1)$ **27.** $B(4, 3)$

PRACTICE AND PROBLEM SOLVING

Name the quadrant where each ordered pair is located.

28. $(3, -1)$ **29.** $(2, 1)$ **30.** $(-2, 3)$ **31.** $(-4, -3)$

32. $\left(4\frac{1}{2}, -3\right)$ **33.** $\left(10, -7\frac{1}{2}\right)$ **34.** $\left(-6, 2\frac{1}{3}\right)$ **35.** $\left(-8\frac{1}{3}, -\frac{1}{2}\right)$

Graph each ordered pair.

36. $(0, -5)$ **37.** $(-4, -4)$ **38.** $(5, 0)$ **39.** $(3, 2)$

40. $(-2, 2)$ **41.** $(0, -3)$ **42.** $(1, -4)$ **43.** $(0, 0)$

44. $\left(-2\frac{1}{2}, 3\right)$ **45.** $\left(5, 3\frac{1}{2}\right)$ **46.** $\left(-4\frac{1}{3}, 0\right)$ **47.** $\left(0, -\frac{1}{2}\right)$

48. **Geometry** Graph points $A(-1, -1)$, $B(2, 1)$, $C(2, -2)$, and $D(-1, -2)$. Connect the points. What type of quadrilateral do the points form?

○ = WORKED-OUT SOLUTIONS
on p. WS12

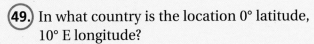
We use a coordinate system on Earth to find exact locations. The *equator* is like the *x*-axis, and the *prime meridian* is like the *y*-axis.

The lines that run east-west are *lines of latitude.* They are measured in degrees north and south of the equator.

The lines that run north-south are *lines of longitude.* They are measured in degrees east and west of the prime meridian.

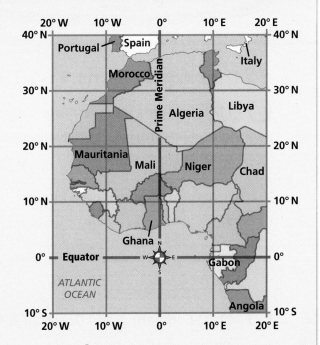

49. In what country is the location 0° latitude, 10° E longitude?

50. Give the coordinates of a location in Algeria.

51. Name two countries that lie along the 30° N line of latitude.

52. Where would you be if you were located at 10° S latitude, 10° W longitude?

53. ✎ **Write About It** How is the coordinate system we use to locate places on Earth different from the coordinate plane? How is it similar?

54. ⭐ **Challenge** Begin at 10° S latitude, 20° E longitude. Travel 40° north and 20° west. What country would you be in now?

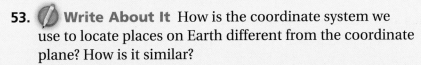

Florida Spiral Review
MA.6.A.5.1, MA.6.A.5.2

55. Multiple Choice In which quadrant is the point $(-1, 2)$ located?

A. Quadrant I   **B.** Quadrant II   **C.** Quadrant III   **D.** Quadrant IV

56. Multiple Choice Which of the following coordinates is the farthest to the right of the origin on a coordinate plane?

F. $(-19, 7)$ **G.** $(0, 12)$ **H.** $(4, 15)$ **I.** $(7, 0)$

Write each fraction or mixed number as a decimal. (Lesson 4-5)

57. $4\frac{2}{5}$ **58.** $\frac{9}{10}$ **59.** $5\frac{3}{4}$ **60.** $\frac{9}{20}$ **61.** $\frac{1}{5}$

Compare. Write <, >, or =. (Lesson 7-5)

62. $\frac{7}{8}$ ▮ 90%   **63.** 0.30 ▮ $\frac{3}{10}$ **64.** 45% ▮ 4.5   **65.** $\frac{2}{7}$ ▮ 26%

Quiz for Lessons 11-1 Through 11-3

11-1 Integers and Absolute Value

Name a positive or negative number to represent each situation.

1. a gain of 10 yards

2. 45 feet below sea level

Write the opposite of each integer.

3. 9   **4.** -17 **5.** 1   **6.** -20

Write the absolute value of each integer.

7. $|7|$ **8.** $|-6|$ **9.** $|-8|$ **10.** $|-9|$

11-2 Comparing and Ordering Integers

Compare. Write $<$ or $>$.

11. 9 ▨ -22 **12.** -7 ▨ 4   **13.** -10 ▨ -19

Order the integers in each set from least to greatest.

14. $2, -7, 14$ **15.** $25, -9, 4, -21$ **16.** $10, 0, -23, -17, 8$

17. The table shows the monthly record low temperatures in Minneapolis, Minnesota. Order the months from the highest temperature to the lowest temperature.

Month	Jan	Feb	Mar	Apr	May	Jun	Jul	Aug	Sep	Oct	Nov	Dec
Temperature (°F)	-41	-33	-32	2	18	34	43	39	26	10	-25	-39

11-3 The Coordinate Plane

Use the coordinate plane for Problems 18–25.

Name the quadrant where each point is located.

18. A **19.** Y **20.** J **21.** C

Give the coordinates of each point.

22. H **23.** I **24.** W **25.** B

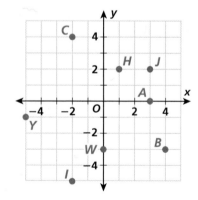

Graph each point on a coordinate plane.

26. $N(-5, -2)$ **27.** $S(0, 4)$ **28.** $R(-2, 6)$ **29.** $M(2, 2)$

30. Graph the points $A(-4, 4)$, $B(-2, 4)$, $C(-1, 1)$, and $D(-3, 1)$ on a coordinate plane. Then connect the points in the order given, and connect point D to point A. What type of quadrilateral do the connected points form?

Focus on Problem Solving

 Understand the Problem

• **Restate the question**

After reading a real-world problem (perhaps several times), look at the question in the problem. Rewrite the question as a statement in your own words. For example, if the question is "How much money did the museum earn?" you could write, "Find the amount of money the museum earned."

Now you have a simple sentence telling you what you must do. This can help you understand and remember what the problem is about. This can also help you find the necessary information in the problem.

 Read the problems below. Rewrite each question as a statement in your own words.

1 Israel is one of the hottest countries in Asia. A temperature of 129 °F was once recorded there. This is the opposite of the coldest recorded temperature in Antarctica. How cold has it been in Antarctica?

2 The average recorded temperature in Fairbanks, Alaska, in January is about −10 °F. In February, the average temperature is about −4 °F. Is the average temperature lower in January or in February?

3 The south pole on Mars is made of frozen carbon dioxide, which has a temperature of −193 °F. The coldest day recorded on Earth was −129 °F, in Antarctica. Which temperature is lower?

4 The pirate Blackbeard's ship, the *Queen Anne's Revenge,* sank at Beauford Inlet, North Carolina, in 1718. In 1996, divers discovered a shipwreck believed to be the *Queen Anne's Revenge.* The ship's cannons were found 21 feet below the water's surface, and the ship's bell was found 20 feet below the surface. Were the cannons or the bell closer to the surface?

In this photo of Mars, different colors represent different temperature ranges. When the photo was taken, it was summer in the northern hemisphere and winter in the southern hemisphere.

−65 °C   −120 °C

Adding Integers

Preview of MA.7.A.3.1 Use and justify the rules for adding . . . integers.
Preview of MA.7.A.3.2 Add . . . integers, . . . including solving problems in everyday contexts.

One of the world's most active volcanoes is Kilauea, in Hawaii. Kilauea's base is 9 km below sea level. The top of Kilauea is 10 km above the base of the mountain.

You can add the integers −9 and 10 to find the height of Kilauea above sea level.

Adding Integers on a Number Line

Move **right** on a number line to add a **positive** integer.

Move **left** on a number line to add a **negative** integer.

EXAMPLE 1

Animated Math
@ thinkcentral.com

Writing Integer Addition

Write the addition modeled on each number line.

Writing Math

Parentheses are used to separate addition, subtraction, multiplication, and division signs from negative integers.
−2 + (−5) = −7

A

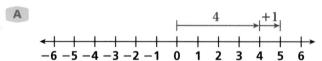

The addition modeled is $4 + 1 = 5$.

B

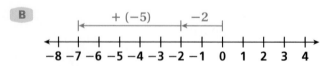

The addition modeled is $-2 + (-5) = -7$.

C

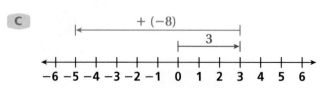

The addition modeled is $3 + (-8) = -5$.

Video **Lesson Tutorial Videos @ thinkcentral.com**

EXAMPLE 2 Adding Integers

Find each sum.

A 6 + (−5)

Think:

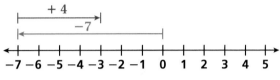

6 + (−5) = 1

B −7 + 4

Think:

−7 + 4 = −3

EXAMPLE 3 Evaluating Integer Expressions

Evaluate x + 3 for x = −9.

x + 3	*Write the expression.*
−9 + 3	*Substitute −9 for x.*
−6	*Add.*

Think:

EXAMPLE 4 *Earth Science Application*

The base of Kilauea is 9 km below sea level. The top is 10 km above the base. How high above sea level is Kilauea?

The base is 9 km below sea level and the top is 10 km above the base.

−9 + 10

1

Kilauea is 1 km above sea level.

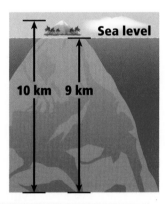

Think and Discuss

1. Tell if the sum of a positive integer and −8 is greater than −8 or less than −8. Explain.

2. Give the sum of a number and its opposite.

Exercises

Preview MA.7.A.3.1,
MA.7.A.3.2

GUIDED PRACTICE

See Example 1 Write the addition modeled on the number line.

1.

See Example 2 Find each sum.

2. $-5 + 9$ **3.** $-3 + (-2)$ **4.** $8 + (-7)$

5. $10 + (-3)$ **6.** $-4 + (-8)$ **7.** $-1 + 5$

See Example 3 Evaluate $n + (-2)$ for each value of n.

8. $n = -10$ **9.** $n = 2$ **10.** $n = -2$

11. $n = -15$ **12.** $n = 12$ **13.** $n = -20$

See Example 4 **14.** A submarine at the water's surface dropped down 100 feet. After thirty minutes at that depth, it dove an additional 500 feet. What was its depth after the second dive?

INDEPENDENT PRACTICE

See Example 1 Write the addition modeled on each number line.

15.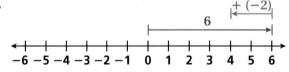

16.

See Example 2 Find each sum.

17. $4 + 7$ **18.** $2 + (-12)$ **19.** $9 + (-9)$ **20.** $10 + (-21)$

21. $-8 + 2$ **22.** $-2 + 8$ **23.** $-1 + (-6)$ **24.** $-25 + (14)$

See Example 3 Evaluate $-6 + a$ for each value of a.

25. $a = -10$ **26.** $a = 7$ **27.** $a = -2$ **28.** $a = -6$

29. $a = 4$ **30.** $a = -9$ **31.** $a = 8$ **32.** $a = -20$

See Example 4 **33.** Jon works on a cruise ship and sleeps in a cabin that is 6 feet below sea level. The main deck is 35 feet above Jon's cabin. How far above sea level is the main deck?

34. Recreation Preston dives to a depth of 15 feet. He stops briefly and then dives an additional 17 feet. What is Preston's depth after his second dive?

Model each addition problem on a number line.

35. $3 + (-1)$ **36.** $-2 + (-4)$ **37.** $-6 + 5$ **38.** $1 + (-2)$

39. $-1 + 6$ **40.** $5 + (-3)$ **41.** $-3 + (-1)$ **42.** $0 + (-5)$

Find each sum.

43. $-18 + 25$ **44.** $8 + (-2)$ **45.** $-5 + (-6)$ **46.** $-12 + (-7)$

47. $-6 + (-3)$ **48.** $4 + (-1)$ **49.** $20 + (-3)$ **50.** $30 + (-25)$

Evaluate each expression for the given value of the variable.

51. $x + (-3); x = 7$ **52.** $-9 + n; n = 7$ **53.** $a + 5; a = -6$

54. $m + (-2); m = -4$ **55.** $-10 + x; x = -7$ **56.** $n + 19; n = -5$

57. **Earth Science** The temperature at midnight was -2 °F. During the next 4 hours, a decrease of 4 °F was recorded. What was the temperature at 4 A.M.?

58. **Sports** In the 2001 U.S. Women's Open, Cristie Kerr had the following scores for the four rounds of golf: $-1, +3, +1,$ and 0. What was her total score?

59. **Choose a Strategy** The first Roman emperor, Augustus, was born in 63 B.C.E. and died in 14 C.E. How many years did he live? (*Hint*: Years B.C.E. are like negative numbers. Years C.E. are like positive numbers. There was no year 0.)

60. **Critical Thinking** Will the expression $-7 + 10$ have the same sum as $10 + (-7)$? Justify your answer.

61. **Write About It** When adding two integers, what will the sign of the answer be when one integer is positive and the other is negative? Explain.

62. **Challenge** Evaluate $-3 + (-2) + (-1) + 0 + 1 + 2 + 3 + 4$. Then use this pattern to find the sum of the integers from -10 to 11 and from -100 to 101.

Link

History

Augustus, originally named Octavian, ruled the Roman Empire for more than 40 years.

Florida Spiral Review

MA.6.A.3.2, MA.6.A.3.4, MA.6.G.4.3

63. **Multiple Choice** Julie earned $1,350 at her part-time job. Her paycheck showed deductions of $148.50. What was the total amount of her paycheck?

A. $1,165.50 **B.** $1,201.50 **C.** $1,498.50 **D.** $1,534.50

64. **Multiple Choice** Which sum is NOT negative?

F. $-38 + (-24)$ **G.** $-61 + 43$ **H.** $-54 + 68$ **I.** $-29 + 11$

65. **Short Response** What is the value of $b + 7$ for $b = -2, -4,$ and -8?

66. A rectangular prism has a volume of 76.68 ft^3. The length of the prism is 7.1 ft and the width is 4 ft. What is the height of the prism? *(Lesson 9-6)*

Solve each equation. *(Lesson 10-3)*

67. $\frac{x}{5} + 8 = 15$ **68.** $3m - 12 = 60$ **69.** $\frac{r + 6}{4} = 11$

Preview of MA.7.A.3.1 Use and justify the rules for . . . subtracting . . . integers.
Preview of MA.7.A.3.2 . . . Subtract . . . integers, . . . including solving problems in everyday contexts.

On a number line, integer subtraction is the opposite of integer addition. Integer subtraction "undoes" integer addition.

Subtracting Integers on a Number Line
Move **left** on a number line to subtract a **positive** integer.
Move **right** on a number line to subtract a **negative** integer.

EXAMPLE 1 **Writing Integer Subtraction**

Animated Math
@ thinkcentral.com

Write the subtraction modeled on each number line.

A
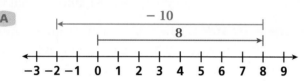

The subtraction modeled is $8 - 10 = -2$.

B
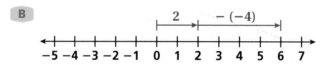

The subtraction modeled is $2 - (-4) = 6$.

EXAMPLE 2 **Subtracting Integers**

Find each difference.

A $7 - 4$

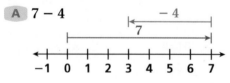

Think:

$7 - 4 = 3$

B $-8 - (-2)$

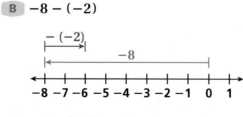

Think:

$-8 - (-2) = -6$

Video **Lesson Tutorial Videos** @ **thinkcentral.com**

EXAMPLE 3 **Evaluating Integer Expressions**

Evaluate $x - (-4)$ for $x = -5$.

$x - (-4)$	*Write the expression.*
$-5 - (-4)$	*Substitute −5 for x.*
-1	*Subtract.*

Think:

Think and Discuss

1. Describe the direction you would move to add a positive integer.

2. Explain how the answers to Example 1 help show that addition and subtraction are inverses.

11-5 Exercises

GUIDED PRACTICE

See Example 1
1. Write the subtraction modeled on the number line.

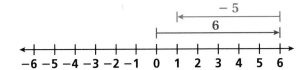

See Example 2
Find each difference.

2. $6 - 3$ **3.** $3 - 6$ **4.** $10 - (-4)$ **5.** $-12 - (-4)$

See Example 3
Evaluate $n - (-6)$ for each value of n.

6. $n = -4$ **7.** $n = 2$ **8.** $n = -15$ **9.** $n = 7$

INDEPENDENT PRACTICE

See Example 1
10. Write the subtraction modeled on the number line.

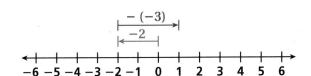

See Example 2
Find each difference.

11. $3 - 7$ **12.** $-4 - 9$ **13.** $2 - (-9)$ **14.** $-22 - (-2)$

See Example 3
Evaluate $m - (-3)$ for each value of m.

15. $m = -1$ **16.** $m = 7$ **17.** $m = -8$ **18.** $m = -5$

19. $m = 4$ **20.** $m = -9$ **21.** $m = -15$ **22.** $m = 13$

Video **Lesson Tutorial Videos @ thinkcentral.com**

Find each difference.

23. $-12 - (-6)$ **24.** $7 - (-3)$ **25.** $-4 - (-3)$ **26.** $8 - (-2)$

27. $19 - (-2)$ **28.** $-5 - 10$ **29.** $50 - 20$ **30.** $-2 - 7$

Evaluate each expression for the given value of the variable.

31. $n - (-10); n = 2$ **32.** $-6 - m; m = -9$ **33.** $x - 2; x = 6$

34. $4 - y; y = 9$ **35.** $j - 21; j = -17$ **36.** $101 - h; h = -75$

37. **Earth Science** The surface of an underground water supply was 10 m below sea level. After one year, the depth of the water supply has decreased by 9 m. How far below sea level is the water's surface now?

38. **Construction** A 200-foot column holds an oil rig platform above the ocean's surface. The column rests on the ocean floor 175 feet below sea level. How high is the platform above sea level?

39. **Earth Science** During summer 1997, NASA landed the *Pathfinder* on Mars. On July 9, *Pathfinder* reported a temperature of -1 °F on the planet's surface. On July 10, it reported a temperature of 8 °F. What is the difference between the temperature on July 10 and the temperature on July 9?

40. **What's the Error?** Ty says that $0 - (-4) = -4$. Explain why this is incorrect.

41. **Write About It** Will the difference between two negative numbers ever be positive? Use examples to support your answer.

42. **Challenge** This pyramid was built by subtracting integers. Two integers are subtracted from left to right, and their difference is centered above them. Find the missing numbers.

Florida Spiral Review   MA.6.A.3.2, MA.6.A.5.1

43. **Multiple Choice** What is the value of $h - (-8)$ when $h = 3$?

   A. -11 **B.** -5 **C.** 5   **D.** 11

44. **Multiple Choice** Trina's score on a game show was -250 points. Gwen's score was -320 points. By how many points was Trina ahead of Gwen?

   F. 570 points   **G.** 70 points   **H.** -70 points   **I.** -570 points

Write each decimal as a percent. (Lesson 7-5)

45. 0.02   **46.** 0.53   **47.** 0.26   **48.** 0.44   **49.** 3.1

50. Raul earned a 72 on his first test. He needs at least 160 points on his first two tests to get a B in the class. What score must Raul make on his second test to ensure a B in the class? Write an inequality to represent the situation. (Lesson 10-4)

○ = **WORKED-OUT SOLUTIONS**
on p. WS12

11-6 ⟩ Multiplying Integers

Preview of MA.7.A.3.1 Use and justify the rules for . . . multiplying . . . integers.
Preview of MA.7.A.3.2 . . . Multiply . . . integers, . . . including solving problems in everyday contexts.

You have seen that you can multiply whole numbers to count items in equally sized groups.

There are three sets of twins in the sixth grade. How many sixth graders are twins?

A set of twins is 2 people.

$3 \cdot 2 = 6$ *3 sets of 2 is 6.*

So 6 students in the sixth grade are twins.

The table shows how to use reasoning about equally sized groups to multiply integers.

Numbers	$3 \cdot 2$	$-3 \cdot 2$	$3 \cdot (-2)$	$-3 \cdot (-2)$
Words	3 groups of 2	the opposite of 3 groups of 2	3 groups of –2	the opposite of 3 groups of –2
Addition	$2 + 2 + 2$	$-(2 + 2 + 2)$	$(-2) + (-2) + (-2)$	$-[(-2) + (-2) + (-2)]$
Product	6	-6	-6	6

EXAMPLE 1   Multiplying Integers

Find each product.

A $4 \cdot 3$

$4 \cdot 3 = 12$ *Think: 4 groups of 3*

B $2 \cdot (-4)$

$2 \cdot (-4) = -8$ *Think: 2 groups of −4*

C $-5 \cdot 2$

$-5 \cdot 2 = -10$ *Think: **the opposite of** 5 groups of 2*

D $-3 \cdot (-4)$

$-3 \cdot (-4) = 12$ *Think: **the opposite of** 3 groups of −4*

Remember!

To find the opposite of a number, change the sign. The opposite of 6 is −6. The opposite of −4 is 4.

 Lesson Tutorial Videos @ thinkcentral.com

11-6 Multiplying Integers   **505**

MULTIPLYING INTEGERS

If the signs are the same, the product is positive.

$$4 \cdot 3 = 12 \qquad -6 \cdot (-3) = 18$$

If the signs are different, the product is negative.

$$-2 \cdot 5 = -10 \qquad 7 \cdot (-8) = -56$$

The product of any number and 0 is 0.

$$0 \cdot 9 = 0 \qquad (-12) \cdot 0 = 0$$

EXAMPLE 2 **Evaluating Integer Expressions**

Evaluate $5x$ for each value of x.

Remember!

$5x$ means $5 \cdot x$.

A $x = -4$

$5x$ *Write the expression.*

$5 \cdot (-4)$ *Substitute −4 for x.*

-20 *The signs are different, so the answer is negative.*

B $x = 0$

$5x$ *Write the expression.*

$5 \cdot 0$ *Substitute 0 for x.*

0 *Any number times 0 is 0.*

Think and Discuss

1. Explain whether the product of two integers is greater than, less than, or between the two factors.

 11-6

Exercises

 Preview MA.7.A.3.1, MA.7.A.3.2

 **Homework Help** THINK central

Go to thinkcentral.com
Exercises 1–32, 33, 35, 37, 39

GUIDED PRACTICE

See Example 1 **Find each product.**

1. $6 \cdot 4$ **2.** $5 \cdot (-2)$ **3.** $-3 \cdot 7$ **4.** $-2 \cdot 3$

5. $-9 \cdot (-1)$ **6.** $13 \cdot 0$ **7.** $-8 \cdot (-2)$ **8.** $-6 \cdot (-6)$

See Example 2 **Evaluate $3n$ for each value of n.**

9. $n = 3$ **10.** $n = -2$ **11.** $n = 11$ **12.** $n = -5$

13. $n = -8$ **14.** $n = -12$ **15.** $n = 6$ **16.** $n = 10$

Video **Lesson Tutorial Videos** @ thinkcentral.com

See Example 1 **Find each product.**

17. $5 \cdot 9$ **18.** $-7 \cdot 6$ **19.** $8 \cdot (-4)$ **20.** $-6 \cdot (-9)$

21. $-13 \cdot (-3)$ **22.** $4 \cdot 12$ **23.** $6 \cdot (-12)$ **24.** $-7 \cdot (-11)$

See Example 2 **Evaluate $-4a$ for each value of a.**

25. $a = 6$ **26.** $a = 12$ **27.** $a = 3$ **28.** $a = -7$

29. $a = -10$ **30.** $a = 7$ **31.** $a = -15$ **32.** $a = -22$

PRACTICE AND PROBLEM SOLVING

Evaluate each expression for the given value of the variable.

33. $n \cdot (-7); n = -2$ **34.** $-6 \cdot m; m = 4$ **35.** $9x; x = 6$

36. $-5m; m = 5$ **37.** $x \cdot 10; x = -9$ **38.** $-8 \cdot n; n = -1$

39. Earth Science When the Moon, the Sun, and Earth are in a straight line, spring tides occur on Earth. Spring tides may cause high and low tides to be two times as great as normal. If high tides at a certain location are usually 2 ft and low tides are usually -2 ft, what might the spring tides be?

40. Critical Thinking What number property is true for integer multiplication?

41. What's the Error? Ava says the value of $-6b$ when $b = -6$ is -36. What is her error? What is the correct answer?

42. Write About It What is the sign of the product when you multiply three negative integers? four negative integers? Use examples to explain.

43. Challenge Name two integers whose product is -36 and whose sum is 0.

Florida Spiral Review

MA.6.A.1.2, MA.6.A.1.3

44. Multiple Choice During a game, Frieda scored -10 points for each question she missed. She missed 5 questions. What was the total number of points she scored on missed questions?

    A. -50 **B.** -2 **C.** 2   **D.** 50

45. Extended Response What is the sign of the product when 4 negative integers are multiplied? when 5 negative integers are multiplied? Describe a rule that can be used to determine the sign of the product when the number of negative integers is even and when the number of negative integers is odd.

46. Kim cut $6\frac{1}{3}$ yards of ribbon into $\frac{1}{3}$-yard pieces. How many pieces of ribbon did Kim have? (Lesson 5-8)

Solve each inequality. (Lesson 10-5)

47. $\frac{a - 5}{4} \geq 6$ **48.** $17 + 2f \leq 30$ **49.** $\frac{n}{10} - 8 < 5$

Dividing Integers

Preview of MA.7.A.3.1 Use and justify the rules for . . . dividing . . . integers.
Preview of MA.7.A.3.2 . . . Divide integers, . . . including solving problems in everyday contexts.

Mona is a biologist studying an endangered species of wombat. Each year she records the change in the wombat population.

Year	Change in Population
1	−2
2	−5
3	−1
4	−4

Australian wombat

One way to describe the change in the wombat population over time is to find the mean of the data in the table.

$$\frac{-2 + (-5) + (-1) + (-4)}{4} = \frac{-12}{4} = -12 \div 4 = \blacksquare$$

Multiplication and division are inverse operations. To solve a division problem, think of the related multiplication.

To solve −12 ÷ 4, think: What number times 4 equals −12?

$$-3 \cdot 4 = -12, \text{ so } -12 \div 4 = -3.$$

The mean change in the wombat population is −3. So on average, the population **decreased by 3 wombats** per year.

Remember!

To find the mean of a list of numbers:
1. Add all the numbers together.
2. Divide by how many numbers are in the list.

See page 252.

EXAMPLE **1**   **Dividing Integers**

Find each quotient.

A $12 \div (-3)$

Think: What number times −3 equals 12?

$-4 \cdot (-3) = 12$, so $12 \div (-3) = -4$.

B $-15 \div (-3)$

Think: What number times −3 equals −15?

$5 \cdot (-3) = -15$, so $-15 \div (-3) = 5$.

Video **Lesson Tutorial Videos** @ thinkcentral.com

Because division is the inverse of multiplication, the rules for dividing integers are the same as the rules for multiplying integers.

DIVIDING INTEGERS

If the signs are the same, the quotient is positive.
$$24 \div 3 = 8 \qquad -6 \div (-3) = 2$$

If the signs are different, the quotient is negative.
$$-20 \div 5 = -4 \qquad 72 \div (-8) = -9$$

Zero divided by any integer equals 0.
$$\frac{0}{14} = 0 \qquad \frac{0}{-11} = 0$$

You cannot divide any integer by 0.

EXAMPLE 2 **Evaluating Integer Expressions**

Evaluate $\frac{x}{3}$ for each value of x.

Remember!

$\frac{x}{3}$ means $x \div 3$.

A $x = 6$

$\frac{x}{3}$	*Write the expression.*
$\frac{6}{3} = 6 \div 3$	*Substitute 6 for x.*
$= 2$	*The signs are the same, so the answer is positive.*

B $x = -18$

$\frac{x}{3}$	*Write the expression.*
$\frac{-18}{3} = -18 \div 3$	*Substitute −18 for x.*
$= -6$	*The signs are different, so the answer is negative.*

C $x = -12$

$\frac{x}{3}$	*Write the expression.*
$\frac{-12}{3} = -12 \div 3$	*Substitute −12 for x.*
$= -4$	*The signs are different, so the answer is negative.*

Think and Discuss

1. Describe the sign of the quotient of two integers with like signs.

2. Describe the sign of the quotient of two integers with unlike signs.

Preview MA.7.A.3.1,
MA.7.A.3.2

Homework Help **THINK** central

Go to thinkcentral.com
Exercises 1–24, 27, 29, 31, 33, 37, 39, 43

GUIDED PRACTICE

See Example **1** Find each quotient.

1. $64 \div 8$
2. $10 \div (-2)$
3. $-21 \div (-7)$
4. $-64 \div 2$

See Example **2** Evaluate $\frac{m}{2}$ for each value of m.

5. $m = -4$
6. $m = 20$
7. $m = -30$
8. $m = 50$

INDEPENDENT PRACTICE

See Example **1** Find each quotient.

9. $45 \div 9$
10. $-42 \div 6$
11. $32 \div (-4)$
12. $54 \div (-6)$

13. $-60 \div (-10)$
14. $-75 \div 15$
15. $22 \div 11$
16. $-48 \div (-4)$

See Example **2** Evaluate $\frac{n}{4}$ for each value of n.

17. $n = 4$
18. $n = -32$
19. $n = 12$
20. $n = -24$

21. $n = 64$
22. $n = -92$
23. $n = 56$
24. $n = -28$

PRACTICE AND PROBLEM SOLVING

Divide.

25. $-12 \div 2$
26. $\frac{16}{-4}$
27. $-6 \div (-6)$
28. $-56 \div (-7)$

29. $\frac{-30}{-3}$
30. $-45 \div 9$
31. $\frac{-35}{5}$
32. $\frac{-63}{9}$

Evaluate each expression for the given value of the variable.

33. $n \div (-7)$; $n = -21$
34. $\frac{m}{3}$; $m = -15$
35. $\frac{x}{4}$; $x = 32$

36. $y \div (-3)$; $y = -6$
37. $\frac{a}{3}$; $a = -9$
38. $w \div (-2)$; $w = -18$

39. $-48 \div n$; $n = -8$
40. $\frac{p}{-2}$; $p = -20$
41. $j \div 9$; $j = -99$

42. The graph shows the low temperatures for 5 days in Fairbanks, Alaska.

   a. What is the mean low temperature for Monday, Tuesday, and Wednesday?

   b. What is the mean low temperature for all 5 days?

   c. **Critical Thinking** Which mean low temperature was higher? Justify your answer.

   d. What is the range of the data?

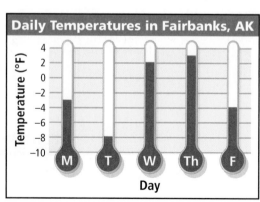

Daily Temperatures in Fairbanks, AK

○ = WORKED-OUT SOLUTIONS
on p. WS12

The Mediterranean monk seal is one of the world's rarest mammals. Monk seals have become endangered largely because divers hunt them for their skin and disturb their habitat.

Annette found this table in a science article about monk seals.

Changes in Population of Monk Seals							
Years	1971–1975	1976–1980	1981–1985	1986–1990	1991–1995	1996–2000	2001–2005
Change	550	−300	−150	−50	100	200	−100

43. **a.** According to the table, what was the change in the monk seal population from 1976 to 1980?

b. What does this number mean?

44. Find the mean change per year from 1971 to 1975. (*Hint:* This is a range of 5 years, so divide by 5.) What does your answer mean?

45. Find the mean change per year from 1981 to 1990. What does your answer mean?

46. **Write About It** Why is it important to use both positive and negative numbers when tracking the changes in a population?

47. **Challenge** Suppose that there were 250 monk seals in 1971. How many seals were there in 2005?

48. Multiple Choice Which quotient is greatest?

A. $-8 \div (-2)$ **B.** $-10 \div 5$ **C.** $-10 \div (-5)$ **D.** $15 \div (-5)$

49. Multiple Choice The change in population for a species is recorded in the table. What is the mean of the data?

Year	1	2	3	4
Change in Population	−2	+5	−7	−4

F. -4 **H.** 1
G. -2 **I.** 3

50. Sabina read 36% of her book on Monday. On Wednesday, she read $\frac{3}{8}$ of the book. Sabina finished the book on Saturday. What percent of the book did she read on Saturday? (Lesson 7-6)

Find the missing measurement for each rectangular prism. (Lesson 9-6)

51. $\ell = 9$ cm; $w = 24$ cm; $h = \underline{\ ?\ }$; $V = 1{,}296$ cm^3 **52.** $\ell = 8$ m; $w = \underline{\ ?\ }$; $h = 13$ m; $V = 728$ m^3

11-8 Solving Integer Equations

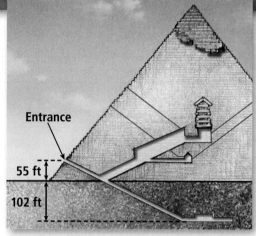

Preview of MA.7.A.3.3
Formulate and use different strategies to solve one-step . . . linear equations . . .
Also **Preview of MA.7.A.3.2**

Vocabulary
Identity Property

The entrance to the Great Pyramid of Khufu is 55 feet above ground. The underground chamber is 102 feet below ground. From the entrance, what is the distance to the underground chamber?

To solve this problem, you can use an equation containing integers.

Entrance

55 ft

102 ft

$$55 + d = -102$$ *Write the equation.*
$$\underline{-55 \qquad\quad -55}$$ *Subtract 55 from both sides to undo the addition.*
$$0 + d = -157$$
$$d = -157$$ *Identity Property of Addition: $0 + d = d$*

It is -157 **feet** from the entrance to the underground chamber. The sign is negative, which means you **go down 157 feet.**

The **Identity Property** of Addition allows you to simplify $0 + d$ to d in the last step of the example above.

Identity Properties		
Words	**Numbers**	**Algebra**
Addition: The sum of 0 and any number is the number.	$6 + 0 = 6$	$d + 0 = d$
Multiplication: The product of 1 and any number is the number.	$5 \cdot 1 = 5$	$d \cdot 1 = d$

EXAMPLE 1   Adding and Subtracting to Solve Equations

A Solve $4 + x = -2$. Check your answer.

$$4 + x = -2$$ *x is added to 4.*
$$\underline{-4 \qquad\quad -4}$$ *Subtract 4 from both sides to undo the addition.*
$$0 + x = -6$$
$$x = -6$$ *Identity Property of Addition: $0 + x = x$*

Check
$$4 + x = -2$$ *Write the equation.*
$$4 + (-6) \overset{?}{=} -2$$ *Substitute -6 for x.*
$$-2 \overset{?}{=} -2 \checkmark$$ *-6 is a solution.*

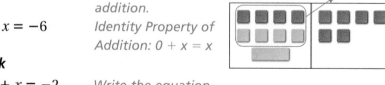

Helpful Hint

Subtracting a number is the same as adding its opposite. To solve this equation using algebra tiles, you can add four red tiles to both sides and then remove zero pairs.

Video   **Lesson Tutorial Videos** @ **thinkcentral.com**

B Solve $y - 6 = -5$. Check your answer.

$$y - 6 = -5$$ *6 is subtracted from y.*

$$\underline{+6 \quad +6}$$ *Add 6 to both sides to*

$$y + 0 = 1$$ *undo the subtraction.*

$$y \quad\quad = 1$$ *Identity Property of*
                           Addition: y + 0 = y

Check

$$y - 6 = -5$$ *Write the equation.*

$$1 - 6 \overset{?}{=} -5$$ *Substitute 1 for y.*

$$-5 \overset{?}{=} -5 ✔$$ *1 is a solution.*

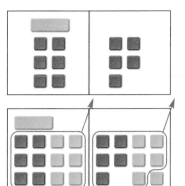

E X A M P L E **2** **Multiplying and Dividing to Solve Equations**

Solve each equation. Check your answers.

A $-3a = 15$

$$\frac{-3a}{-3} = \frac{15}{-3}$$ *a is multiplied by −3. Divide both sides*
                       by −3 to undo the multiplication.

$$1a = -5$$

$$a = -5$$ *Identity Property of Multiplication: 1a = a*

Check

$$-3a = 15$$ *Write the equation.*

$$-3(-5) \overset{?}{=} 15$$ *Substitute −5 for a.*

$$15 \overset{?}{=} 15 ✔$$ *−5 is a solution.*

B $$\frac{b}{-4} = -2$$

$$-4 \cdot \frac{b}{-4} = -4 \cdot (-2)$$ *b is divided by −4. Multiply both sides*
                           by −4 to undo the division.

$$1b = 8$$

$$b = 8$$ *Identity Property of Multiplication: 1b = b*

Check

$$\frac{b}{-4} = -2$$ *Write the equation.*

$$8 \div (-4) \overset{?}{=} -2$$ *Substitute 8 for b.*

$$-2 \overset{?}{=} -2 ✔$$ *8 is a solution.*

Think and Discuss

1. Tell what operation you would use to solve $x + 12 = -32$.

2. Tell whether the solution to $-9t = -27$ will be positive or negative without actually solving the equation.

Homework Help

Go to thinkcentral.com
Exercises 1–32, 47, 51, 55, 57, 59, 61, 67

Preview MA.7.A.3.3,
MA.7.A.3.2

GUIDED PRACTICE

See Example **1** Solve each equation. Check your answers.

1. $m - 3 = 9$ **2.** $a - 8 = -13$ **3.** $z - 12 = -3$ **4.** $j - 2 = 7$

5. $p + 2 = -7$ **6.** $k - 9 = 21$ **7.** $g - 10 = -2$ **8.** $h + 15 = 25$

See Example **2** **9.** $-4b = 32$ **10.** $\frac{w}{3} = 18$ **11.** $5c = -35$ **12.** $\frac{p}{-5} = 10$

13. $6f = -36$ **14.** $-2c = 72$ **15.** $\frac{r}{10} = -90$ **16.** $\frac{d}{-12} = 144$

INDEPENDENT PRACTICE

See Example **1** Solve each equation. Check your answers.

17. $g - 9 = -5$ **18.** $v - 7 = 19$ **19.** $t - 13 = -27$ **20.** $s - 4 = -21$

21. $x + 2 = -12$ **22.** $y + 9 = -10$ **23.** $20 + w = 10$ **24.** $z + 15 = 50$

See Example **2** **25.** $6j = 48$ **26.** $7s = -49$ **27.** $\frac{a}{-2} = 26$ **28.** $-2r = 10$

29. $\frac{m}{-12} = 4$ **30.** $\frac{k}{5} = -4$ **31.** $u \div 6 = -10$ **32.** $6t = -36$

PRACTICE AND PROBLEM SOLVING

Solve each equation. Check your answers.

33. $x - 12 = 5$ **34.** $w - 3 = -2$ **35.** $-7k = 28$ **36.** $g \div 7 = -2$

37. $\frac{m}{-3} = 5$ **38.** $a - 10 = 9$ **39.** $n - 19 = -22$ **40.** $2h = 42$

41. $13g = -39$ **42.** $s \div 6 = -3$ **43.** $24 + f = 16$ **44.** $q - 15 = -4$

45. $d - 26 = 7$ **46.** $-6c = 54$ **47.** $h \div (-4) = 21$ **48.** $7k = 70$

49. $b - 17 = 15$ **50.** $u - 82 = -7$ **51.** $-8a = -64$ **52.** $v + 1 = -9$

53. $\frac{t}{11} = -5$ **54.** $31 + j = -14$ **55.** $c + 23 = 10$ **56.** $\frac{r}{-2} = -8$

57. $15n = -60$ **58.** $z \div (-5) = -9$ **59.** $j - 20 = -23$ **60.** $f + 20 = -60$

61. A deep-sea submersible follows this diving course: dive 200 ft, stop, and then dive another 200 ft. If this pattern is continued, how many dives will be necessary to reach a location 14,000 ft below sea level?

62. Physical Science While exploring a cave, Lin noticed that the temperature dropped 4 °F for every 30 ft that she descended. What is Lin's depth if the temperature is 8° lower than the temperature at the surface?

63. Sports After two rounds in the 2001 LPGA Champions Classic, Wendy Doolan had a score of -12. Her score in the second round was -8. What was her score in the first round?

64. Critical Thinking If the product of a variable and a number is positive and the number is negative, what is the sign of the value of the variable?

○ = **WORKED-OUT SOLUTIONS**
on p. WS12

Use the graph for Exercises 65 and 66.

65. **Life Science** Scientists have found live bacteria at altitudes of 135,000 ft. This is 153,500 ft above one of the animals in the graph. Which one? (*Hint:* Solve $x + 153,500 = 135,000$.)

66. **Social Studies** The world's highest capital city is La Paz, Bolivia, with an elevation of 11,808 ft. The highest altitude that a yak has been found at is how much higher than La Paz? (*Hint:* Solve $11,808 + x = 20,000$.)

67. **Recreation** Carla is a diver. On Friday, she dove 5 times as deep as she dove on Monday. If she dove to −120 ft on Friday, how deep did she dive on Monday?

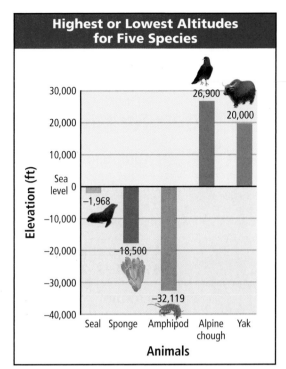

Highest or Lowest Altitudes for Five Species

68. **Write A Problem** Write a word problem that could be solved by using the equation $x − 3 = −15$.

69. **Write About It** Is the solution to $3n = −12$ positive or negative? How could you tell without solving the equation?

70. **Challenge** Find each answer.

　　a. $12 \div (−3 \cdot 2) \div 2$　　　　　　b. $12 \div (−3 \cdot 2 \div 2)$

　　Why are the answers different even though the numbers are the same?

Florida Spiral Review　　　　　　　　　　　　　　　　　　MA.6.A.3.6, MA.6.G.4.1

71. **Multiple Choice** Kathie and her three friends each owe $24 for dinner. Solve the equation $\frac{t}{4} = 24$ to determine the total amount t of the dinner.

　　A. $96　　　　　**B.** $28　　　　　**C.** $20　　　　　**D.** $6

72. **Short Response** David is 12 years younger than his sister Candace. David is 9 years old. Write an equation for the situation. Let c be Candace's age. Then solve the equation to find her age.

73. The circumference of a circle is 20.41 inches. What is the diameter of the circle? What is the radius? Use 3.14 for π. (Lesson 8-7)

Determine whether each ordered pair is a solution of the given equation. (Lesson 10-2)

74. $(5, 18)$; $y = 3x + 1$　　　　　　　　　75. $(12, 19)$; $y = 2x − 5$

Ready To Go On?

SECTION 11B

Ready To Go On? **THINK** central

Go to **thinkcentral.com**

Quiz for Lessons 11-4 Through 11-8

11-4 Adding Integers

Write the addition modeled on each number line.

1.
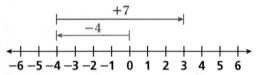

2.
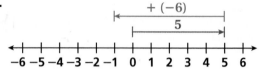

Find each sum.

3. $7 + (-3)$

4. $-10 + 6$

5. $-7 + (-3)$

6. Evaluate $-5 + x$ for $x = 7$.

11-5 Subtracting Integers

Write the subtraction modeled on each number line.

7.
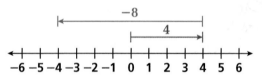

8.
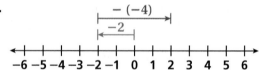

9. Evaluate $x - (-7)$ for $x = -2$.

11-6 Multiplying Integers

Evaluate $6x$ for each value of x.

10. $x = -2$

11. $x = 1$

12. $x = -7$

Find each product.

13. $3 \cdot (-7)$

14. $-10 \cdot 8$

15. $-12 \cdot (-5)$

11-7 Dividing Integers

Evaluate $\frac{x}{4}$ for each value of x.

16. $x = -24$

17. $x = 44$

18. $x = -124$

Find each quotient.

19. $72 \div (-9)$

20. $-15 \div (-3)$

21. $-40 \div 10$

11-8 Solving Integer Equations

Solve each equation. Check your answers.

22. $5 + x = -20$

23. $3a = -27$

24. $p \div 2 = -16$

25. $c - 2 = -7$

Real-World CONNECTIONS

Shipwreck Diving   The ocean floor along the Florida coast is dotted with shipwrecks. By some estimates, there are more than 2,100 shipwrecks in the area. This makes the Florida coast a favorite spot for scuba divers who enjoy exploring the mysterious remains of sunken ships.

The graph shows the depths of several shipwrecks. Use the graph for 1–4.

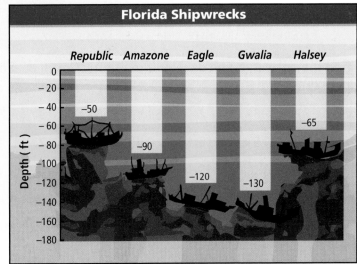

Florida Shipwrecks

Republic Amazone Eagle Gwalia Halsey

Depth (ft)

−50 (Republic)
−90 (Amazone)
−120 (Eagle)
−130 (Gwalia)
−65 (Halsey)

1. The wreck of the *Trio Bravo* is 3 times as deep as that of the *Republic*. While descending to the *Trio Bravo*, a scuba diver stops to check her equipment every 20 feet. How many times will she check her equipment before reaching the *Trio Bravo*?

2. Carlos is diving to the *Eagle*. He dives $\frac{1}{5}$ of the distance and stops to watch a school of fish. Then he descends another 30 feet and stops to rest. How many more feet must he descend in order to reach the *Eagle*?

3. The depth of the *Princess Anne* is $\frac{1}{2}$ that of the *Mystic Isle*. The *Mystic Isle* is 70 feet deeper than the *Gwalia*. What is the depth of the *Princess Anne*?

4. A diver explores the *Halsey*. When he is finished exploring, he ascends at a rate of 4 feet per minute. What is the diver's depth after 7 minutes?

Real-World Connections

Game Time

A Math Riddle

What coin doubles in value when half is subtracted?

To find the answer, graph each pair of points. Connect each pair with a straight line.

1. $(-8, 3)$ $(-6, 3)$	**2.** $(-9, 1)$ $(-7, 5)$	**3.** $(-7, 5)$ $(-5, 1)$	**4.** $(-3, 1)$ $(-3, 5)$
5. $(-1, 1)$ $(-1, 5)$	**6.** $(-3, 3)$ $(-1, 3)$	**7.** $(1, 1)$ $(3, 5)$	**8.** $(3, 5)$ $(5, 1)$
9. $(2, 3)$ $(4, 3)$	**10.** $(6, 1)$ $(6, 5)$	**11.** $(6, 1)$ $(8, 1)$	**12.** $(9, 1)$ $(9, 5)$
13. $(9, 5)$ $(11, 5)$	**14.** $(9, 3)$ $(11, 3)$	**15.** $(-9, -5)$ $(-9, -1)$	**16.** $(-9, -1)$ $(-7, -3)$
17. $(-7, -3)$ $(-9, -5)$	**18.** $(-6, -1)$ $(-6, -5)$	**19.** $(-6, -5)$ $(-4, -5)$	**20.** $(-4, -5)(-4, -1)$
21. $(-4, -1)$ $(-6, -1)$	**22.** $(-3, -1)$ $(-3, -5)$	**23.** $(-3, -5)$ $(-1, -5)$	**24.** $(1, -1)$ $(1, -5)$
25. $(1, -5)$ $(3, -5)$	**26.** $(4, -5)$ $(6, -1)$	**27.** $(6, -1)$ $(8, -5)$	**28.** $(5, -3)$ $(7, -3)$
29. $(9, -5)$ $(9, -1)$	**30.** $(9, -1)$ $(11, -3)$	**31.** $(11, -3)$ $(9, -3)$	**32.** $(9, -3)$ $(11, -5)$

Zero Sum

Each card contains either a positive number, a negative number, or 0. The dealer deals three cards to each player. On your turn, you may exchange one or two of your cards for new ones, or you may keep your three original cards. After everyone has had a turn, the player whose sum is closest to 0 wins the round and receives everyone's cards. The dealer deals a new round and the game continues until the dealer runs out of cards. The winner is the player with the most cards at the end of the game.

Games

THiNK central

Go to thinkcentral.com

A complete copy of the rules and game pieces are available online.

Materials

- business-size envelope
- ruler
- scissors
- tape
- hole punch
- chenille stem
- adding-machine tape

PROJECT ## Positive-Negative Pull-Out

Pull questions and answers out of the bag to check your knowledge of integers and functions.

Directions

1. Seal the envelope. Then cut it in half.

2. Hold the envelope with the opening at the top. Lightly draw lines $\frac{3}{4}$ inch from the bottom and from each side. Fold the envelope back and forth along these lines until the envelope is flexible and easy to work with. **Figure A**

3. Put your hand into the envelope and push out the sides and bottom to form a bag. There will be two triangular points at the bottom of the bag. Tape these to the bottom so that the bag sits flat. **Figure B**

4. Make a 2-inch slit on the front of the bag about an inch from the bottom. Punch two holes at the top of each side of the bag and insert half of a chenile stem to make handles. **Figure C**

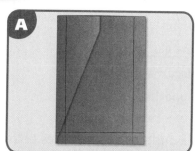

Taking Note of the Math

Starting at the end of the adding-machine tape, write a question about integers and functions, and then write the answer. After you have written several questions and answers, roll up the tape, place it in the bag, and pull the end through the slit.

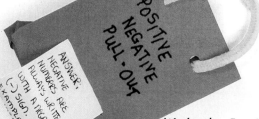

Study Guide: Review

Multi–Language Glossary

THINK central

Go to thinkcentral.com

Vocabulary

Complete the sentences below with vocabulary words from the list above.

1. The ___?___ of –12 is 12.

2. The axes separate the ___?___ into four ___?___.

EXAMPLES

EXERCISES

11-1 **Integers and Absolute Value** (pp. 484–487)

 Preview MA.7.A.3.1

■ **Name a positive or negative number to represent each situation.**

15 feet below sea level: −15
a bank deposit of $10: +10

■ **Use the number line to find the absolute value of −4.**

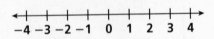

4   *−4 is 4 units from zero.*

Name a positive or negative number to represent each situation.

3. a raise of $10   **4.** a loss of $50

Graph each integer and its opposite on a number line.

5. −3   **6.** 1   **7.** −9   **8.** 0

Write the absolute value of each integer.

9. |37| **10.** |−14| **11.** |97| **12.** |−13|

11-2 **Comparing and Ordering Integers** (pp. 488–491)

 Preview MA.7.A.3.1

■ **Use the number line to compare −2 and 3. Write < or >.**

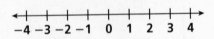

−2 < 3   *−2 is left of 3 on the number line.*

Compare. Write < or >.

13. 3 ▨ 4   **14.** −2 ▨ 5   **15.** 0 ▨ 6

Order the integers in each set from least to greatest.

16. 2, −1, 4   **17.** −3, 0, 4   **18.** −6, −8, 0

Video **Lesson Tutorial Videos @ thinkcentral.com**

Study Guide: Review

11-3 The Coordinate Plane (pp. 492–495)

■ Give the coordinates of A and name the quadrant where it is located.

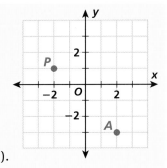

A is in Quadrant IV with coordinates $(2, -3)$.

Preview MA.7.G.4.3

Give the coordinates of each point.

19. A **20.** C

Name the quadrant where each point is located.

21. A **22.** B

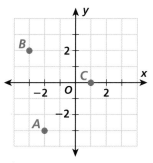

11-4 Adding Integers (pp. 498–501)

■ Find the sum: $3 + (-2)$.

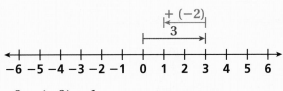

$3 + (-2) = 1$

■ Evaluate $n - 5$ for $n = 2$.

$n - 5$	*Write the expression.*
$2 - 5$	*Substitute 2 for n.*
-3	*Subtract.*

Preview MA.7.A.3.1, MA.7.A.3.2

Find each sum.

23. $-4 + 2$ **24.** $4 + (-4)$

25. $3 + (-2)$ **26.** $-3 + (-2)$

Evaluate $x + 3$ for each value of x.

27. $x = -20$ **28.** $x = 5$

29. $x = -1$ **30.** $x = -3$

31. Bactrian camels who live in the Gobi Desert must endure temperatures as low as $-45\ °F$ and as high as $100\ °F$ in an average year. By how many degrees do the extreme temperatures in the Bactrian's habitat vary throughout the year?

11-5 Subtracting Integers (pp. 502–504)

■ Find the difference: $-4 - 2$.

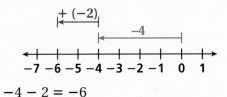

$-4 - 2 = -6$

■ Evaluate $n - 4$ for $n = -1$.

$n - 4$	*Write the expression.*
$-1 - 4$	*Substitute −1 for n.*
-5	*Subtract.*

 Preview MA.7.A.3.1, MA.7.A.3.2

Find each difference.

32. $-6 - 2$ **33.** $5 - (-4)$

34. $-8 - (-5)$ **35.** $14 - 20$

Evaluate $x - (-1)$ for each value of x.

36. $x = 12$ **37.** $x = -7$

38. $x = -3$ **39.** $x = 1$

40. On December 1, the high temperature was $32\ °F$ and the low temperature was $-4\ °F$. What was the difference in the temperatures?

Study Guide: Review

11-6 **Multiplying Integers** (pp. 505–507)

Preview MA.7.A.3.1, MA.7.A.3.2

■ **Find the product: $3 \cdot (-2)$.**

Think: 3 groups of −2

$3 \cdot (-2) = -6$ $(-2) + (-2) + (-2)$

■ **Evaluate $-2x$ for $x = -4$.**

$-2x$ *Write the expression.*

$-2(-4)$ *Substitute −4 for x.*

8 *Multiply. The signs are the same, so the answer is positive.*

Find each product.

41. $5 \cdot (-2)$ **42.** $3 \cdot 2$

43. $-3 \cdot (-2)$ **44.** $-4 \cdot 2$

Evaluate $-9y$ for each value of y.

45. $y = 2$ **46.** $y = -5$

47. $y = -11$ **48.** $y = 1$

49. Over the course of two golf tournaments, Alphonse averaged a score of −5 for each of the 6 rounds he played. How many strokes under par was Alphonse's combined score?

11-7 **Dividing Integers** (pp. 508–511)

Preview MA.7.A.3.1, MA.7.A.3.2

■ **Find the quotient: $-24 \div 4$.**

Think: What number times 4 equals −24?

$-6 \cdot 4 = -24$, so $-24 \div 4 = -6$.

■ **Evaluate $\dfrac{m}{-3}$ for $m = 27$.**

$\dfrac{m}{-3}$ *Write the expression.*

$\dfrac{27}{-3} = 27 \div (-3)$ *Substitute 27 for m.*

$= -9$ *Divide. The signs are different, so the answer is negative.*

Find each quotient.

50. $6 \div (-2)$ **51.** $9 \div 3$

52. $-14 \div (-7)$ **53.** $-4 \div 2$

Evaluate $\dfrac{t}{4}$ for each value of t.

54. $t = -4$ **55.** $t = 24$

56. $t = 0$ **57.** $t = -32$

11-8 **Solving Integer Equations** (pp. 512–515)

Preview MA.7.A.3.3, MA.7.A.3.2

■ **Solve $x + 4 = 18$.**

$x + 4 = 18$ *4 is added to x.*

$\underline{-4 \quad -4}$ *Subtract 4 from both sides.*

$x \quad\quad = 14$

Solve each equation. Check your answers.

58. $w - 5 = -1$ **59.** $\dfrac{a}{-4} = 3$

60. $2q = -14$ **61.** $x + 3 = -2$

62. While touring a cavern, Marcus began in a chamber that was 35 feet above sea level. The middle of the tour was in a chamber that was 103 feet below sea level. How far did Marcus descend?

Chapter Test

Name a positive or negative number to represent each situation.

1. 30° below zero

2. a bank deposit of $75

3. a loss of 5 yards

Write the absolute value of each integer.

4. $|99|$

5. $|-115|$

6. $|-50|$

7. $|522|$

Compare. Write $<$ or $>$.

8. $-4 \quad \blacksquare \quad 4$

9. $2 \quad \blacksquare \quad -9$

10. $-10 \quad \blacksquare \quad 8$

11. $-2 \quad \blacksquare \quad -12$

Order the integers in each set from least to greatest.

12. $21, -19, 34$

13. $-16, -2, 13, 46$

14. $-10, 0, 25, -7, 18$

15. During a week in Cleveland, Ohio, the daily high temperatures were $-4\,°F, -2\,°F, -12\,°F, 5\,°F, 12\,°F, 20\,°F$, and $16\,°F$. Order these temperatures from greatest to least.

Graph each point on a coordinate plane.

16. $A(2, 3)$

17. $B(3, -2)$

18. $C(-1, 3)$

19. $D\left(-1, 2\frac{1}{2}\right)$

20. $E(0, 1)$

Add, subtract, multiply, or divide.

21. $-4 + 4$

22. $-2 - 9$

23. $-3 \cdot 8$

24. $12 \div (-3)$

25. $-48 \div (-4)$

26. $13 + (-9)$

27. $8 - (-11)$

28. $-7 \cdot (-6)$

29. Keisha's watch is water resistant to a maximum of –15 feet. Landon's watch is water resistant up to 6 times the maximum depth of Keisha's watch. Landon's watch is water resistant to what maximum depth?

Evaluate each expression for the given value of the variable.

30. $n + 3; n = -10$

31. $9 - x; x = -9$

32. $4m; m = -6$

33. $\frac{15}{a}; a = -3$

34. $(-11) + z; z = 28$

35. $w - (-8); w = 13$

Solve each equation.

36. $\frac{b}{7} = -3$

37. $-9 \cdot f = -81$

38. $r - 14 = -32$

39. $y + 17 = 22$

40. The three angles of a triangle have equal measures. The sum of their measures is 180°. What is the measure of each angle?

Multiple Choice: Identifying Keywords and Context Clues

When reading a test item, pay attention to keywords and context clues given in the problem. These clues will guide you in providing a correct response.

EXAMPLE 1

Kaulen is building a rectangular dog run that is 12.5 feet by 9 feet. How much fencing will Kaulen need to enclose the dog run?

 A. 21.5 feet   **B.** 43 feet   **C.** 112.5 square feet   **D.** 156.25 square feet

• Look for context clues. Identify what they mean.
• In this test item, **enclose** is a context clue. It means to *surround*.

Find the choice that gives the amount of fencing that surrounds the dog run. To find this amount, you need to find the perimeter of the dog run.
A: This gives the amount of fencing needed for only two sides of the dog run—the length and the width.
B: This is the perimeter of the dog run, which gives the amount of fencing needed to enclose the dog run.
C: This is the area of the dog run, not the perimeter. Area is given in square units, while perimeter is given in units.
D: This is the area of a square dog run with 12.5-foot sides.

The correct answer is B.

EXAMPLE 2

Kenneth delivers flowers along Oak Street. He starts at the flower shop on Oak Street. His first delivery is 8 blocks directly west of the shop. His second delivery takes him 4 blocks directly east of his first delivery. His third delivery takes him 5 blocks east of his second delivery. Which of the following integer expressions models this siutation?

 F. $-4 + 5 + 8$ **G.** $8 + 4 - 5$ **H.** $-8 - 4 - 5$ **I.** $-8 + 4 + 5$

• Look for keywords.
• In this test item, the keywords are **expressions** and **integer.**

Find the choice that shows the correct **integer expression** to model the situation.
F: The first delivery is 8 blocks west. This expression does not begin with -8.
G: The first delivery is 8 blocks west. This expression does not begin with -8.
H: The expression begins with -8, but 4 blocks east would be $+4$.
 I: This expression's integers correctly correspond to the deliveries.

The correct answer is I.

If you do not understand what a word means, reread the sentences that surround the word and make a logical guess.

Read each test item and answer the questions that follow.

Item A
Multiple Choice Jenny is trimming the edges of a card with ribbon. The rectangular card measures 8 inches by 12 inches. How much ribbon does Jenny need to trim the card?

A. 36 inches   C. 64 inches

B. 40 inches   D. 72 inches

1. What are the dimensions of the card?

2. Which words in the problem statement are clues that you need to find the perimeter of the card?

3. When you calculate the perimeter, why are the units not given in square units?

Item B
Multiple Choice Sam has two cylinders. One cylinder has a height of 25 cm and a diameter of 8 cm. The other cylinder has a height of 15 cm and a diameter of 20 cm. What is the difference between the volumes of the two cylinders?

F. 400π cubic centimeters

G. $1,100\pi$ cubic centimeters

H. $1,500\pi$ cubic centimeters

I. $4,400\pi$ cubic centimeters

4. Make a list of the keywords given in the problem statement and link each word to its mathematical meaning.

5. Which choice, if any, can be eliminated? Why?

Item C
Multiple Choice Anna is an interior designer who charges a consultation fee of $60 plus $17.50 per hour. Carolyn and Raja hire Anna for 8 hours. How much must they pay Anna for her work?

A. $77.50   C. $200.00

B. $140.00   D. $1,050.00

6. What other word in the problem can help you guess the meaning of consultation?

7. Identify the keywords in this problem statement.

Item D
Multiple Choice An office supply store states that 4 out of 5 customers would recommend the store to another person. Given this information, what percent of customers would NOT recommend the office supply store to someone else?

F. 10%   H. 40%

G. 20%   I. 80%

8. What information is needed to solve this problem?

9. Which choice can be eliminated immediately? Why?

10. Write a proportion to find the percent of customers who would recommend the office store to someone else.

11. Describe two different ways to solve this problem.

Mastering the Standards

Cumulative Assessment, Chapters 1–11

Multiple Choice

1. Marla bought a shirt on sale for $22, which was $\frac{1}{8}$ off the original price. What decimal represents the discount received?

A. 0.125
C. 0.725
B. 0.225
D. 0.825

2. Which is the greatest number in the following list of numbers?

$$0.31, \frac{13}{25}, 48\%, \frac{7}{20}$$

F. 0.31
H. 48%
G. $\frac{13}{25}$
I. $\frac{7}{20}$

3. The radius of a circle is 2.5 meters. What is the approximate area of the circle in centimeters squared?

A. 15.7
C. 1,570
B. 19.63
D. 196,250

4. At 5:30 P.M., 75% of the people at company A had gone home. What fraction of people had NOT yet gone home?

F. $\frac{3}{4}$
H. $\frac{1}{4}$
G. $\frac{1}{2}$
I. $\frac{1}{25}$

5. A rectangular prism has a volume of 73.2 cubic inches. The width of the prism is 4.8 inches, and the height of the prism is 2.5 inches. What is the length of the prism?

A. 6.1 inches
B. 12.2 inches
C. 29.3 inches
D. 65.9 inches

6. What is the ratio, in simplest form, of the number of students who play the drums to the number of students who play the trumpet?

School Band	
Instrument	**Number of Students**
Drums	10
Trombone	14
Trumpet	8
Tuba	3

F. 10 to 3
H. 5 to 7
G. 5 to 4
I. 10 to 27

7. Monique wants to divide $\frac{16}{25}$ by $1\frac{3}{5}$. What is the reciprocal of $1\frac{3}{5}$?

A. $-1\frac{3}{5}$
C. $\frac{8}{5}$
B. $\frac{5}{8}$
D. 8

8. The cost for a group of 3 adults to see a movie is $18.75. The cost for a group of 6 adults is $37.50, and the cost for 9 adults is $56.25. If all of the tickets are priced the same, which equation represents the function? Let c equal the cost of the group and t represent the number of tickets.

F. $c = 6.25t$
G. $c = 18.75t$
H. $c = 37.50t$
I. $c = 56.25t$

9. Louie buys a baseball bat for $125, a catcher's mitt for $55, and a baseball for $3. The tax rate is 5%. If Louie gives the cashier $200, how much change should he get back?

A. $6.15   C. $9.25

B. $7.85   D. $10.75

10. Sergio constructs a table for the function $y = 5x + 1$. He uses whole numbers for the x-values. Which of the following cannot appear as one of the y-values?

F. 11   H. 32

G. 26   I. 61

 When adding integers on a number line, move right to add a positive number and move left to add a negative number.

Gridded Response

11. On Monday, the balance in June's checking account is $176.39. On Tuesday, she deposits a check for $25.00. On Friday, June withdraws $109.23 to buy a winter coat. How much money, in dollars, is left in June's account on Friday?

12. Wyatt has received the following scores on his chapter spelling tests: 92, 98, 90, 97, and 92. What is the mean score of Wyatt's spelling tests?

13. Mrs. Thomas is covering the tops of 5 cardboard rectangles with foil to use in a cake display. Each rectangle is 12 in. long by 10 in. wide. How many square inches of foil will she need to cover the cardboard rectangles?

14. What is 6,500 centimeters expressed in kilometers?

Short Response

S1. On Monday, the balance in Graham's account was $32. On Tuesday, he wrote three $18 checks. After a deposit on Wednesday, his balance was $15.

a. Find Graham's balance on Tuesday.

b. Write and solve an equation to find the amount of Graham's deposit on Wednesday. Let d equal the amount of the deposit. Show your work.

S2. A job advertisement states that the position pays $11.50 an hour.

a. Write an equation that shows the relationship between the salary s and the number of hours worked, h. Justify your answer.

b. How many hours would you need to work per week to earn $375? Show your work.

S3. A circle has a circumference of 21.98 meters.

a. What is the diameter of the circle in centimeters? Use 3.14 for π. Show your work.

b. What is the area of the circle in square meters? Show your work.

Extended Response

E1. A store sold 44 art masks in September for $528. In October, the store sold 41 art masks for $492. In November, the store sold 38 art masks for $456. All the masks cost the same.

a. Construct a table to organize the data, and then graph the data. Is the function linear? Explain.

b. Write an equation to represent the function. What does each variable represent?

c. In December, the store sold 67 masks. What were the total mask sales in December?

Student Resources

Draw a Diagram

When problems involve objects, distances, or places, you can **draw a diagram** to make the problem easier to understand. You will often be able to use your diagram to solve the problem.

Problem Solving Strategies

Draw a Diagram
Make a Model
Guess and Test
Work Backward
Find a Pattern

Make a Table
Solve a Simpler Problem
Use Logical Reasoning
Use a Venn Diagram
Make an Organized List

All city blocks in Sunnydale are the same size. Tina starts her paper route at the corner of two streets. She travels 8 blocks south, 13 blocks west, 8 blocks north, and 6 blocks east. How far is she from her starting point when she finishes her route?

Understand the Problem

Identify the important information.

- Each block is the same size.
- You are given Tina's route.

The answer will be the distance from her starting point.

Make a Plan

Use the information in the problem to **draw a diagram** showing Tina's route. Label her starting and ending points.

Solve

The diagram shows that at the end of Tina's route she is 13 − 6 blocks from her starting point.

$13 - 6 = 7$

When Tina finishes, she is 7 blocks from her starting point.

Look Back

Be sure that you have drawn your diagram correctly. Does it match the information given in the problem?

PRACTICE

1. Laurence drives a carpool to school every Monday. He starts at his house and travels 4 miles south to pick up two children. Then he drives 9 miles west to pick up two more children, and then he drives 4 miles north to pick up one more child. Finally, he drives 5 miles east to get to the school. How far does he have to travel to get back home?

2. The roots of a tree reach 12 feet into the ground. A kitten is stuck 5 feet from the top of the tree. From the treetop to the root bottom, the tree measures 32 feet. How far above the ground is the kitten?

Problem Solving Handbook

Make a Model

If a problem involves objects, you can sometimes **make a model** using those objects or similar objects to act out the problem. This can help you understand the problem and find the solution.

Problem Solving Strategies

Draw a Diagram	Make a Table
Make a Model	Solve a Simpler Problem
Guess and Test	Use Logical Reasoning
Work Backward	Use a Venn Diagram
Find a Pattern	Make an Organized List

Alice has three pieces of ribbon. Their lengths are 7 inches, 10 inches, and 12 inches. Alice does not have a ruler or scissors. How can she use these ribbons to measure a length of 15 inches?

Understand the Problem

Identify the important information.

- The ribbons are 7 inches, 10 inches, and 12 inches long.

The answer will show how to use the ribbons to measure 15 inches.

Make a Plan

Measure and cut three ribbons or strips of paper to **make a model.** One ribbon should be 7 inches long, one should be 10 inches long, and one should be 12 inches long. Try different combinations of the ribbons to form new lengths.

Solve

When you put any two ribbons together end to end, you can form lengths of 17, 19, and 22 inches. All of these are too long.

Try placing the 10-inch ribbon and the 12-inch ribbon end to end to make 22 inches. Now place the 7-inch ribbon above them. The remaining length that is **not** underneath the 7-inch ribbon will measure 15 inches.

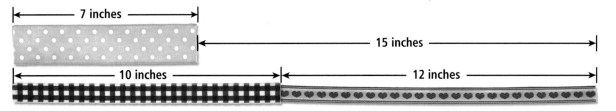

Look Back

Use another strategy. Without using ribbon, you could have **guessed** different ways to add or subtract 7, 10, and 12. Then you could have **tested** to see if any of these gave an answer of 15:

$10 + 12 - 7 = 15$

PRACTICE

1. Find other lengths that you can measure with the three pieces of ribbon.

2. Andy stacks four cubes, one on top of the other, and paints the outside of the stack (not the bottom). How many faces of the cubes are painted?

Problem Solving Handbook

Guess and Test

If you do not know how to solve a problem, you can always make a **guess**. Then **test** your guess using the information in the problem. Use the result to make a better guess. Repeat until you find the correct answer.

Problem Solving Strategies

Draw a Diagram	Make a Table
Make a Model	Solve a Simpler Problem
Guess and Test	Use Logical Reasoning
Work Backward	Use a Venn Diagram
Find a Pattern	Make an Organized List

There were 25 problems on a test. For each correct answer, 4 points were given. For each incorrect answer, 1 point was subtracted. Tania answered all 25 problems. Her score was 85. How many correct and incorrect answers did she have?

 **Understand the Problem**

Identify the important information.

- There were 25 problems on the test.
- A correct answer received 4 points, and an incorrect answer lost 1 point.
- Tania answered all of the problems and her score was 85.

The answer will be the number of problems that Tania got correct and incorrect.

 **Make a Plan**

Start with a **guess** for the number of correct answers. Then **test** to see whether the total score is 85.

 Solve

Make a first guess of 20 correct answers.

Correct	Incorrect	Score	Result
20	5	$(20 \times 4) - (5 \times 1) = 80 - 5 = 75$	Too low—guess higher
23	2	$(23 \times 4) - (2 \times 1) = 92 - 2 = 90$	Too high—guess lower
22	3	$(22 \times 4) - (3 \times 1) = 88 - 3 = 85$	Correct ✓

Tania had 22 correct answers and 3 incorrect answers.

 **Look Back**

Notice that the guesses made while solving this problem were not just "wild" guesses. Guessing and testing in an organized way will often lead you to the correct answer.

PRACTICE

1. The sum of Joe's age and his younger brother's age is 38. The difference between their ages is 8. How old are Joe and his brother?

2. Amy bought some used books for $4.95. She paid $0.50 each for some books and $0.35 each for the others. She bought fewer than 8 books at each price. How many books did Amy buy? How many cost $0.50?

Problem Solving Handbook

Work Backward

Some problems give you a sequence of information and ask you to find something that happened at the beginning. To solve a problem like this, you may want to start at the end of the problem and **work backward.**

 Problem Solving Strategies

Draw a Diagram	Make a Table
Make a Model	Solve a Simpler Problem
Guess and Test	Use Logical Reasoning
Work Backward	Use a Venn Diagram
Find a Pattern	Make an Organized List

Jaclyn and her twin sister, Bailey, received money for their birthday. They used half of their money to buy a video game. Then they spent half of the money they had left on a pizza. Finally, they spent half of the remaining money to rent a movie. At the end of the day, they had $4.50. How much money did they have to start out with?

 **Understand the Problem**

Identify the important information.

- The girls ended with $4.50.
- They spent half of their money at each of three stops.

The answer will be the amount of money they started with.

 **Make a Plan**

Start with the amount you know the girls have left, $4.50, and **work backward** through the information given in the problem.

Solve

Jaclyn and Bailey had $4.50 at the end of the day.

They had twice that amount before renting a movie. $2 \times \$4.50 = \$9$

They had twice that amount before buying a pizza. $2 \times \$9 = \$18$

They had twice that amount before buying a video game. $2 \times \$18 = \$36$

The girls started with $36.

Look Back

Using the starting amount of $36, work from the beginning of the problem. Find the amount they spent at each location and see whether they are left with $4.50.

Start: $36
Video game: $36 ÷ 2 = $18
Pizza: $18 ÷ 2 = $9
Movie rental: $9 ÷ 2 = $4.50 ✓

PRACTICE

1. Chris is 5 years younger than Mark. Justin is half as old as Chris. Mary, who is 10, is 3 years younger than Justin. How old is Mark?

2. If you divide a mystery number by 4, add 8, and multiply by 3, you get 42. What is the mystery number?

Find a Pattern

In some problems, there is a relationship between different pieces of information. Examine this relationship and try to **find a pattern.** You can then use this pattern to find more information and the solution to the problem.

Problem Solving Strategies

Draw a Diagram
Make a Model
Guess and Test
Work Backward
Find a Pattern

Make a Table
Solve a Simpler Problem
Use Logical Reasoning
Use a Venn Diagram
Make an Organized List

Students are using the pattern at right to build stairways for a model house. How many blocks are needed to build a stairway with seven steps?

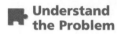 **Understand the Problem**

The answer will be the total number of blocks in a stairway with seven steps.

 **Make a Plan**

Try to **find a pattern** between the number of steps and the number of blocks needed.

The first step is one block. The second step is two blocks, the third step is three blocks, and the fourth step is four blocks.

Step	Number of Blocks in Step	Total Number of Blocks in Stairway
2	2	$1 + 2 = 3$
3	3	$1 + 2 + 3 = 6$
4	4	$1 + 2 + 3 + 4 = 10$

To find the total number of blocks, add the number of blocks in the first step, the second step, the third step, and so on.

Solve

The seventh step will be made of seven blocks. The total number of blocks will be $1 + 2 + 3 + 4 + 5 + 6 + 7 = 28$.

Look Back

Use another strategy. You can **draw a diagram** of a stairway with 7 steps. Count the number of blocks in your diagram. There are 28 blocks.

 **PRACTICE**

1. A cereal company adds baseball cards to the 3rd box, the 6th box, the 11th box, the 18th box, and so on of each case of cereal. In a case of 40 boxes, how many boxes will have baseball cards?

2. Describe the pattern and find the missing numbers.

1; 4; 16; 64; 256; ▮; ▮; 16,384

Problem Solving Handbook

Make a Table

When you are given a lot of information in a problem, it may be helpful to organize that information. One way to organize information is to **make a table.**

Problem Solving Strategies

Draw a Diagram	**Make a Table**
Make a Model	Solve a Simpler Problem
Guess and Test	Use Logical Reasoning
Work Backward	Use a Venn Diagram
Find a Pattern	Make an Organized List

Mrs. Melo's students scored the following on their math test: 90, 80, 77, 78, 91, 92, 73, 62, 83, 79, 72, 85, 93, 84, 75, 68, 82, 94, 98, and 82. An A is given for 90 to 100 points, a B for 80 to 89 points, a C for 70 to 79 points, a D for 60 to 69 points, and an F for less than 60 points. Find the number of students who scored each letter grade.

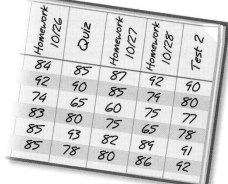

Homework 10/26	Quiz	Homework 10/27	Homework 10/28	Test 2
84	85	87	92	90
92	90	85	79	80
74	65	60	75	77
83	80	75	65	78
85	93	82	89	91
85	78	80	86	92

Understand the Problem

Identify the important information.

* You have been given the list of scores and the letter grades that go with each score.

The answer will be the number of each letter grade.

Make a Plan

Make a table to organize the scores. Use the information in the problem to set up your table. Make one row for each letter grade.

Solve

Read through the list of scores. As you read each score, make a tally in the appropriate place in your table. There are 20 test scores, so be sure you have 20 tallies in all.

Mrs. Melo gave out six A's, six B's, six C's, two D's, and no F's.

Letter Grade	Number
A (90–100)	JHT I
B (80–89)	JHT I
C (70–79)	JHT I
D (60–69)	II
F (below 60)	

Look Back

Use another strategy. Another way you could solve this problem is to **make an organized list.** Order the scores from least to greatest, and count how many scores are in each range.

62, 68, 72, 73, 75, 77, 78, 79, 80, 82, 82, 83, 84, 85, 90, 91, 92, 93, 94, 98
  D   C   B   A

PRACTICE

1. The debate club has 6 members. Each member will debate each of the other members exactly once. How many total debates will there be?

2. At the library, there are three story-telling sessions. Each one lasts 45 minutes, with 30 minutes between sessions. If the first session begins at 10:00 A.M., what time does the last session end?

Solve a Simpler Problem

Sometimes a problem contains large numbers or requires many steps. Try to **solve a simpler problem** that is similar. Solve the simpler problem first, and then try the same steps to solve the original problem.

Problem Solving Strategies

Draw a Diagram	Make a Table
Make a Model	**Solve a Simpler Problem**
Guess and Test	Use Logical Reasoning
Work Backward	Use a Venn Diagram
Find a Pattern	Make an Organized List

At the end of a soccer game, each player shakes hands with every player on the opposing team. How many handshakes are there at the end of a game between two teams that each have 20 players?

Understand the Problem

Identify the important information.

- There are 20 players on each team.
- Each player will shake hands with every player on the opposing team.

The answer will be the total number of handshakes exchanged.

 **Make a Plan**

Solve a simpler problem. For example, suppose each team had just one player. Then there would only be one handshake between the two players. Expand the number of players to two and then three.

 Solve

When there is 1 player, there is $1 \times 1 = 1$ handshake. For 2 players, there are $2 \times 2 = 4$ handshakes. And for 3 players, there are $3 \times 3 = 9$ handshakes.

Players Per Team	Diagram	Handshakes
1		1
2		4
3		9

If each team has 20 players, there will be $20 \times 20 = 400$ handshakes.

Look Back

If the pattern is correct, for 4 players there will be 16 handshakes and for 5 players there will be 25 handshakes. Complete the next two rows of the table to check these answers.

PRACTICE

1. Martha has 5 pairs of pants and 4 blouses that she can wear to school. How many different outfits can she make?

2. What is the smallest 5-digit number that can be divided by 50 with a remainder of 17?

Problem Solving Handbook

Use Logical Reasoning

Sometimes a problem may provide clues and facts that you must use to answer a question. You can **use logical reasoning** to solve this kind of problem.

Problem Solving Strategies

Draw a Diagram	Make a Table
Make a Model	Solve a Simpler Problem
Guess and Test	**Use Logical Reasoning**
Work Backward	Use a Venn Diagram
Find a Pattern	Make an Organized List

Kevin, Ellie, and Jillian play three different sports. One person plays soccer, one likes to run track, and the other swims. Ellie is the sister of the swimmer. Kevin once went shopping with the swimmer and the track runner. Match each student with his or her sport.

 **Understand the Problem**

Identify the important information.

- There are three people, and each person plays a different sport.
- Ellie is the sister of the swimmer.
- Kevin once went shopping with the swimmer and the track runner.

The answer will tell which student plays each sport.

 **Make a Plan**

Start with clues given in the problem, and **use logical reasoning** to find the answer.

 Solve

Make a table with a column for each sport and a row for each person. Work with the clues one at a time. Write "yes" in a box if the clue applies to that person. Write "no" if the clue does not apply.

	Soccer	Track	Swim
Kevin		no	no
Ellie			no
Jillian			

- Ellie is the sister of the swimmer, so she is not the swimmer.
- Kevin went shopping with the swimmer and the track runner. He is not the swimmer or the track runner.

So Kevin must be the soccer player, and Jillian must be the swimmer. This leaves Ellie as the track runner.

 **Look Back**

Compare your answer to the clues in the problem. Make sure none of your conclusions conflict with the clues.

PRACTICE

1. Karin, Brent, and Lola each ordered a different slice of pizza: pepperoni, plain cheese, and ham-pineapple. Karin is allergic to pepperoni. Lola likes more than one topping. Which kind of pizza did each person order?

2. Leo, Jamal, and Kara are in fourth, fifth, and sixth grades. Kara is not in fourth grade. The sixth-grader is in chorus with Kara and has the same lunch time as Leo. Match the students with their grades.

Use a Venn Diagram

You can **use a Venn diagram** to display relationships among sets in a problem. Use ovals, circles, or other shapes to represent individual sets.

Problem Solving Strategies

Draw a Diagram	Make a Table
Make a Model	Solve a Simpler Problem
Guess and Test	Use Logical Reasoning
Work Backward	**Use a Venn Diagram**
Find a Pattern	Make an Organized List

Robert is taking a survey to see what kinds of pets students have. He found that 70 students have dogs, 45 have goldfish, and 60 have birds. Some students have two kinds of pets: 17 students have dogs and goldfish, 22 students have dogs and birds, and 15 students have birds and goldfish. Five students have all three kinds of pets. How many students in the survey have only birds?

Understand the Problem

List the important information.

- You know that 70 students have dogs, 45 have goldfish, and 60 have birds.

The answer will be the number of students who have only birds.

Make a Plan

Use a Venn diagram to show the sets of students who have dogs, students who have goldfish, and students who have birds.

Solve

Draw and label three overlapping circles. Work from the inside out. Write "5" in the area where all three circles overlap. This represents the number of students who have a dog, a goldfish, and a bird.

Use the information in the problem to fill in other sections of the diagram. You know that 60 students have birds, so the numbers within the bird circle will add to 60.

So 18 students have only pet birds.

Look Back

When your Venn diagram is complete, check it carefully against the information in the problem. Make sure your diagram agrees with the facts given.

PRACTICE

1. How many students have only dogs?

2. How many students have only goldfish?

Make an Organized List

 Problem Solving Strategies

Draw a Diagram	Make a Table
Make a Model	Solve a Simpler Problem
Guess and Test	Use Logical Reasoning
Work Backward	Use a Venn Diagram
Find a Pattern	**Make an Organized List**

In some problems, you will need to find how many different ways something can happen. It is often helpful to **make an organized list.** This will help you count the outcomes and be sure that you have included all of them.

In a game at an amusement park, players throw 3 darts at a target to score points and win prizes. If each dart lands within the target area, how many different total scores are possible?

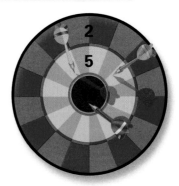

 **Understand the Problem**

Identify the important information.

- A player throws three darts at the target.

The answer will be the number of different scores a player could earn.

Make a Plan

Make an organized list to determine all possible outcomes and score totals. List the value of each dart and the point total for all three darts.

 Solve

You can organize your list by the number of darts that land in the center. All three darts could hit the center circle. Or, two darts could hit the center circle and the third could hit a different circle. One dart could hit the center circle, or no darts could hit the center circle.

3 Darts Hit Center	2 Darts Hit Center	1 Dart Hits Center	0 Darts Hit Center
10 + 10 + 10 = 30	10 + 10 + 5 = 25	10 + 5 + 5 = 20	5 + 5 + 5 = 15
	10 + 10 + 2 = 22	10 + 5 + 2 = 17	5 + 5 + 2 = 12
		10 + 2 + 2 = 14	5 + 2 + 2 = 9
			2 + 2 + 2 = 6

Count the different outcomes. There are 10 possible scores.

Look Back

You could have listed outcomes in random order, but because your list is organized, you can be sure that you have not missed any possibilities. Check to be sure that every score is different.

 **PRACTICE**

1. A restaurant has three different kinds of pancakes: cinnamon, blueberry, and apple. If you order one of each kind, how many different ways can the three pancakes be stacked?

2. How many ways can you make change for a quarter using dimes, nickels, and pennies?

Problem Solving Handbook

Skills Bank . . .

Place Value—Trillions Through Thousandths

You can use a place-value chart to read and write numbers.

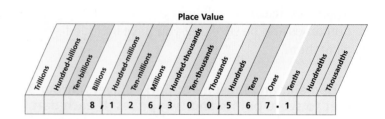

EXAMPLE

What is the place value of the digit 3 in 8,126,300,567.1?

The digit 3 is in the hundred-thousands place.

PRACTICE

Write the place value of the underlined digit.

1. 14,536,992.1
2. 34.071
3. 6,190.05
4. 5,027,549,757,202
5. 103.526
6. 3.721
7. 65,331,040,421
8. 75,983.009

Compare and Order Whole Numbers

As you read a number line from left to right, the numbers are ordered from least to greatest.

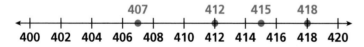

You can use a number line and place value to compare whole numbers.
Use the symbols > (is greater than) and < (is less than).

EXAMPLE

Compare. Write <, >, or =.

A 412 ▮ 418
418 is to the right of 412 on a number line.
412 < 418

B 415 ▮ 407
1 ten is greater than 0 tens.
415 > 407

PRACTICE

Compare. Write <, >, or =.

1. 419 ▮ 410
2. 9,161 ▮ 8,957
3. 5,036 ▮ 5,402
4. 617 ▮ 681
5. 700 ▮ 698
6. 1,611 ▮ 1,489

Round Whole Numbers and Decimals

You can use a number line or rounding rules to round whole numbers to the nearest 10, 100, 1,000, or 10,000.

EXAMPLE 1

Round 547 to the nearest 10.

Look at the number line.

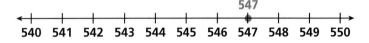

547 is closer to 550 than to 540. So 547 rounded to the nearest 10 is 550.

You can use rounding rules to round whole numbers and decimals to any place value.

> ### ROUNDING RULES
>
> If the digit to the right is 5 or greater, increase the digit in the rounding place by 1.
>
> If the digit to the right is less than 5, keep the digit in the rounding place the same.

EXAMPLE 2

Round each number to the given place value.

A 12,573; thousands

12,573   *Find the digit in the thousands place.*
  ↑ *Digit is 5 or greater. Add 1.*   *Look at the digit to its right.*

12,573 rounded to the nearest 1,000 is 13,000.

B 5.16; whole number

1 < 5   So 5.16 rounds to 5.

C 13.45605; ten-thousandth

5 ≥ 5   So 13.45605 rounds to 13.4561.

PRACTICE

Round each number to the given place value.

1. 15,638; hundreds   **2.** 37,519; thousands   **3.** 9,298; tens

4. 69,504; ten thousands   **5.** 852; thousands   **6.** 33,449; hundreds

7. 3.982; tenth   **8.** 6.3174; hundredth   **9.** 1.471; whole number

10. 48.1526; hundredth   **11.** 5.03654; ten-thousandth   **12.** 0.083; tenth

Roman Numerals

Instead of using place value, as with the decimal system, combinations of letters are used to represent numbers in the Roman numeral system.

I = 1	V = 5	X = 10
L = 50	C = 100	D = 500
M = 1,000		

No letter can be written more than three times in a row. If a letter is written before a letter that represents a larger value, then subtract the first letter's value from the second letter's value.

EXAMPLE

Write each decimal number as a Roman numeral and each Roman numeral as a decimal number.

A 9

$9 = X - I = IX$

B CLV

$CLV = 100 + 50 + 5 = 155$

PRACTICE

Write each decimal number as a Roman numeral and each Roman numeral as a decimal number.

1. 12   **2.** 25   **3.** 209   **4.** 54

5. VIII   **6.** LXXII   **7.** XIX   **8.** MMIV

Multiply Whole Numbers

Multiplication is used to combine groups of equal amounts. The answer to a multiplication problem is called the *product*.

EXAMPLE

105×214

Step 1: Think of 214 as 2 hundreds, 1 ten, and 4 ones. Multiply by 4 ones.	**Step 2:** Multiply by 1 ten, or 10.	**Step 3:** Multiply by 2 hundreds, or 200.	**Step 4:** Add the partial products.
$\begin{array}{r} 2 \\ 105 \\ \times\ 214 \\ \hline 420 \end{array}$ ← 4 × 105	$\begin{array}{r} 105 \\ \times\ 214 \\ \hline 420 \\ 1050 \end{array}$ ← 10 × 105	$\begin{array}{r} 1 \\ 105 \\ \times\ 214 \\ \hline 420 \\ 1050 \\ 21000 \end{array}$ ← 200 × 105	$\begin{array}{r} 105 \\ \times\ 214 \\ \hline 420 \\ 1050 \\ +21000 \\ \hline 22,470 \end{array}$

The product is 22,470.

PRACTICE

Find the product.

1. 350 × 112   **2.** 3,218 × 231   **3.** 187 × 136

4. 5,028 × 225   **5.** 642 × 428   **6.** 2,039 × 570

Divide Whole Numbers

Division is used to separate a quantity into equal groups. The answer to a division problem is known as the *quotient*.

EXAMPLE

672 ÷ 16

Step 1: Write the first number inside the long division symbol and the second number to the left. Place the first digit of the quotient. 16)672 *16 cannot go into 6, so try 67.*	**Step 2:** Multiply 4 by 16, and place the product under 67. 4 16)672 *Subtract 64* −64 *from 67.* 3	**Step 3:** Bring down the next digit of the dividend. 42 16)672 *Divide 32* −64↓ *by 16.* 32 −32 0

The quotient is 42.

PRACTICE

Find the quotient.

1. $578 \div 34$
2. $736 \div 8$
3. $826 \div 118$
4. $945 \div 45$
5. $6,312 \div 263$
6. $5,989 \div 53$

Divide with Zeros in the Quotient

Sometimes when dividing, you need to use zeros in the quotient as placeholders.

EXAMPLE

3,648 ÷ 12

Step 1: Divide 36 by 12 because 12 > 3. 3 12)3,648	**Step 2:** Place a zero in the quotient because 12 > 4. 30 12)3,648 −36↓ 04	**Step 3:** Bring down the 8. 304 12)3,648 −36 ↓ 048 −48 0

The quotient is 304.

PRACTICE

Find the quotient.

1. $424 \div 4$
2. $5,796 \div 28$
3. $540 \div 18$
4. $7,380 \div 123$
5. $12,045 \div 3$
6. $10,626 \div 21$

Fractional Part of a Region

You can use fractions to name parts of a whole. The denominator tells how many equal parts are in the whole. The numerator tells how many of those parts are being considered.

EXAMPLE

Tell what fraction of each region is shaded.

A $\frac{1}{2}$

B $\frac{1}{3}$

C $\frac{3}{4}$

PRACTICE

Tell what fraction of each region is shaded.

1.

2.

3.

4.

5.

6.

Fractional Part of a Set

You can use fractions to name part of a set. The denominator tells how many items are in the set. The numerator tells how many of those items are being used.

EXAMPLE

Tell what fraction of each set are stars.

A ☐★☐★●★●☐☐☐

3 out of 10 shapes are stars.

$\frac{3}{10}$

B ★●★★●★★

5 out of 7 shapes are stars.

$\frac{5}{7}$

PRACTICE

Tell what fraction of each set is shaded.

1. ☆☆☆☆☆☆

2. ◼◼◼◼☐

3. ●☆○○☆○

4. ◼◼◼☐☐

5. ●○☐☐

6. ☆⬡◼○◻△♡

Mental Math

You can use mental math to multiply by powers of ten.

EXAMPLE 1

$4,000 \times 100$

Step 1: Look for a basic fact using the nonzero part of the factors.
$4 \times 1 = 4$
Step 2: Add the number of zeros in the factors. Place that number of zeros in the product.
$4,000 \times 100 = 400,000$

The product is 400,000.

You can use basic facts and place value to solve math problems mentally.

EXAMPLE 2

Solve mentally.

A $300 + 200$
Basic fact: $3 + 2 = 5$ *Think: 3 hundreds + 2 hundreds*
$300 + 200 = 500$

B 200×600
Basic fact: $2 \times 6 = 12$ *Think: There are four zeros in the factors,*
$200 \times 600 = 120,000$ *so place four zeros in the product.*

PRACTICE

Multiply.

1. 600×100
2. $90 \times 1,000$
3. $2,000 \times 10$
4. 400×10
5. $10,000 \times 1,000$
6. $7,100 \times 1,000$

Solve mentally.

7. $500 + 400$
8. $80 - 50$
9. 700×30
10. $2,500 \div 50$
11. $1,200 + 600$
12. $20 \times 9,000$
13. $650 - 300$
14. $320 \div 8$
15. 90×90

Measure with Nonstandard Units

You can create your own units of measurement to approximate measures when you do not have standard measuring tools. You can measure distances like your stride, foot length, hand width, and finger width and use these units to estimate lengths.

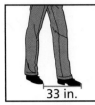

Stride

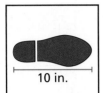

Foot length

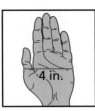

Hand width

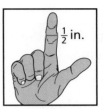

Finger width

EXAMPLES

A The width of your desk is about 7 hand widths. Estimate the width of your desk in inches.

$$\frac{1 \text{ hand width}}{4 \text{ in.}} = \frac{7 \text{ hand widths}}{x \text{ in.}}$$ *Set up a proportion to find the distance in inches.*

$4 \times 7 = 1 \times x$ *Find cross-products.*

$28 = x$ *Multiply.*

The width of your desk is about 28 inches.

B The distance from your classroom to the library is about 24 strides. Estimate the distance from your classroom to the library in feet.

$$\frac{1 \text{ stride}}{33 \text{ in.}} = \frac{24 \text{ strides}}{x \text{ in.}}$$ *Set up a proportion to find the distance in inches.*

$24 \times 33 = 1 \times x$ *Find cross-products.*

$792 = x$ *Multiply.*

$792 \text{ in.} \times \frac{1 \text{ ft}}{12 \text{ in.}}$ *Use a conversion factor.*

66 ft

It is about 66 feet from your classroom to the library.

PRACTICE

Measure your stride, foot length, hand width, and finger width. Choose an appropriate unit for each object, and give an approximate measure for each object.

1. Width of a classroom

2. Diameter of a CD

3. Height of a classroom door

4. Height of a desk

5. Width of your textbook

6. Length of an unsharpened pencil

Building Blocks of Geometry

Points, lines, and planes are the most basic figures in geometry.

A **point** is an exact location. It is represented by a dot, but it has no size at all.	• P	point P or P
A **line** is a straight path that has no thickness and extends forever in opposite directions.	ℓ $\overset{\longleftrightarrow}{\underset{A \qquad B}{\bullet \qquad \bullet}}$	line AB, line BA, $\overleftrightarrow{AB}$, $\overleftrightarrow{BA}$, or ℓ
A **plane** is a flat surface that has no thickness and extends forever.	• J $\quad$ L • K •	plane JKL, plane KLJ

EXAMPLE 1

Use the diagram to name each geometric figure.

A **three points**

P, T, and S *Use capital letters to name the points.*

B **two lines**

$\overleftrightarrow{QS}$, $\overleftrightarrow{RT}$ *Choose any two points on a line to name the line.*

C **a plane**

plane PQR *Choose any three points not all on the same line to name a plane.*

Other geometric figures are defined in terms of points, lines, and planes.

A **ray** is a part of a line. It has one endpoint and extends forever in one direction.	$M \qquad N$ $\bullet \qquad \bullet \longrightarrow$	ray MN or $\overrightarrow{MN}$
A **line segment** is a part of a line or a ray that extends from one endpoint to another.	$E \qquad\qquad F$ $\bullet \qquad\qquad \bullet$	segment EF, segment FE, $\overline{EF}$, or $\overline{FE}$

EXAMPLE 2

Use the diagram to name each geometric figure.

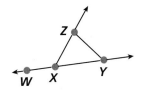

A **three rays**

$\overrightarrow{XW}$, $\overrightarrow{XZ}$, $\overrightarrow{YW}$

B **three line segments**

$\overline{XW}$, $\overline{WY}$, $\overline{YZ}$

PRACTICE

Use the diagram to name each geometric figure.

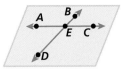

1. three points
2. two lines
3. a plane
4. three rays
5. three line segments

Measure and Draw Angles

An **angle** is formed by two rays with a common endpoint, called the **vertex.** An angle can be named by its vertex or by its vertex and a point on each ray. The middle point of the name must be the vertex. The angle at right may be named ∠K, ∠JKL, or ∠LKJ

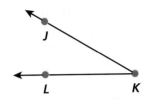

Angles are measured in degrees (°).

EXAMPLE 1

Use a protractor to measure ∠ABC.
- Place the center point of the protractor on the vertex of the angle.
- Place the protractor so that $\overrightarrow{BC}$ passes through the 0° mark.
- Using the scale that starts with 0° along $\overrightarrow{BC}$, read the measure where $\overrightarrow{BA}$ crosses the scale.
- The measure of ∠ABC is 55°. Write this as m∠ABC = 55°.

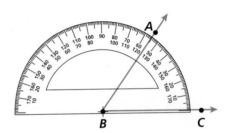

EXAMPLE 2

Use a protractor to draw an angle that measures 130°.
- Draw a ray. Place the center point of the protractor on the endpoint of the ray.
- Place the protractor so that the ray passes through the 0° mark.
- Make a mark at 130° above the scale on the protractor.
- Draw a ray from the endpoint of the first ray through the mark at 130°.

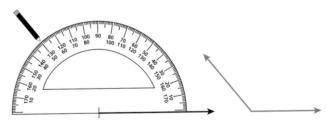

PRACTICE

Use a protractor to measure each angle.

1.   **2.**  **3.**

Use a protractor to draw an angle with each given measure.

4. 35°   **5.** 90°   **6.** 145°   **7.** 60°   **8.** 12°

Skills Bank

Classify Angles

You can classify an angle by its measure.

An **acute angle** measures greater than 0° and less than 90°.	
A **right angle** measures exactly 90°. Right angles are usually marked with a ⌐ symbol.	
An **obtuse angle** measures greater than 90° and less than 180°.	
A **straight angle** measures exactly 180°.	

EXAMPLE

Classify each angle as acute, right, obtuse, or straight.

A

The angle measures less than 90°, so it is an acute angle.

B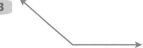

The angle measures greater than 90° and less than 180°, so it is an obtuse angle.

PRACTICE

Classify each angle as acute, right, obtuse, or straight.

1.

2.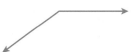

3.

4.

5. an angle with measure 75°

6. an angle with measure 100°

7. The sum of the measures of the angles of a triangle is 180°. What types of angles are possible for the three angles in a triangle? Use the terms acute, right, obtuse, or straight.

Classify Triangles

You can classify a triangle by its angle measures. An **acute triangle** has only acute angles. An **obtuse triangle** has one obtuse angle. A **right triangle** has one right angle.

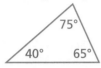
Acute Triangle

Obtuse Triangle

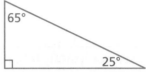
Right Triangle

EXAMPLE 1

Classify each triangle by its angle measures.

 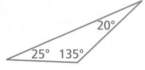

The triangle has one obtuse angle, so it is an obtuse triangle.

B

The triangle has only acute angles, so it is an acute triangle.

You can also classify a triangle by its side lengths. A **scalene triangle** has no sides of equal length. An **isosceles triangle** has at least two sides of equal length. An **equilateral triangle** has three sides of equal length. Note that tick marks are used to mark sides of equal length.

Scalene Triangle

Isosceles Triangle

Equilateral Triangle

EXAMPLE 2

Classify each triangle by its side lengths.

The triangle has two sides of equal length, so it is an isosceles triangle.

B
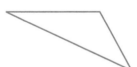

The triangle has no sides of equal length, so it is a scalene triangle.

PRACTICE

Classify each triangle by its angle measures and by its side lengths.

1.

2.
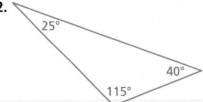

3.
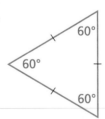

Skills Bank

Classify Polygons

A **polygon** is a closed plane figure formed by three or more line segments.
A **regular polygon** is a polygon in which all the sides are of equal length and all the angles have the same measure.

Polygons are named by the number of sides and angles they have.

	Triangle	Quadrilateral	Pentagon	Hexagon
Number of Sides and Angles	3	4	5	6
Regular	△	□	⬠	⬡
Not Regular				

	Heptagon	Octagon	Nonagon	Decagon
Number of Sides and Angles	7	8	9	10
Regular				
Not Regular				

EXAMPLE

Tell whether each shape is a polygon. If so, give its name and tell whether it appears to be regular or not regular.

A

There are 4 sides and 4 angles. The sides and angles appear congruent.
regular quadrilateral

B

There are 6 sides and 6 angles. The sides do not appear to have the same length.
non-regular hexagon

C

The figure is not closed.
not a polygon

PRACTICE

Tell whether each shape is a polygon. If so, give its name and tell whether it appears to be regular or not regular.

1.

2.

3.

Congruent Figures

Congruent figures have the same shape and same size. Line segments are congruent if they have the same length. Angles are congruent if they have the same measure. Polygons are congruent if the corresponding sides and angles are congruent.

EXAMPLE

Decide whether the figures in each pair are congruent.

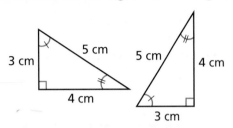

The tick marks show that corresponding angles are congruent.
Each triangle has a 3 cm side, a 4 cm side, and a 5 cm side.

The triangles are congruent.

PRACTICE

Tell whether the figures in each pair are congruent. Explain.

1.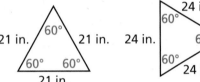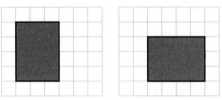

2.

Line Symmetry

A figure has **line symmetry** if it can be folded or reflected so that the two parts of the figure match. The line of reflection is called the **line of symmetry.**

EXAMPLE

Find all the lines of symmetry in the figure.

Count the lines of symmetry.

5 lines of symmetry

PRACTICE

Find all the lines of symmetry in each figure.

1. 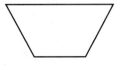 **2.** 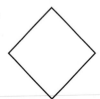 **3.**  **4.**

Skills Bank

Tessellations

A **tessellation** is a repeating pattern of one or more shapes that completely covers a plane without gaps or overlaps. The figure at right shows one way to make a tessellation using rectangles.

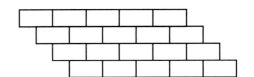

You can cut out a shape and trace it to determine whether the shape can be used to form a tessellation.

EXAMPLE

Determine whether each shape can be used to form a tessellation. If so, sketch the tessellation.

A

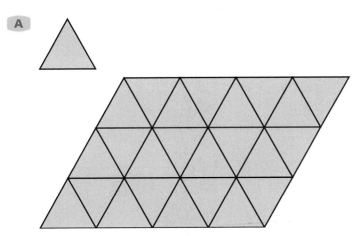

*Cut out the triangle.
Trace around the triangle.
Translate, reflect, or rotate the triangle to a new position and trace it.
Continue the process to create a pattern without gaps or overlaps.*

The triangle can be used to form a tessellation.

B

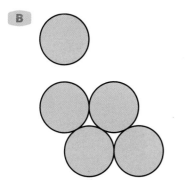
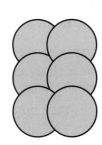

*Cut out the circle.
Trace around the circle.
Every pattern of circles has gaps or overlaps.*

The circle cannot be used to form a tessellation.

PRACTICE

Determine whether each shape can be used to form a tessellation. If so, sketch the tessellation.

1.   2.   3.   4.

Accuracy and Precision

Accuracy is the closeness of a measured value to the actual value. Since it is generally impossible to measure an object with complete accuracy, nearly all measurements are approximations.

Precision is the level of detail an instrument can measure. The smaller the unit an instrument can measure, the more precise its measurements will be.

EXAMPLE 1

Measure the segment to each level of precision.

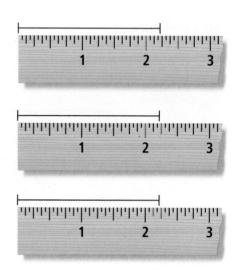

A The nearest $\frac{1}{2}$ inch

The length is slightly closer to 2 in. than $2\frac{1}{2}$ in.

2 inches

B The nearest $\frac{1}{4}$ inch

The length is closer to $2\frac{1}{4}$ in. than 2 in.

$2\frac{1}{4}$ inches

C The nearest $\frac{1}{8}$ inch

The length is slightly closer to $2\frac{1}{4}$ in. than $2\frac{1}{8}$ in.

$2\frac{1}{4}$ inches

EXAMPLE 2

Esteban measured the weight of a lamp as 2 pounds. Linda measured its weight as 34 ounces. The manufacturer lists the weight of the lamp as 32.5 ounces. Which student's measurement is more accurate? more precise?

Esteban's is more accurate.

2 lb = 32 oz, and 32 oz is closer to the accepted weight of the lamp.

Linda's is more precise.

Ounces are smaller units than pounds.

PRACTICE

Measure each segment to the nearest $\frac{1}{2}$ inch, $\frac{1}{4}$ inch, and $\frac{1}{8}$ inch.

1. ├────────────────────────────┤   **2.** ├──────────┤

Measure each segment to the nearest centimeter and nearest millimeter.

3. ├──────────────────────┤   **4.** ├────────────────┤

5. Kit measured the length of a skateboard as 156 cm. Lynn measured the length of the skateboard as 1.5 m. The manufacturer lists the length as 158 cm. Which student's measurement is more accurate? more precise?

Continuous and Discrete Data

The graph on the left shows how the temperature of tea in a mug changes over time. The data shows an example of a **continuous** graph because the graph consists of connected points that form a curve.

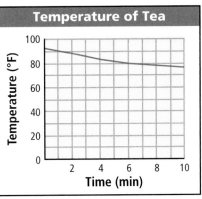

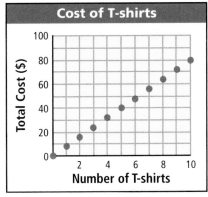

The graph on the right shows the cost of different numbers of T-shirts. This data shows an example of a **discrete** graph because the graph consists of unconnected points. The number of shirts must be a whole number.

EXAMPLE

Graph each set of data. Determine whether the data is continuous or discrete.

A

Amount of Water in a Bathtub				
Time (min)	2	4	6	8
Amount (gal)	10	20	30	40

Plot the points on a coordinate plane.

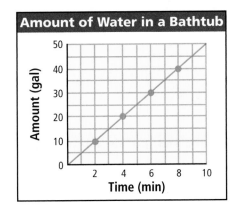

The amount of water changes continuously with time. Connect the points.

The data is continuous.

B

Passengers in Shuttle Buses				
Number of Buses	1	3	5	7
Number of Passengers	12	36	60	84

Plot the points on a coordinate plane.

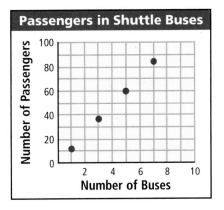

The number of buses and the number of passengers must be whole numbers.

The data is discrete.

PRACTICE

Graph each set of data. Determine whether the data is continuous or discrete.

1.

Number of Refrigerators Installed				
Time (days)	1	2	3	4
Number of Refrigerators	5	10	15	20

2.

Height of a Hot Air Balloon				
Time (min)	3	4	5	6
Height (ft)	100	80	60	40

Worked-Out Solutions ...

Chapter 1

1-1 **Exercises** (pp. 6–9)

17. 9,179 + 2,206; thousands

$$
\begin{array}{r}
9,000 \\
+\ 2,000 \\
\hline
11,000
\end{array}
$$

27. Area of Lake Huron rounded to the nearest ten thousand: 70,000 square miles

Area of Lake Ontario rounded to the nearest ten thousand: 30,000 square miles

70,000 − 30,000 = 40,000 square miles

1-2 **Exercises** (pp. 10–13)

49. $2^9 = 2 \times 2 \times 2 \times 2 \times 2 \times 2 \times 2 \times 2 \times 2 = 512$

57. $5^5 \ \blacksquare\ 25^1$

$5 \times 5 \times 5 \times 5 \times 5 \ \blacksquare\ 25$

$3125 \ \blacksquare\ 25$

$3125 > 25$

1-3 **Exercises** (pp. 16–19)

25. $60 \div (10 + 2) \times 4^2 - 23$

$60 \div 12 \times 4^2 - 23$

$60 \div 12 \times 16 - 23$

$5 \times 16 - 23$

$80 - 23$

57

39. $9^2 - 2 \times (15 + 16) - 8 = 11$

$9^2 - 2 \times 31 - 8 = 11$

$81 - 2 \times 31 - 8 = 11$

$81 - 62 - 8 = 11$

$19 - 8 = 11$

$11 = 11$

$9^2 - 2 \times (15 + 16) - 8 = 11$

1-4 **Exercises** (pp. 20–23)

7. Use pencil and paper.

$$
\begin{array}{r}
5 \\
24 \\
7 \\
1 \\
64 \\
2 \\
+\ 8 \\
\hline
111
\end{array}
$$

13. Use a calculator.

$828 \times 623 = 515{,}844$

1-5 **Exercises** (pp. 24–27)

17. Start with five; add 9.

$5 + 9 = \underline{14}$

$14 + 9 = \underline{23}$

$23 + 9 = \underline{32}$

$32 + 9 = \underline{41}$

5, 14, 23, 32, 41

21. no; A pattern is to subtract 4 from one term and add 5 to the next term.

$60 - 4 = 56$

$56 + 5 = 61$

$61 - 4 = 57$

$57 + 5 = 62$

Chapter 2

2-1 **Exercises** (pp. 44–47)

41. $58 + 4 + 2 + 6$

$58 + 2 + 4 + 6$

$(58 + 2) + (4 + 6)$

$60 + 10$

70 °F

45. $11 \times 18 = 11 \times (10 + 8)$

$= (11 \times 10) + (11 \times 8)$

$= 110 + 88$

$= 198$

2-2 **Exercises** (pp. 48–51)

9. Substitute for x in $9x \div 5 + 32$.

$x = 0;\ 9 \times 0 \div 5 + 32 = 0 \div 5 + 32$

$= 0 + 32$

$= 32$ °F

$x = 10;\ 9 \times 10 \div 5 + 32 = 90 \div 5 + 32$

$= 18 + 32$

$= 50$ °F

$x = 25;\ 9 \times 25 \div 5 + 32$

$= 225 \div 5 + 32$

$= 45 + 32$

$= 77$ °F

17. Evaluate $3x + 17$ for $x = 13$.

$3 \times 13 + 17$

$39 + 17$

56

2-3 Exercises (pp. 52–55)

33. $678 - 319$

37. On the graph, the number of U.S. space missions between 1986 and 1990 is 4. To separate the total cost, d, into cost per mission, divide the total cost by 4. $d \div 4$

2-4 Exercises (pp. 56–59)

9.

Position	1	2	3	4	n
Value of Term	6	7	8	9	$n + 5$

The sum of the position and five is the value of the next term.

Position + 5 = Value of Term

$1 + 5 = 6$

$2 + 5 = 7$

$3 + 5 = 8$

$4 + 5 = 9$

$n + 5$

11. The expression for the number of days it takes Mercury to make n orbits is $88n$.

$1 \times 88 = 88$

$2 \times 88 = 176$

$3 \times 88 = 264$

$n \times 88 = 88n$

$88n$

2-5 Exercises (pp. 62–65)

29. $v + 79 = 167$ for $v = 88$

$88 + 79 \stackrel{?}{=} 167$

$167 = 167$

Yes, 88 is a solution.

35. There are 20 nickels in a dollar.

$350 \div 20 = \$17.50$

$\$17.50 \neq \$17.00$

$17 \neq 350 \div 20$; No, they do not have the same amount of money.

2-6 Exercises (pp. 66–69)

29. $\quad 25 + m = \quad 47$

$\quad \underline{-25 \qquad\quad -25}$

$\qquad\quad m = \quad 22$

33. Let x represent how much more rope Magellan needed.

$x + 370 \text{ m} = 1{,}250 \text{ m}$

$\underline{-370 \text{ m} \qquad -370 \text{ m}}$

$x \qquad = \quad 880 \text{ m}$

Magellan needed another 880 m of rope to reach the ocean floor.

2-7 Exercises (pp. 70–72)

21. $f - 12 = \quad 2$

$\underline{+12 \qquad +12}$

$\quad f \quad = \quad 14$

29. $\quad 8 = s - 5$

$\underline{+5 \qquad +5}$

$\quad 13 = s$

$\quad s = 13$

The population of Shanghai is 13 million.

2-8 Exercises (pp. 73–76)

27. $161 = 7y$

$\dfrac{161}{7} = \dfrac{7y}{7}$

$23 = y$

$y = 23$

39. Let s represent the number of segments.

$2s = 30$

$\dfrac{2s}{2} = \dfrac{30}{2}$

$s = 15$

$2s = 354$

$\dfrac{2s}{2} = \dfrac{354}{2}$

$s = 177$

Centipedes can have from 15 to 177 segments.

2-9 Exercises (pp. 77–79)

21. $\dfrac{c}{15} = 11$

$\dfrac{c}{15} \cdot 15 = 11 \cdot 15$

$c = 165$

27. $\dfrac{w}{381} = 76$

$\dfrac{w}{381} \cdot 381 = 76 \cdot 381$

$w = 28{,}956$

The width of the Grand Canyon is 28,956 meters.

Chapter 3

3-1 Exercises (pp. 94–97)

29. $10.01 < 10.100$, so ten and one hundredth $<$ 10.100

41. Alpha Centauri (4.35), Proxima Centauri (4.22)

3-2 Exercises (pp. 98–101)

25. $67.55 \div 3.83$

$68 \div 4$

17

Worked-Out Solutions **WS3**

Worked-Out Solutions

29. 7.9¢ rounds to 8¢

3.7¢ rounds to 4¢

8¢ × 12 = 96¢

4¢ × 18 = 72¢

96¢ − 72¢

24¢

It costs about 24 cents more to call Japan for 12 minutes than within the United States for 18 minutes.

3-3 **Exercises** (pp. 102–105)

33. 0.0679 + 3.7500 = 3.8179

43. 135.00 − (14.83 + 15.35 + 32.40)

135.00 − 62.58

72.42

Logan needs $72.42 more to buy the bike.

3-4 **Exercises** (pp. 108–111)

39. 1.98 × 0.4 × 5.2

0.792 × 5.2

4.1184

51. Neptune = 9 × 1.2 = 10.8 pounds

Mars = 9 × 0.38 = 3.42 pounds

10.8 − 3.42 = 7.38 pounds

3-5 **Exercises** (pp. 112–114)

21. (13.28 − 7.9) ÷ 4

5.38 ÷ 4

1.345

23. Evaluate $x \div 4$ for $x = 0.944$.

0.944 ÷ 4

0.236

3-6 **Exercises** (pp. 115–118)

27. Evaluate $0.732 \div n$ for $n = 0.06$.

0.732 ÷ 0.06

12.2

35. $2.76 \times 10^2 \div 0.3$

276 ÷ 0.3

920

3-7 **Exercises** (pp. 119–121)

5. 36 ÷ 5 = 7.2

Tina will need 8 bunches.

7. 15 ÷ 6 = 2.5

Nick will need to buy 3 packs of cards.

3-8 **Exercises** (pp. 122–125)

29. a.
$$\begin{aligned} s - 3.5 &= 10 \\ + 3.5 \quad &+3.5 \\ \hline s &= 13.5 \end{aligned}$$

$s + 6 =$ side 1

13.5 + 6 = side 1

19.5 = side 1

$s + 7.5 =$ side 2

13.5 + 7.5 = side 2

21 = side 2

The other two sides of the triangle are 19.5 units and 21 units.

b. 10 + 19.5 + 21 = 50.5

The perimeter of the triangle is 50.5 units.

33. 210 ÷ 25 = 8.4

9 capsules are needed for 210 people.

Chapter 4

4-1 **Exercises** (pp. 142–145)

33. 3: The sum of the digits, 20, is not divisible by 3. 4: The last two digits, 77, do not form a number divisible by 4. 6: 677 is not divisible by 2 and 3. 9: The sum of the digits, 20, is not divisible by 3.

	2	3	4	5	6	9	10
677	no	no	no	no	no	no	no

41. To be divisible by 3, the sum of the digits must also be divisible by 3. 7 + 4 + 1 = 12, which is divisible by 3, so 1 is a possible answer. Other possible answers include 4, because 7 + 4 + 4 = 15, and 7, because 7 + 4 + 7 = 18.

4-2 **Exercises** (pp. 146–149)

35. The prime factorization of 99 is 3 × 3 × 11, or $3^2 \times 11$.

45. 343 = 7 × 7 × 7, or 7^3

4-3 **Exercises** (pp. 150–153)

25. factors of 75: 1, 3, 5, 15, 25, 75

factors of 225: 1, 3, 5, 9, 25, 45, 75, 225

factors of 150: 1, 2, 3, 5, 6, 10, 15, 25, 30, 50, 75, 150

The GCF of 75, 225, and 150 is 75.

29. factors of 30: 1, 2, 3, 5, 6, 10, 15, 30

factors of 24: 1, 2, 3, 4, 6, 8, 12, 24

factors of 12: 1, 2, 3, 4, 6, 12

The GCF of 30, 24, and 12 is 6, so Pam can make at most 6 fruit baskets.

41. The GCF of 28 and 70 is 14, so $\frac{28}{70}$ is not in simplest form.

$\frac{28 \div 14}{70 \div 14} = \frac{2}{5}$ This is $\frac{28}{70}$ in simplest form.

28 and 70 are also divisible by 7: $\frac{28 \div 7}{70 \div 7} = \frac{4}{10}$.

So $\frac{2}{5}$ and $\frac{4}{10}$ are two simplified versions of $\frac{28}{70}$.

45. $12 + 12 + 32 + 16 = 72$ total booths

Baskets & wreaths are $\frac{12}{72} = \frac{1}{6}$; jewelry is $\frac{32}{72} = \frac{4}{9}$;

glass & pottery are $\frac{16}{72} = \frac{2}{9}$; paintings are $\frac{12}{72} = \frac{1}{6}$.

37. $\frac{5}{12} = 0.41\overline{6}$; repeats

55. Rewrite $4\frac{1}{2}$ as 4.5.

$4.5 > 4.48$

$4.48 > 3.92$

The numbers in order from greatest to least are $4\frac{1}{2}$, 4.48, 3.92.

31. $(x \cdot 9) + 1 = 118$

$x \cdot 9 = 117$

$x = 13$

$13\frac{1}{9} = \frac{118}{9}$

35.
$$9\overline{)256}$$
$$28$$
$$-18$$
$$\overline{76}$$
$$-72$$
$$\overline{4}$$

$28\frac{4}{9}$ yards

43. Laura: $\frac{3 \cdot 7}{5 \cdot 7} = \frac{21}{35}$

Kim: $\frac{4 \cdot 5}{7 \cdot 5} = \frac{20}{35}$

$\frac{21}{35} > \frac{20}{35}$, so Laura spent more then Kim.

45. $1\frac{2}{5} = \frac{(1 \cdot 5) + 2}{5} = \frac{5 + 2}{5} = \frac{7}{5} = \frac{7 \cdot 8}{5 \cdot 8} = \frac{56}{40}$

$1\frac{1}{8} = \frac{(1 \cdot 8) + 1}{8} = \frac{8 + 1}{8} = \frac{9}{8} = \frac{9 \cdot 5}{8 \cdot 5} = \frac{45}{40}$

$3\frac{4}{5} = \frac{(3 \cdot 5) + 4}{5} = \frac{15 + 4}{5} = \frac{19}{5} = \frac{19 \cdot 8}{5 \cdot 8} = \frac{152}{40}$

$3 = \frac{3 \cdot 40}{1 \cdot 40} = \frac{120}{40}$

$3\frac{2}{5} = \frac{(3 \cdot 5) + 2}{5} = \frac{15 + 2}{5} = \frac{17}{5} = \frac{17 \cdot 8}{5 \cdot 8} = \frac{136}{40}$

$\frac{45}{40} < \frac{56}{40} < \frac{120}{40} < \frac{136}{40} < \frac{152}{40}$, so $1\frac{1}{8} < 1\frac{2}{5} < 3$

$< 3\frac{2}{5} < 3\frac{4}{5}$

The numbers in order from least to greatest are $1\frac{1}{8}$, $1\frac{2}{5}$, 3, $3\frac{2}{5}$, $3\frac{4}{5}$.

25. $37\frac{13}{18} - 24\frac{7}{18}$

$(37 - 24) + \left(\frac{13}{18} - \frac{7}{18}\right) = 13\frac{6}{18}$, or $13\frac{1}{3}$

39. $\frac{7}{12} + \frac{5}{12} = \frac{12}{12} = 1$

The plants' combined height is 1 foot.

21. $1\frac{1}{2} - 1 = \frac{1}{2}$

$\frac{1}{2} < 1$

29. $5 + 3 + 5\frac{1}{2} = 13\frac{1}{2}$

about $13\frac{1}{2}$

Chapter 5

31. $6 = 2 \cdot 3$

$12 = 2 \cdot 2 \cdot 3$

$2 \cdot 2 \cdot 3 = 12$

LCM: 12

35. factors of 48: 1, 2, 3, 4, 6, 8, 12, 16, 24, 48

pairs of factors of 48 with a sum of 28: 4 and 24, 12 and 16

The LCM of 4 and 24 is 24. The LCM of 12 and 16 is 48.

12 and 16

25. $\frac{8}{9} - b$ for $b = \frac{1}{2}$

$\frac{8}{9} - \frac{1}{2} = \frac{16}{18} - \frac{9}{18} = \frac{7}{18}$

37. $\frac{2}{3} + \frac{1}{4} - \frac{1}{6} = \frac{8}{12} + \frac{3}{12} - \frac{2}{12} = \frac{9}{12} = \frac{3}{4}$

27. $14\frac{1}{4} + 9.5 = 14\frac{1}{4} + 9\frac{1}{2} = 14\frac{1}{4} + 9\frac{2}{4} = 23\frac{3}{4}$

37. $n - 1\frac{1}{4}$ for $n = 2\frac{1}{3}$

$2\frac{1}{3} - 1\frac{1}{4} = 2\frac{4}{12} - 1\frac{3}{12} = 1\frac{1}{12}$

27. $12\frac{5}{9} - 6\frac{2}{3} + 1\frac{4}{9}$

$12\frac{5}{9} - 6\frac{6}{9} + 1\frac{4}{9} = 11\frac{14}{9} - 6\frac{6}{9} + 1\frac{4}{9}$

$= 5\frac{8}{9} + 1\frac{4}{9} = 7\frac{3}{9} = 7\frac{1}{3}$

37. $b - (a + c)$ for $a = 6\frac{2}{3}$, $b = 8\frac{1}{2}$,

and $c = 1\frac{3}{4}$

$8\frac{1}{2} - \left(6\frac{2}{3} + 1\frac{3}{4}\right) = 8\frac{6}{12} - \left(6\frac{8}{12} + 1\frac{9}{12}\right) =$

$8\frac{6}{12} - 7\frac{17}{12} = 8\frac{6}{12} - 8\frac{5}{12} = \frac{1}{12}$

5-5 Exercises (pp. 212–215)

37. $\frac{4}{5}c$ for $c = 12$

$\frac{4}{5} \cdot \frac{12}{1} = \frac{48}{5} = 9\frac{3}{5}$

43. $3 \cdot \frac{2}{9} \,\blacksquare\, \frac{2}{3}$

$\frac{6}{9} = \frac{6}{9}$

5-6 Exercises (pp. 216–219)

27. $\frac{2}{5} \cdot \frac{2}{7} \cdot \frac{5}{8} = \frac{2 \cdot 2 \cdot 5}{5 \cdot 7 \cdot 8} = \frac{20}{280} = \frac{1}{14}$

37. $\frac{5}{6} \cdot \frac{2}{3} \,\blacksquare\, \frac{1}{3} \cdot \frac{2}{3}$

$\frac{5 \cdot 2}{6 \cdot 3} \,\blacksquare\, \frac{1 \cdot 2}{3 \cdot 3}$

$\frac{10}{18} \,\blacksquare\, \frac{2}{9}$

$\frac{5}{9} > \frac{2}{9}$

5-7 Exercises (pp. 220–223)

37. $2 \cdot \frac{4}{5} \cdot 1\frac{2}{3} = \frac{2}{1} \cdot \frac{4}{5} \cdot \frac{5}{3} = \frac{2 \cdot 4 \cdot 5}{1 \cdot 5 \cdot 3} = \frac{40}{15}$

$= 2\frac{10}{15} = 2\frac{2}{3}$

49. $3\frac{3}{4} \cdot p$ for $p = \frac{1}{2}$

$3\frac{3}{4} \cdot \frac{1}{2} = \frac{15}{4} \cdot \frac{1}{2} = \frac{15 \cdot 1}{4 \cdot 2} = \frac{15}{8} = 1\frac{7}{8}$

5-8 Exercises (pp. 224–227)

43. $\frac{12}{1} \div \frac{3}{4} = \frac{12}{1} \cdot \frac{4}{3} = \frac{12 \cdot 4}{1 \cdot 3} = \frac{48}{3} = 16$ bags

55. $2\frac{3}{4} \cdot 1\frac{2}{3} \div 5 = \frac{11}{4} \cdot \frac{5}{3} \cdot \frac{1}{5} = \frac{11 \cdot 5 \cdot 1}{4 \cdot 3 \cdot 5} = \frac{55}{60} = \frac{11}{12}$

5-9 Exercises (pp. 228–231)

23. Let s be the initial amount of shampoo.

$s - 2\frac{5}{8} = 13\frac{3}{8}$

$s - 2\frac{5}{8} + 2\frac{5}{8} = 13\frac{3}{8} + 2\frac{5}{8}$

$s = 16$

There were 16 ounces of shampoo in the bottle before she washed her dog.

27. $3\frac{2}{9} - 1\frac{1}{3} = p - 5\frac{1}{2}$

$3\frac{4}{18} - 1\frac{6}{18} = p - 5\frac{9}{18}$

$2\frac{22}{18} - 1\frac{6}{18} = p - 5\frac{9}{18}$

$1\frac{16}{18} = p - 5\frac{9}{18}$

$1\frac{16}{18} + 5\frac{9}{18} = p - 5\frac{9}{18} + 5\frac{9}{18}$

$6\frac{25}{18} = p$

$7\frac{7}{18} = p$

5-10 Exercises (pp. 232–235)

27. $2y = \frac{4}{5} \div \frac{3}{5}$

$2y = \frac{4}{5} \cdot \frac{5}{3}$

$2y = \frac{20}{15}$

$2y \cdot \frac{1}{2} = \frac{20}{15} \cdot \frac{1}{2}$

$y = \frac{20}{15} \cdot \frac{1}{2}$

$y = \frac{20}{30}$

$y = \frac{2}{3}$

29. $\frac{3}{2}n = 9$

$\frac{3}{2}n \cdot \frac{2}{3} = 9 \cdot \frac{2}{3}$

$n = 9 \cdot \frac{2}{3}$

$n = \frac{18}{3}$

$n = 6$

Chapter 6

6-1 Exercises (pp. 252–255)

7.

State	Mean Score
Connecticut	509
Maine	500
Massachusetts	513
New Hampshire	519
Rhode Island	500
Vermont	508

Data in numerical order: 500, 500, **508**, **509**, 513, 519

mean: $500 + 500 + 508 + 509 + 513 + 519 = 3{,}049$

$3{,}049 \div 6 \approx 508.2$

median: $(508 + 509) \div 2 = 1{,}017 \div 2 = 508.5$

mode: 500

range: $519 - 500 = 19$

11. Given data in numerical order: 4, 4, 7, 8, 8, 9, 10
The mode of the given data is 4 and 8. The mode of the whole set of data is 4, so the missing data is 4.
4

6-2 **Exercises** (pp. 256–259)

5. with Maine: 41, 702, **810**, 1,003, 1,138
mean: 41 + 702 + 810 + 1,003 + 1,138 = 3,694
    3,694 ÷ 5 = 738.8
median: 810
mode: no mode
without Maine: 702, **810**, **1,003**, 1,138
mean: 702 + 810 + 1,003 + 1,138 = 3,653
    3,653 ÷ 4 = 913.25
median: (810 + 1,003) ÷ 2 = 906.5
mode: no mode

7. 59, 120, 122, **128**, 129, 134, 136
mean: 59 + 120 + 122 + 128 + 129 + 134 + 136 = 828
    828 ÷ 7 ≈ 118.29
median: 128
mode: no mode

6-3 **Exercises** (pp. 262–265)

9. $17 - 3 = 14$ million mi^2
11. 3 + 4 + 5 + 7 + 9 + 12 + 17 = 57
    57 ÷ 7 ≈ 8.14 million mi^2

6-4 **Exercises** (pp. 266–268)

7.

Populations of Australia's States and Territories	
Census	**Frequency**
0–999,999	3
1,000,000–1,999,999	2
2,000,000–2,999,999	0
3,000,000–3,999,999	1
4,000,000–4,999,999	1
5,000,000–5,999,999	0
6,000,000–6,999,999	1

9. No; intervals cannot contain the same values.

6-5 **Exercises** (pp. 269–271)

23. $(1, 7)$: A
29. D: $(9, 8)$

6-6 **Exercises** (pp. 272–275)

7. 200 million
9.

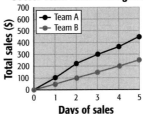

Soccer Team Fund-Raising Efforts

6-7 **Exercises** (pp. 276–278)

7. The graph is misleading because the yearly increments have changed.

9.

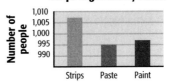

Strips' Significantly Better

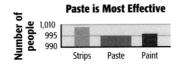

Paste is Most Effective

6-8 **Exercises** (pp. 279–281)

15. A: mode: 21
B: mode: no mode
C: mode: no mode
A has a mode of 21

17. Number of Cars with One Passenger

Stems	Leaves
8	0 1 2 3 7 8 9
9	2 4 4 5 9
10	0 1 3 9
11	
12	4 5

Key: 8|0 means 80

Chapter 7

7-1 **Exercises** (pp. 296–299)

15. Possible answer: 7 to 10, 7:10
27. Monday: $\dfrac{1,020\,\text{m}}{6\,\text{min}} = \dfrac{1,020\,\text{m} \div 6}{6\,\text{min} \div 6} = \dfrac{170\,\text{m}}{1\,\text{min}}$
Wednesday: $\dfrac{1,554\,\text{m}}{9\,\text{min}} = \dfrac{1,554\,\text{m} \div 9}{9\,\text{min} \div 9} = \dfrac{172.\overline{6}\,\text{m}}{1\,\text{min}}$

Alfonso ran faster on Wednesday.

21. The ratio of the bat's wing span to the bat's body length is 8:3.

$\frac{8}{3}$

23.

$6 \cdot 4 = 24$

$5 \cdot 3 = 15$

24; 15

17. $\frac{p}{10} = \frac{15}{50}$

$50 \cdot p = 10 \cdot 15$

$50p = 150$

$\frac{50p}{50} = \frac{150}{50}$

$p = 3$

23. $\frac{7 \cdot 3}{2 \cdot 3} = \frac{21}{6}$

41. $8\% = \frac{8}{100}$

$\frac{8 \div 4}{100 \div 4} = \frac{2}{25}$

$8 \div 100 = 0.08$

47. $52\% = \frac{52}{100}$

$\frac{52 \div 4}{100 \div 4} = \frac{13}{25}$

$52 \div 100 = 0.52$

43. $25\overline{)1.00}$ quotient 0.04

$0.04 \cdot 100$

4%; 0.04

59. $\frac{7}{25} = \frac{7 \cdot 4}{25 \cdot 4} = \frac{28}{100} = 28\%$

$0.21 = \frac{21}{100} = 21\%$

21%, 28%, 38%

$0.21, \frac{7}{25}, 38\%$

21. 13% of 40

$13\% = 0.13$

$0.13 \cdot 40 = 5.2$

33. Glucose has 24 atoms per molecule.

Hydrogen: Find 50% of 24.

$50\% = 0.50$

$0.50 \cdot 24 = 12$

Carbon: Find 25% of 24

$25\% = 0.25$

$0.25 \cdot 24 = 6$

Oxygen: Find 25% of 24

$25\% = 0.25$

$0.25 \cdot 24 = 6$

12 atoms of hydrogen, 6 atoms of carbon, and 6 atoms of oxygen

9. Step 1: First round $52.75 \approx \$53$

Step 2: Think: $5\% = 5 \cdot 1\%$

1% of $\$53 = 0.01 \cdot \$53 = \$0.53$

Step 3: $5\% = 5 \cdot 1\%$

$5 \cdot \$0.53 = \$2.65$

The approximate sales tax is $2.65.

$\$53 + \$2.65 = \$55.65$

13. $\$649 + \$199 = \$848$

$60\% = 0.60$

$848 \cdot 0.60$

$\$848 - \$508.80 = \$339.20$

5. Sides: $\overline{WX}$ and $\overline{BA}$; $\overline{XY}$ and $\overline{AC}$; $\overline{YW}$ and $\overline{CB}$

Angles: $\angle W$ and $\angle B$; $\angle X$ and $\angle A$; $\angle Y$ and $\angle C$

9. $\angle Z$ corresponds to $\angle I$, so m$\angle Z = 100°$.

$\angle H$ corresponds to $\angle Y$, so m$\angle H = 80°$.

$\angle J$ corresponds to $\angle W$, so m$\angle J = 80°$.

$\overline{WZ}$ is congruent to $\overline{XY}$, so the length of $\overline{WZ}$ is 4 yards.

$\frac{GH}{XY} = \frac{JG}{WX}$

$\frac{8}{4} = \frac{11}{x}$

$8 \cdot x = 4 \cdot 11$

$8x = 44$

$\frac{8x}{8} = \frac{44}{8}$

$x = 5.5$

The length of $\overline{WX}$ is 5.5 yards.

$\overline{YZ}$ is congruent to $\overline{WX}$, so the length of $\overline{YZ}$ is 5.5 yards.

Worked-Out Solutions

5. $\dfrac{h}{84} = \dfrac{130}{105}$

$105 \cdot h = 84 \cdot 130$

$105h = 10{,}920$

$\dfrac{105h}{105} = \dfrac{10{,}920}{105}$

$h = 104$

The tree is 104 inches tall.

7. $\dfrac{h}{2} = \dfrac{360}{6}$

$6 \cdot h = 2 \cdot 360$

$6h = 720$

$\dfrac{6h}{6} = \dfrac{720}{6}$

$h = 120$

The statue is 120 meters tall.

7-10 **Exercises** (pp. 333–335)

5. $\dfrac{1\,\text{in.}}{20\,\text{mi}} = \dfrac{x\,\text{in.}}{50\,\text{mi}}$

$20 \cdot x = 1 \cdot 50$

$20x = 50$

$\dfrac{20x}{20} = \dfrac{50}{20}$

$x = 2.5$

On the map, the distance between Riverside and Los Angeles should be 2.5 inches.

7. $\dfrac{1\,\text{ft}}{87\,\text{ft}} = \dfrac{3\,\text{ft}}{x\,\text{ft}}$

$1 \cdot x = 87 \cdot 3$

$x = 261$

The actual length of the train is 261 feet.

Chapter 8

8-1 **Exercises** (pp. 352–355)

9. Foot; possible answer: The height of a flagpole is more than the distance from my elbow to my wrist but less than the distance of four times around a track.

21. $8\frac{1}{4}$lb

8-2 **Exercises** (pp. 356–359)

13. kilometers (km); the distance around a city block

17. milliliter (mL); a drop of water

8-3 **Exercises** (pp. 360–363)

31. 12 pt ▇ 3 gal

$12\,\text{pt} \times \dfrac{1\,\text{gal}}{8\,\text{pt}} = 1.5\,\text{gal}$

$1.5\,\text{gal} < 3\,\text{gal}$

$12\,\text{pt} < 3\,\text{gal}$

37. $1{,}302\,\text{ft} \times \dfrac{1\,\text{yd}}{3\,\text{ft}} = 434\,\text{yd}$

The depth of Lake superior is about 434 yards.

8-4 **Exercises** (pp. 364–367)

23. $28\,\text{L} = (28 \times 1{,}000)\,\text{mL} = 28{,}000\,\text{mL}$

$16 \times 400 = 6{,}400$

$28{,}000 - 6{,}400 = 21{,}600\,\text{mL}$

There are 21,600 mL, or 21.6 L, of soup left in the pot.

29. 1,000 mm ▇ 1 m

$1{,}000\,\text{mm} \times \dfrac{1\,\text{m}}{1{,}000\,\text{mm}} = 1\,\text{m}$

$1\,\text{m} = 1\,\text{m}$

$1{,}000\,\text{mm} = 1\,\text{m}$

8-5 **Exercises** (pp. 368–371)

23. 21 hr ▇ $\frac{5}{6}$ day

$24\,\text{hr} \cdot \dfrac{5}{6} = \dfrac{120}{6} = 20$

$20 \text{ hours} = \frac{5}{6}$ day

$21\,\text{hr} > \frac{5}{6}$ day

29. $C = \frac{5}{9}(F - 32)$

$C \approx \frac{1}{2}(86 - 30)$

$C = \frac{1}{2}(56)$

$C = 28$

86°F is about 28°C

8-6 **Exercises** (pp. 374–377)

13. $FE = CD - AG$

$= 8 - 2$

$= 6$

Side FE is 6 in. long.

17. $P = 5s$

$P = 5 \cdot \dfrac{2}{5}$

$P = \dfrac{5}{1} \cdot \dfrac{2}{5}$

$P = \dfrac{10}{5}$

$P = 2$

The perimeter is 2 km.

11. $d = ?; C = 1.57$ in.

$$C = \pi d$$
$$1.57 \approx 3.14d$$
$$\frac{1.57}{3.14} \approx \frac{3.14d}{3.14}$$
$$0.5 \text{ in.} \approx d$$

13. $r = ?; d = 11.5$ ft; $C = ?$

$$C = \pi d$$
$$d = 2r$$
$$11.5 = 2r$$
$$\frac{11.5}{2} = \frac{2r}{2}$$
$$5.75 = r$$
$$C \approx 3.14 \cdot 11.5$$
$$C \approx 36.11 \text{ ft}$$

If $d = 11.5$ ft, then $r = 5.75$ ft, and $C = 36.11$ ft.

Chapter 9

11. There are 4 full or almost full squares and 4 half-full squares. The area of the figure is about 6 square units.

19. $A = bh$

$$A = 1.5 \cdot 0.5$$
$$A = 0.75$$

The area is 0.75 cm^2.

17. $A = \frac{1}{2}(5)(2) = \frac{1}{2}(10) = 5$ square units

21. $A = \frac{1}{2}h\left(b_1 + b_2\right)$

$$A = \frac{1}{2}(15.4)(18 + 27)$$
$$A = \frac{1}{2}(15.4)(45) = 346.5$$

The area is 346.5 m^2.

15. $r = 5.7$ cm

$$d = 2r$$
$$= 2 \cdot 5.7$$
$$= 11.4 \text{ cm}$$
$$C = \pi d$$
$$C \approx 3.14 \cdot 11.4$$
$$C \approx 35.8 \text{ cm}$$
$$A = \pi r^2$$
$$A \approx 3.14 \cdot 5.7^2$$
$$A \approx 3.14 \cdot 32.49$$
$$A \approx 102.02 \text{ cm}^2$$

17. $d = 14.9$ in.

$$r = d \div 2$$
$$= 14.9 \div 2$$
$$= 7.45 \text{ in.}$$
$$C = \pi d$$
$$C \approx 3.14 \cdot 14.9$$
$$C \approx 46.79 \text{ in.}$$
$$A = \pi r^2$$
$$A \approx 3.14 \cdot 7.45^2$$
$$A \approx 3.14 \cdot 55.5$$
$$A \approx 174.28 \text{ in}^2$$

9. Subtract the area of the triangle from the area of the rectangle.

area of rectangle:
$$A = bh = 12(6) = 72 \text{ cm}^2$$

area of triangle:
$$A = \frac{1}{2}bh = \frac{1}{2}(12)(3) = 18 \text{ cm}^2$$

shaded area:
$$A = 72 - 18 = 54 \text{ cm}^2$$

11. Subtract the area of the circle from the area of the square.

area of square:
$$A = s^2 = 6^2 = 36 \text{ in}^2$$

area of circle:
$$A = \pi r^2 = \pi(2)^2$$
$$\approx (3.14)(4) \approx 12.56 \text{ in}^2$$

area of wood:
$$A \approx 36 - 12.56 \approx 23.44 \text{ in}^2$$

The area of the remaining piece of wood is 23.4 in^2.

13. All faces are polygons. The base is a square, and the sides are triangles; square pyramid; Yes, it is a polyhedron.

19. B

17. $V = Bh$

$$V = \left(\frac{1}{2} \cdot 11 \cdot 7.5\right) \cdot 11.5$$
$$V = 41.25 \cdot 11.5$$
$$V = 474.375 \text{ km}^3$$

19.
$$V = \ell w h$$
$$900 = 9 \cdot w \cdot 5$$
$$900 = 45 \cdot w$$
$$900 \div 45 = 45w \div 45$$
$$20 \text{ ft} = w$$

9-7 Exercises (pp. 422–425)

11. $V = \pi r^2 h$

$V \approx 3.14 \times 2.8^2 \times 5.6$

$V \approx 138 \text{ in}^3$

15. $4 \text{ ft} \div 2 = 2 \text{ ft}$

$V = \pi r^2 h$

$V \approx 3.14 \times 2^2 \times 8$

$V \approx 100.48 \text{ in}^3$

9-8 Exercises (pp. 426–429)

15. $S = $ area of square $+ 4 \times$ (area of triangular face)

$S = s^2 + 4 \times \left(\frac{1}{2}bh\right)$

$S = 1^2 + 4 \times \left(\frac{1}{2} \times 1 \times 5\right)$

$S = 1 + 4 \times \frac{5}{2}$

$S = 1 + \frac{20}{2}$

$S = 1 + 10$

$S = 11$

The surface area is 11 km^2.

17. $S = $ area of lateral surface

$\quad\quad + 2 \times$ (area of each base)

$S = h \times (2\pi r) + 2 \times (\pi r^2)$

$S = 6.75 \times (2 \times \pi \times 7.8) + 2 \times (\pi \times 7.8^2)$

$S = 6.75 \times 15.6\pi + 2 \times 60.84\pi$

$S \approx 6.75 \times 15.6(3.14) + 2 \times 60.84(3.14)$

$S \approx 6.75 \times 48.984 + 2 \times 191.0376$

$S \approx 330.642 + 382.0752$

$S \approx 712.7172$

The surface area is 712.72 m^2.

Chapter 10

10-1 Exercises (pp. 446–449)

11. For each consecutive x value, the y values increase by 4. So $4x$ is in the equation.

$4(2) = 8$

$4(3) = 12$

$4(5) = 20$

$4(9) = 36$, etc.

All the y values in the table are 2 less than 4 times the corresponding x value. The equation is $y = 4x - 2$.

$y = 4(14) - 2 = 54$

15. $h = $ hours of playing, $c = $ total cost,

$125 + 55h = c$

10-2 Exercises (pp. 450–453)

27. $y = 4(1) + 9 = 13$

(1, 14) is not a solution.

31.

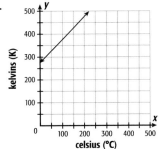

10-3 Exercises (pp. 456–460)

19. $118 = 6x + 16$

$102 = 6x$

$17 = x$

$17 per ticket

23. $4x - 3 = 25$

$\quad\quad \underline{+3 \quad +3}$

$\quad 4x \quad = 28$

$\quad \dfrac{4x}{4} = \dfrac{28}{4}$

$\quad\quad x = 7$

10-4 Exercises (pp. 461–465)

31. $c \leq 2$

```
←—●—+—+—+—+—+—+—+—+—→
  0 1 2 3 4 5 6 7 8 9 10
```

35. All trout that are kept must be 10 inches or greater, so $t \geq 10$.

10-5 Exercises (pp. 466–469)

39. $12p + 15 \leq 120$

$\quad \underline{-15 \quad -15}$

$\quad 12p \quad\quad \leq 105$

$\quad \dfrac{12p}{12} \leq \dfrac{105}{12}$

$\quad\quad p \leq 8.75$

Peter can buy no more than 8 pizzas.

41. $\dfrac{x}{2} + 4 < 6$

$\quad \underline{-4 \quad -4}$

$\quad \dfrac{x}{2} \quad < 2$

$\quad 2 \cdot \dfrac{x}{2} < 2 \cdot 2$

$\quad\quad x < 4$

```
←—+—+—+—+—⊕—+—+—+—+—→
  0 1 2 3 4 5 6 7 8 9 10
```

Chapter 11

11-1 Exercises (pp. 484–487)

29. +92

33. 0

11-2 Exercises (pp. 488–491)

21. $-16 \blacksquare -51$

$-16 > -51$

35. $-2,189 < -1,296 < 14,410 < 19,000 < 29,022$; So, the features in order from least to greatest are: San Augustin Cave, Dead Sea, Mt. Rainier, Kilimanjaro, Mt. Everest.

11-3 Exercises (pp. 492–495)

37.

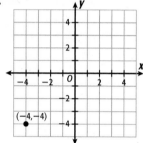

49. Gabon

11-4 Exercises (pp. 498–501)

35.

57. $-2 + -4 = -6$

The temperature at 4 A.M. was $-6\,°F$.

11-5 Exercises (pp. 502–504)

23. $-12 - (-6) = -6$

37. $-10 - 9 = -19$

The water's surface is now 19 meters below sea level.

11-6 Exercises (pp. 505–507)

33. Evaluate $n \cdot (-7)$ for $n = -2$.

$n \cdot (-7)$

$-2 \cdot (-7)$

14

39. The spring tides are two times as great as normal, so multiply the values for the high and low tides by 2.

$2 \cdot 2 = 4$

$2 \cdot (-2) = -4$

The spring tides might be 4 feet to -4 feet.

11-7 Exercises (pp. 508–511)

33. Evaluate $n \div (-7)$ for $n = -21$.

$n \div (-7)$

$-21 \div (-7)$

3

43. a. -300

b. A decrease of 300 seals from 1976 to 1980.

11-8 Exercises (pp. 512–515)

47. $\qquad h \div (-4) = 21$

$h \div (-4) \cdot (-4) = 21 \cdot (-4)$

$\qquad\qquad h = -84$

61. $-200x = -14,000$

$\dfrac{-200x}{-200} = \dfrac{-14,000}{-200}$

$\qquad x = 70$

At a rate of -200 ft per dive, the submarine will need to take 70 dives to reach $-14,000$ ft.

Selected Answers . . .

Chapter 1

1-1 Exercises

1. 7,000 **3.** 1,500 bottles of water
5. about 2 gallons **7.** 40,000
9. 20,000 **11.** 40 golf balls **13.** 500
15. 0 **17.** 11,000 **19.** 40,000
21. 70,000 **23.** 400,000 **25.** 10
square miles **27.** 40,000 square
miles **33.** 400; 36 rounds to 40,
and 8 rounds to 10 **35.** 2,615
37. 2,496 **39.** 1,000 + 300 + 50 + 4
41. 400,000 + 10,000 + 6,000 + 700
+ 3

1-2 Exercises

1. 8^3 **3.** 6^5 **5.** 5^5 **7.** 16 **9.** 625
11. 343 **13.** 2^6 **15.** 8^2 **17.** 6^5
19. 7^7 **21.** 4^2 **23.** 243 **25.** 81
27. 512 **29.** 256 **31.** 144
33. $16 \times 16 \times 16$ **35.** $31 \times 31 \times 31$
$\times 31 \times 31 \times 31$ **37.** $50 \times 50 \times 50$
39. $1 \times 1 \times 1 \times 1 \times 1 \times 1 \times 1$
$\times 1 \times 1$ **41.** $8 \times 8 \times 8 \times 8 \times 8$
43. 1,000,000 **45.** 6,561
47. 100,000 **49.** 512 **51.** 125
53. > **55.** < **57.** > **59.** 1,024
cells **61.** 8; 2^8, or 256 **65.** D
67. 8,245; 8,452; 8,732 **69.** 11,901;
12,681; 12,751 **71.** 50,000

1-3 Exercises

1. 33 **3.** 50 **5.** 4 **7.** $138 **9.** 10
11. 32 **13.** 14 **15.** 25 **17.** 40
19. 24 **21.** 1,250 pages **23.** 18
25. 57 **27.** 1 **29.** 22 **31.** 64 **33.** 22
35. $(7 + 2) \times 6 - (4 - 3) = 53$
37. $5^2 - 10 + (5 + 4^2) = 36$
39. $9^2 - 2 \times (15 + 16) - 8 = 11$
41. $4^2 \times (3 - 2) \div 4 = 4$ **43.** 30 m^2
45. 300 m^3 **49.** I **51.** 3,273
53. 70,007 **55.** 125 **57.** 256

1-4 Exercises

1. paper and pencil; 364
3. calculator; 64,890 **5.** mental
math; middle row **7.** 111
9. mental math; 430
11. calculator; 35,511
13. calculator; 515,844 **15.** mental
math; 210 **17.** mental math; 350
19. calculator; 264 **21.** 11,822,400
miles **23.** 25 taste buds **29.** A
31. 900 **33.** 8,200 **35.** 2 **37.** 60

1-5 Exercises

1. add 12; 60; 72; 84 **3.** add 11; 51;
62 **5.** add 7 and subtract 2; 12; 19
7. multiply by 6 and divide by 2; 9;
162 **9.** subtract 14; 28; 14; 0
11. add 3; 20; 23 **13.** add 21 and
subtract 4; 41; 62; 58 **15.** divide by
4 and multiply by 2; 100; 25
17. 5, 14, 23, 32, 41 **19a.** 2018
b. 1994 **c.** yes; 2006 + 2(12) =
2030 **21.** subtract 4 and add 5
27. A **29.** 5^6 **31.** 7^5

Chapter 1 Study Guide: Review

1. sequence, term **2.** base,
exponent **3.** order of operations
4. simplify **5.** 1,000 **6.** 6,000
7. 20,000 **8.** 800 **9.** 5^3 **10.** 3^5
11. 7^4 **12.** 8^2 **13.** 4^4 **14.** 1^3
15. 256 **16.** 16 **17.** 216
18. 27 **19.** 1 **20.** 2,401 **21.** 125
22. 100 **23.** 81 **24.** 32 organisms
25. 1,024 people **26.** 59 **27.** 11
28. 26 **29.** 17 **30.** 5 **31.** 45
32. $149 **33.** $396 **34.** 62°
35. Possible answer: You can use
the Distributive Property to break
up 14 and then use mental math;
$(10 \times 5) + (4 \times 5) = 70$.
36. Possible answer: Since
the numbers are so big, it
is best to use a calculator;
$8,951,056,150,180.66 \div$
$302,634,238 = $29,577.14$.
37. Possible answer: Since the
numbers are easy, you can use

mental math; 69 °F − 41 °F =
28 °F. **38.** Add 5; 24, 29.
39. Subtract 2; 13, 11. **40.** Add 4
and subtract 2; 20, 22.
41. Multiply by 3; 81, 243.
42. Add 5 and subtract 2; 71, 74.

Chapter 2

2-1 Exercises

1. 40 **3.** 50 **5.** 320 **7.** 120 **9.** 156
11. 99 **13.** 108 **15.** 40 **17.** 50
19. 640 **21.** 108 **23.** 426 **25.** 138
27. 372 **29.** 328 **31.** 40 **33.** 60
35. 198 **37.** 111 **39.** 70 **41.** 70°F
43. 153 **45.** 198 **51.** 108 eggs
53. $208

2-2 Exercises

1. 56; 65 **3.** 24; 28; 32; 36
5. 23; 25 **7a.** 2 hr: 100 − 120
miles; 3 hr: 150 − 180 miles; 4 hr:
200 − 240 miles; 5 hr: 250 − 300
miles **b.** between 350 and 420
miles **9.** 32° F; 50° F; 77° F **11.** 32
13. 13 **15.** 8 **17.** 56 **19.** 10
21. 110 **23.** 24 zlotys **29.** 38
31. The Distributive Property; 294

2-3 Exercises

1. $4,028 - m$ **3.** $15x$ **5.** $\frac{p}{5}$
7. $(149)(2)$ **9.** the product of 345
and 196; 345 times 196 **11.** the
difference of d and 5; 5 less than d
13. $5x$ **15.** $325 \div 25$ **17.** $137 + 675$
19. $j - 14$ **21.** take away 19 from
243; 243 minus 19 **23.** 342
multiplied by 75; the product of
342 and 75 **25.** the product of 45
and 23; 45 times 23 **27.** the
difference of 228 and b; b less than
228 **29.** $15 \div d$ **31.** $67m$
33. $678 - 319$ **37.** $d \div 4$ **41.** C
43. 14 **45.** 123 **47.** III; this
illustrates the Associative
Property.

2-4 Exercises

1. $4n$ **3.** $5w$ **5.** $7n$ **7.** s^2 **9.** $n + 5$
11. $88n$ **13.** $n + 7; 3n + 1$ **17.** G

2-5 Exercises

1. no **3.** yes **5.** yes **7.** 53 feet is
equal to 636 inches. **9.** no **11.** yes
13. no **15.** yes **17.** no **19.** yes
21. 300 m is equal to 30,000 cm.
23. yes **25.** no **27.** no **29.** yes
31. no **33.** yes **35.** $17 \neq 350 \div 20$;
no, they do not have the same
amount of money. **37.** 6 **39.** 2
41. 3 **47.** H **49.** 27 **51.** 2

2-6 Exercises

1. $x = 36$ **3.** $n = 19$ **5.** $p = 18$
7. 6 blocks **9.** $r = 7$ **11.** $b = 25$
13. $z = 9$ **15.** $g = 16$ **17.** 6 meters
19. $n = 7$ **21.** $y = 19$ **23.** $h = 78$
25. $b = 69$ **27.** $t = 26$ **29.** $m = 22$
31. $p + 20 = 36$ **33.** 880 m **37.** B
39. 54; 63; 72 **41.** I: this illustrates
the Commutative Property.

2-7 Exercises

1. $p = 17$ **3.** $a = 31$ **5.** $n = 33$
7. $y = 25$ **9.** $a = 38$ **11.** $a = 97$
13. $p = 33$ **15.** $s = 31$ **17.** $x = 36$
19. $a = 21$ **21.** $f = 14$ **23.** $r = 154$
25. $g = 143$ **27.** $m = 18$
29. 13 million **33.** D
35. Distributive Prop.
37. Associative Prop. **39.** $y = 38$
41. $b = 56$

2-8 Exercises

1. $x = 3$ **3.** $a = 9$ **5.** $c = 11$
7. 45 feet **9.** $a = 4$ **11.** $x = 4$
13. $t = 7$ **15.** $m = 11$ **17.** 6 feet
19. $y = 9$ **21.** $y = 8$ **23.** $y = 20$
25. $z = 40$ **27.** $y = 23$ **29.** $y = 18$
31. $y = 8$ **33.** $a = 14$ **35.** $x = 3$
37. $t = 6$ **39.** 15 to 177 segments
41. 4,000 light-sensitive cells **45.** C
47. $18 + x$ **49.** $a = 440$ **51.** $w = 75$

2-9 Exercises

1. $y = 12$ **3.** $r = 63$ **5.** $j = 36$
7. $f = 60$ **9.** 90 min **11.** $c = 26$
13. $g = 98$ **15.** $x = 144$ **17.** $r = 81$
19. $c = 96$ **21.** $c = 165$ **23.** $c = 70$
25. $c = 60$ **27.** $\frac{w}{381} = 76$;
$w = 28{,}956$ m **33.** I **35.** $r = 13$
37. $p = 9$

Chapter 2 Study Guide: Review

1. Commutative Property
2. algebraic expression
3. equation **4.** variable
5. Associative Property **6.** 30
7. 520 **8.** 80 **9.** 1,080 **10.** 40
11. 320 **12.** 168 **13.** 135
14. 204 **15.** 152 **16.** 7, 6 **17.** 6, 10
18. 9, 18, 27, 36 **19.** $15 + b$
20. $2 - k$ **21.** 6×5 **22.** $g \div 9$
23. the product of 4 and z; 4 times z
24. 15 plus x; the sum of 15 and x
25. 54 divided by 6; the quotient
of 54 and 6
26. m divided by 20; the quotient
of m and 20 **27.** $3n + 1$ **28.** yes
29. no **30.** yes **31.** yes **32.** $x = 6$
33. $n = 14$ **34.** $c = 29$ **35.** $y = 6$
36. $p = 27$ **37.** $w = 9$
38. 67 channels **39.** $k = 45$
40. $d = 9$ **41.** $p = 63$ **42.** $n = 67$
43. $r = 14$ **44.** $w = 144$
45. 31 sports **46.** $v = 8$ **47.** $y = 9$
48. $c = 7$ **49.** $n = 2$ **50.** $s = 8$
51. $t = 10$ **52.** 4 people
53. $r = 42$ **54.** $t = 15$ **55.** $y = 18$
56. $n = 72$ **57.** $z = 52$
58. $b = 100$

Chapter 3

3-1 Exercises

1. $1 + 0.9 + 0.08$; one and
ninety-eight hundredths

3. 0.0765; seven hundred sixty-five
ten-thousandths **5.** Osmium
7. 4.09, 4.1, 4.18 **9.** $7 + 0.08 +$
$0.009 + 0.0003$; seven and
eight hundred ninety-three
ten-thousandths **11.** 7.15; 7 +
0.1 + 0.05 **13.** the Chupaderos
meteorite **15.** 1.5, 1.56, 1.62
17. nine and seven thousandths
19. ten and twenty-two
thousandths **21.** one hundred
forty-two and six thousand
five hundred forty-one ten-
thousandths **23.** ninety-two
thousand, seven hundred fifty-five
hundred thousandths **25.** <
27. < **29.** < **31.** three
hundredths **33.** one tenth
35. 4.034, 1.43, 1.424, 1.043, 0.34
37. 652.12, 65.213, 65.135, 61.53
39. Ross 154 **41.** Alpha Centauri,
Proxima Centauri **45.** B **47.** 40
49. 75 **51.** $n = 123$ **53.** $c = 52$

3-2 Exercises

1. about 12 miles **3.** 12 **5.** 5.4988
7. 120 **9.** from 44 to 46.5
11. about 450 miles **13.** 3.4
15. 5.157 **17.** 20 **19.** 6 **21.** from
14 to 17 **23.** 48 **25.** 17 **27.** $0.22,
$0.10, $0.08, $0.04 **29.** $(12 \times 8) -$
$(18 \times 4) = 24$, or about 24 cents
37. 6 inches in April, 10 inches in
May, 2 inches in June **39.** $x = 69$
41. 8.009, 8.05, 8.304 **43.** 30.211,
30.709, 30.75

3-3 Exercises

1. 20.2 miles **3.** 12.65 miles
5. 5.6 **7.** 4.9 **9.** 3.55 **11.** 4.948
13. $567.38 **15.** 1.5 **17.** 18 **19.** 4.3
21. 2.3 **23.** 5.87 **25.** 9.035
27. 8.669 **29.** 0.143 **31.** 3.778
33. 3.8179 **35.** 1 **37.** 52.836
39. 29.376 **41.** 84.966 **43.** $72.42
45. 0.196 **49.** C **51.** $s = 70$
53. $t = 1{,}464$ **55.** 60

3-4 Exercises

1. $1.68 **3.** 0.24 **5.** 0.21 **7.** 16.52
9. 35.63 **11.** 2.59 km **13.** 0.027
15. 0.217 **17.** 0.00042 **19.** 0.012
21. 13.321 **23.** 26.04 **25.** 1.148
27. 2.5914 **29.** 0.009 **31.** 0.0612
33. 26.46 **35.** 1.6632 **37.** 0.2444
39. 4.1184 **41.** 14.06 **43.** 37.38
45. 62.1 **47.** 5.8 **49.** 4.65 pounds
51. 7.38 lb **55.** B **57.** $x = 32$
59. $t = 51$ **61.** > **63.** =

3-5 Exercises

1. 0.23 **3.** 0.35 **5.** 0.078 **7.** 0.104
9. $8.82 **11.** 0.22 **13.** 0.27
15. 0.171 **17.** 0.076 **19.** 0.107
21. 1.345 **23.** 0.236 **25.** 0.412
31. C **33.** $y = 6$ **35.** $a = 23$
37. 32.314 **39.** 5.358

3-6 Exercises

1. 5 **3.** 17 **5.** 6 **7.** 54.6 mi/h **9.** 6
11. 8 **13.** 217.5 **15.** 11 **17.** 5
19. 11.6 gallons of gas **21.** 6.3
23. 191.1 **25.** 184.74 **27.** 12.2
29. 12.2 **31.** 1,270 **33.** 1,125
35. 920 **37.** 21,500,000
39. about 232 bills; about $4,640
45. C **47.** $x + 12$ **49.** $15 - a$
51. 16.06 **53.** 3.12

3-7 Exercises

1. 10 belts **3.** 2.25 meters
5. 8 bunches **7.** 3 packs
13. C **15.** $y = 63$ **17.** $y = 17$
19. 9.1 **21.** 14

3-8 Exercises

1. $a = 7.1$ **3.** $c = 12.8$ **5.** $d = 3.488$
7. 60.375 m^2 **9.** $b = 9.3$
11. $r = 20.8$ **13.** $a = 10.7$
15. $f = 6.56$ **17.** $z = 4$
19a. 1.6 meters **b.** $14.40
21. $q = 24.7$ **23.** $b = 4.2$
25. $a = 13.9$ **27.** $z = 13$
29a. 19.5 units, 21 units
b. 50.5 units **31.** 1,900,000 kg

33. 9 capsules **39.** H **41.** $7z$
43. 5.1 **45.** 16.08

Chapter 3 Study Guide: Review

1. front-end estimation
2. clustering **3.** $5 + 0.6 + 0.08$;
five and sixty-eight hundredths
4. $1 + 0.007 + 0.0006$; one and
seventy-six ten-thousandths
5. $1 + 0.2 + 0.003$; one and two
hundred three thousandths
6. $20 + 3 + 0.005$; twenty-three
and five thousandths **7.** $70 +$
$1 + 0.03 + 0.008$; seventy-one and
thirty-eight thousandths
8. $90 + 9 + 0.9 + 0.09 + 0.009 +$
0.0009; ninety-nine and nine
thousand, nine hundred ninety-
nine ten thousandths **9.** 1.12, 1.2,
1.3 **10.** 11.07, 11.17, 11.7
11. 0.033, 0.3, 0.303 **12.** 5.009,
5.5, 5.950 **13.** 101.025, 101.25,
101.52 **14.** 11.32 **15.** 2.3 **16.** 14
17. 80 **18.** 9 **19.** 2,000 **20.** 24.85
21. 5.3 **22.** 33.02 **23.** 4.9225
24. 2.58 **25.** 2.8718 **26.** 1.47
27. 6.423 **28.** $41.73 **29.** 9.44
30. 0.865 **31.** 0.0072 **32.** 24.416
33. 0.54 **34.** 10.5148 **35.** 5,678.4
lbs **36.** 15.24 **37.** 5.125 **38.** 1.462
39. 11.04 **40.** 4.75 **41.** 1.03
42. 0.72 **43.** 3.85 **44.** 2.59
45. $3.64 **46.** 8.1 **47.** $6.1\overline{6}$
48. $3.87\overline{6}$ **49.** 52.275 **50.** 0.75
meter **51.** 14 bookmarks
52. 8 plants **53.** 14 containers
54. 9 cars **55.** 5.5 ft **56.** 10 pages
57. $a = 13.38$ **58.** $y = 2.62$
59. $n = 2.29$ **60.** $p = 60.2$
61. $5.00

Chapter 4

4-1 Exercises

1. 2, 4 **3.** none **5.** composite
7. composite **9.** composite
11. composite **13.** 3 **15.** 3, 5, 9

17. 2, 4 **19.** 2 **21.** composite
23. prime **25.** composite
27. prime **29.** composite
31. prime **33.** no, no, no, no
35. yes, no, yes, no, no, no, no
37. True **39.** True **41.** 1, 4, or 7
43. 1, 4, or 7 **45.** 0, 3, 6, or 9
47. The prime numbers from 50
to 100 are 53, 59, 61, 67, 71, 73,
79, 83, 89, and 97. **49.** Mackinac
Straits **55.** D **57.** 36 **59.** 5
61. 0.7 **63.** 0.105

4-2 Exercises

1. 1, 2, 3, 4, 6, 12 **3.** 1, 2, 4, 13, 26,
52 **5.** $2^4 \cdot 3$ **7.** $2 \cdot 3 \cdot 11$ **9.** 1, 2, 3,
4, 6, 8, 12, 24 **11.** 1, 2, 3, 6, 7, 14, 21,
42 **13.** 1, 67 **15.** 1, 5, 17, 85 **17.** 7^2
19. $2^2 \cdot 19$ **21.** 3^4 **23.** $2^2 \cdot 5 \cdot 7$
33a. 15 boys per team **b.** 5 teams
of 9 players **35.** $3^2 \cdot 11$ **37.** $2^2 \cdot 71$
39. $2^3 \cdot 3 \cdot 5 \cdot 7$ **41.** $2^2 \cdot 5 \cdot 37$
43. $2^2 \cdot 5^2$ **45.** 7^3 **47.** Birds **53.** 60
55. no **57.** no

4-3 Exercises

1. 9 **3.** 7 **5.** 6 **7.** 4 arrangements
9. 14 **11.** 2 **13.** 4 **15.** 12
17. 3 teams **19.** 12 **21.** 5 **23.** 2
25. 75 **27.** 4 **29.** 6 baskets
31. 2 **33.** 9 **35.** 6 **37.** 6 rows
39. 4 groups **43.** A **45.** $c = 24$
47. $m = 34$ **49.** 70.1, 71.03, 71.3,
73.7

4-4 Exercises

1. $\frac{2}{3}, \frac{8}{12}$ **3.** $\frac{1}{2}, \frac{5}{10}$ **5.** 25 **7.** 21 **9.** $\frac{1}{5}$
11. $\frac{1}{4}$ **21.** 15 **23.** 70 **25.** 6 **27.** 140
29. $\frac{1}{4}$ **31.** $\frac{1}{5}$ **33.** $\frac{3}{4}$ **35.** $\frac{1}{2}$
37a. $\frac{16}{24}, \frac{14}{20}$; No **b.** Yes **39.** $\frac{5}{20}; \frac{1}{4}$
41. $\frac{14}{35}; \frac{2}{5}$ **45.** Baskets and wreaths
are $\frac{12}{72} = \frac{1}{6}$; jewelry is $\frac{32}{72} = \frac{4}{9}$; glass
and pottery are $\frac{16}{72} = \frac{2}{9}$; paintings
are $\frac{12}{72} = \frac{1}{6}$. **49.** B **51.** $x = 45$
53. $w = 18$ **55.** 3 weeks

4-5 Exercises
1. $\frac{3}{20}$ 3. $\frac{43}{100}$ 5. 0.4 7. 0.125
9. 0.21, $\frac{2}{3}$, 0.78 11. $\frac{1}{9}$, 0.3, 0.52
13. $5\frac{71}{100}$ 15. $3\frac{23}{100}$ 17. $2\frac{7}{10}$
19. $6\frac{3}{10}$ 21. 1.6 23. 3.275
25. 0.375 27. 0.625 29. $\frac{1}{9}$, 0.29, $\frac{3}{8}$
31. $\frac{1}{10}$, 0.11, 0.13 33. 0.31, $\frac{3}{7}$, 0.76
35. $0.1\overline{6}$; repeats 37. $0.41\overline{6}$; repeats 39. 0.8; terminates
41. $0.8\overline{3}$; repeats 43. $0.91\overline{6}$; repeats
45. > 47. < 49. < 51. <
53. 1.5 m; 0.1 cm, 150 cm
55. $4\frac{1}{2}$, 4.48, 3.92 57. 125.25, 125.205, $125\frac{1}{5}$ 59. Jill 61. $\frac{1}{20}$
65. D 67. $p \div 4$ 69. 0.06 71. 79.3

4-6 Exercises
1. $2\frac{2}{5}$ 3. $\frac{8}{3}$ 5. $\frac{12}{5}$ 7. $8\frac{3}{5}$ 9. $\frac{20}{9}$
11. $\frac{13}{3}$ 13. $\frac{25}{6}$ 15. $\frac{19}{5}$ 17. 4; whole number 19. $8\frac{3}{5}$; mixed number 21. $8\frac{7}{10}$; mixed number
23. 15; whole number 25. $\frac{53}{11}$
27. $\frac{93}{5}$ 29. 3; 5 31. 13; 9 33. 2; 10
35. $28\frac{4}{9}$ yards 37. = 39. <
41. $40\frac{1}{2}$; $50\frac{1}{2}$ 43. $\frac{9}{5}$ 49. I 51. 100 minutes, or 1 hour 40 minutes

4-7 Exercises
1. > 3. = 5. yes 7. $\frac{1}{4}$, $\frac{1}{3}$, $\frac{2}{5}$
9. $\frac{1}{6}$, $\frac{1}{2}$, $\frac{2}{3}$ 11. < 13. > 15. =
17. > 19. $\frac{3}{7}$, $\frac{1}{2}$, $\frac{3}{8}$ 21. $\frac{1}{3}$, $\frac{3}{8}$, $\frac{4}{9}$
23. $\frac{2}{3}$, $\frac{7}{10}$, $\frac{3}{4}$ 25. $\frac{1}{4}$, $\frac{3}{8}$, $\frac{2}{3}$ 27. <
29. > 31. > 33. > 35. $\frac{3}{10}$, $\frac{2}{5}$, $\frac{1}{2}$
37. $\frac{1}{5}$, $\frac{7}{15}$, $\frac{2}{3}$ 39. $\frac{2}{5}$, $\frac{4}{9}$, $\frac{11}{15}$
41. $\frac{5}{12}$, $\frac{5}{8}$, $\frac{3}{4}$ 43. Laura; $\frac{3}{5} > \frac{4}{7}$
45. $1\frac{1}{8}$, $1\frac{2}{5}$, 3, $3\frac{2}{5}$, $3\frac{4}{5}$
47. $\frac{1}{3}$, $\frac{3}{4}$, $3\frac{1}{15}$, $3\frac{1}{10}$, $3\frac{3}{5}$ 49. $3\frac{5}{7}$, $4\frac{2}{3}$, $4\frac{3}{4}$, 5, $5\frac{1}{3}$ 51a. United States, China, Canada b. more than 53. 5 57. C
59. $f = 28$ 61. $n = 35$ 63. $3.19

4-8 Exercises
1. $\frac{1}{2}$ foot 3. $7\frac{1}{7}$ 5. $5\frac{1}{6}$ 7. $\frac{2}{5}$ 9. $\frac{1}{5}$
11. $\frac{2}{7}$ 13. $1\frac{3}{5}$ 15. $\frac{6}{5}$ or $1\frac{1}{5}$ 17. $\frac{1}{10}$
19. $\frac{5}{8}$ 21. $\frac{14}{33}$ 23. $\frac{2}{3}$ 25. $13\frac{1}{3}$

27. $\frac{17}{24}$ 29. $\frac{4}{9}$ 31. $\frac{5}{7}$ 33. $8\frac{2}{3}$
35. $\frac{3}{4}$ hour 37. $1\frac{3}{4}$ hr 39. 1 foot
47. $a = 45$ 49. $y = 12$
51. $\frac{4}{11}$, $\frac{5}{8}$, $\frac{2}{3}$

4-9 Exercises
1. about 1 3. about $\frac{1}{2}$ 5. 16 miles
7. about $\frac{1}{2}$ 9. about 0
11. about $1\frac{1}{2}$ 13. about 2
15. 4 tons 17. $3\frac{1}{2}$ tons 19. >
21. < 23. > 25. about 2
27. about 3 29. about $13\frac{1}{2}$
31. $\frac{3}{4}$ in. 33. about $9\frac{1}{2}$ in. 37. B
39. $7n$ 41. 0.2

Chapter 4 Study Guide: Review
1. improper fraction; mixed number 2. repeating decimal; terminating decimal 3. prime number; composite number 4. 2
5. 2, 3, 5, 6, 9, 10 6. 2, 3, 6, 9 7. 2, 4
8. 2, 5, 10 9. 3 10. composite
11. composite 12. prime
13. composite 14. prime
15. composite 16. composite
17. prime 18. composite
19. prime 20. 1, 2, 3, 4, 5, 6, 10, 12, 15, 20, 30, 60 21. 1, 2, 3, 4, 6, 8, 9, 12, 18, 24, 36, 72 22. 1, 29 23. 1, 2, 4, 7, 8, 14, 28, 56 24. 1, 5, 17, 85
25. 1, 71 26. $5 \cdot 13$ 27. $2 \cdot 5 \cdot 11$
28. 3^4 29. $3^2 \cdot 11$ 30. $7 \cdot 11$
31. $2 \cdot 23$ 32. 12 33. 8 34. 25
35. 18 36. 9 37. 7 38. Possible answer: $\frac{2}{3}$; $\frac{8}{12}$ 39. Possible answer: $\frac{8}{10}$; $\frac{16}{20}$ 40. Possible answer: $\frac{1}{4}$; $\frac{2}{8}$ 41. $\frac{7}{8}$ 42. $\frac{3}{10}$ 43. $\frac{7}{10}$
44. $\frac{37}{100}$ 45. $1\frac{4}{5}$ 46. $\frac{2}{5}$ 47. 0.875
48. 0.4 49. $0.\overline{7}$ 50. the $1\frac{7}{16}$ ft board 51. $\frac{34}{9}$ 52. $\frac{29}{12}$ 53. $\frac{37}{7}$
54. $3\frac{5}{6}$ 55. $3\frac{2}{5}$ 56. $5\frac{1}{8}$ 57. the $4\frac{3}{4}$ in. envelope 58. > 59. >
60. = 61. < 62. $\frac{3}{8}$, $\frac{2}{3}$, $\frac{7}{8}$
63. $\frac{3}{12}$, $\frac{1}{4}$, $\frac{4}{6}$ 64. $\frac{1}{3}$, $\frac{3}{8}$, $\frac{1}{2}$ 65. $\frac{5}{6}$, $\frac{7}{8}$, $\frac{9}{10}$
66. 1 67. $\frac{3}{4}$ 68. $\frac{3}{5}$ 69. $6\frac{5}{7}$ 70. $\frac{5}{8}$
71. 1 72. $\frac{1}{2}$ 73. 11 74. $2\frac{1}{2}$

Chapter 5

5-1 Exercises
1. 3 packs of pencils and 4 packs of erasers 3. 36 5. 20 7. 48
9. 40 11. 63 13. 150 15. 8
17. 20 19. 18 21. 12 23. 24
25. 66 27. 60 29. 140 31. 12
33c. 12 d. Possible answer: 120, 144, 132 35. 12 and 16 37a. 120
b. 120 c. 4 41. B 43. no
45. yes 47. 0.08 49. 6.3 51. =

5-2 Exercises
1. $\frac{5}{12}$ ton 3. $\frac{3}{10}$ 5. $\frac{13}{14}$ 7. $\frac{1}{6}$ cup
9. $\frac{7}{12}$ 11. $\frac{9}{20}$ 13. $1\frac{2}{15}$ 15. $1\frac{1}{8}$
17. $\frac{7}{15}$ 19. $\frac{7}{8}$ 21. $\frac{1}{3}$ 23. $\frac{28}{33}$
25. $\frac{7}{18}$ 27. $\frac{1}{5}$ 29. $\frac{2}{2}$ or 1 31. $1\frac{1}{8}$
33. $\frac{1}{2}$ 35. $\frac{4}{7}$ 37. $\frac{3}{4}$ 39. $\frac{7}{8}$
41. $\frac{1}{6}$ gallon 43. $\frac{9}{40}$ lb 51. $d = 6$
53. $f = 7$ 55. 1.1 57. 0.125

5-3 Exercises
1. $10\frac{5}{12}$ 3. $6\frac{1}{12}$ 5. $4\frac{1}{4}$ 7. $6\frac{7}{12}$
9. $6\frac{1}{4}$ 11. $8\frac{7}{12}$ 13. $29\frac{3}{5}$ 15. $34\frac{1}{2}$
17. $3\frac{17}{30}$ 19. $20\frac{13}{36}$ 21. $12\frac{5}{24}$
23a. $26\frac{3}{5}$ lb b. $2\frac{1}{10}$ lb c. $11\frac{1}{10}$ lb
25. $1\frac{7}{10}$ 27. $23\frac{3}{4}$ 29. $13\frac{1}{4}$ 31. $18\frac{1}{5}$
33. $\frac{1}{2}$ mi 35. 5 37. $1\frac{1}{12}$ 39. $8\frac{1}{9}$
41. 0 43. $9\frac{3}{8}$ km 45. $16\frac{1}{2}$ yards
51. I 53. 1.6 55. 2.3 57. $1\frac{1}{2}$
59. $1\frac{2}{5}$

5-4 Exercises
1. $\frac{3}{4}$ 3. $1\frac{2}{3}$ 5. $2\frac{3}{5}$ pounds 7. $3\frac{4}{5}$
9. $7\frac{7}{8}$ 11. $4\frac{13}{18}$ 13. $1\frac{4}{5}$ 15. $6\frac{2}{3}$ pounds 17. $1\frac{4}{9}$ 19. $8\frac{9}{11}$ 21. $11\frac{2}{9}$
23. $12\frac{13}{18}$ 25. $7\frac{1}{4}$ in. 27. $7\frac{1}{3}$
29. $3\frac{8}{11}$ 31. $11\frac{4}{5}$ 33. $4\frac{11}{12}$ 35. $1\frac{5}{6}$
37. $\frac{1}{12}$ 39. $13\frac{5}{12}$ 41. $1\frac{1}{12}$ yards^2
43. $1\frac{11}{12}$ yards^2 47. C 49. $2n + 2$
51. 0.306 53. 3.85

5-5 Exercises
1. $\frac{8}{9}$ 3. 3 5. $\frac{3}{7}$ 7. 6 9. 8 11. 9
13. 27 boys 15. $\frac{3}{4}$ 17. $\frac{4}{5}$ 19. $\frac{6}{11}$

21. 10 **23.** 6 **25.** 2 **27.** $5\frac{5}{7}$ **29.** $3\frac{5}{9}$
31. 7 **33.** 15 **35.** 5 **37.** $\frac{48}{5}$ or $9\frac{3}{5}$
39. 45 **41.** > **43.** = **45.** < **47.** >
49. $33 **51.** 165 feet tall **55.** C
57. $75 - w$ **59.** $p \div 7$

5-6 Exercises

1. $\frac{1}{6}$ **3.** $\frac{3}{7}$ **5.** $\frac{2}{15}$ **7.** $\frac{1}{20}$ **9.** $\frac{2}{21}$
11. $\frac{5}{9}$ **13.** $\frac{1}{4}$ **15.** $\frac{5}{11}$ **17.** $\frac{2}{15}$ **19.** $\frac{1}{8}$
21. $\frac{4}{27}$ **23.** $\frac{5}{48}$ **25.** $\frac{4}{15}$ **27.** $\frac{1}{14}$
29. $\frac{27}{35}$ **31.** $\frac{9}{55}$ **33.** $\frac{1}{4}$ cup **35.** <
37. > **39.** < **41a.** Multiply by $\frac{1}{4}$.
b. $\frac{1}{12}$ **43.** $\frac{3}{8}$ lb **45a.** $\frac{3}{8}$ **b.** 360
49. D **51.** $n = 3$ **53.** $a = 13$
55. 2 **57.** 5

5-7 Exercises

1. $\frac{5}{6}$ **3.** $\frac{11}{14}$ **5.** $\frac{13}{15}$ **7.** $2\frac{1}{16}$ **9.** $21\frac{5}{7}$
11. $12\frac{7}{20}$ **13.** $\frac{15}{16}$ **15.** $\frac{7}{15}$ **17.** $1\frac{1}{18}$
19. $\frac{13}{14}$ **21.** $2\frac{2}{7}$ **23.** $15\frac{1}{2}$ **25.** $23\frac{1}{2}$
27. $3\frac{3}{5}$ **29.** $\frac{10}{27}$ **31.** $1\frac{1}{4}$ **33.** $\frac{1}{6}$
35. $13\frac{3}{4}$ **37.** $2\frac{2}{3}$ **39.** $17\frac{1}{2}$
41. $1\frac{17}{25}$ bags **45.** $1\frac{3}{7}$
47. 28 **49.** $1\frac{7}{8}$ **51.** $21\frac{3}{4}$
53. $3\frac{1}{2}$ cups of flour; 5 teaspoons
of baking powder **55a.** $6\frac{1}{8}$ cups
b. $1\frac{1}{6}$ cups **c.** $1\frac{3}{4}$ teaspoons
57. 12 **59.** $1\frac{2}{3}$ **61.** $a = 5$
63. $g = 11$ **65.** $\frac{1}{2}$ **67.** 4

5-8 Exercises

1. $\frac{7}{2}$ **3.** 9 **5.** $\frac{5}{13}$ **7.** $1\frac{5}{7}$ **9.** $2\frac{1}{6}$
11. $\frac{9}{50}$ **13.** $4\frac{4}{7}$ **15.** 10 **17.** $\frac{12}{11}$
19. $\frac{11}{8}$ **21.** $\frac{7}{6}$ **23.** $\frac{4}{21}$ **25.** $1\frac{5}{14}$
27. 12 **29.** $\frac{3}{10}$ **31.** $2\frac{22}{45}$ **33.** $\frac{2}{3}$
35. $\frac{1}{40}$ **37.** $1\frac{17}{25}$ **39.** $4\frac{2}{3}$ **41.** $\frac{3}{28}$
43. 16 bags **45.** yes **47.** yes
49. $\frac{5}{2}, \frac{25}{4}$ **51.** $\frac{1}{5}, \frac{1}{5}$ **55.** $\frac{11}{12}$ **57.** $1\frac{1}{14}$
59. $41\frac{19}{75}$ **61.** $24\frac{2}{9}$ in. **67.** H
69. 1; 9.5 **71.** 2; 0.04 **73.** $\frac{7}{8}$
75. $5\frac{13}{15}$

5-9 Exercises

1. $4\frac{1}{2}$ **3.** $5\frac{5}{8}$ **5.** $4\frac{1}{10}$ **7.** $57\frac{3}{4}$ in.
9. $3\frac{5}{8}$ **11.** $4\frac{5}{6}$ **13.** $8\frac{7}{9}$ **15.** $6\frac{1}{4}$ feet
17. $5\frac{1}{10}$ **19.** $7\frac{9}{10}$ **21.** $\frac{1}{3}$

---

23. 16 ounces **25.** $\frac{3}{8}$ in. **27.** $7\frac{7}{18}$
29. $5\frac{5}{12}$ **31.** $4\frac{1}{4}$ **37.** B **39.** $b = 18$
41. $s = 144$ **43.** $\frac{2}{7}$ **45.** $\frac{1}{5}$

5-10 Exercises

1. $z = 16$ **3.** $x = 7\frac{1}{2}$ **5.** 24 **7.** $x = 9$
9. $t = \frac{1}{10}$ **11.** $y = 20$ **13.** $j = 12\frac{6}{7}$
15. $10 **17.** $y = 10$ **19.** $t = 16$
21. $b = 14$ **23.** $x = 9\frac{1}{3}$ **25.** $n = 12$
27. $y = \frac{2}{3}$ **29.** $\frac{3}{2}n = 9$; $n = 6$
31. 4 minutes **33.** 11 dresses
35. 20 more pages **41.** B **43.** 35
45. $3\frac{3}{4}$ **47.** $6\frac{1}{2}$ **49.** $1\frac{1}{5}$ **51.** $\frac{15}{28}$

Chapter 5 Study Guide: Review

1. reciprocals **2.** least common
denominator **3.** 30 **4.** 48 **5.** 27
6. 60 **7.** 225 **8.** 660 **9.** $\frac{33}{40}$ **10.** $\frac{3}{4}$
11. $\frac{1}{15}$ **12.** $\frac{5}{24}$ **13.** $4\frac{7}{10}$ **14.** $3\frac{1}{18}$
15. $\frac{11}{30}$ **16.** $3\frac{2}{3}$ **17.** $1\frac{1}{2}$ **18.** $5\frac{2}{3}$
19. $2\frac{5}{8}$ **20.** $6\frac{13}{14}$ **21.** $1\frac{1}{8}$
22. $4\frac{3}{4}$ feet **23.** $\frac{5}{7}$ **24.** $\frac{3}{4}$
25. $2\frac{4}{7}$ **26.** $2\frac{1}{2}$ **27.** 3 **28.** $1\frac{1}{5}$
29. 21 members **30.** $\frac{1}{3}$ **31.** $\frac{15}{28}$
32. $\frac{1}{10}$ **33.** $\frac{7}{25}$ **34.** $\frac{5}{81}$ **35.** $\frac{3}{14}$
36. $\frac{8}{15}$ **37.** $\frac{9}{10}$ **38.** $1\frac{1}{4}$ **39.** 2 **40.** $\frac{1}{3}$
41. $3\frac{3}{5}$ **42.** $6\frac{5}{12}$ **43.** $\frac{4}{21}$ **44.** $\frac{3}{20}$
45. $\frac{5}{9}$ **46.** 8 times **47.** $30\frac{3}{20}$
48. $14\frac{11}{12}$ **49.** $5\frac{5}{12}$ **50.** $3\frac{4}{9}$
51. $5\frac{7}{15}$ **52.** $3\frac{3}{10}$ **53.** $1\frac{2}{3}$ miles
54. $a = \frac{1}{8}$ **55.** $b = 2$ **56.** $m = 17\frac{1}{2}$
57. $g = \frac{2}{15}$ **58.** $r = 10\frac{4}{5}$
59. $s = 50$ **60.** $p = \frac{1}{9}$ **61.** $j = 1\frac{53}{64}$
62. 80 inches

Chapter 6

6-1 Exercises

1. mean = 22 **3.** mean = 6.5
5. mean = 57, median = 54, no
mode, range = 23 **7.** range = 19,
mean = 508.2, median = 508.5,
mode = 500 **9.** 11 **11.** 4 **13.** 70
15. 6, 7, 12, 15, 15 **19.** $\frac{n+1}{2}$
21. 25 **23.** 4

6-2 Exercises

1a. mean = 4.75, median = 5, no
mode **b.** mean = 10, median =
7, no mode **3.** mean = 225,
median = 187.5, mode = 240;
median **5.** with: mean = 738.8,
median = 810, no mode
without: mean = 913.25, median
= 906.5, no mode **7.** mean ≈
118.29, median = 128, no mode
13. 34.5 mi/h **15.** 31 **17.** median:
35; no mode; range = 45

6-3 Exercises

1. green

3.

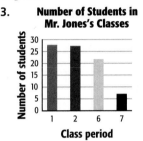

Number of Students in
Mr. Jones's Classes

5. orange

7.

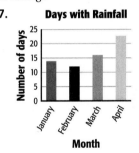

Days with Rainfall

9. 14 million mi^2
11. ≈ 8.14 million mi^2
13a.

Scores of Practice Games

b. Blue: mean ≈ 47.3, range = 26;
Green: mean = 47.3, range = 16
c. Possible answer: The green
squad; their performance is more
consistent, and their scores have
steadily increased over time.
17. I **19.** <

6-4 Exercises

1. mode = B

3.

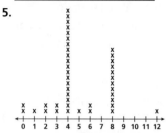

Number of Years of Each Presidential Term				
Number (Intervals)	0–3	4–7	8–11	12-15
Frequency	7	22	12	1

5.

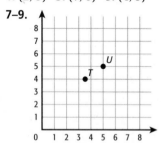

7.

Populations of Australia's States and Territories	
Census	Frequency
0–999,999	3
1,000,000–1,999,999	2
2,000,000–2,999,999	0
3,000,000–3,999,999	1
4,000,000–4,999,999	1
5,000,000–5,999,999	0
6,000,000–6,999,999	1

9. no   **11.** 1.7   **13.** 0.6, $\frac{2}{3}$, $\frac{5}{6}$
15. 0.16, $\frac{5}{8}$, $\frac{13}{16}$

6-5 Exercises

1. (2, 3)   **3.** (7, 6)   **5.** (4, 5)
7–9.

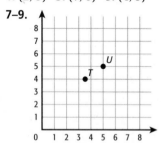

11. (3, 0)   **13.** (1, 4)   **15.** (11, 7)
17–21.

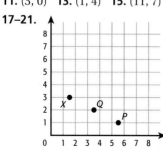

23. A **25.** C **27.** P **29.** (9, 8)

31. (1, 5)   **33.** (9, 0)   **35.** $\left(5\frac{1}{2}, 0\right)$
39. D   **41.** 14.48   **43.** 10.4
45. $\frac{2}{15}$ **47.** $\frac{1}{12}$

6-6 Exercises

1.

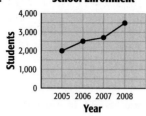

School Enrollment

3. 125

5.

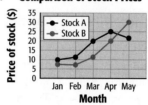

Comparison of Stock Prices

7. 200 million

9.

Soccer Team Fund-Raising Efforts

11. Max   **15.** C   **17.** $s = 18$
19. $m = 15$ **21.** 32 questions

6-7 Exercises

5. The vertical axis begins at 430 rather than zero.   **7.** the yearly increments changed

9.

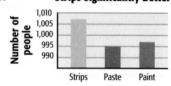

Strips Significantly Better

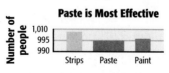

Paste is Most Effective

11. D   **13.** $x = 2$

6-8 Exercises

1.   **Daily High Temperatures (°F)**

Stems	Leaves
3	7 9
4	0 5 8
5	1 6

Key: 3|7 means 37

3. 44   **5.** 32   **7.** 34   **9.** 41   **11.** 52
13. 42   **15.** A
17.   **Number of Cars with One Passenger**

Stems	Leaves
8	0 1 2 3 7 8 9
9	2 4 4 5 9
10	0 1 3 9
11	
12	4 5

Key: 8|0 means 80

21. 2,000   **23.** 15   **25.** 25 sandwiches

Chapter 6 Study Guide: Review

1. line plot   **2.** ordered pair
3. mode   **4.** mean: 37; median: 38; mode: 39; range: 7   **5.** mean: 62.5; median: 50; mode: 50; range: 90   **6.** with outlier: mean ≈ 14.29; median = 11; mode = 12; without outlier: mean ≈ 10.33; median = 10.5; mode = 12
7. with outlier: mean = 31; median = 32; mode = 32; without outlier: mean = 35.75; median = 33; mode = 32   **8.** with outlier: mean ≈ 19.67; median = 14; mode = none; without outlier: mean = 13.2; median = 13; mode = none   **9.** 8th grade

10.

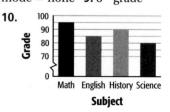

11. mean = 87.5; median = 90; no mode

12.

Points Scored		
Points (Intervals)	1–4	5–8	9–12
Frequency	2	3	1

13. 5.5 points **14.** 4 points
15. (4, 1) **16.** (3, 3) **17.** (6, 5)
18. Bob; she is only 1 unit to the right from Bob's house.
19.

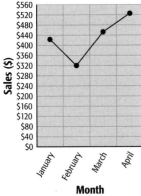

Bookstore Sales

20. April **21.** Sales decreased from January to February and then increased from February to April. **22.** The scale starts out in increments of one mile and then it changes to 5 miles.

23. Basketball Scores

Stems	Leaves
2	0 2 6 8
3	4
4	0 4 6

Key: 2|0 means 20

24. smallest value: 20, largest value: 46, mean: 32.5, median: 31, no mode, range: 26 **25.** median: 32, mode: 34

Chapter 7

7-1 Exercises

1. 3:10 **3.** 41:16 **5.** the 8-ounce bag **7.** 19:3 **11.** the 15 lb bag **13.** 24 to 11, 24:11 **15.** 7 to 10, 7:10 **17.** 5 to 9, 5:9 **19.** $\frac{100}{101}$, 100:101 **21.** 8:5 **23.** 5:8 **25.** 8:16 **27.** Wednesday **33.** The 24-ounce box is the better deal. **35.** 0.4, $\frac{4}{9}$, 0.45 **37.** $1\frac{1}{4}$ **39.** 1

7-2 Exercises

1.

2	4	6	16
7	14	21	56

3.

96	48	24	12
48	24	12	6

5.

120	60	30	15
8	4	2	1

7.

0.15	0.3	0.45	0.6
1	2	3	4

9. Beth

11.

200	400	600	800
2	4	6	8

13.

12	24	36	48
4	8	12	16

15.

13	26	39	52
20	40	60	80

17.

2,400	4,800	7,200	9,600
1	2	3	4

19. Leslin **21.** $\frac{8}{3}$ **23.** 24; 15
29. about 70,000,000 **33.** B
35. 448.5; 447; 452; 94

7-3 Exercises

1. $90 **3.** 4 **5.** 2 **7.** $26.25 **9.** 6 lb
11. 15 **13.** 55 **15.** 2 **17.** 3 **19.** 7
21. 3 **23.** $\frac{21}{6}$ **25.** $23.63 **29.** C
31. < **33.** = **35.** 4 to 9, $\frac{4}{9}$
37. 6:13, 6 to 13

7-4 Exercises

1.

3.

5. $\frac{4}{5}$ **7.** $\frac{23}{25}$ **9.** 0.04 **11.** 0.64
13.

15.

17. $\frac{3}{4}$ **19.** $\frac{18}{25}$ **21.** $\frac{16}{25}$ **23.** $\frac{17}{20}$
25. 0.44 **27.** 0.29 **29.** 0.6
31. 0.07 **33.** 0.02 **35.** $\frac{1}{100}$, 0.01
37. $\frac{7}{10}$, 0.7 **39.** $\frac{37}{100}$, 0.37
41. $\frac{2}{25}$, 0.08 **43.** $\frac{3}{4}$, 0.75 **45.** 1, 1
47. $\frac{13}{25}$, 0.52 **49.** $\frac{3}{20}$, $\frac{13}{25}$, $\frac{71}{100}$, 1
51. 11% = 0.11 **53.** No **59.** H
61. $x = 7$ **63.** Grass Cutters

7-5 Exercises

1. 39% **3.** 80% **5.** 44% **7.** 70%
9. 60% **11.** 60% **13.** 34% **15.** 62%
17. 30% **19.** 45% **21.** 12.5%
23. 74% **25.** 40% **27.** 4%, $\frac{1}{25}$
29. 45%, $\frac{9}{20}$ **31.** 1%, $\frac{1}{100}$
33. 60%, $\frac{3}{5}$ **35.** 14%, $\frac{7}{50}$
37. 80%, 0.8 **39.** 83.33%, 0.83
41. 34%, 0.34 **43.** 4%, 0.04
45. 26.67%, 0.27 **47.** < **49.** =
51. > **53.** < **55.** about 48%; about 52% **57.** 0.098, $\frac{7}{8}$, 90%
59. 0.21, $\frac{7}{25}$, 38% **61.** 17%, $\frac{5}{9}$, 0.605 **67.** D **69.** $\frac{1}{3}$
71. $\frac{1}{4}$ **73.** 12; 12

7-6 Exercises

1. 44 T-shirts **3.** 6.72 **5.** 0.4
7. 37.8 **9.** 6 dolls **11.** 30 minutes
13. 28.6 **15.** 18.2 **17.** 94.5
19. 2.28 **21.** 5.2 **23.** 12.32
25. 40.56 **27.** 31 **29.** 12
31a. 9 feet **b.** 108 square feet
33. 12 atoms of hydrogen, 6 atoms of carbon, and 6 atoms of oxygen
39. $57.60 **41.** $\frac{39}{50}$ **43.** $\frac{99}{100}$
45. 87.5%

7-7 Exercises

1. about $7.65 **3.** about $151.20
5. about $18.75 **7.** about $11.10
9. about $55.65 **11.** Yes
13. $339.20 **19.** Music Palace CDs sell for $11.97. Awesome Sound CDs sell for $11.69. Awesome

Sound has the better deal. **21.** yes
23. 3 **25.** 13 **27.** 600

7-8 Exercises

1. The length of the missing side is
4 cm; m∠G = 37° **3.** The length
of the missing side, n, is 3 inches;
m∠M = 110° **5.** sides: $\overline{AC}$ and $\overline{XY}$;
$\overline{XW}$ and $\overline{AB}$; $\overline{BC}$ and $\overline{WY}$; angles:
X and A; W and B; Y and C
9. m∠H = 80°, m∠J = 80°,
m∠Z = 100°; the length of $\overline{WX}$ is
5.5 yd, the length of $\overline{ZY}$ is 5.5 yd,
and the length of $\overline{WZ}$ is 4 yd.
11. No; the corresponding sides
are not in proportion. **17.** G
19. Distributive Property **21.** 5
23. 0.7

7-9 Exercises

1. 15 ft **3.** 18 ft **5.** 104 in. **7.** 120 m
11. 14.2 **13.** 4.9 **15.** > **17.** >

7-10 Exercises

1. 300 ft **3.** No **5.** 2.5 inches
7. 261 ft **11.** 64 in. **13.** b = 4
15. a = 24

Chapter 7 Study Guide: Review

1. discount **2.** percent
3. corresponding angles
4. Possible answers: 2:4; 3:6; 6:12
5. 12 oz for $2.64
6. Possible answers:

3	6	9	12
10	20	30	40

7. Possible answers:

5	10	15	20
21	42	63	84

8. Possible answers:

15	30	45	60
7	14	21	28

9. $47.25 **10.** n = 9 **11.** n = 3
12. n = 14 **13.** n = 2 **14.** 6 cups
of bananas **15.** $\frac{3}{4}$ **16.** $\frac{3}{50}$

17. $\frac{3}{10}$ **18.** 0.08 **19.** 0.65 **20.** 0.2
21. 89.6% **22.** 70% **23.** 5.7%
24. 12% **25.** 70% **26.** 25%
27. 87.5% **28.** 80% **29.** 6.25%
30. 65% **31.** 12 **32.** 5.94
33. 117 tickets **34.** about $1.80
35. about $19.20 **36.** about $4.35
37. about $1.08 **38.** n = inches;
m∠A = 90° **39.** 94 ft
40. 43.75 miles **41.** 3 inches

Chapter 8

8-1 Exercises

1. in. **3.** gal **5.** mi **7.** qt **9.** ft
11. gal **13.** oz **21.** about
$8\frac{1}{4}$ lb **23.** about $\frac{3}{4}$ c **27.** Possible
answers: *rod*: a unit of length
equal to $5\frac{1}{2}$ yards; *peck*: a dry
measure of capacity equal to 8
quarts; *dram*: a very small unit
of weight equal to 0.0625 ounce
29. F **31.** 9 **33.** $\frac{3}{4}$ **35.** mean = 14,
median = 14, mode = 5

8-2 Exercises

1. m **3.** L **5.** about 7 cm **7.** g
9. L **11.** the width of his fist
13. km **15.** g **17.** mL **19.** Yes;
possible answer: The balloon's
mass is 0.8 g greater with the air.
23. C **25.** y = 72 **27.** r = 35
29. $0.49/lb

8-3 Exercises

1. 108 **3.** 7 **5.** 3 **7.** 8 **9.** 3 **11.** 22
13. about 24 cups **15.** 48 **17.** 2
19. 2 **21.** 6,000 **23.** 3 **25.** 20
27. < **29.** = **31.** < **33.** = **35.** >
37. about 434 yards **39a.** 9 yd
b. 324 in. **41.** 3,520; 2 **43.** 8; 16
45. $0.03 **47.** 4 pints **51.** A
53. x = 9 **55.** d = 17 **57.** 5.84
59. 0.006 **61.** 7.7%

8-4 Exercises

1. 0.115 km **3.** 0.852 **5.** 3,500
7. 4,400 **9.** 0.05 **11.** 0.006

13. 0.110 **15.** 22,500 **17.** 2.460
19. 9.68 **21.** 0.782 **23.** 21.6 L;
21,600 mL **25.** x = 0.23850
27. 7,000 **29.** = **31.** < **33.** =
35. St. Louis Gateway Arch; 18 m
39. approximately 55 cups
41. 0.452 kg; 452,000 mg; 0.136 kg
43. > **45.** = **47.** 7 **49.** 5,000

8-5 Exercises

1. 1,200 **3.** $2\frac{1}{2}$ **5.** 480 **7.** 2:15 P.M.
9. 54 **11.** 60 **13.** 4 **15.** 2 **17.** 26
19. 12:10 P.M. **21.** 198
23. > **25.** < **27.** 480; 470
29. about 28 °C **31.** about
14 hours **35.** C **37.** >
39. < **41.** 1,600 **43.** 510

8-6 Exercises

1. 2 in. **3.** 40 m **5.** 7 yd **7.** 96 in.
9. 7 cm **11.** 42 m **13.** 6 in.
15. 42 in. **17.** 2 km **19a.** 44 ft ×
20 ft **b.** 128 ft **23.** A
25. 28 questions **27.** 160 °C

8-7 Exercises

1. circle G, chords $\overline{EF}$ and $\overline{HI}$,
diameter $\overline{EF}$, and radii $\overline{GF}$, $\overline{GE}$,
and $\overline{GD}$ **3.** 12 ft **5.** 12.56 in.
7. 15 yd **9.** 4.71 m **11.** 0.5 in.
13. 5.75 ft, 36.11 ft **15.** 5.4 in.,
2.7 in. **17.** 9.42 ft **21.** 48.8 cm
23. 880 times **25.** $\frac{10}{12}, \frac{3}{4}, \frac{1}{12}$
27. $\frac{3}{4}, \frac{5}{8}, \frac{7}{16}$ **29.** 0.05 **31.** 1

Chapter 8 Study Guide: Review

1. perimeter; circumference
2. diameter **3.** customary system
4. in.; about five widths of your
thumb **5.** mi; about 3,200 times
around a track **6.** lb; about 2
loaves of bread **7.** fl oz; about a
spoonful **8.** $\frac{1}{8}$ in. **9.** mm; about
32 times the thickness of a dime
10. mg; about 5 very small insects
11. kg; about two textbooks
12. L; about two water pitchers
13. 2 cm **14.** 15,840 ft **15.** 6 yd

16. 12 c **17.** 3 gal **18.** 8 lb
19. 4 T **20.** 4 lb **21.** 144 in.
22. 4 qt **23.** 99 ft **24.** 250 yd
25. 3,200 mL **26.** 0.007 L
27. 0.342 km **28.** 0.042 kg
29. 0.051 m **30.** 71,000 m
31. 681,296 g **32.** 1 h **33.** 59,400 s
34. 105 days **35.** 12:10 P.M.
36. 5 °C **37.** 94 °F **38.** 50 °C
39. 33.9 in. **40.** 10 cm **41.** 20 ft
42. 31.4 ft **43.** 9 m **44.** 50.24 cm
45. 11 ft

Chapter 9

9-1 Exercises

1. about 8.5 square units **3.** about
6 square units **5.** 100.1 in²
7. 48 ft² **9.** 10 in² **11.** about
6 square units **13.** about 4 square
units **15.** 12.75 m² **17.** 260 ft²
19. 0.75 cm² **25.** B **27.** 7 ft
29. $2\frac{5}{8}$ **31.** $\frac{3}{10}$

9-2 Exercises

1. 3 yd² **3.** 27 m² **5.** 26 ft²
7. 88 cm² **9.** 3 ft² **11.** 72 in²
13. 16 yd² **15.** 96 m²
17. 5 square units **19.** 15 square
units **21.** 346.5 m² **31.** 175
33. $\frac{12}{5}$ **35.** $\frac{15}{2}$

9-3 Exercises

1. 48 ft² **3.** 243 in² **5.** 616 cm²
7. 12.56 ft² **9.** 768 in² **11.** 38.5 yd²
13. 2,464 ft² **15.** $A = 102.02$ cm²,
$C = 35.8$ cm **17.** $A = 174.28$ in²,
$C = 46.79$ in. **19.** 1.13 km² **25.** C
27. $\frac{1}{6}$ **29.** $\frac{5}{18}$ **31.** no

9-4 Exercises

1. 48 m² **3.** 109.5 cm² **5.** 59.6 in²
7. 88.1 ft² **9.** 54 cm² **11.** 23.4 in²
13. 4 in. **17.** B **19.** Tom, Fred,
Nadia, Marie

9-5 Exercises

1. 5 faces, 8 edges, 5 vertices
3. 5 faces, 8 edges, 5 vertices

5. Possible answer: rectangular
pyramid **7.** 5 faces, 9 edges,
6 vertices **9.** 6 faces, 12 edges,
8 vertices **11.** sphere
13. rectangular pyramid, yes
15. cone, no **17.** B, C and D
19. B **21.** true **23.** true
25. 8; octagonal pyramid **29.** C
31. Associative Property
33. 24 pages

9-6 Exercises

1. 162 cm³ **3.** 10 ft³ **5.** 320 ft³
7. 1 × 1 × 10 and 2 × 5 × 1
9. 79.36 in³ **11.** 54 m³ **13.** 71.72 ft³
15. 480 in³ **17.** 474.375 km³
19. 20 ft **21.** 10 cm³, 1 cm³,
3.5 cm³, 300 cm³, 20 cm³ **23.** pine
25. Alicia does not have gold.
29. 77.4 **31.** 77 in²

9-7 Exercises

1. 754 m³ **3.** 3,140 in³
5. Cylinder B **7.** 314 ft³ **9.** 31 cm³
and 283 cm³ **11.** 138 in³ **13.** 4 m³
15. 100.48 in³ **17.** 1,987.03 ft³
19. 12,560 mm³ **21.** 923 ft³
23. It cannot hold 200 cm³ of juice
because it only has a volume of
196.25 cm³. **29.** the tomato soup
can holds more soup **31.** 5
33. 3 **35.** 40

9-8 Exercises

1. 94 in² **3.** 56 cm² **5.** 2,640 cm²
7. 326.56 ft² **9.** 376.8 m²
11. $16\frac{1}{2}$ m² **13.** 133 cm²
15. 11 km² **17.** 712.72 m²
21. about 96 ft² **23.** about 190 cm²
27. D **29.** $y = 11$ **31.** $y = 154$
33. $3\frac{3}{10}$ **35.** $17\frac{25}{48}$

Chapter 9 Study Guide: Review

1. polyhedron **2.** volume
3. vertex **4.** 18 ft² **5.** 7 m²
6. 12 in² **7.** 12 in² **8.** 154 in²
9. 12 cm² **10.** 30 cm² **11.** 12 ft²
12. 78.5 ft² **13.** 200.96 cm²
14. 12.56 m² **15.** 113.04 ft²

16. 154 ft² **17.** 57 m²
18. 47.56 ft² **19.** 73.5 cm²
20. 5 faces, 8 edges, 5 vertices;
rectangular pyramid **21.** 6 faces,
12 edges, 8 vertices; rectangular
prism **22.** 384 cm³ **23.** 6,300 in³
24. 353 m³ **25.** 2,308 ft³
26. 125 m² **27.** 102 cm²

Chapter 10

10-1 Exercises

1. $y = x + 6$; 15 **3.** $j = b - 6$
7. $c = 12s - 2$ **9.** $p = 150m$
11. $y = 4x - 2$; 54 **13.** $y = 2x - 1$;
5; 15 **15.** Let c be the total cost
and h be the number of hours.
$c = \$125 + \$55h$ **17.** $a = 7h$; \$63
23. G **25.** 1.1 **27.** 0.4
29. 29.75 ft³

10-2 Exercises

1. (1, 8); (2, 14); (3, 20); (4, 26)
3. no **5.** 2 **7.** 4

9.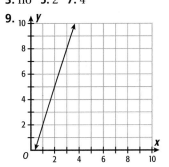

11. (1, 3); (2, 7); (3, 11);
(4, 15) **13.** yes **15.** 5 **17.** 3
21.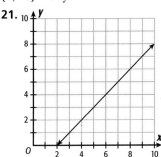

23.

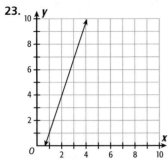

25. 0; 1; 2; 3 **27.** (1, 14)

29.

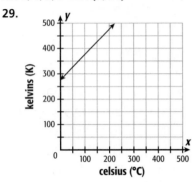

31. 293 kelvins **37.** H **39.** $p = 19$
41. $m = 4$ **43.** 6

10-3 Exercises

1. $x = 8$ **3.** $x = 7$ **5.** 20
7. $x = 6$ **9.** $x = 6$ **11.** $x = 70$
13. $x = 12$ **15a.** $32x + 84 = 180$ **b.** $x = 3$; Rachel can pay a magician for 3 hours. **17.** 3
19. \$17 **21a.** $y = x + 4$ **b.** $x = 11$
23. $4x - 3 = 25$; $x = 7$ **25.** $5x + 1 = 41$; $x = 8$ **29.** $x = 20$
31. $x = 1$ **33.** $x = 6$ **39.** 9
41. 0.95, 1.1, $\frac{4}{3}$ **43.** 0.35, 0.5, $\frac{3}{5}$
45. $y = 3x$; 15

10-4 Exercises

1. $w \geq 0$

3. $z \geq 9$

5. $x < 6$

7. $t \leq 9$

9. $d \geq 6$

11. $n \geq 5$

13. $q \leq 7$

15. $y \leq 1$

17. $g \geq 10$

19. $w < 5$

21. $x < 9$

23. $a \leq 3$

25. $r \geq 8$

27. $n > 30$
29. $3c < 60$; $c < \$20$
31. $c \leq 2$

33. $2r < 14$; $r < 7$

35. $t \geq 10$ **41.** D **43.** 19
45. 9 **47.** 208

10-5 Exercises

1. $x \geq 6$;

3. $x \geq 3$;

5. $x \geq 6$;

7. $x \leq 4$;

9. $x > 15$;

11. $x \leq 2$;

13. $x < 3$;

15. $x < 3$;

17. $x < 6$;

19. $700 + 0.05x \geq 2,800$; $x \geq 42,000$; the salesman must sell \$42,000 or more.

21. $x < 6$;

23. $x \geq 2$;

25. $x \leq 8$;

27. $x > 10$;

29. $x \geq 4$;

31. $x \leq 2$;

33. $x \geq 0$;

35. $x > 10$;

37. $x < 1$;

39. $12p + 15 \leq 120$; $p \leq 8.75$; Peter can buy no more than 8 pizzas.

41. $\frac{x}{2} + 4 < 6$; $x < 4$;

43. $\frac{x - 2}{3} \geq 1$; $x \geq 5$;

45. $g \leq 2$;

47. $x < 7$;

0 1 2 3 4 5 6 7 8 9 10

49. $y < 35$;

30 31 32 33 34 35 36 37 38 39 40

51. at least 45 tickets   **55.** A
57. 6   **59.** 38.4   **61.** 6 m^2
63. 112.5 ft^2

Chapter 10 Study Guide: Review

1. inequality   **2.** linear equation
3. function   **4.** $y = 2x + 2$; 18
5. $y = x - 5$; 9   **6.** $y = 2x + 5$; 25
7. $\ell = 4w$, ℓ = length, w = width
8. $h = b - 2$; h = Hunter's age;
b = Blake's age, **9.** $t = 3c$;
t = number of songs on Thomas's
MP3 player; c = number of songs
on Cynthia's MP3 player
10. $p = 7g - 3$; p = number of
penguins; g = number of giraffes
11. (1, 7), (2, 9), (3, 11), (4, 13)
12. (1, 8), (2, 9), (3, 10), (4, 11)
13. yes   **14.** no

15.

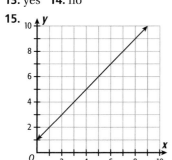

16.

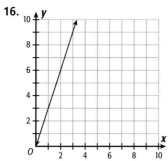

17.

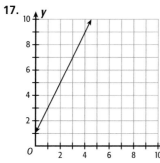

18.

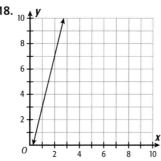

19.

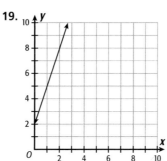

20.

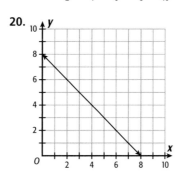

21. $z = 10$ **22.** $a = 3$
23. $b = 2$ **24.** $b = 75$
25. $c = 600$ **26.** $d = 2$
27. $h = 8$ **28.** $j = 112$
29. 28 pizzas   **30.** 10
31. $n > 30$;

25   27   30   33   35

32. $p \le 1$;

0 1 2 3 4 5 6 7 8 9 10

33. $s \ge 5$;

0   2   5   8   10

34. $r > 14$;

10   12   14   16   18   20

35. $q \le 60$;

55   57   60   63   65

36. $u < 11$;

5   7   9   11   13   15

37. $t \le 9$;

3   5   7   9   11   13

38. $v > 4$;

0   2   4   6   8   10

39. $w > 4$;

0   2   4   6   8   10

40. $x > 3$;

1   3   5   7   9   11

41. $x \ge 3$; at least 3 more projects
42. $x \le 387$; 387 more tickets at most
43. $a < 8$;

0   2   4   6   8   10

44. $b \le 64$;

60   62   64   66   68   70

45. $c \ge 88$;

80   82   84   86   88   90

46. $d < 3$;

0 1 2 3 4 5 6 7 8 9 10

47. $g > 12$;

5   7   9   12   15

48. $h \ge 28$;

26   28   30   32   34   36

49. $j \le 77$;

74   77   80   82   84

50. $k < 9$;

3   5   7   9   11   13

51. $x \ge 84$; a score of at least 84
52. $x \ge 5$; at least 5 miles each day

Chapter 11

11-1 Exercises

1. +5
3.

−4   −2   0   2   4

5.

−7 −5 −3 −1   1   3   5   7

7. 10 **9.** 3   **11.** +50   **13.** +7   **21.** 1
23. 2   **25.** Possible answer:
spending $83   **27.** Possible
answer: earning $15   **29.** +92
31. +25   **33.** 0   **35.** 105   **37.** 55
41. +45   **43.** +2; −2   **45.** C
49. D **51.** 1.7   **53.** 6.215

11-2 Exercises

1. > **3.** < **5.** −5, −4, 3, 7
7a. 3:30 A.M. **b.** 1 °F **9.** > **11.** <
13. −8, 7, 15 **15.** −16, −9, −1, 13
17. −19, −3, 0, 8, 22 **19.** < **21.** >
23. < **25.** < **27.** −39, 14, 21
29. −26, −12, 0, 43
31. −73, −67, −10, 20, 82 **33.** C
35. San Augustin Cave, Dead
Sea, Mt. Rainier, Kilimanjaro, Mt.
Everest **39.** C **41.** 7.60 ft, 47.73 ft

11-3 Exercises

1. III **3.** I **5.** (1, 2)
7, 9.

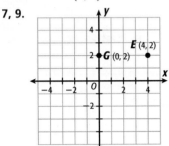

11. II **13.** I **15.** IV **17.** (−2, 4)
19. (4, 4) **21.** (−3, 0)
29. I **31.** III **33.** IV **35.** III
37, 39, 41, 43, 45, 47.

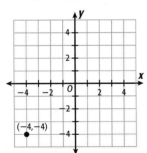

49. Gabon **51.** Possible answers:
Morocco, Libya, Algeria **55.** B
57. 4.4 **59.** 5.75 **61.** 0.2 **63.** =
65. >

11-4 Exercises

1. 3 + 2 = 5 **3.** −5 **5.** 7 **7.** 4 **9.** 0
11. −17 **13.** −22 **15.** 6 + (−2) = 4
17. 11 **19.** 0 **21.** −6 **23.** −7
25. −16 **27.** −8 **29.** −2 **31.** 2
33. 29 feet

35.

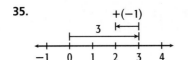

37.

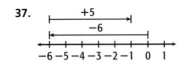

39.

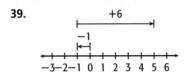

41.

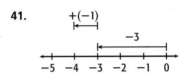

43. 7 **45.** −11 **47.** −9 **49.** 17
51. 4 **53.** −1 **55.** −17 **57.** −6 °F
63. B **65.** 5, 3, −1 **67.** $x = 35$
69. $r = 38$

11-5 Exercises

1. 6 − 5 = 1 **3.** −3 **5.** −8 **7.** 8
9. 13 **11.** −4 **13.** 11 **15.** 2
17. −5 **19.** 7 **21.** −12 **23.** −6
25. −1 **27.** 21 **29.** 30 **31.** 12
33. 4 **35.** −38 **37.** −19 m
39. 9 °F **43.** D **45.** 2% **47.** 26%
49. 310%

11-6 Exercises

1. 24 **3.** −21 **5.** 9 **7.** 16 **9.** 9
11. 33 **13.** −24 **15.** 18 **17.** 45
19. −32 **21.** 39 **23.** −72 **25.** −24
27. −12 **29.** 40 **31.** 60 **33.** 14
35. 54 **37.** −90 **39.** 4 ft to −4 ft
41. A negative multiplied by a
negative is positive; 36.
43. 6 and −6 **45.** positive;
negative **47.** $a \geq 29$ **49.** $n = 130$

11-7 Exercises

1. 8 **3.** 3 **5.** −2 **7.** −15 **9.** 5
11. −8 **13.** 6 **15.** 2 **17.** 1 **19.** 3
21. 16 **23.** 14 **25.** −6 **27.** 1
29. 10 **31.** −7 **33.** 3 **35.** 8
37. −3 **39.** 6 **41.** −11 **43a.** −300
b. a decrease of 300 seals from

1976 to 1980 **45.** −20; a decrease
of 20 seals per year from 1981 to
1990 **49.** G **51.** 6 cm

11-8 Exercises

1. $m = 12$ **3.** $z = 9$ **5.** $p = −9$
7. $g = 8$ **9.** $b = −8$ **11.** $c = −7$
13. $f = −6$ **15.** $r = −900$
17. $g = 4$ **19.** $t = −14$
21. $x = −14$ **23.** $w = −10$
25. $j = 8$ **27.** $a = −52$
29. $m = −48$ **31.** $u = −60$
33. $x = 17$ **35.** $k = −4$
37. $m = −15$ **39.** $n = −3$
41. $g = −3$ **43.** $f = −8$ **45.** $d = 33$
47. $h = −84$ **49.** $b = 32$ **51.** $a = 8$
53. $t = −55$ **55.** $c = −13$
57. $n = −4$ **59.** $j = −3$
61. 70 dives **63.** −4
65. $x = −18,500$; sponge
67. −24 ft **69.** Negative; a
negative number divided by a
positive number gives a negative
quotient. **71.** A **73.** 6.5 in.,
3.25 in. **75.** yes

Chapter 11 Study Guide: Review

1. absolute value **2.** coordinate
plane, quadrants **3.** +10 **4.** −50

5.

6.

7.

8.

9. 37 **10.** 14 **11.** 97 **12.** 13
13. < **14.** < **15.** <
16. −1, 2, 4 **17.** −3, 0, 4
18. −8, −6, 0 **19.** (−2, −3)
20. (1, 0) **21.** III **22.** II
23. −2 **24.** 0 **25.** 1 **26.** −5
27. −17 **28.** 8 **29.** 2 **30.** 0
31. 145 degrees **32.** −8
33. 9 **34.** −3 **35.** −6 **36.** 13
37. −6 **38.** −2 **39.** 2 **40.** 36 °F
41. −10 **42.** 6 **43.** 6 **44.** −8
45. −18 **46.** 45 **47.** 99 **48.** −9

49. –30 **50.** –3 **51.** 3 **52.** 2
53. –2 **54.** –1 **55.** 6 **56.** 0
57. –8 **58.** $w = 4$ **59.** $a = -12$
60. $q = -7$ **61.** $x = -5$ **62.** 138 ft

Glossary/Glosario · · ·

ENGLISH	SPANISH	EXAMPLES
absolute value The distance of a number from zero on a number line; shown by | |. (p. 485)	**valor absoluto** Distancia a la que está un número de 0 en una recta numérica. El símbolo del valor absoluto es | |.	$\|-5\| = 5$
accuracy The closeness of a given measurement or value to the actual measurement or value. (p. SB16)	**exactitud** Cercanía de una medida o un valor a la medida o el valor real.	
acute angle An angle that measures greater than 0° and less than 90°. (p. SB11)	**ángulo agudo** Ángulo que mide más do 0° y menos de 90°.	
acute triangle A triangle with all angles measuring less than 90°. (p. SB12)	**triángulo acutángulo** Triángulo en el que todos los ángulos miden menos de 90°.	
addend A number added to one or more other numbers to form a sum.	**sumando** Número que se suma a uno o más números para formar una suma.	In the expression 4 + 6 + 7, the numbers 4, 6, and 7 are addends.
Addition Property of Opposites The property that states that the sum of a number and its opposite equals zero.	**Propiedad de la suma de los opuestos** Propiedad que establece que la suma de un número y su opuesto es cero.	$12 + (-12) = 0$
algebraic expression An expression that contains at least one variable. (p. 48)	**expresión algebraica** Expresión que contiene al menos una variable.	$x + 8$ $4(m - b)$
algebraic inequality An inequality that contains at least one variable.	**desigualdad algebraica** Desigualdad que contiene al menos una variable.	$x + 3 > 10$ $5a > b + 3$
angle A figure formed by two rays with a common endpoint called the vertex. (p. SB10)	**ángulo** Figura formada por dos rayos con un extremo común llamado vértice.	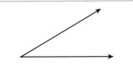
area The number of square units needed to cover a given surface. (p. 396)	**área** El número de unidades cuadradas que se necesitan para cubrir una superficie dada.	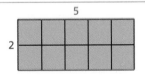 The area is 10 square units.

ENGLISH	SPANISH	EXAMPLES
arithmetic sequence A sequence in which the terms change by the same amount each time. (p. 24)	**sucesión aritmética** Una sucesión en la que los términos cambian la misma cantidad cada vez.	The sequence 2, 5, 8, 11, 14. . . is an arthmetic sequence.
Associative Property of Addition The property that states that for three or more numbers, their sum is always the same, regardless of their grouping. (p. 44)	**Propiedad asociativa de la suma** Propiedad que establece que agrupar tres o más números en cualquier orden siempre da como resultado la misma suma.	$2 + 3 + 8 = (2 + 3) + 8 = 2 + (3 + 8)$
Associative Property of Multiplication The property that states that for three or more numbers, their product is always the same, regardless of their grouping. (p. 44)	**Propiedad asociativa de la multiplicación** Propiedad que establece que agrupar tres o más números en cualquier orden siempre da como resultado el mismo producto.	$2 \cdot 3 \cdot 8 = (2 \cdot 3) \cdot 8 = 2 \cdot (3 \cdot 8)$
asymmetrical Not identical on either side of a central line; not symmetrical.	**asimétrico** Que no es idéntico a ambos lados de una línea central; no simétrico.	
average The sum of the items in a set of data divided by the number of items in the set; also called *mean*. (p. 252)	**promedio** La suma de los elementos de un conjunto de datos dividida entre el número de elementos del conjunto. También se le llama *media*.	Data set: 4, 6, 7, 8, 10 Average: $\frac{4 + 6 + 7 + 8 + 10}{5} = \frac{35}{5} = 7$
axes The two perpendicular lines of a coordinate plane that intersect at the origin. (p. 492)	**ejes** Las dos rectas numéricas perpendiculares del plano cartesiano que se intersecan en el origen.	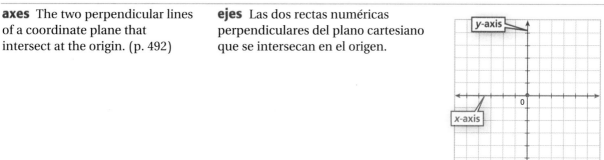

B

bar graph A graph that uses vertical or horizontal bars to display data. (p. 262)	**gráfica de barras** Gráfica en la que se usan barras verticales u horizontales para presentar datos.	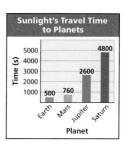
base (in numeration) When a number is raised to a power, the number that is used as a factor is the base. (p. 10)	**base (en numeración)** Cuando un número es elevado a una potencia, el número que se usa como factor es la base.	$3^5 = 3 \cdot 3 \cdot 3 \cdot 3 \cdot 3$; 3 is the base.

base (of a polygon or three-dimensional figure) A side of a polygon; a face of a three-dimensional figure by which the figure is measured or classified. (p. 414)

base (de un polígono o figura tridimensional) Lado de un polígono; la cara de una figura tridimensional, a partir de la cual se mide o se clasifica la figura.

Bases of a cylinder   Bases of a prism

Base of a cone   Base of a pyramid

break (graph) A zigzag on a horizontal or vertical scale of a graph that indicates that some of the numbers on the scale have been omitted. (p. 263)

discontinuidad (gráfica) Zig-zag en la escala horizontal o vertical de una gráfica que indica la omisión de algunos de los números de la escala.

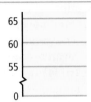

capacity The amount a container can hold when filled.

capacidad Cantidad que cabe en un recipiente cuando se llena.

A large milk container has a capacity of 1 gallon.

Celsius A metric scale for measuring temperature in which 0°C is the freezing point of water and 100°C is the boiling point of water.

Celsius Escala métrica para medir la temperatura, en la que 0° C es el punto de congelación del agua y 100° C es el punto de ebullición.

center (of a circle) The point inside a circle that is the same distance from all the points on the circle. (p. 378)

centro (de un círculo) Punto interior de un círculo que se encuentra a la misma distancia de todos los puntos de la circunferencia.

chord A segment whose endpoints lie on a circle. (p. 378)

cuerda Segmento cuyos extremos se encuentran en un círculo.

circle The set of all points in a plane that are the same distance from a given point called the center. (p. 378)

círculo Conjunto de todos los puntos en un plano que se encuentran a la misma distancia de un punto dado llamado centro.

circumference The distance around a circle. (p. 378)

circunferencia Distancia alrededor de un círculo.

Circumference

clustering A method used to estimate a sum when all addends are close to the same value. (p. 98)

aproximación Método que se usa para estimar una suma cuando todos los sumandos se aproximan al mismo valor.

27, 29, 24, and 23 all cluster around 25.

ENGLISH	SPANISH	EXAMPLES
common denominator A denominator that is the same in two or more fractions. (p. 169)	**denominador común** Denominador que es común a dos o más fracciones.	The common denominator of $\frac{5}{8}$ and $\frac{2}{8}$ is 8.
common factor A number that is a factor of two or more numbers.	**factor común** Número que es factor de dos o más números.	8 is a common factor of 16 and 40.
common multiple A number that is a multiple of each of two or more numbers.	**múltiplo común** Un número que es múltiplo de dos o más números.	15 is a common multiple of 3 and 5.
Commutative Property of Addition The property that states that two or more numbers can be added in any order without changing the sum. (p. 44)	**Propiedad conmutativa de la suma** Propiedad que establece que sumar dos o más números en cualquier orden no altera la suma.	$8 + 20 = 20 + 8$
Commutative Property of Multiplication The property that states that two or more numbers can be multiplied in any order without changing the product. (p. 44)	**Propiedad conmutativa de la multiplicación** Propiedad que establece que multiplicar dos o más números en cualquier orden no altera el producto.	$6 \cdot 12 = 12 \cdot 6$
compatible numbers Numbers that are close to the given numbers that make estimation or mental calculation easier. (p. 6)	**números compatibles** Números que están cerca de los números dados y hacen más fácil la estimación o el cálculo mental.	To estimate $7,957 + 5,009$, use the compatible numbers 8,000 and 5,000: $8,000 + 5,000 = 13,000$
compensation When a number in a problem is close to another number that is easier to calculate with, the easier number is used to find the answer. Then the answer is adjusted by adding to it or subtracting from it. (p. 26)	**compensación** Cuando un número de un problema está cerca de otro con el que es más fácil hacer cálculos, se usa el número más fácil para hallar la respuesta. Luego, se ajusta la respuesta sumando o restando.	
composite number A number greater than 1 that has more than two whole-number factors. (p. 143)	**número compuesto** Número mayor que 1 que tiene más de dos factores que son números cabales.	4, 6, 8, and 9 are composite numbers.
cone A three-dimensional figure with one vertex and one circular base. (p. 414)	**cono** Figura tridimensional con un vértice y una base circular.	
congruent Having the same size and shape.	**congruentes** Que tienen la misma forma y el mismo tamaño.	
congruent figures Two figures whose corresponding sides and angles are congruent. (p. SB14)	**figuras congruentes** Figuras que tienen el mismo tamaño y forma.	
conjecture A statement that is believed to be true.	**conjetura** Enunciado que se supone verdadero.	

ENGLISH	SPANISH	EXAMPLES
constant A value that does not change. (p. 48)	**constante** Valor que no cambia.	3, 0, π
continuous graph A graph made up of connected lines or curves. (p. SB17)	**gráfica continua** Gráfica compuesta por líneas rectas *o* curvas conectadas.	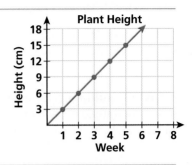
coordinates The numbers of an ordered pair that locate a point on a coordinate graph. (p. 492)	**coordenadas** Los números de un par ordenado que ubican un punto en una gráfica de coordenadas.	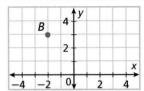 The coordinates of *B* are (−2, 3).
coordinate grid A grid formed by the intersection of horizontal and vertical lines that is used to locate points. (p. 269)	**cuadrícula de coordenadas** Cuadricula formado por la intersección de líneas horizontales y líneas verticales que se usando por localizar puntos.	
coordinate plane A plane formed by the intersection of a horizontal number line called the *x*-axis and a vertical number line called the *y*-axis. (p. 492)	**plano cartesiano** Plano formado por la intersección de una recta numérica horizontal llamada eje *x* y otra vertical llamada eje *y*.	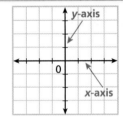
correspondence The relationship between two or more objects that are matched.	**correspondencia** La relación entre dos o más objetos que coinciden.	
corresponding angles (in polygons) Angles in the same relative position in polygons with an equal number of sides. (p. 326)	**ángulos correspondientes (en polígonos)** Ángulos que se ubican en la misma posición relativa en polígonos que tienen el mismo número de lados.	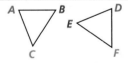 ∠*A* and ∠*D* are corresponding angles.
corresponding sides Sides in the same relative position in polygons with an equal number of sides. (p. 326)	**lados correspondientes** Lados que se ubican en la misma posición relativa en polígonos que tienen el mismo número de lados.	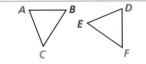 $\overline{AB}$ and $\overline{DE}$ are corresponding sides.
cross product The product of numbers on the diagonal when comparing two ratios. (p. 305)	**producto cruzado** El producto de los números multiplicados en diagonal cuando se comparan dos razones.	For the proportion $\frac{2}{3} = \frac{4}{6}$, the cross products are 2 · 6 = 12 and 3 · 4 = 12.
cube (geometric figure) A rectangular prism with six congruent square faces.	**cubo (figura geométrica)** Prisma rectangular con seis caras cuadradas congruentes.	

Glossary/Glosario

ENGLISH	SPANISH	EXAMPLES
cube (in numeration) A number raised to the third power.	**cubo (en numeración)** Número elevado a la tercera potencia.	$5^3 = 5 \cdot 5 \cdot 5 = 125$
customary system The measurement system often used in the United States. (p. 352)	**sistema usual de medidas** El sistema de medidas que se usa comúnmente en Estados Unidos.	inches, feet, miles, ounces, pounds, tons, cups, quarts, gallons
cylinder A three-dimensional figure with two parallel, congruent circular bases connected by a curved lateral surface. (p. 414)	**cilindro** Figura tridimensional con dos bases circulares paralelas y congruentes, unidas por una superficie lateral curva.	

decagon A polygon with ten sides.	**decágono** Polígono de diez lados.	
degree The unit of measure for angles or temperature.	**grado** Unidad de medida para ángulos y temperaturas.	
denominator The bottom number of a fraction that tells how many equal parts are in the whole.	**denominador** Número de abajo en una fracción que indica en cuántas partes iguales se divide el entero.	$\frac{3}{4}$ ◄—— denominator
diameter A line segment that passes through the center of a circle and has endpoints on the circle, or the length of that segment. (p. 378)	**diámetro** Segmento de recta que pasa por el centro de un círculo y tiene sus extremos en la circunferencia, o bien la longitud de ese segmento.	
difference The result when one number is subtracted from another.	**diferencia** El resultado de restar un número de otro.	
dimension The length, width, or height of a figure.	**dimensión** Longitud, ancho o altura de una figura.	
discount The amount by which the original price is reduced. (p. 322)	**descuento** Cantidad que se resta del precio original de un artículo.	
discrete graph A graph made up of unconnected points. (p. SB17)	**gráfica discreta** Gráfica compuesta de puntos no conectados.	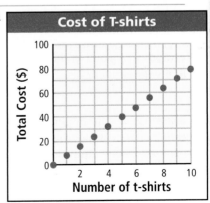

ENGLISH	SPANISH	EXAMPLES
Distributive Property The property that states if you multiply a sum by a number, you will get the same result if you multiply each addend by that number and then add the products. (p. 45)	**Propiedad distributiva** Propiedad que establece que, si multiplicas una suma por un número, obtendrás el mismo resultado que si multiplicas cada sumando por ese número y luego sumas los productos.	$5(20 + 1) = 5 \cdot 20 + 5 \cdot 1$
dividend The number to be divided in a division problem.	**dividendo** Número que se divide en un problema de división.	In $8 \div 4 = 2$, 8 is the dividend.
divisible Can be divided by a number without leaving a remainder. (p. 142)	**divisible** Que se puede dividir entre un número sin dejar residuo.	18 is divisible by 3.
divisor The number you are dividing by in a division problem.	**divisor** El número entre el que se divide en un problema de división.	In $8 \div 4 = 2$, 4 is the divisor.
dodecagon A polygon with 12 sides.	**dodecágono** Polígono de 12 lados.	
double-bar graph A bar graph that compares two related sets of data. (p. 263)	**gráfica de doble barra** Gráfica de barras que compara dos conjuntos de datos relacionados.	
double-line graph A graph that shows how two related sets of data change over time. (p. 273)	**gráfica de doble línea** Gráfica lineal que muestra cómo cambian con el tiempo dos conjuntos de datos relacionados.	

E

edge The line segment along which two faces of a polyhedron intersect. (p. 414)	**arista** Segmento de recta donde se intersecan dos caras de un poliedro.	
endpoint A point at the end of a line segment or ray.	**extremo** Un punto ubicado al final de un segmento de recta o rayo.	
equation A mathematical sentence that shows that two expressions are equivalent. (p. 62)	**ecuación** Enunciado matemático que indica que dos expresiones son equivalentes.	$x + 4 = 7$ $6 + 1 = 10 - 3$

equilateral triangle A triangle with three congruent sides. (p. SB12)

triángulo equilátero Triángulo con tres lados congruentes.

---

equivalent Having the same value.

equivalentes Que tienen el mismo valor.

---

equivalent fractions Fractions that name the same amount or part. (p. 156)

fracciones equivalentes Fracciones que representan la misma cantidad o parte.

$\frac{1}{2}$ and $\frac{2}{4}$ are equivalent fractions.

---

equivalent ratios Ratios that name the same comparison. (p. 296)

razones equivalentes Razones que representan la misma comparación.

$\frac{1}{2}$ and $\frac{2}{4}$ are equivalent ratios.

---

estimate (n) An answer that is close to the exact answer and is found by rounding or other methods. (p. 6)

estimación (s) Una solución aproximada a la respuesta exacta que se halla mediante el redondeo u otros métodos.

---

estimate (v) To find an answer close to the exact answer by rounding or other methods.

estimar (v) Hallar una solución aproximada a la respuesta exacta mediante el redondeo u otros métodos.

---

evaluate To find the value of a numerical or algebraic expression. (p. 48)

evaluar Hallar el valor de una expresión numérica o algebraica.

Evaluate $2x + 7$ for $x = 3$.
$2x + 7$
$2(3) + 7$
$6 + 7$
13

---

even number A whole number that is divisible by two.

número par Un número cabal que es divisible entre dos.

---

expanded form A number written as the sum of the values of its digits.

forma desarrollada Número escrito como suma de los valores de sus dígitos.

236,536 written in expanded form is $200,000 + 30,000 + 6,000 + 500 + 30 + 6$.

---

exponent The number that indicates how many times the base is used as a factor. (p. 10)

exponente Número que indica cuántas veces se usa la base como factor.

$2^3 = 2 \cdot 2 \cdot 2 = 8$; 3 is the exponent.

---

exponential form A number is in exponential form when it is written with a base and an exponent. (p. 10)

forma exponencial Cuando se escribe un número con una base y un exponente, está en forma exponencial.

4^2 is the exponential form for $4 \cdot 4$.

---

expression A mathematical phrase that contains operations, numbers, and/or variables.

expresión Enunciado matemático que contiene operaciones, números y/o variables.

$6x + 1$

---

face A flat surface of a polyhedron. (p. 414)

cara Lado plano de un poliedro.

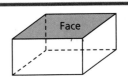

Face

ENGLISH	SPANISH	EXAMPLES
factor A number that is multiplied by another number to get a product. (p. 146)	**factor** Número que se multiplica por otro para hallar un producto.	7 is a factor of 21 since $7 \cdot 3 = 21$.
factor tree A diagram showing how a whole number breaks down into its prime factors. (p. 147)	**árbol de factores** Diagrama que muestra cómo se descompone un número cabal en sus factores primos.	$$\begin{array}{c} 12 \\ / \ \backslash \\ 3 \cdot 4 \\ \quad / \ \backslash \\ 2 \cdot 2 \end{array}$$ $12 = 3 \cdot 2 \cdot 2$
fahrenheit A temperature scale in which 32°F is the freezing point of water and 212°F is the boiling point of water.	**Fahrenheit** Escala de temperatura en la que 32° F es el punto de congelación del agua y 212° F es el punto de ebullición.	
formula A rule showing relationships among quantities.	**fórmula** Regla que muestra relaciones entre cantidades.	$A = \ell w$ is the formula for the area of a rectangle.
fraction A number in the form $\frac{a}{b}$, where $b \neq 0$.	**fracción** Número escrito en la forma $\frac{a}{b}$, donde $b \neq 0$.	
frequency The number of times a data value occurs. (p. 266)	**frecuencia** Cantidad de veces que aparece el valor en un conjunto de datos.	In the data set 5, 6, 6, 8, 9, the data value 6 has a frequency of 2.
frequency table A table that lists items together according to the number of times, or frequency, that the items occur. (p. 266)	**tabla de frecuencia** Una tabla en la que se organizan los datos de acuerdo con el número de veces que aparece cada valor (o la frecuencia).	Data set: 1, 1, 2, 2, 3, 4, 5, 5, 5, 6, 6 Frequency table: 	Data	Frequency	 |---|---| 	1	2	 	2	2	 	3	1	 	4	1	 	5	3	 	6	2	
front-end estimation An estimating technique in which the front digits of the addends are added. (p. 99)	**estimación por partes** Técnica en la que se suman sólo los números enteros de los sumandos. y luego se ajusta la suma para tener una estimacion mas exacta.	Estimate $25.05 + 14.671$ with the sum $25 + 14 = 39$. The actual value is 39 or greater.
function An input-output relationship that has exactly one output for each input. (p. 446)	**función** Relación de entrada-salida en la que a cada valor de entrada corresponde un valor de salida.	
function table A table of ordered pairs that represent solutions of a function. (p. 446)	**tabla de función** Tabla de pares ordenados que representan soluciones de una función.		x	3	4	5	6	 	---	---	---	---	---	 	y	7	9	11	13	

graph of an equation A graph of the set of ordered pairs that are solutions of the equation.

gráfica de una ecuación Gráfica del conjunto de pares ordenados que son soluciones de la ecuación.

greatest common factor (GCF) The largest common factor of two or more given numbers. (p. 150)

máximo común divisor (MCD) El mayor de los factores comunes compartidos por dos o más números dados.

The GCF of 27 and 45 is 9.

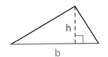

height In a triangle or quadrilateral, the perpendicular distance from the base to the opposite vertex or side. (p. 401) In a prism or cylinder, the perpendicular distance between the bases. (pp. 422, 426)

altura En un triángulo o cuadrilátero, la distancia perpendicular desde la base de la figura al vértice o lado opuesto. En un prisma o cilindro, la distancia perpendicular entre las bases.

heptagon A seven-sided polygon.

heptágono Polígono de siete lados.

hexagon A six-sided polygon.

hexágono Polígono de seis lados.

Identity Property (for Addition) The property that states the sum of zero and any number is that number. (p. 512)

Propiedad de identidad (de la suma) Propiedad que establece que la suma de cero y cualquier número es ese número.

$7 + 0 = 7$
$-9 + 0 = -9$

Identity Property (for Multiplication) The property that states that the product of 1 and any number is that number. (p. 512)

Propiedad de identidad (de la multiplicación) Propiedad que establece que el producto de 1 y cualquier número es ese número.

$5 \times 1 = 5$
$-8 \times 1 = -8$

improper fraction A fraction in which the numerator is greater than or equal to the denominator. (p. 164)

fracción impropia Fracción cuyo numerador es mayor que o igual al denominador.

$\frac{5}{5}$
$\frac{7}{3}$

indirect measurement The technique of using similar figures and proportions to find a measure. (p. 330)

medición indirecta La técnica de usar figuras semejantes y proporciones para hallar una medida.

ENGLISH	SPANISH	EXAMPLES
inequality A mathematical sentence that shows the relationship between quantities that are not equal. (p. 461)	**desigualdad** Enunciado matemático que muestra una relación entre cantidades que no son iguales.	$5 < 8$ $5x + 2 \geq 12$
input The value substituted into an expression or function. (p. 446)	**valor de entrada** Valor que se usa para sustituir una variable en una expresión o función.	For the rule $y = 6x$, the input 4 produces an output of 24.
integer A member of the set of whole numbers and their opposites. (p. 484)	**entero** Un miembro del conjunto de los números cabales y sus opuestos.	. . . $-3, -2, -1, 0, 1, 2, 3, . . .$
interval The space between marked values on a number line or the scale of a graph.	**intervalo** El espacio entre los valores marcados en una recta numérica o en la escala de una gráfica.	
inverse operations Operations that undo each other: addition and subtraction, or multiplication and division. (p. 66)	**operaciones inversas** Operaciones que se cancelan mutuamente: suma y resta, o multiplicación y división.	
isosceles triangle A triangle with at least two congruent sides. (p. SB12)	**triángulo isósceles** Triángulo que tiene al menos dos lados congruentes.	

L

lateral surface In a cylinder, the curved surface connecting the circular bases; in a cone, the curved surface that is not a base.	**superficie lateral** En un cilindro, superficie curva que une las bases circulares; en un cono, la superficie curva que no es la base.	
least common denominator (LCD) The least common multiple of two or more denominators. (p. 198)	**mínimo común denominador (mcd)** El mínimo común múltiplo de dos o más denominadores.	The LCD of $\frac{3}{4}$ and $\frac{5}{6}$ is 12.
least common multiple (LCM) The smallest number, other than zero, that is a multiple of two or more given numbers. (p. 194)	**mínimo común múltiplo (mcm)** El menor de los múltiplos (distinto de cero) de dos o más números.	The LCM of 10 and 18 is 90.
like fractions Fractions that have the same denominator. (p. 168)	**fracciones semejantes** Fracciones que tienen el mismo denominador.	$\frac{5}{12}$ and $\frac{3}{12}$ are like fractions.
line A straight path that has no thickness and extends forever. (p. SB9)	**rectas** Trayectoria recta que no tiene ningún grueso y que se extiende por siempre.	
line graph A graph that uses line segments to show how data changes. (p. 272)	**gráfica lineal** Gráfica que muestra cómo cambian los datos mediante segmentos de recta.	

ENGLISH	SPANISH	EXAMPLES

line plot A number line with marks or dots that show frequency. (p. 266)

diagrama de acumulación Recta numérica con marcas o puntos que indican la frecuencia.

Number of pets

---

line of symmetry The imaginary "mirror" in line symmetry. (p. SB14)

eje de simetría El "espejo" imaginario en la simetría axial.

---

line segment A part of a line between two endpoints. (p. SB9)

segmento de recta Parte de una línea con dos extremos.

---

line symmetry A figure has line symmetry if one half is a mirror-image of the other half. (p. SB14)

simetría axial Una figura tiene simetría axial si una de sus mitades es la imagen reflejada de la otra.

---

linear equation An equation whose solutions form a straight line on a coordinate plane. (p. 451)

ecuación lineal Ecuación en la que las soluciones forman una línea recta en un plano cartesiano.

$y = 2x + 1$

---

mean The sum of the items in a set of data divided by the number of items in the set; also called *average*. (p. 252)

media La suma de todos los elementos de un conjunto de datos dividida entre el número de elementos del conjunto.

Data set: 4, 6, 7, 8, 10

Mean: $\frac{4 + 6 + 7 + 8 + 10}{5} = \frac{35}{5} = 7$

---

median The middle number or the mean (average) of the two middle numbers in an ordered set of data. (p. 253)

mediana El número intermedio o la media (el promedio) de los dos números intermedios en un conjunto ordenado de datos.

Data set: 4, 6, 7, 8, 10

Median: 7

---

metric system A decimal system of weights and measures that is used universally in science and commonly throughout the world. (p. 356)

sistema métrico Sistema decimal de pesos y medidas empleado universalmente en las ciencias y por lo general en todo el mundo.

centimeters, meters, kilometers, grams, kilograms, milliliters, liters

---

mixed number A number made up of a whole number that is not zero and a fraction. (p. 160)

número mixto Número compuesto por un número cabal distinto de cero y una fracción.

$5\frac{1}{8}$

---

mode The number or numbers that occur most frequently in a set of data; when no value is repeated in the set, we say there is no mode. (p. 253)

moda Número o números más frecuentes en un conjunto de datos; si ningun valor no repita en el conjunto, no hay moda.

Data set: 3, 5, 8, 8, 10

Mode: 8

---

multiple A multiple of a number is the product of the number and any nonzero whole number.

múltiplo El producto de un número y cualquier número cabal distinto de cero es un múltiplo de ese número.

ENGLISH	SPANISH	EXAMPLES

Multiplication Property of Zero The property that states that the product of any number and 0 is 0.

Propiedad de multiplicación del cero Propiedad que establece que el producto de cualquier número y 0 es 0.

$6 \times 0 = 0$
$-5 \times 0 = 0$

---

multiplicative inverse One of two numbers whose product is 1. (p. 224)

inverso multiplicativo Uno de dos números cuyo producto es igual a 1.

The multiplicative inverse of $\frac{3}{4}$ is $\frac{4}{3}$.

---

negative number A number less than zero. (p. 484)

número negativo Número menor que cero.

-2 is a negative number.

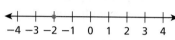

---

net An arrangement of two-dimensional figures that can be folded to form a polyhedron. (p. 426)

plantilla Arreglo de figuras bidimensionales que se doblan para formar un poliedro.

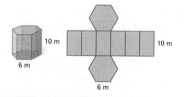

---

numerator The top number of a fraction that tells how many parts of a whole are being considered.

numerador El número de arriba de una fracción; indica cuántas partes de un entero se consideran.

$\frac{3}{4}$ ← numerator

---

numerical expression An expression that contains only numbers and operations. (p. 16)

expresión numérica Expresión que incluye sólo números y operaciones.

$(2 \cdot 3) + 1$

---

obtuse angle An angle whose measure is greater than 90° but less than 180°. (p. SB11)

ángulo obtuso Ángulo que mide más de 90° y menos de 180°.

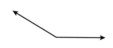

---

obtuse triangle A triangle containing one obtuse angle. (p. SB12)

triángulo obtusángulo Triángulo que tiene un ángulo obtuso.

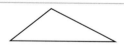

---

odd number A whole number that is not divisible by two.

número impar Un número cabal que no es divisible entre dos.

---

opposites Two numbers that are an equal distance from zero on a number line. (p. 484)

opuestos Dos números que están a la misma distancia de cero en una recta numérica.

5 and -5 are opposites.

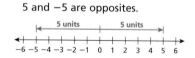

---

order of operations A rule for evaluating expressions: first perform the operations in parentheses, then compute powers and roots, then perform all multiplication and division from left to right, and then perform all addition and subtraction from left to right. (p. 16)

orden de las operaciones Regla para evaluar expresiones: primero se resuelven las operaciones entre paréntesis, luego se hallan las potencias y raíces, después todas las multiplicaciones y divisiones de izquierda a derecha y, por último, todas las sumas y restas de izquierda a derecha.

$3^2 - 12 \div 4$
$9 - 12 \div 4$ Evaluate the power.
$9 - 3$ Divide.
6 Subtract.

	ENGLISH	SPANISH	EXAMPLES

ordered pair A pair of numbers that can be used to locate a point on a coordinate plane. (p. 269)

par ordenado Par de números que sirven para ubicar un punto en un plano cartesiano.

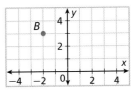

The coordinates of *B* are (−2, 3)

origin The point where the *x*-axis and *y*-axis intersect on the coordinate plane; (0, 0). (p. 492)

origen Punto de intersección entre el eje *x* y el eje *y* en un plano cartesiano: (0, 0).

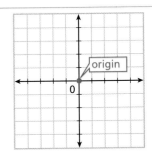

outlier A value much greater or much less than the others in a data set. (p. 256)

valor extremo Un valor mucho mayor o menor que los demás valores de un conjunto de datos.

Most of data Mean   Outlier

output The value that results from the substitution of a given input into an expression or function. (p. 446)

valor de salida Valor que resulta después de sustituir un valor de entrada determinado en una expresión o función.

For the rule $y = 6x$, the input 4 produces an output of 24.

overestimate An estimate that is greater than the exact answer. (p. 6)

estimación alta Estimación mayor que la respuesta exacta.

100 is an overestimate for the sum 23 + 24 + 21 + 22.

 P

parallelogram A quadrilateral with two pairs of parallel sides.

paralelogramo Cuadrilátero con dos pares de lados paralelos.

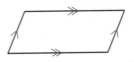

pentagon A five-sided polygon.

pentágono Polígono de cinco lados.

percent A ratio comparing a number to 100. (p. 310)

porcentaje Razón que compara un número con el número 100.

$45\% = \frac{45}{100}$

perfect square A square of a whole number.

cuadrado perfecto El cuadrado de un número cabal.

$5^2 = 25$, so 25 is a perfect square.

perimeter The distance around a polygon. (p. 374)

perímetro Distancia alrededor de un polígono.

18 ft

6 ft

perimeter = 48 ft

pi (π) The ratio of the circumference of a circle to the length of its diameter; $\pi \approx 3.14$ or $\frac{22}{7}$. (p. 378)

pi (π) Razón de la circunferencia de un círculo a la longitud de su diámetro; $\pi \approx 3.14$ ó $\frac{22}{7}$

ENGLISH	SPANISH	EXAMPLES
plane A flat surface that has no thickness and extends forever. (p. SB9)	**plano** Superficie plana que no tiene ningún grueso y que se extiende por siempre.	 plane *R* or plane *ABC*
point An exact location that has no size. (p. SB9)	**punto** Ubicación exacta que no tiene ningún tamaño.	*P* • point *P*
polygon A closed plane figure formed by three or more line segments that intersect only at their endpoints. (p. SB13)	**polígono** Figura plana cerrada, formada por tres o más segmentos de recta que se intersecan sólo en sus extremos.	
polyhedron A three-dimensional figure in which all the surfaces or faces are polygons. (p. 414)	**poliedro** Figura tridimensional cuyas superficies o caras tienen forma de polígonos.	
positive number A number greater than zero. (p. 484)	**número positivo** Número mayor que cero.	2 is a positive number. −4 −3 −2 −1 0 1 2 3 4
power A number produced by raising a base to an exponent.	**potencia** Número que resulta al elevar una base a un exponente.	$2^3 = 8$, so 2 to the 3rd power is 8.
precision The level of detail an instrument can measure. (p. SB16)	**precisión** El grado de detalle con que mide un instrumento.	
prime factorization A number written as the product of its prime factors. (p. 146)	**factorización prima** Un número escrito como el producto de sus factores primos.	$10 = 2 \cdot 5$ $24 = 2^3 \cdot 3$
prime number A whole number greater than 1 that has exactly two factors, itself and 1. (p. 143)	**número primo** Número cabal mayor que 1 que sólo es divisible entre 1 y él mismo.	5 is prime because its only factors are 5 and 1.
prism A polyhedron that has two congruent, polygon-shaped bases and other faces that are all rectangles. (p. 414)	**prisma** Poliedro con dos bases congruentes con forma de polígono y caras con forma de rectángulos.	
product The result when two or more numbers are multiplied.	**producto** Resultado de multiplicar dos o más números.	The product of 4 and 8 is 32.
proper fraction A fraction in which the numerator is less than the denominator. (p. 164)	**fracción propia** Fracción en la que el numerador es menor que el denominador.	$\frac{3}{4}, \frac{1}{13}, \frac{7}{8}$
proportion An equation that states that two ratios are equivalent. (p. 304)	**proporción** Ecuación que establece que dos razones son equivalentes.	$\frac{2}{3} = \frac{4}{6}$
protractor A tool for measuring angles.	**transportador** Instrumento para medir ángulos.	
pyramid A polyhedron with a polygon base and triangular sides that all meet at a common vertex. (p. 415)	**pirámide** Poliedro cuya base es un polígono; tiene caras triangulares que se juntan en un vértice común.	

Glossary/Glosario

Q

quadrant The *x*- and *y*-axes divide the coordinate plane into four regions. Each region is called a quadrant. (p. 492)

cuadrante El eje *x* y el eje *y* dividen el plano cartesiano en cuatro regiones. Cada región recibe el nombre de cuadrante.

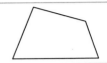

quadrilateral A four-sided polygon.

cuadrilátero Polígono de cuatro lados.

quotient The result when one number is divided by another.

cociente Resultado de dividir un número entre otro.

In 8 ÷ 4 = 2, 2 is the quotient.

R

radius A line segment with one endpoint at the center of a circle and the other endpoint on the circle, or the length of that segment. (p. 378)

radio Segmento de recta con un extremo en el centro de un círculo y el otro en la circunferencia, o bien la longitud de ese segmento.

range (in statistics) The difference between the greatest and least values in a data set. (p. 253)

rango (en estadística) Diferencia entre los valores máximo y mínimo de un conjunto de datos.

Data set: 3, 5, 7, 7, 12
Range: 12 − 3 = 9

rate A ratio that compares two quantities measured in different units. (p. 297)

tasa Una razón que compara dos cantidades medidas en diferentes unidades.

The speed limit is 55 miles per hour or 55 mi/h.

ratio A comparison of two quantities by division. (p. 296)

razón Comparación de dos cantidades mediante una división.

12 to 25, 12:25, $\frac{12}{25}$

rational number A number that can be written in the form $\frac{a}{b}$, where *a* and *b* are integers and $b \neq 0$.

número racional Número que se puede expresar como $\frac{a}{b}$, donde *a* y *b* son números enteros y $b \neq 0$.

3, 1.75, 0.$\overline{3}$, $-\frac{2}{3}$, 0

ray A part of a line that starts at one endpoint and extends forever in one direction. (p. SB9)

rayo Parte de una línea que comienza en un extremo y se extiende siempre en una dirección.

reciprocal One of two numbers whose product is 1. (p. 224)

recíproco Uno de dos números cuyo producto es igual a 1.

The reciprocal of $\frac{2}{3}$ is $\frac{3}{2}$.

rectangle A parallelogram with four right angles.

rectángulo Paralelogramo con cuatro ángulos rectos.

rectangular prism A polyhedron whose bases are rectangles and whose other faces are rectangles.

prisma rectangular Poliedro cuyas bases son rectángulos y cuyas caras tienen forma de rectángulos.

Glossary/Glosario **G17**

Glossary/Glosario

regular polygon A polygon with congruent sides and angles. (p. SB13)

polígono regular Polígono con lados y ángulos congruentes.

---

repeating decimal A decimal in which one or more digits repeat infinitely. (p. 161)

decimal periódico Decimal en el que uno o más dígitos se repiten infinitamente.

$0.75757575\ldots = 0.\overline{75}$

---

rhombus A parallelogram with all sides congruent.

rombo Paralelogramo en el que todos los lados son congruentes.

---

right angle An angle that measures 90°. (p. SB11)

ángulo recto Ángulo que mide exactamente 90°.

---

right triangle A triangle containing a right angle. (p. SB12)

triángulo rectángulo Triángulo que tiene un ángulo recto.

---

rounding Replacing a number with an estimate of that number to a given place value.

redondear Sustituir un número por una estimación de ese número hasta cierto valor posicional.

2,354 rounded to the nearest thousand is 2,000; 2,354 rounded to the nearest 100 is 2,400.

---

sales tax A percent of the cost of an item, which is charged by governments to raise money. (p. 322)

impuesto sobre la venta Porcentaje del costo de un artículo que los gobiernos cobran para recaudar fondos.

---

scale The ratio between two sets of measurements. (p. 333)

escala La razón entre dos conjuntos de medidas.

1 cm: 5 mi

---

scale drawing A drawing that uses a scale to make an object proportionally smaller than or larger than the real object. (p. 333)

dibujo a escala Dibujo en el que se usa una escala para que un objeto se vea proporcionalmente mayor o menor que el objeto real al que representa.

A blueprint is an example of a scale drawing.

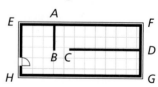

---

scale model A proportional model of a three-dimensional object.

modelo a escala Modelo proporcional de un objeto tridimensional.

---

scalene triangle A triangle with no congruent sides. (p. SB12)

triángulo escaleno Triángulo que no tiene lados congruentes.

---

sequence An ordered list of numbers. (p. 24)

sucesión Lista ordenada de números.

2, 4, 6, 8, 10, . . .

ENGLISH	SPANISH	EXAMPLES
side A line segment that connects consecutive vertices of a polygon.	**lado** Uno de los segmentos que forman un polígono.	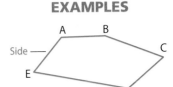
similar Figures with the same shape but not necessarily the same size are similar. (p. 326)	**semejantes** Figuras que tienen la misma forma, pero no necesariamente el mismo tamaño.	
simplest form (of a fraction) A fraction is in simplest form when the numerator and denominator have no common factors other than 1. (p. 157)	**mínima expresión (de una fracción)** Una fracción está en su mínima expresión cuando el numerador y el denominador no tienen más factor común que 1.	Fraction: $\frac{8}{12}$ Simplest form: $\frac{2}{3}$
simplify To write a fraction or expression in simplest form. (p. 16)	**simplificar** Escribir una fracción o expresión numérica en su mínima expresión.	
solid figure A three-dimensional figure.	**cuerpo geométrico** Figura tridimensional.	
solution of an equation A value or values that make an equation true. (p. 62)	**solución de una ecuación** Valor o valores que hacen verdadera una ecuación.	Equation: $x + 2 = 6$ Solution: $x = 4$
solution of an inequality A value or values that make an inequality true. (p. 461)	**solución de una desigualdad** Valor o valores que hacen verdadera una desigualdad.	Inequality: $x + 3 \geq 10$ Solution: $x \geq 7$
solve To find an answer or a solution.	**resolver** Hallar una respuesta o solución.	
sphere A three-dimensional figure with all points the same distance from the center. (p. 415)	**esfera** Figura tridimensional en la que todos los puntos están a la misma distancia del centro.	
square (geometry) A rectangle with four congruent sides.	**cuadrado (en geometría)** Rectángulo con cuatro lados congruentes.	
square (numeration) A number raised to the second power.	**cuadrado (en numeración)** Número elevado a la segunda potencia.	In 5^2, the number 5 is squared.

ENGLISH	SPANISH	EXAMPLES
standard form (in numeration) A number written using digits.	**forma estándar** Una forma de escribir números por medio de dígitos.	Five thousand, two hundred ten in standard form is 5,210.
stem-and-leaf plot A graph used to organize and display data so that the frequencies can be compared. (p. 279)	**diagrama de tallo y hojas** Gráfica que muestra y ordena los datos, y que sirve para comparar las frecuencias.	Stem | Leaves 3 | 2 3 4 4 7 9 4 | 0 1 5 7 7 7 8 5 | 1 2 2 3 *Key: 3|2 means 3.2*
straight angle An angle that measures 180°. (p. SB11)	**ángulo llano** Ángulo que mide exactamente 180°.	
substitute To replace a variable with a number or another expression in an algebraic expression.	**sustituir** Reemplazar una variable por un número u otra expresión en una expresión algebraica.	
sum The result when two or more numbers are added.	**suma** Resultado de sumar dos o más números.	
surface area The sum of the areas of the faces, or surfaces, of a three-dimensional figure. (p. 426)	**área total** Suma de las áreas de las caras, o superficies, de una figura tridimensional.	12 cm 6 cm 8 cm Surface area = 2(8)(12) + 2(8)(6) + 2(12)(6) = 432 cm²

T

term (in a sequence) An element or number in a sequence. (p. 24)	**término (en una sucesión)** Elemento o número de una sucesión.	5 is the third term in the sequence 1, 3, 5, 7, 9, . . .
terminating decimal A decimal number that ends, or terminates. (p. 161)	**decimal finito** Decimal con un número determinado de posiciones decimales.	6.75
tessellation A repeating pattern of plane figures that completely cover a plane with no gaps or overlaps. (p. SB15)	**teselado** Patrón repetido de figuras planas que cubren totalmente un plano sin superponerse ni dejar huecos.	
tip The amount of money added to a bill for service; usually a percent of the bill. (p. 322)	**propina** Cantidad que se agrega al total de una factura por servicios. Por lo general, es un porcentaje del total de la factura.	
trapezoid A quadrilateral with exactly one pair of parallel sides.	**trapecio** Cuadrilátero con un par de lados paralelos.	B C A D

ENGLISH	**SPANISH**	**EXAMPLES**
triangle A three-sided polygon.	**triángulo** Polígono de tres lados.	
triangular prism A polyhedron whose bases are triangles and whose other faces are rectangles.	**prisma triangular** Poliedro cuyas bases son triángulos y cuyas demás caras tienen forma de rectángulos.	

underestimate An estimate that is less than the exact answer. (p. 6)	**estimación baja** Estimación menor que la respuesta exacta.	100 is an underestimate for the sum 26 + 29 + 31 + 27.
unit conversion The process of changing one unit of measure to another.	**conversión de unidades** Proceso que consiste en cambiar una unidad de medida por otra.	
unit rate A rate in which the second quantity in the comparison is one unit. (p. 297)	**tasa unitaria** Una tasa en la que la segunda cantidad de la comparación es una unidad.	10 cm per minute
unlike fractions Fractions with different denominators. (p. 168)	**fracciones distintas** Fracciones con distinto denominador.	$\frac{3}{4}$ and $\frac{1}{2}$ are unlike fractions.

variable A symbol used to represent a quantity that can change. (p. 48)	**variable** Símbolo que representa una cantidad que puede cambiar.	In the expression $2x + 3$, x is the variable.
Venn diagram A diagram that is used to show relationships between sets.	**diagrama de Venn** Diagrama que muestra las relaciones entre conjuntos.	Transformations / Rotations
vertex On an angle or polygon, the point where two sides intersect. (p. 414, SB10)	**vértice** En un ángulo o polígono, el punto de intersección de dos lados	A is the vertex of $\angle CAB$.
volume The number of cubic units needed to fill a given space. (p. 418)	**volumen** Número de unidades cúbicas que se necesitan para llenar un espacio.	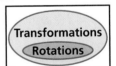 Volume = $3 \cdot 4 \cdot 12 = 144$ ft³

x-axis The horizontal axis on a coordinate plane. (p. 492)

eje x El eje horizontal del plano cartesiano.

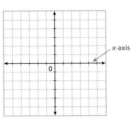

x-coordinate The first number in an ordered pair; it tells the distance to move right or left from the origin, (0, 0). (p. 492)

coordenada x El primer número en un par ordenado; indica la distancia que debes avanzar hacia la izquierda o hacia la derecha desde el origen, (0, 0).

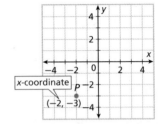

y-axis The vertical axis on a coordinate plane. (p. 492)

eje y El eje vertical del plano cartesiano.

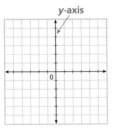

y-coordinate The second number in an ordered pair; it tells the distance to move up or down from the origin, (0, 0). (p. 492)

coordenada y El segundo número en un par ordenado; indica la distancia que debes avanzar hacia arriba o hacia abajo desde el origen, (0, 0).

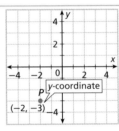

zero pair A number and its opposite, which add to 0.

par nulo Un número y su opuesto, que sumados dan 0.

18 and −18

Index

Index

Index

Index

Credits ...

Credits

Table of Measures

METRIC (SI)	U.S. CUSTOMARY

Length

1 kilometer (km) = 1000 meters (m)

1 meter = 100 centimeters (cm)

1 meter = 1000 millimeters (mm)

Length

1 mile (mi) = 1,760 yards (yd)

= 5,280 feet (ft)

1 yard = 3 feet

Capacity

1 liter (L) = 1000 milliliters (mL)

= 1000 cubic centimeters (cm^3)

Capacity

1 gallon (gal) = 4 quarts (qt)

1 quart = 2 pints (pt)

1 pint = 2 cups (c)

1 cup = 8 fluid ounces (fl oz)

Mass

1 kilogram (kg) = 1000 grams (g)

1 gram = 1000 milligrams (mg)

Weight

1 ton (T) = 2,000 pounds (lb)

1 pound = 16 ounces (oz)

TIME

1 year (yr) = 52 weeks (wk)

= 365 days

1 hour = 60 minutes (min)

1 minute = 60 seconds (s)

TEMPERATURE

Celsius (°C) $\qquad C = \frac{5}{9}(F - 32)$ $\qquad$ Fahrenheit (°F) $\qquad F = \frac{9}{5}C + 32$

Symbols

<	is less than	=	is equal to
>	is greater than	≠	is not equal to
≤	is less than or equal to	≈	is approximately equal to
≥	is greater than or equal to		

Centimeters